PENGUIN  CLASSICS

PENGUIN ENGLISH POETS
GENERAL EDITOR: CHRISTOPHER RICKS

JOHN MILTON: PARADISE LOST

JOHN MILTON was born in 1608. The son of a scrivener (a notary and money-lender), he was educated by private tutors and attended St Paul's School and Christ's College, Cambridge. He left Cambridge in 1632 and spent the next six years in scholarly retirement. *A Masque* and *Lycidas* belong to this period. Following his Italian journey (1638–9), he took up the cause of Presbyterianism in a series of hard-hitting anti-prelatical pamphlets (1641–2). His divorce pamphlets (1643–5), written after his first wife had temporarily deserted him, earned him much notoriety and contributed to his breach with the Presbyterians. In 1649 he took up the cause of the new Commonwealth. As Secretary for Foreign Tongues to the Council of State, he defended the English revolution both in English and Latin – and sacrificed his eyesight in the process. He risked his life by publishing *The Ready and Easy Way to Establish a Free Commonwealth* on the eve of the Restoration (1660). His great poems were published after this political defeat. A ten-book version of *Paradise Lost* appeared in 1667, and *Paradise Regained* and *Samson Agonistes* were published together in 1671. An expanded version of his shorter poems (first published in 1646) was brought out in 1673, and the twelve-book *Paradise Lost* appeared in 1674, the year of his death.

JOHN LEONARD has taught at the universities of Cambridge, Ottawa and Western Ontario. He has published widely on Milton, and his book *Naming in Paradise* (Clarendon Press, 1990) was a co-winner of the Milton Society's James Holly Hanford Award. He also won the Hanford Award for best article on Milton published in 2001. He is a Professor of English at the University of Western Ontario, where he has taught since 1987.

JOHN MILTON

PARADISE LOST

Edited with an Introduction and Notes by
JOHN LEONARD

0292267938O

PENGUIN BOOKS

PENGUIN BOOKS

Published by the Penguin Group
Penguin Books Ltd, 80 Strand, London WC2R ORL, England
Penguin Putnam Inc., 375 Hudson Street, New York, New York 10014, USA
Penguin Books Australia Ltd, 250 Camberwell Road, Camberwell, Victoria 3124, Australia
Penguin Books Canada Ltd, 10 Alcorn Avenue, Toronto, Ontario, Canada M4V 3B2
Penguin Books India (P) Ltd, 11 Community Centre, Panchsheel Park, New Delhi – 110 017, India
Penguin Books (NZ) Ltd, Cnr Rosedale and Airborne Roads, Albany, Auckland, New Zealand
Penguin Books (South Africa) (Pty) Ltd, 24 Sturdee Avenue, Rosebank 2196, South Africa

Penguin Books Ltd, Registered Offices: 80 Strand, London WC2R ORL, England

www.penguin.com

First published 2000
Published in Penguin Classics 2000
Reprinted with corrections and updated Further Reading 2003
022

Introduction and Notes copyright © John Leonard, 2000
All rights reserved

The moral right of the editor has been asserted

Set in 10/11.5 pt Monotype Ehrhardt
Typeset by Rowland Phototypesetting Ltd, Bury St Edmunds, Suffolk
Printed in England by Clays Ltd, St Ives plc

www.greenpenguin.co.uk

MIX
Paper from
responsible sources
FSC
www.fsc.org   FSC™ C018179

Penguin Books is committed to a sustainable
future for our business, our readers and our planet.
This book is made from Forest Stewardship
Council™ certified paper.

ALWAYS LEARNING   **PEARSON**

CONTENTS

INTRODUCTION

John Milton was nearly sixty when he published *Paradise Lost* in 1667. John Aubrey (1626–97) tells us that the poem was begun in about 1658 and finished in about 1663. But parts were almost certainly written earlier, and its roots lie in Milton's earliest youth. He had wanted to write a great poem for several decades, but the Civil War had intervened. His hope was to write an epic that would rival those of Homer, Virgil, and Tasso or a tragedy that would rival those of Aeschylus, Sophocles and Euripides. He had spent much of his life preparing for this task. The aspiring epic poet, following a pattern established by Virgil, was to begin with pastoral apprentice work before graduating to the sublimity of heroic verse. Like Spenser before him, Milton consciously followed this career. His pastoral elegies 'Lycidas' (1638) and 'Epitaphium Damonis' (1640) solicit comparison with pastoral poems by Virgil and Spenser, and 'Epitaphium Damonis' mentions plans for an epic about ancient Britain. Many of Milton's early poems voice the hope that greater things will follow. As early as 1628, when he was only nineteen, Milton announced his epic ambitions in an English poem that he delivered at Christ's College, Cambridge. 'At a Vacation Exercise' was part of a public oration on an academic topic, but Milton turns the occasion to higher things. He says that he will one day write on 'some graver subject' that will permit his 'transported mind' to 'soar / Above the wheeling poles, and at Heav'n's door / Look in, and see each blissful deity' (33–34). Already we see the kind of imagination that Milton will display in *Paradise Lost* when he describes himself as 'rapt above the pole' (vii 23). The young Milton goes on to say that he will 'sing of secret things that came to pass / When beldam Nature in her cradle was' (45–46). From earliest youth, Milton aspired to write an epic that would encompass all space and time.

He did not at first plan to write a biblical epic. In 'At a Vacation Exercise' he assumes that pagan gods are the proper epic deities, and that 'kings and queens and heroes old' (47) are the proper epic subject. Epic poems were expected to express the spirit of a nation, and Milton's initial aim was to write an epic for England. For several years he imagined that his hero would be a British or Saxon king. 'Epitaphium Damonis' names Brennus, Belinus, Arviragus and Arthur as possible heroes, while 'Mansus' (another Latin poem, written a few months earlier) mentions Arthur's Saxon wars as a potential subject. In *The Reason of Church Government* (1642) Milton wonders what king or knight 'before the conquest might be chosen in whom to lay the pattern of a Christian *Heroe*'. He plans to write in English and so do for England what the Greeks, Romans, Italians, and 'Hebrews of old did for their country'.[1] Milton achieved his goal of writing an epic in English, but in the event he did not write about England. Arthur was too fabulous a hero for high epic seriousness, and British history was too narrow a subject. Despite his claim to be 'content with these British Ilands as my world',[2] Milton was a man of European culture for whom a British or Saxon subject would have seemed provincial. He might also have had a political reason for abandoning his Arthuriad. National epics were traditionally monarchist, and an epic about King Arthur would be inescapably so. Milton could have had little use for Arthur after the outbreak of the English Civil War in 1642.

Milton did not fight in the war, but he did write political pamphlets throughout the 1640s and 1650s. His first pamphlets, published in 1641–2, were his five anti-episcopal tracts, urging the cause of Presbyterianism against Church government by bishops. Early in the summer of 1642, when he was thirty-three, Milton unwisely married Mary Powell, a woman half his age. The marriage was unhappy and Mary returned to her parents' house after only a few weeks. (She would not be reconciled with Milton until 1645.) Between 1643 and 1645 Milton published four pamphlets in defence of divorce. He boldly addressed three of them to Parliament, which was then dominated by the Presbyterians, Milton's old allies against the bishops. Parliament was scandalized and in June 1643 introduced pre-publication censorship in an attempt to forestall pamphlets like Milton's. In *Areopagitica* (1644) Milton urged Parliament to repeal its new Licensing Order, but to no avail. He became disillusioned with Presbyterianism. By 1648 Parliament had won the war, but the Presbyterians were unwilling to try or execute the king. The victorious army therefore purged Parliament. Charles I was beheaded on 30 January 1649. The event horrified most English people and shook all Europe. But Milton approved of it and in *The Tenure of Kings and Magistrates* (February 1649) he defended the right of subjects to depose their king. One month later he was appointed Secretary for Foreign Tongues to the Council of State. In this capacity he defended the English Commonwealth in English and Latin, and won fame throughout Europe.

Milton did not abandon his poetic plans during the 1640s and 1650s, but the only original English poems that he finished in this period were a few sonnets. Critics have often wondered why he did not write more poetry at this time. Some have argued that he did and that either or both of *Samson Agonistes* and *Paradise Regained* (which are usually dated after *Paradise Lost*) really belong to this period. Other critics have conjectured that Milton suffered from some kind of writer's block that was lifted only after he became totally blind in 1652. Milton most likely deferred his poetic ambitions because he thought that his political pamphlets served a more urgent need. He certainly took pride in his pamphlets. In *The Reason of Church Government* (1642) he had disparaged prose as an inferior medium in which 'I have the use, as I may account it, but of my left hand' (1:808). Many readers have agreed with this verdict, but it would be rash to lift it out of context as if it applied with equal force to all of Milton's prose works, early or late, English or Latin. Thomas Hobbes loathed Milton's politics, but even Hobbes grudgingly conceded that Milton was a master of Latin prose. If Milton aspired to be the Homer or Virgil of his age, he also aspired to be the Demosthenes or Cicero. He was willing to sacrifice much for his political pamphlets. He believed – perhaps rightly – that they had cost him his eyesight, and he was willing, if need be, to sacrifice more. On the very eve of the Restoration, he risked his life (and his unfinished epic) by publishing *The Ready and Easy Way to Establish a Free Commonwealth* (March 1660). All of Milton's political hopes collapsed with the Restoration of King Charles II in May 1660. As a defender of regicide, Milton was in brief but real danger of being hanged, drawn and quartered (a fate to which he obliquely refers in *Paradise Lost* vii 24–38). His blindness may have helped to save him. Royalists were able to point to it as a sign of God's judgement.

Milton suffered other personal crises in the 1650s and 1660s. His

[margin annotation: Indicative of Milton's writing being purposeful]

first wife died in childbirth in May 1652, just a few weeks after Milton had lost his sight. His infant son John died about six weeks later. In November 1656 Milton married his second wife, Katherine Woodcock, whom he dearly loved, but she died in February 1658, and their five-month-old daughter died soon after her. In 1663 Milton married his third wife, Elizabeth Minshull, but relations with his three surviving daughters (all by Mary Powell) became strained. In 1671 Milton published *Samson Agonistes* and *Paradise Regained*, and in 1673 he published a revised edition of his shorter poems (many of which had been written in the 1630s and published in an earlier edition, dated 1645). In 1674 he published the second edition of *Paradise Lost*. He died in November 1674 in his house in Bunhill Fields. His friend Cyriack Skinner relates that 'Hee dy'd in a fitt of the Gout, but with so little pain or Emotion, that the time of his expiring was not perceiv'd by those in the room'.[3]

Tragedy or Epic?

We do not know when Milton decided to make the Fall of Man the subject of his epic. His initial plan had been to treat this subject in a tragedy. Four drafts for such a tragedy (one with the title 'Paradise Lost') survive in a manuscript in Trinity College, Cambridge. The drafts resemble the completed *Paradise Lost* in some details, and it is possible that some parts of the poem we have were first written for a tragedy. Edward Phillips, Milton's nephew and biographer, reports that the opening lines of Satan's address to the sun (iv 32–41) were shown to him as 'the very beginning' of a tragedy 'several Years before the Poem was begun'.[4] Aubrey says that Phillips saw the lines in about 1642.[5] If this is right, Milton was writing a tragedy on the Fall at the very time that he was planning an Arthurian epic. At some later date he realized that the subject he had intended for his tragedy was better suited to his epic. Milton was 'long choosing, and beginning late' (ix 26), but he eventually matched the right subject with the right genre. War, the traditional epic subject, did not suit his poetic temperament or his exalted notions of moral heroism. *Paradise Lost* does include some fighting, but its main action is very simple: two people eat an apple in a garden. This would have seemed absurd to Homer or Virgil. Even the Christian poet Torquato Tasso (1544–95) chose a military subject (the First Crusade) for his epic *Gerusalemme Liberata* (*Jerusalem Delivered*). Rejecting this long tradition, Milton claims that his own subject is 'Not less but more heroic than the wrath / Of stern Achilles' (ix 14–15). *Paradise Lost* attains epic sublimity. The epic form gave Milton a licence to cover vast tracts of space and time. Spatially, the action ranges over the whole earth, throughout the universe, and beyond the universe to Heaven, Chaos, and Hell. The action extends back in time before the creation of our universe to the begetting of the Son of God (v 575ff.) and forward to the Second Coming (xii 458–65). Milton would have forfeited this cosmic sweep had he presented the action on a stage. The drafts in the Trinity manuscript follow the classic limitation to a single place. The War in Heaven is related in a chorus, the temptation takes place off-stage, and God and the Son never appear or speak. As Helen Gardner points out, the great advantage of handling this story in epic form 'was that it made possible a far more dramatic treatment' than would have been possible 'within the limits of drama'.[6]

Milton did well to choose the epic form, but it would be rash to suppose that his original plan left no trace on the poem we have. More than any epic poet before him, Milton makes use of soliloquy – a characteristic feature of Elizabethan and Jacobean tragedy. The lines that he showed Phillips are part of a soliloquy. Originally intended for 'the very beginning' of a tragedy, they resemble the opening lines of Aeschylus's *Prometheus Bound* and Euripides's *The Phoenician Women* – both of which begin with an address to the sun. Satan has five soliloquies in *Paradise Lost* (iv 32–113, 358–92, 505–35, ix 99–178, 473–93), and Adam and Eve speak soliloquies when they are fallen or about to fall (ix 745–79, 795–833, 896–916, x 720–844). Critics often say that the characters of *Paradise Lost* do not soliloquize until they are fallen, but the good angel Abdiel soliloquizes (vi 114–126) and Adam's first words on waking into life are an address to the sun (viii 273–82). The very structure of the first edition of *Paradise Lost* (1667) might owe something to English tragedy. This edition was printed as a poem of ten books. (The ten books became twelve in the second edition when the original books seven and ten were split in two.) Critics sometimes see the original ten books as forming five dramatic acts of two books each. There might be something to this, but a ten-book epic would not have looked odd in the

Renaissance. Camões's Portugese epic *The Lusíads* (1572) has ten cantos, and Tasso's *Jerusalem Delivered* (1580–81) has twenty books. Homer's *Iliad* and *Odyssey* have twenty-four books each, so a ten-book epic would have the same relation to Tasso that a twelve-book epic has to Homer. Milton frequently alludes to Tasso in *Paradise Lost*, and his devils have many features in common with Tasso's Saracens. But it is Virgil's *Aeneid* that provides the clearest model for the twelve-book structure that Milton eventually chose.

Milton continually alludes to his epic predecessors, but there is disagreement among critics as to how, or even whether, he sets his poem within the epic tradition. Some critics see *Paradise Lost* as an 'anti-epic' that pointedly rejects the martial and imperialist values traditionally associated with the epic genre. Others see Milton as renovating a tradition that he loves. The question is closely related to that of Satan's heroism, for much of the traditional epic material in *Paradise Lost* clusters around Milton's Devil. In the first two books especially it seems that Satan will be the hero of a poem like Virgil's *Aeneid*; but Milton then takes this poem back in Book III and offers a different kind of heroism in the Son of God. The Son's offer to die for mankind when no one else will do so (iii 214ff.) clearly looks back to the moment when Satan alone volunteers to seek out the new creation and destroy its human inhabitants (ii 430ff.). Both episodes are loosely modelled on *Iliad* vii 92–3, where Ajax alone will accept Hector's challenge to single combat. Satan's speech also echoes Sarpedon's praise of duty (*Iliad* xii 310–16). Milton certainly exalts Christian above pagan heroism, but it need not follow that he therefore scorns pagan epic. Readers must finally decide for themselves whether Milton Satanizes the epic or measures Satan against an epic standard and finds him wanting.

Nakedness

Had Milton stuck with his plan to present the Fall as a tragedy he would have faced one insuperable obstacle. Adam and Eve could not have appeared naked on stage. Milton would have had either to garb them in flesh-coloured robes or keep them off-stage until after the Fall. He probably intended to use flesh-coloured robes when he prepared his first outline for a tragedy. This early draft (a bare list of *dramatis personae*) names Adam and Eve 'with the serpent'. The later drafts keep Adam and Eve off-stage until they are fallen and clothed. The third outline ('Paradise Lost') has Moses explain in a prologue that sinful mortals cannot see Adam 'in the state of innocence'. The final outline ('Adam Unparadiz'd') has Adam and Eve make their first entrance 'confusedly cover'd with leaves', 'having by this time bin seduc't by the serpent'.[7] These later outlines escape the absurdity of flesh-coloured robes, but only at the price of limiting the dramatic action. By choosing the epic form, Milton gave himself the freedom to portray Adam and Eve before, during, and after the Fall, and to make 'naked majesty' (iv 290) a major theme of his poem. This was a bold decision and we should not take it for granted. One of the most remarkable things about the poem we have is that the two main characters (and the angels[8]) are naked for most of the action.

Milton gives nakedness a heroic treatment. In this he is strangely close to Marlowe. Marlowe's comic, erotic poem *Hero and Leander* (1598) is worlds away from *Paradise Lost* in tone and mood, but it supplied Milton with some felicitous raw materials. Leander is unembarrassedly in the raw for much of Marlowe's poem, and even the bashful Hero stays 'not for her robes' when she leaps from bed to welcome naked Leander at her door (ii 235). Hero's robes warrant a closer look:

> Her wide sleeves green, and bordered with a grove
> Where Venus in her naked glory strove
> To please the careless and disdainful eyes
> Of proud Adonis that before her lies.   (i 11–14)[9]

Milton alludes to these lines twice in *Paradise Lost*. He borrows the phrase 'naked glory' when he tells how the fallen Adam and Eve cover themselves with leaves: 'O how unlike / To that first naked glory!' (ix 1114–15). His other allusion occurs when he likens Eve to 'the fairest goddess feigned / Of three that in Mount Ida naked strove' (v 381–2). This refers to the beauty contest in which Juno, Minerva and Venus strove naked for the apple of discord. Paris awarded Venus the apple and so precipitated Troy's fall. Eve too will win an apple and bring about a fall. The simile is ominous, but the allusion to Marlowe, signalled by 'naked strove', still credits Eve's nakedness with heroic splendour.

There is a difference between the two poets. Marlowe evokes a sense of grandeur only to mock it: 'Venus in her naked glory strove / To please'. David Lee Miller sees a comic deflation here:

'Strove' appears in the emphatic position at line's end, its sense of power and exertion amplified by 'naked glory'. But what follows the line break is an ironically inappropriate complement to the verb; the sense of mighty contest collapses into mere exhibition as we discover that 'Venus in her naked glory strove' only to be gloriously naked.[10]

Nakedness, for Marlowe, is exhilarating *and* ridiculous. Milton borrows Marlowe's exhilaration and discards his ridicule. There is nothing 'mere' about Eve's naked majesty:

> but Eve
> Undecked, save with herself more lovely fair
> Than wood-nymph, or the fairest goddess feigned
> Of three that in Mount Ida naked strove,
> Stood to entertain her guest from Heav'n (v 379–83)

Where Marlowe's mighty line collapses, Milton's stands firm, the heroic 'strove' reinforced, not mocked, by the alliterating 'Stood'. 'Stood' implies moral as well as physical demeanour, for standing (especially in Milton) is the opposite of falling.[11] The heart of the passage is that superb phrase 'Undecked, save with herself'. This too might glance at Marlowe, for Hero was quite literally bedecked with Venus's 'naked glory'; Eve wears *her* glory in her own person.

Milton gives Adam's nakedness an even more exalted treatment. At one point he makes it a vehicle for his most cherished political convictions:

> Meanwhile our primitive great sire, to meet
> His god-like guest, walks forth, without more train
> Accompanied than with his own complete
> Perfections; in himself was all his state,
> More solemn than the tedious pomp that waits
> On princes, when their rich retinue long
> Of horses led, and grooms besmeared with gold
> Dazzles the crowd and sets them all agape. (v 350–57)

Satirists have often used nakedness to puncture princely pretension, but Milton's satire is sharper for not equating nakedness with shame, and not stripping the emperors of their new clothes. Here the exhibitionist royals bring shame on themselves by flashing flashy habiliments. It is naked Adam who is truly 'solemn' ('grand, imposing'). Milton drives the point home with a lovely pun on 'state'. When kings parade in 'state', they flaunt themselves 'with great pomp and solemnity; with a great train; with splendid or honorific trappings and insignia' (*OED* 17c). Milton plays on that sense, but the 'state' that Adam carries 'in himself' is all the more magnificent for meaning 'bodily form' (*OED* 9a) and 'stateliness of bearing' (*OED* 18a).

There might be a topical reference in these lines. The most spectacular display of royal pomp in all of English history occurred on 29 May 1660 when the restored King Charles II made his triumphant entry into London. One historian calls it the 'most momentous day of the century'.[12] Tens of thousands of people lined the royal route from Rochester to London, some climbing trees to see over the crowds. Flowers and herbs were strewn before the royal coach, and the streets of every town were hung with garlands. Fifty thousand horse and foot acclaimed the King at Blackheath, and at St George's Fields the royal train was joined by the Lord Mayor of London and the aldermen, wearing scarlet robes and golden chains. The 'rich retínue long' crossed London Bridge at half-past four in the afternoon. A troop of three hundred horse dressed in cloth of silver doublets led the way, followed by other uniformed regiments and two trumpeters with His Majesty's arms. Next came eighty sheriff's men in red cloaks laced with silver, six hundred liveried horsemen with a kettledrum and five trumpets, the City Marshal with eight liveried footmen, the sheriffs and aldermen in their scarlet robes, heralds with trumpets and maces, and the Lord Mayor with drawn sword. The King followed on a white horse, sporting a plume of scarlet feathers in his cap. More regiments stretched behind as far as the eye could see. Stands for spectators had been erected all along the procession route, and people watched from every window. The streets were hung with tapestries. Fountains ran claret. The dazzled crowd was 'all agape'. The shouting, the cannonades, the cries of 'God save the King!' were deafening. For John Milton, then hiding in Bartholomew Close in peril for his life, it must have been a barbarous dissonance. How typical of this poet to recall Charles's triumph and mock it with one naked man. But even as he mocks, Milton takes the nakedness entirely seriously.

Milton's Cosmos

For Renaissance literary theorists a defining feature of epic was *maraviglia*, 'the marvellous'. In his *Discourses on the Heroic Poem* (1594), Tasso argued that epic has the specific 'purpose of moving the mind to wonder'.[13] No epic has been more celebrated for sublimity than *Paradise Lost*. Milton's 'peculiar power', writes Samuel Johnson, is 'to astonish':

> He seems to have been well acquainted with his own genius, and to know what it was that Nature had bestowed upon him more bountifully than upon others: the power of displaying the vast, illuminating the splendid, enforcing the awful, darkening the gloomy, and aggravating the dreadful.[14]

The power Johnson describes is most evident in Milton's vast, splendid, gloomy cosmos. This contains much else beside the created universe of stars and planets. Heaven, Hell, Chaos, and Night all lie outside the stellar universe in Milton's scheme of things. Milton's cosmos is infinite; his universe large, but finite. Milton usually depicts the universe as earth-centred, but he often hints that it is sun-centred, and at one point he boldly suggests that every star might be a sun with its own solar system (viii 148–52). The universe is spherical in shape and is surrounded by a 'firm opacous globe' (iii 418) or hard outer shell that protects it from Chaos. All around our universe lies the infinite void of Night in which the atoms of Chaos collide at random for all eternity. Heaven lies far above our universe, Hell far below it. The universe hangs suspended from Heaven's floor by a golden chain (ii 1051) which later turns out to be a retractable moving staircase like Jacob's ladder (iii 510–20). Hell is not at first linked to any other world. Sin and Death join it to our universe at the time of man's Fall by building a bridge across Chaos (x 282–320).

From this brief map one might suppose that Heaven and the universe correspond to 'the splendid' in Johnson's terms, while Hell, Chaos, and Night correspond to 'the dreadful' and 'the gloomy'. This is the case, to some extent, but Milton's Hell is not without some splendour, and his Heaven is not untouched by sullen dread. Hell's flames cast 'no light' (i 63), but when the fallen angels rally their forces, 'Millions of flaming swords, drawn from the thighs / Of mighty Cherubim' send forth a 'sudden blaze' that 'Far round illumined Hell' (i 664–6). If Hell has brief moments of brilliance, Heaven has long periods of gloom. God hides himself 'oft amidst / Thick clouds and dark . . . And with the majesty of darkness round / Covers his throne' so 'Heav'n resembles Hell' (ii 263–8). The speaker here is the devil Mammon, who has his own dark reasons for likening Heaven to Hell, but we cannot simply dismiss Mammon's picture, for the Bible also avers that God has 'made darkness his secret place' (Psalms 18.11). The vast, the splendid, the dreadful and the gloomy are richly portrayed in *Paradise Lost*, then, but we do not always find them where we might expect.

Our earth is 'a spot, a grain, / An atom' in the universe (viii 17–18), but the entire universe may be no more than a speck in cosmic space. I say 'may be' for Milton is inconsistent on this point. Sometimes he writes as if the universe loomed large in the void. Satan describes the universe as 'vast and round' (ii 832), and Milton in his own voice says that Hell is 'As far removed from God and light of Heav'n / As from the centre thrice to th' utmost pole' (i 73–4). 'The centre' is the earth, and 'th' utmost pole' a celestial pole, so Milton here measures the distance between Heaven and Hell as three times the radius of our universe. A universe as large as that would be a significant encroachment on Chaos. The allegorical person Chaos certainly resents the new creation. Satan finds him encamped on the 'frontiers' of his realm, determined to defend 'That little which is left' (ii 1000). But the relative dimensions of universe and cosmos undergo an abrupt change at the end of Book II, when Satan emerges from Chaos and sees Heaven far above him. Heaven is so large that Satan cannot tell whether it is square or round, but a tiny spherical object hangs just below it:

> And fast by hanging in a golden chain,
> This pendent world, in bigness as a star
> Of smallest magnitude close by the moon. (ii 1051–3)

'This pendent world' is the entire universe, not the earth. Viewed across cosmic space, our universe with all its stars looks as small as one of its own faint stars.

Milton calls his universe 'the universe' or 'the world'. He never uses the word 'cosmos'. I use it here for convenience only. The word can be misleading, for it means 'order'. Much of Milton's cosmos consists of Chaos, which is conspicuous for disorder. Milton never sums his cosmos up in one word. He repeatedly refers to the infinite space outside our universe as 'the deep', 'the abyss', 'the void' or simply 'space'. When Satan says 'Space may produce new worlds' (i 650), 'worlds' means 'universes', not 'planets'. The *Oxford English Dictionary* credits Milton with coining the astronomical sense of 'space'. Milton probably took it from the Roman poet Lucretius (*c*. 98–55 BC), who in *De Rerum Natura* refers to outer space as *spatium*. Milton's cosmos owes much to Lucretius. Both poets depict our universe as a finite sphere in an infinite void, both suppose that the universe was formed from chaotic atoms, both imagine the possibility of multiple universes, and both imagine that Chaos is still out there in the void. Milton's Chaos seems hostile partly because it continues to exist. (The more usual view was that Chaos was all used up in creation.) Lucretius had theorized that our universe would at last be overwhelmed from outside. Milton imagines such a cataclysm at ii 924–7 and vii 210–15. In a line that is a direct translation of Lucretius, he calls Chaos 'The womb of Nature and perhaps her grave' (ii 911). But there is a key difference between Lucretius and Milton. Lucretius's universe came about by chance; Milton's was created by God.

God created Hell at the time of Satan's rebellion, and he created the universe soon after that. For nine days Satan's legions fell through Chaos (vi 871) and they 'Lay vanquished, rolling in the fiery gulf' for a further nine days (i 52). God created our universe in six days at some time during this second nine-day period (vii 131–5). He created Hell and our universe out of Chaos, not nothing. We are never told whether he created Heaven. Chaos resents Hell and our universe as encroachments, but he never lays claim to Heaven (ii 1000–4). In his theological treatise *De Doctrina Christiana*, Milton conjectures that God must have dwelt in a place of light from all eternity. He inclines to the same view in his invocation to Light in *Paradise Lost* (iii 1–5), so it is likely that he thought of Heaven as God's eternal, uncreated abode.

Many critics infer that Hell is the absolute bottom of Milton's cosmos, but two memorable moments tell against this view. One occurs when Satan stands in the open gateway of Hell and looks out into the 'wild abyss' (ii 910, 917). The repeated word 'abyss' (which literally means 'bottomless') raises the daunting possibility that Night has no bottom, and that 'up' and 'down' are indistinguishable in the void. But the most telling sign that Hell is not an absolute bottom is to be found just after this, when Satan takes the plunge into Chaos. At first Satan makes good progress, soaring aloft with 'sail-broad' (ii 927) wings. Then he encounters a 'vast vacuity' and promptly plummets:

> all unawares
> Flutt'ring his pennons vain plumb down he drops
> Ten thousand fathom deep, and to this hour
> Down had been falling, had not by ill chance
> The strong rebuff of some tumultuous cloud
> Instinct with fire and nitre hurried him
> As many miles aloft.   (ii 932–8)

We should not miss the implications of 'to this hour'. Satan's fall from Heaven to Hell had lasted nine days. Now Milton imagines a fall that might last for thousands of years. The prospect of an infinite fall through an infinite abyss dislodges Hell from its position as rock bottom. Such a fall is terrifying for Satan, but it also poses a roundabout threat to God because it makes his notions of moral and physical distance seem paltry.

For this reason, some critics are reluctant to admit that Milton's cosmos is infinite. They argue that terms like 'infinite abyss' (ii 405) and 'vast infinitude' (iii 711) express 'merely an hyperbolical infinitude'. Such terms, we are told, 'must not be taken literally' since 'only God is infinite'.[15] The problem with this is that it diminishes the sublimity of Milton's imagination. Astronomers and philosophers in Milton's own time were divided on the question of whether space was infinite. Johannes Kepler (1571–1630) believed that space could not be infinite, for infinity belonged to God alone. Giordano Bruno (1548–1600), Galileo Galilei (1564–1642), and Henry More (1614–87), took a broader view and argued that an infinite universe would redound to God's glory. Milton has much in common with these three thinkers, but there is a difference between his universe and theirs. They imagined that the stellar universe itself was infinite. Milton is unusual in that he places a finite universe in an infinite abyss and shuts infinity out by enclosing his universe with a protective shell. Critics have been hard-pressed to find precedents for this shell. The traditional Ptolemaic universe was spherical in shape, but nothing, not even space or time, existed outside it. Milton's fortified universe is besieged by a Chaos that Milton in his own voice calls 'hostile' (ii 1040).

The hostility of Chaos raises troubling questions about God. If God is good, all-powerful, and the ultimate source of matter (as Raphael affirms at v 469f. and as *De Doctrina Christiana* also argues), how can we account for the existence of an evil Chaos? An evil Chaos would suggest either that God is not good or that he is not all-powerful. Many critics try to get around this problem by arguing that Milton's Chaos (despite appearances) is not evil but good. This argument does have the appeal of making *Paradise Lost* accord with *De Doctrina Christiana*, which argues that all matter is good. Critics who see Milton's Chaos as good usually employ either or both of two arguments.[16] Some argue that Chaos is the material equivalent of free will. Chaos and free will both preclude determinism, and atomist philosophers like Lucretius and Pierre Gassendi (1592–1655) had invoked the unpredictability of atomic motion to argue for human freedom. Since human beings are made of atoms, which are unpredictable, human decisions must also be unpredictable. At first sight, this does sound like Milton, but there is a difference. Atomist philosophers reduce freedom to a chance matter of colliding atoms. Milton equates freedom with responsible moral choice. When Raphael tells Adam that the decision 'to stand or fall' lies free in his 'own arbitrament' (viii 640–41), he is not inviting Adam to follow random caprice. He is urging him to choose wisely. For Milton, freedom is a matter of choice, not chance. In Chaos, 'Chance', not choice, is the 'high arbiter' that 'governs all' (ii 909–10).

The second argument for the goodness of Chaos stresses its fecundity as a womb. Milton does refer to 'the wide womb of uncreated Night' (ii 150), but that is no indication that Night's womb is healthy or fertile. Night is an 'abortive gulf' (ii 441). It breeds 'embryon atoms' (ii 900) but fails to give them form. The very sight of Night's womb threatens 'utter loss of being' (ii 440). When Satan beholds 'The secrets of the hoary deep' (ii 891), 'secrets' contains a pun on 'privy parts' (*OED* 'secret' B 6), while 'hoary' ('old, grey-haired') contains puns on 'hory' ('filthy') and 'whorish'. George Chapman had written a hymn to Night in which primal Night '(Most harlot-like) her naked secrets shows'.[17] Lying behind the sexual imagery is a silent pun on 'nothing' (a slang term for female genitals). Milton's Night is a real void. As Regina Schwartz remarks, 'it is as Nothing' that the abyss 'is most threatening'.[18]

Night outside our universe is unremittingly dark. This will not surprise the modern reader, who is accustomed to think of outer space as black. But the interstellar space within Milton's universe is bright. In *Paradise Lost* as in his Ludlow *Masque* (also known as *Comus*), Milton depicts the stellar heavens as a region 'where day never shuts his eye' (*A Masque* 978). How then can he account for the fact that terrestrial nights are visibly dark? The old astronomy held that the darkness of night was an illusion. The darkness is not really out there between the stars. The night sky just looks dark because we see it through our earth's shadow. This view of the universe was standard in ancient and medieval times and it survived into the Renaissance. The celestial heavens above and around the earth's shadow are a brilliant blue, with sun, moon, planets and stars all visible at once. As C. S. Lewis puts it, an observer of the night sky in the old astronomy looks 'through darkness but not at darkness'.[19] Satan enters our universe through a hole in its outer shell (iii 526f.). Standing on the rim of this opening, Satan looks down into a bright universe: 'Round he surveys, and well might, where he stood / So high above the circling canopy / Of night's extended shade' (iii 555–7). The 'circling canopy / Of night's extended shade' is the earth's shadow rotating around the universe like the hand of a clock. From where Satan stands, all the stellar heavens are bathed in light, and he 'Looks down with wonder at the sudden view / Of all this world [i.e. 'universe'] at once' (iii 542–3). A few lines later he glides down through 'the pure marble air' (564). 'Marble' (from Greek *marmareos*) means 'gleaming'.

Apparently it was 'the invention of the telescope at the dawn of the scientific age' that 'destroyed the old belief in celestial light and plunged the heavens in darkness'.[20] Milton's bright universe was out of date by the time *Paradise Lost* was published. Even Milton's universe is not always bright. Some forty lines after his descent through the 'marble air', Satan lands on the sun. There he disguises himself as a good angel and asks Uriel, the angelic 'regent of the sun', for directions to earth. Uriel replies:

> Look downward on that globe whose hither side
> With light from hence, though but reflected, shines;
> That place is earth the seat of man, that light

> His day, which else as th' other hemisphere
> Night would invade, but there the neighbouring moon
> (So call that opposite fair star) her aid
> Timely interposes.   (iii 723–8)

Suddenly it is day, not night, which is the merely local phenomenon ('that light / His day'). The 'pure marble air' has become a pitch-black void.

This contradiction is never resolved in *Paradise Lost*. When Raphael descends to earth, he sails 'between worlds and worlds' like an Aegean pilot sailing through the Cyclades (v 264–8). This lovely simile implies that the 'vast ethereal sky' (v 267) is as blue as the Mediterranean, with planets inviting the island-hopping space-traveller to rest. But when Eve asks Adam why the stars shine, Adam's answer assumes a dark universe. The stars shine, he says, 'Lest total darkness should by night regain / Her old possession' (iv 665–6). Here, as in Uriel's lines, darkness is primal, not just privative. Yet one hundred lines later Milton once again equates night with the earth's shadow when he refers to night's 'shadowy cone' (iv 776). How can we explain the contradiction? The simple answer is that Milton has it both ways because he does not know which is right. But we should not assume that he doesn't care, or that nothing is at stake. What is at stake is the relation of our universe to ancient Night. A bright universe would be wholly distinct from outer darkness. A dark universe would be uncomfortably like 'the void profound / Of unessential Night' (ii 438–9). Milton wanted very much to believe in a bright universe, illumined by God's love, and to that end he banished Hell and Night beyond the walls of the universe. But Night creeps back in his despite.

Whatever his fears about outer space, Milton shows surprising equanimity about one question that troubled many of his contemporaries. He has no difficulty in accepting the existence of life on other worlds. It is the thought of unpeopled emptiness that chills him. He even hints at a solution to a problem that had tormented others. The possibility of life on other worlds raises awkward questions for Christianity. The problem is this: did extraterrestrials fall with Adam? If they did, God's decision to punish them for Adam's sin looks unjust. But if aliens were untouched by Adam's fall, Christ's redemption of one small world looks cosmically insignificant. In

1600 the Church of Rome burned Giordano Bruno alive because he had argued that the universe was infinite and contained an infinite number of inhabited worlds. Milton never engages directly with the question of extraterrestrial life and its implications for Christianity, but he does hint at a possible answer. As Satan passes other planets, they resemble 'those Hesperian gardens famed of old' (iii 568). The Hesperian gardens of myth contained forbidden apples. Editors sometimes take the line as a foreshadowing of Adam and Eve's fall, but Milton might instead be hinting that every planet has its own forbidden tree, and that aliens have their own contracts with God. We cannot know, and are not encouraged to ask, whether aliens fell. Since Satan 'stayed not to inquire' (iii 571), we cannot even know whether they exist. But the angel Raphael later gives a strong hint that they do (viii 151–8).

Milton's God

Paradise Lost is, among other things, a poem about a civil war. Satan raises 'impious war in Heav'n' (i 43) by leading a third of the angels in revolt against God. The term 'impious war' (punning on Latin *bellum impium*, 'internecine war') implies that civil war is impious. But Milton applauded the English people for having the courage to depose and execute King Charles I. In his poem, however, he takes the side of 'Heav'n's awful Monarch' (iv 960). Critics have long wrestled with the question of why an antimonarchist and defender of regicide should have chosen a subject that obliged him to defend monarchical authority. C. S. Lewis was dismissive of the problem. Arguing from the principle that 'the goodness, happiness, and dignity of every being consists in obeying its natural superior and ruling its natural inferiors', Lewis claims there is no contradiction between Milton's poem and his politics. Milton believed that God was his 'natural superior' and that Charles Stuart was not. When Charles claimed to rule by divine right he was merely playing God; God *is* God. Milton is therefore consistent in arguing that we should obey God and disobey Charles.[21] Within its own terms, this is a satisfying answer, perhaps the best that can be given. But Lewis's emphasis on hierarchy is unfashionable these days, and some critics try to reconcile Milton's poem with his politics in a different way. They argue that Milton's God is a constitutional ruler, accountable to his subjects.[22] The problem with this, as Robert Fallon succinctly remarks, is that Milton's God is 'every inch a king'. He demands absolute obedience and rules by personal decree (as Charles I did between 1629 and 1640). He is accountable to no Parliament.[23] Other critics argue that God is a just ruler because he abides by his own decrees.[24] Fallon counters this by pointing out that 'the difficulty, of course, lies in those decrees'. The real question is 'whether *they* are just or not'. God decrees that Adam and Eve will die if they eat the apple. They do eat the apple, and God does kill them (and us). God abides by his decree, then, but is that enough to justify him? Fallon draws a devastating analogy:

God may certainly be said to keep his word and so may be absolved of arbitrariness; but the same may be said of any tyrant. In January 1655, the duke of Savoy issued the Edict of Gastaldo, directing that his Waldensian subjects either vacate their homes or convert to Catholicism; and three months later he adhered resolutely to his decree by massacring those who refused.[25]

Like the Duke of Savoy, God does what he said he would do, 'but it is precisely his merciless adherence to the law that stands most in need of justification'.[26] The Waldensian massacre moved Milton to write Sonnet XV 'On the Late Massacre in Piedmont' in angry protest ('Avenge, O Lord, thy slaughtered saints'). Is it not possible that some note of angry protest creeps into his account of God's doings in *Paradise Lost*?

The declared purpose of Milton's epic is to 'justify the ways of God to men' (i 26). Many have thought this a presumptuous aim, and many have thought that Milton fails to achieve it. Most critics assume that the poem's success as a poem must depend upon the success of its theodicy, its justification of God. 'If one is left at the end in any doubt as to God's justice and love,' writes Alastair Fowler, 'the poem has failed, not on a single count, but altogether.'[27] Dennis Danielson agrees: 'If Milton presents a God who is wicked, or untruthful, or manipulative, or feeble, or unwise, then his epic poem must suffer accordingly.'[28] Not everyone sees it that way. 'The reason why the poem is so good', says William Empson, 'is that it makes God so bad.'[29] Like others before him, Empson sees Milton's God as arid, legalistic, tyrannical, and cruel, but he does not conclude that the poem is therefore bad. In Empson's view,

Milton deserves credit for making God wicked, since the God of Christianity is (for Empson) 'a wicked God'.[30] A God who kills Adam and Eve and all their descendants for eating an apple, and then takes 'rigid satisfaction' (iii 212) in the death (by torture) of his own Son, must be a merciless tyrant, Empson believes. Rejecting the old view that Milton made God bad 'by getting into muddles', Empson insists that Milton's God 'is merely the traditional Christian God'.[31] This brings Empson strangely close to C. S. Lewis, who had averred that 'Many of those who say that they dislike Milton's God only mean that they dislike God.'[32] Lewis and Empson are often seen as mighty opposites in the debate about Milton's God, and in some ways that is what they are. But they are in agreement as to what the debate is about.

Empson stands in the tradition of Blake and Shelley. Blake famously and notoriously declared that 'The reason Milton wrote in fetters when he wrote of Angels & God, and at liberty when of Devils & Hell, is because he was a true Poet and of the Devils party without knowing it.'[33] Shelley held that 'Milton's Devil as a moral being is . . . far superior to his God'.[34] Empson agrees that Satan is morally superior to God, but his emphasis differs from Shelley's. Shelley had thrilled to 'the energy and magnificence of the character of Satan'. Empson's prime concern is not with Satan, but God. His thesis is not that Satan is good but that God is bad. Miltonists often overlook this distinction. Some even call Empson a 'Satanist'. But Empson's case against God does not stand or fall with such case as he is willing to make for Satan. Empson does not applaud all of Satan's deeds. He concedes that Satan's character 'rots away' when he strikes at God through Adam and Eve, and he acknowledges that 'Milton felt a personal dislike for Satan'.[35] Empson never denies that Satan's plan is wicked. What he does deny is that God is innocent of its wickedness: 'Milton steadily drives home that the inmost counsel of God was the Fortunate Fall of man; however wicked Satan's plan may be, it is God's plan too.'[36]

This is a powerful argument and it deserves to be considered seriously. It threatens to circumvent Milton's theodicy, which is built on the 'free-will defence'. Milton claims that Adam and Eve fell by their own free will and so have no one to blame but themselves. God made them 'Sufficient to have stood, though free to fall' (iii 99). Empson's argument calls this freedom into question. A God who plans (not just plans around) man's Fall must be the author of sin – must, in Empson's terms, be 'wicked'. So does God plan the Fall? Many readers of *Paradise Lost* have thought that he does, and not all of them have thought the Fall 'Fortunate'. (We shall return in a moment to the question of a 'Fortunate Fall'.) The first and perhaps most serious obstacle that the 'free will defence' must face is the problem of God's foreknowledge. How can Adam and Eve be free when God foresees their every act and speaks of their Fall as a certainty even before it has happened (iii 93–7)? Milton addresses this problem in *De Doctrina Christiana*. He there draws a distinction between certainty and necessity. Because God has foreseen the Fall from all eternity, and because his foreknowledge is infallible, the Fall was always a certainty. But it was not necessitated by any divine decree. It was a free act in the moment of its occurrence. God foresaw the Fall, and permitted it, but he did not make it happen. He therefore has every right to hold Adam and Eve responsible for their disobedience. Milton goes out of his way to test this argument in the details of his poem. Several events and episodes in the poem tempt the reader with the disturbing possibility that God is actively working for man's ruin. To cite just a few instances: it is God who frees Satan from his chains in Hell (i 210–16); it is God who places the key to Hell in the hands of Satan's daughter Sin, even though he knows that she will let Satan out (ii 774–7); and it is God who prompts the good angels to release Satan when they have arrested him in Paradise (iv 995 f.). For many readers, this is enough to convict God. But the 'free-will defence' can answer these difficulties. So long as Adam and Eve are free to resist Satan's temptation, his act of tempting them does not necessitate their Fall. One might even argue that God aids and abets Satan's arrival in Paradise for the benign reason that he respects Adam and Eve's freedom, and does not want to censor their experience. Milton had adopted this line of argument in *Areopagitica*. Applying the principles of that pamphlet to *Paradise Lost*, one might argue that the temptation itself is good – or would have been if only Adam and Eve had not failed God's test.

So far so good, but the case is altered once we introduce the Fortunate Fall. In an influential article published in 1937, Arthur Lovejoy invoked the medieval notion of a *felix culpa* or Fortunate Fall to argue that Adam and Eve's sin is paradoxically a cause for celebration. Lovejoy sees Milton's God as working for the Fall all along. God wants humankind to fall so that he can then show his goodness by restoring us. Our final state will be even happier than that from which we fell. God contrives the Fall, then, but his motives are benign. Empson seizes on this argument and pushes it to its logical conclusion. If God contrives the Fall, he must be what Milton says he is not: the author of sin. The doctrine of the Fortunate Fall would place God in the awkward position of secretly wanting Adam and Eve to do what he tells them not to do, and condemns them for doing. Worse, the doctrine would make all of God's warnings hypocritical. In Book V God sends the angel Raphael to Paradise to warn Adam about Satan. On the face of it, God's intent is benign, but the Argument to Book V tells us that his real motive is 'to render man inexcusable'. Malevolent or not, this is Machiavellian.

Empson's view of God has not gone unanswered. Dennis Danielson in *Milton's Good God* (1982) challenges Empson's premises. Acknowledging that a Fortunate Fall would implicate God, Danielson questions Empson's assumption that the Fall is fortunate. The term 'Fortunate Fall' can be confusing, for critics often use it in a loose way to refer to what undoubtedly is a major theme of *Paradise Lost*: the bringing of good out of evil. This theme, implicit in the poem's opening (i 4–5), soon becomes explicit (i 159–68, 211–20), and Milton repeatedly returns to it (see for example ii 385–6, iv 110–12, vii 188–91). God brings good out of evil, but that is not enough to make the Fall fortunate. The Fall can be fortunate only if the good that comes from it could not have come about in any other way. The key question is whether God needs evil. Does God require Adam and Eve to eat the apple as a necessary pre-condition for the ultimate and supreme happiness of those few human beings who will enjoy it? (Most of us will of course be tormented for all eternity in Hell.) Many critics have seen evidence for a Fortunate Fall in the following lines, spoken by Adam when he hears about the Messiah's ultimate triumph:

O goodness infinite, goodness immense!
That all this good of evil shall produce,
And evil turn to good; more wonderful
Than that which by creation first brought forth
Light out of darkness! full of doubt I stand,

> Whether I should repent me now of sin
> By me done and occasioned, or rejoice
> Much more, that much more good thereof shall spring,
> To God more glory, more good will to men
> From God, and over wrath grace shall abound. (xii 469–78)

There is an ambiguity here. Does Adam's word 'more' ('more good', 'more glory', 'more good will') mean 'additional' or 'greater'? Adam is delighted to receive additional blessings, but he does not state unequivocally that he is better off for sinning. Even if we do put that construction on his words, it is significant that the angel Michael does not encourage him. Michael elsewhere applauds Adam for making the correct response (see for example xi 884, xii 79), but here he gives no sign of approval. One might expect more of a nudge if Milton were really concerned to argue 'that the inmost counsel of God was the Fortunate Fall of man' (Empson).

The notion of a fortunate fall can take many forms. Some Church Fathers saw the Fall as fortunate because it made possible our ascent to Heaven. Had Adam and Eve not eaten the apple (so the argument goes) they and their descendants would have lived for ever in the earthly Paradise. By disobeying God, Adam and Eve bring death into the world, but they also open the way to Heaven. Whatever other version of the Fortunate Fall Milton may or may not entertain, he certainly does not entertain this one. His God never intended that human beings stay for ever in the Garden of Eden. From the moment of their creation God intends that they should work their way up to Heaven 'under long obedience tried' (vii 159). Once they got there, earth would be 'changed to Heav'n, and Heav'n to earth,/ One Kingdom, joy and union without end' (vii 160–61). This plan remains unchanged after the Fall (xii 463–5), so the Fall cannot be a pre-condition for the plan. The one significant difference is that fallen man will be saved by the Incarnate Son of God. This enables Lovejoy to make a point that has convinced many: if the Fall 'had never occurred, the Incarnation and Redemption could never have occurred'.[37] But there is a problem with this. As Danielson points out, the Redemption and Incarnation are different things. The Incarnation is Christ's embodiment in human flesh. The Redemption is our deliverance from sin by Christ's sacrifice. The Redemption clearly presupposes a Fall. There would be no one to redeem had there not been a Fall. But the Incarnation might have occurred even in a sinless world. As Danielson observes, the Fall seems fortunate 'only when the Redemption is considered together with the Incarnation'.[38] Danielson finds hints in the poem that the Son of God might have become incarnate even without man's Fall. There is some theological precedent for this view. Duns Scotus had argued that Christ would have taken on human form even if angels and men had kept their blessed state.[39]

The beauty of Danielson's argument is that it frees God from the taint of working for the Fall. Despite Empson, Satan's wicked plan need not be God's plan too. Danielson shows that Empson's book is written against (one particular form of) a Calvinist God – a God who needs sin and actively works for it. This is ironic because Milton went to great lengths in *Paradise Lost* to refute Calvinist beliefs. But we should not suppose that Empson's argument is utterly discredited. Milton, Empson and Danielson agree about one thing: a God who decrees the Fall would be wicked. The question then becomes: has Milton created a Calvinist God in spite of himself? It is not enough for Milton simply to declare for free will. If he is truly to justify God's ways he must make his theodicy convincing in the poem. The question of free will clearly troubled Milton, and his anxiety sometimes infiltrates the poem in awkward ways. We feel it especially strongly when God plays the triple role of judge, jury and the accused. The problem is not just one of tone. In his anxiety to acquit himself, God sometimes says things that he could not possibly mean but which ring all too awkwardly true. Foreseeing Adam and Eve's Fall, he says:

> they themselves decreed
> Their own revolt, not I: if I foreknew,
> Foreknowledge had no influence on their fault,
> Which had no less proved certain unforeknown. (iii 116–19)

Critics usually paraphrase that last line as if it were a simple expression of Milton's belief that the Fall was foreknown but not foreordained. God no doubt intends such a statement, and he very nearly pulls it off in line 118. But then, in his eagerness to acquit himself, he asserts that the Fall was bound to happen anyway: 'Which had no less proved certain unforeknown'. This is a false step because it concedes the very point that Milton's theodicy exists to deny. We have seen that Milton draws a distinction between certainty and necessity. The Fall was always a certainty (since God foresaw it), but it was not necessitated by God's decree. If this argument is to work, the certainty of future events must be rooted in nothing other than God's foreknowledge. In the moment that we root the certainty of the Fall in something (anything) other than divine foreknowledge, the distinction between certainty and necessity breaks down. That is exactly what happens in the lines just quoted. In his haste to allay suspicion about his foreknowledge, God says that the Fall would have 'proved certain' even if he had not foreknown it. At one stroke this undoes Milton's theodicy and concedes that the Fall was necessitated. God does not mean to say this, but he says it.

The point is not to gloat over one of Milton's slips. The question is whether slips of this kind (and there are many in *Paradise Lost*) manifest an unconscious hostility toward the God that Milton claims to be justifying. Danielson shows that Empson is often overconfident in his theological pronouncements, but many parts of the poem remain troubling even after Danielson has illuminated them. One such is the speech in which God declares the Son to be Messiah and so provokes Satan's revolt:

> This day I have begot whom I declare
> My only Son, and on this holy hill
> Him have anointed, whom ye now behold
> At my right hand; your head I him appoint;
> And by myself have sworn to him shall bow
> All knees in Heav'n, and shall confess him Lord:
> Under his great vicegerent reign abide
> United as one individual soul
> For ever happy: him who disobeys
> Me disobeys, breaks union, and that day
> Cast out from God and blessèd vision, falls
> Into utter darkness, deep engulfed, his place
> Ordained without redemption, without end. (v 603–15)

These lines sound especially provocative to the modern reader, who is prone to give 'begot' its literal meaning and so conclude that the Son of God did not exist before this day. We know from *De Doctrina Christiana* i 5 and Milton's translation of Psalm 2 that 'begot' means 'made a king'. The Son of God is older than the angels, whom he created (v 835–40). But the lines are troubling even with this sense of 'begot'. Danielson (following a hint by Abdiel at v 842–3) infers that the Son is 'begotten' in the sense that he becomes an incarnate angel.[40] One would expect such an event to be a blessing of the angels. Lewis does hear God's lines as 'a compliment to the angels',[41] but God's edict does not sound like a compliment. It sounds like a threat. True, God knows that some angels will rebel and he wants to make the penalty clear so that no angel will be able to say that he wasn't warned. God's warning certainly is clear. But in giving it he imparts an unseasonable air of hostility and suspicion to what ought to be a joyous, festive occasion. One cannot blame God for knowing that some angels will rebel, but his speech is so aggressive as to excite the suspicion that he is deliberately provoking a rebellion. It is at moments like this that one has most sympathy with Blake, Shelley and Empson.

Innocence and Knowledge

God's threats are especially unseasonable when we consider that the as-yet-unfallen angels have never heard a threat before. When Michael encounters Satan on the battlefield he tells him that the word 'evil' was 'unknown till thy revolt, / Unnamed in Heav'n' (vi 262–3). It is impossible to imagine how words like 'disobeys' and 'breaks union' might sound to ears that have never heard 'evil'. It is no small tribute to Empson's acuteness that he should wonder whether Satan even understands God's vague hints about Hell.[42] We touch here on a difficult topic: Milton's representation of innocence. According to one extreme view, Adam and Eve would have to be fallen even to understand God's command not to eat from the tree of knowledge of good and evil. Milton never goes that far. His Adam and Eve know what is required of them. But they do not understand what is at stake. Recalling the prohibition, Adam is puzzled by one of its terms. He reminds Eve that God requires

From us no other service than to keep
This one, this easy charge, of all the trees
In Paradise that bear delicious fruit
So various, not to taste that only Tree
Of Knowledge, planted by the Tree of Life,

> So near grows death to life, whate'er death is,
> Some dreadful thing no doubt; for well thou know'st
> God hath pronounced it death to taste that Tree. (iv 420–27)

Adam knows that 'death' is something to be feared, but he does not know what it is. Milton captures his bewilderment in 'pronounced' which here means 'produced a vocal sound' as well as 'delivered a legal sentence'.

Adam's failure to comprehend 'death' invites closer scrutiny, for Adam was supposed to have instant knowledge of whatever he named. The scriptural source of this idea is Genesis 2.19, where Adam names the animals and 'whatsoever Adam called every living creature, that was the name thereof'. Recalling his naming of the animals in *Paradise Lost*, Adam says: 'I named them, as they passed, and understood / Their nature, with such knowledge God endued / My sudden apprehension' (viii 352–4). But Adam has no 'sudden apprehension' of 'death'. Eve is also at a loss to make sense of the word. The serpent turns her innocence to his advantage when he tells her not to fear death, 'whatever thing death be' (ix 695). This is a perversion of Adam's words, for Adam had at least recognized that death is 'dreadful'. The serpent implies that death is nothing to worry about.

In each of these instances Milton presents innocence as a state of blissful unacquaintance with evil. But there are other places in *Paradise Lost* where he has a different notion of what innocence is. At the beginning of Book V Eve tells Adam about a troubling dream she has had, in which she was prompted to eat the fruit. Not knowing that Satan has inspired the dream, Adam tries to comfort Eve:

> The trouble of thy thoughts this night in sleep
> Affects me equally; nor can I like
> This uncouth dream, of evil sprung I fear;
> Yet evil whence? In thee can harbour none,
> Created pure ...   (v 96–100)

>   yet be not sad.
> Evil into the mind of god or man
> May come and go, so unapproved, and leave
> No spot or blame behind.   (v 116–19)

It is odd that Adam should know so much about evil. The very word had been 'unnamed in Heav'n' until Satan's revolt. Adam when he speaks these lines has heard God name the tree of knowledge of good and evil (viii 323–4), but he knows nothing of Satan, and has had no experience of evil. The problem is not that Milton's picture of innocence is inherently absurd; the problem is that Milton presents two pictures of innocence. Both are philosophically respectable, but they coexist uneasily in the same poem. The Adam who recognizes and checks 'evil' in himself looks very different from the Adam who draws a blank with 'death'.

A related difficulty attends the meaning of the tree of knowledge. Lewis speaks for most critics when he says that 'the apple has no intrinsic magic' but is simply a pledge of man's obedience.[43] This is the standard Christian view, expressed by Augustine and countless others, and Milton adopts it in *Paradise Lost*. But he adopts it with a difference. While the apple brings Adam and Eve no *useful* knowledge, it does bring knowledge. We have seen that Eve has no answer to Satan's 'whatever thing death be' (ix 695). But once she eats the fruit she suddenly gains a new insight:

> what if God hath seen,
> And death ensue? then I shall be no more,
> And Adam wedded to another Eve,
> Shall live with her enjoying, I extinct. (ix 826–9)

Eve had no notion of death as extinction earlier in the poem. Can it be that the fruit has enlightened her? Some might think that Milton has merely slipped here, but it is more likely that he is being subtle. Eve's acquisition of knowledge is consistent with what God says about the fruit. Eve and Adam gain knowledge, but not of God's creation. They gain knowledge of the darkness into which creation falls when it is deprived of God's goodness. Saint Augustine had argued that evil has no real existence but is only the privation of good. Adam and Eve gain knowledge of privation. Put simply, they come to realize what it is that they have lost. As Adam puts it after the Fall:

> our eyes
> Opened we find indeed, and find we know
> Both good and evil, good lost, and evil got,
> Bad fruit of knowledge if this be to know,

> Which leaves us naked thus, of honour void,
> Of innocence, of faith, of purity. (ix 1070–75)

Even nakedness, once a living embodiment of 'complete / Perfections' (v 352–3), statelier than the pomp of kings, is now felt as shameful privation. Death is of course the greatest privation of all, so it is fitting that Eve should gain knowledge of that. Lewis oversimplifies when he says 'the apple has no intrinsic magic'. The word 'magic' is rhetorically convenient, but it does not do justice to Adam's lines, which are the more potent for their recognition that he and Eve have 'got' something by eating. The matter is complicated, for Eve's new understanding of 'death' is not complete. She imagines death to be extinction. The truth, for Milton, is darker than that, for 'death' includes 'the second death': eternal damnation.

Closely related to the problem of the tree's name is the question of whether one can know one's happiness in Paradise. Milton often implies that Adam and Eve lose their happiness in the moment they gain knowledge of it. On first waking into life, Adam says 'I . . . feel that I am happier than I know' (viii 282). Milton in his own voice counsels the sleeping Adam and Eve: 'O yet happiest if ye seek / No happier state, and know to know no more' (iv 774–5). Adam and Eve gain knowledge of their happiness when they lose it ('Bad fruit of knowledge if this be to know'). Statements like this imply that the innocent cannot know their bliss. But on the sixth day of Creation the angelic choir sings a hymn that ends with this blessing of mankind: 'thrice happy if they know / Their happiness, and persevere upright' (vii 631–2). A contradiction? *Paradise Lost* does have contradictions, some of which raise troubling questions about God. But this one might be resolvable. We have seen that God did not intend Adam and Eve to stay in Paradise for ever. Paradise is a place of (sometimes strenuous) trial where Adam and Eve grow and develop. Adam is put to the test when God pretends that he will not create a companion for him (viii 369f.). The newly-created Eve experiences danger and trial when she is attracted by her own reflection in a lake (iv 460f.). On these occasions Adam and Eve grow in knowledge *and* happiness. In the event, they know their happiness by losing it. But had they remained obedient they might have continued to grow in knowledge and happiness until they finally achieved a happy self-knowledge that did not involve privation.

Allusion and Intertextuality

The scholarly tradition of noting Milton's biblical and classical allusions began in 1695 with the publication of Patrick Hume's commentary on *Paradise Lost*. Each new annotated edition is indebted to its predecessors, but it would be a mistake to suppose that all allusions in the editorial tradition are the straightforward accumulation of centuries of disinterested enquiry. Editors inevitably engage in an interpretative act when they decide what does or does not count as an allusion. Milton's editors have tended to privilege those source texts that support the poem's orthodox morality. Allusions that would introduce unwanted complications have, for the most part, been suppressed or explained away. The impression has therefore arisen that Milton's allusions are dry, pedantic, scholarly and safe. This is a pity, for *Paradise Lost* draws much of its power from intertextual relationships that are disquieting, unexpected, or unsafe.

An example of what I mean may be found when Satan, spying on Adam and Eve, utters this in a soliloquy:

> Hell shall unfold,
> To entertain you two, her widest gates,
> And send forth all her kings; there will be room,
> Not like these narrow limits, to receive
> Your numerous offspring.   (iv 381–4)

Most critics believe that Satan is being malevolent. Editors usually (and quite rightly) hear an allusion to Isaiah's prophecy of the Fall of Babylon: 'Hell from beneath is moved for thee to meet thee at thy coming: it stirreth up the dead for thee, even all the chief ones of the earth; it hath raised up from their thrones all the kings of the nations' (Isaiah 14.9). This makes Satan sound cruelly ironic, but ironic statements (as Empson always maintained) have no point unless they are true, to some degree, in both senses. Empson notoriously believed that Satan was sincere in offering Adam and Eve high honour in Hell. He points out that the devils are able to live there 'comfortably', so Satan might not know that Hell will be a place of excruciating torture for humans. He concludes that the irony 'belongs only to the God who made Hell'.[44]

Miltonists usually dismiss Empson's reading, but it draws some support from a second possible allusion – one that editors have not noted. If Satan echoes Isaiah, he also echoes Pluto in Claudian's *De Raptu Proserpinae* (*The Rape of Proserpine*). This late classical Latin poem (a favourite of Milton's) tells the familiar story of how Pluto, god of the underworld, abducted the maiden goddess Proserpine while she was gathering flowers in the fair field of Henna in Sicily. As the earth closes over them, Pluto tries to console Proserpine by describing the honours that await her as Queen of Hades. He tells her not to miss the earth, for Hades is roomy ('*immensum*') and even has its own sun and stars. This is close to Satan's contrast between earth's 'narrow limits' and Hell's 'room'. Pluto concludes: '*sub tua purpurei venient vestigia reges*', 'To thy feet shall come purple-robed kings' (ii 300). This is as close to 'send forth all her kings' as the verse from Isaiah is. Both possible sources are appropriate to the moment, but they call forth different responses. The biblical allusion makes Satan seem cruel; the classical one suggests that he is capable of finer feelings even when he knowingly commits a wrong. An allusion to Claudian would not be far-fetched. Earlier in the same book Milton had likened Paradise to

> that fair field
> Of Enna, where Prosérpine gath'ring flow'rs
> Herself a fairer flow'r by gloomy Dis
> Was gathered. (iv 268–71)

After this beautiful and memorable simile, it takes only a nudge to make us see Satan as Pluto (Dis) and Eve as Proserpine. Empson pushes Satan's soliloquy too far in the direction of generosity, but his intuition shows real insight. To call Satan's speech 'sarcastic', as many critics have done, is to coarsen the poem.

There is admittedly a danger of subjectivity with questions like this. Not everyone will agree about the pertinence of every supposed allusion. But allusion is in this respect no different from any other effect in poetry. The objection that allusions are subjective in any case cuts both ways. If awkward or troubling allusions are vulnerable to this objection, so too are safe, traditional ones. It is not the case that safe allusions are always more obvious or accessible than unsafe ones. Sometimes it is the unwelcome or disturbing allusion that lies more readily to hand. In Book IV Milton describes Adam and Eve's embrace:

> half her swelling breast
> Naked met his under the flowing gold
> Of her loose tresses hid: he in delight
> Both of her beauty and submissive charms
> Smiled with superior love, as Jupiter
> On Juno smiles, when he impregns the clouds
> That shed May flowers.   (iv 495–501)

'Impregns the clouds': Roy Flannagan bravely admits that this may 'jar' on 'some readers', but then he explains the difficulty away by invoking an allegorical tradition in which Jupiter was the aether and Juno the air.[45] Fowler cites Natale Conti's *Mythologiae* (1616), which tells how Jupiter makes rain by agitating the air (Juno's realm). This is pertinent, but it does not account for Milton's graphic sexual image. A more obvious source (Conti himself cites it) is Hera's seduction of Zeus in the *Iliad*:

> the son of Kronos caught his wife in his arms. There
> underneath them the divine earth broke into young, fresh
> grass, and into dewy clover, crocus and hyacinth
> so thick and soft it held the hard ground deep away from them.
> There they lay down together and drew about them a golden
> wonderful cloud, and from it the glimmering dew descended.
>
> (xiv 346–51)[46]

Like Milton, Homer portrays an erotic moment involving Zeus (Jupiter), Hera (Juno) and a cloud. But Milton's threesome is different from Homer's. As Homer tells the story, Zeus gathers a cloud so that he and Hera can secretly make love to *each other* inside it. Milton's Jupiter 'smiles' at Juno while he makes love to 'the clouds'. What could Milton have been thinking of? There is a mythical precedent for cloudy coitus. Ixion, the would-be seducer of Juno, sired the monstrous race of centaurs on a cloud that Jupiter formed in Juno's shape. Jupiter then bound Ixion to a fiery wheel in Tartarus. In Milton it is Jupiter himself, not his would-be cuckolder, who 'impregns the clouds', but the proximity of that phrase to 'Juno' still strongly suggests Ixion. Other poems by Milton trigger an allusion to Ixion with less than this. The unfinished poem 'The Passion' falters and dies when Milton likens himself to one who has 'got a race of mourners on some pregnant cloud' (56). In

Paradise Regained Jesus scorns pagan philosophy as Wisdom's 'false resemblance . . . / An empty cloud' (iv 320–21). Editors readily direct readers to Ixion in these cases, but they are silent about him in the *Paradise Lost* simile. One can understand this reticence. Adam and Eve's embrace is one of their most tender moments. The intrusion of Ixion's cloud into this domestic scene would detract from the tenderness. Could Milton have really intended the allusion?

It would not be alien to his imagination. He had explicitly compared Eve to Ixion's cloud in his divorce pamphlet *Tetrachordon* (1645). He there insists that God had wholly benign motives for creating Eve. To suppose otherwise would be blasphemous:

Nay such an unbounteous giver we should make him, as in the fables *Jupiter* was to *Ixion*, giving him a *cloud* instead of *Juno*, giving him a monstrous issue by her, the breed of *Centaures* a neglected and unlov'd race, the fruits of a delusive mariage, and lastly giving him her with a damnation to that wheele in hell, from a life thrown into the midst of temptations and disorders.[47]

The whole point of this allusion is that we should *not* think of Eve as a cloud-Juno, but there is a note of self-doubt amidst the earnest protestations. Milton here writes as if the Fall had never happened. It is especially odd that he should write the words 'temptations', 'damnation' and 'fruits' as if they had no relevance for Adam and Eve. What, then, are we to make of the *Paradise Lost* simile? Does Milton once again evoke Ixion in order to exclude him? Does the substitution of 'May flowers' for centaurs imply that Adam has nothing to fear from *this* cloud-Juno? Perhaps, but it is still disconcerting that Jupiter's affections should wander from 'Juno' to 'clouds' in the very moment that Adam kisses Eve. It is not an editor's business to interpret allusions, but I have, in this edition, made a conscious effort not to exclude or discount allusions that would raise awkward or troubling questions.

From the foregoing examples it should be clear that the noting of allusions is a difficult and delicate task. This is especially true of those similes which are borrowed from earlier epics, and so enter Milton's poem with a cluster of ready-made associations. At the end of Book IV Milton likens the good angels (who are preparing to fight Satan) to wind-tossed corn:

> th' angelic squadron bright
> Turned fiery red, sharp'ning in moonèd horns
> Their phalanx, and began to hem him round
> With ported spears, as thick as when a field
> Of Ceres ripe for harvest waving bends
> Her bearded grove of ears, which way the wind
> Sways them; the careful ploughman doubting stands
> Lest on the threshing floor his hopeful sheaves
> Prove chaff. (iv 977–85)

'It certainly makes the good angels look weak', Empson remarks of this simile[48] – and epic precedent supports his view. Homer, Apollonius Rhodius, Ariosto and Tasso all compare armed warriors to wind-tossed grain, and in every case the army so described is demoralized, routed, or about to be cut down. Homer uses the simile of the Greeks when they flee to their ships:

> As when the west wind moves across the grain deep standing,
> boisterously, and shakes and sweeps it till the tassels lean, so
> all of that assembly was shaken, and the men in tumult
> swept to the ships. (*Iliad* ii 147–50)

Milton's angels intend to stand and fight, but the words 'which way the wind / Sways them' do not bode well for their prowess. A seventeenth-century reader might recall that Tasso had used the simile of wind and cornfield to describe Rinaldo cutting down the pagan host. Milton's wording recalls Edward Fairfax's translation (1600):

> He brake their pikes, and brake their close array,
> Entred their battaile, feld them downe around,
> So winde or tempest with impetious sway
> The eares of ripened corn strikes flat to ground. (xx 60)

Editors have been reluctant to acknowledge these parallels. Fowler notes that the 'comparison of an excited army to wind-stirred corn is Homeric', and (in his 1998 edition) he admits that Homer's simile implies 'defeatism'. But even Fowler prefers not to dwell on the implications. He locates the heart of Milton's simile not in the cornfield but the threshing-floor. Noting that this was a biblical metaphor for divine judgement, Fowler pertinently cites Jeremiah 51. 33: 'Babylon is like a threshingfloor, it is time to thresh her: yet a little while, and the time of her harvest shall come'. From this, Fowler concludes that God as ploughman 'is *careful* that the final judgement 'should not be premature'. Attractive at first sight, this reading encounters an obstacle in 'ripe for harvest'. These words clearly state that the time of reckoning is now, not later. Pursuing the notion of judgement, Flannagan sees an allusion to Matthew 3. 12 where John the Baptist prophesies Christ's final separation of the wheat from the chaff. Milton employs exactly this image in his translation of Psalm 1. 4 where 'the wicked' are 'as chaff which fanned/The wind drives'. But we still face the difficulty that Milton has likened the *good* angels to 'a field/Of Ceres', so it is they, not Satan, who are in danger of becoming chaff.

Milton's allusions often work like this. Much as we editors would like to regulate them, they escape our control. My own candidate for a safe source (were I forced to choose one), would be Phineas Fletcher's *The Locusts* (1627). Like Milton, Fletcher is describing Satan, who has just broken out of Hell, accompanied by a host of devils. These descend on our world as when the South wind

> sweeps with his dropping beard
> The ayer, earth, and Ocean; downe he flings
> The laden trees, the Plowmans hopes new-eard
> Swimme on the playne.   (ii 40)

The connection with Milton is fortified by the ploughman, who here represents the peaceful world threatened by Satan's invasion. Critics have long debated whether Milton's ploughman is God or Satan, but I suspect that Milton intended him to have much the same significance as Fletcher's. This does not mean that Fletcher's simile drives all subversive possibilities from Milton's. Whatever Milton's conscious intentions, the classical and biblical precedents complicate his simile in ways that both trouble and enrich it. Throughout this edition I have endeavoured to annotate Milton's allusions in a way that opens rather than closes a reader's interpretative choice. I do this not because I am determined on indeterminacy, but because I want to provide readers with the materials that will enable them to determine interpretative matters for themselves.

Throughout my notes I assume that Milton wrote *De Doctrina Christiana*, even though William B. Hunter has argued that the traditional ascription of that work to Milton is unsafe.[49] Although

I am unpersuaded by Hunter's arguments, I value them both for their own sake and for the excellent replies they have elicited from (among others) Christopher Hill, Maurice Kelley, John Shawcross, Gordon Campbell and Barbara Lewalski.[50]

In preparing this edition I have received valuable help and guidance from many learned colleagues, as well as from graduate and undergraduate students at the University of Western Ontario. I owe a special debt to Gordon Campbell, John Creaser, Roy Flannagan and Christopher Ricks, both for their own work as editors and for their advice on numerous points of detail. I have also received generous assistance from Christopher Brown, Gardner Campbell, Dennis Danielson, Stephen Fallon, Richard Green, John Hale, the late Jeremy Maule, Diane McColley, Earl Miner, Alan Rudrum and John Rumrich. I much regret that in preparing my text and notes I did not have the benefit of the second edition of Alastair Fowler's Longman Annotated English Poets *Paradise Lost* (1998). My text and notes are taken from my Penguin English Poets edition of Milton's *Complete Poems*, which was published a few weeks before Fowler's new edition. My work has been assisted by a grant from the Social Sciences and Research Council of Canada. To the Council I extend my sincerest thanks.

Notes

1. John Milton, *Complete Prose Works*, ed. Don M. Wolfe *et al.* 8 vols (Yale University Press: New Haven, Connecticut, 1953–84), 1:812–14.
2. Ibid., p. 812.
3. *The Early Lives of Milton*, ed. Helen Darbishire (Constable: London, 1932), p. 33. Darbishire erroneously attributes this anonymous Life to Milton's nephew, John Phillips.
4. *Ibid.*, p. 72.
5. *Ibid.*, p. 13.
6. Helen Gardner, *A Reading of 'Paradise Lost'* (Oxford University Press: Oxford, 1965), 31.
7. John Milton, *Complete Prose Works*, 8:554, 560.
8. The angel Raphael is covered by 'mantling' wings (v 277–87), but he wears no clothes. After the Fall, Michael puts off 'his shape celestial' and visits Adam 'as man / Clad to meet man' (xi 239–40).
9. Christopher Marlowe, *The Complete Poems and Translations*, ed. Stephen Orgel (Penguin: Harmondsworth, 1971).

10. David Lee Miller, 'The Death of the Modern: Gender and Desire in *Hero and Leander*', in *South Atlantic Quarterly* 88 (Fall 1989), 757–87 (pp. 766–7).

11. Milton repeatedly opposes standing to falling in *Paradise Lost*. To cite just a few instances: 'Freely they stood who stood, and fell who fell' (iii 102), 'other Powers as great / Fell not, but stand' (iv 63–4), 'stand fast; to stand or fall / Free in thine own arbitrament it lies' (viii 640–41).

12. Patrick Morrah, *1660: the Year of Restoration* (Chatto & Windus: London, 1960), p. 150. The following description of Charles's procession is condensed from pp. 150–53 of Morrah's book.

13. Torquato Tasso, *Discourses on the Heroic Poem*, trans. Mariella Cavalchini and Irene Samuel (Clarendon Press: Oxford, 1973), 21.

14. Samuel Johnson, *Lives of the English Poets*, ed. G. B. Hill, 3 vols. (Octagon: New York, New York, 1967), vol. 1, p. 177.

15. Walter Clyde Curry, *Milton's Ontology Cosmogony and Physics* (University of Kentucky Press: Lexington, Kentucky, 1957), p. 77, p. 145.

16. John P. Rumrich defends Chaos in Chapter 6 of *Milton Unbound* (Cambridge University Press: Cambridge, 1996), where he employs both of the arguments summarized here. Although I find his argument unpersuasive, it clarifies the issues with admirable eloquence and precision.

17. George Chapman, *The Shadow of Night* (*Hymnus in Noctem* 73–4), in *The Poems of George Chapman*, ed. Phyllis Brooks Bartlett (Oxford University Press: London, 1941), p. 21.

18. Regina M. Schwartz, *Remembering and Repeating: Biblical Creation in 'Paradise Lost'* (Cambridge University Press: Cambridge, 1988), p. 19.

19. C. S. Lewis, *The Discarded Image* (Cambridge University Press: Cambridge, 1964), pp. 111–12.

20. Edward Harrison, *Darkness at Night: a Riddle of the Universe* (Harvard University Press: Cambridge, Massachusetts, 1987), p. 42.

21. C. S. Lewis, *A Preface to 'Paradise Lost'* (Oxford University Press: Oxford, 1942), p. 73.

22. See for example Stevie Davies, *Images of Kingship in 'Paradise Lost': Milton's Politics and Christian Liberty* (University of Missouri Press, Columbia, Missouri, 1983), p. 162.

23. Robert Fallon, *Divided Empire: Milton's Political Imagery* (Pennsylvania State University Press: University Park, Pennsylvania, 1995), p. 27.

24. See for example Joan Bennett, *Reviving Liberty: Radical Christian Humanism in Milton's Great Poems* (Harvard University Press: Cambridge, Massachusetts, 1989), p. 9, p. 60.

25. Robert Fallon, *Divided Empire: Milton's Political Imagery* pp. 33–34.

26. *Ibid.*, p. 34.

27. *John Milton: 'Paradise Lost'*, ed. Alastair Fowler, second edition (Longman: London, 1998), p. 39.

28. Dennis Danielson, *Milton's Good God* (Cambridge University Press: Cambridge, 1982), p. ix

29. William Empson, *Milton's God* (Cambridge University Press: Cambridge, 1961), revised edition (1981), p. 13.

30. *Ibid.*, p. 11.

31. *Ibid.*, p. 12, p. 25.

32. C. S. Lewis, *A Preface to 'Paradise Lost'*, p. 130.

33. William Blake, *The Marriage of Heaven and Hell* (1793), in *The Complete Poetry and Prose of William Blake*, ed. David V. Erdman (1965), revised edition (University of California Press: Berkley, California, 1982), p. 35.

34. Shelley wrote these words for his *Essay on the Devil and Devils* (1819) and repeated them verbatim in *A Defence of Poetry* (1821). See *Shelley's Prose*, ed. David Lee Clark (New Amsterdam: New York, 1988), p. 267, p. 290.

35. William Empson, *Milton's God*, p. 44.

36. *Ibid.*, p. 39.

37. A. O. Lovejoy, 'Milton and the Paradox of the Fortunate Fall', *ELH* 4 (1937), repeated in *Critical Essays on Milton from 'ELH'* (Johns Hopkins Press: Baltimore, Maryland, 1969), pp. 163–81.

38. Dennis Danielson, *Milton's Good God*, p. 215.

39. *Ibid.*, pp. 215–16.

40. *Ibid.*, p. 223.

41. C. S. Lewis *A Preface to 'Paradise Lost'*, p. 96.

42. William Empson, *Milton's God*, p. 158.

43. C.S. Lewis *A Preface to 'Paradise Lost'*, p. 69.

44. William Empson *Milton's God*, p. 68. Empson develops the point in all three of his major works on Milton. See *Some Versions of Pastoral* (Chatto & Windus: London, 1935) p. 168, and *The Structure of Complex Words* (Chatto & Windus: London, 1951) p. 103.

45. Roy Flannagan, ed., *The Riverside Milton* (Houghton Mifflin: Boston, Massachusetts, 1998), p. 457.

46. *The Iliad of Homer*, trans. Richmond Lattimore (University of Chicago Press: Chicago, Illinois, 1951).

47. John Milton, *Complete Prose Works*, 2:597–8.

48. William Empson *Some Versions of Pastoral* (1935) p. 172.

49. Hunter makes his case against Milton's authorship of *De Doctrina Christiana* in *SEL* 32 (1992), pp. 129–42; *SEL* 33 (1994), pp. 191–207; *SEL* 34 (1994), pp. 195–203; and in *Visitation Unimplor'd: Milton and the Authorship of 'De Doctrina Christiana'* Duquesne University Press: Pittsburgh, Pennsylvania, 1998).

50. See Christopher Hill in *SEL* 34 (1994), pp. 165–93; Maurice Kelley in *SEL* 34 (1994), pp. 195–203; John Shawcross in *SEL* 32 (1992), pp. 155–62; Gordon Campbell *et al.* in *MQ* 31 (1997), pp. 67–119; and Barbara Lewalski in *SEL* 32 (1992), pp. 143–54 and *MS* 36 (1998), pp. 203–28.

TABLE OF DATES

Unless otherwise stated, Milton's works are listed by date of publication.

1608 (9 December) M. born in his father's house, Bread Street, Cheapside, London.

1615 (24 November) Brother Christopher born.

1620 (?) Enters St Paul's School. Friendship with Charles Diodati begins. Thomas Young begins to tutor M. at home at about this time.

1625 (12 February) Matriculates at Christ's College, Cambridge. March: Charles I becomes King.

1626 Probably rusticated (suspended) from Cambridge for part of the Lent term.

1629 (March) BA degree. December: writes *On the Morning of Christ's Nativity*.

1632 *On Shakespeare* published in second Shakespeare folio. July: MA degree.

1632–8 Life of scholarly retirement at family homes in Hammersmith and Horton.

1633 William Laud becomes Archbishop of Canterbury.

1634 (29 September) *A Masque* performed at Ludlow Castle.

1637 *A Masque* published. 3 April: mother dies. 30 June: Bastwick, Burton and Prynne lose their ears for writing anti-prelatical pamphlets. They are confined in prison ships on the Irish Sea throughout the autumn. 10 August: M.'s classmate Edward King drowns on the Irish Sea. November: writes *Lycidas*.

1638 (April)–1639 (August) Continental tour.

1638 *Lycidas* published in a volume of elegies for Edward King. August: Charles Diodati dies.

1639 (March) War with Scotland (First Bishops' War).

1639–40 Settles in London where he takes pupils, including his nephews Edward and John Phillips.

1640 (August) Second Bishops' War. 3 November: Long Parliament convened. Laud and Strafford impeached.

1641 Publication of first anti-prelatical pamphlets: *Of Reformation, Of Prelatical Episcopacy, Animadversions upon the Remonstrant's Defence.* Rebellion in Ireland.

1642 More anti-prelatical pamphlets: *The Reason of Church Government, An Apology for Smectymnuus.* May–June: marries Mary Powell, who left him a month or two later. 22 August: Civil War begins.

1643 *The Doctrine and Discipline of Divorce* (first edition).

1644 (February) *The Doctrine and Discipline of Divorce* (second edition). Thomas Young, M.'s old tutor, warns Parliament against advocates of 'digamy'. June: *Of Education.* August: *Judgement of Martin Bucer Concerning Divorce.* Herbert Palmer denounces M. in sermon before Parliament. Further attacks from the Stationers' Company, from Prynne and other Presbyterians. November: *Areopagitica.* December: M. summoned before the House of Lords, but soon dismissed.

1645 *Tetrachordon* and *Colasterion* published. June: Cromwell's New Model Army victorious at Naseby. July or August: M.'s wife returns. September(?): moves to a larger house in the Barbican.

1646 (January) *Poems of Mr. John Milton* published (dated 1645). 29 July: daughter Anne born.

1647 (13 March) Father dies.

1648 (25 October) Daughter Mary born. 6 December: Colonel Pride's Purge of Long Parliament.

1649 (30 January) Charles I executed. *Eikon Basilike* (then given out as by the King) published one week later. 13 February: *The Tenure of Kings and Magistrates.* March: M. appointed Secretary for Foreign Tongues by the Council of State. 11 May: Salmasius's *Defensio Regia* appears in England. 16 May: *Observations on the Articles of Peace.* 6 October: *Eikonoklastes* (M.'s answer to *Eikon Basilike*).

1651 (24 February) *Pro Populo Anglicano Defensio* (M.'s answer to Salmasius). 16 March: son John born.

1652 Becomes totally blind. 2 May: daughter Deborah born. Wife dies three days later. June: son John dies.

1653 (20 April) Cromwell forcibly dissolves Rump Parliament.

3 September: Salmasius dies. 12 December: dissolution of Nominated Parliament. Cromwell becomes Lord Protector.

1654 (30 May) *Defensio Secunda*.

1655 (8 August) *Defensio Pro Se*.

1656 (12 November) Marries Katherine Woodcock.

1657 (19 October) Daughter Katherine born.

1658 (3 February) Wife dies. 17 March: daughter Katherine dies. 3 September: Oliver Cromwell dies.

1659 (16 February) *A Treatise of Civil Power*. August: *Considerations Touching the Likeliest Means to Remove Hirelings out of the Church*. May: Richard Cromwell abdicates.

1660 (3 March) *Ready and Easy Way to Establish a Free Commonwealth*. April: *Brief Notes upon a Late Sermon*. May: M. goes into hiding in a friend's house in Bartholomew Close. Charles II enters London in triumph. August: M.'s books burned by hangman, but M. is exempted from the death-list. October: M. arrested and imprisoned until December.

1662 Sir Henry Vane executed. M.'s sonnet to Vane published.

1663 (24 February) Marries Elizabeth Minshull. Moves to a house in Artillery Walk, Bunhill Fields.

1665 M. takes house in Chalfont St Giles to escape the plague.

1666 Great Fire of London.

1667 *Paradise Lost* published in a ten-book version.

1670 *The History of Britain* published.

1671 *Paradise Regained* and *Samson Agonistes* published.

1673 *Of True Religion* published. Revised and enlarged edition of *Poems* (1645) published.

1674 Second (twelve-book) edition of *Paradise Lost*. M. died on or about 8 November, and was buried on 12 November in St Giles, Cripplegate.

FURTHER READING

Editions

Richard Bentley, *Milton's 'Paradise Lost'*, 1732.

Douglas Bush, *Milton: Poetical Works*, Oxford University Press, 1966.

Gordon Campbell, *John Milton: Complete English Poems, Of Education, Areopagitica*, Dent, 1990.

John Carey and Alastair Fowler, *Poems of John Milton*, Longman, 1968; revised 1980.

Scott Elledge, *John Milton: 'Paradise Lost'*, Norton, 1975; 2nd edn, 1993.

Roy Flannagan, *John Milton: 'Paradise Lost'*, Macmillan, 1993.

——, *The Riverside Milton*, Houghton Mifflin, 1998.

Harris F. Fletcher, *Milton's Complete Poetical Works in Photographic Facsimile*, 4 vols., University of Illinois Press, 1943–8.

Alastair Fowler, *John Milton: Paradise Lost*; 2nd edn, Longman, 1998.

Merritt Y. Hughes, *John Milton: Complete Poems and Major Prose*, Odyssey, 1957.

P[atrick] H[ume], *Annotations on Milton's 'Paradise Lost'*, 1695.

David Masson, *The Poetical Works of John Milton*, 3 vols., 1893.

Thomas Newton, *'Paradise Lost': a Poem in Twelve Books*, 1749.

Stephen Orgel and Jonathan Goldberg, *The Oxford Authors: John Milton*, Oxford University Press, 1990.

Zachary Pearce, *A Review of the Text of 'Paradise Lost'*, 1733.

Jonathan Richardson, sen. and jun., *Explanatory Notes on 'Paradise Lost'*, 1734.

Christopher Ricks, *John Milton: 'Paradise Lost' and 'Paradise Regained'*, Signet Classics, 1968.

John T. Shawcross, *The Complete Poetry of John Milton*, Anchor-Doubleday, 1791.

Don M. Wolfe (general ed.), *The Complete Prose Works of John Milton*, Yale University Press, 1953–82.

Biographies

Cedric Brown, *John Milton: a Literary Life*, St Martin's Press, 1995.

Helen Darbishire (ed.), *The Early Lives of Milton*, Constable, 1932; repr. Scholarly Press, 1972.

Barbara Lewalski, *The Life of John Milton: a Critical Biography*, Basil Blackwell, 2000.

David Masson, *The Life of John Milton: Narrated in Connexion with the Political, Ecclesiastical, and Literary History of His Time*, 7 vols., Macmillan, 1859–94.

William Riley Parker, *Milton: a Biography*, 2 vols., revised version, ed. Gordon Campbell, Oxford University Press, 1996.

Critical Studies

Sharon Achinstein, *Milton and the Revolutionary Reader*, Princeton University Press, 1994.

Robert M. Adams, *Ikon: John Milton and the Modern Critics*, Cornell University Press, 1955.

Don Cameron Allen, *The Harmonious Vision: Studies in Milton's Poetry*, Johns Hopkins Press, 1954.

Michael Bauman, *Milton's Arianism*, Lang, 1987.

Joan Bennett, *Reviving Liberty: Radical Christian Humanism in Milton's Great Poems*, Harvard University Press, 1989.

Francis C. Blessington, *'Paradise Lost' and the Classical Epic*, Routledge and Kegan Paul, 1979.

——, *'Paradise Lost': Ideal and Tragic Epic*, Twayne Publishers, 1988.

John B. Broadbent, *Some Graver Subject*, Chatto and Windus, 1960.

Dennis Burden, *The Logical Epic: a Study of the Argument of 'Paradise Lost'*, Harvard University Press, 1967.

Colin Burrow, *Epic Romance: Homer to Milton*, Clarendon Press, 1993.

Georgia Christopher, *Milton and the Science of the Saints*, Princeton University Press, 1982.

Thomas N. Corns, *Milton's Language*, Basil Blackwell, 1990.

——, ed., *A Companion to Milton*, Basil Blackwell, 2001.

John Creaser, 'Editorial Problems in Milton', *Review of English Studies* n.s. 34 (1983), 279–303 and 35 (1984), 45–60.

Dennis Danielson, *Milton's Good God*, Cambridge University Press, 1982.

——, 'Through the Telescope of Typology: What Adam Should Have Done', *Milton Quarterly* 23 (1989), pp.121-7.

——, ed., *The Cambridge Companion to Milton*, Cambridge University Press, 1989.

——, ed., *The Cambridge Companion to Milton*, Second Edition, Cambridge University Press, 1999.

Stevie Davies, *Images of Kingship in 'Paradise Lost': Milton's Politics and Christian Liberty*, University of Missouri Press, 1983.

——, *Milton*, Harvester Wheatsheaf, 1991.

Stephen B. Dobranski and John P. Rumrich, eds., *Milton and Heresy*, Cambridge University Press, 1998.

Richard J. DuRocher, *Milton and Ovid*, Cornell University Press, 1985.

——, *Milton among the Romans: the Pedagogy and Influence of Milton's Latin Curriculum*, Duquesne Univeristy Press, 2001.

William Empson, *Milton's God*, Chatto & Windus, 1961, rev. edn 1965.

——, *Some Versions of Pastoral*, Chatto & Windus, 1935.

J. Martin Evans, *'Paradise Lost' and the Genesis Tradition*, Clarendon Press, 1968.

——, *Milton's Imperial Epic: 'Paradise Lost' and the Discourse of Colonialism*, Cornell University Press, 1996.

Robert Thomas Fallon, *Captain or Colonel: The Soldier in Milton's Life and Art*, University of Missouri Press, 1984.

——, *Milton in Government*, Pennsylvania State University Press, 1993.

——, *Divided Empire: Milton's Political Imagery*, Pennsylvania State University Press, 1995.

Stephen M. Fallon, *Milton among the Philosophers*, Cornell University Press, 1991.

Stanley Eugene Fish, *Surprised by Sin: the Reader in 'Paradise Lost'*, St Martin's Press, 1967; 2nd edn, Harvard University Press, 1997.

Northrop Frye, *The Return of Eden: Five Essays on Milton's Epics*, University of Toronto Press, 1965.

Roland Mushat Frye, *Milton's Imagery and the Visual Arts: Iconographic Tradition in the Epic Poems*, Princeton University Press, 1978.

Helen Gardner, *A Reading of 'Paradise Lost'*, Oxford University Press, 1965.

Dustin Griffin, *Regaining Paradise: Milton and the Eighteenth Century*, Cambridge University Press, 1986.

Marshall Grossman, *Authors to Themselves: Milton and the Revelation of History*, Cambridge University Press, 1987.

John K. Hale, *Milton's Languages: the Impact of Multilingualism on Style*, Cambridge University Press, 1997.

Dayton Haskin, *Milton's Burden of Interpretation*, University of Pennsylvania Press, 1994.

Christopher Hill, *Milton and the English Revolution*, Faber and Faber, 1977.

William B. Hunter, *The Descent of Urania: Studies in Milton, 1946–1988*, Bucknell University Press, 1989.

——, 'Milton's Arianism Reconsidered', in *Bright Essence: Studies in Milton's Theology*, ed. William B. Hunter, C. A. Patrides and J. H. Adamson, University of Utah Press, 1971.

Maurice Kelley, *This Great Argument: a Study of Milton's 'De Doctrina Christiana' as a Gloss upon 'Paradise Lost'*, Princeton University Press, 1941.

William Kerrigan, *The Sacred Complex: on the Psychogenesis of 'Paradise Lost'*, Harvard University Press, 1983.

Watson Kirkconnell, *The Celestial Cycle: the Theme of 'Paradise Lost' in World Literature with Translations of the Major Analogues*, University of Toronto Press, 1952.

Edward Le Comte, *Milton and Sex*, Columbia University Press, 1978.

John Leonard, *Naming in Paradise: Milton and the Language of Adam and Eve*, Clarendon Press, 1990.

Barbara K. Lewalski, *'Paradise Lost' and the Rhetoric of Literary Forms*, Princeton University Press, 1985.

C. S. Lewis, *A Preface to 'Paradise Lost'*, Oxford University Press, 1942.

Michael Lieb, *Poetics of the Holy: a Reading of 'Paradise Lost'*, University of North Carolina Press, 1981.

——, *Milton and the Culture of Violence*, Cornell University Press, 1994.

David Loewenstein, *Milton and the Drama of History*, Cambridge University Press, 1990.

——, *Milton: 'Paradise Lost'*, Cambridge University Press, 1993.

Isabel MacCaffrey, *'Paradise Lost' as Myth*, Harvard University Press, 1959.

Hugh MacCallum, *Milton and the Sons of God*, University of Toronto Press, 1986.

Harinder S. Marjara, *Contemplation of Created Things: Science in 'Paradise Lost'*, University of Toronto Press, 1992.

Charles Martindale, *John Milton and the Transformation of Ancient Epic*, Barnes & Noble, 1986.

Diane K. McColley, *Milton's Eve*, University of Illinois Press, 1983.

——, *A Gust for Paradise: Milton's Eden and the Visual Arts*, University of Illinois Press, 1993.

R. G. Moyles, *The Text of 'Paradise Lost': a Study in Editorial Procedure*, University of Toronto Press, 1985.

John Mulryan, *Through a Glass Darkly: Milton's Reinvention of the Mythological Tradition*, Duquesne University Press, 1996.

David Norbrook, *Writing the English Republic: Poetry, Rhetoric and Politics, 1627–1660*, Cambridge University Press, 1999.

A. D. Nuttall, *The Alternative Trinity: Gnostic Hersey in Marlowe, Milton, and Blake*, Clarendon Press, 1998.

Mary Nyquist and Margaret W. Ferguson, *Re-Membering Milton: Essays on the Texts and Traditions*, Methuen, 1987, 1988.

Annabel Patterson, ed., *John Milton*, Longman, 1992.

John Peter, *A Critique of 'Paradise Lost'*, Columbia University Press, 1960.

William Porter, *Reading the Classics and 'Paradise Lost'*, Nebraska University Press, 1993.

F. T. Prince, *The Italian Element in Milton's Verse*, Oxford University Press, 1954.

David Quint, *Epic and Empire: Politics and Generic Form from Virgil to Milton*, Princeton University Press, 1993.

Mary Ann Radzinowicz, *Toward 'Samson Agonistes': the Growth of Milton's Mind*, Princeton University Press, 1978.

Balachandra Rajan, *'Paradise Lost' and the Seventeenth-Century Reader*, Chatto & Windus, 1947.

Herman Rapaport, *Milton and the Postmodern*, University of Nebraska Press, 1983.

Stella Purce Revard, *The War in Heaven: 'Paradise Lost' and the Tradition of Satan's Rebellion*, Cornell University Press, 1980.

Christopher Ricks, *Milton's Grand Style*, Clarendon Press, 1963.

——, 'John Milton: Sound and Sense in *Paradise Lost*', in *Essays by Divers Hands: Being the Transactions of the Royal Society of Literature*, new series, 39, ed. John Press, Oxford University Press, 1977. Repr. in *The Force of Poetry*, Clarendon Press, 1984.

John Rogers, *The Matter of Revolution: Science, Poetry, and Politics in the Age of Milton*, Cornell University Press, 1996.

John P. Rumrich, *Matter of Glory: a New Preface to 'Paradise Lost'*, University of Pittsburgh Press, 1987.

——, *Milton Unbound: Controversy and Reinterpretation*, Cambridge University Press, 1996.

Claes Schaar, *The Full Voic'd Quire Below: Vertical Context Systems in 'Paradise Lost'*, CWK Gleerup, 1982.

Regina Schwartz, *Remembering and Repeating: Biblical Creation in 'Paradise Lost'*, Cambridge University Press, 1988.

Harold Skulsky, *Milton and the Death of Man: Humanism on Trial in Paradise Lost*, University of Delaware Press, 2000.

John M. Steadman, *Epic and Tragic Structure in 'Paradise Lost'*, University of Chicago Press, 1976.

——, *Milton and the Renaissance Hero*, Clarendon Press, 1967.

——, *Milton's Biblical and Classical Imagery*, Duquesne University Press, 1984.

——, *Milton's Epic Characters, Image and Idol*, University of North Carolina Press, 1968.

——, *Moral Fiction in Milton and Spenser*, University of Missouri Press, 1995.

Arnold Stein, *Answerable Style: Essays on 'Paradise Lost'*, University of Minnesota Press, 1953.

Joseph Summers, *The Muse's Method: an Introduction to 'Paradise Lost'*, Harvard University Press, 1962.

Kester Svendsen, *Milton and Science*, Harvard University Press, 1956.

John S. Tanner, *Anxiety in Eden: a Kierkegaardian reading of 'Paradise Lost'*, Clarendon Press, 1993.

Mindele Anne Treip, *Allegorical Poetics and the Epic: the Renaissance Tradition to 'Paradise Lost'*, University Press of Kentucky, 1994.

James Grantham Turner, *One Flesh: Paradisal Marriage and Sexual Relations in the Age of Milton*, Clarendon Press, 1987.

A. J. A. Waldock, *'Paradise Lost' and its Critics*, Cambridge University Press, 1947.

Joan M. Webber, *Milton and his Epic Tradition*, University of Washington Press, 1979.

R. H. West, *Milton and the Angels*, University of Georgia Press, 1955.

Arnold Williams, *The Common Expositor: an Account of the Commentaries on Genesis 1527–1633*, University of North Carolina Press, 1948.

NOTE ON THE TEXT

The present text represents a partial modernization. Spelling has been modernized, most capitals reduced, and most italics removed. I have kept many contractions for they can be a helpful guide to scansion (for example i 223 'Driv'n' and xi 432 'I' th' midst'). Most critics now agree that Milton's own punctuation of *Paradise Lost* is irrecoverable, if it even existed. The manuscript of Book I (now in the Pierpont Morgan Library) is for the most part sparsely punctuated; the first and second editions show evidence of normalization at the printing house. I have nevertheless resisted the impulse to modernize the punctuation. The note on 'The Verse' added in 1668 describes the sense as being 'variously drawn out from one verse into another'. The light, flexible pointing of the early texts is admirably suited to Milton's long 'drawn out' periods. It maintains momentum and keeps multiple chains of discourse open. I have most often followed the punctuation of the first edition (1667), but I have freely substituted punctuation from the second edition (1674) when I feel it is superior. I have also drawn on the manuscript of Book I (for example at i 128 and i 229–30). John Creaser has argued for the virtues of eclecticism in choosing between these texts.[1] Convinced by his arguments, I have drawn on the punctuation of all the texts produced in Milton's lifetime.

I have on a very few occasions modernized punctuation that might impede a modern reader, but I have not altered anything that in my judgement conveys a deliberate ambiguity. An example is *Paradise Lost* v 77–81:

> Taste this, and be henceforth among the gods
> Thyself a goddess, not to earth confined,
> But sometimes in the air, as we, sometimes
> Ascend to Heav'n, by merit thine, and see
> What life the gods live there, and such live thou.

Many editors change the comma after 'we' to a semi-colon and so remove a suggestive ambiguity. As Zachary Pearce noted in 1733, Satan's 'as we' is placed so as to refer either to 'Ascend to Heaven' or 'in the air'. Empson discerns 'a natural embarrassment' in the fallen Satan's implied doubt as to whether 'he could go to Heaven himself'.[2] It is not always easy – and is sometimes impossible – to decide when a poet is being deliberately ambiguous, but it is an editor's responsibility to make difficult decisions. The first two editions seldom differ substantively. When they do, I choose the reading that in my judgement makes the best sense, and give the alternative reading in the notes. In most cases my preference coincides with that of the majority of editors, but there are three occasions (vii 366, ix 394 and ix 922) where I find myself in the minority. I give my reasons in the notes.

Attention should be drawn to a liberty I have taken in my use of capitals. The early editions usually capitalize 'Heaven', and they make no typographical distinction between God's empyreal Heaven and the stellar heavens of the created universe. I have used the upper case for God's Heaven and the lower case for the heavens below the *primum mobile*. The justification for this typographical distinction is that it can serve the modern reader as a helpful guide (see for example ii 1004–6 and vii 106–7). Modern-spelling editions invariably make such a distinction between 'God' and 'god', even though the early texts use the upper case for pagan gods as well as God.

Neologisms

Like Shakespeare, Milton introduced many new words and meanings into English. Some of these have since become a familiar part of the language and so do not surprise us. But Milton may have meant them to surprise. We must make an imaginative effort if we are to hear them afresh. The most famous example is 'Pandaemonium' ('seat of all demons') which Milton coined as the name of Hell's capital (i 756). In the notes at the back of this volume I have marked Milton's neologisms with an asterisk. When the *OED* credits Milton with the first use of a word, I place the asterisk before the word, as in my note to *Paradise Lost* i 548:

serried pressed close together, shoulder to shoulder.

When the *OED* credits Milton with using an existing word in a new sense, I place the asterisk before the sense, as in my note to *Paradise Lost* ii 439:

unessential *possessing no essence (*OED* 1).

My asterisks should be used with caution. Although the editors of the *OED* attempted to record the first use of every word, they inevitably made some errors. William B. Hunter has identified some of these in his seminal essay 'New Words in Milton's English Poems'.[3] Hunter nevertheless found the *OED* to be reliable in the vast majority of cases. Out of more than one thousand words and senses 'apparently original in some sense with Milton', Hunter found only twenty-eight cases where the *OED* was in error. Hunter was writing in 1954. Preparing my edition in the 1990s, I have been able to use the enormous searching-power of the *OED* on CD-ROM. With just a few keystrokes it has been possible to check Milton's putative neologisms against all quotations in the *OED*. Sometimes the *OED* credits Milton with a new word, not knowing that it is quoted in an earlier text elsewhere in the dictionary. The *OED* credits Milton with coining 'loquacious' in *Paradise Lost* x 161, but a global search of all *OED* quotations finds an earlier instance from 1656. Sometimes Milton antedates the *OED*'s first instance. The *OED*'s earliest instance of 'self-esteem' is from 1657, but Milton had used the term in *An Apology for Smectymnuus* (1642). In my note to *Paradise Lost* viii 572 I accordingly mark 'self-esteem' with an asterisk and note that Milton may have coined the term in his prose. I have silently omitted any neologism that the *OED* falsely accredits to Milton.

Notes

1. John Creaser, 'Editorial Problems in Milton', *RES* 34 (1983), pp. 279–303 and *RES* 35 (1984), pp. 45–60.
2. William Empson, *Some Versions of Pastoral* (Chatto & Windus: London, 1935), pp. 163.
3. Hunter's essay (first published in *Essays in Honor of Walter Clyde Curry*, 1954) is reprinted in *The Descent of Urania: Studies in Milton, 1946–1988* (Associated University Presses: London and Toronto, 1989), pp. 224–42.

ON *PARADISE LOST*

When I beheld the poet blind, yet bold,
In slender book his vast design unfold,
Messiah crowned, God's reconciled decree,
Rebelling angels, the forbidden tree,
5   Heav'n, Hell, earth, Chaos, all; the argument
Held me a while misdoubting his intent,
That he would ruin (for I saw him strong)
The sacred truths to fable and old song
(So Sampson groped the Temple's posts in spite)
10   The world o'erwhelming to revenge his sight.

Yet as I read, soon growing less severe,
I liked his project, the success did fear;
Through that wide field how he his way should find
O'er which lame faith leads understanding blind;
15   Lest he perplexed the things he would explain,
And what was easy he should render vain.

Or if a work so infinite he spanned,
Jealous I was that some less skilful hand
(Such as disquiet always what is well,
20   And by ill imitating would excel)
Might hence presume the whole Creation's day
To change in scenes, and show it in a play.

Pardon me, mighty poet, nor despise
My causeless, yet not impious, surmise.
25   But I am now convinced, and none will dare
Within thy labours to pretend a share.
Thou hast not missed one thought that could be fit,
And all that was improper dost omit:
So that no room is here for writers left,
30   But to detect their ignorance or theft.

That majesty which through thy work doth reign
Draws the devout, deterring the profane.
And things divine thou treat'st of in such state
As them preserves, and thee, inviolate.

35   At once delight and horror on us seize,
        Thou sing'st with so much gravity and ease;
        And above human flight dost soar aloft
        With plume so strong, so equal, and so soft.
        The bird named from that Paradise you sing
40   So never flags, but always keeps on wing.
            Where couldst thou words of such a compass find?
        Whence furnish such a vast expense of mind?
        Just Heav'n thee like Tiresias to requite
        Rewards with prophecy thy loss of sight.
45   Well might'st thou scorn thy readers to allure
        With tinkling rhyme, of thy own sense secure;
        While the Town-Bayes writes all the while and spells,
        And like a pack-horse tires without his bells:
        Their fancies like our bushy-points appear,
50   The poets tag them, we for fashion wear.
        I too transported by the mode offend,
        And while I meant to praise thee must commend.
        Thy verse created like thy theme sublime,
        In number, weight, and measure, needs not rhyme.
                                    A[ndrew]. M[arvell]

Notes

Andrew Marvell's rhymed tribute was prefaced to the second edition of
Paradise Lost. A Latin tribute (probably by Milton's friend Samuel Barrow)
was printed immediately before it.
5. *argument* subject matter (the 'great argument' of *PL* i 25)
6. *misdoubting his intent* 'fearing that he had taken on too much'.
7. *strong* firm in will or purpose (*OED* 3a), with a glance at Samson's
physical strength, which reduced Dagon's temple to a *ruin*.
9–10. *So Sampson groped . . . revenge his sight* See Judges 16.28–9. The
biblical Samson prays that he may be 'avenged of the Philistines for my
two eyes', but he was not generally supposed to have been motivated by
spite. In M.'s *Samson Agonistes* (1671) it is the Philistines who are 'set on
revenge and spite' (1462). Samson grasping the pillars bows his head 'as
one who prayed, / Or some great matter in his mind revolved' (1637–8).
12. *project* plan.
      success outcome (good or bad).

13–14. *wide field . . . blind* Cp. *PL* vii 17–20 where M. likens himself to blind Bellerophon wandering 'on th' Aleian field', having been thrown from Pegasus (a symbol of poetic daring).

18. *Jealous* zealously protective.

18–22. *some less skilful . . . in a play* A dig at John Dryden, who adapted *Paradise Lost* for the stage in his heroic opera *The State of Innocence* (1677), originally called *The Fall of Angels and Man in Innocence*, and licensed 17 April 1674. Dryden's opera was never performed. See also 47*n* and 50*n* below.

26. *pretend* claim.

35. *horror* including 'awe or reverent fear' (*OED* 4).

38. *plume* quill of the poet and wing of the bird of Paradise.

equal even, tranquil, unruffled (*OED* 9), also 'equal to the challenge', adequately fit (*OED* 3b).

39–40. *The bird named from that Paradise . . . keeps on wing* Birds of Paradise were thought to spend their whole lives in the air.

42. *expense* expenditure (of substance, labour, time etc.) (*OED* 1b).

43–4. *Tiresias . . . loss of sight* Jupiter gave Tiresias the gift of prophecy after Juno had punished him with blindness. M. likens himself to Tiresias in *PL*, iii 36.

45–6. *scorn . . . tinkling rhyme* alluding to M.'s comments on 'the jingling sound of like endings' in his immediately following prefatory remarks on 'The Verse'.

47. *Town-Bayes* glancing at Dryden, who was satirized as 'Bayes' in the Duke of Buckingham's comedy *The Rehearsal* (1672). 'Bay' means 'laurel', and Dryden had been Poet Laureate since 1668. A 'bay' was also a kind of horse (notice *pack-horse*).

spells writes laboriously, letter by letter (in search of rhyme).

49. *bushy-points* A 'point' was 'a tagged lace or cord, of twisted yarn, silk, or leather, for attaching the hose to the doublet' (*OED* sb¹ B5). Points were 'bushy' when tied in tassels. Marvell therefore likens rhyme to a vain fashion. Points were also a byword for 'something of small value' (*OED*).

50. *tag* both 'attach metal tags to points' and 'supply blank verse with rhymes' (*OED* v¹ 1c). John Aubrey reports that M. used the word in conversation with Dryden when the latter asked for his permission to turn 'Paradise-lost into a Drama in Rhyme: Mr. Milton received him civilly, & told him he would give him leave to tagge his Verses' (Darbishire 7).

52. *must commend* Marvell's own poem, written in rhyme, forces him to use the weaker word *commend* where he *meant to praise*.

54. *Number, weight, and measure* Cp. Wisdom 11.20: 'thou hast ordered all things in measure, and number, and weight'. Cp. also M.'s defence of blank verse in his note on 'The Verse': 'true musical delight . . . consists only in apt numbers, fit quantity of syllables, and the sense variously drawn out from one verse into another'.

PARADISE LOST

The Verse

The measure is English heroic verse without rhyme, as that
of Homer in Greek, and of Virgil in Latin; rhyme being no
necessary adjunct or true ornament of poem or good verse,
in longer works especially, but the invention of a barbarous
age, to set off wretched matter and lame metre; graced indeed
since by the use of some famous modern poets, carried away
by custom, but much to their own vexation, hindrance, and
constraint to express many things otherwise, and for the most
part worse than else they would have expressed them. Not
without cause therefore some both Italian and Spanish poets
of prime note have rejected rhyme both in longer and shorter
works, as have also long since our best English tragedies, as
a thing of itself, to all judicious ears, trivial and of no true
musical delight; which consists only in apt numbers, fit quan-
tity of syllables, and the sense variously drawn out from one
verse into another, not in the jingling sound of like endings,
a fault avoided by the learned ancients both in poetry and all
good oratory. This neglect then of rhyme so little is to be
taken for a defect, though it may seem so perhaps to vulgar
readers, that it rather is to be esteemed an example set, the
first in English, of ancient liberty recovered to heroic poem
from the troublesome and modern bondage of rhyming.

BOOK I

The Argument

This first book proposes, first in brief, the whole subject, man's disobedience, and the loss thereupon of Paradise wherein he was placed: then touches the prime cause of his fall, the serpent, or rather Satan in the serpent; who revolting from
5 God, and drawing to his side many legions of angels, was by the command of God driven out of Heaven with all his crew into the great deep. Which action passed over, the poem hastes into the midst of things, presenting Satan with his angels now fallen into Hell, described here, not in the centre (for heaven
10 and earth may be supposed as yet not made, certainly not yet accursed) but in a place of utter darkness, fitliest called Chaos: here Satan with his angels lying on the burning lake, thunder-struck and astonished, after a certain space recovers, as from confusion, calls up him who next in order and dignity lay by
15 him; they confer of their miserable fall, Satan awakens all his legions, who lay till then in the same manner confounded; they rise, their numbers, array of battle, their chief leaders named, according to the idols known afterwards in Canaan and the countries adjoining. To these Satan directs his speech,
20 comforts them with hope yet of regaining Heaven, but tells them lastly of a new world and new kind of creature to be created, according to an ancient prophecy or report in Heaven; for that angels were long before this visible Creation, was the opinion of many ancient Fathers. To find out the truth of
25 this prophecy, and what to determine thereon he refers to a full council. What his associates thence attempt. Pandaemonium the palace of Satan rises, suddenly built out of the deep: the infernal Peers there sit in council.

1. center of earth
2. Our universe was created after Satan fell from Heaven but before he escaped from Hell
3. outer

Of man's first disobedience, and the fruit _pun_
Of that forbidden tree, whose mortal taste
Brought death into the world, and all our woe,
With loss of Eden, till one greater man _Christ_
5   Restore us, and regain the blissful seat,
Sing Heav'nly Muse, that on the secret top   _Holy Spirit_
Of Oreb, or of Sinai, didst inspire
Moses That shepherd, who first taught the chosen seed,
In the beginning how the heav'ns and earth
10 Rose out of Chaos: or if Sion hill
Delight thee more, and Siloa's brook that flowed
Fast by the oracle of God; I thence
Invoke thy aid to my advent'rous song,
That with no middle flight intends to soar
15 Above th' Aonian mount, while it pursues
Things unattempted yet in prose or rhyme.
And chiefly thou O Spirit, that dost prefer
Before all temples th' upright heart and pure,
Instruct me, for thou know'st; thou from the first
20 Wast present, and with mighty wings outspread
Dove-like sat'st brooding on the vast abyss
And mad'st it pregnant: what in me is dark
Illumine, what is low raise and support;
That to the heighth of this great argument
25 I may assert Eternal Providence,
And justify the ways of God to men.
    Say first, for Heav'n hides nothing from thy view
Nor the deep tract of Hell, say first what cause   _Muse is_
Moved our grand parents in that happy state,   _omniscient_
30 Favoured of Heav'n so highly, to fall off
From their Creator and transgress his will
For one restraint, lords of the world besides?
Who first seduced them to that foul revolt?
Th' infernal Serpent; he it was, whose guile   _Blame on_
35 Stirred up with envy and revenge, deceived   _Satan_
The mother of mankind, what time his pride
Had cast him out from Heav'n, with all his host
Of rebel angels, by whose aid aspiring
To set himself in glory above his peers,

40 He trusted to have equalled the Most High,
   If he opposed; and with ambitious aim
   Against the throne and monarchy of God
   Raised impious war in Heav'n and battle proud
   With vain attempt. Him the Almighty Power
45 Hurled headlong flaming from th' ethereal sky
   With hideous ruin and combustion down
   To bottomless perdition, there to dwell
   In adamantine chains and penal fire,
   Who durst defy th' Omnipotent to arms.

Nine days

50 Nine times the space that measures day and night
   To mortal men, he with his horrid crew
   Lay vanquished, rolling in the fiery gulf
   Confounded though immortal: but his doom
   Reserved him to more wrath; for now the thought
55 Both of lost happiness and lasting pain
   Torments him; round he throws his baleful eyes
   That witnessed huge affliction and dismay
   Mixed with obdúrate pride and steadfast hate:
   At once as far as angels' ken he views
60 The dismal situation waste and wild,
   A dungeon horrible, on all sides round
   As one great furnace flamed, yet from those flames
   No light, but rather darkness visible
   Served only to discover sights of woe,

Chaos

65 Regions of sorrow, doleful shades, where peace
   And rest can never dwell, hope never comes
   That comes to all; but torture without end
   Still urges, and a fiery deluge, fed
   With ever-burning sulphur unconsumed:
70 Such place Eternal Justice had prepared
   For those rebellious, here their prison ordained
   In utter darkness, and their portion set
   As far removed from God and light of Heav'n
   As from the centre thrice to th' utmost pole.
75 O how unlike the place from whence they fell!
   There the companions of his fall, o'erwhelmed
   With floods and whirlwinds of tempestuous fire,
   He soon discerns, and welt'ring by his side

One next himself in power, and next in crime,
80 Long after known in Palestine, and named
Beëlzebub. To whom th' Arch-Enemy,
And thence in Heav'n called Satan, with bold words
Breaking the horrid silence thus began.
    If thou beest he; but O how fall'n! how changed
85 From him, who in the happy realms of light
Clothed with transcendent brightness didst outshine
Myriads though bright: if he whom mutual league,
United thoughts and counsels, equal hope
And hazard in the glorious enterprise,
90 Joined with me once, now misery hath joined
In equal ruin: into what pit thou seest
From what heighth fall'n, so much the stronger proved
He with his thunder: and till then who knew
The force of those dire arms? yet not for those,
95 Nor what the potent Victor in his rage
Can else inflict, do I repent or change,
Though changed in outward lustre, that fixed mind
And high disdain, from sense of injured merit,
That with the mightiest raised me to contend,
100 And to the fierce contention brought along
Innumerable force of Spirits armed
That durst dislike his reign, and me preferring,
His utmost power with adverse power opposed
In dubious battle on the plains of Heav'n,
105 And shook his throne. What though the field be lost?
All is not lost; the unconquerable will,
And study of revenge, immortal hate,
And courage never to submit or yield:
And what is else not to be overcome?
110 That glory never shall his wrath or might
Extort from me. To bow and sue for grace
With suppliant knee, and deify his power
Who from the terror of this arm so late
Doubted his empire, that were low indeed,
115 That were an ignominy and shame beneath
This downfall; since by Fate the strength of gods
And this empyreal substance cannot fail,

[handwritten margin notes: "Lord of the Flies"; "Satan pre-Fall"]

Since through experience of this great event
In arms not worse, in foresight much advanced,
120 We may with more successful hope resolve
To wage by force or guile eternal war
Irreconcilable, to our grand Foe,
Who now triúmphs, and in th' excess of joy
Sole reigning holds the tyranny of Heav'n.
125   So spake th' apostate angel, though in pain,
Vaunting aloud, but racked with deep despair:
And him thus answered soon his bold compeer.
      O Prince, O chief of many thronèd Powers
That led th' embattled Seraphim to war
130 Under thy conduct, and in dreadful deeds
Fearless, endangered Heav'n's perpetual King;
And put to proof his high supremacy,
Whether upheld by strength, or Chance, or Fate;
Too well I see and rue the dire event,
135 That with sad overthrow and foul defeat
Hath lost us Heav'n, and all this mighty host
In horrible destruction laid thus low,
As far as gods and Heav'nly essences
Can perish: for the mind and spirit remains
140 Invincible, and vigour soon returns,
Though all our glory extinct, and happy state
Here swallowed up in endless misery.
But what if he our Conqueror, (whom I now
Of force believe Almighty, since no less
145 Than such could have o'erpow'red such force as ours)
Have left us this our spirit and strength entire
Strongly to suffer and support our pains,
That we may so suffice his vengeful ire,
Or do him mightier service as his thralls
150 By right of war, whate'er his business be,
Here in the heart of Hell to work in fire,
Or do his errands in the gloomy deep;
What can it then avail though yet we feel
Strength undiminished, or eternal being
155 To undergo eternal punishment?
Whereto with speedy words th' Arch-Fiend replied.

Fall'n Cherub, to be weak is miserable
Doing or suffering: but of this be sure,
To do aught good never will be our task,
160   But ever to do ill our sole delight,
As being the contrary to his high will
Whom we resist. If then his Providence
Out of our evil seek to bring forth good,
Our labour must be to pervert that end,
165   And out of good still to find means of evil,
Which oft-times may succeed, so as perhaps
Shall grieve him, if I fail not, and disturb
His inmost counsels from their destined aim.
But see the angry Victor hath recalled
170   His ministers of vengeance and pursuit
Back to the gates of Heav'n: the sulphurous hail
Shot after us in storm, o'erblown hath laid
The fiery surge, that from the precipice
Of Heav'n received us falling, and the thunder
175   Winged with red lightning and impetuous rage,
Perhaps hath spent his shafts, and ceases now
To bellow through the vast and boundless deep.
Let us not slip th' occasion, whether scorn,
Or satiate fury yield it from our Foe.
180   Seest thou yon dreary plain, forlorn and wild,
The seat of desolation, void of light,
Save what the glimmering of these livid flames
Casts pale and dreadful? Thither let us tend
From off the tossing of these fiery waves,
185   There rest, if any rest can harbour there,
And reassembling our afflicted powers,
Consult how we may henceforth most offend
Our Enemy, our own loss how repair,
How overcome this dire calamity,
190   What reinforcement we may gain from hope,
If not what resolution from despair.
　　　Thus Satan talking to his nearest mate
With head uplift above the wave, and eyes
That sparkling blazed; his other parts besides
195   Prone on the flood, extended long and large

Lay floating many a rood, in bulk as huge
As whom the fables name of monstrous size,
Titanian, or Earth-born, that warred on Jove,
Briareos or Typhon, whom the den
200 By ancient Tarsus held, or that sea-beast
Leviathan, which God of all his works
Created hugest that swim th' Océan stream:
Him haply slumb'ring on the Norway foam
The pilot of some small night-foundered skiff,
205 Deeming some island, oft, as seamen tell,
With fixèd anchor in his scaly rind
Moors by his side under the lee, while night
Invests the sea, and wishèd morn delays:
So stretched out huge in length the Arch-Fiend lay
210 Chained on the burning lake, nor ever thence
Had ris'n or heaved his head, but that the will
And high permission of all-ruling Heaven
Left him at large to his own dark designs,
That with reiterated crimes he might
215 Heap on himself damnation, while he sought
Evil to others, and enraged might see
How all his malice served but to bring forth
Infinite goodness, grace and mercy shown
On man by him seduced, but on himself
220 Treble confusion, wrath and vengeance poured.
Forthwith upright he rears from off the pool
His mighty stature; on each hand the flames
Driv'n backward slope their pointing spires, and rolled
In billows, leave i' th' midst a horrid vale.
225 Then with expanded wings he steers his flight
Aloft, incumbent on the dusky air
That felt unusual weight, till on dry land
He lights, if it were land that ever burned
With solid, as the lake with liquid fire,
230 And such appeared in hue; as when the force
Of subterranean wind transports a hill
Torn from Pelorus, or the shattered side
Of thund'ring Etna, whose combustible
And fuelled entrails thence conceiving fire,

235   Sublimed with mineral fury, aid the winds,
And leave a singèd bottom all involved
With stench and smoke: such resting found the sole
Of unblest feet. Him followed his next mate,
Both glorying to have 'scaped the Stygian flood
240   As gods, and by their own recovered strength,
Not by the sufferance of supernal power.
     Is this the region, this the soil, the clime,
Said then the lost Archangel, this the seat
That we must change for Heav'n, this mournful gloom
245   For that celestial light? Be it so, since he
Who now is sov'reign can dispose and bid
What shall be right: farthest from him is best
Whom reason hath equalled, force hath made supreme
Above his equals. Farewell happy fields
250   Where joy for ever dwells: hail horrors, hail
Infernal world, and thou profoundest Hell
Receive thy new possessor: one who brings
A mind not to be changed by place or time.
The mind is its own place, and in itself
255   Can make a Heav'n of Hell, a Hell of Heav'n.
What matter where, if I be still the same,
And what I should be, all but less than he
Whom thunder hath made greater? Here at least
We shall be free; th' Almighty hath not built
260   Here for his envy, will not drive us hence:
Here we may reign secure, and in my choice
To reign is worth ambition though in Hell:
Better to reign in Hell, than serve in Heav'n.
But wherefore let we then our faithful friends,
265   Th' associates and copartners of our loss
Lie thus astonished on th' oblivious pool,
And call them not to share with us their part
In this unhappy mansion; or once more
With rallied arms to try what may be yet
270   Regained in Heav'n, or what more lost in Hell?
     So Satan spake, and him Beëlzebub
Thus answered. Leader of those armies bright,
Which but th' Omnipotent none could have foiled,

If once they hear that voice, their liveliest pledge
275 Of hope in fears and dangers, heard so oft
In worst extremes, and on the perilous edge
Of battle when it raged, in all assaults
Their surest signal, they will soon resume
New courage and revive, though now they lie
280 Grovelling and prostrate on yon lake of fire,
As we erewhile, astounded and amazed,
No wonder, fall'n such a pernicious heighth.
    He scarce had ceased when the superior fiend
Was moving toward the shore; his ponderous shield
285 Ethereal temper, massy, large and round,
Behind him cast; the broad circumference
Hung on his shoulders like the moon, whose orb
Through optic glass the Tuscan artist views
At evening from the top of Fesole,
290 Or in Valdarno, to descry new lands,
Rivers or mountains in her spotty globe.
His spear, to equal which the tallest pine
Hewn on Norwegian hills, to be the mast
Of some great ammiral, were but a wand,
295 He walked with to support uneasy steps
Over the burning marl, not like those steps
On Heaven's azure; and the torrid clime
Smote on him sore besides, vaulted with fire;
Nathless he so endured, till on the beach
300 Of that inflamèd sea, he stood and called
His legions, angel forms, who lay entranced
Thick as autumnal leaves that strow the brooks
In Vallombrosa, where th' Etrurian shades
High overarched embow'r; or scattered sedge
305 Afloat, when with fierce winds Orion armed
Hath vexed the Red Sea coast, whose waves o'erthrew
Busiris and his Memphian chivalry,
While with perfidious hatred they pursued
The sojourners of Goshen, who beheld
310 From the safe shore their floating carcasses
And broken chariot wheels. So thick bestrown
Abject and lost lay these, covering the flood,

Under amazement of their hideous change.
He called so loud, that all the hollow deep
315   Of Hell resounded. Princes, Potentates,
Warriors, the flow'r of Heav'n, once yours, now lost,
If such astonishment as this can seize
Eternal Spirits: or have ye chos'n this place
After the toil of battle to repose
320   Your wearied virtue, for the ease you find
To slumber here, as in the vales of Heav'n?
Or in this abject posture have ye sworn
To adore the Conqueror? who now beholds
Cherub and Seraph rolling in the flood
325   With scattered arms and ensigns, till anon
His swift pursuers from Heav'n gates discern
Th' advantage, and descending tread us down
Thus drooping, or with linkèd thunderbolts
Transfix us to the bottom of this gulf.
330   Awake, arise, or be for ever fall'n.
      They heard, and were abashed, and up they sprung
Upon the wing, as when men wont to watch
On duty, sleeping found by whom they dread,
Rouse and bestir themselves ere well awake.
335   Nor did they not perceive the evil plight
In which they were, or the fierce pains not feel;
Yet to their General's voice they soon obeyed
Innumerable. As when the potent rod
Of Amram's son in Egypt's evil day
340   Waved round the coast, up called a pitchy cloud
Of locusts, warping on the eastern wind,
That o'er the realm of impious Pharaoh hung
Like night, and darkened all the land of Nile:
So numberless were those bad angels seen
345   Hovering on wing under the cope of Hell
'Twixt upper, nether, and surrounding fires;
Till, as a signal giv'n, th' uplifted spear
Of their great Sultan waving to direct
Their course, in even balance down they light
350   On the firm brimstone, and fill all the plain;
A multitude, like which the populous North

Poured never from her frozen loins, to pass
Rhene or the Danaw, when her barbarous sons
Came like a deluge on the South, and spread
355   Beneath Gibraltar to the Libyan sands.
Forthwith from every squadron and each band
The heads and leaders thither haste where stood
Their great Commander; godlike shapes and forms
Excelling human, Princely dignities,
360   And Powers that erst in Heaven sat on thrones;
Though of their names in Heav'nly records now
Be no memorial, blotted out and razed
By their rebellion, from the Books of Life.
Nor had they yet among the sons of Eve
365   Got them new names, till wand'ring o'er the earth,
Through God's high sufferance for the trial of man,
By falsities and lies the greatest part
Of mankind they corrupted to forsake
God their Creator, and th' invisible
370   Glory of him that made them to transform
Oft to the image of a brute, adorned
With gay religions full of pomp and gold,
And devils to adore for deities:
Then were they known to men by various names,
375   And various idols through the heathen world.
Say, Muse, their names then known, who first, who last,
Roused from the slumber on that fiery couch,
At their great Emperor's call, as next in worth
Came singly where he stood on the bare strand,
380   While the promiscuous crowd stood yet aloof?
The chief were those who from the pit of Hell
Roaming to seek their prey on earth, durst fix
Their seats, long after, next the seat of God,
Their altars by his altar, gods adored
385   Among the nations round, and durst abide
Jehovah thund'ring out of Sion, throned
Between the Cherubim; yea, often placed
Within his sanctuary itself their shrines,
Abominations; and with cursèd things
390   His holy rites, and solemn feasts profaned,

And with their darkness durst affront his light.
First Moloch, horrid king besmeared with blood
Of human sacrifice, and parents' tears,
Though for the noise of drums and timbrels loud
395   Their children's cries unheard, that passed through fire
To his grim idol. Him the Ammonite
Worshipped in Rabba and her wat'ry plain,
In Argob and in Basan, to the stream
Of utmost Arnon. Nor content with such
400   Audacious neighbourhood, the wisest heart
Of Solomon he led by fraud to build
His temple right against the temple of God
On that opprobrious hill, and made his grove
The pleasant valley of Hinnom, Tophet thence,
405   And black Gehenna called, the type of Hell.
Next Chemos, th' óbscene dread of Moab's sons,
From Aroer to Nebo, and the wild
Of southmost Abarim; in Hesebon
And Horonaim, Seon's realm, beyond
410   The flow'ry dale of Sibma clad with vines,
And Elealè to th' Asphaltic pool.
Peor his other name, when he enticed
Israel in Sittim on their march from Nile
To do him wanton rites, which cost them woe.
415   Yet thence his lustful orgies he enlarged
Even to that hill of scandal, by the grove
Of Moloch homicide, lust hard by hate;
Till good Josiah drove them thence to Hell.
With these came they, who from the bord'ring flood
420   Of old Euphrates to the brook that parts
Egypt from Syrian ground, had general names
Of Baälim and Ashtaroth, those male,
These feminine. For Spirits when they please
Can either sex assume, or both; so soft
425   And uncompounded is their essence pure;
Not tied or manacled with joint or limb,
Nor founded on the brittle strength of bones,
Like cumbrous flesh; but in what shape they choose
Dilated or condensed, bright or obscure,

430 Can execute their airy purposes,
     And works of love or enmity fulfil.
     For these the race of Israel oft forsook
     Their Living Strength, and unfrequented left
     His righteous altar, bowing lowly down
435 To bestial gods; for which their heads as low
     Bowed down in battle, sunk before the spear
     Of déspicable foes. With these in troop
     Came Astoreth, whom the Phoenicians called
     Astarte, queen of Heav'n, with crescent horns;
440 To whose bright image nightly by the moon
     Sidonian virgins paid their vows and songs,
     In Sion also not unsung, where stood
     Her temple on th' offensive mountain, built
     By that uxorious king whose heart though large,
445 Beguiled by fair idolatresses, fell
     To idols foul. Thammuz came next behind,
     Whose annual wound in Lebanon allured
     The Syrian damsels to lament his fate
     In amorous ditties all a summer's day,
450 While smooth Adonis from his native rock
     Ran purple to the sea, supposed with blood
     Of Thammuz yearly wounded: the love-tale
     Infected Sion's daughters with like heat,
     Whose wanton passions in the sacred porch
455 Ezekiel saw, when by the vision led
     His eye surveyed the dark idolatries
     Of alienated Judah. Next came one
     Who mourned in earnest, when the captive ark
     Maimed his brute image, head and hands lopped off
460 In his own temple, on the grunsel edge,
     Where he fell flat, and shamed his worshippers:
     Dagon his name, sea-monster, upward man
     And downward fish: yet had his temple high
     Reared in Azotus, dreaded through the coast
465 Of Palestine, in Gath and Ascalon
     And Accaron and Gaza's frontier bounds.
     Him followed Rimmon, whose delightful seat
     Was fair Damascus, on the fertile banks

Of Abbana and Pharphar, lucid streams.
470 He also against the house of God was bold:
A leper once he lost and gained a king,
Ahaz his sottish conqueror, whom he drew
God's altar to disparage and displace
For one of Syrian mode, whereon to burn
475 His odious off'rings, and adore the gods
Whom he had vanquished. After these appeared
A crew who under names of old renown,
Osiris, Isis, Orus and their train
With monstrous shapes and sorceries abused
480 Fanatic Egypt and her priests, to seek
Their wand'ring gods disguised in brutish forms
Rather than human. Nor did Israel 'scape
Th' infection when their borrowed gold composed
The calf in Oreb: and the rebel king
485 Doubled that sin in Bethel and in Dan,
Lik'ning his Maker to the grazèd ox,
Jehovah, who in one night when he passed
From Egypt marching, equalled with one stroke
Both her first-born and all her bleating gods.
490 Belial came last, than whom a Spirit more lewd
Fell not from Heaven, or more gross to love
Vice for itself: to him no temple stood
Or altar smoked; yet who more oft than he
In temples and at altars, when the priest
495 Turns atheist, as did Eli's sons, who filled
With lust and violence the house of God.
In courts and palaces he also reigns
And in luxurious cities, where the noise
Of riot ascends above their loftiest tow'rs,
500 And injury and outrage: and when night
Darkens the streets, then wander forth the sons
Of Belial, flown with insolence and wine.
Witness the streets of Sodom, and that night
In Gibeah, when the hospitable door
505 Exposed a matron to avoid worse rape.
These were the prime in order and in might;
The rest were long to tell, though far renowned,

Th' Ionian gods, of Javan's issue held
Gods, yet confessed later than Heav'n and Earth
510 Their boasted parents; Titan Heav'n's first-born
With his enormous brood, and birthright seized
By younger Saturn, he from mightier Jove
His own and Rhea's son like measure found;
So Jove usurping reigned: these first in Crete
515 And Ida known, thence on the snowy top
Of cold Olympus ruled the middle air
Their highest heav'n; or on the Delphian cliff,
Or in Dodona, and through all the bounds
Of Doric land; or who with Saturn old
520 Fled over Adria to th' Hesperian fields,
And o'er the Celtic roamed the utmost isles.
All these and more came flocking; but with looks
Downcast and damp, yet such wherein appeared
Obscure some glimpse of joy, to have found their chief
525 Not in despair, to have found themselves not lost
In loss itself; which on his count'nance cast
Like doubtful hue: but he his wonted pride
Soon recollecting, with high words, that bore
Semblance of worth, not substance, gently raised
530 Their fainting courage and dispelled their fears.
Then straight commands that at the warlike sound
Of trumpets loud and clarions be upreared
His mighty standard; that proud honour claimed
Azazel as his right, a Cherub tall:
535 Who forthwith from the glittering staff unfurled
Th' imperial ensign, which full high advanced
Shone like a meteor streaming to the wind
With gems and golden lustre rich emblazed,
Seraphic arms and trophies: all the while
540 Sonórous metal blowing martial sounds:
At which the universal host upsent
A shout that tore Hell's concave, and beyond
Frighted the reign of Chaos and old Night.
All in a moment through the gloom were seen
545 Ten thousand banners rise into the air
With orient colours waving: with them rose

A forest huge of spears: and thronging helms
Appeared, and serried shields in thick array
Of depth immeasurable: anon they move
550 In perfect phalanx to the Dorian mood
Of flutes and soft recorders; such as raised
To heighth of noblest temper heroes old
Arming to battle, and instead of rage
Deliberate valour breathed, firm and unmoved
555 With dread of death to flight or foul retreat,
Nor wanting power to mitigate and swage
With solemn touches, troubled thoughts, and chase
Anguish and doubt and fear and sorrow and pain
From mortal or immortal minds. Thus they
560 Breathing united force with fixèd thought
Moved on in silence to soft pipes that charmed
Their painful steps o'er the burnt soil; and now
Advanced in view they stand, a horrid front
Of dreadful length and dazzling arms, in guise
565 Of warriors old with ordered spear and shield,
Awaiting what command their mighty chief
Had to impose: he through the armèd files
Darts his experienced eye, and soon traverse
The whole battalion views; their order due,
570 Their visages and stature as of gods,
Their number last he sums. And now his heart
Distends with pride, and hard'ning in his strength
Glories: for never since created man,
Met such embodied force, as named with these
575 Could merit more than that small infantry
Warred on by cranes: though all the Giant brood
Of Phlegra with th' heroic race were joined
That fought at Thebes and Ilium, on each side
Mixed with auxiliar gods; and what resounds
580 In fable or romance of Uther's son
Begirt with British and Armoric knights;
And all who since, baptized or infidel
Jousted in Aspramont or Montalban,
Damasco, or Morocco, or Trebizond,
585 Or whom Biserta sent from Afric shore

When Charlemagne with all his peerage fell
By Fontarabbia. Thus far these beyond
Compare of mortal prowess, yet observed
Their dread commander: he above the rest
590 In shape and gesture proudly eminent
Stood like a tow'r; his form had yet not lost
All her original brightness, nor appeared
Less than Archangel ruined, and th' excess
Of glory obscured: as when the sun new ris'n
595 Looks through the horizontal misty air
Shorn of his beams, or from behind the moon
In dim eclipse disastrous twilight sheds
On half the nations, and with fear of change
Perplexes monarchs. Darkened so, yet shone
600 Above them all th' Archangel: but his face
Deep scars of thunder had intrenched, and care
Sat on his faded cheek, but under brows
Of dauntless courage, and considerate pride
Waiting revenge: cruel his eye, but cast
605 Signs of remorse and passion to behold
The fellows of his crime, the followers rather
(Far other once beheld in bliss) condemned
For ever now to have their lot in pain,
Millions of Spirits for his fault amerced
610 Of Heav'n, and from eternal splendours flung
For his revolt, yet faithful how they stood,
Their glory withered. As when Heaven's fire
Hath scathed the forest oaks or mountain pines,
With singèd top their stately growth though bare
615 Stands on the blasted heath. He now prepared
To speak; whereat their doubled ranks they bend
From wing to wing, and half enclose him round
With all his peers: attention held them mute.
Thrice he assayed, and thrice in spite of scorn,
620 Tears such as angels weep, burst forth: at last
Words interwove with sighs found out their way.
   O myriads of immortal Spirits, O Powers
Matchless, but with th' Almighty, and that strife
Was not inglorious, though th' event was dire,

625 As this place testifies, and this dire change
Hateful to utter: but what power of mind
Foreseeing or presaging, from the depth
Of knowledge past or present, could have feared,
How such united force of gods, how such
630 As stood like these, could ever know repulse?
For who can yet believe, though after loss,
That all these puissant legions, whose exile
Hath emptied Heav'n, shall fail to reascend
Self-raised, and repossess their native seat?
635 For me be witness all the host of Heav'n,
If counsels different, or danger shunned
By me, have lost our hopes. But he who reigns
Monarch in Heav'n, till then as one secure
Sat on his throne, upheld by old repute,
640 Consent or custom, and his regal state
Put forth at full, but still his strength concealed,
Which tempted our attempt, and wrought our fall.
Henceforth his might we know, and know our own
So as not either to provoke, or dread
645 New war, provoked; our better part remains
To work in close design, by fraud or guile
What force effected not: that he no less
At length from us may find, who overcomes
By force, hath overcome but half his foe.
650 Space may produce new worlds; whereof so rife
There went a fame in Heav'n that he ere long
Intended to create, and therein plant
A generation, whom his choice regard
Should favour equal to the sons of Heav'n:
655 Thither, if but to pry, shall be perhaps
Our first eruption; thither or elsewhere:
For this infernal pit shall never hold
Celestial Spirits in bondage, nor th' abyss
Long under darkness cover. But these thoughts
660 Full counsel must mature: peace is despaired,
For who can think submission? War then, war
Open or understood must be resolved.
    He spake: and to confirm his words, out flew

Millions of flaming swords, drawn from the thighs
665 Of mighty Cherubim; the sudden blaze
Far round illumined Hell: highly they raged
Against the Highest, and fierce with graspèd arms
Clashed on their sounding shields the din of war,
Hurling defiance toward the vault of Heav'n.
670   There stood a hill not far whose grisly top
Belched fire and rolling smoke; the rest entire
Shone with a glossy scurf, undoubted sign
That in his womb was hid metallic ore,
The work of sulphur. Thither winged with speed
675 A numerous brígade hastened. As when bands
Of pioneers with spade and pickaxe armed
Forerun the royal camp, to trench a field
Or cast a rampart. Mammon led them on,
Mammon, the least erected Spirit that fell
680 From Heav'n, for ev'n in Heav'n his looks and thoughts
Were always downward bent, admiring more
The riches of Heav'n's pavement, trodden gold,
Than aught divine or holy else enjoyed
In vision beatific: by him first
685 Men also, and by his suggestion taught,
Ransacked the centre, and with impious hands
Rifled the bowels of their mother Earth
For treasures better hid. Soon had his crew
Opened into the hill a spacious wound
690 And digged out ribs of gold. Let none admire
That riches grow in Hell; that soil may best
Deserve the precious bane. And here let those
Who boast in mortal things, and wond'ring tell
Of Babel, and the works of Memphian kings,
695 Learn how their greatest monuments of fame,
And strength and art are easily outdone
By Spirits reprobate, and in an hour
What in an age they with incessant toil
And hands innumerable scarce perform.
700 Nigh on the plain in many cells prepared,
That underneath had veins of liquid fire
Sluiced from the lake, a second multitude

With wondrous art founded the massy ore,
Severing each kind, and scummed the bullion dross:
705 A third as soon had formed within the ground
A various mould, and from the boiling cells
By strange conveyance filled each hollow nook,
As in an organ from one blast of wind
To many a row of pipes the sound-board breathes.
710 Anon out of the earth a fabric huge
Rose like an exhalation, with the sound
Of dulcet symphonies and voices sweet,
Built like a temple, where pilasters round
Were set, and Doric pillars overlaid
715 With golden architrave; nor did there want
Cornice or frieze with bossy sculptures grav'n;
The roof was fretted gold. Not Babylon,
Nor great Alcairo such magnificence
Equalled in all their glories, to enshrine
720 Belus or Serapis their gods, or seat
Their kings, when Egypt with Assyria strove
In wealth and luxury. Th' ascending pile
Stood fixed her stately heighth, and straight the doors
Op'ning their brazen folds discover wide
725 Within, her ample spaces, o'er the smooth
And level pavement: from the archèd roof
Pendent by subtle magic many a row
Of starry lamps and blazing cressets fed
With naphtha and asphaltus yielded light
730 As from a sky. The hasty multitude
Admiring entered, and the work some praise
And some the architect: his hand was known
In Heav'n by many a towered structure high,
Where sceptred angels held their residence,
735 And sat as princes, whom the súpreme King
Exalted to such power, and gave to rule,
Each in his hierarchy, the orders bright.
Nor was his name unheard or unadored
In ancient Greece; and in Ausonian land
740 Men called him Mulciber; and how he fell
From Heav'n, they fabled, thrown by angry Jove

Sheer o'er the crystal battlements: from morn
To noon he fell, from noon to dewy eve,
A summer's day: and with the setting sun
745   Dropped from the zenith like a falling star,
On Lemnos th' Aégean isle: thus they relate,
Erring; for he with this rebellious rout
Fell long before; nor aught availed him now
To have built in Heav'n high tow'rs; nor did he 'scape
750   By all his engines, but was headlong sent
With his industrious crew to build in Hell.
Meanwhile the wingèd heralds by command
Of sov'reign power, with awful ceremony
And trumpets' sound throughout the host proclaim
755   A solemn council forthwith to be held
At Pandaemonium, the high capital
Of Satan and his peers: their summons called
From every band and squarèd regiment
By place or choice the worthiest; they anon
760   With hundreds and with thousands trooping came
Attended: all accéss was thronged, the gates
And porches wide, but chief the spacious hall
(Though like a covered field, where champions bold
Wont ride in armed, and at the Soldan's chair
765   Defied the best of paynim chivalry
To mortal combat or career with lance)
Thick swarmed, both on the ground and in the air,
Brushed with the hiss of rustling wings. As bees
In springtime, when the sun with Taurus rides,
770   Pour forth their populous youth about the hive
In clusters; they among fresh dews and flowers
Fly to and fro, or on the smoothèd plank,
The suburb of their straw-built citadel,
New rubbed with balm, expatiate and confer
775   Their state affairs. So thick the airy crowd
Swarmed and were straitened; till the signal giv'n,
Behold a wonder! They but now who seemed
In bigness to surpass Earth's Giant sons
Now less than smallest dwarfs, in narrow room
780   Throng numberless, like that Pygméan race

Beyond the Indian mount, or faery elves,
Whose midnight revels, by a forest side
Or fountain some belated peasant sees,
Or dreams he sees, while overhead the moon
785 Sits arbitress, and nearer to the earth
Wheels her pale course: they on their mirth and dance
Intent, with jocund music charm his ear;
At once with joy and fear his heart rebounds.
Thus incorporeal Spirits to smallest forms
790 Reduced their shapes immense, and were at large,
Though without number still amidst the hall
Of that infernal Court. But far within
And in their own dimensions like themselves
The great Seraphic Lords and Cherubim
795 In close recess and secret conclave sat
A thousand demi-gods on golden seats,
Frequent and full. After short silence then
And summons read, the great consult began.

BOOK II

The Argument

The consultation begun, Satan debates whether another battle
be to be hazarded for the recovery of Heaven: some advise it,
others dissuade: a third proposal is preferred, mentioned
before by Satan, to search the truth of that prophecy or
tradition in Heaven concerning another world, and another
kind of creature equal or not much inferior to themselves,
about this time to be created: their doubt who shall be sent
on this difficult search: Satan their chief undertakes alone the
voyage, is honoured and applauded. The council thus ended,
the rest betake them several ways and to several employments,
as their inclinations lead them, to entertain the time till Satan
return. He passes on his journey to Hell gates, finds them
shut, and who sat there to guard them, by whom at length
they are opened, and discover to him the great gulf between
Hell and Heaven; with what difficulty he passes through,
directed by Chaos, the power of that place, to the sight of
this new world which he sought.

High on a throne of royal state, which far
Outshone the wealth of Ormus and of Ind,
Or where the gorgeous East with richest hand
Show'rs on her kings barbaric pearl and gold,
Satan exalted sat, by merit raised
To that bad eminence; and from despair
Thus high uplifted beyond hope, aspires
Beyond thus high, insatiate to pursue
Vain war with Heav'n, and by success untaught
His proud imaginations thus displayed.
    Powers and Dominions, deities of Heaven,
For since no deep within her gulf can hold
Immortal vigour, though oppressed and fall'n,

I give not Heav'n for lost. From this descent
15 Celestial Virtues rising, will appear
More glorious and more dread than from no fall,
And trust themselves to fear no second fate:
Me though just right, and the fixed laws of Heav'n
Did first create your leader, next, free choice,
20 With what besides, in counsel or in fight,
Hath been achieved of merit, yet this loss
Thus far at least recovered, hath much more
Established in a safe unenvied throne
Yielded with full consent. The happier state
25 In Heav'n, which follows dignity, might draw
Envy from each inferior; but who here
Will envy whom the highest place exposes
Foremost to stand against the Thunderer's aim
Your bulwark, and condemns to greatest share
30 Of endless pain? Where there is then no good
For which to strive, no strife can grow up there
From faction; for none sure will claim in Hell
Precédence, none, whose portion is so small
Of present pain, that with ambitious mind
35 Will covet more. With this advantage then
To union, and firm faith, and firm accord,
More than can be in Heav'n, we now return
To claim our just inheritance of old,
Surer to prosper than prosperity
40 Could have assured us; and by what best way,
Whether of open war or covert guile,
We now debate; who can advise, may speak.
    He ceased, and next him Moloch, sceptred king
Stood up, the strongest and the fiercest Spirit
45 That fought in Heav'n; now fiercer by despair:
His trust was with th' Eternal to be deemed
Equal in strength, and rather than be less
Cared not to be at all; with that care lost
Went all his fear: of God, or Hell, or worse
50 He recked not, and these words thereafter spake.
    My sentence is for open war: of wiles,
More unexpért, I boast not: them let those

Contrive who need, or when they need, not now.
For while they sit contriving, shall the rest,
55   Millions that stand in arms, and longing wait
The signal to ascend, sit ling'ring here
Heav'n's fugitives, and for their dwelling place
Accept this dark opprobrious den of shame,
The prison of his tyranny who reigns
60   By our delay? No, let us rather choose
Armed with Hell flames and fury all at once
O'er Heav'n's high tow'rs to force resistless way,
Turning our tortures into horrid arms
Against the Torturer; when to meet the noise
65   Of his almighty engine he shall hear
Infernal thunder, and for lightning see
Black fire and horror shot with equal rage
Among his angels; and his throne itself
Mixed with Tartarean sulphur, and strange fire,
70   His own invented torments. But perhaps
The way seems difficult and steep to scale
With upright wing against a higher foe.
Let such bethink them, if the sleepy drench
Of that forgetful lake benumb not still,
75   That in our proper motion we ascend
Up to our native seat: descent and fall
To us is adverse. Who but felt of late
When the fierce foe hung on our broken rear
Insulting, and pursued us through the deep,
80   With what compulsion and laborious flight
We sunk thus low? Th' ascent is easy then;
Th' event is feared; should we again provoke
Our stronger, some worse way his wrath may find
To our destruction: if there be in Hell
85   Fear to be worse destroyed: what can be worse
Than to dwell here, driv'n out from bliss, condemned
In this abhorrèd deep to utter woe;
Where pain of unextinguishable fire
Must exercise us without hope of end
90   The vassals of his anger, when the scourge
Inexorably, and the torturing hour

Calls us to penance? More destroyed than thus
We should be quite abolished and expire.
What fear we then? What doubt we to incense
His utmost ire? Which to the heighth enraged,
Will either quite consume us, and reduce
To nothing this essential, happier far
Than miserable to have eternal being:
Or if our substance be indeed divine,
And cannot cease to be, we are at worst
On this side nothing; and by proof we feel
Our power sufficient to disturb his Heav'n,
And with perpetual inroads to alarm,
Though inaccessible, his fatal throne:
Which if not victory is yet revenge.
    He ended frowning, and his look denounced
Desperate revenge, and battle dangerous
To less than gods. On th' other side up rose
Belial, in act more graceful and humane:
A fairer person lost not Heav'n; he seemed
For dignity composed and high explóit:
But all was false and hollow; though his tongue
Dropped manna, and could make the worse appear
The better reason, to perplex and dash
Maturest counsels: for his thoughts were low;
To vice industrious, but to nobler deeds
Timorous and slothful: yet he pleased the ear,
And with persuasive accent thus began.
    I should be much for open war, O Peers,
As not behind in hate; if what was urged
Main reason to persuade immediate war,
Did not dissuade me most, and seem to cast
Ominous conjecture on the whole success:
When he who most excels in fact of arms,
In what he counsels and in what excels
Mistrustful, grounds his courage on despair
And utter dissolution, as the scope
Of all his aim, after some dire revenge.
First, what revenge? The tow'rs of Heav'n are filled
With armèd watch, that render all accéss

Impregnable; oft on the bordering deep
Encamp their legions, or with óbscure wing
Scout far and wide into the realm of Night,
Scorning surprise. Or could we break our way
135 By force, and at our heels all Hell should rise
With blackest insurrection, to confound
Heav'n's purest light, yet our great Enemy
All incorruptible would on his throne
Sit unpolluted, and th' ethereal mould
140 Incapable of stain would soon expel
Her mischief, and purge off the baser fire
Victorious. Thus repulsed, our final hope
Is flat despair: we must exasperate
Th' Almighty Victor to spend all his rage,
145 And that must end us, that must be our cure,
To be no more; sad cure; for who would lose,
Though full of pain, this intellectual being,
Those thoughts that wander through eternity,
To perish rather, swallowed up and lost
150 In the wide womb of uncreated Night,
Devoid of sense and motion? And who knows,
Let this be good, whether our angry Foe
Can give it, or will ever? How he can
Is doubtful; that he never will is sure.
155 Will he, so wise, let loose at once his ire,
Belike through impotence, or unaware,
To give his enemies their wish, and end
Them in his anger, whom his anger saves
To punish endless? Wherefore cease we then?
160 Say they who counsel war, we are decreed,
Reserved and destined to eternal woe;
Whatever doing, what can we suffer more,
What can we suffer worse? Is this then worst,
Thus sitting, thus consulting, thus in arms?
165 What when we fled amain, pursued and strook
With Heav'n's afflicting thunder, and besought
The deep to shelter us? This Hell then seemed
A refuge from those wounds: or when we lay
Chained on the burning lake? That sure was worse.

170   What if the breath that kindled those grim fires
       Awaked should blow them into sevenfold rage
       And plunge us in the flames? Or from above
       Should intermitted vengeance arm again
       His red right hand to plague us? What if all
175   Her stores were opened, and this firmament
       Of Hell should spout her cataracts of fire,
       Impendent horrors, threatening hideous fall
       One day upon our heads; while we perhaps
       Designing or exhorting glorious war,
180   Caught in a fiery tempest shall be hurled
       Each on his rock transfixed, the sport and prey
       Of racking whirlwinds, or for ever sunk
       Under yon boiling ocean, wrapped in chains;
       There to converse with everlasting groans,
185   Unrespited, unpitied, unreprieved,
       Ages of hopeless end; this would be worse.
       War therefore, open or concealed, alike
       My voice dissuades; for what can force or guile
       With him, or who deceive his mind, whose eye
190   Views all things at one view? He from Heav'n's heighth
       All these our motions vain, sees and derides;
       Not more Almighty to resist our might
       Than wise to frustrate all our plots and wiles.
       Shall we then live thus vile, the race of Heav'n
195   Thus trampled, thus expelled to suffer here
       Chains and these torments? Better these than worse
       By my advice: since Fate inevitable
       Subdues us, and omnipotent decree,
       The Victor's will. To suffer, as to do,
200   Our strength is equal, nor the law unjust
       That so ordains: this was at first resolved,
       If we were wise, against so great a foe
       Contending, and so doubtful what might fall.
       I laugh, when those who at the spear are bold
205   And vent'rous, if that fail them, shrink and fear
       What yet they know must follow, to endure
       Exile, or ignominy, or bonds, or pain,
       The sentence of their Conqueror: this is now

Our doom; which if we can sustain and bear,
210 Our súpreme Foe in time may much remit
His anger, and perhaps thus far removed
Not mind us not offending, satisfied
With what is punished; whence these raging fires
Will slacken, if his breath stir not their flames.
215 Our purer essence then will overcome
Their noxious vapour, or inured not feel,
Or changed at length, and to the place conformed
In temper and in nature, will receive
Familiar the fierce heat, and void of pain;
220 This horror will grow mild, this darkness light,
Besides what hope the never-ending flight
Of future days may bring, what chance, what change
Worth waiting, since our present lot appears
For happy though but ill, for ill not worst,
225 If we procure not to ourselves more woe.
     Thus Belial with words clothed in reason's garb
Counselled ignoble ease and peaceful sloth,
Not peace: and after him thus Mammon spake.
     Either to disenthrone the King of Heav'n
230 We war, if war be best, or to regain
Our own right lost: him to unthrone we then
May hope when everlasting Fate shall yield
To fickle Chance, and Chaos judge the strife:
The former vain to hope argues as vain
235 The latter: for what place can be for us
Within Heav'n's bound, unless Heav'n's Lord supreme
We overpower? Suppose he should relent
And publish grace to all, on promise made
Of new subjection; with what eyes could we
240 Stand in his presence humble, and receive
Strict laws imposed, to celebrate his throne
With warbled hymns, and to his Godhead sing
Forced hallelujahs; while he lordly sits
Our envied sov'reign, and his altar breathes
245 Ambrosial odours and ambrosial flowers,
Our servile offerings. This must be our task
In Heav'n, this our delight: how wearisome

Eternity so spent in worship paid
To whom we hate. Let us not then pursue
250 By force impossible, by leave obtained
Unácceptáble, though in Heav'n, our state
Of splendid vassalage, but rather seek
Our own good from ourselves, and from our own
Live to ourselves, though in this vast recess,
255 Free, and to none accountable, preferring
Hard liberty before the easy yoke
Of servile pomp. Our greatness will appear
Then most conspicuous, when great things of small,
Useful of hurtful, prosperous of adverse,
260 We can create, and in what place soe'er
Thrive under evil, and work ease out of pain
Through labour and endurance. This deep world
Of darkness do we dread? How oft amidst
Thick clouds and dark doth Heav'n's all-ruling Sire
265 Choose to reside, his glory unobscured,
And with the majesty of darkness round
Covers his throne; from whence deep thunders roar
Must'ring their rage, and Heav'n resembles Hell?
As he our darkness, cannot we his light
270 Imitate when we please? This desert soil
Wants not her hidden lustre, gems and gold;
Nor want we skill or art, from whence to raise
Magnificence; and what can Heav'n show more?
Our torments also may in length of time
275 Become our elements, these piercing fires
As soft as now severe, our temper changed
Into their temper; which must needs remove
The sensible of pain. All things invite
To peaceful counsels, and the settled state
280 Of order, how in safety best we may
Compose our present evils, with regard
Of what we are and where, dismissing quite
All thoughts of war: ye have what I advise.
    He scarce had finished, when such murmur filled
285 Th' assembly, as when hollow rocks retain
The sound of blust'ring winds, which all night long

Had roused the sea, now with hoarse cadence lull
Seafaring men o'erwatched, whose bark by chance
Or pinnace anchors in a craggy bay
290   After the tempest: such applause was heard
As Mammon ended, and his sentence pleased,
Advising peace: for such another field
They dreaded worse than Hell: so much the fear
Of thunder and the sword of Michaël
295   Wrought still within them; and no less desire
To found this nether empire, which might rise
By policy, and long procéss of time,
In emulation opposite to Heav'n.
Which when Beëlzebub perceived, than whom,
300   Satan except, none higher sat, with grave
Aspéct he rose, and in his rising seemed
A pillar of state; deep on his front engraven
Deliberation sat and public care;
And princely counsel in his face yet shone,
305   Majestic though in ruin: sage he stood
With Atlantéan shoulders fit to bear
The weight of mightiest monarchies; his look
Drew audience and attention still as night
Or summer's noontide air, while thus he spake.
310   Thrones and imperial Powers, offspring of Heav'n
Ethereal Virtues; or these titles now
Must we renounce, and changing style be called
Princes of Hell? For so the popular vote
Inclines, here to continue, and build up here
315   A growing empire; doubtless; while we dream,
And know not that the King of Heav'n hath doomed
This place our dungeon, not our safe retreat
Beyond his potent arm, to live exempt
From Heav'n's high jurisdiction, in new league
320   Banded against his throne, but to remain
In strictest bondage, though thus far removed,
Under th' inevitable curb, reserved
His captive multitude: for he, be sure
In heighth or depth, still first and last will reign
325   Sole King, and of his kingdom lose no part

By our revolt, but over Hell extend
His empire, and with iron sceptre rule
Us here, as with his golden those in Heav'n.
What sit we then projecting peace and war?
330 War hath determined us, and foiled with loss
Irreparable; terms of peace yet none
Vouchsafed or sought; for what peace will be giv'n
To us enslaved, but custody severe,
And stripes, and arbitrary punishment
335 Inflicted? and what peace can we return,
But to our power hostility and hate,
Untamed reluctance, and revenge though slow,
Yet ever plotting how the Conqueror least
May reap his conquest, and may least rejoice
340 In doing what we most in suffering feel?
Nor will occasion want, nor shall we need
With dangerous expedition to invade
Heav'n, whose high walls fear no assault or siege
Or ambush from the deep. What if we find
345 Some easier enterprise? There is a place
(If ancient and prophetic fame in Heav'n
Err not) another world, the happy seat
Of some new race called *Man*, about this time
To be created like to us, though less
350 In power and excellence, but favoured more
Of him who rules above; so was his will
Pronounced among the gods, and by an oath,
That shook Heav'n's whole circumference, confirmed.
Thither let us bend all our thoughts, to learn
355 What creatures there inhabit, of what mould,
Or substance, how endued, and what their power,
And where their weakness, how attempted best,
By force or subtlety: though Heav'n be shut,
And Heav'n's high Arbitrator sit secure
360 In his own strength, this place may lie exposed
The utmost border of his kingdom, left
To their defence who hold it: here perhaps
Some advantageous act may be achieved
By sudden onset, either with Hell fire

365   To waste his whole Creation, or possess
       All as our own, and drive as we were driven,
       The puny habitants, or if not drive,
       Seduce them to our party, that their God
       May prove their foe, and with repenting hand
370   Abolish his own works. This would surpass
       Common revenge, and interrupt his joy
       In our confusion, and our joy upraise
       In his disturbance, when his darling sons
       Hurled headlong to partake with us, shall curse
375   Their frail original, and faded bliss,
       Faded so soon. Advise if this be worth
       Attempting, or to sit in darkness here
       Hatching vain empires. Thus Beëlzebub
       Pleaded his devilish counsel, first devised
380   By Satan, and in part proposed: for whence,
       But from the author of all ill could spring
       So deep a malice, to confound the race
       Of mankind in one root, and earth with Hell
       To mingle and involve, done all to spite
385   The great Creator? But their spite still serves
       His glory to augment. The bold design
       Pleased highly those infernal States, and joy
       Sparkled in all their eyes; with full assent
       They vote: whereat his speech he thus renews.
390   Well have ye judged, well ended long debate,
       Synod of gods, and like to what ye are,
       Great things resolved, which from the lowest deep
       Will once more lift us up, in spite of Fate,
       Nearer our ancient seat; perhaps in view
395   Of those bright confines, whence with neighbouring arms
       And opportune excursion we may chance
       Re-enter Heav'n; or else in some mild zone
       Dwell not unvisited of Heav'n's fair light
       Secure, and at the bright'ning orient beam
400   Purge off this gloom; the soft delicious air,
       To heal the scar of these corrosive fires
       Shall breathe her balm. But first whom shall we send
       In search of this new world, whom shall we find

Sufficient? Who shall tempt with wand'ring feet
405   The dark unbottomed infinite abyss
And through the palpable obscure find out
His uncouth way, or spread his airy flight
Upborne with indefatigable wings
Over the vast abrupt, ere he arrive
410   The happy isle; what strength, what art can then
Suffice, or what evasion bear him safe
Through the strict senteries and stations thick
Of angels watching round? Here he had need
All circumspection, and we now no less
415   Choice in our suffrage; for on whom we send,
The weight of all and our last hope relies.
      This said, he sat; and expectation held
His look suspense, awaiting who appeared
To second, or oppose, or undertake
420   The perilous attempt: but all sat mute,
Pondering the danger with deep thoughts; and each
In other's count'nance read his own dismay
Astonished: none among the choice and prime
Of those Heav'n-warring champions could be found
425   So hardy as to proffer or accept
Alone the dreadful voyage; till at last
Satan, whom now transcendent glory raised
Above his fellows, with monarchal pride
Conscious of highest worth, unmoved thus spake.
430   O progeny of Heav'n, empyreal Thrones,
With reason hath deep silence and demur
Seized us, though undismayed: long is the way
And hard, that out of Hell leads up to light;
Our prison strong, this huge convéx of fire,
435   Outrageous to devour, immures us round
Ninefold, and gates of burning adamant
Barred over us prohibit all egress.
These passed, if any pass, the void profound
Of unessential Night receives him next
440   Wide gaping, and with utter loss of being
Threatens him, plunged in that abortive gulf.
If thence he 'scape into whatever world,

Or unknown region, what remains him less
Than unknown dangers and as hard escape.
445 But I should ill become this throne, O Peers,
And this imperial sov'reignty, adorned
With splendour, armed with power, if aught proposed
And judged of public moment, in the shape
Of difficulty or danger could deter
450 Me from attempting. Wherefore do I assume
These royalties, and not refuse to reign,
Refusing to accept as great a share
Of hazard as of honour, due alike
To him who reigns, and so much to him due
455 Of hazard more, as he above the rest
High honoured sits? Go therefore mighty Powers,
Terror of Heav'n, though fall'n; intend at home,
While here shall be our home, what best may ease
The present misery, and render Hell
460 More tolerable; if there be cure or charm
To respite or deceive, or slack the pain
Of this ill mansion: intermit no watch
Against a wakeful Foe, while I abroad
Through all the coasts of dark destruction seek
465 Deliverance for us all: this enterprise
None shall partake with me. Thus saying rose
The monarch, and prevented all reply,
Prudent, lest from his resolution raised
Others among the chief might offer now
470 (Certain to be refused) what erst they feared;
And so refused might in opinion stand
His rivals, winning cheap the high repute
Which he through hazard huge must earn. But they
Dreaded not more th' adventure than his voice
475 Forbidding; and at once with him they rose;
Their rising all at once was as the sound
Of thunder heard remote. Towards him they bend
With awful reverence prone; and as a god
Extol him equal to the highest in Heav'n.
480 Nor failed they to express how much they praised,
That for the general safety he despised

His own: for neither do the Spirits damned
Lose all their virtue; lest bad men should boast
Their specious deeds on earth, which glory excites,
485 Or close ambition varnished o'er with zeal.
Thus they their doubtful consultations dark
Ended rejoicing in their matchless chief:
As when from mountain tops the dusky clouds
Ascending, while the north wind sleeps, o'erspread
490 Heav'n's cheerful face, the louring element
Scowls o'er the darkened landscape snow, or show'r;
If chance the radiant sun with farewell sweet
Extend his ev'ning beam, the fields revive,
The birds their notes renew, and bleating herds
495 Attest their joy, that hill and valley rings.
O shame to men! Devil with devil damned
Firm concord holds, men only disagree
Of creatures rational, though under hope
Of Heav'nly grace: and God proclaiming peace,
500 Yet live in hatred, enmity, and strife
Among themselves, and levy cruel wars,
Wasting the earth, each other to destroy:
As if (which might induce us to accord)
Man had not Hellish foes enow besides,
505 That day and night for his destruction wait.
    The Stygian Council thus dissolved; and forth
In order came the grand infernal Peers:
Midst came their mighty Paramount, and seemed
Alone th' Antagonist of Heav'n, nor less
510 Than Hell's dread Emperor with pomp supreme,
And God-like imitated state; him round
A globe of fiery Seraphim enclosed
With bright emblazonry, and horrent arms.
Then of their session ended they bid cry
515 With trumpets' regal sound the great result:
Toward the four winds four speedy Cherubim
Put to their mouths the sounding alchemy
By herald's voice explained: the hollow abyss
Heard far and wide, and all the host of Hell
520 With deaf'ning shout, returned them loud acclaim.

Thence more at ease their minds and somewhat raised
By false presumptuous hope, the rangèd powers
Disband, and wand'ring, each his several way
Pursues, as inclination or sad choice
525   Leads him perplexed, where he may likeliest find
Truce to his restless thoughts, and entertain
The irksome hours, till his great chief return.
Part on the plain, or in the air sublime
Upon the wing, or in swift race contend,
530   As at th' Olympian games or Pythian fields;
Part curb their fiery steeds, or shun the goal
With rapid wheels, or fronted brígades form.
As when to warn proud cities war appears
Waged in the troubled sky, and armies rush
535   To battle in the clouds, before each van
Prick forth the airy knights, and couch their spears
Till thickest legions close; with feats of arms
From either end of heav'n the welkin burns.
Others with vast Typhoean rage more fell
540   Rend up both rocks and hills, and ride the air
In whirlwind; Hell scarce holds the wild uproar.
As when Alcides from Oechalia crowned
With conquest, felt th' envenomed robe, and tore
Through pain up by the roots Thessalian pines,
545   And Lichas from the top of Oeta threw
Into th' Euboic Sea. Others more mild,
Retreated in a silent valley, sing
With notes angelical to many a harp
Their own heroic deeds and hapless fall
550   By doom of battle; and complain that Fate
Free virtue should enthrall to Force or Chance.
Their song was partial, but the harmony
(What could it less when Spirits immortal sing?)
Suspended Hell, and took with ravishment
555   The thronging audience. In discourse more sweet
(For eloquence the soul, song charms the sense,)
Others apart sat on a hill retired,
In thoughts more elevate, and reasoned high
Of Providence, Foreknowledge, Will and Fate,

560   Fixed Fate, Free Will, Foreknowledge absolute,
       And found no end, in wand'ring mazes lost.
       Of good and evil much they argued then,
       Of happiness and final misery,
       Passion and apathy, and glory and shame,
565   Vain wisdom all, and false philosophy:
       Yet with a pleasing sorcery could charm
       Pain for a while or anguish, and excite
       Fallacious hope, or arm th' obdurèd breast
       With stubborn patience as with triple steel.
570   Another part in squadrons and gross bands,
       On bold adventure to discover wide
       That dismal world, if any clime perhaps
       Might yield them easier habitation, bend
       Four ways their flying march, along the banks
575   Of four infernal rivers that disgorge
       Into the burning lake their baleful streams;
       Abhorrèd Styx the flood of deadly hate,
       Sad Acheron of sorrow, black and deep;
       Cocytus, named of lamentation loud
580   Heard on the rueful stream; fierce Phlegethon
       Whose waves of torrent fire inflame with rage.
       Far off from these a slow and silent stream,
       Lethe the river of oblivion rolls
       Her wat'ry labyrinth, whereof who drinks,
585   Forthwith his former state and being forgets,
       Forgets both joy and grief, pleasure and pain.
       Beyond this flood a frozen continent
       Lies dark and wild, beat with perpetual storms
       Of whirlwind and dire hail, which on firm land
590   Thaws not, but gathers heap and ruin seems
       Of ancient pile; all else deep snow and ice,
       A gulf profound as that Serbonian bog
       Betwixt Damiata and Mount Casius old,
       Where armies whole have sunk: the parching air
595   Burns frore, and cold performs th' effect of fire.
       Thither by Harpy-footed Furies haled,
       At certain revolutions all the damned
       Are brought: and feel by turns the bitter change

Of fierce extremes, extremes by change more fierce,
600 From beds of raging fire to starve in ice
Their soft ethereal warmth, and there to pine
Immovable, infixed, and frozen round,
Periods of time, thence hurried back to fire.
They ferry over this Lethean sound
605 Both to and fro, their sorrow to augment,
And wish and struggle, as they pass, to reach
The tempting stream, with one small drop to lose
In sweet forgetfulness all pain and woe.
All in one moment, and so near the brink;
610 But Fate withstands, and to oppose th' attempt
Medusa with Gorgonian terror guards
The ford, and of itself the water flies
All taste of living wight, as once it fled
The lip of Tantalus. Thus roving on
615 In cónfused march forlorn, th' adventurous bands
With shudd'ring horror pale, and eyes aghast
Viewed first their lamentable lot, and found
No rest: through many a dark and dreary vale
They passed, and many a region dolorous,
620 O'er many a frozen, many a fiery alp,
Rocks, caves, lakes, fens, bogs, dens, and shades of death,
A universe of death, which God by curse
Created evil, for evil only good,
Where all life dies, death lives, and nature breeds,
625 Perverse, all monstrous, all prodigious things,
Abominable, unutterable, and worse
Than fables yet have feigned, or fear conceived,
Gorgons, and Hydras, and Chimeras dire.
    Meanwhile the Adversary of God and man,
630 Satan with thoughts inflamed of highest design,
Puts on swift wings, and toward the gates of Hell
Explores his solitary flight; sometimes
He scours the right-hand coast, sometimes the left,
Now shaves with level wing the deep, then soars
635 Up to the fiery concave tow'ring high.
As when far off at sea a fleet descried
Hangs in the clouds, by equinoctial winds

Close sailing from Bengala, or the isles
Of Ternate and Tidore, whence merchants bring
640 Their spicy drugs: they on the trading flood
Through the wide Ethiopian to the Cape
Ply stemming nightly toward the pole. So seemed
Far off the flying Fiend: at last appear
Hell bounds high reaching to the horrid roof,
645 And thrice threefold the gates; three folds were brass,
Three iron, three of adamantine rock,
Impenetrable, impaled with circling fire,
Yet unconsumed. Before the gates there sat
On either side a formidable shape;
650 The one seemed woman to the waist, and fair,
But ended foul in many a scaly fold
Voluminous and vast, a serpent armed
With mortal sting: about her middle round
A cry of Hell-hounds never ceasing barked
655 With wide Cerberean mouths full loud, and rung
A hideous peal: yet, when they list, would creep,
If aught disturbed their noise, into her womb,
And kennel there, yet there still barked and howled
Within unseen. Far less abhorred than these
660 Vexed Scylla bathing in the sea that parts
Calabria from the hoarse Trinacrian shore:
Nor uglier follow the night-hag, when called
In secret, riding through the air she comes
Lured with the smell of infant blood, to dance
665 With Lapland witches, while the labouring moon
Eclipses at their charms. The other shape,
If shape it might be called that shape had none
Distinguishable in member, joint, or limb,
Or substance might be called that shadow seemed,
670 For each seemed either; black it stood as Night,
Fierce as ten Furies, terrible as Hell,
And shook a dreadful dart; what seemed his head
The likeness of a kingly crown had on.
Satan was now at hand, and from his seat
675 The monster moving onward came as fast,
With horrid strides, Hell trembled as he strode.

Th' undaunted Fiend what this might be admired,
Admired, not feared; God and his Son except,
Created thing naught valued he nor shunned;
680   And with disdainful look thus first began.
      Whence and what art thou, execrable shape,
That dar'st though grim and terrible, advance
Thy miscreated front athwart my way
To yonder gates? Through them I mean to pass,
685   That be assured, without leave asked of thee:
Retire, or taste thy folly, and learn by proof,
Hell-born, not to contend with Spirits of Heav'n.
      To whom the goblin full of wrath replied,
Art thou that traitor angel, art thou he,
690   Who first broke peace in Heav'n and faith, till then
Unbroken, and in proud rebellious arms
Drew after him the third part of Heav'n's sons
Conjúred against the Highest, for which both thou
And they outcást from God, are here condemned
695   To waste eternal days in woe and pain?
And reckon'st thou thyself with Spirits of Heav'n,
Hell-doomed, and breath'st defiance here and scorn,
Where I reign king, and to enrage thee more,
Thy king and lord? Back to thy punishment,
700   False fugitive, and to thy speed add wings,
Lest with a whip of scorpions I pursue
Thy ling'ring, or with one stroke of this dart
Strange horror seize thee, and pangs unfelt before.
      So spake the grisly terror, and in shape,
705   So speaking and so threat'ning, grew tenfold
More dreadful and deform: on th' other side
Incensed with indignation Satan stood
Unterrified, and like a comet burned,
That fires the length of Ophiucus huge
710   In th' Arctic sky, and from his horrid hair
Shakes pestilence and war. Each at the head
Levelled his deadly aim; their fatal hands
No second stroke intend, and such a frown
Each cast at th' other, as when two black clouds
715   With heav'n's artillery fraught, come rattling on

Over the Caspian, then stand front to front
Hov'ring a space, till winds the signal blow
To join their dark encounter in mid air:
So frowned the mighty combatants, that Hell
720 Grew darker at their frown, so matched they stood;
For never but once more was either like
To meet so great a foe: and now great deeds
Had been achieved, whereof all Hell had rung,
Had not the snaky sorceress that sat
725 Fast by Hell gate, and kept the fatal key,
Ris'n, and with hideous outcry rushed between.
O father, what intends thy hand, she cried,
Against thy only son? What fury O son,
Possesses thee to bend that mortal dart
730 Against thy father's head? and know'st for whom;
For him who sits above and laughs the while
At thee ordained his drudge, to execute
Whate'er his wrath, which he calls justice, bids,
His wrath which one day will destroy ye both.
735 She spake, and at her words the Hellish pest
Forbore, then these to her Satan returned:
So strange thy outcry, and thy words so strange
Thou interposest, that my sudden hand
Prevented spares to tell thee yet by deeds
740 What it intends; till first I know of thee,
What thing thou art, thus double-formed, and why
In this infernal vale first met thou call'st
Me father, and that phantasm call'st my son?
I know thee not, nor ever saw till now
745 Sight more detestable than him and thee.
T' whom thus the portress of Hell gate replied;
Hast thou forgot me then, and do I seem
Now in thine eye so foul, once deemed so fair
In Heav'n, when at th' assembly, and in sight
750 Of all the Seraphim with thee combined
In bold conspiracy against Heav'n's King,
All on a sudden miserable pain
Surprised thee, dim thine eyes, and dizzy swum
In darkness, while thy head flames thick and fast

755   Threw forth, till on the left side op'ning wide,
      Likest to thee in shape and count'nance bright,
      Then shining Heav'nly fair, a goddess armed
      Out of thy head I sprung: amazement seized
      All th' host of Heav'n; back they recoiled afraid
760   At first, and called me *Sin*, and for a Sign
      Portentous held me; but familiar grown,
      I pleased, and with attractive graces won
      The most averse, thee chiefly, who full oft
      Thyself in me thy perfect image viewing
765   Becam'st enamoured, and such joy thou took'st
      With me in secret, that my womb conceived
      A growing burden. Meanwhile war arose,
      And fields were fought in Heav'n; wherein remained
      (For what could else) to our Almighty Foe
770   Clear victory, to our part loss and rout
      Through all the Empyrean: down they fell
      Driv'n headlong from the pitch of Heaven, down
      Into this deep, and in the general fall
      I also; at which time this powerful key
775   Into my hand was giv'n, with charge to keep
      These gates for ever shut, which none can pass
      Without my op'ning. Pensive here I sat
      Alone, but long I sat not, till my womb
      Pregnant by thee, and now excessive grown
780   Prodigious motion felt and rueful throes.
      At last this odious offspring whom thou seest
      Thine own begotten, breaking violent way
      Tore through my entrails, that with fear and pain
      Distorted, all my nether shape thus grew
785   Transformed: but he my inbred enemy
      Forth issued, brandishing his fatal dart
      Made to destroy: I fled, and cried out *Death*;
      Hell trembled at the hideous name, and sighed
      From all her caves, and back resounded *Death*.
790   I fled, but he pursued (though more, it seems,
      Inflamed with lust than rage) and swifter far,
      Me overtook his mother all dismayed,
      And in embraces forcible and foul

Engend'ring with me, of that rape begot
795   These yelling monsters that with ceaseless cry
Surround me, as thou saw'st, hourly conceived
And hourly born, with sorrow infinite
To me, for when they list into the womb
That bred them they return, and howl and gnaw
800   My bowels, their repast; then bursting forth
Afresh with conscious terrors vex me round,
That rest or intermission none I find.
Before mine eyes in opposition sits
Grim Death my son and foe, who sets them on,
805   And me his parent would full soon devour
For want of other prey, but that he knows
His end with mine involved; and knows that I
Should prove a bitter morsel, and his bane,
Whenever that shall be; so Fate pronounced.
810   But thou O father, I forewarn thee, shun
His deadly arrow; neither vainly hope
To be invulnerable in those bright arms,
Though tempered Heav'nly, for that mortal dint,
Save he who reigns above, none can resist.
815   She finished, and the subtle Fiend his lore
Soon learned, now milder, and thus answered smooth.
Dear daughter, since thou claim'st me for thy sire,
And my fair son here show'st me, the dear pledge
Of dalliance had with thee in Heav'n, and joys
820   Then sweet, now sad to mention, through dire change
Befall'n us unforeseen, unthought of, know
I come no enemy, but to set free
From out this dark and dismal house of pain,
Both him and thee, and all the Heav'nly host
825   Of Spirits that in our just pretences armed
Fell with us from on high: from them I go
This uncouth errand sole, and one for all
Myself expose, with lonely steps to tread
Th' unfounded deep, and through the void immense
830   To search with wand'ring quest a place foretold
Should be, and, by concurring signs, ere now
Created vast and round, a place of bliss

In the purlieus of Heav'n, and therein placed
A race of upstart creatures, to supply
835   Perhaps our vacant room, though more removed,
Lest Heav'n surcharged with potent multitude
Might hap to move new broils: be this or aught
Than this more secret now designed, I haste
To know, and this once known, shall soon return,
840   And bring ye to the place where thou and Death
Shall dwell at ease, and up and down unseen
Wing silently the buxom air, embalmed
With odours; there ye shall be fed and filled
Immeasurably, all things shall be your prey.
845   He ceased, for both seemed highly pleased, and Death
Grinned horrible a ghastly smile, to hear
His famine should be filled, and blessed his maw
Destined to that good hour: no less rejoiced
His mother bad, and thus bespake her sire.
850   The key of this infernal pit by due,
And by command of Heav'n's all-powerful King
I keep, by him forbidden to unlock
These adamantine gates: against all force
Death ready stands to interpose his dart,
855   Fearless to be o'ermatched by living might.
But what owe I to his commands above
Who hates me, and hath hither thrust me down
Into this gloom of Tartarus profound,
To sit in hateful office here confined,
860   Inhabitant of Heav'n, and Heav'nly-born,
Here in perpetual agony and pain,
With terrors and with clamours compassed round
Of mine own brood, that on my bowels feed:
Thou art my father, thou my author, thou
865   My being gav'st me; whom should I obey
But thee, whom follow? thou wilt bring me soon
To that new world of light and bliss, among
The gods who live at ease, where I shall reign
At thy right hand voluptuous, as beseems
870   Thy daughter and thy darling, without end.
    Thus saying, from her side the fatal key,

Sad instrument of all our woe, she took;
And towards the gate rolling her bestial train,
Forthwith the huge portcullis high up drew,
875 Which but herself not all the Stygian powers
Could once have moved; then in the key-hole turns
Th' intricate wards, and every bolt and bar
Of massy iron or solid rock with ease
Unfastens: on a sudden open fly
880 With impetuous recoil and jarring sound
Th' infernal doors, and on their hinges grate
Harsh thunder, that the lowest bottom shook
Of Erebus. She opened, but to shut
Excelled her power; the gates wide open stood,
885 That with extended wings a bannered host
Under spread ensigns marching might pass through
With horse and chariots ranked in loose array;
So wide they stood, and like a furnace mouth
Cast forth redounding smoke and ruddy flame.
890 Before their eyes in sudden view appear
The secrets of the hoary deep, a dark
Illimitable Ocean without bound,
Without dimension, where length, breadth, and heighth,
And time and place are lost; where eldest Night
895 And Chaos, ancestors of Nature, hold
Eternal anarchy, amidst the noise
Of endless wars, and by confusion stand.
For Hot, Cold, Moist, and Dry, four champions fierce
Strive here for mast'ry, and to battle bring
900 Their embryon atoms; they around the flag
Of each his faction, in their several clans,
Light-armed or heavy, sharp, smooth, swift or slow,
Swarm populous, unnumbered as the sands
Of Barca or Cyrene's torrid soil,
905 Levied to side with warring winds, and poise
Their lighter wings. To whom these most adhere,
He rules a moment; Chaos umpire sits,
And by decision more embroils the fray
By which he reigns: next him high arbiter
910 Chance governs all. Into this wild abyss,

The womb of Nature and perhaps her grave,
Of neither sea, nor shore, nor air, nor fire,
But all these in their pregnant causes mixed
Confus'dly, and which thus must ever fight,
915   Unless th' Almighty Maker them ordain
His dark materials to create more worlds,
Into this wild abyss the wary Fiend
Stood on the brink of Hell and looked a while,
Pondering his voyage; for no narrow frith
920   He had to cross. Nor was his ear less pealed
With noises loud and ruinous (to compare
Great things with small) than when Bellona storms,
With all her battering engines bent to raze
Some capital city; or less than if this frame
925   Of heav'n were falling, and these elements
In mutiny had from her axle torn
The steadfast earth. At last his sail-broad vans
He spreads for flight, and in the surging smoke
Uplifted spurns the ground, thence many a league
930   As in a cloudy chair ascending rides
Audacious, but that seat soon failing, meets
A vast vacuity: all unawares
Flutt'ring his pennons vain plumb down he drops
Ten thousand fathom deep, and to this hour
935   Down had been falling, had not by ill chance
The strong rebuff of some tumultuous cloud
Instínct with fire and nitre hurried him
As many miles aloft: that fury stayed,
Quenched in a boggy Syrtis, neither sea,
940   Nor good dry land: nigh foundered on he fares,
Treading the crude consistence, half on foot,
Half flying; behooves him now both oar and sail.
As when a gryphon through the wilderness
With wingèd course o'er hill or moory dale,
945   Pursues the Arimaspian, who by stealth
Had from his wakeful custody purloined
The guarded gold: so eagerly the Fiend
O'er bog or steep, through strait, rough, dense, or rare,
With head, hands, wings, or feet pursues his way,

950 And swims or sinks, or wades, or creeps, or flies:
At length a universal hubbub wild
Of stunning sounds and voices all confused
Borne through the hollow dark assaults his ear
With loudest vehemence: thither he plies,
955 Undaunted to meet there whatever Power
Or Spirit of the nethermost abyss
Might in that noise reside, of whom to ask
Which way the nearest coast of darkness lies
Bordering on light; when straight behold the throne
960 Of Chaos, and his dark pavilion spread
Wide on the wasteful deep; with him enthroned
Sat sable-vested Night, eldest of things,
The consort of his reign; and by them stood
Orcus and Ades, and the dreaded name
965 Of Demogorgon; Rumour next and Chance,
And Tumult and Confusion all embroiled,
And Discord with a thousand various mouths.
    T' whom Satan turning boldly, thus. Ye Powers
And Spirits of this nethermost abyss,
970 Chaos and ancient Night, I come no spy,
With purpose to explore or to disturb
The secrets of your realm, but by constraint
Wand'ring this darksome desert, as my way
Lies through your spacious empire up to light,
975 Alone, and without guide, half lost, I seek
What readiest path leads where your gloomy bounds
Confine with Heav'n; or if some other place
From your dominion won, th' Ethereal King
Possesses lately, thither to arrive
980 I travel this profound, direct my course;
Directed, no mean recompense it brings
To your behoof, if I that region lost,
All usurpation thence expelled, reduce
To her original darkness and your sway
985 (Which is my present journey) and once more
Erect the standard there of ancient Night;
Yours be th' advantage all, mine the revenge.
    Thus Satan; and him thus the Anarch old

With falt'ring speech and visage incomposed
990 Answered. I know thee, stranger, who thou art,
That mighty leading angel, who of late
Made head against Heav'n's King, though overthrown.
I saw and heard, for such a numerous host
Fled not in silence through the frighted deep
995 With ruin upon ruin, rout on rout,
Confusion worse confounded; and Heav'n gates
Poured out by millions her victorious bands
Pursuing. I upon my frontiers here
Keep residence; if all I can will serve,
1000 That little which is left so to defend,
Encroached on still through [y]our intestine broils
Weak'ning the sceptre of old Night: first Hell
Your dungeon stretching far and wide beneath;
Now lately heav'n and earth, another world
1005 Hung o'er my realm, linked in a golden chain
To that side Heav'n from whence your legions fell:
If that way be your walk, you have not far;
So much the nearer danger; go and speed;
Havoc and spoil and ruin are my gain.
1010   He ceased; and Satan stayed not to reply,
But glad that now his sea should find a shore,
With fresh alacrity and force renewed
Springs upward like a pyramid of fire
Into the wide expanse, and through the shock
1015 Of fighting elements, on all sides round
Environed wins his way; harder beset
And more endangered, than when Argo passed
Through Bosporus betwixt the justling rocks:
Or when Ulysses on the larboard shunned
1020 Charybdis, and by th' other whirlpool steered.
So he with difficulty and labour hard
Moved on, with difficulty and labour he;
But he once passed, soon after when man fell,
Strange alteration! Sin and Death amain
1025 Following his track, such was the will of Heav'n,
Paved after him a broad and beaten way
Over the dark abyss, whose boiling gulf

Tamely endured a bridge of wondrous length
From Hell continued reaching th' utmost orb
1030 Of this frail world; by which the Spirits perverse
With easy intercourse pass to and fro
To tempt or punish mortals, except whom
God and good angels guard by special grace.
But now at last the sacred influence
1035 Of light appears, and from the walls of Heav'n
Shoots far into the bosom of dim Night
A glimmering dawn; here Nature first begins
Her farthest verge, and Chaos to retire
As from her outmost works a broken foe
1040 With tumult less and with less hostile din,
That Satan with less toil, and now with ease
Wafts on the calmer wave by dubious light
And like a weather-beaten vessel holds
Gladly the port, though shrouds and tackle torn;
1045 Or in the emptier waste, resembling air,
Weighs his spread wings, at leisure to behold
Far off th' empyreal Heav'n, extended wide
In circuit, undetermined square or round,
With opal tow'rs and battlements adorned
1050 Of living sapphire, once his native seat;
And fast by hanging in a golden chain
This pendent world, in bigness as a star
Of smallest magnitude close by the moon.
Thither full fraught with mischievous revenge,
1055 Accursed, and in a cursèd hour he hies.

BOOK III

The Argument

1   God sitting on his throne sees Satan flying towards this world, then newly created; shows him to the Son who sat at his right hand; foretells the success of Satan in perverting mankind; clears his own justice and wisdom from all imputation, having

5   created man free and able enough to have withstood his tempter; yet declares his purpose of grace towards him, in regard he fell not of his own malice, as did Satan, but by him seduced. The Son of God renders praises to his Father for the manifestation of his gracious purpose towards man; but

10   God again declares, that grace cannot be extended towards man without the satisfaction of divine justice; man hath offended the majesty of God by aspiring to Godhead, and therefore with all his progeny devoted to death must die, unless someone can be found sufficient to answer for his

15   offence, and undergo his punishment. The Son of God freely offers himself a ransom for man: the Father accepts him, ordains his Incarnation, pronounces his Exaltation above all names in Heaven and earth; commands all the angels to adore him; they obey, and hymning to their harps in full choir,

20   celebrate the Father and the Son. Meanwhile Satan alights upon the bare convex of this world's outermost orb; where wandering he first finds a place since called the Limbo of Vanity; what persons and things fly up thither; thence comes to the gate of Heaven, described ascending by stairs, and the

25   waters above the firmament that flow about it: his passage thence to the orb of the sun; he finds there Uriel the regent of that orb, but first changes himself into the shape of a meaner angel; and pretending a zealous desire to behold the new Creation and man whom God had placed here, inquires of

30   him the place of his habitation, and is directed; alights first on Mount Niphates.

Hail holy Light, offspring of Heav'n first-born,
Or of th' Eternal co-eternal beam
May I express thee unblamed? Since God is light,
And never but in unapproachèd light
5   Dwelt from eternity, dwelt then in thee,
Bright effluence of bright essence increate.
Or hear'st thou rather pure ethereal stream,
Whose fountain who shall tell? Before the sun,
Before the heavens thou wert, and at the voice
10 Of God, as with a mantle didst invest
The rising world of waters dark and deep,
Won from the void and formless infinite.
Thee I revisit now with bolder wing,
Escaped the Stygian pool, though long detained
15 In that obscure sojóurn, while in my flight
Through utter and through middle darkness borne
With other notes than to th' Orphéan lyre
I sung of Chaos and eternal Night,
Taught by the Heav'nly Muse to venture down
20 The dark descent, and up to reascend,
Though hard and rare: thee I revisit safe,
And feel thy sov'reign vital lamp; but thou
Revisit'st not these eyes, that roll in vain
To find thy piercing ray, and find no dawn;
25 So thick a drop serene hath quenched their orbs,
Or dim suffusion veiled. Yet not the more
Cease I to wander where the Muses haunt
Clear spring, or shady grove, or sunny hill,
Smit with the love of sacred song; but chief
30 Thee Sion and the flow'ry brooks beneath
That wash thy hallowed feet, and warbling flow,
Nightly I visit: nor sometimes forget
Those other two equalled with me in fate,
So were I equalled with them in renown,
35 Blind Thamyris and blind Maeonides,
And Tiresias and Phineus prophets old.
Then feed on thoughts, that voluntary move
Harmonious numbers; as the wakeful bird

Sings darkling, and in shadiest covert hid
40 Tunes her nocturnal note. Thus with the year
Seasons return, but not to me returns
Day, or the sweet approach of ev'n or morn,
Or sight of vernal bloom, or summer's rose,
Or flocks, or herds, or human face divine;
45 But cloud instead, and ever-during dark
Surrounds me, from the cheerful ways of men
Cut off, and for the Book of Knowledge fair
Presented with a universal blank
Of Nature's works to me expunged and razed,
50 And wisdom at one entrance quite shut out.
So much the rather thou celestial Light
Shine inward, and the mind through all her powers
Irradiate, there plant eyes, all mist from thence
Purge and disperse, that I may see and tell
55 Of things invisible to mortal sight.
      Now had th' Almighty Father from above,
From the pure Empyrean where he sits
High throned above all heighth, bent down his eye,
His own works and their works at once to view:
60 About him all the sanctities of Heaven
Stood thick as stars, and from his sight received
Beatitude past utterance; on his right
The radiant image of his glory sat,
His only Son; on earth he first beheld
65 Our two first parents, yet the only two
Of mankind, in the happy garden placed,
Reaping immortal fruits of joy and love,
Uninterrupted joy, unrivalled love
In blissful solitude; he then surveyed
70 Hell and the gulf between, and Satan there
Coasting the wall of Heav'n on this side Night
In the dun air sublime, and ready now
To stoop with wearied wings, and willing feet
On the bare outside of this world, that seemed
75 Firm land imbosomed without firmament,
Uncertain which, in ocean or in air.
Him God beholding from his prospect high,

Wherein past, present, future he beholds,
Thus to his only Son foreseeing spake.
80   Only begotten Son, seest thou what rage
Transports our Adversary, whom no bounds
Prescribed, no bars of Hell, nor all the chains
Heaped on him there, nor yet the main abyss
Wide interrupt can hold; so bent he seems
85   On desperate revenge, that shall redound
Upon his own rebellious head. And now
Through all restraint broke loose he wings his way
Not far off Heav'n, in the precincts of light,
Directly towards the new created world,
90   And man there placed, with purpose to assay
If him by force he can destroy, or worse,
By some false guile pervert; and shall pervert;
For man will hearken to his glozing lies,
And easily transgress the sole command,
95   Sole pledge of his obedience: so will fall
He and his faithless progeny: whose fault?
Whose but his own? Ingrate, he had of me
All he could have; I made him just and right,
Sufficient to have stood, though free to fall.
100   Such I created all th' ethereal Powers
And Spirits, both them who stood and them who failed;
Freely they stood who stood, and fell who fell.
Not free, what proof could they have giv'n sincere
Of true allegiance, constant faith or love,
105   Where only what they needs must do, appeared,
Not what they would? What praise could they receive?
What pleasure I from such obedience paid,
When will and reason (reason also is choice)
Useless and vain, of freedom both despoiled,
110   Made passive both, had served necessity,
Not me. They therefore as to right belonged,
So were created, nor can justly accuse
Their Maker, or their making, or their fate,
As if predestination overruled
115   Their will, disposed by absolute decree
Or high foreknowledge; they themselves decreed

Their own revolt, not I: if I foreknew,
Foreknowledge had no influence on their fault,
Which had no less proved certain unforeknown.
120 So without least impúlse or shadow of Fate,
Or aught by me immutably foreseen,
They trespass, authors to themselves in all
Both what they judge and what they choose; for so
I formed them free, and free they must remain,
125 Till they enthrall themselves: I else must change
Their nature, and revoke the high decree
Unchangeable, eternal, which ordained
Their freedom; they themselves ordained their Fall.
The first sort by their own suggestion fell,
130 Self-tempted, self-depraved: man falls deceived
By the other first: man therefore shall find grace;
The other none: in mercy and justice both,
Through Heav'n and earth, so shall my glory excel,
But mercy first and last shall brightest shine.
135   Thus while God spake, ambrosial fragrance filled
All Heav'n, and in the blessèd Spirits elect
Sense of new joy ineffable diffused:
Beyond compare the Son of God was seen
Most glorious, in him all his Father shone
140 Substantially expressed, and in his face
Divine compassion visibly appeared,
Love without end, and without measure grace,
Which uttering thus he to his Father spake.
    O Father, gracious was that word which closed
145 Thy sov'reign sentence, that man should find grace;
For which both Heav'n and earth shall high extol
Thy praises, with th' innumerable sound
Of hymns and sacred songs, wherewith thy throne
Encompassed shall resound thee ever blest.
150 For should man finally be lost, should man
Thy creature late so loved, thy youngest son
Fall circumvented thus by fraud, though joined
With his own folly? That be from thee far,
That far be from thee, Father, who art judge
155 Of all things made, and judgest only right.

Or shall the Adversary thus obtain
His end, and frustrate thine, shall he fulfil
His malice, and thy goodness bring to naught,
Or proud return though to his heavier doom,
160 Yet with revenge accomplished and to Hell
Draw after him the whole race of mankind,
By him corrupted? Or wilt thou thyself
Abolish thy creation, and unmake,
For him, what for thy glory thou hast made?
165 So should thy goodness and thy greatness both
Be questioned and blasphemed without defence.
    To whom the great Creator thus replied.
O Son, in whom my soul hath chief delight,
Son of my bosom, Son who art alone
170 My Word, my wisdom, and effectual might,
All hast thou spoken as my thoughts are, all
As my eternal purpose hath decreed:
Man shall not quite be lost, but saved who will,
Yet not of will in him, but grace in me
175 Freely vouchsafed; once more I will renew
His lapsèd powers, though forfeit and enthralled
By sin to foul exorbitant desires;
Upheld by me, yet once more he shall stand
On even ground against his mortal foe,
180 By me upheld, that he may know how frail
His fall'n condition is, and to me owe
All his deliverance, and to none but me.
Some I have chosen of peculiar grace
Elect above the rest; so is my will:
185 The rest shall hear me call, and oft be warned
Their sinful state, and to appease betimes
Th' incensèd Deity, while offered grace
Invites; for I will clear their senses dark,
What may suffice, and soften stony hearts
190 To pray, repent, and bring obedience due.
To prayer, repentance, and obedience due,
Though but endeavoured with sincere intent,
Mine ear shall not be slow, mine eye not shut.
And I will place within them as a guide

195   My umpire conscience, whom if they will hear,
       Light after light well-used they shall attain,
       And to the end persisting, safe arrive.
       This my long sufferance and my day of grace
       They who neglect and scorn, shall never taste;
200   But hard be hardened, blind be blinded more,
       That they may stumble on, and deeper fall;
       And none but such from mercy I exclude.
       But yet all is not done; man disobeying,
       Disloyal breaks his fealty, and sins
205   Against the high supremacy of Heav'n,
       Affecting Godhead, and so losing all,
       To expiate his treason hath naught left,
       But to destruction sacred and devote,
       He with his whole posterity must die,
210   Die he or Justice must; unless for him
       Some other able, and as willing, pay
       The rigid satisfaction, death for death.
       Say Heav'nly Powers, where shall we find such love,
       Which of ye will be mortal to redeem
215   Man's mortal crime, and just th' unjust to save,
       Dwells in all Heaven charity so dear?
          He asked, but all the Heav'nly choir stood mute,
       And silence was in Heav'n: on man's behalf
       Patron or intercessor none appeared,
220   Much less that durst upon his own head draw
       The deadly forfeiture, and ransom set.
       And now without redemption all mankind
       Must have been lost, adjudged to death and Hell
       By doom severe, had not the Son of God,
225   In whom the fulness dwells of love divine,
       His dearest mediation thus renewed.
          Father, thy word is past, man shall find grace;
       And shall grace not find means, that finds her way,
       The speediest of thy wingèd messengers,
230   To visit all thy creatures, and to all
       Comes unprevented, unimplored, unsought,
       Happy for man, so coming; he her aid
       Can never seek, once dead in sins and lost;

Atonement for himself or offering meet,
235 Indebted and undone, hath none to bring:
Behold me then, me for him, life for life
I offer, on me let thine anger fall;
Account me man; I for his sake will leave
Thy bosom, and this glory next to thee
240 Freely put off, and for him lastly die
Well pleased, on me let Death wreck all his rage;
Under his gloomy power I shall not long
Lie vanquished; thou hast given me to possess
Life in myself for ever, by thee I live,
245 Though now to Death I yield, and am his due
All that of me can die, yet that debt paid,
Thou wilt not leave me in the loathsome grave
His prey, nor suffer my unspotted soul
For ever with corruption there to dwell;
250 But I shall rise victorious, and subdue
My vanquisher, spoiled of his vaunted spoil;
Death his death's wound shall then receive, and stoop
Inglorious, of his mortal sting disarmed.
I through the ample air in triumph high
255 Shall lead Hell captive maugre Hell, and show
The powers of darkness bound. Thou at the sight
Pleased, out of Heaven shalt look down and smile,
While by thee raised I ruin all my foes,
Death last, and with his carcass glut the grave:
260 Then with the multitude of my redeemed
Shall enter Heaven long absent, and return,
Father, to see thy face, wherein no cloud
Of anger shall remain, but peace assured,
And reconcilement; wrath shall be no more
265 Thenceforth, but in thy presence joy entire.
    His words here ended, but his meek aspéct
Silent yet spake, and breathed immortal love
To mortal men, above which only shone
Filial obedience: as a sacrifice
270 Glad to be offered, he attends the will
Of his great Father. Admiration seized
All Heav'n, what this might mean, and whither tend

Wond'ring; but soon th' Almighty thus replied:
    O thou in Heav'n and earth the only peace
275 Found out for mankind under wrath, O thou
    My sole complacence! Well thou know'st how dear
    To me are all my works, nor man the least
    Though last created, that for him I spare
    Thee from my bosom and right hand, to save,
280 By losing thee a while, the whole race lost.
    Thou therefore whom thou only canst redeem,
    Their nature also to thy nature join;
    And be thyself man among men on earth,
    Made flesh, when time shall be, of virgin seed,
285 By wondrous birth: be thou in Adam's room
    The head of all mankind, though Adam's son.
    As in him perish all men, so in thee
    As from a second root shall be restored,
    As many as are restored, without thee none.
290 His crime makes guilty all his sons; thy merit
    Imputed shall absolve them who renounce
    Their own both righteous and unrighteous deeds,
    And live in thee transplanted, and from thee
    Receive new life. So man, as is most just,
295 Shall satisfy for man, be judged and die,
    And dying rise, and rising with him raise
    His brethren, ransomed with his own dear life.
    So Heav'nly love shall outdo Hellish hate,
    Giving to death, and dying to redeem,
300 So dearly to redeem what Hellish hate
    So easily destroyed, and still destroys
    In those who, when they may, accept not grace.
    Nor shalt thou by descending to assume
    Man's nature, lessen or degrade thine own.
305 Because thou hast, though throned in highest bliss
    Equal to God, and equally enjoying
    God-like fruition, quitted all to save
    A world from utter loss, and hast been found
    By merit more than birthright Son of God,
310 Found worthiest to be so by being good,
    Far more than great or high; because in thee

Love hath abounded more than glory abounds,
Therefore thy humiliation shall exalt
With thee thy manhood also to this throne;
315 Here shalt thou sit incarnate, here shalt reign
Both God and man, Son both of God and man,
Anointed universal King; all power
I give thee, reign for ever, and assume
Thy merits; under thee as Head Supreme
320 Thrones, Princedoms, Powers, Dominions I reduce:
All knees to thee shall bow, of them that bide
In Heaven, or earth, or under earth in Hell;
When thou attended gloriously from Heav'n
Shalt in the sky appear, and from thee send
325 The summoning Archangels to proclaim
Thy dread tribunal: forthwith from all winds
The living, and forthwith the cited dead
Of all past ages to the general doom
Shall hasten, such a peal shall rouse their sleep.
330 Then all thy saints assembled, thou shalt judge
Bad men and angels, they arraigned shall sink
Beneath thy sentence; Hell, her numbers full,
Thenceforth shall be for ever shut. Meanwhile
The world shall burn, and from her ashes spring
335 New heav'n and earth, wherein the just shall dwell,
And after all their tribulations long
See golden days, fruitful of golden deeds,
With joy and love triúmphing, and fair truth.
Then thou thy regal sceptre shalt lay by,
340 For regal sceptre then no more shall need,
God shall be All in All. But all ye gods,
Adore him, who to compass all this dies,
Adore the Son, and honour him as me.
    No sooner had th' Almighty ceased, but all
345 The multitude of angels with a shout
Loud as from numbers without number, sweet
As from blest voices, uttering joy, Heav'n rung
With jubilee, and loud hosannas filled
Th' eternal regions: lowly reverent
350 Towards either throne they bow, and to the ground

With solemn adoration down they cast
Their crowns inwove with amarant and gold,
Immortal amarant, a flow'r which once
In Paradise, fast by the Tree of Life
355   Began to bloom, but soon for man's offence
To Heav'n removed where first it grew, there grows,
And flow'rs aloft shading the Fount of Life,
And where the river of bliss through midst of Heav'n
Rolls o'er Elysian flow'rs her amber stream;
360   With these that never fade the Spirits elect
Bind their resplendent locks inwreathed with beams;
Now in loose garlands thick thrown off, the bright
Pavement that like a sea of jasper shone
Impurpled with celestial roses smiled.
365   Then crowned again their golden harps they took,
Harps ever tuned, that glittering by their side
Like quivers hung, and with preamble sweet
Of charming symphony they introduce
Their sacred song, and waken raptures high;
370   No voice exempt, no voice but well could join
Melodious part, such concord is in Heav'n.
    Thee Father first they sung omnipotent,
Immutable, immortal, infinite,
Eternal King; thee Author of all being,
375   Fountain of light, thyself invisible
Amidst the glorious brightness where thou sitt'st
Throned inaccessible, but when thou shad'st
The full blaze of thy beams, and through a cloud
Drawn round about thee like a radiant shrine,
380   Dark with excessive bright thy skirts appear,
Yet dazzle Heav'n, that brightest Seraphim
Approach not, but with both wings veil their eyes.
Thee next they sang of all Creation first,
Begotten Son, Divine Similitude,
385   In whose conspicuous count'nance, without cloud
Made visible, th' Almighty Father shines,
Whom else no creature can behold; on thee
Impressed th' effulgence of his glory abides,
Transfused on thee his ample Spirit rests.

390 He Heav'n of Heav'ns and all the Powers therein
By thee created, and by thee threw down
Th' aspiring Dominations: thou that day
Thy Father's dreadful thunder didst not spare,
Nor stop thy flaming chariot wheels, that shook
395 Heav'n's everlasting frame, while o'er the necks
Thou drov'st of warring angels disarrayed.
Back from pursuit thy Powers with loud acclaim
Thee only extolled, Son of thy Father's might,
To execute fierce vengeance on his foes,
400 Not so on man; him through their malice fall'n,
Father of mercy and grace, thou didst not doom
So strictly, but much more to pity incline:
No sooner did thy dear and only Son
Perceive thee purposed not to doom frail man
405 So strictly, but much more to pity inclined,
He to appease thy wrath, and end the strife
Of mercy and justice in thy face discerned,
Regardless of the bliss wherein he sat
Second to thee, offered himself to die
410 For man's offence. O unexampled love,
Love nowhere to be found less than divine!
Hail Son of God, Saviour of men, thy name
Shall be the copious matter of my song
Henceforth, and never shall my harp thy praise
415 Forget, nor from thy Father's praise disjoin.
    Thus they in Heav'n, above the starry sphere,
Their happy hours in joy and hymning spent.
Meanwhile upon the firm opacous globe
Of this round world, whose first convéx divides
420 The luminous inferior orbs, enclosed
From Chaos and th' inroad of Darkness old,
Satan alighted walks: a globe far off
It seemed, now seems a boundless continent
Dark, waste, and wild, under the frown of Night
425 Starless exposed, and ever-threat'ning storms
Of Chaos blust'ring round, inclement sky;
Save on that side which from the wall of Heav'n
Though distant far some small reflection gains

Of glimmering air less vexed with tempest loud:
430 Here walked the Fiend at large in spacious field.
As when a vulture on Imaus bred,
Whose snowy ridge the roving Tartar bounds,
Dislodging from a region scarce of prey
To gorge the flesh of lambs or yeanling kids
435 On hills where flocks are fed, flies toward the springs
Of Ganges or Hydaspes, Indian streams;
But in his way lights on the barren plains
Of Sericana, where Chineses drive
With sails and wind their cany wagons light:
440 So on this windy sea of land, the Fiend
Walked up and down alone bent on his prey,
Alone, for other creature in this place
Living or lifeless to be found was none,
None yet, but store hereafter from the earth
445 Up hither like aërial vapours flew
Of all things transitory and vain, when sin
With vanity had filled the works of men:
Both all things vain, and all who in vain things
Built their fond hopes of glory or lasting fame,
450 Or happiness in this or th' other life;
All who have their reward on earth, the fruits
Of painful superstition and blind zeal,
Naught seeking but the praise of men, here find
Fit retribution, empty as their deeds;
455 All th' unaccomplished works of Nature's hand,
Abortive, monstrous, or unkindly mixed,
Dissolved on earth, fleet hither, and in vain,
Till final dissolution, wander here,
Not in the neighbouring moon, as some have dreamed;
460 Those argent fields more likely habitants,
Translated saints, or middle Spirits hold
Betwixt th' angelical and human kind:
Hither of ill-joined sons and daughters born
First from the ancient world those Giants came
465 With many a vain explóit, though then renowned:
The builders next of Babel on the plain
Of Sennaär, and still with vain design

New Babels, had they wherewithal, would build:
Others came single; he who to be deemed
470   A god, leaped fondly into Etna flames,
Empedocles, and he who to enjoy
Plato's Elysium, leaped into the sea,
Cleombrotus, and many more too long,
Embryos and idiots, eremites and friars
475   White, black and grey, with all their trumpery.
Here pilgrims roam, that strayed so far to seek
In Golgotha him dead, who lives in Heav'n;
And they who to be sure of Paradise
Dying put on the weeds of Dominic,
480   Or in Franciscan think to pass disguised;
They pass the planets seven, and pass the fixed,
And that crystálline sphere whose balance weighs
The trepidation talked, and that first moved;
And now Saint Peter at Heav'n's wicket seems
485   To wait them with his keys, and now at foot
Of Heav'n's ascent they lift their feet, when lo
A violent crosswind from either coast
Blows them transverse ten thousand leagues awry
Into the devious air; then might ye see
490   Cowls, hoods and habits with their wearers tossed
And fluttered into rags; then relics, beads,
Indulgences, dispenses, pardons, bulls,
The sport of winds: all these upwhirled aloft
Fly o'er the backside of the world far off
495   Into a Limbo large and broad, since called
The Paradise of Fools, to few unknown
Long after, now unpeopled, and untrod;
All this dark globe the Fiend found as he passed,
And long he wandered, till at last a gleam
500   Of dawning light turned thitherward in haste
His travelled steps; far distant he descries
Ascending by degrees magnificent
Up to the wall of Heaven a structure high,
At top whereof, but far more rich appeared
505   The work as of a kingly palace gate
With frontispiece of diamond and gold

Embellished; thick with sparkling orient gems
The portal shone, inimitable on earth
By model, or by shading pencil drawn.
510   The stairs were such as whereon Jacob saw
Angels ascending and descending, bands
Of guardians bright, when he from Esau fled
To Padan-Aram, in the field of Luz
Dreaming by night under the open sky,
515   And waking cried, *This is the gate of Heav'n.*
Each stair mysteriously was meant, nor stood
There always, but drawn up to Heav'n sometimes
Viewless, and underneath a bright sea flowed
Of jasper, or of liquid pearl, whereon
520   Who after came from earth, sailing arrived,
Wafted by angels, or flew o'er the lake
Rapt in a chariot drawn by fiery steeds.
The stairs were then let down, whether to dare
The Fiend by easy ascent, or aggravate
525   His sad exclusion from the doors of bliss.
Direct against which opened from beneath,
Just o'er the blissful seat of Paradise,
A passage down to th' earth, a passage wide,
Wider by far than that of aftertimes
530   Over Mount Sion, and, though that were large,
Over the Promised Land to God so dear,
By which to visit oft those happy tribes,
On high behests his angels to and fro
Passed frequent, and his eye with choice regard
535   From Paneas the fount of Jordan's flood
To Beërsaba, where the Holy Land
Borders on Egypt and the Arabian shore;
So wide the op'ning seemed, where bounds were set
To darkness, such as bound the ocean wave.
540   Satan from hence now on the lower stair
That scaled by steps of gold to Heaven gate
Looks down with wonder at the sudden view
Of all this world at once. As when a scout
Through dark and desert ways with peril gone
545   All night; at last by break of cheerful dawn

Obtains the brow of some high-climbing hill,
Which to his eye discovers unaware
The goodly prospect of some foreign land
First seen, or some renowned metropolis
550   With glistering spires and pinnacles adorned,
Which now the rising sun gilds with his beams.
Such wonder seized, though after Heaven seen,
The Spirit malign, but much more envy seized
At sight of all this world beheld so fair.
555   Round he surveys, and well might, where he stood
So high above the circling canopy
Of night's extended shade; from eastern point
Of Libra to the fleecy star that bears
Andromeda far off Atlantic seas
560   Beyond th' horizon; then from pole to pole
He views in breadth, and without longer pause
Down right into the world's first region throws
His flight precipitant, and winds with ease
Through the pure marble air his óblique way
565   Amongst innumerable stars, that shone
Stars distant, but nigh hand seemed other worlds;
Or other worlds they seemed, or happy isles,
Like those Hesperian gardens famed of old,
Fortunate fields, and groves and flow'ry vales,
570   Thrice happy isles, but who dwelt happy there
He stayed not to inquire: above them all
The golden sun in splendour likest Heaven
Allured his eye: thither his course he bends
Through the calm firmament; but up or down
575   By centre or eccentric, hard to tell,
Or longitude, where the great luminary
Aloof the vulgar constellations thick,
That from his lordly eye keep distance due,
Dispenses light from far; they as they move
580   Their starry dance in numbers that compute
Days, months, and years, towards his all-cheering lamp
Turn swift their various motions, or are turned
By his magnetic beam, that gently warms
The universe, and to each inward part

585 With gentle penetration, though unseen,
     Shoots invisible virtue even to the deep:
     So wondrously was set his station bright.
     There lands the Fiend, a spot like which perhaps
     Astronomer in the sun's lucent orb
590 Through his glazed optic tube yet never saw.
     The place he found beyond expression bright,
     Compared with aught on earth, metal or stone;
     Not all parts like, but all alike informed
     With radiant light, as glowing iron with fire;
595 If metal, part seemed gold, part silver clear;
     If stone, carbuncle most or chrysolite,
     Ruby or topaz, to the twelve that shone
     In Aaron's breastplate, and a stone besides
     Imagined rather oft than elsewhere seen,
600 That stone, or like to that which here below
     Philosophers in vain so long have sought,
     In vain, though by their powerful art they bind
     Volátile Hermes, and call up unbound
     In various shapes old Proteus from the sea,
605 Drained through a limbeck to his native form.
     What wonder then if fields and regions here
     Breathe forth elixir pure, and rivers run
     Potable gold, when with one virtuous touch
     Th' arch-chemic sun so far from us remote
610 Produces with terrestrial humour mixed
     Here in the dark so many precious things
     Of colour glorious and effect so rare?
     Here matter new to gaze the Devil met
     Undazzled; far and wide his eye commands,
615 For sight no obstacle found here, nor shade,
     But all sunshine, as when his beams at noon
     Culminate from th' equator, as they now
     Shot upward still direct, whence no way round
     Shadow from body opaque can fall, and the air,
620 Nowhere so clear, sharpened his visual ray
     To objects distant far, whereby he soon
     Saw within ken a glorious angel stand,
     The same whom John saw also in the sun:

His back was turned, but not his brightness hid;
625   Of beaming sunny rays, a golden tiar
Circled his head, nor less his locks behind
Illustrious on his shoulders fledge with wings
Lay waving round; on some great charge employed
He seemed, or fixed in cogitation deep.
630   Glad was the Spirit impure; as now in hope
To find who might direct his wand'ring flight
To Paradise the happy seat of man,
His journey's end and our beginning woe.
But first he casts to change his proper shape,
635   Which else might work him danger or delay:
And now a stripling Cherub he appears,
Not of the prime, yet such as in his face
Youth smiled celestial, and to every limb
Suitable grace diffused, so well he feigned;
640   Under a coronet his flowing hair
In curls on either cheek played, wings he wore
Of many a coloured plume sprinkled with gold,
His habit fit for speed succinct, and held
Before his decent steps a silver wand.
645   He drew not nigh unheard, the angel bright,
Ere he drew nigh, his radiant visage turned,
Admonished by his ear, and straight was known
Th' Archangel Uriel, one of the seven
Who in God's presence, nearest to his throne
650   Stand ready at command, and are his eyes
That run through all the heavens, or down to the earth
Bear his swift errands over moist and dry,
O'er sea and land: him Satan thus accosts.
    Uriel, for thou of those sev'n Spirits that stand
655   In sight of God's high throne, gloriously bright,
The first art wont his great authentic will
Interpreter through highest Heav'n to bring,
Where all his sons thy embassy attend;
And here art likeliest by supreme decree
660   Like honour to obtain, and as his eye
To visit oft this new Creation round;
Unspeakable desire to see, and know

All these his wondrous works, but chiefly man,
His chief delight and favour, him for whom
665   All these his works so wondrous he ordained,
Hath brought me from the choirs of Cherubim
Alone thus wand'ring. Brightest Seraph tell
In which of all these shining orbs hath man
His fixèd seat, or fixèd seat hath none,
670   But all these shining orbs his choice to dwell;
That I may find him, and with secret gaze,
Or open admiration him behold
On whom the great Creator hath bestowed
Worlds, and on whom hath all these graces poured;
675   That both in him and all things, as is meet,
The Universal Maker we may praise;
Who justly hath driv'n out his rebel foes
To deepest Hell, and to repair that loss
Created this new happy race of men
680   To serve him better: wise are all his ways.
　　So spake the false dissembler unperceived;
For neither man nor angel can discern
Hypocrisy, the only evil that walks
Invisible, except to God alone,
685   By his permissive will, through Heav'n and earth:
And oft though wisdom wake, suspicion sleeps
At wisdom's gate, and to simplicity
Resigns her charge, while goodness thinks no ill
Where no ill seems: which now for once beguiled
690   Uriel, though regent of the sun, and held
The sharpest sighted Spirit of all in Heav'n;
Who to the fraudulent impostor foul
In his uprightness answer thus returned.
Fair angel, thy desire which tends to know
695   The works of God, thereby to glorify
The great Work-Master, leads to no excess
That reaches blame, but rather merits praise
The more it seems excess, that led thee hither
From thy empyreal mansion thus alone,
700   To witness with thine eyes what some perhaps

Contented with report hear only in Heav'n:
For wonderful indeed are all his works,
Pleasant to know, and worthiest to be all
Had in remembrance always with delight;
705 But what created mind can comprehend
Their number, or the wisdom infinite
That brought them forth, but hid their causes deep.
I saw when at his word the formless mass,
This world's material mould, came to a heap:
710 Confusion heard his voice, and wild uproar
Stood ruled, stood vast infinitude confined;
Till at his second bidding darkness fled,
Light shone, and order from disorder sprung:
Swift to their several quarters hasted then
715 The cumbrous elements, earth, flood, air, fire
And this ethereal quintessence of heav'n
Flew upward, spirited with various forms,
That rolled orbicular, and turned to stars
Numberless, as thou seest, and how they move;
720 Each had his place appointed, each his course,
The rest in circuit walls this universe.
Look downward on that globe whose hither side
With light from hence, though but reflected, shines;
That place is earth the seat of man, that light
725 His day, which else as th' other hemisphere
Night would invade, but there the neighbouring moon
(So call that opposite fair star) her aid
Timely interposes, and her monthly round
Still ending, still renewing, through mid heav'n,
730 With borrowed light her countenance triform
Hence fills and empties to enlighten th' earth,
And in her pale dominion checks the night.
That spot to which I point is Paradise,
Adam's abode, those lofty shades his bower.
735 Thy way thou canst not miss, me mine requires.
        Thus said, he turned, and Satan bowing low,
As to superior Spirits is wont in Heav'n,
Where honour due and reverence none neglects,

Took leave, and toward the coast of earth beneath,
740 Down from th' ecliptic, sped with hoped success,
Throws his steep flight in many an airy wheel,
Nor stayed, till on Niphates' top he lights.

BOOK IV

The Argument

Satan now in prospect of Eden, and nigh the place where he must now attempt the bold enterprise which he undertook alone against God and man, falls into many doubts with himself, and many passions, fear, envy, and despair; but at length confirms himself in evil, journeys on to Paradise, whose outward prospect and situation is described, overleaps the bounds, sits in the shape of a cormorant on the Tree of Life, as highest in the garden to look about him. The garden described; Satan's first sight of Adam and Eve; his wonder at their excellent form and happy state, but with resolution to work their Fall; overhears their discourse, thence gathers that the Tree of Knowledge was forbidden them to eat of, under penalty of death; and thereon intends to found his Temptation, by seducing them to transgress: then leaves them a while, to know further of their state by some other means. Meanwhile Uriel descending on a sunbeam warns Gabriel, who had in charge the gate of Paradise, that some evil Spirit had escaped the deep, and passed at noon by his sphere in the shape of a good angel down to Paradise, discovered after by his furious gestures in the mount. Gabriel promises to find him ere morning. Night coming on, Adam and Eve, discourse of going to their rest: their bower described; their evening worship. Gabriel drawing forth his bands of night-watch to walk the round of Paradise, appoints two strong angels to Adam's bower, lest the evil spirit should be there doing some harm to Adam or Eve sleeping; there they find him at the ear of Eve, tempting her in a dream, and bring him, though unwilling, to Gabriel; by whom questioned, he scornfully answers, prepares resistance, but hindered by a sign from Heaven, flies out of Paradise.

O for that warning voice, which he who saw
Th' Apocalypse, heard cry in Heav'n aloud,
Then when the Dragon, put to second rout,
Came furious down to be revenged on men,
5 *Woe to the inhabitants on earth!* that now,
While time was, our first parents had been warned
The coming of their secret foe, and 'scaped
Haply so 'scaped his mortal snare; for now
Satan, now first inflamed with rage, came down,
10 The Tempter ere th' Accuser of mankind,
To wreck on innocent frail man his loss
Of that first battle, and his flight to Hell:
Yet not rejoicing in his speed, though bold,
Far off and fearless, nor with cause to boast,
15 Begins his dire attempt, which nigh the birth
Now rolling, boils in his tumultuous breast,
And like a devilish engine back recoils
Upon himself; horror and doubt distract
His troubled thoughts, and from the bottom stir
20 The Hell within him, for within him Hell
He brings, and round about him, nor from Hell
One step no more than from himself can fly
By change of place: now conscience wakes despair
That slumbered, wakes the bitter memory
25 Of what he was, what is, and what must be
Worse; of worse deeds worse sufferings must ensue.
Sometimes towards Eden which now in his view
Lay pleasant, his grieved look he fixes sad,
Sometimes towards heav'n and the full-blazing sun,
30 Which now sat high in his meridian tower:
Then much revolving, thus in sighs began.
   O thou that with surpassing glory crowned,
Look'st from thy sole dominion like the God
Of this new world; at whose sight all the stars
35 Hide their diminished heads; to thee I call,
But with no friendly voice, and add thy name
O sun, to tell thee how I hate thy beams
That bring to my remembrance from what state
I fell, how glorious once above thy sphere;

40   Till pride and worse ambition threw me down
      Warring in Heav'n against Heav'n's matchless King:
      Ah wherefore! he deserved no such return
      From me, whom he created what I was
      In that bright eminence, and with his good
45   Upbraided none; nor was his service hard.
      What could be less than to afford him praise,
      The easiest recompense, and pay him thanks,
      How due! Yet all his good proved ill in me,
      And wrought but malice; lifted up so high
50   I 'sdained subjection, and thought one step higher
      Would set me highest, and in a moment quit
      The debt immense of endless gratitude,
      So burdensome, still paying, still to owe;
      Forgetful what from him I still received,
55   And understood not that a grateful mind
      By owing owes not, but still pays, at once
      Indebted and discharged; what burden then?
      O had his powerful destiny ordained
      Me some inferior angel, I had stood
60   Then happy; no unbounded hope had raised
      Ambition. Yet why not? Some other Power
      As great might have aspired, and me though mean
      Drawn to his part; but other Powers as great
      Fell not, but stand unshaken, from within
65   Or from without, to all temptations armed.
      Hadst thou the same free will and power to stand?
      Thou hadst: whom hast thou then or what to accuse,
      But Heav'n's free love dealt equally to all?
      Be then his love accursed, since love or hate,
70   To me alike, it deals eternal woe.
      Nay cursed be thou; since against his thy will
      Chose freely what it now so justly rues.
      Me miserable! Which way shall I fly
      Infinite wrath, and infinite despair?
75   Which way I fly is Hell; myself am Hell;
      And in the lowest deep a lower deep
      Still threat'ning to devour me opens wide,
      To which the Hell I suffer seems a Heav'n.

O then at last relent: is there no place
80   Left for repentance, none for pardon left?
None left but by submission; and that word
Disdain forbids me, and my dread of shame
Among the Spirits beneath, whom I seduced
With other promises and other vaunts
85   Than to submit, boasting I could subdue
Th' Omnipotent. Ay me, they little know
How dearly I abide that boast so vain,
Under what torments inwardly I groan;
While they adore me on the throne of Hell,
90   With diadem and sceptre high advanced
The lower still I fall, only supreme
In misery; such joy ambition finds.
But say I could repent and could obtain
By act of grace my former state; how soon
95   Would heighth recall high thoughts, how soon unsay
What feigned submission swore: ease would recant
Vows made in pain, as violent and void.
For never can true reconcilement grow
Where wounds of deadly hate have pierced so deep:
100   Which would but lead me to a worse relapse
And heavier fall: so should I purchase dear
Short intermission bought with double smart.
This knows my punisher; therefore as far
From granting he, as I from begging peace:
105   All hope excluded thus, behold instead
Of us outcást, exíled, his new delight,
Mankind created, and for him this world.
So farewell hope, and with hope farewell fear,
Farewell remorse: all good to me is lost;
110   Evil be thou my good; by thee at least
Divided empire with Heav'n's King I hold
By thee, and more than half perhaps will reign;
As man ere long, and this new world shall know.
    Thus while he spake, each passion dimmed his face
115   Thrice changed with pale, ire, envy and despair,
Which marred his borrowed visage, and betrayed
Him counterfeit, if any eye beheld.

For Heav'nly minds from such distempers foul
Are ever clear. Whereof he soon aware,
120 Each perturbation smoothed with outward calm,
Artificer of fraud; and was the first
That practised falsehood under saintly show,
Deep malice to conceal, couched with revenge:
Yet not enough had practised to deceive
125 Uriel once warned; whose eye pursued him down
The way he went, and on th' Assyrian mount
Saw him disfigured, more than could befall
Spirit of happy sort: his gestures fierce
He marked and mad demeanour, then alone,
130 As he supposed, all unobserved, unseen.
So on he fares, and to the border comes
Of Eden, where delicious Paradise,
Now nearer, crowns with her enclosure green,
As with a rural mound the champaign head
135 Of a steep wilderness, whose hairy sides
With thicket overgrown, grotesque and wild,
Access denied; and overhead up grew
Insuperable heighth of loftiest shade,
Cedar, and pine, and fir, and branching palm,
140 A sylvan scene, and as the ranks ascend
Shade above shade, a woody theatre
Of stateliest view. Yet higher than their tops
The verdurous wall of Paradise up sprung:
Which to our general sire gave prospect large
145 Into his nether empire neighbouring round.
And higher than that wall a circling row
Of goodliest trees loaden with fairest fruit,
Blossoms and fruits at once of golden hue
Appeared, with gay enamelled colours mixed:
150 On which the sun more glad impressed his beams
Than in fair evening cloud, or humid bow,
When God hath show'red the earth; so lovely seemed
That landscape: and of pure now purer air
Meets his approach, and to the heart inspires
155 Vernal delight and joy, able to drive
All sadness but despair: now gentle gales

Fanning their odoriferous wings dispense
Native perfumes and whisper whence they stole
Those balmy spoils. As when to them who sail
160   Beyond the Cape of Hope, and now are past
Mozámbique, off at sea northeast winds blow
Sabéan odours from the spicy shore
Of Araby the blest, with such delay
Well pleased they slack their course, and many a league
165   Cheered with the grateful smell old Ocean smiles.
So entertained those odorous sweets the Fiend
Who came their bane, though with them better pleased
Than Asmodéus with the fishy fume,
That drove him, though enamoured, from the spouse
170   Of Tobit's son, and with a vengeance sent
From Media post to Egypt, there fast bound.
    Now to th' ascent of that steep savage hill
Satan had journeyed on, pensive and slow;
But further way found none, so thick entwined,
175   As one continued brake, the undergrowth
Of shrubs and tangling bushes had perplexed
All path of man or beast that passed that way:
One gate there only was, and that looked east
On th' other side: which when th' Arch-felon saw
180   Due entrance he disdained, and in contempt,
At one slight bound high overleaped all bound
Of hill or highest wall, and sheer within
Lights on his feet. As when a prowling wolf,
Whom hunger drives to seek new haunt for prey,
185   Watching where shepherds pen their flocks at eve
In hurdled cotes amid the field secure,
Leaps o'er the fence with ease into the fold:
Or as a thief bent to unhoard the cash
Of some rich burgher, whose substantial doors,
190   Cross-barred and bolted fast, fear no assault,
In at the window climbs, or o'er the tiles;
So clomb this first grand thief into God's fold:
So since into his Church lewd hirelings climb.
Thence up he flew, and on the Tree of Life,
195   The middle tree and highest there that grew,

Sat like a cormorant; yet not true life
Thereby regained, but sat devising death
To them who lived; nor on the virtue thought
Of that life-giving plant, but only used
200 For prospect, what well used had been the pledge
Of immortality. So little knows
Any, but God alone, to value right
The good before him, but perverts best things
To worst abuse, or to their meanest use.
205 Beneath him with new wonder now he views
To all delight of human sense exposed
In narrow room Nature's whole wealth, yea more,
A Heav'n on earth, for blissful Paradise
Of God the garden was, by him in the east
210 Of Eden planted; Eden stretched her line
From Auran eastward to the royal towers
Of great Seleucia, built by Grecian kings,
Or where the sons of Eden long before
Dwelt in Telassar: in this pleasant soil
215 His far more pleasant garden God ordained;
Out of the fertile ground he caused to grow
All trees of noblest kind for sight, smell, taste;
And all amid them stood the Tree of Life,
High eminent, blooming ambrosial fruit
220 Of vegetable gold; and next to life
Our death the Tree of Knowledge grew fast by,
Knowledge of Good bought dear by knowing ill.
Southward through Eden went a river large,
Nor changed his course, but through the shaggy hill
225 Passed underneath ingulfed, for God had thrown
That mountain as his garden mould high raised
Upon the rapid current, which through veins
Of porous earth with kindly thirst up drawn,
Rose a fresh fountain, and with many a rill
230 Watered the garden; thence united fell
Down the steep glade, and met the nether flood,
Which from his darksome passage now appears,
And now divided into four main streams,
Runs diverse, wand'ring many a famous realm

235 And country whereof here needs no account,
  But rather to tell how, if art could tell,
  How from that sapphire fount the crispèd brooks,
  Rolling on orient pearl and sands of gold,
  With mazy error under pendent shades
240 Ran nectar, visiting each plant, and fed
  Flow'rs worthy of Paradise which not nice art
  In beds and curious knots, but Nature boon
  Poured forth profuse on hill and dale and plain,
  Both where the morning sun first warmly smote
245 The open field, and where the unpierced shade
  Embrowned the noontide bowers: thus was this place,
  A happy rural seat of various view;
  Groves whose rich trees wept odorous gums and balm,
  Others whose fruit burnished with golden rind
250 Hung amiable, Hesperian fables true,
  If true, here only, and of delicious taste:
  Betwixt them lawns, or level downs, and flocks
  Grazing the tender herb, were interposed,
  Or palmy hillock, or the flow'ry lap
255 Of some irriguous valley spread her store,
  Flow'rs of all hue, and without thorn the rose:
  Another side, umbrageous grots and caves
  Of cool recess, o'er which the mantling vine
  Lays forth her purple grape, and gently creeps
260 Luxuriant; meanwhile murmuring waters fall
  Down the slope hills, dispersed, or in a lake,
  That to the fringèd bank with myrtle crowned,
  Her crystal mirror holds, unite their streams.
  The birds their choir apply; airs, vernal airs,
265 Breathing the smell of field and grove, attune
  The trembling leaves, while univcrsal Pan
  Knit with the Graces and the Hours in dance
  Led on th' eternal spring. Not that fair field
  Of Enna, where Prosérpine gath'ring flow'rs
270 Herself a fairer flow'r by gloomy Dis
  Was gathered, which cost Ceres all that pain
  To seek her through the world; nor that sweet grove
  Of Daphne by Orontes, and th' inspired

Castalian spring, might with this Paradise
275 Of Eden strive; nor that Nyseian isle
Girt with the river Triton, where old Cham,
Whom Gentiles Ammon call and Libyan Jove,
Hid Amalthea and her florid son
Young Bacchus from his stepdame Rhea's eye;
280 Nor where Abássin kings their issue guard,
Mount Amara, though this by some supposed
True Paradise under the Ethiop line
By Nilus' head, enclosed with shining rock,
A whole day's journey high, but wide remote
285 From this Assyrian garden, where the Fiend
Saw undelighted all delight, all kind
Of living creatures new to sight and strange:
Two of far nobler shape erect and tall,
Godlike erect, with native honour clad
290 In naked majesty seemed lords of all,
And worthy seemed, for in their looks divine
The image of their glorious Maker shone,
Truth, wisdom, sanctitude severe and pure,
Severe, but in true filial freedom placed;
295 Whence true authority in men; though both
Not equal, as their sex not equal seemed;
For contemplation he and valour formed,
For softness she and sweet attractive grace,
He for God only, she for God in him:
300 His fair large front and eye sublime declared
Absolute rule; and hyacinthine locks
Round from his parted forelock manly hung
Clust'ring, but not beneath his shoulders broad:
She as a veil down to the slender waist
305 Her unadornèd golden tresses wore
Dishevelled, but in wanton ringlets waved
As the vine curls her tendrils, which implied
Subjection, but required with gentle sway,
And by her yielded, by him best received,
310 Yielded with coy submission, modest pride,
And sweet reluctant amorous delay.
Nor those mysterious parts were then concealed;

Then was not guilty shame, dishonest shame
Of nature's works, honour dishonourable,
315   Sin-bred, how have ye troubled all mankind
With shows instead, mere shows of seeming pure,
And banished from man's life his happiest life,
Simplicity and spotless innocence.
So passed they naked on, nor shunned the sight
320   Of God or angel, for they thought no ill:
So hand in hand they passed, the loveliest pair
That ever since in love's embraces met,
Adam the goodliest man of men since born
His sons, the fairest of her daughters Eve.
325   Under a tuft of shade that on a green
Stood whispering soft, by a fresh fountain side
They sat them down, and after no more toil
Of their sweet gard'ning labour than sufficed
To recommend cool Zephyr, and made ease
330   More easy, wholesome thirst and appetite
More grateful, to their supper fruits they fell,
Nectarine fruits which the compliant boughs
Yielded them, sidelong as they sat recline
On the soft downy bank damasked with flow'rs:
335   The savoury pulp they chew, and in the rind
Still as they thirsted scoop the brimming stream;
Nor gentle purpose, nor endearing smiles
Wanted, nor youthful dalliance as beseems
Fair couple, linked in happy nuptial league,
340   Alone as they. About them frisking played
All beasts of th' earth, since wild, and of all chase
In wood or wilderness, forest or den;
Sporting the lion ramped, and in his paw
Dandled the kid; bears, tigers, ounces, pards
345   Gambolled before them, th' unwieldy elephant
To make them mirth used all his might, and wreathed
His lithe proboscis; close the serpent sly
Insinuating, wove with Gordian twine
His braided train, and of his fatal guile
350   Gave proof unheeded; others on the grass
Couched, and now filled with pasture gazing sat,

Or bedward ruminating: for the sun
Declined was hasting now with prone career
To th' Ocean Isles, and in th' ascending Scale
355 Of Heav'n the stars that usher evening rose:
When Satan still in gaze, as first he stood,
Scarce thus at length failed speech recovered sad.
　　O Hell! What do mine eyes with grief behold,
Into our room of bliss thus high advanced
360 Creatures of other mould, earth-born perhaps,
Not Spirits, yet to Heav'nly Spirits bright
Little inferior; whom my thoughts pursue
With wonder, and could love, so lively shines
In them divine resemblance, and such grace
365 The hand that formed them on their shape hath poured.
Ah gentle pair, ye little think how nigh
Your change approaches, when all these delights
Will vanish and deliver ye to woe,
More woe, the more your taste is now of joy;
370 Happy, but for so happy ill secured
Long to continue, and this high seat your Heav'n
Ill fenced for Heav'n to keep out such a foe
As now is entered; yet no purposed foe
To you whom I could pity thus forlorn
375 Though I unpitied: league with you I seek,
And mutual amity so strait, so close,
That I with you must dwell, or you with me
Henceforth; my dwelling haply may not please
Like this fair Paradise, your sense, yet such
380 Accept your Maker's work; he gave it me,
Which I as freely give; Hell shall unfold,
To entertain you two, her widest gates,
And send forth all her kings; there will be room,
Not like these narrow limits, to receive
385 Your numerous offspring; if no better place,
Thank him who puts me loath to this revenge
On you who wrong me not for him who wronged.
And should I at your harmless innocence
Melt, as I do, yet public reason just,
390 Honour and empire with revenge enlarged,

By conquering this new world, compels me now
To do what else though damned I should abhor.
      So spake the Fiend, and with necessity,
The tyrant's plea, excused his devilish deeds.
395 Then from his lofty stand on that high tree
Down he alights among the sportful herd
Of those four-footed kinds, himself now one,
Now other, as their shape served best his end
Nearer to view his prey, and unespied
400 To mark what of their state he more might learn
By word or action marked: about them round
A lion now he stalks with fiery glare,
Then as a tiger, who by chance hath spied
In some purlieu two gentle fawns at play,
405 Straight couches close, then rising changes oft
His couchant watch, as one who chose his ground
Whence rushing he might surest seize them both
Gripped in each paw: when Adam first of men
To first of women Eve thus moving speech,
410 Turned him all ear to hear new utterance flow.
      Sole partner and sole part of all these joys,
Dearer thyself than all; needs must the power
That made us, and for us this ample world
Be infinitely good, and of his good
415 As liberal and free as infinite,
That raised us from the dust and placed us here
In all this happiness, who at his hand
Have nothing merited, nor can perform
Aught whereof he hath need, he who requires
420 From us no other service than to keep
This one, this easy charge, of all the trees
In Paradise that bear delicious fruit
So various, not to taste that only Tree
Of Knowledge, planted by the Tree of Life,
425 So near grows death to life, whate'er death is,
Some dreadful thing no doubt; for well thou know'st
God hath pronounced it death to taste that Tree,
The only sign of our obedience left
Among so many signs of power and rule

430 Conferred upon us, and dominion giv'n
     Over all other creatures that possess
     Earth, air, and sea. Then let us not think hard
     One easy prohibition, who enjoy
     Free leave so large to all things else, and choice
435 Unlimited of manifold delights:
     But let us ever praise him, and extol
     His bounty, following our delightful task
     To prune these growing plants, and tend these flow'rs,
     Which were it toilsome, yet with thee were sweet.
440   To whom thus Eve replied. O thou for whom
     And from whom I was formed flesh of thy flesh,
     And without whom am to no end, my guide
     And head, what thou hast said is just and right.
     For we to him indeed all praises owe,
445 And daily thanks, I chiefly who enjoy
     So far the happier lot, enjoying thee
     Pre-eminent by so much odds, while thou
     Like consort to thyself canst nowhere find.
     That day I oft remember, when from sleep
450 I first awaked, and found myself reposed
     Under a shade of flow'rs, much wond'ring where
     And what I was, whence thither brought, and how.
     Not distant far from thence a murmuring sound
     Of waters issued from a cave and spread
455 Into a liquid plain, then stood unmoved
     Pure as th' expanse of heav'n; I thither went
     With unexperienced thought, and laid me down
     On the green bank, to look into the clear
     Smooth lake, that to me seemed another sky.
460 As I bent down to look, just opposite,
     A shape within the wat'ry gleam appeared
     Bending to look on me: I started back,
     It started back, but pleased I soon returned,
     Pleased it returned as soon with answering looks
465 Of sympathy and love; there I had fixed
     Mine eyes till now, and pined with vain desire,
     Had not a voice thus warned me, What thou seest,
     What there thou seest fair creature is thyself,

With thee it came and goes: but follow me,
470   And I will bring thee where no shadow stays
Thy coming, and thy soft embraces, he
Whose image thou art, him thou shall enjoy
Inseparably thine, to him shalt bear
Multitudes like thyself, and thence be called
475   Mother of human race: what could I do,
But follow straight, invisibly thus led?
Till I espied thee, fair indeed and tall,
Under a platan, yet methought less fair,
Less winning soft, less amiably mild,
480   Than that smooth wat'ry image; back I turned,
Thou following cried'st aloud, Return, fair Eve;
Whom fli'st thou? Whom thou fli'st, of him thou art,
His flesh, his bone; to give thee being I lent
Out of my side to thee, nearest my heart
485   Substantial life, to have thee by my side
Henceforth an individual solace dear;
Part of my soul I seek thee, and thee claim
My other half: with that thy gentle hand
Seized mine, I yielded, and from that time see
490   How beauty is excelled by manly grace
And wisdom, which alone is truly fair.
    So spake our general mother, and with eyes
Of conjugal attraction unreproved,
And meek surrender, half embracing leaned
495   On our first father; half her swelling breast
Naked met his under the flowing gold
Of her loose tresses hid: he in delight
Both of her beauty and submissive charms
Smiled with superior love, as Jupiter
500   On Juno smiles, when he impregns the clouds
That shed May flowers; and pressed her matron lip
With kisses pure: aside the Devil turned
For envy, yet with jealous leer malign
Eyed them askance, and to himself thus plained.
505   Sight hateful, sight tormenting! Thus these two
Imparadised in one another's arms
The happier Eden, shall enjoy their fill

Of bliss on bliss, while I to Hell am thrust,
Where neither joy nor love, but fierce desire,
510 Among our other torments not the least,
Still unfulfilled with pain of longing pines;
Yet let me not forget what I have gained
From their own mouths; all is not theirs it seems:
One fatal Tree there stands of Knowledge called,
515 Forbidden them to taste: knowledge forbidd'n?
Suspicious, reasonless. Why should their Lord
Envy them that? Can it be sin to know,
Can it be death? And do they only stand
By ignorance, is that their happy state,
520 The proof of their obedience and their faith?
O fair foundation laid whereon to build
Their ruin! Hence I will excite their minds
With more desire to know, and to reject
Envious commands, invented with design
525 To keep them low whom knowledge might exalt
Equal with gods; aspiring to be such,
They taste and die: what likelier can ensue?
But first with narrow search I must walk round
This garden, and no corner leave unspied;
530 A chance but chance may lead where I may meet
Some wand'ring Spirit of Heav'n, by fountain side,
Or in thick shade retired, from him to draw
What further would be learnt. Live while ye may,
Yet happy pair; enjoy, till I return,
535 Short pleasures, for long woes are to succeed.
   So saying, his proud step he scornful turned,
But with sly circumspection, and began
Through wood, through waste, o'er hill, o'er dale his roam.
Meanwhile in utmost longitude, where heav'n
540 With earth and Ocean meets, the setting sun
Slowly descended, and with right aspéct
Against the eastern gate of Paradise
Levelled his evening rays: it was a rock
Of alabaster, piled up to the clouds,
545 Conspicuous far, winding with one ascent
Accessible from earth, one entrance high;

The rest was craggy cliff, that overhung
Still as it rose, impossible to climb.
Betwixt these rocky pillars Gabriel sat
550   Chief of th' angelic guards, awaiting night;
About him exercised heroic games
Th' unarmèd youth of Heav'n, but nigh at hand
Celestial armoury, shields, helms, and spears,
Hung high with diamond flaming, and with gold.
555   Thither came Uriel, gliding through the even
On a sunbeam, swift as a shooting star
In autumn thwarts the night, when vapours fired
Impress the air, and shows the mariner
From what point of his compass to beware
560   Impetuous winds: he thus began in haste.
        Gabriel, to thee thy course by lot hath giv'n
Charge and strict watch that to this happy place
No evil thing approach or enter in;
This day at heighth of noon came to my sphere
565   A Spirit, zealous, as he seemed, to know
More of th' Almighty's works, and chiefly man
God's latest image: I described his way
Bent all on speed, and marked his airy gait;
But in the mount that lies from Eden north,
570   Where he first lighted, soon discerned his looks
Alien from Heav'n, with passions foul obscured:
Mine eye pursued him still, but under shade
Lost sight of him; one of the banished crew
I fear, hath ventured from the deep, to raise
575   New troubles; him thy care must be to find.
        To whom the wingèd warrior thus returned:
Uriel, no wonder if thy perfect sight,
Amid the sun's bright circle where thou sitt'st,
See far and wide: in at this gate none pass
580   The vigilance here placed, but such as come
Well known from Heav'n; and since meridian hour
No creature thence: if Spirit of other sort,
So minded, have o'erleaped these earthy bounds
On purpose, hard thou know'st it to exclude
585   Spiritual substance with corporeal bar.

But if within the circuit of these walks,
In whatsoever shape he lurk, of whom
Thou tell'st, by morrow dawning I shall know.
       So promised he, and Uriel to his charge
590 Returned on that bright beam, whose point now raised
Bore him slope downward to the sun now fall'n
Beneath the Azores; whether the prime orb,
Incredible how swift, had thither rolled
Diurnal, or this less volúble earth
595 By shorter flight to th' east, had left him there
Arraying with reflected purple and gold
The clouds that on his western throne attend:
Now came still ev'ning on, and twilight grey
Had in her sober livery all things clad;
600 Silence accompanied, for beast and bird,
They to their grassy couch, these to their nests
Were slunk, all but the wakeful nightingale;
She all night long her amorous descant sung;
Silence was pleased: now glowed the firmament
605 With living sapphires: Hesperus that led
The starry host, rode brightest, till the moon
Rising in clouded majesty, at length
Apparent queen unveiled her peerless light,
And o'er the dark her silver mantle threw.
610   When Adam thus to Eve: Fair consort, th' hour
Of night, and all things now retired to rest
Mind us of like repose, since God hath set
Labour and rest, as day and night to men
Successive, and the timely dew of sleep
615 Now falling with soft slumb'rous weight inclines
Our eye-lids; other creatures all day long
Rove idle unemployed, and less need rest;
Man hath his daily work of body or mind
Appointed, which declares his dignity,
620 And the regard of Heav'n on all his ways;
While other animals unactive range,
And of their doings God takes no account.
Tomorrow ere fresh morning streak the east
With first approach of light, we must be ris'n,

625 And at our pleasant labour, to reform
    Yon flow'ry arbours, yonder alleys green,
    Our walk at noon, with branches overgrown,
    That mock our scant manuring, and require
    More hands than ours to lop their wanton growth:
630 Those blossoms also, and those dropping gums,
    That lie bestrewn unsightly and unsmooth,
    Ask riddance, if we mean to tread with ease;
    Meanwhile, as nature wills, night bids us rest.
        To whom thus Eve with perfect beauty adorned.
635 My author and disposer, what thou bidd'st
    Unargued I obey; so God ordains,
    God is thy law, thou mine: to know no more
    Is woman's happiest knowledge and her praise.
    With thee conversing I forget all time,
640 All seasons and their change, all please alike.
    Sweet is the breath of morn, her rising sweet,
    With charm of earliest birds; pleasant the sun
    When first on this delightful land he spreads
    His orient beams, on herb, tree, fruit, and flow'r,
645 Glist'ring with dew; fragrant the fertile earth
    After soft showers; and sweet the coming on
    Of grateful ev'ning mild, then silent night
    With this her solemn bird and this fair moon,
    And these the gems of heav'n, her starry train:
650 But neither breath of morn when she ascends
    With charm of earliest birds, nor rising sun
    On this delightful land, nor herb, fruit, flow'r,
    Glist'ring with dew, nor fragrance after showers,
    Nor grateful ev'ning mild, nor silent night
655 With this her solemn bird, nor walk by moon,
    Or glittering starlight without thee is sweet.
    But wherefore all night long shine these, for whom
    This glorious sight, when sleep hath shut all eyes?
        To whom our general ancestor replied.
660 Daughter of God and man, accomplished Eve,
    Those have their course to finish, round the earth,
    By morrow ev'ning, and from land to land
    In order, though to nations yet unborn,

Minist'ring light prepared, they set and rise;
665 Lest total darkness should by night regain
Her old possession, and extinguish life
In nature and all things, which these soft fires
Not only enlighten, but with kindly heat
Of various influence foment and warm,
670 Temper or nourish, or in part shed down
Their stellar virtue on all kinds that grow
On earth, made hereby apter to receive
Perfection from the sun's more potent ray.
These then, though unbeheld in deep of night,
675 Shine not in vain, nor think, though men were none,
That heav'n would want spectators, God want praise;
Millions of spiritual creatures walk the earth
Unseen, both when we wake, and when we sleep:
All these with ceaseless praise his works behold
680 Both day and night: how often from the steep
Of echoing hill or thicket have we heard
Celestial voices to the midnight air,
Sole, or responsive each to other's note
Singing their great Creator: oft in bands
685 While they keep watch, or nightly rounding walk
With Heav'nly touch of instrumental sounds
In full harmonic number joined, their songs
Divide the night, and lift our thoughts to Heaven.
       Thus talking hand in hand alone they passed
690 On to their blissful bower; it was a place
Chos'n by the sov'reign Planter, when he framed
All things to man's delightful use; the roof
Of thickest covert was inwoven shade
Laurel and myrtle, and what higher grew
695 Of firm and fragrant leaf; on either side
Acanthus, and each odorous bushy shrub
Fenced up the verdant wall; each beauteous flow'r,
Iris all hues, roses, and jessamine
Reared high their flourished heads between, and wrought
700 Mosaic; underfoot the violet,
Crocus, and hyacinth with rich inlay
Broidered the ground, more coloured than with stone

Of costliest emblem: other creature here
Beast, bird, insect, or worm durst enter none;
705 Such was their awe of man. In shadier bower
More sacred and sequestered, though but feigned,
Pan or Silvanus never slept, nor nymph,
Nor Faunus haunted. Here in close recess
With flowers, garlands, and sweet-smelling herbs
710 Espousèd Eve decked first her nuptial bed,
And Heav'nly choirs the hymenean sung,
What day the genial angel to our sire
Brought her in naked beauty more adorned,
More lovely than Pandora, whom the gods
715 Endowed with all their gifts, and O too like
In sad event, when to th' unwiser son
Of Japhet brought by Hermes, she ensnared
Mankind with her fair looks, to be avenged
On him who had stole Jove's authentic fire.
720   Thus at their shady lodge arrived, both stood,
Both turned, and under open sky adored
The God that made both sky, air, earth and heav'n
Which they beheld, the moon's resplendent globe
And starry pole: Thou also mad'st the night,
725 Maker omnipotent, and thou the day,
Which we in our appointed work employed
Have finished happy in our mutual help
And mutual love, the crown of all our bliss
Ordained by thee, and this delicious place
730 For us too large, where thy abundance wants
Partakers, and uncropped falls to the ground.
But thou hast promised from us two a race
To fill the earth, who shall with us extol
Thy goodness infinite, both when we wake,
735 And when we seek, as now, thy gift of sleep.
        This said unanimous, and other rites
Observing none, but adoration pure
Which God likes best, into their inmost bower
Handed they went; and eased the putting off
740 These troublesome disguises which we wear,
Straight side by side were laid, nor turned I ween

Adam from his fair spouse, nor Eve the rites
Mysterious of connubial love refused:
Whatever hypocrites austerely talk
745 Of purity and place and innocence,
Defaming as impure what God declares
Pure, and commands to some, leaves free to all.
Our Maker bids increase, who bids abstain
But our destroyer, foe to God and man?
750 Hail wedded love, mysterious law, true source
Of human offspring, sole propriety,
In Paradise of all things common else.
By thee adulterous lust was driv'n from men
Among the bestial herds to range, by thee
755 Founded in reason, loyal, just, and pure,
Relations dear, and all the charities
Of father, son, and brother first were known.
Far be it, that I should write thee sin or blame,
Or think thee unbefitting holiest place,
760 Perpetual fountain of domestic sweets,
Whose bed is undefiled and chaste pronounced,
Present, or past, as saints and patriarchs used.
Here Love his golden shafts employs, here lights
His constant lamp, and waves his purple wings,
765 Reigns here and revels; not in the bought smile
Of harlots, loveless, joyless, unendeared,
Casual fruition, nor in court amours
Mixed dance, or wanton masque, or midnight ball,
Or serenade, which the starved lover sings
770 To his proud fair, best quitted with disdain.
These lulled by nightingales embracing slept,
And on their naked limbs the flow'ry roof
Show'red roses, which the morn repaired. Sleep on,
Blest pair; and O yet happiest if ye seek
775 No happier state, and know to know no more.
     Now had night measured with her shadowy cone
Half way up hill this vast sublunar vault,
And from their ivory port the Cherubim
Forth issuing at th' accustomed hour stood armed
780 To their night watches in warlike parade,

When Gabriel to his next in power thus spake.
    Uzziel, half these draw off, and coast the south
With strictest watch; these other wheel the north,
Our circuit meets full west. As flame they part
785 Half wheeling to the shield, half to the spear.
From these, two strong and subtle Spirits he called
That near him stood, and gave them thus in charge.
    Ithuriel and Zephon, with winged speed
Search through this garden, leave unsearched no nook,
790 But chiefly where those two fair creatures lodge,
Now laid perhaps asleep secure of harm.
This ev'ning from the sun's decline arrived
Who tells of some infernal Spirit seen
Hitherward bent (who could have thought?) escaped
795 The bars of Hell, on errand bad no doubt:
Such where ye find, seize fast, and hither bring.
    So saying, on he led his radiant files,
Dazzling the moon; these to the bower direct
In search of whom they sought: him there they found
800 Squat like a toad, close at the ear of Eve;
Assaying by his devilish art to reach
The organs of her Fancy, and with them forge
Illusions as he list, phantasms and dreams,
Or if, inspiring venom, he might taint
805 Th' animal spirits that from pure blood arise
Like gentle breaths from rivers pure, thence raise
At least distempered, discontented thoughts,
Vain hopes, vain aims, inordinate desires
Blown up with high conceits engend'ring pride.
810 Him thus intent Ithuriel with his spear
Touched lightly; for no falsehood can endure
Touch of celestial temper, but returns
Of force to its own likeness: up he starts
Discovered and surprised. As when a spark
815 Lights on a heap of nitrous powder, laid
Fit for the tun some magazine to store
Against a rumoured war, the smutty grain
With sudden blaze diffused, inflames the air:
So started up in his own shape the Fiend.

820   Back stepped those two fair angels half amazed
       So sudden to behold the grisly King;
       Yet thus, unmoved with fear, accost him soon.
           Which of those rebel Spirits adjudged to Hell
       Com'st thou, escaped thy prison, and transformed,
825   Why sat'st thou like an enemy in wait
       Here watching at the head of these that sleep?
           Know ye not then said Satan, filled with scorn,
       Know ye not me? Ye knew me once no mate
       For you, there sitting where ye durst not soar;
830   Not to know me argues yourselves unknown,
       The lowest of your throng; or if ye know,
       Why ask ye, and superfluous begin
       Your message, like to end as much in vain?
       To whom thus Zephon, answering scorn with scorn.
835   Think not, revolted Spirit, thy shape the same,
       Or undiminished brightness, to be known
       As when thou stood'st in Heav'n upright and pure;
       That glory then, when thou no more wast good,
       Departed from thee, and thou resemblest now
840   Thy sin and place of doom obscure and foul.
       But come, for thou, be sure, shalt give account
       To him who sent us, whose charge is to keep
       This place inviolable, and these from harm.
           So spake the Cherub, and his grave rebuke
845   Severe in youthful beauty, added grace
       Invincible: abashed the Devil stood,
       And felt how awful goodness is, and saw
       Virtue in her shape how lovely, saw, and pined
       His loss; but chiefly to find here observed
850   His lustre visibly impaired; yet seemed
       Undaunted. If I must contend, said he,
       Best with the best, the sender not the sent,
       Or all at once; more glory will be won,
       Or less be lost. Thy fear, said Zephon bold,
855   Will save us trial what the least can do
       Single against thee wicked, and thence weak.
           The Fiend replied not, overcome with rage;
       But like a proud steed reined, went haughty on,

Champing his iron curb: to strive or fly
860 He held it vain; awe from above had quelled
His heart, not else dismayed. Now drew they nigh
The western point, where those half-rounding guards
Just met, and closing stood in squadron joined
Awaiting next command. To whom their chief
865 Gabriel from the front thus called aloud.
O friends, I hear the tread of nimble feet
Hasting this way, and now by glimpse discern
Ithuriel and Zephon through the shade,
And with them comes a third of regal port,
870 But faded splendour wan; who by his gait
And fierce demeanour seems the Prince of Hell,
Not likely to part hence without contést;
Stand firm, for in his look defiance lours.
He scarce had ended, when those two approached
875 And brief related whom they brought, where found,
How busied, in what form and posture couched.
To whom with stern regard thus Gabriel spake.
Why hast thou, Satan, broke the bounds prescribed
To thy transgressions, and disturbed the charge
880 Of others, who approve not to transgress
By thy example, but have power and right
To question thy bold entrance on this place;
Employed it seems to violate sleep, and those
Whose dwelling God hath planted here in bliss?
885 To whom thus Satan with contemptuous brow.
Gabriel, thou hadst in Heav'n th' esteem of wise,
And such I held thee; but this question asked
Puts me in doubt. Lives there who loves his pain?
Who would not, finding way, break loose from Hell,
890 Though thither doomed? Thou wouldst thyself, no doubt,
And boldly venture to whatever place
Farthest from pain, where thou might'st hope to change
Torment with ease, and soonest recompense
Dole with delight, which in this place I sought;
895 To thee no reason; who know'st only good,
But evil hast not tried: and wilt object

His will who bound us? Let him surer bar
His iron gates, if he intends our stay
In that dark durance: thus much what was asked.
900 The rest is true, they found me where they say;
But that implies not violence or harm.
    Thus he in scorn. The warlike angel moved,
Disdainfully half smiling thus replied.
O loss of one in Heav'n to judge of wise,
905 Since Satan fell, whom folly overthrew,
And now returns him from his prison 'scaped,
Gravely in doubt whether to hold them wise
Or not, who ask what boldness brought him hither
Unlicensed from his bounds in Hell prescribed;
910 So wise he judges it to fly from pain
However, and to 'scape his punishment.
So judge thou still, presumptuous, till the wrath,
Which thou incurr'st by flying, meet thy flight
Sevenfold, and scourge that wisdom back to Hell,
915 Which taught thee yet no better, that no pain
Can equal anger infinite provoked.
But wherefore thou alone? Wherefore with thee
Came not all Hell broke loose? Is pain to them
Less pain, less to be fled, or thou than they
920 Less hardy to endure? Courageous chief,
The first in flight from pain, hadst thou alleged
To thy deserted host this cause of flight,
Thou surely hadst not come sole fugitive.
    To which the Fiend thus answered frowning stern.
925 Not that I less endure, or shrink from pain,
Insulting angel, well thou know'st I stood
Thy fiercest, when in battle to thy aid
The blasting volleyed thunder made all speed
And seconded thy else not dreaded spear.
930 But still thy words at random, as before,
Argue thy inexperience what behooves
From hard assays and ill successes past
A faithful leader, not to hazard all
Through ways of danger by himself untried.

935 I therefore, I alone first undertook
To wing the desolate abyss, and spy
This new-created world, whereof in Hell
Fame is not silent, here in hope to find
Better abode, and my afflicted powers
940 To settle here on earth, or in mid air;
Though for possession put to try once more
What thou and thy gay legions dare against;
Whose easier business were to serve their Lord
High up in Heav'n, with songs to hymn his throne,
945 And practised distances to cringe, not fight.
    To whom the warrior angel soon replied.
To say and straight unsay, pretending first
Wise to fly pain, professing next the spy,
Argues no leader but a liar traced,
950 Satan, and couldst thou faithful add? O name,
O sacred name of faithfulness profaned!
Faithful to whom? To thy rebellious crew?
Army of fiends, fit body to fit head;
Was this your discipline and faith engaged,
955 Your military obedience, to dissolve
Allegiance to th' acknowledged Power Supreme?
And thou sly hypocrite, who now wouldst seem
Patron of liberty, who more than thou
Once fawned, and cringed, and servilely adored
960 Heav'n's awful Monarch? Wherefore but in hope
To dispossess him, and thyself to reign?
But mark what I aread thee now, avaunt;
Fly thither whence thou fledd'st: if from this hour
Within these hallowed limits thou appear,
965 Back to th' infernal pit I drag thee chained,
And seal thee so, as henceforth not to scorn
The facile gates of Hell too slightly barred.
    So threatened he, but Satan to no threats
Gave heed, but waxing more in rage replied.
970   Then when I am thy captive talk of chains,
Proud limitary Cherub, but ere then
Far heavier load thyself expect to feel

From my prevailing arm, though Heaven's King
Ride on thy wings, and thou with thy compeers,
975   Used to the yoke, draw'st his triumphant wheels
In progress through the road of Heav'n star-paved.
 While thus he spake, th' angelic squadron bright
Turned fiery red, sharp'ning in moonèd horns
Their phalanx, and began to hem him round
980   With ported spears, as thick as when a field
Of Ceres ripe for harvest waving bends
Her bearded grove of ears, which way the wind
Sways them; the careful ploughman doubting stands
Lest on the threshing floor his hopeful sheaves
985   Prove chaff. On th' other side Satan alarmed
Collecting all his might dilated stood,
Like Teneriffe or Atlas unremoved:
His stature reached the sky, and on his crest
Sat Horror plumed; nor wanted in his grasp
990   What seemed both spear and shield: now dreadful deeds
Might have ensued, nor only Paradise
In this commotion, but the starry cope
Of heav'n perhaps, or all the elements
At least had gone to wrack, disturbed and torn
995   With violence of this conflict, had not soon
Th' Eternal to prevent such horrid fray
Hung forth in heav'n his golden Scales, yet seen
Betwixt Astraea and the Scorpion sign,
Wherein all things created first he weighed,
1000   The pendulous round earth with balanced air
In counterpoise, now ponders all events,
Battles and realms: in these he put two weights
The sequel each of parting and of fight;
The latter quick up flew, and kicked the beam;
1005   Which Gabriel spying, thus bespake the Fiend.
 Satan, I know thy strength, and thou know'st mine,
Neither our own but giv'n; what folly then
To boast what arms can do, since thine no more
Than Heav'n permits, nor mine, though doubled now
1010   To trample thee as mire: for proof look up,

And read thy lot in yon celestial sign
Where thou art weighed, and shown how light, how weak,
If thou resist. The Fiend looked up and knew
His mounted scale aloft: nor more; but fled
1015 Murmuring, and with him fled the shades of night.

BOOK V

The Argument

Morning approached, Eve relates to Adam her troublesome
dream; he likes it not, yet comforts her: they come forth to
their day labours: their morning hymn at the door of their
bower. God to render man inexcusable sends Raphael to
admonish him of his obedience, of his free estate, of his enemy
near at hand; who he is, and why his enemy, and whatever
else may avail Adam to know. Raphael comes down to Paradise,
his appearance described, his coming discerned by Adam afar
off sitting at the door of his bower; he goes out to meet him,
brings him to his lodge, entertains him with the choicest fruits
of Paradise got together by Eve; their discourse at table:
Raphael performs his message, minds Adam of his state and
of his enemy; relates at Adam's request who that enemy is,
and how he came to be so, beginning from his first revolt in
Heaven and the occasion thereof; how he drew his legions
after him to the parts of the North, and there incited them
to rebel with him, persuading all but only Abdiel a Seraph,
who in argument dissuades and opposes him, then forsakes
him.

Now Morn her rosy steps in th' eastern clime
Advancing, sowed the earth with orient pearl,
When Adam waked, so customed, for his sleep
Was airy light, from pure digestion bred,
And temperate vapours bland, which th' only sound
Of leaves and fuming rills, Aurora's fan,
Lightly dispersed, and the shrill matin song
Of birds on every bough; so much the more
His wonder was to find unwakened Eve
With tresses discomposed, and glowing cheek,
As through unquiet rest: he on his side

Leaning half-raised, with looks of cordial love
Hung over her enamoured, and beheld
Beauty, which whether waking or asleep,
15   Shot forth peculiar graces; then with voice
Mild, as when Zephyrus on Flora breathes,
Her hand soft touching, whispered thus. Awake
My fairest, my espoused, my latest found,
Heav'n's last best gift, my ever new delight,
20   Awake, the morning shines, and the fresh field
Calls us; we lose the prime, to mark how spring
Our tended plants, how blows the citron grove,
What drops the myrrh, and what the balmy reed,
How Nature paints her colours, how the bee
25   Sits on the bloom extracting liquid sweet.
    Such whispering waked her, but with startled eye
On Adam, whom embracing, thus she spake.
    O sole in whom my thoughts find all repose,
My glory, my perfection, glad I see
30   Thy face, and morn returned, for I this night,
Such night till this I never passed, have dreamed,
If dreamed, not as I oft am wont, of thee,
Works of day past, or morrow's next design,
But of offence and trouble, which my mind
35   Knew never till this irksome night; methought
Close at mine ear one called me forth to walk
With gentle voice, I thought it thine; it said,
Why sleep'st thou Eve? Now is the pleasant time,
The cool, the silent, save where silence yields
40   To the night-warbling bird, that now awake
Tunes sweetest his love-laboured song; now reigns
Full orbed the moon, and with more pleasing light
Shadowy sets off the face of things; in vain,
If none regard; heav'n wakes with all his eyes,
45   Whom to behold but thee, Nature's desire,
In whose sight all things joy, with ravishment
Attracted by thy beauty still to gaze.
I rose as at thy call, but found thee not;
To find thee I directed then my walk;
50   And on, methought, alone I passed through ways

That brought me on a sudden to the Tree
Of interdicted Knowledge: fair it seemed,
Much fairer to my Fancy than by day:
And as I wond'ring looked, beside it stood
55 One shaped and winged like one of those from Heav'n
By us oft seen; his dewy locks distilled
Ambrosia; on that tree he also gazed;
And O fair plant, said he, with fruit surcharged,
Deigns none to ease thy load and taste thy sweet,
60 Nor god, nor man; is knowledge so despised?
Or envy, or what reserve forbids to taste?
Forbid who will, none shall from me withhold
Longer thy offered good, why else set here?
This said he paused not, but with vent'rous arm
65 He plucked, he tasted; me damp horror chilled
At such bold words vouched with a deed so bold:
But he thus overjoyed, O fruit divine,
Sweet of thyself, but much more sweet thus cropped,
Forbidden here, it seems, as only fit
70 For gods, yet able to make gods of men:
And why not gods of men, since good, the more
Communicated, more abundant grows,
The Author not impaired, but honoured more?
Here, happy creature, fair angelic Eve,
75 Partake thou also; happy though thou art,
Happier thou may'st be, worthier canst not be:
Taste this, and be henceforth among the gods
Thyself a goddess, not to earth confined,
But sometimes in the air, as we, sometimes
80 Ascend to Heav'n, by merit thine, and see
What life the gods live there, and such live thou.
So saying, he drew nigh, and to me held,
Even to my mouth of that same fruit held part
Which he had plucked; the pleasant savoury smell
85 So quickened appetite, that I, methought,
Could not but taste. Forthwith up to the clouds
With him I flew, and underneath beheld
The earth outstretched immense, a prospect wide
And various: wond'ring at my flight and change

90   To this high exaltation; suddenly
My guide was gone, and I, methought, sunk down,
And fell asleep; but O how glad I waked
To find this but a dream! Thus Eve her night
Related, and thus Adam answered sad.

95   Best image of myself and dearer half,
The trouble of thy thoughts this night in sleep
Affects me equally; nor can I like
This uncouth dream, of evil sprung I fear;
Yet evil whence? In thee can harbour none,

100   Created pure. But know that in the soul
Are many lesser faculties that serve
Reason as chief; among these Fancy next
Her office holds; of all external things,
Which the five watchful senses represent,

105   She forms imaginations, airy shapes,
Which Reason joining or disjoining, frames
All what we affirm or what deny, and call
Our knowledge or opinion; then retires
Into her private cell when nature rests.

110   Oft in her absence mimic Fancy wakes
To imitate her; but misjoining shapes,
Wild work produces oft, and most in dreams,
Ill matching words and deeds long past or late.
Some such resemblances methinks I find

115   Of our last ev'ning's talk, in this thy dream,
But with addition strange; yet be not sad.
Evil into the mind of god or man
May come and go, so unapproved, and leave
No spot or blame behind: which gives me hope

120   That what in sleep thou didst abhor to dream,
Waking thou never wilt consent to do.
Be not disheartened then, nor cloud those looks
That wont to be more cheerful and serene
Than when fair morning first smiles on the world,

125   And let us to our fresh employments rise
Among the groves, the fountains, and the flow'rs
That open now their choicest bosomed smells
Reserved from night, and kept for thee in store.

So cheered he his fair spouse, and she was cheered,
130 But silently a gentle tear let fall
From either eye, and wiped them with her hair;
Two other precious drops that ready stood,
Each in their crystal sluice, he ere they fell
Kissed as the gracious signs of sweet remorse
135 And pious awe, that feared to have offended.
So all was cleared, and to the field they haste.
But first from under shady arborous roof,
Soon as they forth were come to open sight
Of day-spring, and the sun, who scarce up risen
140 With wheels yet hov'ring o'er the ocean brim,
Shot parallel to the earth his dewy ray,
Discovering in wide landscape all the east
Of Paradise and Eden's happy plains,
Lowly they bowed adoring, and began
145 Their orisons, each morning duly paid
In various style, for neither various style
Nor holy rapture wanted they to praise
Their Maker, in fit strains pronounced or sung
Unmeditated, such prompt eloquence
150 Flowed from their lips, in prose or numerous verse,
More tuneable than needed lute or harp
To add more sweetness, and they thus began.
These are thy glorious works, Parent of good,
Almighty, thine this universal frame,
155 Thus wondrous fair; thyself how wondrous then!
Unspeakable, who sitt'st above these heavens
To us invisible or dimly seen
In these thy lowest works, yet these declare
Thy goodness beyond thought, and power divine:
160 Speak ye who best can tell, ye sons of light,
Angels, for ye behold him, and with songs
And choral symphonies, day without night,
Circle his throne rejoicing, ye in Heav'n,
On earth join all ye creatures to extol
165 Him first, him last, him midst, and without end.
Fairest of stars, last in the train of night,
If better thou belong not to the dawn,

Sure pledge of day, that crown'st the smiling morn
With thy bright circlet, praise him in thy sphere
170   While day arises, that sweet hour of prime.
Thou sun, of this great world both eye and soul,
Acknowledge him thy greater, sound his praise
In thy eternal course, both when thou climb'st,
And when high noon hast gained, and when thou fall'st.
175   Moon, that now meet'st the orient sun, now fli'st
With the fixed stars, fixed in their orb that flies,
And ye five other wand'ring fires that move
In mystic dance not without song, resound
His praise who out of darkness called up light.
180   Air, and ye elements the eldest birth
Of Nature's womb, that in quaternion run
Perpetual circle multiform; and mix
And nourish all things, let your ceaseless change
Vary to our great Maker still new praise.
185   Ye mists and exhalations that now rise
From hill or steaming lake, dusky or grey,
Till the sun paint your fleecy skirts with gold,
In honour to the world's great Author rise,
Whether to deck with clouds the uncoloured sky,
190   Or wet the thirsty earth with falling showers,
Rising or falling still advance his praise.
His praise ye winds, that from four quarters blow,
Breathe soft or loud; and wave your tops, ye pines,
With every plant, in sign of worship wave.
195   Fountains and ye, that warble, as ye flow,
Melodious murmurs, warbling tune his praise.
Join voices all ye living souls, ye birds,
That singing up to heaven gate ascend,
Bear on your wings and in your notes his praise;
200   Ye that in waters glide, and ye that walk
The earth, and stately tread, or lowly creep;
Witness if I be silent, morn or even,
To hill, or valley, fountain, or fresh shade
Made vocal by my song, and taught his praise.
205   Hail universal Lord, be bounteous still
To give us only good; and if the night

Have gathered aught of evil or concealed,
Disperse it, as now light dispels the dark.
  So prayed they innocent, and to their thoughts
210   Firm peace recovered soon and wonted calm.
On to their morning's rural work they haste
Among sweet dews and flow'rs; where any row
Of fruit-trees overwoody reached too far
Their pampered boughs, and needed hands to check
215   Fruitless embraces: or they led the vine
To wed her elm; she spoused about him twines
Her marriageable arms, and with her brings
Her dow'r th' adopted clusters, to adorn
His barren leaves. Them thus employed beheld
220   With pity Heav'n's high King, and to him called
Raphael, the sociable Spirit, that deigned
To travel with Tobias, and secured
His marriage with the seven-times-wedded maid.
  Raphael, said he, thou hear'st what stir on earth
225   Satan from Hell 'scaped through the darksome gulf
Hath raised in Paradise, and how disturbed
This night the human pair, how he designs
In them at once to ruin all mankind.
Go therefore, half this day as friend with friend
230   Converse with Adam, in what bow'r or shade
Thou find'st him from the heat of noon retired,
To respite his day-labour with repast,
Or with repose; and such discourse bring on,
As may advise him of his happy state,
235   Happiness in his power left free to will,
Left to his own free will, his will though free,
Yet mutable; whence warn him to beware
He swerve not too secure: tell him withal
His danger, and from whom, what enemy
240   Late fall'n himself from Heav'n, is plotting now
The fall of others from like state of bliss;
By violence, no, for that shall be withstood,
But by deceit and lies; this let him know,
Lest wilfully transgressing he pretend
245   Surprisal, unadmonished, unforewarned.

So spake th' Eternal Father, and fulfilled
All justice: nor delayed the wingèd saint
After his charge received; but from among
Thousand celestial ardours, where he stood
250   Veiled with his gorgeous wings, up springing light
Flew through the midst of Heav'n; th' angelic choirs
On each hand parting, to his speed gave way
Through all th' empyreal road; till at the gate
Of Heav'n arrived, the gate self-opened wide
255   On golden hinges turning, as by work
Divine the sov'reign Architect had framed.
From hence, no cloud, or, to obstruct his sight,
Star interposed, however small he sees,
Not unconform to other shining globes,
260   Earth and the gard'n of God, with cedars crowned
Above all hills. As when by night the glass
Of Galileo, less assured, observes
Imagined lands and regions in the moon:
Or pilot from amidst the Cyclades
265   Delos or Samos first appearing kens
A cloudy spot. Down thither prone in flight
He speeds, and through the vast ethereal sky
Sails between worlds and worlds, with steady wing
Now on the polar winds, then with quick fan
270   Winnows the buxom air; till within soar
Of tow'ring eagles, to all the fowls he seems
A phoenix, gazed by all, as that sole bird
When to enshrine his relics in the sun's
Bright temple, to Egyptian Thebes he flies.
275   At once on th' eastern cliff of Paradise
He lights, and to his proper shape returns
A Seraph winged; six wings he wore, to shade
His lineaments divine; the pair that clad
Each shoulder broad, came mantling o'er his breast
280   With regal ornament; the middle pair
Girt like a starry zone his waist, and round
Skirted his loins and thighs with downy gold
And colours dipped in Heav'n; the third his feet
Shadowed from either heel with feathered mail

285　Sky-tinctured grain. Like Maia's son he stood,
　　　And shook his plumes, that Heav'nly fragrance filled
　　　The circuit wide. Straight knew him all the bands
　　　Of angels under watch; and to his state,
　　　And to his message high in honour rise;
290　For on some message high they guessed him bound.
　　　Their glittering tents he passed, and now is come
　　　Into the blissful field, through groves of myrrh,
　　　And flow'ring odours, cassia, nard, and balm;
　　　A wilderness of sweets; for Nature here
295　Wantoned as in her prime, and played at will
　　　Her virgin fancies, pouring forth more sweet,
　　　Wild above rule or art; enormous bliss.
　　　Him through the spicy forest onward come
　　　Adam discerned, as in the door he sat
300　Of his cool bow'r, while now the mounted sun
　　　Shot down direct his fervid rays to warm
　　　Earth's inmost womb, more warmth than Adam needs;
　　　And Eve within, due at her hour prepared
　　　For dinner savoury fruits, of taste to please
305　True appetite, and not disrelish thirst
　　　Of nectarous draughts between, from milky stream,
　　　Berry or grape: to whom thus Adam called.
　　　　Haste hither Eve, and worth thy sight behold
　　　Eastward among those trees, what glorious shape
310　Comes this way moving; seems another morn
　　　Ris'n on mid-noon; some great behest from Heav'n
　　　To us perhaps he brings, and will vouchsafe
　　　This day to be our guest. But go with speed,
　　　And what thy stores contain, bring forth and pour
315　Abundance, fit to honour and receive
　　　Our Heav'nly stranger; well we may afford
　　　Our givers their own gifts, and large bestow
　　　From large bestowed, where Nature multiplies
　　　Her fertile growth, and by disburd'ning grows
320　More fruitful, which instructs us not to spare.
　　　　To whom thus Eve, Adam, earth's hallowed mould,
　　　Of God inspired, small store will serve, where store,
　　　All seasons, ripe for use hangs on the stalk;

Save what by frugal storing firmness gains
325   To nourish, and superfluous moist consumes:
But I will haste and from each bough and brake,
Each plant and juiciest gourd will pluck such choice
To entertain our angel guest, as he
Beholding shall confess that here on earth
330   God hath dispensed his bounties as in Heav'n.
     So saying, with dispatchful looks in haste
She turns, on hospitable thoughts intent
What choice to choose for delicacy best,
What order, so contrived as not to mix
335   Tastes, not well joined, inelegant, but bring
Taste after taste upheld with kindliest change;
Bestirs her then, and from each tender stalk
Whatever Earth all-bearing Mother yields
In India east or west, or middle shore
340   In Pontus or the Punic coast, or where
Alcinous reigned, fruit of all kinds, in coat,
Rough, or smooth rined, or bearded husk, or shell
She gathers, tribute large, and on the board
Heaps with unsparing hand; for drink the grape
345   She crushes, inoffensive must, and meaths
From many a berry, and from sweet kernels pressed
She tempers dulcet creams, nor these to hold
Wants her fit vessels pure, then strews the ground
With rose and odours from the shrub unfumed.
350   Meanwhile our primitive great sire, to meet
His god-like guest, walks forth, without more train
Accompanied than with his own complete
Perfections; in himself was all his state,
More solemn than the tedious pomp that waits
355   On princes, when their rich retinue long
Of horses led, and grooms besmeared with gold
Dazzles the crowd, and sets them all agape.
Nearer his presence Adam though not awed,
Yet with submiss approach and reverence meek,
360   As to a superior nature, bowing low,
     Thus said. Native of Heav'n, for other place
None can than Heav'n such glorious shape contain;

Since by descending from the thrones above,
Those happy places thou hast deigned a while
365   To want, and honour these, vouchsafe with us
Two only, who yet by sov'reign gift possess
This spacious ground, in yonder shady bow'r
To rest, and what the garden choicest bears
To sit and taste, till this meridian heat
370   Be over, and the sun more cool decline.
    Whom thus the angelic Virtue answered mild.
Adam, I therefore came, nor art thou such
Created, or such place hast here to dwell,
As may not oft invite, though Spirits of Heav'n
375   To visit thee; lead on then where thy bow'r
O'ershades; for these mid-hours, till ev'ning rise
I have at will. So to the sylvan lodge
They came, that like Pomona's arbour smiled
With flow'rets decked and fragrant smells; but Eve
380   Undecked, save with herself more lovely fair
Than wood-nymph, or the fairest goddess feigned
Of three that in Mount Ida naked strove,
Stood to entertain her guest from Heav'n; no veil
She needed, virtue-proof, no thought infirm
385   Altered her cheek. On whom the angel Hail
Bestowed, the holy salutation used
Long after to blest Mary, second Eve.
    Hail mother of mankind, whose fruitful womb
Shall fill the world more numerous with thy sons
390   Than with these various fruits the trees of God
Have heaped this table. Raised of grassy turf
Their table was, and mossy seats had round,
And on her ample square from side to side
All autumn piled, though spring and autumn here
395   Danced hand in hand. A while discourse they hold;
No fear lest dinner cool; when thus began
Our author. Heav'nly stranger, please to taste
These bounties which our Nourisher, from whom
All perfect good unmeasured out, descends,
400   To us for food and for delight hath caused
The earth to yield; unsavoury food perhaps

To spiritual natures; only this I know,
That one celestial Father gives to all.
   To whom the angel. Therefore what he gives
405   (Whose praise be ever sung) to man in part
Spiritual, may of purest Spirits be found
No ingrateful food: and food alike those pure
Intelligential substances require
As doth your rational; and both contain
410   Within them every lower faculty
Of sense, whereby they hear, see, smell, touch, taste,
Tasting concoct, digest, assimilate,
And corporeal to incorporeal turn.
For know, whatever was created, needs
415   To be sustained and fed; of elements
The grosser feeds the purer, earth the sea,
Earth and the sea feed air, the air those fires
Ethereal, and as lowest first the moon;
Whence in her visage round those spots, unpurged
420   Vapours not yet into her substance turned.
Nor doth the moon no nourishment exhale
From her moist continent to higher orbs.
The sun that light imparts to all, receives
From all his alimental recompense
425   In humid exhalations, and at even
Sups with the ocean: though in Heav'n the trees
Of life ambrosial fruitage bear, and vines
Yield nectar, though from off the boughs each morn
We brush mellifluous dews, and find the ground
430   Covered with pearly grain: yet God hath here
Varied his bounty so with new delights,
As may compare with Heaven; and to taste
Think not I shall be nice. So down they sat,
And to their viands fell, nor seemingly
435   The angel, nor in mist, the common gloss
Of theologians, but with keen dispatch
Of real hunger, and concoctive heat
To transubstantiate; what redounds, transpires
Through Spirits with ease; nor wonder; if by fire
440   Of sooty coal th' empiric alchemist

Can turn, or holds it possible to turn
Metals of drossiest ore to perfect gold
As from the mine. Meanwhile at table Eve
Ministered naked, and their flowing cups
445 With pleasant liquors crowned: O innocence
Deserving Paradise! if ever, then,
Then had the sons of God excuse to have been
Enamoured at that sight; but in those hearts
Love unlibidinous reigned, nor jealousy
450 Was understood, the injured lover's Hell.
    Thus when with meats and drinks they had sufficed,
Not burdened nature, sudden mind arose
In Adam, not to let th' occasion pass
Given him by this great conference to know
455 Of things above his world, and of their being
Who dwell in Heav'n, whose excellence he saw
Transcend his own so far, whose radiant forms'
Divine effulgence, whose high power so far
Exceeded human, and his wary speech
460 Thus to th' empyreal minister he framed.
    Inhabitant with God, now know I well
Thy favour, in this honour done to man,
Under whose lowly roof thou hast vouchsafed
To enter, and these earthly fruits to taste,
465 Food not of angels, yet accepted so,
As that more willingly thou couldst not seem
At Heav'n's high feasts to have fed: yet what compare?
    To whom the wingèd hierarch replied.
O Adam, one Almighty is, from whom
470 All things proceed, and up to him return,
If not depraved from good, created all
Such to perfection, one first matter all,
Endued with various forms, various degrees
Of substance, and in things that live, of life;
475 But more refined, more spiritous, and pure,
As nearer to him placed or nearer tending
Each in their several active spheres assigned,
Till body up to spirit work, in bounds
Proportioned to each kind. So from the root

480 Springs lighter the green stalk, from thence the leaves
More airy, last the bright consummate flow'r
Spirits odórous breathes: flow'rs and their fruit
Man's nourishment, by gradual scale sublimed
To vital spirits aspire, to animal,
485 To intellectual, give both life and sense,
Fancy and understanding, whence the soul
Reason receives, and reason is her being,
Discursive, or intuitive; discourse
Is oftest yours, the latter most is ours,
490 Differing but in degree, of kind the same.
Wonder not then, what God for you saw good
If I refuse not, but convert, as you,
To proper substance; time may come when men
With angels may participate, and find
495 No inconvenient diet, nor too light fare:
And from these corporal nutriments perhaps
Your bodies may at last turn all to Spirit,
Improved by tract of time, and winged ascend
Ethereal, as we, or may at choice
500 Here or in Heav'nly Paradises dwell;
If ye be found obedient, and retain
Unalterably firm his love entire
Whose progeny you are. Meanwhile enjoy
Your fill what happiness this happy state
505 Can comprehend, incapable of more.
    To whom the patriarch of mankind replied.
O favourable Spirit, propitious guest,
Well hast thou taught the way that might direct
Our knowledge, and the scale of Nature set
510 From centre to circumference, whereon
In contemplation of created things
By steps we may ascend to God. But say,
What meant that caution joined, *if ye be found*
Obedient? can we want obedience then
515 To him, or possibly his love desert
Who formed us from the dust, and placed us here
Full to the utmost measure of what bliss
Human desires can seek or apprehend?

To whom the angel. Son of Heav'n and earth,
520 Attend: that thou art happy, owe to God;
That thou continuest such, owe to thyself,
That is, to thy obedience; therein stand.
This was that caution giv'n thee; be advised.
God made thee perfect, not immutable;
525 And good he made thee, but to persevere
He left it in thy power, ordained thy will
By nature free, not overruled by Fate
Inextricable, or strict necessity;
Our voluntary service he requires,
530 Not our necessitated, such with him
Finds no acceptance, nor can find, for how
Can hearts, not free, be tried whether they serve
Willing or no, who will but what they must
By destiny, and can no other choose?
535 Myself and all th' angelic host that stand
In sight of God enthroned, our happy state
Hold, as you yours, while our obedience holds;
On other surety none; freely we serve,
Because we freely love, as in our will
540 To love or not; in this we stand or fall:
And some are fall'n, to disobedience fall'n,
And so from Heav'n to deepest Hell; O fall
From what high state of bliss into what woe!
To whom our great progenitor. Thy words
545 Attentive, and with more delighted ear,
Divine instructor, I have heard, than when
Cherubic songs by night from neighbouring hills
Aërial music send: nor knew I not
To be both will and deed created free;
550 Yet that we never shall forget to love
Our Maker, and obey him whose command
Single, is yet so just, my constant thoughts
Assured me, and still assure: though what thou tell'st
Hath passed in Heav'n, some doubt within me move,
555 But more desire to hear, if thou consent,
The full relation, which must needs be strange,
Worthy of sacred silence to be heard;

And we have yet large day, for scarce the sun
Hath finished half his journey, and scarce begins
His other half in the great zone of heav'n.
    Thus Adam made request, and Raphael
After short pause assenting, thus began.
    High matter thou enjoin'st me, O prime of men,
Sad task and hard, for how shall I relate
To human sense th' invisible explóits
Of warring Spirits; how without remorse
The ruin of so many glorious once
And perfect while they stood; how last unfold
The secrets of another world, perhaps
Not lawful to reveal? yet for thy good
This is dispensed, and what surmounts the reach
Of human sense, I shall delineate so,
By lik'ning spiritual to corporal forms,
As may express them best, though what if earth
Be but the shadow of Heav'n, and things therein
Each to other like, more than on earth is thought?
    As yet this world was not, and Chaos wild
Reigned where these heav'ns now roll, where earth now
       rests
Upon her centre poised, when on a day
(For time, though in eternity, applied
To motion, measures all things durable
By present, past, and future) on such day
As Heav'n's Great Year brings forth, th' empyreal host
Of angels by imperial summons called,
Innumerable before th' Almighty's throne
Forthwith from all the ends of Heav'n appeared
Under their hierarchs in orders bright:
Ten thousand thousand ensigns high advanced,
Standards, and gonfalons 'twixt van and rear
Stream in the air, and for distinction serve
Of hierarchies, of orders, and degrees;
Or in their glittering tissues bear imblazed
Holy memorials, acts of zeal and love
Recorded eminent. Thus when in orbs
Of circuit inexpressible they stood,

Orb within orb, the Father infinite,
By whom in bliss embosomed sat the Son,
Amidst as from a flaming Mount, whose top
Brightness had made invisible, thus spake.
600   Hear all ye angels, progeny of Light,
Thrones, Dominations, Princedoms, Virtues, Powers,
Hear my decree, which unrevoked shall stand.
This day I have begot whom I declare
My only Son, and on this holy hill
605   Him have anointed, whom ye now behold
At my right hand; your head I him appoint;
And by myself have sworn to him shall bow
All knees in Heav'n, and shall confess him Lord:
Under his great vicegerent reign abide
610   United as one individual soul
For ever happy: him who disobeys
Me disobeys, breaks union, and that day
Cast out from God and blessèd vision, falls
Into utter darkness, deep engulfed, his place
615   Ordained without redemption, without end.
      So spake th' Omnipotent, and with his words
All seemed well pleased; all seemed, but were not all.
That day, as other solemn days, they spent
In song and dance about the sacred hill,
620   Mystical dance, which yonder starry sphere
Of planets and of fixed in all her wheels
Resembles nearest, mazes intricate,
Eccentric, intervolved, yet regular
Then most, when most irregular they seem,
625   And in their motions harmony divine
So smooths her charming tones, that God's own ear
Listens delighted. Ev'ning now approached
(For we have also our ev'ning and our morn,
We ours for change delectable, not need);
630   Forthwith from dance to sweet repast they turn
Desirous; all in circles as they stood,
Tables are set, and on a sudden piled
With angels' food, and rubied nectar flows
In pearl, in diamond, and massy gold,

635   Fruit of delicious vines, the growth of Heav'n.
       On flow'rs reposed, and with fresh flow'rets crowned,
       They eat, they drink, and in communion sweet
       Quaff immortality and joy, secure
       Of surfeit where full measure only bounds
640   Excess, before th' all-bounteous King, who show'red
       With copious hand, rejoicing in their joy.
       Now when ambrosial night with clouds exhaled
       From that high Mount of God, whence light and shade
       Spring both, the face of brightest Heav'n had changed
645   To grateful twilight (for night comes not there
       In darker veil) and roseate dews disposed
       All but the unsleeping eyes of God to rest,
       Wide over all the plain, and wider far
       Than all this globous earth in plain outspread,
650   (Such are the courts of God) th' angelic throng
       Dispersed in bands and files their camp extend
       By living streams among the Trees of Life,
       Pavilions numberless, and sudden reared,
       Celestial tabernacles, where they slept
655   Fanned with cool winds, save those who in their course
       Melodious hymns about the sov'reign throne
       Alternate all night long: but not so waked
       Satan, so call him now, his former name
       Is heard no more in Heav'n; he of the first,
660   If not the first Archangel, great in power,
       In favour and pre-eminence, yet fraught
       With envy against the Son of God, that day
       Honoured by his great Father, and proclaimed
       Messiah King anointed, could not bear
665   Through pride that sight, and thought himself impaired.
       Deep malice thence conceiving and disdain,
       Soon as midnight brought on the dusky hour
       Friendliest to sleep and silence, he resolved
       With all his legions to dislodge, and leave
670   Unworshipped, unobeyed the throne supreme
       Contemptuous, and his next subordinate
       Awak'ning, thus to him in secret spake.
           Sleep'st thou companion dear, what sleep can close

Thy eye-lids? and remember'st what decree
675 Of yesterday, so late hath passed the lips
Of Heav'n's Almighty. Thou to me thy thoughts
Wast wont, I mine to thee was wont to impart;
Both waking we were one; how then can now
Thy sleep dissent? New laws thou seest imposed;
680 New laws from him who reigns, new minds may raise
In us who serve, new counsels, to debate
What doubtful may ensue; more in this place
To utter is not safe. Assemble thou
Of all those myriads which we lead the chief;
685 Tell them that by command, ere yet dim night
Her shadowy cloud withdraws, I am to haste,
And all who under me their banners wave,
Homeward with flying march where we possess
The quarters of the North, there to prepare
690 Fit entertainment to receive our King
The great Messiah, and his new commands,
Who speedily through all the hierarchies
Intends to pass triumphant, and give laws.
        So spake the false Archangel, and infused
695 Bad influence into th' unwary breast
Of his associate; he together calls,
Or several one by one, the regent Powers,
Under him regent, tells, as he was taught,
That the Most High commanding, now ere night,
700 Now ere dim night had disencumbered Heav'n,
The great hierarchal standard was to move;
Tells the suggested cause, and casts between
Ambiguous words and jealousies, to sound
Or taint integrity; but all obeyed
705 The wonted signal, and superior voice
Of their great Potentate; for great indeed
His name, and high was his degree in Heav'n;
His count'nance, as the morning star that guides
The starry flock, allured them, and with lies
710 Drew after him the third part of Heav'n's host:
Meanwhile th' Eternal eye, whose sight discerns
Abstrusest thoughts, from forth his holy Mount

And from within the golden lamps that burn
Nightly before him, saw without their light
715 Rebellion rising, saw in whom, how spread
Among the sons of morn, what multitudes
Were banded to oppose his high decree;
And smiling to his only Son thus said.
        Son, thou in whom my glory I behold
720 In full resplendence, heir of all my might,
Nearly it now concerns us to be sure
Of our omnipotence, and with what arms
We mean to hold what anciently we claim
Of deity or empire, such a foe
725 Is rising, who intends to erect his throne
Equal to ours, throughout the spacious North;
Nor so content, hath in his thought to try
In battle what our power is, or our right.
Let us advise, and to this hazard draw
730 With speed what force is left, and all employ
In our defence, lest unawares we lose
This our high place, our sanctuary, our hill.
        To whom the Son with calm aspéct and clear
Light'ning divine, ineffable, serene,
735 Made answer. Mighty Father, thou thy foes
Justly hast in derision, and secure
Laugh'st at their vain designs and tumults vain,
Matter to me of glory, whom their hate
Illústrates, when they see all regal power
740 Giv'n me to quell their pride, and in event
Know whether I be dextrous to subdue
Thy rebels, or be found the worst in Heav'n.
        So spake the Son, but Satan with his powers
Far was advanced on wingèd speed, an host
745 Innumerable as the stars of night,
Or stars of morning, dew-drops, which the sun
Impearls on every leaf and every flow'r.
Regions they passed, the mighty regencies
Of Seraphim and Potentates and Thrones
750 In their triple degrees, regions to which
All thy dominion, Adam, is no more

Than what this garden is to all the earth,
And all the sea, from one entire globose
Stretched into longitude; which having passed
755 At length into the limits of the North
They came, and Satan to his royal seat
High on a hill, far blazing, as a mount
Raised on a mount, with pyramids and tow'rs
From diamond quarries hewn, and rocks of gold,
760 The palace of great Lucifer, (so call
That structure in the dialect of men
Interpreted) which not long after, he
Affecting all equality with God,
In imitation of that Mount whereon
765 Messiah was declared in sight of Heav'n,
The Mountain of the Congregation called;
For thither he assembled all his train,
Pretending so commanded to consult
About the great reception of their King,
770 Thither to come, and with calumnious art
Of counterfeited truth thus held their ears.
    Thrones, Dominations, Princedoms, Virtues, Powers,
If these magnific titles yet remain
Not merely titular, since by decree
775 Another now hath to himself engrossed
All power, and us eclipsed under the name
Of King anointed, for whom all this haste
Of midnight march, and hurried meeting here,
This only to consult how we may best
780 With what may be devised of honours new
Receive him coming to receive from us
Knee-tribute yet unpaid, prostration vile,
Too much to one, but double how endured,
To one and to his image now proclaimed?
785 But what if better counsels might erect
Our minds and teach us to cast off this yoke?
Will ye submit your necks, and choose to bend
The supple knee? ye will not, if I trust
To know ye right, or if ye know yourselves
790 Natives and sons of Heav'n possessed before

By none, and if not equal all, yet free,
Equally free; for orders and degrees
Jar not with liberty, but well consist.
Who can in reason then or right assume
795   Monarchy over such as live by right
His equals, if in power and splendour less,
In freedom equal? or can introduce
Law and edíct on us, who without law
Err not, much less for this to be our Lord,
800   And look for adoration to th' abuse
Of those imperial titles which assert
Our being ordained to govern, not to serve?
    Thus far his bold discourse without control
Had audience, when among the Seraphim
805   Abdiel, than whom none with more zeal adored
The Deity, and divine commands obeyed,
Stood up, and in a flame of zeal severe
The current of his fury thus opposed.
    O argument blasphémous, false and proud!
810   Words which no ear ever to hear in Heav'n
Expected, least of all from thee, ingrate
In place thyself so high above thy peers.
Canst thou with impious obloquy condemn
The just decree of God, pronounced and sworn,
815   That to his only Son by right endued
With regal sceptre, every soul in Heav'n
Shall bend the knee, and in that honour due
Confess him rightful King? unjust thou say'st
Flatly unjust, to bind with laws the free,
820   And equal over equals to let reign,
One over all with unsucceeded power.
Shalt thou give law to God, shalt thou dispute
With him the points of liberty, who made
Thee what thou art, and formed the Powers of Heav'n
825   Such as he pleased, and circumscribed their being?
Yet by experience taught we know how good,
And of our good, and of our dignity
How provident he is, how far from thought
To make us less, bent rather to exalt

830 Our happy state under one head more near
     United. But to grant it thee unjust,
     That equal over equals monarch reign:
     Thyself though great and glorious dost thou count,
     Or all angelic nature joined in one,
835 Equal to him begotten Son, by whom
     As by his Word the mighty Father made
     All things, ev'n thee, and all the Spirits of Heav'n
     By him created in their bright degrees,
     Crowned them with glory, and to their glory named
840 Thrones, Dominations, Princedoms, Virtues, Powers,
     Essential Powers, nor by his reign obscured,
     But more illustrious made, since he the head
     One of our number thus reduced becomes,
     His laws our laws, all honour to him done
845 Returns our own. Cease then this impious rage,
     And tempt not these; but hasten to appease
     Th' incensèd Father, and th' incensèd Son,
     While pardon may be found in time besought.
         So spake the fervent angel, but his zeal
850 None seconded, as out of season judged,
     Or singular and rash, whereat rejoiced
     Th' Apostate, and more haughty thus replied.
     That we were formed then say'st thou? and the work
     Of secondary hands, by task transferred
855 From Father to his Son? strange point and new!
     Doctrine which we would know whence learnt: who saw
     When this creation was? remember'st thou
     Thy making, while the Maker gave thee being?
     We know no time when we were not as now;
860 Know none before us, self-begot, self-raised
     By our own quick'ning power, when fatal course
     Had circled his full orb, the birth mature
     Of this our native Heav'n, ethereal sons.
     Our puissance is our own, our own right hand
865 Shall teach us highest deeds, by proof to try
     Who is our equal: then thou shalt behold
     Whether by supplication we intend
     Address, and to begirt th' Almighty throne

Beseeching or besieging. This report,
870 These tidings carry to th' anointed King;
And fly, ere evil intercept thy flight.
　　He said, and as the sound of waters deep
Hoarse murmur echoed to his words applause
Through the infinite host, nor less for that
875 The flaming Seraph fearless, though alone
Encompassed round with foes, thus answered bold.
　　O alienate from God, O Spirit accursed,
Forsaken of all good; I see thy fall
Determined, and thy hapless crew involved
880 In this perfidious fraud, contagion spread
Both of thy crime and punishment: henceforth
No more be troubled how to quit the yoke
Of God's Messiah; those indulgent laws
Will not be now vouchsafed, other decrees
885 Against thee are gone forth without recall;
That golden sceptre which thou didst reject
Is now an iron rod to bruise and break
Thy disobedience. Well thou didst advise,
Yet not for thy advice or threats I fly
890 These wicked tents devoted, lest the wrath
Impendent, raging into sudden flame
Distinguish not: for soon expect to feel
His thunder on thy head, devouring fire.
Then who created thee lamenting learn,
895 When who can uncreate thee thou shalt know.
　　So spake the Seraph Abdiel faithful found,
Among the faithless, faithful only he;
Among innumerable false, unmoved,
Unshaken, unseduced, unterrified,
900 His loyalty he kept, his love, his zeal;
Nor number, nor example with him wrought
To swerve from truth, or change his constant mind
Though single. From amidst them forth he passed,
Long way through hostile scorn, which he sustained
905 Superior, nor of violence feared aught;
And with retorted scorn his back he turned
On those proud tow'rs to swift destruction doomed.

BOOK VI

The Argument

Raphael continues to relate how Michael and Gabriel were
sent forth to battle against Satan and his angels. The first
fight described: Satan and his powers retire under night: he
calls a council, invents devilish engines, which in the second
5   day's fight put Michael and his angels to some disorder; but
they at length pulling up mountains overwhelmed both the
force and machines of Satan: yet the tumult not so ending,
God on the third day sends Messiah his Son, for whom he
had reserved the glory of that victory: he in the power of his
10 Father coming to the place, and causing all his legions to
stand still on either side, with his chariot and thunder driving
into the midst of his enemies, pursues them unable to resist
towards the wall of Heaven; which opening, they leap down
with horror and confusion into the place of punishment pre-
15 pared for them in the deep: Messiah returns with triumph to
his Father.

All night the dreadless angel unpursued
Through Heav'n's wide champaign held his way, till Morn,
Waked by the circling Hours, with rosy hand
Unbarred the gates of light. There is a cave
5   Within the Mount of God, fast by his throne,
Where light and darkness in perpetual round
Lodge and dislodge by turns, which makes through Heav'n
Grateful vicissitude, like day and night;
Light issues forth, and at the other door
10 Obsequious darkness enters, till her hour
To veil the Heav'n, though darkness there might well
Seem twilight here; and now went forth the Morn
Such as in highest Heav'n, arrayed in gold
Empyreal; from before her vanished night,

15   Shot through with orient beams: when all the plain
      Covered with thick embattled squadrons bright,
      Chariots and flaming arms, and fiery steeds
      Reflecting blaze on blaze, first met his view:
      War he perceived, war in procinct, and found
20   Already known what he for news had thought
      To have reported: gladly then he mixed
      Among those friendly Powers who him received
      With joy and acclamations loud, that one
      That of so many myriads fall'n, yet one
25   Returned not lost: on to the sacred hill
      They led him high applauded, and present
      Before the seat supreme; from whence a voice
      From midst a golden cloud thus mild was heard.
          Servant of God, well done, well hast thou fought
30   The better fight, who single hast maintained
      Against revolted multitudes the cause
      Of truth, in word mightier than they in arms;
      And for the testimony of truth hast borne
      Universal reproach, far worse to bear
35   Than violence: for this was all thy care
      To stand approved in sight of God, though worlds
      Judged thee perverse: the easier conquest now
      Remains thee, aided by this host of friends,
      Back on thy foes more glorious to return
40   Than scorned thou didst depart, and to subdue
      By force, who reason for their law refuse,
      Right reason for their law, and for their King
      Messiah, who by right of merit reigns.
      Go Michael of celestial armies prince,
45   And thou in military prowess next,
      Gabriel, lead forth to battle these my sons
      Invincible, lead forth my armèd saints
      By thousands and by millions ranged for fight;
      Equal in number to that Godless crew
50   Rebellious, them with fire and hostile arms
      Fearless assault, and to the brow of Heav'n
      Pursuing drive them out from God and bliss,
      Into their place of punishment, the gulf

Of Tartarus, which ready opens wide
55　His fiery Chaos to receive their fall.
　　So spake the sov'reign voice, and clouds began
To darken all the hill, and smoke to roll
In dusky wreaths, reluctant flames, the sign
Of wrath awaked: nor with less dread the loud
60　Ethereal trumpet from on high gan blow:
At which command the powers militant,
That stood for Heav'n, in mighty quadrate joined
Of union irresistible, moved on
In silence their bright legions, to the sound
65　Of instrumental harmony that breathed
Heroic ardour to advent'rous deeds
Under their godlike leaders, in the cause
Of God and his Messiah. On they move
Indissolúbly firm; nor obvious hill,
70　Nor strait'ning vale, nor wood, nor stream divides
Their perfect ranks; for high above the ground
Their march was, and the passive air upbore
Their nimble tread; as when the total kind
Of birds in orderly array on wing
75　Came summoned over Eden to receive
Their names of thee; so over many a tract
Of Heav'n they marched, and many a province wide
Tenfold the length of this terrene: at last
Far in th' horizon to the North appeared
80　From skirt to skirt a fiery region, stretched
In battailous aspéct, and nearer view
Bristled with upright beams innumerable
Of rigid spears, and helmets thronged, and shields
Various, with boastful argument portrayed,
85　The banded powers of Satan hasting on
With furious expedition; for they weened
That selfsame day by fight, or by surprise
To win the Mount of God, and on his throne
To set the envier of his state, the proud
90　Aspirer, but their thoughts proved fond and vain
In the mid way: though strange to us it seemed
At first, that angel should with angel war,

And in fierce hosting meet, who wont to meet
So oft in festivals of joy and love
95 Unanimous, as sons of one great Sire,
Hymning th' Eternal Father: but the shout
Of battle now began, and rushing sound
Of onset ended soon each milder thought.
High in the midst exalted as a god
100 Th' Apostate in his sun-bright chariot sat
Idol of majesty divine, enclosed
With flaming Cherubim, and golden shields;
Then lighted from his gorgeous throne, for now
'Twixt host and host but narrow space was left,
105 A dreadful interval, and front to front
Presented stood in terrible array
Of hideous length: before the cloudy van,
On the rough edge of battle ere it joined
Satan with vast and haughty strides advanced,
110 Came tow'ring, armed in adamant and gold;
Abdiel that sight endured not, where he stood
Among the mightiest, bent on highest deeds,
And thus his own undaunted heart explores.
   O Heav'n! that such resemblance of the Highest
115 Should yet remain, where faith and realty
Remain not; wherefore should not strength and might
There fail where virtue fails, or weakest prove
Where boldest; though to sight unconquerable?
His puissance, trusting in th' Almighty's aid,
120 I mean to try, whose reason I have tried
Unsound and false; nor is it aught but just,
That he who in debate of truth hath won,
Should win in arms, in both disputes alike
Victor; though brutish that contést and foul,
125 When reason hath to deal with force, yet so
Most reason is that reason overcome.
   So pondering, and from his armèd peers
Forth stepping opposite, half way he met
His daring foe, at this prevention more
130 Incensed, and thus securely him defied.
   Proud, art thou met? thy hope was to have reached

The heighth of thy aspiring unopposed,
The throne of God unguarded, and his side
Abandoned at the terror of thy power
135   Or potent tongue; fool, not to think how vain
Against th' Omnipotent to rise in arms;
Who out of smallest things could without end
Have raised incessant armies to defeat
Thy folly; or with solitary hand
140   Reaching beyond all limit, at one blow
Unaided could have finished thee, and whelmed
Thy legions under darkness; but thou seest
All are not of thy train; there be who faith
Prefer, and piety to God, though then
145   To thee not visible, when I alone
Seemed in thy world erroneous to dissent
From all: my sect thou seest, now learn too late
How few sometimes may know, when thousands err.
    Whom the grand Foe with scornful eye askance
150   Thus answered. Ill for thee, but in wished hour
Of my revenge, first sought for thou return'st
From flight, seditious angel, to receive
Thy merited reward, the first assay
Of this right hand provoked, since first that tongue
155   Inspired with contradiction durst oppose
A third part of the gods, in synod met
Their deities to assert, who while they feel
Vigour divine within them, can allow
Omnipotence to none. But well thou com'st
160   Before thy fellows, ambitious to win
From me some plume, that thy success may show
Destruction to the rest: this pause between
(Unanswered lest thou boast) to let thee know;
At first I thought that liberty and Heav'n
165   To Heav'nly souls had been all one; but now
I see that most through sloth had rather serve,
Minist'ring Spirits, trained up in feast and song;
Such hast thou armed, the minstrelsy of Heav'n,
Servility with freedom to contend,
170   As both their deeds compared this day shall prove.

To whom in brief thus Abdiel stern replied.
Apostate, still thou err'st, nor end wilt find
Of erring, from the path of truth remote:
Unjustly thou deprav'st it with the name
175 Of servitude to serve whom God ordains,
Or Nature; God and Nature bid the same,
When he who rules is worthiest, and excels
Them whom he governs. This is servitude,
To serve th' unwise, or him who hath rebelled
180 Against his worthier, as thine now serve thee,
Thyself not free, but to thyself enthralled;
Yet lewdly dar'st our minist'ring upbraid.
Reign thou in Hell thy Kingdom, let me serve
In Heav'n God ever blest, and his divine
185 Behests obey, worthiest to be obeyed;
Yet chains in Hell, not realms expect: meanwhile
From me returned, as erst thou saidst, from flight,
This greeting on thy impious crest receive.
So saying, a noble stroke he lifted high,
190 Which hung not, but so swift with tempest fell
On the proud crest of Satan, that no sight,
Nor motion of swift thought, less could his shield
Such ruin intercept: ten paces huge
He back recoiled; the tenth on bended knee
195 His massy spear upstayed; as if on earth
Winds under ground or waters forcing way
Sidelong, had pushed a mountain from his seat
Half sunk with all his pines. Amazement seized
The rebel Thrones, but greater rage to see
200 Thus foiled their mightiest; ours joy filled, and shout,
Presage of victory and fierce desire
Of battle: whereat Michaël bid sound
Th' Archangel trumpet; through the vast of Heav'n
It sounded, and the faithful armies rung
205 Hosanna to the Highest: nor stood at gaze
The adverse legions, nor less hideous joined
The horrid shock: now storming fury rose,
And clamour such as heard in Heav'n till now
Was never; arms on armour clashing brayed

210 Horrible discord, and the madding wheels
Of brazen chariots raged; dire was the noise
Of conflict; overhead the dismal hiss
Of fiery darts in flaming volleys flew,
And flying vaulted either host with fire.
215 So under fiery cope together rushed
Both battles main, with ruinous assault
And inextinguishable rage; all Heav'n
Resounded, and had earth been then, all earth
Had to her centre shook. What wonder? when
220 Millions of fierce encount'ring angels fought
On either side, the least of whom could wield
These elements, and arm him with the force
Of all their regions: how much more of power
Army against army numberless to raise
225 Dreadful combustion warring, and disturb,
Though not destroy, their happy native seat;
Had not th' Eternal King Omnipotent
From his stronghold of Heav'n high overruled
And limited their might; though numbered such
230 As each divided legion might have seemed
A numerous host, in strength each armèd hand
A legion; led in fight, yet leader seemed
Each warrior single as in chief, expért
When to advance, or stand, or turn the sway
235 Of battle, open when, and when to close
The ridges of grim war; no thought of flight,
None of retreat, no unbecoming deed
That argued fear; each on himself relied,
As only in his arm the moment lay
240 Of victory; deeds of eternal fame
Were done, but infinite: for wide was spread
That war and various; sometimes on firm ground
A standing fight, then soaring on main wing
Tormented all the air; all air seemed then
245 Conflicting fire: long time in even scale
The battle hung; till Satan, who that day
Prodigious power had shown, and met in arms
No equal, ranging through the dire attack

Of fighting Seraphim confused, at length
250 Saw where the sword of Michael smote, and felled
Squadrons at once, with huge two-handed sway
Brandished aloft the horrid edge came down
Wide wasting; such destruction to withstand
He hasted, and opposed the rocky orb
255 Of tenfold adamant, his ample shield
A vast circumference: at his approach
The great Archangel from his warlike toil
Surceased, and glad as hoping here to end
Intestine war in Heav'n, the Arch-foe subdued
260 Or captive dragged in chains, with hostile frown
And visage all inflamed first thus began.
Author of evil, unknown till thy revolt,
Unnamed in Heav'n, now plenteous, as thou seest
These acts of hateful strife, hateful to all,
265 Though heaviest by just measure on thyself
And thy adherents: how hast thou disturbed
Heav'n's blessèd peace, and into Nature brought
Misery, uncreated till the crime
Of thy rebellion? how hast thou instilled
270 Thy malice into thousands, once upright
And faithful, now proved false. But think not here
To trouble holy rest; Heav'n casts thee out
From all her confines. Heav'n the seat of bliss
Brooks not the works of violence and war.
275 Hence then, and evil go with thee along
Thy offspring, to the place of evil, Hell,
Thou and thy wicked crew; there mingle broils,
Ere this avenging sword begin thy doom,
Or some more sudden vengeance winged from God
280 Precipitate thee with augmented pain.
So spake the Prince of angels; to whom thus
The Adversary. Nor think thou with wind
Of airy threats to awe whom yet with deeds
Thou canst not. Hast thou turned the least of these
285 To flight, or if to fall, but that they rise
Unvanquished, easier to transact with me
That thou shouldst hope, imperious, and with threats

To chase me hence? err not that so shall end
The strife which thou call'st evil, but we style
290   The strife of glory: which we mean to win,
Or turn this Heav'n itself into the Hell
Thou fablest; here however to dwell free,
If not to reign: meanwhile thy utmost force,
And join him named Almighty to thy aid,
295   I fly not, but have sought thee far and nigh.
They ended parle, and both addressed for fight
Unspeakable; for who, though with the tongue
Of angels, can relate, or to what things
Liken on earth conspicuous, that may lift
300   Human imagination to such heighth
Of godlike power: for likest gods they seemed,
Stood they or moved, in stature, motion, arms
Fit to decide the empire of great Heav'n.
Now waved their fiery swords, and in the air
305   Made horrid circles; two broad suns their shields
Blazed opposite, while Expectation stood
In horror; from each hand with speed retired
Where erst was thickest fight, th' angelic throng,
And left large field, unsafe within the wind
310   Of such commotion, such as to set forth
Great things by small, if Nature's concord broke,
Among the constellations war were sprung,
Two plancts rushing from aspéct malign
Of fiercest opposition in mid sky,
315   Should combat, and their jarring spheres confound.
Together both with next to Almighty arm,
Uplifted imminent one stroke they aimed
That might determine, and not need repeat,
As not of power, at once; nor odds appeared
320   In might or swift prevention; but the sword
Of Michael from the armoury of God
Was giv'n him tempered so, that neither keen
Nor solid might resist that edge: it met
The sword of Satan with steep force to smite
325   Descending, and in half cut sheer, nor stayed,
But with swift wheel reverse, deep ent'ring shared

All his right side; then Satan first knew pain,
And writhed him to and fro convolved; so sore
The griding sword with discontinuous wound
330 Passed through him, but th' ethereal substance closed
Not long divisible, and from the gash
A stream of nectarous humour issuing flowed
Sanguine, such as celestial Spirits may bleed,
And all his armour stained erewhile so bright.
335 Forthwith on all sides to his aid was run
By angels many and strong, who interposed
Defence, while others bore him on their shields
Back to his chariot, where it stood retired
From off the files of war; there they him laid
340 Gnashing for anguish and despite and shame
To find himself not matchless, and his pride
Humbled by such rebuke, so far beneath
His confidence to equal God in power.
Yet soon he healed; for Spirits that live throughout
345 Vital in every part, not as frail man
In entrails, heart or head, liver or reins,
Cannot but by annihilating die;
Nor in their liquid texture mortal wound
Receive, no more than can the fluid air:
350 All heart they live, all head, all eye, all ear,
All intellect, all sense, and as they please,
They limb themselves, and colour, shape or size
Assume, as likes them best, condense or rare.
      Meanwhile in other parts like deeds deserved
355 Memorial, where the might of Gabriel fought,
And with fierce ensigns pierced the deep array
Of Moloch furious king, who him defied,
And at his chariot wheels to drag him bound
Threatened, nor from the Holy One of Heav'n
360 Refrained his tongue blasphémous; but anon
Down cloven to the waist, with shattered arms
And uncouth pain fled bellowing. On each wing
Uriel and Raphaël his vaunting foe,
Though huge, and in a rock of diamond armed,
365 Vanquished Adramelech, and Asmadai,

Two potent Thrones, that to be less than gods
Disdained, but meaner thoughts learned in their flight,
Mangled with ghastly wounds through plate and mail.
Nor stood unmindful Abdiel to annoy
370   The atheist crew, but with redoubled blow
Ariel and Arioch, and the violence
Of Ramiel scorched and blasted overthrew.
I might relate of thousands, and their names
Eternize here on earth; but those elect
375   Angels contented with their fame in Heav'n
Seek not the praise of men: the other sort
In might though wondrous and in acts of war,
Nor of renown less eager, yet by doom
Cancelled from Heav'n and sacred memory,
380   Nameless in dark oblivion let them dwell.
For strength from Truth divided and from Just,
Illaudable, naught merits but dispraise
And ignominy, yet to glory aspires
Vainglorious, and through infamy seeks fame:
385   Therefore eternal silence be their doom.
    And now their mightiest quelled, the battle swerved,
With many an inroad gored; deformèd rout
Entered, and foul disorder; all the ground
With shivered armour strewn, and on a heap
390   Chariot and charioteer lay overturned
And fiery foaming steeds; what stood, recoiled
O'er-wearied, through the faint Satanic host
Defensive scarce, or with pale fear surprised,
Then first with fear surprised and sense of pain,
395   Fled ignominious, to such evil brought
By sin of disobedience, till that hour
Not liable to fear or flight or pain.
Far otherwise th' inviolable saints
In cubic phalanx firm advanced entire,
400   Invulnerable, impenetrably armed:
Such high advantages their innocence
Gave them above their foes, not to have sinned,
Not to have disobeyed; in fight they stood
Unwearied, unobnoxious to be pained

405 By wound, though from their place by violence moved.
　　　Now night her course began, and over Heav'n
　　Inducing darkness, grateful truce imposed,
　　And silence on the odious din of war:
　　Under her cloudy covert both retired,
410 Victor and vanquished: on the foughten field
　　Michaël and his angels prevalent
　　Encamping, placed in guard their watches round,
　　Cherubic waving fires: on th' other part
　　Satan with his rebellious disappeared,
415 Far in the dark dislodged, and void of rest,
　　His Potentates to council called by night;
　　And in the midst thus undismayed began.
　　　O now in danger tried, now known in arms
　　Not to be overpowered, companions dear,
420 Found worthy not of liberty alone,
　　Too mean pretence, but what we more affect,
　　Honour, dominion, glory, and renown,
　　Who have sustained one day in doubtful fight
　　(And if one day, why not eternal days?)
425 What Heaven's Lord had powerfullest to send
　　Against us from about his throne, and judged
　　Sufficient to subdue us to his will,
　　But proves not so: then fallible, it seems,
　　Of future we may deem him, though till now
430 Omniscient thought. True is, less firmly armed,
　　Some disadvantage we endured and pain,
　　Till now not known, but known as soon contemned,
　　Since now we find this our empyreal form
　　Incapable of mortal injury
435 Imperishable, and though pierced with wound,
　　Soon closing, and by native vigour healed.
　　Of evil then so small as easy think
　　The remedy; perhaps more valid arms,
　　Weapons more violent, when next we meet,
440 May serve to better us, and worse our foes,
　　Or equal what between us made the odds,
　　In nature none: if other hidden cause
　　Left them superior, while we can preserve

Unhurt our minds, and understanding sound,
445 Due search and consultation will disclose.
       He sat; and in th' assembly next upstood
Nisroch, of Principalities the prime;
As one he stood escaped from cruel fight,
Sore toiled, his riven arms to havoc hewn,
450 And cloudy in aspéct thus answering spake.
Deliverer from new Lords, leader to free
Enjoyment of our right as gods; yet hard
For gods, and too unequal work we find
Against unequal arms to fight in pain,
455 Against unpained, impassive; from which evil
Ruin must needs ensue; for what avails
Valour or strength, though matchless, quelled with pain
Which all subdues, and makes remiss the hands
Of mightiest. Sense of pleasure we may well
460 Spare out of life perhaps, and not repine,
But live content, which is the calmest life:
But pain is perfect misery, the worst
Of evils, and excessive, overturns
All patience. He who therefore can invent
465 With what more forcible we may offend
Our yet unwounded enemies, or arm
Ourselves with like defence, to me deserves
No less than for deliverance what we owe.
       Whereto with look composed Satan replied.
470 Not uninvented that, which thou aright
Believ'st so main to our success, I bring;
Which of us who beholds the bright surfáce
Of this ethereous mould whereon we stand,
This continent of spacious Heav'n, adorned
475 With plant, fruit, flow'r ambrosial, gems and gold,
Whose eye so superficially surveys
These things, as not to mind from whence they grow
Deep under ground, materials dark and crude,
Of spiritous and fiery spume, till touched
480 With Heav'n's ray, and tempered they shoot forth
So beauteous, op'ning to the ambient light.
These in their dark nativity the deep

Shall yield us, pregnant with infernal flame,
Which into hollow engines long and round
485   Thick-rammed, at th' other bore with touch of fire
Dilated and infuriate shall send forth
From far with thund'ring noise among our foes
Such implements of mischief as shall dash
To pieces, and o'erwhelm whatever stands
490   Adverse, that they shall fear we have disarmed
The Thunderer of his only dreaded bolt.
Nor long shall be our labour, yet ere dawn,
Effect shall end our wish. Meanwhile revive;
Abandon fear; to strength and counsel joined
495   Think nothing hard, much less to be despaired.
He ended, and his words their drooping cheer
Enlightened, and their languished hope revived.
Th' invention all admired, and each, how he
To be th' inventor missed, so easy it seemed
500   Once found, which yet unfound most would have thought
Impossible: yet haply of thy race
In future days, if malice should abound,
Someone intent on mischief, or inspired
With dev'lish machination might devise
505   Like instrument to plague the sons of men
For sin, on war and mutual slaughter bent.
Forthwith from council to the work they flew,
None arguing stood, innumerable hands
Were ready; in a moment up they turned
510   Wide the celestial soil, and saw beneath
Th' originals of nature in their crude
Conception; sulphurous and nitrous foam
They found, they mingled, and with subtle art,
Concocted and adusted they reduced
515   To blackest grain, and into store conveyed:
Part hidden veins digged up (nor hath this earth
Entrails unlike) of mineral and stone,
Whereof to found their engines and their balls
Of missive ruin; part incentive reed
520   Provide, pernicious with one touch to fire.
So all ere day-spring, under conscious night

Secret they finished, and in order set,
With silent circumspection unespied.
Now when fair morn orient in Heav'n appeared
525 Up rose the victor angels, and to arms
The matin trumpet sung: in arms they stood
Of golden panoply, refulgent host,
Soon banded; others from the dawning hills
Looked round, and scouts each coast light-armèd scour,
530 Each quarter, to descry the distant foe,
Where lodged, or whither fled, or if for fight,
In motion or in halt: him soon they met
Under spread ensigns moving nigh, in slow
But firm battalion; back with speediest sail
535 Zophiel, of Cherubim the swiftest wing,
Came flying, and in mid air aloud thus cried.

Arm, warriors, arm for fight, the foe at hand,
Whom fled we thought, will save us long pursuit
This day, fear not his flight; so thick a cloud
540 He comes, and settled in his face I see
Sad resolution and secure: let each
His adamantine coat gird well, and each
Fit well his helm, grip fast his orbèd shield,
Borne ev'n or high, for this day will pour down,
545 If I conjecture aught, no drizzling show'r,
But rattling storm of arrows barbed with fire.
So warned he them aware themselves, and soon
In order, quit of all impediment;
Instant without disturb they took alarm,
550 And onward move embattled; when behold
Not distant far with heavy pace the foe
Approaching gross and huge; in hollow cube
Training his devilish enginery, impaled
On every side with shadowing squadrons deep,
555 To hide the fraud. At interview both stood
A while, but suddenly at head appeared
Satan: and thus was heard commanding loud.

Vanguard, to right and left the front unfold;
That all may see who hate us, how we seek
560 Peace and composure, and with open breast

Stand ready to receive them, if they like
Our overture, and turn not back perverse;
But that I doubt; however witness Heaven,
Heav'n witness thou anon, while we discharge
565   Freely our part; ye who appointed stand
Do as you have in charge, and briefly touch
What we propound, and loud that all may hear.
       So scoffing in ambiguous words, he scarce
Had ended; when to right and left the front
570   Divided, and to either flank retired.
Which to our eyes discovered new and strange,
A triple-mounted row of pillars laid
On wheels (for like to pillars most they seemed
Or hollowed bodies made of oak or fir
575   With branches lopped, in wood or mountain felled),
Brass, iron, stony mould, had not their mouths
With hideous orifice gaped on us wide,
Portending hollow truce; at each behind
A Seraph stood, and in his hand a reed
580   Stood waving tipped with fire; while we suspense,
Collected stood within our thoughts amused,
Not long, for sudden all at once their reeds
Put forth, and to a narrow vent applied
With nicest touch. Immediate in a flame,
585   But soon obscured with smoke, all Heav'n appeared,
From those deep-throated engines belched, whose roar
Embowelled with outrageous noise the air,
And all her entrails tore, disgorging foul
Their devilish glut, chained thunderbolts and hail
590   Of iron globes, which on the victor host
Levelled, with such impetuous fury smote,
That whom they hit, none on their feet might stand,
Though standing else as rocks, but down they fell
By thousands, Angel on Archangel rolled,
595   The sooner for their arms; unarmed they might
Have easily as Spirits evaded swift
By quick contraction or remove; but now
Foul dissipation followed and forced rout;
Nor served it to relax their serried files.

600 What should they do? if on they rushed, repulse
     Repeated, and indecent overthrow
     Doubled, would render them yet more despised,
     And to their foes a laughter; for in view
     Stood ranked of Seraphim another row
605 In posture to displode their second tire
     Of thunder: back defeated to return
     They worse abhorred. Satan beheld their plight,
     And to his mates thus in derision called.
         O friends, why come not on these victors proud?
610 Erewhile they fierce were coming, and when we,
     To entertain them fair with open front
     And breast, (what could we more?) propounded terms
     Of composition, straight they changed their minds,
     Flew off, and into strange vagáries fell,
615 As they would dance, yet for a dance they seemed
     Somewhat extravagant and wild, perhaps
     For joy of offered peace: but I suppose
     If our proposals once again were heard
     We should compel them to a quick result.
620   To whom thus Belial in like gamesome mood.
     Leader, the terms we sent were terms of weight,
     Of hard conténts, and full of force urged home,
     Such as we might perceive amused them all,
     And stumbled many; who receives them right,
625 Had need from head to foot well understand;
     Not understood, this gift they have besides,
     They show us when our foes walk not upright.
         So they among themselves in pleasant vein
     Stood scoffing, heightened in their thoughts beyond
630 All doubt of victory; eternal might
     To match with their inventions they presumed
     So easy, and of his thunder made a scorn,
     And all his host derided, while they stood
     Awhile in trouble; but they stood not long,
635 Rage prompted them at length, and found them arms
     Against such Hellish mischief fit to oppose.
     Forthwith (behold the excellence, the power
     Which God hath in his mighty angels placed)

Their arms away they threw, and to the hills
640 (For earth hath this variety from Heav'n
Of pleasure situate in hill and dale)
Light as the lightning glimpse they ran, they flew,
From their foundations loos'ning to and fro
They plucked the seated hills with all their load,
645 Rocks, waters, woods, and by the shaggy tops
Uplifting bore them in their hands: amaze,
Be sure, and terror seized the rebel host,
When coming towards them so dread they saw
The bottom of the mountains upward turned,
650 Till on those cursèd engines' triple-row
They saw them whelmed, and all their confidence
Under the weight of mountains buried deep,
Themselves invaded next, and on their heads
Main promontories flung, which in the air
655 Came shadowing, and oppressed whole legions armed;
Their armour helped their harm, crushed in and bruised
Into their substance pent, which wrought them pain
Implacable, and many a dolorous groan,
Long struggling underneath, ere they could wind
660 Out of such prison, though Spirits of purest light,
Purest at first, now gross by sinning grown.
The rest in imitation to like arms
Betook them, and the neighbouring hills uptore;
So hills amid the air encountered hills
665 Hurled to and fro with jaculation dire,
That under ground they fought in dismal shade;
Infernal noise; war seemed a civil game
To this uproar; horrid confusion heaped
Upon confusion rose: and now all Heav'n
670 Had gone to wrack, with ruin overspread,
Had not th' Almighty Father where he sits
Shrined in his sanctuary of Heav'n secure,
Consulting on the sum of things, foreseen
This tumult, and permitted all, advised:
675 That his great purpose he might so fulfil,
To honour his Anointed Son avenged
Upon his enemies, and to declare

All power on him transferred: whence to his Son
Th' Assessor of his throne he thus began.
680   Effulgence of my Glory, Son beloved,
Son in whose face invisible is beheld
Visibly, what by Deity I am,
And in whose hand what by decree I do,
Second Omnipotence, two days are passed,
685 Two days, as we compute the days of Heav'n,
Since Michael and his powers went forth to tame
These disobedient; sore hath been their fight,
As likeliest was, when two such foes met armed;
For to themselves I left them, and thou know'st,
690 Equal in their creation they were formed,
Save what sin hath impaired, which yet hath wrought
Insensibly, for I suspend their doom;
Whence in perpetual fight they needs must last
Endless, and no solution will be found:
695 War wearied hath performed what war can do,
And to disordered rage let loose the reins,
With mountains as with weapons armed, which makes
Wild work in Heav'n, and dangerous to the main.
Two days are therefore passed, the third is thine;
700 For thee I have ordained it, and thus far
Have suffered, that the glory may be thine
Of ending this great war, since none but thou
Can end it. Into thee such virtue and grace
Immense I have transfused, that all may know
705 In Heav'n and Hell thy power above compare,
And this perverse commotion governed thus,
To manifest thee worthiest to be heir
Of all things, to be heir and to be King
By sacred unction, thy deservèd right.
710 Go then thou Mightiest in thy Father's might,
Ascend my chariot, guide the rapid wheels
That shake Heav'n's basis, bring forth all my war,
My bow and thunder, my almighty arms
Gird on, and sword upon thy puissant thigh;
715 Pursue these sons of darkness, drive them out
From all Heav'n's bounds into the utter deep:

There let them learn, as likes them, to despise
God and Messiah his anointed King.
    He said, and on his Son with rays direct
720 Shone full; he all his Father full expressed
Ineffably into his face received,
And thus the filial Godhead answering spake.
    O Father, O Supreme of Heav'nly thrones,
First, highest, holiest, best, thou always seek'st
725 To glorify thy Son, I always thee,
As is most just; this I my glory account,
My exaltation, and my whole delight,
That thou in me well pleased, declar'st thy will
Fulfilled, which to fulfil is all my bliss.
730 Sceptre and power, thy giving, I assume,
And gladlier shall resign, when in the end
Thou shalt be All in All, and I in thee
For ever, and in me all whom thou lov'st:
But whom thou hat'st, I hate, and can put on
735 Thy terrors, as I put thy mildness on,
Image of thee in all things; and shall soon,
Armed with thy might, rid Heav'n of these rebelled,
To their prepared ill mansion driven down
To chains of darkness, and th' undying worm,
740 That from thy just obedience could revolt,
Whom to obey is happiness entire.
Then shall thy saints unmixed, and from th' impure
Far separate, circling thy holy Mount
Unfeignèd hallelujahs to thee sing,
745 Hymns of high praise, and I among them chief.
So said, he o'er his sceptre bowing, rose
From the right hand of Glory where he sat,
And the third sacred morn began to shine
Dawning through Heav'n: forth rushed with whirlwind
        sound
750 The chariot of Paternal Deity,
Flashing thick flames, wheel within wheel undrawn,
Itself instínct with Spirit, but convóyed
By four Cherubic shapes; four faces each
Had wondrous; as with stars their bodies all

755 And wings were set with eyes, with eyes the wheels
Of beryl, and careering fires between;
Over their heads a crystal firmament,
Whereon a sapphire throne, inlaid with pure
Amber, and colours of the show'ry arch.
760 He in celestial panoply all armed
Of radiant urim, work divinely wrought,
Ascended, at his right hand Victory
Sat eagle-winged, beside him hung his bow
And quiver with three-bolted thunder stored,
765 And from about him fierce effusion rolled
Of smoke and bickering flame, and sparkles dire;
Attended with ten thousand thousand saints,
He onward came, far off his coming shone,
And twenty thousand (I their number heard)
770 Chariots of God, half on each hand were seen:
He on the wings of Cherub rode sublime
On the crystálline sky, in sapphire throned.
Illustrious far and wide, but by his own
First seen; them unexpected joy surprised,
775 When the great ensign of Messiah blazed
Aloft by angels borne, his sign in Heav'n:
Under whose conduct Michael soon reduced
His army, circumfused on either wing,
Under their Head embodied all in one.
780 Before him Power Divine his way prepared;
At his command the uprooted hills retired
Each to his place, they heard his voice and went
Obsequious; Heav'n his wonted face renewed,
And with fresh flow'rets hill and valley smiled.
785 This saw his hapless foes but stood obdured,
And to rebellious fight rallied their powers
Insensate, hope conceiving from despair.
In Heav'nly Spirits could such perverseness dwell?
But to convince the proud what signs avail,
790 Or wonders move th' obdúrate to relent?
They hardened more by what might most reclaim,
Grieving to see his glory, at the sight
Took envy, and aspiring to his heighth,

Stood re-embattled fierce, by force or fraud
795 Weening to prosper, and at length prevail
Against God and Messiah, or to fall
In universal ruin last, and now
To final battle drew, disdaining flight,
Or faint retreat; when the great Son of God
800 To all his host on either hand thus spake.
　　Stand still in bright array ye saints, here stand
Ye angels armed, this day from battle rest;
Faithful hath been your warfare, and of God
Accepted, fearless in his righteous cause,
805 And as ye have received, so have ye done
Invincibly; but of this cursèd crew
The punishment to other hand belongs;
Vengeance is his, or whose he sole appoints;
Number to this day's work is not ordained
810 Nor multitude; stand only and behold
God's indignation on these Godless poured
By me; not you but me they have despised,
Yet envied; against me is all their rage,
Because the Father, t' whom in Heav'n supreme
815 Kingdom and power and glory appertains,
Hath honoured me according to his will.
Therefore to me their doom he hath assigned;
That they may have their wish, to try with me
In battle which the stronger proves, they all,
820 Or I alone against them, since by strength
They measure all, of other excellence
Not emulous, nor care who them excels;
Nor other strife with them do I vouchsafe.
　　So spake the Son, and into terror changed
825 His count'nance too severe to be beheld
And full of wrath bent on his enemies.
At once the Four spread out their starry wings
With dreadful shade contiguous, and the orbs
Of his fierce chariot rolled, as with the sound
830 Of torrent floods, or of a numerous host.
He on his impious foes right onward drove,

Gloomy as Night; under his burning wheels
The steadfast Empyrean shook throughout,
All but the throne itself of God. Full soon
835 Among them he arrived; in his right hand
Grasping ten thousand thunders, which he sent
Before him, such as in their souls infixed
Plagues; they astonished all resistance lost,
All courage; down their idle weapons dropped;
840 O'er shields and helms, and helmèd heads he rode
Of Thrones and mighty Seraphim prostrate,
That wished the mountains now might be again
Thrown on them as a shelter from his ire.
Nor less on either side tempestuous fell
845 His arrows, from the fourfold-visaged four,
Distinct with eyes, and from the living wheels,
Distinct alike with multitude of eyes;
One spirit in them ruled, and every eye
Glared lightning, and shot forth pernicious fire
850 Among th' accursed, that withered all their strength,
And of their wonted vigour left them drained,
Exhausted, spiritless, afflicted, fall'n.
Yet half his strength he put not forth, but checked
His thunder in mid volley, for he meant
855 Not to destroy, but root them out of Heav'n:
The overthrown he raised, and as a herd
Of goats or timorous flock together thronged
Drove them before him thunderstruck, pursued
With terrors and with furies to the bounds
860 And crystal wall of Heav'n, which op'ning wide,
Rolled inward, and a spacious gap disclosed
Into the wasteful deep; the monstrous sight
Strook them with horror backward, but far worse
Urged them behind; headlong themselves they threw
865 Down from the verge of Heav'n; eternal wrath
Burnt after them to the bottomless pit.
    Hell heard th' unsufferable noise, Hell saw
Heav'n ruining from Heav'n and would have fled
Affrighted; but strict Fate had cast too deep

870   Her dark foundations, and too fast had bound.
       Nine days they fell; confounded Chaos roared,
       And felt tenfold confusion in their fall
       Through his wide anarchy, so huge a rout
       Encumbered him with ruin: Hell at last
875   Yawning received them whole, and on them closed,
       Hell their fit habitation fraught with fire
       Unquenchable, the house of woe and pain.
       Disburdened Heav'n rejoiced, and soon repaired
       Her mural breach, returning whence it rolled.
880   Sole Victor from th' expulsion of his foes
       Messiah his triumphal chariot turned:
       To meet him all his saints, who silent stood
       Eye witnesses of his almighty acts,
       With jubilee advanced; and as they went,
885   Shaded with branching palm, each order bright,
       Sung triumph, and him sung victorious King,
       Son, heir, and Lord, to him dominion giv'n,
       Worthiest to reign: he celebrated rode
       Triumphant through mid Heav'n, into the courts
890   And temple of his mighty Father throned
       On high; who into glory him received,
       Where now he sits at the right hand of bliss.
           Thus measuring things in Heav'n by things on earth
       At thy request, and that thou may'st beware
895   By what is past, to thee I have revealed
       What might have else to human race been hid;
       The discord which befell, and war in Heav'n
       Among th' angelic Powers, and the deep fall
       Of those too high aspiring, who rebelled
900   With Satan, he who envies now thy state,
       Who now is plotting how he may seduce
       Thee also from obedience, that with him
       Bereaved of happiness thou may'st partake
       His punishment, eternal misery;
905   Which would be all his solace and revenge,
       As a despite done against the Most High,
       Thee once to gain companion of his woe.

But listen not to his temptations, warn
Thy weaker; let it profit thee to have heard
910 By terrible example the reward
Of disobedience; firm they might have stood,
Yet fell; remember, and fear to transgress.

BOOK VII

The Argument

Raphael at the request of Adam relates how and wherefore
this world was first created; that God, after the expelling of
Satan and his angels out of Heaven, declared his pleasure to
create another world and other creatures to dwell therein;
5 sends his Son with glory and attendance of angels to perform
the work of Creation in six days: the angels celebrate with
hymns the performance thereof, and his reascension into
Heaven.

Descend from Heav'n Urania, by that name
If rightly thou art called, whose voice divine
Following, above th' Olympian hill I soar,
Above the flight of Pegasean wing.
5 The meaning, not the name I call: for thou
Nor of the Muses nine, nor on the top
Of old Olympus dwell'st, but Heav'nly born,
Before the hills appeared, or fountain flowed,
Thou with eternal Wisdom didst converse,
10 Wisdom thy sister, and with her didst play
In presence of th' Almighty Father, pleased
With thy celestial song. Up led by thee
Into the Heav'n of Heav'ns I have presumed,
An earthly guest, and drawn empyreal air,
15 Thy temp'ring; with like safety guided down
Return me to my native element:
Lest from this flying steed unreined, (as once
Bellerophon, though from a lower clime)
Dismounted, on th' Aleian field I fall
20 Erroneous there to wander and forlorn.
Half yet remains unsung, but narrower bound
Within the visible diurnal sphere;

Standing on earth, not rapt above the pole,
More safe I sing with mortal voice, unchanged
25 To hoarse or mute, though fall'n on evil days,
On evil days though fall'n, and evil tongues;
In darkness, and with dangers compassed round,
And solitude; yet not alone, while thou
Visit'st my slumbers nightly, or when Morn
30 Purples the east: still govern thou my song,
Urania, and fit audience find, though few.
But drive far off the barbarous dissonance
Of Bacchus and his revellers, the race
Of that wild rout that tore the Thracian bard
35 In Rhodope, where woods and rocks had ears
To rapture, till the savage clamour drowned
Both harp and voice; nor could the Muse defend
Her son. So fail not thou, who thee implores:
For thou art Heav'nly, she an empty dream.
40 　　Say Goddess, what ensued when Raphael,
The affable Archangel, had forewarned
Adam by dire example to beware
Apostasy, by what befell in Heaven
To those apostates, lest the like befall
45 In Paradise to Adam or his race,
Charged not to touch the interdicted Tree,
If they transgress, and slight that sole command,
So easily obeyed amid the choice
Of all tastes else to please their appetite,
50 Though wand'ring. He with his consorted Eve
The story heard attentive, and was filled
With admiration, and deep muse to hear
Of things so high and strange, things to their thought
So unimaginable as hate in Heav'n,
55 And war so near the peace of God in bliss
With such confusion: but the evil soon
Driv'n back redounded as a flood on those
From whom it sprung, impossible to mix
With blessedness. Whence Adam soon repealed
60 The doubts that in his heart arose: and now
Led on, yet sinless, with desire to know

What nearer might concern him, how this world
Of heav'n and earth conspicuous first began,
When, and whereof created, for what cause,
65   What within Eden or without was done
Before his memory, as one whose drouth
Yet scarce allayed still eyes the current stream,
Whose liquid murmur heard new thirst excites,
Proceeded thus to ask his Heav'nly guest.
70   Great things and full of wonder in our ears,
Far differing from this world, thou hast revealed
Divine interpreter, by favour sent
Down from the Empyrean to forewarn
Us timely of what might else have been our loss,
75   Unknown, which human knowledge could not reach:
For which to the infinitely Good we owe
Immortal thanks, and his admonishment
Receive with solemn purpose to observe
Immutably his sov'reign will, the end
80   Of what we are. But since thou hast vouchsafed
Gently for our instruction to impart
Things above earthly thought, which yet concerned
Our knowing, as to highest Wisdom seemed,
Deign to descend now lower, and relate
85   What may no less perhaps avail us known,
How first began this heav'n which we behold
Distant so high, with moving fires adorned
Innumerable, and this which yields or fills
All space, the ambient air wide interfused
90   Embracing round this florid earth; what cause
Moved the Creator in his holy rest
Through all eternity so late to build
In Chaos, and the work begun, how soon
Absolved, if unforbid thou may'st unfold
95   What we, not to explore the secrets ask
Of his eternal empire, but the more
To magnify his works, the more we know.
And the great light of day yet wants to run
Much of his race though steep, suspense in heav'n
100 Held by thy voice, thy potent voice he hears,

And longer will delay to hear thee tell
His generation, and the rising birth
Of Nature from the unapparent deep:
Or if the star of ev'ning and the moon
105   Haste to thy audience, night with her will bring
Silence, and sleep list'ning to thee will watch,
Or we can bid his absence, till thy song
End, and dismiss thee ere the morning shine.
    Thus Adam his illustrious guest besought:
110   And thus the godlike angel answered mild.
This also thy request with caution asked
Obtain: though to recount Almighty works
What words or tongue of Seraph can suffice,
Or heart of man suffice to comprehend?
115   Yet what thou canst attain, which best may serve
To glorify the Maker, and infer
Thee also happier, shall not be withheld
Thy hearing, such commission from above
I have received, to answer thy desire
120   Of knowledge within bounds; beyond abstain
To ask, nor let thine own inventions hope
Things not revealed, which th' invisible King,
Only omniscient, hath suppressed in night,
To none communicable in earth or Heaven:
125   Enough is left besides to search and know.
But knowledge is as food, and needs no less
Her temperance over appetite, to know
In measure what the mind may well contain,
Oppresses else with surfeit, and soon turns
130   Wisdom to folly, as nourishment to wind.
    Know then, that after Lucifer from Heav'n
(So call him, brighter once amidst the host
Of angels, than that star the stars among)
Fell with his flaming legions through the deep
135   Into his place, and the great Son returned
Victorious with his saints, th' Omnipotent
Eternal Father from his throne beheld
Their multitude, and to his Son thus spake.
    At least our envious Foe hath failed, who thought

140   All like himself rebellious, by whose aid
       This inaccessible high strength, the seat
       Of Deity supreme, us dispossessed,
       He trusted to have seized, and into fraud
       Drew many, whom their place knows here no more;
145   Yet far the greater part have kept, I see,
       Their station, Heav'n yet populous retains
       Number sufficient to possess her realms
       Though wide, and this high temple to frequent
       With ministeries due and solemn rites:
150   But lest his heart exalt him in the harm
       Already done, to have dispeopled Heav'n,
       My damage fondly deemed, I can repair
       That detriment, if such it be to lose
       Self-lost, and in a moment will create
155   Another world, out of one man a race
       Of men innumerable, there to dwell,
       Not here, till by degrees of merit raised
       They open to themselves at length the way
       Up hither, under long obedience tried,
160   And earth be changed to Heav'n, and Heav'n to earth,
       One Kingdom, joy and union without end.
       Meanwhile inhabit lax, ye Powers of Heav'n,
       And thou my Word, begotten Son, by thee
       This I perform, speak thou, and be it done:
165   My overshadowing Spirit and might with thee
       I send along, ride forth, and bid the deep
       Within appointed bounds be heav'n and earth;
       Boundless the deep, because I am who fill
       Infinitude, nor vacuous the space.
170   Though I uncircumscribed myself retire,
       And put not forth my goodness, which is free
       To act or not, Necessity and Chance
       Approach not me, and what I will is Fate.
          So spake th' Almighty, and to what he spake
175   His Word, the filial Godhead, gave effect.
       Immediate are the acts of God, more swift
       Than time or motion, but to human ears
       Cannot without procéss of speech be told,

So told as earthly notion can receive.
180 Great triumph and rejoicing was in Heav'n
When such was heard declared the Almighty's will;
Glory they sung to the Most High, good will
To future men, and in their dwellings peace:
Glory to him whose just avenging ire
185 Had driven out th' ungodly from his sight
And th' habitations of the just; to him
Glory and praise, whose wisdom had ordained
Good out of evil to create, instead
Of Spirits malign a better race to bring
190 Into their vacant room, and thence diffuse
His good to worlds and ages infinite.
So sang the hierarchies: meanwhile the Son
On his great expedition now appeared,
Girt with omnipotence, with radiance crowned
195 Of majesty divine, sapience and love
Immense, and all his Father in him shone.
About his chariot numberless were poured
Cherub and Seraph, Potentates and Thrones,
And Virtues, wingèd Spirits, and chariots winged,
200 From the armoury of God, where stand of old
Myriads between two brazen mountains lodged
Against a solemn day, harnessed at hand,
Celestial equipage; and now came forth
Spontaneous, for within them Spirit lived,
205 Attendant on their Lord: Heav'n opened wide
Her ever-during gates, harmonious sound
On golden hinges moving, to let forth
The King of Glory in his powerful Word
And Spirit coming to create new worlds.
210 On Heav'nly ground they stood, and from the shore
They viewed the vast immeasurable abyss
Outrageous as a sea, dark, wasteful, wild,
Up from the bottom turned by furious winds
And surging waves, as mountains to assault
215 Heav'n's heighth, and with the centre mix the pole.
     Silence, ye troubled waves, and thou deep, peace
Said then th' omnific Word, your discord end:

Nor stayed, but on the wings of Cherubim
Uplifted, in paternal glory rode
220 Far into Chaos, and the world unborn;
For Chaos heard his voice: him all his train
Followed in bright procession to behold
Creation, and the wonders of his might.
Then stayed the fervid wheels, and in his hand
225 He took the golden compasses, prepared
In God's eternal store, to circumscribe
This universe, and all created things:
One foot he centred, and the other turned
Round through the vast profundity obscure,
230 And said, Thus far extend, thus far thy bounds,
This be thy just circumference, O world.
Thus God the heav'n created, thus the earth,
Matter unformed and void: darkness profound
Covered th' abyss: but on the wat'ry calm
235 His brooding wings the Spirit of God outspread,
And vital virtue infused, and vital warmth
Throughout the fluid mass, but downward purged
The black tartareous cold infernal dregs
Adverse to life: then founded, then conglobed
240 Like things to like, the rest to several place
Disparted, and between spun out the air,
And earth self-balanced on her centre hung.
    Let there be light, said God, and forthwith light
Ethereal, first of things, quintessence pure
245 Sprung from the deep, and from her native east
To journey through the airy gloom began,
Sphered in a radiant cloud, for yet the sun
Was not; she in a cloudy tabernacle
Sojourned the while. God saw the light was good;
250 And light from darkness by the hemisphere
Divided: light the day, and darkness night
He named. Thus was the first day ev'n and morn:
Nor passed uncelebrated, nor unsung
By the celestial choirs, when orient light
255 Exhaling first from darkness they beheld;
Birthday of heav'n and earth; with joy and shout

The hollow universal orb they filled,
And touched their golden harps, and hymning praised
God and his works; Creator him they sung,
260 Both when first ev'ning was, and when first morn.
    Again, God said, let there be firmament
Amid the waters, and let it divide
The waters from the waters: and God made
The firmament, expanse of liquid, pure,
265 Transparent, elemental air, diffused
In circuit to the uttermost convéx
Of this great round: partition firm and sure,
The waters underneath from those above
Dividing: for as earth, so he the world
270 Built on circumfluous waters calm, in wide
Crystálline ocean, and the loud misrule
Of Chaos far removed, lest fierce extremes
Contiguous might distemper the whole frame:
And heav'n he named the firmament: so ev'n
275 And morning chorus sung the second day.
    The earth was formed, but in the womb as yet
Of waters, embryon immature involved,
Appeared not: over all the face of earth
Main ocean flowed, not idle, but with warm
280 Prolific humour soft'ning all her globe,
Fermented the Great Mother to conceive,
Satiate with genial moisture, when God said
Be gathered now ye waters under heav'n
Into one place, and let dry land appear.
285 Immediately the mountains huge appear
Emergent, and their broad bare backs upheave
Into the clouds, their tops ascend the sky:
So high as heaved the tumid hills, so low
Down sunk a hollow bottom broad and deep,
290 Capacious bed of waters: thither they
Hasted with glad precipitance, uprolled
As drops on dust conglobing from the dry;
Part rise in crystal wall, or ridge direct,
For haste; such flight the great command impressed
295 On the swift floods: as armies at the call

Of trumpet (for of armies thou hast heard)
Troop to their standard, so the wat'ry throng,
Wave rolling after wave, where way they found,
If steep, with torrent rapture, if through plain,
300 Soft-ebbing; nor withstood them rock or hill,
But they, or under ground, or circuit wide
With serpent error wand'ring, found their way,
And on the washy ooze deep channels wore;
Easy, ere God had bid the ground be dry.
305 All but within those banks, where rivers now
Stream, and perpetual draw their humid train.
The dry land, earth, and the great receptacle
Of congregated waters he called seas:
And saw that it was good, and said, Let th' earth
310 Put forth the verdant grass, herb yielding seed,
And fruit tree yielding fruit after her kind;
Whose seed is in herself upon the earth.
He scarce had said, when the bare earth, till then
Desert and bare, unsightly, unadorned,
315 Brought forth the tender grass, whose verdure clad
Her universal face with pleasant green,
Then herbs of every leaf, that sudden flow'red
Op'ning their various colours, and made gay
Her bosom smelling sweet: and these scarce blown,
320 Forth flourished thick the clust'ring vine, forth crept
The swelling gourd, up stood the corny reed
Embattled in her field: and the humble shrub,
And bush with frizzled hair implicit: last
Rose as in dance the stately trees, and spread
325 Their branches hung with copious fruit; or gemmed
Their blossoms: with high woods the hills were crowned,
With tufts the valleys and each fountain side,
With borders long the rivers. That earth now
Seemed like to Heav'n, a seat where gods might dwell,
330 Or wander with delight, and love to haunt
Her sacred shades: though God had yet not rained
Upon the earth, and man to till the ground
None was, but from the earth a dewy mist
Went up and watered all the ground, and each

335   Plant of the field, which ere it was in the earth
God made, and every herb, before it grew
On the green stem; God saw that it was good:
So ev'n and morn recorded the third day.
    Again th' Almighty spake: Let there be lights
340   High in th' expanse of heaven to divide
The day from night; and let them be for signs,
For seasons, and for days, and circling years,
And let them be for lights as I ordain
Their office in the firmament of heav'n
345   To give light on the earth; and it was so.
And God made two great lights, great for their use
To man, the greater to have rule by day,
The less by night altern: and made the stars,
And set them in the firmament of heav'n
350   To illuminate the earth, and rule the day
In their vicissitude, and rule the night,
And light from darkness to divide. God saw,
Surveying his great work, that it was good:
For of celestial bodies first the sun
355   A mighty sphere he framed, unlightsome first,
Though of ethereal mould: then formed the moon
Globose, and every magnitude of stars,
And sowed with stars the heaven thick as a field:
Of light by far the greater part he took,
360   Transplanted from her cloudy shrine, and placed
In the sun's orb, made porous to receive
And drink the liquid light, firm to retain
Her gathered beams, great palace now of light.
Hither as to their fountain other stars
365   Repairing, in their golden urns draw light,
And hence the morning planet gilds his horns;
By tincture or reflection they augment
Their small peculiar, though from human sight
So far remote, with diminution seen.
370   First in his east the glorious lamp was seen,
Regent of day, and all th' horizon round
Invested with bright rays, jocund to run
His longitude through heav'n's high road: the grey

Dawn, and the Pleiades before him danced
375   Shedding sweet influence: less bright the moon,
But opposite in levelled west was set
His mirror, with full face borrowing her light
From him, for other light she needed none
In that aspéct, and still that distance keeps
380   Till night, then in the east her turn she shines,
Revolved on heaven's great axle, and her reign
With thousand lesser lights dividual holds,
With thousand thousand stars, that then appeared
Spangling the hemisphere: then first adorned
385   With their bright luminaries that set and rose,
Glad ev'ning and glad morn crowned the fourth day.
    And God said, Let the waters generate
Reptile with spawn abundant, living soul:
And let fowl fly above the earth, with wings
390   Displayed on the op'n firmament of heav'n.
And God created the great whales, and each
Soul living, each that crept, which plenteously
The waters generated by their kinds,
And every bird of wing after his kind;
395   And saw that it was good, and blessed them, saying,
Be fruitful, multiply, and in the seas
And lakes and running streams the waters fill;
And let the fowl be multiplied on the earth.
Forthwith the sounds and seas, each creek and bay
400   With fry innumerable swarm, and shoals
Of fish that with their fins and shining scales
Glide under the green wave, in schools that oft
Bank the mid sea: part single or with mate
Graze the sea-weed their pasture, and through groves
405   Of coral stray, or sporting with quick glance
Show to the sun their waved coats dropped with gold,
Or in their pearly shells at ease, attend
Moist nutriment, or under rocks their food
In jointed armour watch: on smooth the seal,
410   And bended dolphins play: part huge of bulk
Wallowing unwieldy, enormous in their gait
Tempest the ocean: there Leviathan

Hugest of living creatures, on the deep
Stretched like a promontory sleeps or swims,
415 And seems a moving land, and at his gills
Draws in, and at his trunk spouts out a sea.
Meanwhile the tepid caves, and fens and shores
Their brood as numerous hatch, from the egg that soon
Bursting with kindly rupture forth disclosed
420 Their callow young, but feathered soon and fledge
They summed their pens, and soaring th' air sublime
With clang despised the ground, under a cloud
In prospect; there the eagle and the stork
On cliffs and cedar tops their eyries build:
425 Part loosely wing the region, part more wise
In common, ranged in figure wedge their way,
Intelligent of seasons, and set forth
Their airy caravan high over seas
Flying, and over lands with mutual wing
430 Easing their flight; so steers the prudent crane
Her annual voyage, borne on winds; the air
Floats, as they pass, fanned with unnumbered plumes:
From branch to branch the smaller birds with song
Solaced the woods, and spread their painted wings
435 Till ev'n, nor then the solemn nightingale
Ceased warbling, but all night tuned her soft lays:
Others on silver lakes and rivers bathed
Their downy breast; the swan with archèd neck
Between her white wings mantling proudly, rows
440 Her state with oary feet: yet oft they quit
The dank, and rising on stiff pennons, tow'r
The mid aërial sky: others on ground
Walked firm; the crested cock whose clarion sounds
The silent hours, and th' other whose gay train
445 Adorns him, coloured with the florid hue
Of rainbows and starry eyes. The waters thus
With fish replenished, and the air with fowl,
Ev'ning and morn solémnized the fifth day.
    The sixth, and of Creation last arose
450 With ev'ning harps and matin, when God said,
Let the earth bring forth soul living in her kind,

Cattle and creeping things, and beast of the earth,
Each in their kind. The earth obeyed, and straight
Op'ning her fertile womb teemed at a birth
455   Innumerous living creatures, perfect forms,
Limbed and full-grown: out of the ground uprose
As from his lair the wild beast where he wons
In forest wild, in thicket, brake, or den;
Among the trees in pairs they rose, they walked:
460   The cattle in the fields and meadows green:
Those rare and solitary, these in flocks
Pasturing at once, and in broad herds upsprung.
The grassy clods now calved, now half appeared
The tawny lion, pawing to get free
465   His hinder parts, then springs as broke from bonds,
And rampant shakes his brinded mane; the ounce,
The libbard and the tiger, as the mole
Rising, the crumbled earth above them threw
In hillocks; the swift stag from under ground
470   Bore up his branching head: scarce from his mould
Behemoth biggest born of earth upheaved
His vastness: fleeced the flocks and bleating rose,
As plants: ambiguous between sea and land
The river horse and scaly crocodile.
475   At once came forth whatever creeps the ground,
Insect or worm; those waved their limber fans
For wings, and smallest lineaments exact
In all the liveries decked of summer's pride
With spots of gold and purple, azure and green:
480   These as a line their long dimension drew,
Streaking the ground with sinuous trace; not all
Minims of nature; some of serpent kind
Wondrous in length and corpulence involved
Their snaky folds, and added wings. First crept
485   The parsimonious emmet, provident
Of future, in small room large heart enclosed,
Pattern of just equality perhaps
Hereafter, joined in her popular tribes
Of commonalty: swarming next appeared
490   The female bee that feeds her husband drone

Deliciously, and builds her waxen cells
With honey stored: the rest are numberless,
And thou their natures know'st, and gav'st them names,
Needless to thee repeated; nor unknown
495 The serpent subtlest beast of all the field,
Of huge extent sometimes, with brazen eyes
And hairy mane terrific, though to thee
Not noxious, but obedient at thy call.
Now heav'n in all her glory shone, and rolled
500 Her motions, as the great First Mover's hand
First wheeled their course; earth in her rich attire
Consummate lovely smiled; air, water, earth,
By fowl, fish, beast, was flown, was swum, was walked
Frequent; and of the sixth day yet remained;
505 There wanted yet the master work, the end
Of all yet done; a creature who not prone
And brute as other creatures, but endued
With sanctity of reason, might erect
His stature, and upright with front serene
510 Govern the rest, self-knowing, and from thence
Magnanimous to correspond with Heav'n,
But grateful to acknowledge whence his good
Descends, thither with heart and voice and eyes
Directed in devotion, to adore
515 And worship God supreme, who made him chief
Of all his works: therefore the Omnipotent
Eternal Father (for where is not he
Present) thus to his Son audibly spake.
    Let us make now man in our image, man
520 In our similitude, and let them rule
Over the fish and fowl of sea and air,
Beast of the field, and over all the earth,
And every creeping thing that creeps the ground.
This said, he formed thee, Adam, thee O man
525 Dust of the ground, and in thy nostrils breathed
The breath of life; in his own image he
Created thee, in the image of God
Express, and thou becam'st a living soul.
Male he created thee, but thy consórt

530   Female for race; then blessed mankind, and said,
       Be fruitful, multiply, and fill the earth,
       Subdue it, and throughout dominion hold
       Over fish of the sea, and fowl of the air,
       And every living thing that moves on the earth.
535   Wherever thus created, for no place
       Is yet distinct by name, thence, as thou know'st
       He brought thee into this delicious grove,
       This garden, planted with the trees of God,
       Delectable both to behold and taste;
540   And freely all their pleasant fruit for food
       Gave thee, all sorts are here that all th' earth yields,
       Variety without end; but of the Tree
       Which tasted works Knowledge of Good and Evil,
       Thou may'st not; in the day thou eat'st, thou diest;
545   Death is the penalty imposed, beware,
       And govern well thy appetite, lest Sin
       Surprise thee, and her black attendant Death.
       Here finished he, and all that he had made
       Viewed, and behold all was entirely good;
550   So ev'n and morn accomplished the sixth day:
       Yet not till the Creator from his work
       Desisting, though unwearied, up returned
       Up to the Heav'n of Heav'ns his high abode,
       Thence to behold this new created world
555   Th' addition of his empire, how it showed
       In prospect from his throne, how good, how fair,
       Answering his great Idea. Up he rode
       Followed with acclamation and the sound
       Symphonious of ten thousand harps that tuned
560   Angelic harmonies: the earth, the air
       Resounded, (thou remember'st, for thou heard'st)
       The heav'ns and all the constellations rung,
       The planets in their stations list'ning stood,
       While the bright pomp ascended jubilant.
565   Open, ye everlasting gates, they sung,
       Open, ye Heav'ns, your living doors; let in
       The great Creator from his work returned
       Magnificent, his six days' work, a world;

Open, and henceforth oft; for God will deign
570   To visit oft the dwellings of just men
Delighted, and with frequent intercourse
Thither will send his wingèd messengers
On errands of supernal grace. So sung
The glorious train ascending: he through Heav'n,
575   That opened wide her blazing portals, led
To God's eternal house direct the way,
A broad and ample road, whose dust is gold
And pavement stars, as stars to thee appear,
Seen in the Galaxy, that Milky Way
580   Which nightly as a circling zone thou seest
Powdered with stars. And now on earth the seventh
Ev'ning arose in Eden, for the sun
Was set, and twilight from the east came on,
Forerunning night; when at the holy Mount
585   Of Heav'n's high-seated top, th' imperial throne
Of Godhead, fixed for ever firm and sure,
The Filial Power arrived, and sat him down
With his great Father (for he also went
Invisible, yet stayed: such privilege
590   Hath Omnipresence) and the work ordained,
Author and end of all things, and from work
Now resting, blessed and hallowed the seventh day,
As resting on that day from all his work,
But not in silence holy kept; the harp
595   Had work and rested not, the solemn pipe,
And dulcimer, all organs of sweet stop,
All sounds on fret by string or golden wire
Tempered soft tunings, intermixed with voice
Choral or unison: of incense clouds
600   Fuming from golden censers hid the Mount.
Creation and the six days' acts they sung,
Great are thy works, Jehovah, infinite
Thy power; what thought can measure thee or tongue
Relate thee; greater now in thy return
605   Than from the Giant angels; thee that day
Thy thunders magnified; but to create
Is greater than created to destroy.

Who can impair thee, mighty King, or bound
Thy empire? easily the proud attempt
610 Of Spirits apostate and their counsels vain
Thou hast repelled, while impiously they thought
Thee to diminish, and from thee withdraw
The number of thy worshippers. Who seeks
To lessen thee, against his purpose serves
615 To manifest the more thy might: his evil
Thou usest, and from thence creat'st more good.
Witness this new-made world, another Heav'n
From Heaven gate not far, founded in view
On the clear hyaline, the glassy sea;
620 Of amplitude almost immense, with stars
Numerous, and every star perhaps a world
Of destined habitation; but thou know'st
Their seasons: among these the seat of men,
Earth with her nether Ocean circumfused,
625 Their pleasant dwelling place. Thrice happy men,
And sons of men, whom God hath thus advanced,
Created in his image, there to dwell
And worship him, and in reward to rule
Over his works, on earth, in sea, or air,
630 And multiply a race of worshippers
Holy and just: thrice happy if they know
Their happiness, and persevere upright.
    So sung they, and the Empyrean rung,
With hallelujahs: thus was Sabbath kept.
635 And thy request think now fulfilled, that asked
How first this world and face of things began,
And what before thy memory was done
From the beginning, that posterity
Informed by thee might know; if else thou seek'st
640 Aught, not surpassing human measure, say.

BOOK VIII

The Argument

Adam inquires concerning celestial motions, is doubtfully
answered, and exhorted to search rather things more worthy
of knowledge: Adam assents, and still desirous to detain
Raphael, relates to him what he remembered since his own
creation, his placing in Paradise, his talk with God concerning
solitude and fit society, his first meeting and nuptials with Eve,
his discourse with the angel thereupon; who after admonitions
repeated departs.

The angel ended, and in Adam's ear
So charming left his voice, that he a while
Thought him still speaking, still stood fixed to hear;
Then as new waked thus gratefully replied.
What thanks sufficient, or what recompense
Equal have I to render thee, divine
Historian, who thus largely hast allayed
The thirst I had of knowledge, and vouchsafed
This friendly condescension to relate
Things else by me unsearchable, now heard
With wonder, but delight, and, as is due,
With glory áttribúted to the high
Creator; something yet of doubt remains,
Which only thy solution can resolve.
When I behold this goodly frame, this world
Of heav'n and earth consisting, and compute
Their magnitudes, this earth a spot, a grain,
An atom, with the firmament compared
And all her numbered stars, that seem to roll
Spaces incomprehensible (for such
Their distance argues and their swift return
Diurnal) merely to officiate light

Round this opacous earth, this punctual spot,
One day and night; in all their vast survéy
25 Useless besides, reasoning I oft admire,
How Nature wise and frugal could commit
Such disproportions, with superfluous hand
So many nobler bodies to create,
Greater so manifold, to this one use,
30 For aught appears, and on their orbs impose
Such restless revolution day by day
Repeated, while the sedentary earth,
That better might with far less compass move,
Served by more noble than herself, attains
35 Her end without least motion, and receives,
As tribute such a sumless journey brought
Of incorporeal speed, her warmth and light;
Speed, to describe whose swiftness number fails.
  So spake our sire, and by his count'nance seemed
40 Ent'ring on studious thoughts abstruse, which Eve
Perceiving where she sat retired in sight,
With lowliness majestic from her seat,
And grace that won who saw to wish her stay,
Rose, and went forth among her fruits and flow'rs,
45 To visit how they prospered, bud and bloom,
Her nursery; they at her coming sprung
And touched by her fair tendance gladlier grew.
Yet went she not, as not with such discourse
Delighted, or not capable her ear
50 Of what was high: such pleasure she reserved,
Adam relating, she sole auditress;
Her husband the relater she preferred
Before the angel, and of him to ask
Chose rather; he, she knew would intermix
55 Grateful digressions, and solve high dispute
With conjugal caresses; from his lip
Not words alone pleased her. O when meet now
Such pairs, in love and mutual honour joined?
With goddess-like demeanour forth she went;
60 Not unattended, for on her as queen
A pomp of winning Graces waited still,

And from about her shot darts of desire
Into all eyes to wish her still in sight.
And Raphael now to Adam's doubt proposed
65   Benevolent and facile thus replied.
      To ask or search I blame thee not, for heav'n
Is as the Book of God before thee set,
Wherein to read his wondrous works, and learn
His seasons, hours, or days, or months, or years:
70   This to attain, whether heav'n move or earth,
Imports not, if thou reckon right; the rest
From man or angel the great Architect
Did wisely to conceal, and not divulge
His secrets to be scanned by them who ought
75   Rather admire; or if they list to try
Conjecture, he his fabric of the heav'ns
Hath left to their disputes, perhaps to move
His laughter at their quaint opinions wide
Hereafter, when they come to model heav'n
80   And calculate the stars, how they will wield
The mighty frame, how build, unbuild, contrive
To save appearances, how gird the sphere
With centric and eccentric scribbled o'er,
Cycle and epicycle, orb in orb:
85   Already by thy reasoning this I guess,
Who art to lead thy offspring, and supposest
That bodies bright and greater should not serve
The less not bright, nor heav'n such journeys run,
Earth sitting still, when she alone receives
90   The benefit: consider first, that great
Or bright infers not excellence; the earth
Though, in comparison of heav'n, so small,
Nor glistering, may of solid good contain
More plenty than the sun that barren shines,
95   Whose virtue on itself works no effect,
But in the fruitful earth; there first received
His beams, unactive else, their vigour find.
Yet not to earth are those bright luminaries
Officious, but to thee earth's habitant.
100 And for the heav'n's wide circuit, let it speak

The Maker's high magnificence, who built
So spacious, and his line stretched out so far;
That man may know he dwells not in his own;
An edifice too large for him to fill,
105   Lodged in a small partition, and the rest
Ordained for uses to his Lord best known.
The swiftness of those circles áttribúte,
Though numberless, to his Omnipotence,
That to corporeal substances could add
110   Speed almost spiritual; me thou think'st not slow,
Who since the morning hour set out from Heav'n
Where God resides, and ere mid-day arrived
In Eden, distance inexpressible
By numbers that have name. But this I urge,
115   Admitting motion in the heav'ns, to show
Invalid that which thee to doubt it moved;
Not that I so affirm, though so it seem
To thee who hast thy dwelling here on earth.
God to remove his ways from human sense,
120   Placed heav'n from earth so far, that earthly sight,
If it presume, might err in things too high,
And no advantage gain. What if the sun
Be centre to the world, and other stars
By his attractive virtue and their own
125   Incited, dance about him various rounds?
Their wand'ring course now high, now low, then hid,
Progressive, retrograde, or standing still,
In six thou seest, and what if seventh to these
The planet earth, so steadfast though she seem,
130   Insensibly three different motions move?
Which else to several spheres thou must ascribe,
Moved contrary with thwart obliquities,
Or save the sun his labour, and that swift
Nocturnal and diurnal rhomb supposed,
135   Invisible else above all stars, the wheel
Of day and night; which needs not thy belief,
If earth industrious of herself fetch day
Travelling east, and with her part averse
From the sun's beam meet night, her other part

140 Still luminous by his ray. What if that light
Sent from her through the wide transpicuous air,
To the terrestrial moon be as a star
Enlight'ning her by day, as she by night
This earth? reciprocal, if land be there,
145 Fields and inhabitants: her spots thou seest
As clouds, and clouds may rain, and rain produce
Fruits in her softened soil, for some to eat
Allotted there; and other suns perhaps
With their attendant moons thou wilt descry
150 Communicating male and female light,
Which two great sexes animate the world,
Stored in each orb perhaps with some that live.
For such vast room in Nature unpossessed
By living soul, desért and desolate,
155 Only to shine, yet scarce to cóntribute
Each orb a glimpse of light, conveyed so far
Down to this habitable, which returns
Light back to them, is obvious to dispute.
But whether thus these things, or whether not,
160 Whether the sun predominant in heav'n
Rise on the earth, or earth rise on the sun,
He from the east his flaming road begin,
Or she from west her silent course advance
With inoffensive pace that spinning sleeps
165 On her soft axle, while she paces ev'n,
And bears thee soft with the smooth air along,
Solicit not thy thoughts with matters hid,
Leave them to God above, him serve and fear;
Of other creatures, as him pleases best,
170 Wherever placed, let him dispose: joy thou
In what he gives to thee, this Paradise
And thy fair Eve; heav'n is for thee too high
To know what passes there; be lowly wise:
Think only what concerns thee and thy being;
175 Dream not of other worlds, what creatures there
Live, in what state, condition or degree,
Contented that thus far hath been revealed
Not of earth only but of highest Heav'n.

     To whom thus Adam cleared of doubt, replied.
180 How fully hast thou satisfied me, pure
     Intelligence of Heav'n, angel serene,
     And freed from intricacies, taught to live,
     The easiest way, nor with perplexing thoughts
     To interrupt the sweet of life, from which
185 God hath bid dwell far off all anxious cares,
     And not molest us, unless we ourselves
     Seek them with wand'ring thoughts, and notions vain.
     But apt the mind or fancy is to rove
     Unchecked, and of her roving is no end;
190 Till warned, or by experience taught, she learn,
     That not to know at large of things remote
     From use, obscure and subtle, but to know
     That which before us lies in daily life,
     Is the prime wisdom; what is more, is fume,
195 Or emptiness, or fond impertinence,
     And renders us in things that most concern
     Unpractised, unprepared, and still to seek.
     Therefore from this high pitch let us descend
     A lower flight, and speak of things at hand
200 Useful, whence haply mention may arise
     Of something not unseasonable to ask
     By sufferance, and thy wonted favour deigned.
     Thee I have heard relating what was done
     Ere my remembrance: now hear me relate
205 My story, which perhaps thou hast not heard;
     And day is yet not spent; till then thou seest
     How subtly to detain thee I devise,
     Inviting thee to hear while I relate,
     Fond, were it not in hope of thy reply:
210 For while I sit with thee, I seem in Heav'n,
     And sweeter thy discourse is to my ear
     Than fruits of palm-tree pleasantest to thirst
     And hunger both, from labour, at the hour
     Of sweet repast; they satiate, and soon fill,
215 Though pleasant, but thy words with grace divine
     Imbued, bring to their sweetness no satiety.
     To whom thus Raphael answered Heav'nly meek.

Nor are thy lips ungraceful, sire of men,
Nor tongue ineloquent; for God on thee
220 Abundantly his gifts hath also poured
Inward and outward both, his image fair:
Speaking or mute all comeliness and grace
Attends thee, and each word, each motion forms.
Nor less think we in Heav'n of thee on earth
225 Than of our fellow servant, and inquire
Gladly into the ways of God with man:
For God we see hath honoured thee, and set
On man his equal love: say therefore on;
For I that day was absent, as befell,
230 Bound on a voyage uncouth and obscure,
Far on excursion toward the gates of Hell;
Squared in full legion (such command we had)
To see that none thence issued forth a spy,
Or enemy, while God was in his work,
235 Lest he incensed at such eruption bold,
Destruction with Creation might have mixed.
Not that they durst without his leave attempt,
But us he sends upon his high behests
For state, as sov'reign King, and to inure
240 Our prompt obedience. Fast we found, fast shut
The dismal gates, and barricadoed strong;
But long ere our approaching heard within
Noise, other than the sound of dance or song,
Torment, and loud lament, and furious rage.
245 Glad we returned up to the coasts of light
Ere sabbath ev'ning: so we had in charge.
But thy relation now; for I attend,
Pleased with thy words no less than thou with mine.
    So spake the Godlike Power, and thus our sire.
250 For man to tell how human life began
Is hard; for who himself beginning knew?
Desire with thee still longer to converse
Induced me. As new waked from soundest sleep
Soft on the flow'ry herb I found me laid
255 In balmy sweat, which with his beams the sun
Soon dried, and on the reeking moisture fed.

Straight toward heav'n my wond'ring eyes I turned,
And gazed a while the ample sky, till raised
By quick instinctive motion up I sprung,
260   As thitherward endeavouring, and upright
Stood on my feet; about me round I saw
Hill, dale, and shady woods, and sunny plains,
And liquid lapse of murmuring streams; by these,
Creatures that lived, and moved, and walked, or flew,
265   Birds on the branches warbling; all things smiled,
With fragrance and with joy my heart o'erflowed.
Myself I then perused, and limb by limb
Surveyed, and sometimes went, and sometimes ran
With supple joints, as lively vigour led:
270   But who I was, or where, or from what cause,
Knew not; to speak I tried, and forthwith spake,
My tongue obeyed and readily could name
Whate'er I saw. Thou sun, said I, fair light,
And thou enlightened earth, so fresh and gay,
275   Ye hills and dales, ye rivers, woods, and plains,
And ye that live and move, fair creatures, tell,
Tell, if ye saw, how came I thus, how here?
Not of myself; by some great Maker then,
In goodness and in power pre-eminent;
280   Tell me, how may I know him, how adore,
From whom I have that thus I move and live,
And feel that I am happier than I know.
While thus I called, and strayed I knew not whither,
From where I first drew air, and first beheld
285   This happy light, when answer none returned,
On a green shady bank profuse of flow'rs
Pensive I sat me down; there gentle sleep
First found me, and with soft oppression seized
My drowsèd sense, untroubled, though I thought
290   I then was passing to my former state
Insensible, and forthwith to dissolve:
When suddenly stood at my head a dream,
Whose inward apparition gently moved
My fancy to believe I yet had being,
295   And lived: one came, methought, of shape divine,

And said, thy mansion wants thee, Adam, rise,
First man, of men innumerable ordained
First father, called by thee I come thy guide
To the garden of bliss, thy seat prepared.
300 So saying, by the hand he took me raised,
And over fields and waters, as in air
Smooth sliding without step, last led me up
A woody mountain; whose high top was plain,
A circuit wide, enclosed, with goodliest trees
305 Planted, with walks, and bowers, that what I saw
Of earth before scarce pleasant seemed. Each tree
Loaden with fairest fruit that hung to the eye
Tempting, stirred in me sudden appetite
To pluck and eat; whereat I waked, and found
310 Before mine eyes all real, as the dream
Had lively shadowed: here had new begun
My wand'ring, had not he who was my guide
Up hither, from among the trees appeared,
Presence divine. Rejoicing, but with awe
315 In adoration at his feet I fell
Submiss: he reared me, and Whom thou sought'st I am,
Said mildly, Author of all this thou seest
Above, or round about thee or beneath.
This Paradise I give thee, count it thine
320 To till and keep, and of the fruit to eat:
Of every tree that in the garden grows
Eat freely with glad heart; fear here no dearth:
But of the tree whose operation brings
Knowledge of good and ill, which I have set
325 The pledge of thy obedience and thy faith,
Amid the garden by the Tree of Life,
Remember what I warn thee, shun to taste,
And shun the bitter consequence: for know,
The day thou eat'st thereof, my sole command
330 Transgressed, inevitably thou shalt die;
From that day mortal, and this happy state
Shalt lose, expelled from hence into a world
Of woe and sorrow. Sternly he pronounced
The rigid interdiction, which resounds

335 Yet dreadful in mine ear, though in my choice
     Not to incur; but soon his clear aspéct
     Returned and gracious purpose thus renewed.
     Not only these fair bounds, but all the earth
     To thee and to thy race I give; as lords
340 Possess it, and all things that therein live,
     Or live in sea, or air, beast, fish, and fowl.
     In sign whereof each bird and beast behold
     After their kinds; I bring them to receive
     From thee their names, and pay thee fealty
345 With low subjection; understand the same
     Of fish within their wat'ry residence,
     Not hither summoned, since they cannot change
     Their element to draw the thinner air.
     As thus he spake, each bird and beast behold
350 Approaching two and two, these cow'ring low
     With blandishment, each bird stooped on his wing.
     I named them, as they passed, and understood
     Their nature, with such knowledge God endued
     My sudden apprehension: but in these
355 I found not what methought I wanted still;
     And to the Heav'nly vision thus presumed.
          O by what name, for thou above all these,
     Above mankind, or aught than mankind higher,
     Surpassest far my naming, how may I
360 Adore thee, Author of this universe,
     And all this good to man, for whose well-being
     So amply, and with hands so liberal
     Thou hast provided all things: but with me
     I see not who partakes. In solitude
365 What happiness, who can enjoy alone,
     Or all enjoying, what contentment find?
     Thus I presumptuous; and the vision bright,
     As with a smile more brightened, thus replied.
          What call'st thou solitude, is not the earth
370 With various living creatures, and the air
     Replenished, and all these at thy command
     To come and play before thee? Know'st thou not
     Their language and their ways? They also know,

And reason not contemptibly; with these
375 Find pastime, and bear rule; thy realm is large.
So spake the Universal Lord, and seemed
So ordering. I with leave of speech implored,
And humble deprecation thus replied.
　　Let not my words offend thee, Heav'nly Power,
380 My Maker, be propitious while I speak.
Hast thou not made me here thy substitute,
And these inferior far beneath me set?
Among unequals what society
Can sort, what harmony or true delight?
385 Which must be mutual, in proportion due
Giv'n and received; but in disparity
The one intense, the other still remiss
Cannot well suit with either, but soon prove
Tedious alike: of fellowship I speak
390 Such as I seek, fit to participate
All rational delight, wherein the brute
Cannot be human consort; they rejoice
Each with their kind, lion with lioness;
So fitly them in pairs thou hast combined;
395 Much less can bird with beast, or fish with fowl
So well converse, nor with the ox the ape;
Worse then can man with beast, and least of all.
　　Whereto th' Almighty answered, not displeased.
A nice and subtle happiness I see
400 Thou to thyself proposest, in the choice
Of thy associates, Adam, and wilt taste
No pleasure, though in pleasure, solitary.
What think'st thou then of me, and this my state?
Seem I to thee sufficiently possessed
405 Of happiness, or not? who am alone
From all eternity, for none I know
Second to me or like, equal much less.
How have I then with whom to hold converse
Save with the creatures which I made, and those
410 To me inferior, infinite descents
Beneath what other creatures are to thee?
　　He ceased, I lowly answered. To attain

The heighth and depth of thy eternal ways
All human thoughts come short, supreme of things;
Thou in thy self art perfect, and in thee
Is no deficience found; not so is man,
But in degree, the cause of his desire
By conversation with his like to help,
Or solace his defects. No need that thou
Shouldst propagate, already infinite;
And through all numbers absolute, though One;
But man by number is to manifest
His single imperfection, and beget
Like of his like, his image multiplied,
In unity defective, which requires
Collateral love, and dearest amity.
Thou in thy secrecy although alone,
Best with thyself accompanied, seek'st not
Social communication, yet so pleased,
Canst raise thy creature to what heighth thou wilt
Of union or communion, deified;
I by conversing cannot these erect
From prone, nor in their ways complacence find.
Thus I emboldened spake, and freedom used
Permissive, and acceptance found, which gained
This answer from the gracious voice divine.
     Thus far to try thee, Adam, I was pleased,
And find thee knowing not of beasts alone,
Which thou hast rightly named, but of thyself,
Expressing well the spirit within thee free,
My image, not imparted to the brute,
Whose fellowship therefore unmeet for thee
Good reason was thou freely shouldst dislike,
And be so minded still; I, ere thou spak'st,
Knew it not good for man to be alone,
And no such company as then thou saw'st
Intended thee, for trial only brought,
To see how thou could'st judge of fit and meet:
What next I bring shall please thee, be assured,
Thy likeness, thy fit help, thy other self,
Thy wish exactly to thy heart's desire.

He ended, or I heard no more, for now
My earthly by his Heav'nly overpowered,
Which it had long stood under, strained to the heighth
455   In that celestial colloquy sublime,
As with an object that excels the sense,
Dazzled and spent, sunk down, and sought repair
Of sleep, which instantly fell on me, called
By nature as in aid, and closed mine eyes.
460   Mine eyes he closed, but open left the cell
Of Fancy my internal sight, by which
Abstráct as in a trance methought I saw,
Though sleeping, where I lay, and saw the shape
Still glorious before whom awake I stood,
465   Who stooping opened my left side, and took
From thence a rib, with cordial spirits warm,
And life-blood streaming fresh; wide was the wound,
But suddenly with flesh filled up and healed:
The rib he formed and fashioned with his hands;
470   Under his forming hands a creature grew,
Manlike, but different sex, so lovely fair,
That what seemed fair in all the world, seemed now
Mean, or in her summed up, in her contained
And in her looks, which from that time infused
475   Sweetness into my heart, unfelt before,
And into all things from her air inspired
The spirit of love and amorous delight.
She disappeared, and left me dark, I waked
To find her, or for ever to deplore
480   Her loss, and other pleasures all abjure:
When out of hope, behold her, not far off,
Such as I saw her in my dream, adorned
With what all earth or Heaven could bestow
To make her amiable: on she came,
485   Led by her Heav'nly Maker, though unseen,
And guided by his voice, nor uninformed
Of nuptial sanctity and marriage rites:
Grace was in all her steps, Heav'n in her eye,
In every gesture dignity and love.
490   I overjoyed could not forbear aloud.

This turn hath made amends; thou hast fulfilled
Thy words, Creator bounteous and benign,
Giver of all things fair, but fairest this
Of all thy gifts, nor enviest. I now see
495 Bone of my bone, flesh of my flesh, my self
Before me; woman is her name, of man
Extracted; for this cause he shall forgo
Father and mother, and to his wife adhere;
And they shall be one flesh, one heart, one soul.
500   She heard me thus, and though divinely brought,
Yet innocence and virgin modesty,
Her virtue and the conscience of her worth,
That would be wooed, and not unsought be won,
Not obvious, not obtrusive, but retired,
505 The more desirable, or to say all,
Nature herself, though pure of sinful thought,
Wrought in her so, that seeing me, she turned;
I followed her, she what was honour knew,
And with obsequious majesty approved
510 My pleaded reason. To the nuptial bow'r
I led her blushing like the Morn: all Heav'n,
And happy constellations on that hour
Shed their selectest influence; the earth
Gave sign of gratulation, and each hill;
515 Joyous the birds; fresh gales and gentle airs
Whispered it to the woods, and from their wings
Flung rose, flung odours from the spicy shrub,
Disporting, till the amorous bird of night
Sung spousal, and bid haste the ev'ning star
520 On his hill top, to light the bridal lamp.
Thus have I told thee all my state, and brought
My story to the sum of earthly bliss
Which I enjoy, and must confess to find
In all things else delight indeed, but such
525 As used or not, works in the mind no change,
Nor vehement desire, these delicacies
I mean of taste, sight, smell, herbs, fruits and flow'rs,
Walks, and the melody of birds; but here
Far otherwise, transported I behold,

530 Transported touch; here passion first I felt,
     Commotion strange, in all enjoyments else
     Superior and unmoved, here only weak
     Against the charm of beauty's powerful glance.
     Or Nature failed in me, and left some part
535 Not proof enough such object to sustain,
     Or from my side subducting, took perhaps
     More than enough; at least on her bestowed
     Too much of ornament, in outward show
     Elaborate, of inward less exact.
540 For well I understand in the prime end
     Of Nature her th' inferior, in the mind
     And inward faculties, which most excel,
     In outward also her resembling less
     His image who made both, and less expressing
545 The character of that dominion giv'n
     O'er other creatures; yet when I approach
     Her loveliness, so absolute she seems
     And in herself complete, so well to know
     Her own, that what she wills to do or say,
550 Seems wisest, virtuousest, discreetest, best;
     All higher knowledge in her presence falls
     Degraded, wisdom in discourse with her
     Looses discount'nanced and like folly shows;
     Authority and reason on her wait,
555 As one intended first, not after made
     Occasionally; and to consúmmate all,
     Greatness of mind and nobleness their seat
     Build in her loveliest, and create an awe
     About her, as a guard angelic placed.
560 To whom the angel with contracted brow.
         Accuse not Nature, she hath done her part;
     Do thou but thine, and be not diffident
     Of Wisdom; she deserts thee not, if thou
     Dismiss not her, when most thou need'st her nigh,
565 By áttribúting overmuch to things
     Less excellent, as thou thyself perceiv'st.
     For what admir'st thou, what transports thee so,
     An outside? fair no doubt, and worthy well

Thy cherishing, thy honouring, and thy love,
570 Not thy subjection: weigh with her thyself;
Then value: oft times nothing profits more
Than self-esteem, grounded on just and right
Well managed; of that skill the more thou know'st,
The more she will acknowledge thee her head,
575 And to realities yield all her shows:
Made so adorn for thy delight the more,
So awful, that with honour thou may'st love
Thy mate, who sees when thou art seen least wise.
But if the sense of touch whereby mankind
580 Is propagated seem such dear delight
Beyond all other, think the same vouchsafed
To cattle and each beast; which would not be
To them made common and divulged, if aught
Therein enjoyed were worthy to subdue
585 The soul of man, or passion in him move.
What higher in her society thou find'st
Attractive, human, rational, love still;
In loving thou dost well, in passion not,
Wherein true love consists not; love refines
590 The thoughts, and heart enlarges, hath his seat
In reason, and is judicious, is the scale
By which to Heav'nly love thou may'st ascend,
Not sunk in carnal pleasure, for which cause
Among the beasts no mate for thee was found.
595   To whom thus half abashed Adam replied.
Neither her outside formed so fair, nor aught
In procreation common to all kinds
(Though higher of the genial bed by far,
And with mysterious reverence I deem)
600 So much delights me as those graceful acts,
Those thousand decencies that daily flow
From all her words and actions, mixed with love
And sweet compliance, which declare unfeigned
Union of mind, or in us both one soul;
605 Harmony to behold in wedded pair
More grateful than harmonious sound to the ear.
Yet these subject not; I to thee disclose

What inward thence I feel, not therefore foiled,
Who meet with various objects, from the sense
610   Variously representing; yet still free
Approve the best, and follow what I approve.
To love thou blam'st me not, for love thou say'st
Leads up to Heav'n, is both the way and guide;
Bear with me then, if lawful what I ask;
615   Love not the Heav'nly Spirits, and how their love
Express they, by looks only, or do they mix
Irradiance, virtual or immediate touch?

    To whom the angel with a smile that glowed
Celestial rosy red, love's proper hue,
620   Answered. Let it suffice thee that thou know'st
Us happy, and without love no happiness.
Whatever pure thou in the body enjoy'st
(And pure thou wert created) we enjoy
In eminence, and obstacle find none
625   Of membrane, joint, or limb, exclusive bars:
Easier than air with air, if Spirits embrace,
Total they mix, union of pure with pure
Desiring; nor restrained conveyance need
As flesh to mix with flesh, or soul with soul.
630   But I can now no more; the parting sun
Beyond the earth's green cape and verdant isles
Hesperian sets, my signal to depart.
Be strong, live happy, and love, but first of all
Him whom to love is to obey, and keep
635   His great command; take heed lest passion sway
Thy judgement to do aught, which else free will
Would not admit; thine and of all thy sons
The weal or woe in thee is placed; beware.
I in thy persevering shall rejoice,
640   And all the blest: stand fast; to stand or fall
Free in thine own arbitrament it lies.
Perfect within, no outward aid require;
And all temptation to transgress repel.

    So saying, he arose; whom Adam thus
645   Followed with benediction. Since to part,
Go Heavenly guest, ethereal messenger,

Sent from whose sov'reign goodness I adore.
Gentle to me and affable hath been
Thy condescension, and shall be honoured ever
650   With grateful memory: thou to mankind
Be good and friendly still, and oft return.
    So parted they, the angel up to Heav'n
From the thick shade, and Adam to his bow'r.

BOOK IX

Satan having compassed the earth, with meditated guile
returns as a mist by night into Paradise, enters into the serpent
sleeping. Adam and Eve in the morning go forth to their
labours, which Eve proposes to divide in several places, each
5 labouring apart: Adam consents not, alleging the danger, lest
that Enemy, of whom they were forewarned, should attempt
her found alone: Eve loath to be thought not circumspect or
firm enough, urges her going apart, the rather desirous to
make trial of her strength; Adam at last yields: the serpent
10 finds her alone; his subtle approach, first gazing, then speaking,
with much flattery extolling Eve above all other creatures.
Eve wondering to hear the serpent speak, asks how he attained
to human speech and such understanding not till now; the
serpent answers, that by tasting of a certain tree in the garden
15 he attained both to speech and reason, till then void of both:
Eve requires him to bring her to that tree, and finds it to be
the Tree of Knowledge forbidden: the serpent now grown
bolder, with many wiles and arguments induces her at length
to eat; she pleased with the taste deliberates a while whether
20 to impart thereof to Adam or not, at last brings him of the
fruit, relates what persuaded her to eat thereof: Adam at first
amazed, but perceiving her lost, resolves through vehemence
of love to perish with her; and extenuating the trespass eats
also of the fruit: the effects thereof in them both; they seek
25 to cover their nakedness; then fall to variance and accusation
of one another.

No more of talk where God or angel guest
With man, as with his friend, familiar used
To sit indulgent, and with him partake
Rural repast, permitting him the while

5   Venial discourse unblamed: I now must change
Those notes to tragic; foul distrust, and breach
Disloyal on the part of man, revolt,
And disobedience: on the part of Heav'n
Now alienated, distance and distaste,
10   Anger and just rebuke, and judgement giv'n,
That brought into this world a world of woe,
Sin and her shadow Death, and misery
Death's harbinger: sad task, yet argument
Not less but more heroic than the wrath
15   Of stern Achilles on his foe pursued
Thrice fugitive about Troy wall; or rage
Of Turnus for Lavinia disespoused,
Or Neptune's ire or Juno's, that so long
Perplexed the Greek and Cytherea's son;
20   If answerable style I can obtain
Of my celestial patroness, who deigns
Her nightly visitation unimplored,
And díctates to me slumb'ring, or inspires
Easy my unpremeditated verse:
25   Since first this subject for heroic song
Pleased me long choosing, and beginning late;
Not sedulous by nature to indite
Wars, hitherto the only argument
Heroic deemed, chief mast'ry to dissect
30   With long and tedious havoc fabled knights
In battles feigned; the better fortitude
Of patience and heroic martyrdom
Unsung; or to describe races and games,
Or tilting furniture, emblazoned shields,
35   Impreses quaint, caparisons and steeds;
Bases and tinsel trappings, gorgeous knights
At joust and tournament; then marshalled feast
Served up in hall with sewers, and seneschals;
The skill of artifice or office mean,
40   Not that which justly gives heroic name
To person or to poem. Me of these
Nor skilled nor studious, higher argument
Remains, sufficient of itself to raise

That name, unless an age too late, or cold
45 Climate, or years damp my intended wing
Depressed, and much they may, if all be mine,
Not hers who brings it nightly to my ear.
    The sun was sunk, and after him the star
Of Hesperus, whose office is to bring
50 Twilight upon the earth, short arbiter
'Twixt day and night, and now from end to end
Night's hemisphere had veiled the horizon round:
When Satan who late fled before the threats
Of Gabriel out of Eden, now improved
55 In meditated fraud and malice, bent
On man's destruction, maugre what might hap
Of heavier on himself, fearless returned.
By night he fled, and at midnight returned
From compassing the earth, cautious of day,
60 Since Uriel regent of the sun descried
His entrance, and forewarned the Cherubim
That kept their watch; thence full of anguish driv'n,
The space of seven continued nights he rode
With darkness, thrice the equinoctial line
65 He circled, four times crossed the car of Night
From pole to pole, traversing each colure;
On the eighth returned, and on the coast averse
From entrance or Cherubic watch, by stealth
Found unsuspected way. There was a place,
70 Now not, though sin, not time, first wrought the change,
Where Tigris at the foot of Paradise
Into a gulf shot under ground, till part
Rose up a fountain by the Tree of Life;
In with the river sunk, and with it rose
75 Satan involved in rising mist, then sought
Where to lie hid; sea he had searched and land
From Eden over Pontus, and the pool
Maeotis, up beyond the river Ob;
Downward as far Antarctic; and in length
80 West from Orontes to the ocean barred
At Darien, thence to the land where flows
Ganges and Indus: thus the orb he roamed

With narrow search; and with inspection deep
Considered every creature, which of all
85   Most opportune might serve his wiles, and found
The serpent subtlest beast of all the field.
Him after long debate, irresolute
Of thoughts revolved, his final sentence chose
Fit vessel, fittest imp of fraud, in whom
90   To enter, and his dark suggestions hide
From sharpest sight: for in the wily snake,
Whatever sleights none would suspicious mark,
As from his wit and native subtlety
Proceeding, which in other beasts observed
95   Doubt might beget of diabolic pow'r
Active within beyond the sense of brute.
Thus he resolved, but first from inward grief
His bursting passion into plaints thus poured.
    O earth, how like to Heav'n, if not preferred
100   More justly, seat worthier of gods, as built
With second thoughts, reforming what was old!
For what god after better worse would build?
Terrestrial Heav'n, danced round by other heav'ns
That shine, yet bear their bright officious lamps,
105   Light above light, for thee alone, as seems,
In thee concentring all their precious beams
Of sacred influence: as God in Heav'n
Is centre, yet extends to all, so thou
Centring receiv'st from all those orbs; in thee,
110   Not in themselves, all their known virtue appears
Productive in herb, plant, and nobler birth
Of creatures animate with gradual life
Of growth, sense, reason, all summed up in man.
With what delight could I have walked thee round,
115   If I could joy in aught, sweet interchange
Of hill and valley, rivers, woods and plains,
Now land, now sea, and shores with forest crowned,
Rocks, dens, and caves; but I in none of these
Find place or refuge; and the more I see
120   Pleasures about me, so much more I feel
Torment within me, as from the hateful siege

Of contraries; all good to me becomes
Bane, and in Heav'n much worse would be my state.
But neither here seek I, no nor in Heav'n
125 To dwell, unless by mast'ring Heav'n's Supreme;
Nor hope to be myself less miserable
By what I seek, but others to make such
As I, though thereby worse to me redound:
For only in destroying I find ease
130 To my relentless thoughts; and him destroyed,
Or won to what may work his utter loss,
For whom all this was made, all this will soon
Follow, as to him linked in weal or woe;
In woe then; that destruction wide may range:
135 To me shall be the glory sole among
The infernal Powers, in one day to have marred
What he Almighty styled, six nights and days
Continued making, and who knows how long
Before had been contriving, though perhaps
140 Not longer than since I in one night freed
From servitude inglorious well nigh half
Th' angelic name, and thinner left the throng
Of his adorers: he to be avenged,
And to repair his numbers thus impaired,
145 Whether such virtue spent of old now failed
More angels to create, if they at least
Are his created, or to spite us more,
Determined to advance into our room
A creature formed of earth, and him endow,
150 Exalted from so base original,
With Heav'nly spoils, our spoils: what he decreed
He effected; man he made, and for him built
Magnificent this world, and earth his seat,
Him lord pronounced, and, O indignity!
155 Subjected to his service angel wings,
And flaming ministers to watch and tend
Their earthy charge: of these the vigilance
I dread, and to elude, thus wrapped in mist
Of midnight vapour glide obscure, and pry
160 In every bush and brake, where hap may find

The serpent sleeping, in whose mazy folds
To hide me, and the dark intent I bring.
O foul descent! that I who erst contended
With Gods to sit the highest, am now constrained
165   Into a beast, and mixed with bestial slime,
This essence to incarnate and imbrute,
That to the heighth of Deity aspired;
But what will not ambition and revenge
Descend to? who aspires must down as low
170   As high he soared, obnoxious first or last
To basest things. Revenge, at first though sweet,
Bitter ere long back on itself recoils;
Let it; I reck not, so it light well aimed,
Since higher I fall short, on him who next
175   Provokes my envy, this new favourite
Of Heav'n, this man of clay, son of despite,
Whom us the more to spite his Maker raised
From dust: spite then with spite is best repaid.
    So saying, through each thicket dank or dry,
180   Like a black mist low creeping, he held on
His midnight search, where soonest he might find
The serpent: him fast sleeping soon he found
In labyrinth of many a round self-rolled,
His head the midst, well stored with subtle wiles:
185   Not yet in horrid shade or dismal den,
Nor nocent yet, but on the grassy herb
Fearless unfeared he slept: in at his mouth
The Devil entered, and his brutal sense,
In heart or head, possessing soon inspired
190   With act intelligential; but his sleep
Disturbed not, waiting close th' approach of morn.
Now when as sacred light began to dawn
In Eden on the humid flow'rs, that breathed
Their morning incense, when all things that breathe,
195   From th' earth's great altar send up silent praise
To the Creator, and his nostrils fill
With grateful smell, forth came the human pair
And joined their vocal worship to the choir
Of creatures wanting voice; that done, partake

200   The season, prime for sweetest scents and airs:
       Then cómmune how that day they best may ply
       Their growing work: for much their work outgrew
       The hands' dispatch of two gard'ning so wide.
       And Eve first to her husband thus began.
205   Adam, well may we labour still to dress
       This garden, still to tend plant, herb and flow'r,
       Our pleasant task enjoined, but till more hands
       Aid us, the work under our labour grows,
       Luxurious by restraint; what we by day
210   Lop overgrown, or prune, or prop, or bind,
       One night or two with wanton growth derides
       Tending to wild. Thou therefore now advise
       Or hear what to my mind first thoughts present;
       Let us divide our labours, thou where choice
215   Leads thee, or where most needs, whether to wind
       The woodbine round this arbour, or direct
       The clasping ivy where to climb, while I
       In yonder spring of roses intermixed
       With myrtle, find what to redress till noon:
220   For while so near each other thus all day
       Our task we choose, what wonder if so near
       Looks intervene and smiles, or object new
       Casual discourse draw on, which intermits
       Our day's work brought to little, though begun
225   Early, and th' hour of supper comes unearned.
           To whom mild answer Adam thus returned.
       Sole Eve, associate sole, to me beyond
       Compare above all living creatures dear,
       Well hast thou motioned, well thy thoughts employed
230   How we might best fulfil the work which here
       God hath assigned us, nor of me shalt pass
       Unpraised: for nothing lovelier can be found
       In woman, than to study household good,
       And good works in her husband to promote.
235   Yet not so strictly hath our Lord imposed
       Labour, as to debar us when we need
       Refreshment, whether food, or talk between,
       Food of the mind, or this sweet intercourse

Of looks and smiles, for smiles from reason flow,
240 To brute denied, and are of love the food,
Love not the lowest end of human life.
For not to irksome toil, but to delight
He made us, and delight to reason joined.
These paths and bowers doubt not but our joint hands
245 Will keep from wilderness with ease, as wide
As we need walk, till younger hands ere long
Assist us: but if much convérse perhaps
Thee satiate, to short absence I could yield.
For solitude sometimes is best society,
250 And short retirement urges sweet return.
But other doubt possesses me, lest harm
Befall thee severed from me; for thou know'st
What hath been warned us, what malicious Foe
Envying our happiness, and of his own
255 Despairing, seeks to work us woe and shame
By sly assault; and somewhere nigh at hand
Watches, no doubt, with greedy hope to find
His wish and best advantage, us asunder,
Hopeless to circumvent us joined, where each
260 To other speedy aid might lend at need;
Whether his first design be to withdraw
Our fealty from God, or to disturb
Conjugal love, than which perhaps no bliss
Enjoyed by us excites his envy more;
265 Or this, or worse, leave not the faithful side
That gave thee being, still shades thee and protects.
The wife, where danger or dishonour lurks,
Safest and seemliest by her husband stays,
Who guards her, or with her the worst endures.
270   To whom the virgin majesty of Eve,
As one who loves, and some unkindness meets,
With sweet austere composure thus replied.
    Offspring of Heav'n and earth, and all earth's lord,
That such an Enemy we have, who seeks
275 Our ruin, both by thee informed I learn,
And from the parting angel overheard
As in a shady nook I stood behind,

Just then returned at shut of evening flow'rs.
But that thou shouldst my firmness therefore doubt
280 To God or thee, because we have a foe
May tempt it, I expected not to hear.
His violence thou fear'st not, being such,
As we, not capable of death or pain,
Can either not receive, or can repel.
285 His fraud is then thy fear, which plain infers
Thy equal fear that my firm faith and love
Can by his fraud be shaken or seduced;
Thoughts, which how found they harbour in thy breast,
Adam, misthought of her to thee so dear?
290   To whom with healing words Adam replied.
Daughter of God and man, immortal Eve,
For such thou art, from sin and blame entire:
Not diffident of thee do I dissuade
Thy absence from my sight, but to avoid
295 Th' attempt itself, intended by our Foe.
For he who tempts, though in vain, at least asperses
The tempted with dishonour foul, supposed
Not incorruptible of faith, not proof
Against temptation: thou thyself with scorn
300 And anger wouldst resent the offered wrong,
Though ineffectual found: misdeem not then,
If such affront I labour to avert
From thee alone, which on us both at once
The Enemy, though bold, will hardly dare,
305 Or daring, first on me th' assault shall light.
Nor thou his malice and false guile contemn;
Subtle he needs must be, who could seduce
Angels, nor think superfluous others' aid.
I from the influence of thy looks receive
310 Accéss in every virtue, in thy sight
More wise, more watchful, stronger, if need were
Of outward strength; while shame, thou looking on,
Shame to be overcome or overreached
Would utmost vigour raise, and raised unite.
315 Why shouldst not thou like sense within thee feel
When I am present, and thy trial choose

With me, best witness of thy virtue tried.
 So spake domestic Adam in his care
And matrimonial love; but Eve, who thought
320 Less áttribúted to her faith sincere,
Thus her reply with accent sweet renewed.
 If this be our condition, thus to dwell
In narrow circuit straitened by a Foe,
Subtle or violent, we not endued
325 Single with like defence, wherever met,
How are we happy, still in fear of harm?
But harm precedes not sin: only our Foe
Tempting affronts us with his foul esteem
Of our integrity: his foul esteem
330 Sticks no dishonour on our front, but turns
Foul on himself; then wherefore shunned or feared
By us? Who rather double honour gain
From his surmise proved false, find peace within,
Favour from Heav'n, our witness from th' event.
335 And what is faith, love, virtue unassayed
Alone, without exterior help sustained?
Let us not then suspect our happy state
Left so imperfect by the Maker wise,
As not secure to single or combined.
340 Frail is our happiness, if this be so,
And Eden were no Eden thus exposed.
 To whom thus Adam fervently replied.
O woman, best are all things as the will
Of God ordained them; his creating hand
345 Nothing imperfect or deficient left
Of all that he created, much less man,
Or aught that might his happy state secure,
Secure from outward force; within himself
The danger lies, yet lies within his power:
350 Against his will he can receive no harm.
But God left free the will, for what obeys
Reason, is free, and reason he made right,
But bid her well beware, and still erect,
Lest by some fair appearing good surprised
355 She díctate false, and misinform the will

To do what God expressly hath forbid.
Not then mistrust, but tender love enjoins,
That I should mind thee oft, and mind thou me.
Firm we subsist, yet possible to swerve,
360 Since reason not impossibly may meet
Some specious object by the Foe suborned,
And fall into deception unaware,
Not keeping strictest watch, as she was warned.
Seek not temptation then, which to avoid
365 Were better, and most likely if from me
Thou sever not: trial will come unsought.
Wouldst thou approve thy constancy, approve
First thy obedience; th' other who can know,
Not seeing thee attempted, who attest?
370 But if thou think, trial unsought may find
Us both securer than thus warned thou seem'st,
Go; for thy stay, not free, absents thee more;
Go in thy native innocence, rely
On what thou hast of virtue, summon all,
375 For God towards thee hath done his part, do thine.
　　So spake the patriarch of mankind, but Eve
Persisted, yet submiss, though last, replied.
　　With thy permission, then, and thus forewarned
Chiefly by what thy own last reasoning words
380 Touched only, that our trial, when least sought,
May find us both perhaps far less prepared,
The willinger I go, nor much expect
A Foe so proud will first the weaker seek;
So bent, the more shall shame him his repulse.
385 Thus saying, from her husband's hand her hand
Soft she withdrew, and like a wood-nymph light
Oread or Dryad, or of Delia's train,
Betook her to the groves, but Delia's self
In gait surpassed and goddess-like deport,
390 Though not as she with bow and quiver armed,
But with such gard'ning tools as art yet rude,
Guiltless of fire had formed, or angels brought.
To Pales, or Pomona thus adorned,
Likeliest she seemed, Pomona when she fled

395   Vertumnus, or to Ceres in her prime,
       Yet virgin of Proserpina from Jove.
       Her long with ardent look his eye pursued
       Delighted, but desiring more her stay.
       Oft he to her his charge of quick return
400   Repeated, she to him as oft engaged
       To be returned by noon amid the bow'r,
       And all things in best order to invite
       Noontide repast, or afternoon's repose.
       O much deceived, much failing, hapless Eve,
405   Of thy presumed return! event perverse!
       Thou never from that hour in Paradise
       Found'st either sweet repast, or sound repose;
       Such ambush hid among sweet flow'rs and shades
       Waited with Hellish rancour imminent
410   To intercept thy way, or send thee back
       Despoiled of innocence, of faith, of bliss.
       For now, and since first break of dawn the Fiend,
       Mere serpent in appearance, forth was come,
       And on his quest, where likeliest he might find
415   The only two of mankind, but in them
       The whole included race, his purposed prey.
       In bow'r and field he sought, where any tuft
       Of grove or garden-plot more pleasant lay,
       Their tendance or plantation for delight;
420   By fountain or by shady rivulet
       He sought them both, but wished his hap might find
       Eve separate; he wished, but not with hope
       Of what so seldom chanced, when to his wish,
       Beyond his hope, Eve separate he spies,
425   Veiled in a cloud of fragrance, where she stood,
       Half spied, so thick the roses bushing round
       About her glowed, oft stooping to support
       Each flow'r of slender stalk, whose head though gay
       Carnation, purple, azure, or specked with gold,
430   Hung drooping unsustained; them she upstays
       Gently with myrtle band, mindless the while,
       Herself, though fairest unsupported flow'r,
       From her best prop so far, and storm so nigh.

Nearer he drew, and many a walk traversed
435   Of stateliest covert, cedar, pine, or palm,
Then voluble and bold, now hid, now seen
Among thick-woven arborets and flow'rs
Embordered on each bank, the hand of Eve:
Spot more delicious than those gardens feigned
440   Or of revived Adonis, or renowned
Alcinous, host of old Laertes' son,
Or that, not mystic, where the sapient king
Held dalliance with his fair Egyptian spouse.
Much he the place admired, the person more.
445   As one who long in populous city pent,
Where houses thick and sewers annoy the air,
Forth issuing on a summer's morn to breathe
Among the pleasant villages and farms
Adjoined, from each thing met conceives delight,
450   The smell of grain, or tedded grass, or kine,
Or dairy, each rural sight, each rural sound;
If chance with nymph-like step fair virgin pass,
What pleasing seemed, for her now pleases more,
She most, and in her look sums all delight.
455   Such pleasure took the serpent to behold
This flow'ry plat, the sweet recess of Eve
Thus early, thus alone; her Heav'nly form
Angelic, but more soft, and feminine,
Her graceful innocence, her every air
460   Of gesture or least action overawed
His malice, and with rapine sweet bereaved
His fierceness of the fierce intent it brought:
That space the Evil One abstracted stood
From his own evil, and for the time remained
465   Stupidly good, of enmity disarmed,
Of guile, of hate, of envy, of revenge;
But the hot Hell that always in him burns,
Though in mid-Heav'n, soon ended his delight,
And tortures him now more, the more he sees
470   Of pleasure not for him ordained: then soon
Fierce hate he recollects, and all his thoughts
Of mischief, gratulating, thus excites.

Thoughts, whither have ye led me, with what sweet
Compulsion thus transported to forget
475 What hither brought us, hate, not love, nor hope
Of Paradise for Hell, hope here to taste
Of pleasure, but all pleasure to destroy,
Save what is in destroying; other joy
To me is lost. Then let me not let pass
480 Occasion which now smiles; behold alone
The woman, opportune to all attempts,
Her husband, for I view far round, not nigh,
Whose higher intellectual more I shun,
And strength, of courage haughty, and of limb
485 Heroic built, though of terrestrial mould,
Foe not informidable, exempt from wound,
I not; so much hath Hell debased, and pain
Enfeebled me, to what I was in Heav'n.
She fair, divinely fair, fit love for gods,
490 Not terrible, though terror be in love
And beauty, not approached by stronger hate,
Hate stronger, under show of love well-feigned,
The way which to her ruin now I tend.
So spake the Enemy of mankind, enclosed
495 In serpent, inmate bad, and toward Eve
Addressed his way, not with indented wave,
Prone on the ground, as since, but on his rear,
Circular base of rising folds, that tow'red
Fold above fold, a surging maze, his head
500 Crested aloft, and carbuncle his eyes;
With burnished neck of verdant gold, erect
Amidst his circling spires, that on the grass
Floated redundant: pleasing was his shape,
And lovely, never since of serpent kind
505 Lovelier, not those that in Illyria changed
Hermione and Cadmus, or the god
In Epidaurus; nor to which transformed
Ammonian Jove, or Capitoline was seen,
He with Olympias, this with her who bore
510 Scipio the heighth of Rome. With tract oblique
At first, as one who sought accéss, but feared

To interrupt, sidelong he works his way.
As when a ship by skilful steersman wrought
Nigh river's mouth or foreland, where the wind
515 Veers oft, as oft so steers, and shifts her sail;
So varied he, and of his tortuous train
Curled many a wanton wreath in sight of Eve,
To lure her eye; she busied heard the sound
Of rustling leaves, but minded not, as used
520 To such disport before her through the field,
From every beast, more duteous at her call,
Than at Circean call the herd disguised.
He bolder now, uncalled before her stood;
But as in gaze admiring: oft he bowed
525 His turret crest, and sleek enamelled neck,
Fawning, and licked the ground whereon she trod.
His gentle dumb expression turned at length
The eye of Eve to mark his play; he glad
Of her attention gained, with serpent tongue
530 Organic, or impúlse of vocal air,
His fraudulent temptation thus began.
      Wonder not, sov'reign mistress, if perhaps
Thou canst, who art sole wonder, much less arm
Thy looks, the Heav'n of mildness, with disdain,
535 Displeased that I approach thee thus, and gaze
Insatiate, I thus single, nor have feared
Thy awful brow, more awful thus retired.
Fairest resemblance of thy Maker fair,
Thee all things living gaze on, all things thine
540 By gift, and thy celestial beauty adore
With ravishment beheld, there best beheld
Where universally admired; but here
In this enclosure wild, these beasts among,
Beholders rude, and shallow to discern
545 Half what in thee is fair, one man except,
Who sees thee? (and what is one?) who shouldst be seen
A goddess among gods, adored and served
By angels numberless, thy daily train.
      So glozed the Tempter, and his proem tuned;
550 Into the heart of Eve his words made way,

Though at the voice much marvelling; at length
Not unamazed she thus in answer spake.
What may this mean? Language of man pronounced
By tongue of brute, and human sense expressed?
555   The first at least of these I thought denied
To beasts, whom God on their Creation-day
Created mute to all articulate sound;
The latter I demur, for in their looks
Much reason, and in their actions oft appears.
560   Thee, serpent, subtlest beast of all the field
I knew, but not with human voice endued;
Redouble then this miracle, and say,
How cam'st thou speakable of mute, and how
To me so friendly grown above the rest
565   Of brutal kind, that daily are in sight?
Say, for such wonder claims attention due.
   To whom the guileful Tempter thus replied.
Empress of this fair world, resplendent Eve,
Easy to me it is to tell thee all
570   What thou command'st, and right thou shouldst be obeyed:
I was at first as other beasts that graze
The trodden herb, of abject thoughts and low,
As was my food, nor aught but food discerned
Or sex, and apprehended nothing high:
575   Till on a day roving the field, I chanced
A goodly tree far distant to behold
Loaden with fruit of fairest colours mixed,
Ruddy and gold: I nearer drew to gaze;
When from the boughs a savoury odour blown,
580   Grateful to appetite, more pleased my sense
Than smell of sweetest fennel, or the teats
Of ewe or goat dropping with milk at ev'n,
Unsucked of lamb or kid, that tend their play.
To satisfy the sharp desire I had
585   Of tasting those fair apples, I resolved
Not to defer; hunger and thirst at once,
Powerful persuaders, quickened at the scent
Of that alluring fruit, urged me so keen.
About the mossy trunk I wound me soon,

590 For high from ground the branches would require
Thy utmost reach or Adam's: round the tree
All other beasts that saw, with like desire
Longing and envying stood, but could not reach.
Amid the tree now got, where plenty hung
595 Tempting so nigh, to pluck and eat my fill
I spared not, for such pleasure till that hour
At feed or fountain never had I found.
Sated at length, ere long I might perceive
Strange alteration in me, to degree
600 Of reason in my inward powers, and speech
Wanted not long, though to this shape retained.
Thenceforth to speculations high or deep
I turned my thoughts, and with capacious mind
Considered all things visible in heav'n,
605 Or earth, or middle, all things fair and good;
But all that fair and good in thy divine
Semblance, and in thy beauty's Heav'nly ray
United I beheld; no fair to thine
Equivalent or second, which compelled
610 Me thus, though importune perhaps, to come
And gaze, and worship thee of right declared
Sov'reign of creatures, universal dame.
　　So talked the spirited sly snake; and Eve
Yet more amazed unwary thus replied.
615 　　Serpent, thy overpraising leaves in doubt
The virtue of that fruit, in thee first proved:
But say, where grows the tree, from hence how far?
For many are the trees of God that grow
In Paradise, and various, yet unknown
620 To us, in such abundance lies our choice,
As leaves a greater store of fruit untouched,
Still hanging incorruptible, till men
Grow up to their provision, and more hands
Help to disburden Nature of her bearth.
625 　　To whom the wily adder, blithe and glad.
Empress, the way is ready, and not long,
Beyond a row of myrtles, on a flat,
Fast by a fountain, one small thicket past

       Of blowing myrrh and balm; if thou accept

630   My conduct, I can bring thee thither soon.

          Lead then, said Eve. He leading swiftly rolled

       In tangles, and made intricate seem straight,

       To mischief swift. Hope elevates, and joy

       Brightens his crest, as when a wand'ring fire,

635   Compact of unctuous vapour, which the night

       Condenses, and the cold environs round,

       Kindled through agitation to a flame,

       Which oft, they say, some evil Spirit attends

       Hovering and blazing with delusive light,

640   Misleads th' amazed night-wanderer from his way

       To bogs and mires, and oft through pond or pool,

       There swallowed up and lost, from succour far.

       So glistered the dire snake, and into fraud

       Led Eve our credulous mother, to the tree

645   Of prohibition, root of all our woe;

       Which when she saw, thus to her guide she spake.

          Serpent, we might have spared our coming hither,

       Fruitless to me, though fruit be here to excess,

       The credit of whose virtue rest with thee,

650   Wondrous indeed, if cause of such effects.

       But of this tree we may not taste nor touch;

       God so commanded, and left that command

       Sole daughter of his voice; the rest, we live

       Law to ourselves, our reason is our law.

655   To whom the Tempter guilefully replied.

       Indeed? hath God then said that of the fruit

       Of all these garden trees ye shall not eat,

       Yet lords declared of all in earth or air?

          To whom thus Eve yet sinless. Of the fruit

660   Of each tree in the garden we may eat,

       But of the fruit of this fair tree amidst

       The garden, God hath said, Ye shall not eat

       Thereof, nor shall ye touch it, lest ye die.

          She scarce had said, though brief, when now more bold

665   The Tempter, but with show of zeal and love

       To man, and indignation at his wrong,

       New part puts on, and as to passion moved,

Fluctuates disturbed, yet comely, and in act
Raised, as of some great matter to begin.
670 As when of old some orator renowned
In Athens or free Rome, where eloquence
Flourished, since mute, to some great cause addressed,
Stood in himself collected, while each part,
Motion, each act won audience ere the tongue,
675 Sometimes in heighth began, as no delay
Of preface brooking through his zeal of right.
So standing, moving, or to heighth upgrown
The Tempter all impassioned thus began.

O sacred, wise, and wisdom-giving plant,
680 Mother of science, now I feel thy power
Within me clear, not only to discern
Things in their causes, but to trace the ways
Of highest agents, deemed however wise.
Queen of this universe, do not believe
685 Those rigid threats of death; ye shall not die:
How should ye? by the fruit? it gives you life
To knowledge. By the Threat'ner? look on me,
Me who have touched and tasted, yet both live,
And life more perfect have attained than Fate
690 Meant me, by vent'ring higher than my lot.
Shall that be shut to man, which to the beast
Is open? or will God incense his ire
For such a petty trespass, and not praise
Rather your dauntless virtue, whom the pain
695 Of death denounced, whatever thing death be,
Deterred not from achieving what might lead
To happier life, knowledge of good and evil;
Of good, how just? of evil, if what is evil
Be real, why not known, since easier shunned?
700 God therefore cannot hurt ye, and be just;
Not just, not God; not feared then, nor obeyed:
Your fear itself of death removes the fear.
Why then was this forbid? Why but to awe,
Why but to keep ye low and ignorant,
705 His worshippers; he knows that in the day
Ye eat thereof, your eyes that seem so clear,

Yet are but dim, shall perfectly be then
Opened and cleared, and ye shall be as gods,
Knowing both good and evil as they know.
710 That ye should be as gods, since I as man,
Internal man, is but proportion meet,
I of brute human, ye of human gods.
So ye shall die perhaps, by putting off
Human, to put on gods, death to be wished,
715 Though threatened, which no worse than this can bring.
And what are gods that man may not become
As they, participating god-like food?
The gods are first, and that advantage use
On our belief, that all from them proceeds;
720 I question it, for this fair earth I see,
Warmed by the sun, producing every kind,
Them nothing: if they all things, who enclosed
Knowledge of good and evil in this tree,
That whoso eats thereof, forthwith attains
725 Wisdom without their leave? and wherein lies
Th' offence, that man should thus attain to know?
What can your knowledge hurt him, or this tree
Impart against his will if all be his?
Or is it envy, and can envy dwell
730 In Heav'nly breasts? these, these and many more
Causes import your need of this fair fruit.
Goddess humane, reach then, and freely taste.
    He ended, and his words replete with guile
Into her heart too easy entrance won:
735 Fixed on the fruit she gazed, which to behold
Might tempt alone, and in her ears the sound
Yet rung of his persuasive words, impregned
With reason, to her seeming, and with truth;
Meanwhile the hour of noon drew on, and waked
740 An eager appetite, raised by the smell
So savoury of that fruit, which with desire,
Inclinable now grown to touch or taste,
Solicited her longing eye; yet first
Pausing a while, thus to herself she mused.
745   Great are thy virtues, doubtless, best of fruits,

Though kept from man, and worthy to be admired,
Whose taste, too long forborne, at first assay
Gave elocution to the mute, and taught
The tongue not made for speech to speak thy praise:
750 Thy praise he also who forbids thy use,
Conceals not from us, naming thee the Tree
Of Knowledge, knowledge both of good and evil;
Forbids us then to taste, but his forbidding
Commends thee more, while it infers the good
755 By thee communicated, and our want:
For good unknown, sure is not had, or had
And yet unknown, is as not had at all.
In plain then, what forbids he but to know,
Forbids us good, forbids us to be wise?
760 Such prohibitions bind not. But if death
Bind us with after-bands, what profits then
Our inward freedom? In the day we eat
Of this fair fruit, our doom is, we shall die.
How dies the serpent? he hath eat'n and lives,
765 And knows, and speaks, and reasons, and discerns,
Irrational till then. For us alone
Was death invented? or to us denied
This intellectual food, for beasts reserved?
For beasts it seems: yet that one beast which first
770 Hath tasted, envies not, but brings with joy
The good befall'n him, author unsuspect,
Friendly to man, far from deceit or guile.
What fear I then, rather what know to fear
Under this ignorance of good and evil,
775 Of God or death, of law or penalty?
Here grows the cure of all, this fruit divine,
Fair to the eye, inviting to the taste,
Of virtue to make wise: what hinders then
To reach, and feed at once both body and mind?
780   So saying, her rash hand in evil hour
Forth reaching to the fruit, she plucked, she ate:
Earth felt the wound, and Nature from her seat
Sighing through all her works gave signs of woe,
That all was lost. Back to the thicket slunk

785 The guilty serpent, and well might, for Eve
Intent now wholly on her taste, naught else
Regarded, such delight till then, as seemed,
In fruit she never tasted, whether true
Or fancied so, through expectation high
790 Of knowledge, nor was Godhead from her thought.
Greedily she engorged without restraint,
And knew not eating death: satiate at length,
And heightened as with wine, jocund and boon,
Thus to herself she pleasingly began.

795 O sov'reign, virtuous, precious of all trees
In Paradise, of operation blest
To sapience, hitherto obscured, infamed,
And thy fair fruit let hang, as to no end
Created; but henceforth my early care,
800 Not without song, each morning, and due praise
Shall tend thee, and the fertile burden ease
Of thy full branches offered free to all;
Till dieted by thee I grow mature
In knowledge, as the gods who all things know;
805 Though others envy what they cannot give;
For had the gift been theirs, it had not here
Thus grown. Experience, next to thee I owe,
Best guide; not following thee, I had remained
In ignorance, thou open'st wisdom's way,
810 And giv'st accéss, though secret she retire.
And I perhaps am secret; Heav'n is high,
High and remote to see from thence distinct
Each thing on earth; and other care perhaps
May have diverted from continual watch
815 Our great Forbidder, safe with all his spies
About him. But to Adam in what sort
Shall I appear? shall I to him make known
As yet my change, and give him to partake
Full happiness with me, or rather not,
820 But keep the odds of knowledge in my power
Without copartner? so to add what wants
In female sex, the more to draw his love,
And render me more equal, and perhaps,

A thing not undesirable, sometime
825   Superior; for inferior who is free?
This may be well: but what if God have seen,
And death ensue? then I shall be no more,
And Adam wedded to another Eve,
Shall live with her enjoying, I extinct;
830   A death to think. Confirmed then I resolve,
Adam shall share with me in bliss or woe:
So dear I love him, that with him all deaths
I could endure, without him live no life.
      So saying, from the tree her step she turned,
835   But first low reverence done, as to the power
That dwelt within, whose presence had infused
Into the plant sciential sap, derived
From nectar, drink of gods. Adam the while
Waiting desirous her return, had wove
840   Of choicest flow'rs a garland to adorn
Her tresses, and her rural labours crown,
As reapers oft are wont their harvest queen.
Great joy he promised to his thoughts, and new
Solace in her return, so long delayed;
845   Yet oft his heart, divine of something ill,
Misgave him; he the falt'ring measure felt;
And forth to meet her went, the way she took
That morn when first they parted; by the Tree
Of Knowledge he must pass, there he her met,
850   Scarce from the tree returning; in her hand
A bough of fairest fruit that downy smiled,
New gathered, and ambrosial smell diffused.
To him she hasted, in her face excuse
Came prologue, and apology to prompt,
855   Which with bland words at will she thus addressed.
      Hast thou not wondered, Adam, at my stay?
Thee I have missed, and thought it long, deprived
Thy presence, agony of love till now
Not felt, nor shall be twice, for never more
860   Mean I to try, what rash untried I sought,
The pain of absence from thy sight. But strange
Hath been the cause, and wonderful to hear:

This tree is not as we are told, a tree
Of danger tasted, nor to evil unknown
865   Op'ning the way, but of divine effect
To open eyes, and make them gods who taste;
And hath been tasted such: the serpent wise,
Or not restrained as we, or not obeying,
Hath eaten of the fruit, and is become,
870   Not dead, as we are threatened, but thenceforth
Endued with human voice and human sense,
Reasoning to admiration, and with me
Persuasively hath so prevailed, that I
Have also tasted, and have also found
875   Th' effects to correspond, opener mine eyes,
Dim erst, dilated spirits, ampler heart,
And growing up to godhead; which for thee
Chiefly I sought, without thee can despise.
For bliss, as thou hast part, to me is bliss,
880   Tedious, unshared with thee, and odious soon.
Thou therefore also taste, that equal lot
May join us, equal joy, as equal love;
Lest thou not tasting, different degree
Disjoin us, and I then too late renounce
885   Deity for thee, when Fate will not permit.
      Thus Eve with count'nance blithe her story told;
But in her cheek distemper flushing glowed.
On th' other side, Adam, soon as he heard
The fatal trespass done by Eve, amazed,
890   Astonied stood and blank, while horror chill
Ran through his veins, and all his joints relaxed;
From his slack hand the garland wreathed for Eve
Down dropped, and all the faded roses shed:
Speechless he stood and pale, till thus at length
895   First to himself he inward silence broke.
      O fairest of Creation, last and best
Of all God's works, creature in whom excelled
Whatever can to sight or thought be formed,
Holy, divine, good, amiable or sweet!
900   How art thou lost, how on a sudden lost,
Defaced, deflow'red, and now to death devote?

Rather how hast thou yielded to transgress
The strict forbiddance, how to violate
The sacred fruit forbidd'n! Some cursèd fraud
905   Of Enemy hath beguiled thee, yet unknown,
And me with thee hath ruined, for with thee
Certain my resolution is to die;
How can I live without thee, how forgo
Thy sweet convérse and love so dearly joined,
910   To live again in these wild woods forlorn?
Should God create another Eve, and I
Another rib afford, yet loss of thee
Would never from my heart; no no, I feel
The link of nature draw me: flesh of flesh,
915   Bone of my bone thou art, and from thy state
Mine never shall be parted, bliss or woe.
    So having said, as one from sad dismay
Recomforted, and after thoughts disturbed
Submitting to what seemed remédiless,
920   Thus in calm mood his words to Eve he turned.
    Bold deed thou hast presumed, advent'rous Eve,
And peril great provoked, who thus hath dared
Had it been only coveting to eye
That sacred fruit, sacred to abstinence,
925   Much more to taste it under ban to touch.
But past who can recall, or done undo?
Not God omnipotent, nor Fate, yet so
Perhaps thou shalt not die, perhaps the fact
Is not so heinous now, foretasted fruit,
930   Profaned first by the serpent, by him first
Made common and unhallowed ere our taste;
Nor yet on him found deadly; he yet lives,
Lives, as thou saidst, and gains to live as man
Higher degree of life, inducement strong
935   To us, as likely tasting to attain
Proportional ascent, which cannot be
But to be gods, or angels demi-gods.
Nor can I think that God, Creator wise,
Though threat'ning, will in earnest so destroy
940   Us his prime creatures, dignified so high,

Set over all his works, which in our Fall,
For us created, needs with us must fail,
Dependent made; so God shall uncreate,
Be frustrate, do, undo, and labour lose,
945   Not well conceived of God, who though his power
Creation could repeat, yet would be loath
Us to abolish, lest the Adversary
Triúmph and say; Fickle their state whom God
Most favours, who can please him long? Me first
950   He ruined, now mankind; whom will he next?
Matter of scorn, not to be given the Foe.
However I with thee have fixed my lot,
Certain to undergo like doom; if death
Consort with thee, death is to me as life;
955   So forcible within my heart I feel
The bond of nature draw me to my own,
My own in thee, for what thou art is mine;
Our state cannot be severed, we are one,
One flesh; to lose thee were to lose myself.
960   So Adam, and thus Eve to him replied.
O glorious trial of exceeding love,
Illustrious evidence, example high!
Engaging me to emulate, but short
Of thy perfection, how shall I attain,
965   Adam, from whose dear side I boast me sprung,
And gladly of our union hear thee speak,
One heart, one soul in both; whereof good proof
This day affords, declaring thee resolved,
Rather than death or aught than death more dread
970   Shall separate us, linked in love so dear,
To undergo with me one guilt, one crime,
If any be, of tasting this fair fruit,
Whose virtue, for of good still good proceeds,
Direct, or by occasion hath presented
975   This happy trial of thy love, which else
So eminently never had been known.
Were it I thought death menaced would ensue
This my attempt, I would sustain alone
The worst, and not persuade thee, rather die

980 Deserted, than oblige thee with a fact
      Pernicious to thy peace, chiefly assured
      Remarkably so late of thy so true,
      So faithful love unequalled; but I feel
      Far otherwise th' event, not death, but life
985 Augmented, opened eyes, new hopes, new joys,
      Taste so divine, that what of sweet before
      Hath touched my sense, flat seems to this, and harsh.
      On my experience, Adam, freely taste,
      And fear of death deliver to the winds.
990   So saying, she embraced him, and for joy
      Tenderly wept, much won that he his love
      Had so ennobled, as of choice to incur
      Divine displeasure for her sake, or death.
      In recompense (for such compliance bad
995 Such recompense best merits) from the bough
      She gave him of that fair enticing fruit
      With liberal hand: he scrupled not to eat
      Against his better knowledge, not deceived,
      But fondly overcome with female charm.
1000 Earth trembled from her entrails, as again
      In pangs, and Nature gave a second groan;
      Sky loured, and muttering thunder, some sad drops
      Wept at completing of the mortal sin
      Original; while Adam took no thought,
1005 Eating his fill, nor Eve to iterate
      Her former trespass feared, the more to soothe
      Him with her loved society, that now
      As with new wine intoxicated both
      They swim in mirth, and fancy that they feel
1010 Divinity within them breeding wings
      Wherewith to scorn the earth: but that false fruit
      Far other operation first displayed,
      Carnal desire inflaming; he on Eve
      Began to cast lascivious eyes, she him
1015 As wantonly repaid; in lust they burn:
      Till Adam thus gan Eve to dalliance move.
          Eve, now I see thou art exact of taste,
      And elegant, of sapience no small part,

Since to each meaning savour we apply,
1020 And palate call judicious; I the praise
Yield thee, so well this day thou hast purveyed.
Much pleasure we have lost, while we abstained
From this delightful fruit, nor known till now
True relish, tasting; if such pleasure be
1025 In things to us forbidden, it might be wished,
For this one tree had been forbidden ten.
But come, so well refreshed, now let us play,
As meet is, after such delicious fare;
For never did thy beauty since the day
1030 I saw thee first and wedded thee, adorned
With all perfections, so inflame my sense
With ardour to enjoy thee, fairer now
Than ever, bounty of this virtuous tree.
     So said he, and forbore not glance or toy
1035 Of amorous intent, well understood
Of Eve, whose eye darted contagious fire.
Her hand he seized, and to a shady bank,
Thick overhead with verdant roof embow'red
He led her nothing loath; flow'rs were the couch,
1040 Pansies, and violets, and asphodel,
And hyacinth, earth's freshest softest lap.
There they their fill of love and love's disport
Took largely, of their mutual guilt the seal,
The solace of their sin, till dewy sleep
1045 Oppressed them, wearied with their amorous play.
Soon as the force of that fallacious fruit,
That with exhilarating vapour bland
About their spirits had played, and inmost powers
Made err, was now exhaled, and grosser sleep
1050 Bred of unkindly fumes, with conscious dreams
Encumbered, now had left them, up they rose
As from unrest, and each the other viewing,
Soon found their eyes how opened, and their minds
How darkened; innocence, that as a veil
1055 Had shadowed them from knowing ill, was gone;
Just confidence, and native righteousness
And honour from about them, naked left

To guilty Shame: he covered, but his robe
Uncovered more. So rose the Danite strong
1060   Hercúlean Samson from the harlot-lap
Of Phílistéan Dálila, and waked
Shorn of his strength, they destitute and bare
Of all their virtue: silent, and in face
Confounded long they sat, as strucken mute,
1065   Till Adam, though not less than Eve abashed,
At length gave utterance to these words constrained.
O Eve, in evil hour thou didst give ear
To that false worm, of whomsoever taught
To counterfeit man's voice, true in our Fall,
1070   False in our promised rising; since our eyes
Opened we find indeed, and find we know
Both good and evil, good lost, and evil got,
Bad fruit of knowledge, if this be to know,
Which leaves us naked thus, of honour void,
1075   Of innocence, of faith, of purity,
Our wonted ornaments now soiled and stained,
And in our faces evident the signs
Of foul concupiscence; whence evil store;
Even shame, the last of evils; of the first
1080   Be sure then. How shall I behold the face
Henceforth of God or angel, erst with joy
And rapture so oft beheld? those Heav'nly shapes
Will dazzle now this earthly, with their blaze
Insufferably bright. O might I here
1085   In solitude live savage, in some glade
Obscured, where highest woods impenetrable
To star or sunlight, spread their umbrage broad
And brown as evening: cover me ye pines,
Ye cedars, with innumerable boughs
1090   Hide me, where I may never see them more.
But let us now, as in bad plight, devise
What best may for the present serve to hide
The parts of each from other, that seem most
To shame obnoxious, and unseemliest seen;
1095   Some tree whose broad smooth leaves together sewed,
And girded on our loins, may cover round

Those middle parts, that this new comer, Shame,
There sit not, and reproach us as unclean.
　　So counselled he, and both together went
1100 Into the thickest wood, there soon they chose
The fig-tree, not that kind for fruit renowned,
But such as at this day to Indians known
In Malabar or Deccan spreads her arms
Branching so broad and long, that in the ground
1105 The bended twigs take root, and daughters grow
About the mother tree, a pillared shade
High overarched, and echoing walks between;
There oft the Indian herdsman shunning heat
Shelters in cool, and tends his pasturing herds
1110 At loopholes cut through thickest shade: those leaves
They gathered, broad as Amazonian targe,
And with what skill they had, together sewed,
To gird their waist, vain covering if to hide
Their guilt and dreaded shame; O how unlike
1115 To that first naked glory. Such of late
Columbus found th' American so girt
With feathered cincture, naked else and wild
Among the trees on isles and woody shores.
Thus fenced, and as they thought, their shame in part
1120 Covered, but not at rest or ease of mind,
They sat them down to weep, nor only tears
Rained at their eyes, but high winds worse within
Began to rise, high passions, anger, hate,
Mistrust, suspicion, discord, and shook sore
1125 Their inward state of mind, calm region once
And full of peace, now tossed and turbulent:
For understanding ruled not, and the will
Heard not her lore, both in subjection now
To sensual appetite, who from beneath
1130 Usurping over sov'reign reason claimed
Superior sway: from thus distempered breast,
Adam, estranged in look and altered style,
Speech intermitted thus to Eve renewed.
　　Would thou hadst hearkened to my words, and stayed
1135 With me, as I besought thee, when that strange

Desire of wand'ring this unhappy morn,
I know not whence possessed thee; we had then
Remained still happy, not as now, despoiled
Of all our good, shamed, naked, miserable.

1140 Let none henceforth seek needless cause to approve
The faith they owe; when earnestly they seek
Such proof, conclude, they then begin to fail.
        To whom soon moved with touch of blame thus Eve.
What words have passed thy lips, Adam severe,

1145 Imput'st thou that to my default, or will
Of wand'ring, as thou call'st it, which who knows
But might as ill have happened thou being by,
Or to thyself perhaps: hadst thou been there,
Or here th' attempt, thou couldst not have discerned

1150 Fraud in the serpent, speaking as he spake;
No ground of enmity between us known,
Why he should mean me ill, or seek to harm.
Was I to have never parted from thy side?
As good have grown there still a lifeless rib.

1155 Being as I am, why didst not thou the head
Command me absolutely not to go,
Going into such danger as thou saidst?
Too facile then thou didst not much gainsay,
Nay, didst permit, approve, and fair dismiss.

1160 Hadst thou been firm and fixed in thy dissent,
Neither had I transgressed, nor thou with me.
        To whom then first incensed Adam replied.
Is this the love, is this the recompense
Of mine to thee, ingrateful Eve, expressed

1165 Immutable when thou wert lost, not I,
Who might have lived and joyed immortal bliss,
Yet willingly chose rather death with thee:
And am I now upbraided, as the cause
Of thy transgressing? not enough severe,

1170 It seems, in thy restraint: what could I more?
I warned thee, I admonished thee, foretold
The danger, and the lurking Enemy
That lay in wait; beyond this had been force,
And force upon free will hath here no place.

1175 But confidence then bore thee on, secure
Either to meet no danger, or to find
Matter of glorious trial, and perhaps
I also erred in overmuch admiring
What seemed in thee so perfect, that I thought
1180 No evil durst attempt thee, but I rue
That error now, which is become my crime,
And thou th' accuser. Thus it shall befall
Him who to worth in women overtrusting
Lets her will rule; restraint she will not brook,
1185 And left to herself, if evil thence ensue,
She first his weak indulgence will accuse.
Thus they in mutual accusation spent
The fruitless hours, but neither self-condemning,
And of their vain contést appeared no end.

BOOK X

The Argument

Man's transgression known, the guardian angels forsake Paradise, and return up to Heaven to approve their vigilance, and are approved, God declaring that the entrance of Satan could not be by them prevented. He sends his Son to judge the transgressors, who descends and gives sentence accordingly; then in pity clothes them both, and reascends. Sin and Death sitting till then at the gates of Hell, by wondrous sympathy feeling the success of Satan in this new world, and the sin by man there committed, resolve to sit no longer confined in Hell, but to follow Satan their sire up to the place of man: to make the way easier from Hell to this world to and fro, they pave a broad highway or bridge over Chaos, according to the track that Satan first made; then preparing for earth, they meet him proud of his success returning to Hell; their mutual gratulation. Satan arrives at Pandaemonium, in full assembly relates with boasting his success against man; instead of applause is entertained with a general hiss by all his audience, transformed with himself also suddenly into serpents, according to his doom given in Paradise; then deluded with a show of the Forbidden Tree springing up before them, they greedily reaching to take of the fruit, chew dust and bitter ashes. The proceedings of Sin and Death; God foretells the final victory of his Son over them, and the renewing of all things; but for the present commands his angels to make several alterations in the heavens and elements. Adam more and more perceiving his fallen condition heavily bewails, rejects the condolement of Eve; she persists and at length appeases him: then to evade the curse likely to fall on their offspring, proposes to Adam violent ways which he approves not, but conceiving better hope, puts her in mind of the late promise made them, that her seed should be revenged on the serpent, and exhorts her

with him to seek peace of the offended Deity, by repentance
and supplication.

Meanwhile the heinous and despiteful act
Of Satan done in Paradise, and how
He in the serpent had perverted Eve,
Her husband she, to taste the fatal fruit,
Was known in Heav'n; for what can 'scape the eye
Of God all-seeing, or deceive his heart
Omniscient, who in all things wise and just,
Hindered not Satan to attempt the mind
Of man, with strength entire, and free will armed,
Complete to have discovered and repulsed
Whatever wiles of foe or seeming friend.
For still they knew, and ought to have still remembered
The high injunction not to taste that fruit,
Whoever tempted; which they not obeying,
Incurred, what could they less, the penalty,
And manifold in sin, deserved to fall.
Up into Heav'n from Paradise in haste
Th' angelic guards ascended, mute and sad
For man, for of his state by this they knew,
Much wond'ring how the subtle Fiend had stol'n
Entrance unseen. Soon as th' unwelcome news
From earth arrived at Heaven gate, displeased
All were who heard, dim sadness did not spare
That time celestial visages, yet mixed
With pity, violated not their bliss.
About the new-arrived, in multitudes
Th' ethereal people ran, to hear and know
How all befell: they towards the throne supreme
Accountable made haste to make appear
With righteous plea, their utmost vigilance,
And easily approved; when the Most High
Eternal Father from his secret cloud,
Amidst in thunder uttered thus his voice.
     Assembled angels, and ye Powers returned
From unsuccessful charge, be not dismayed,

Nor troubled at these tidings from the earth,
Which your sincerest care could not prevent,
Foretold so lately what would come to pass,
When first this Tempter crossed the gulf from Hell.
40   I told ye then he should prevail and speed
On his bad errand, man should be seduced
And flattered out of all, believing lies
Against his Maker; no decree of mine
Concurring to necessitate his Fall,
45   Or touch with lightest moment of impúlse
His free will, to her own inclining left
In even scale. But fall'n he is, and now
What rests but that the mortal sentence pass
On his transgression, death denounced that day,
50   Which he presumes already vain and void,
Because not yet inflicted, as he feared,
By some immediate stroke; but soon shall find
Forbearance no acquittance ere day end.
Justice shall not return as bounty scorned.
55   But whom send I to judge them? whom but thee
Vicegerent Son, to thee I have transferred
All judgement, whether in Heav'n, or earth, or Hell.
Easy it might be seen that I intend
Mercy colléague with justice, sending thee
60   Man's friend, his Mediator, his designed
Both ransom and Redeemer voluntary,
And destined man himself to judge man fall'n.
    So spake the Father, and unfolding bright
Toward the right hand his glory, on the Son
65   Blazed forth unclouded deity; he full
Resplendent all his Father manifest
Expressed, and thus divinely answered mild.
    Father Eternal, thine is to decree,
Mine both in Heav'n and earth to do thy will
70   Supreme, that thou in me thy Son beloved
May'st ever rest well pleased. I go to judge
On earth these thy transgressors, but thou know'st,
Whoever judged, the worst on me must light,
When time shall be, for so I undertook

75   Before thee; and not repenting, this obtain
       Of right, that I may mitigate their doom
       On me derived; yet I shall temper so
       Justice with mercy, as may illústrate most
       Them fully satisfied, and thee appease.
80   Attendance none shall need, nor train, where none
       Are to behold the judgement, but the judged,
       Those two; the third best absent is condemned,
       Convíct by flight, and rebel to all law;
       Conviction to the serpent none belongs.
85   Thus saying, from his radiant seat he rose
       Of high collateral glory: him Thrones and Powers,
       Princedoms, and Dominations ministrant
       Accompanied to Heaven gate, from whence
       Eden and all the coast in prospect lay.
90   Down he descended straight; the speed of Gods
       Time counts not, though with swiftest minutes winged.
       Now was the sun in western cadence low
       From noon, and gentle airs due at their hour
       To fan the earth now waked, and usher in
95   The ev'ning cool when he from wrath more cool
       Came the mild Judge and Intercessor both
       To sentence man: the voice of God they heard
       Now walking in the garden, by soft winds
       Brought to their ears, while day declined; they heard
100   And from his presence hid themselves among
       The thickest trees, both man and wife, till God
       Approaching, thus to Adam called aloud.
            Where art thou Adam, wont with joy to meet
       My coming seen far off? I miss thee here,
105   Not pleased, thus entertained with solitude,
       Where obvious duty erewhile appeared unsought:
       Or come I less conspicuous, or what change
       Absents thee, or what chance detains? Come forth.
       He came, and with him Eve, more loath, though first
110   To offend, discount'nanced both, and discomposed;
       Love was not in their looks, either to God
       Or to each other, but apparent guilt,
       And shame, and perturbation, and despair,

Anger, and obstinacy, and hate, and guile.
115 Whence Adam falt'ring long, thus answered brief.
 I heard thee in the garden, and of thy voice
Afraid, being naked, hid myself. To whom
The gracious Judge without revile replied.
 My voice thou oft hast heard, and hast not feared,
120 But still rejoiced, how is it now become
So dreadful to thee? that thou art naked, who
Hath told thee? hast thou eaten of the tree
Whereof I gave thee charge thou shouldst not eat?
 To whom thus Adam sore beset replied.
125 O Heav'n! in evil strait this day I stand
Before my Judge, either to undergo
Myself the total crime, or to accuse
My other self, the partner of my life;
Whose failing, while her faith to me remains,
130 I should conceal, and not expose to blame
By my complaint; but strict necessity
Subdues me, and calamitous constraint,
Lest on my head both sin and punishment,
However insupportable, be all
135 Devolved; though should I hold my peace, yet thou
Wouldst easily detect what I conceal.
This woman whom thou mad'st to be my help,
And gav'st me as thy perfect gift, so good,
So fit, so ácceptáble, so divine,
140 That from her hand I could suspect no ill,
And what she did, whatever in itself,
Her doing seemed to justify the deed;
She gave me of the tree, and I did eat.
 To whom the sov'reign Presence thus replied.
145 Was she thy God, that her thou didst obey
Before his voice, or was she made thy guide,
Superior, or but equal, that to her
Thou didst resign thy manhood, and the place
Wherein God set thee above her made of thee,
150 And for thee, whose perfection far excelled
Hers in all real dignity: adorned
She was indeed, and lovely to attract

Thy love, not thy subjection, and her gifts
Were such as under government well seemed,
155 Unseemly to bear rule, which was thy part
And person, hadst thou known thyself aright.
    So having said, he thus to Eve in few:
Say woman, what is this which thou hast done?
    To whom sad Eve with shame nigh overwhelmed,
160 Confessing soon, yet not before her Judge
Bold or loquacious, thus abashed replied.
    The serpent me beguiled and I did eat.
    Which when the Lord God heard, without delay
To judgement he proceeded on th' accused
165 Serpent though brute, unable to transfer
The guilt on him who made him instrument
Of mischief, and polluted from the end
Of his creation; justly then accursed,
As vitiated in nature: more to know
170 Concerned not man (since he no further knew)
Nor altered his offence; yet God at last
To Satan first in sin his doom applied,
Though in mysterious terms, judged as then best:
And on the serpent thus his curse let fall.
175   Because thou hast done this, thou art accursed
Above all cattle, each beast of the field;
Upon thy belly grovelling thou shalt go,
And dust shalt eat all the days of thy life.
Between thee and the woman I will put
180 Enmity, and between thine and her seed;
Her seed shall bruise thy head, thou bruise his heel.
    So spake this oracle, then verified
When Jesus son of Mary second Eve,
Saw Satan fall like lightning down from Heav'n,
185 Prince of the Air; then rising from his grave
Spoiled Principalities and Powers, triúmphed
In open show, and with ascension bright
Captivity led captive through the air,
The realm itself of Satan long usurped,
190 Whom he shall tread at last under our feet;
Ev'n he who now foretold his fatal bruise,

And to the woman thus his sentence turned.
    Thy sorrow I will greatly multiply
By thy conception; children thou shalt bring
195 In sorrow forth, and to thy husband's will
Thine shall submit, he over thee shall rule.
    On Adam last thus judgement he pronounced.
Because thou hast hearkened to the voice of thy wife,
And eaten of the tree concerning which
200 I charged thee, saying: Thou shalt not eat thereof,
Cursed is the ground for thy sake, thou in sorrow
Shalt eat thereof all the days of thy life;
Thorns also and thistles it shall bring thee forth
Unbid, and thou shalt eat the herb of the field,
205 In the sweat of thy face shalt thou eat bread,
Till thou return unto the ground, for thou
Out of the ground wast taken; know thy birth,
For dust thou art, and shalt to dust return.
    So judged he man, both Judge and Saviour sent,
210 And th' instant stroke of death denounced that day
Removed far off; then pitying how they stood
Before him naked to the air, that now
Must suffer change, disdained not to begin
Thenceforth the form of servant to assume,
215 As when he washed his servants' feet, so now
As father of his family he clad
Their nakedness with skins of beasts, or slain,
Or as the snake with youthful coat repaid;
And thought not much to clothe his enemies:
220 Nor he their outward only with the skins
Of beasts, but inward nakedness, much more
Opprobrious, with his robe of righteousness,
Arraying covered from his Father's sight.
To him with swift ascent he up returned,
225 Into his blissful bosom reassumed
In glory as of old, to him appeased,
All, though all-knowing, what had passed with man
Recounted, mixing intercession sweet.
    Meanwhile ere thus was sinned and judged on earth,
230 Within the gates of Hell sat Sin and Death,

In counterview within the gates, that now
Stood open wide, belching outrageous flame
Far into Chaos, since the Fiend passed through,
Sin opening, who thus now to Death began.
235   O Son, why sit we here each other viewing
Idly, while Satan our great author thrives
In other worlds, and happier seat provides
For us his offspring dear? It cannot be
But that success attends him; if mishap,
240   Ere this he had returned, with fury driv'n
By his avengers, since no place like this
Can fit his punishment, or their revenge.
Methinks I feel new strength within me rise,
Wings growing, and dominion giv'n me large
245   Beyond this deep; whatever draws me on,
Or sympathy, or some connatural force
Powerful at greatest distance to unite
With secret amity things of like kind
By secretest conveyance. Thou my shade
250   Inseparable must with me along:
For Death from Sin no power can separate.
But lest the difficulty of passing back
Stay his return perhaps over this gulf
Impassable, impervious, let us try
255   Advent'rous work, yet to thy power and mine
Not unagreeable, to found a path
Over this main from Hell to that new world
Where Satan now prevails, a monument
Of merit high to all th' infernal host,
260   Easing their passage hence, for intercourse,
Or transmigration, as their lot shall lead.
Nor can I miss the way, so strongly drawn
By this new felt attraction and instinct.
      Whom thus the meagre Shadow answered soon.
265   Go whither Fate and inclination strong
Leads thee, I shall not lag behind, nor err
The way, thou leading, such a scent I draw
Of carnage, prey innumerable, and taste
The savour of death from all things there that live:

270 Nor shall I to the work thou enterprisest
     Be wanting, but afford thee equal aid.
         So saying, with delight he snuffed the smell
     Of mortal change on earth. As when a flock
     Of ravenous fowl, though many a league remote,
275 Against the day of battle, to a field,
     Where armies lie encamped, come flying, lured
     With scent of living carcasses designed
     For death, the following day, in bloody fight.
     So scented the grim feature, and upturned
280 His nostril wide into the murky air,
     Sagacious of his quarry from so far.
     Then both from out Hell gates into the waste
     Wide anarchy of Chaos damp and dark
     Flew diverse, and with power (their power was great)
285 Hovering upon the waters; what they met
     Solid or slimy, as in raging sea
     Tossed up and down, together crowded drove
     From each side shoaling towards the mouth of Hell.
     As when two polar winds blowing adverse
290 Upon the Cronian Sea, together drive
     Mountains of ice, that stop th' imagined way
     Beyond Petsora eastward, to the rich
     Cathayan coast. The aggregated soil
     Death with his mace petrific, cold and dry,
295 As with a trident smote, and fixed as firm
     As Delos floating once; the rest his look
     Bound with Gorgonian rigor not to move,
     And with asphaltic slime; broad as the gate,
     Deep to the roots of Hell the gathered beach
300 They fastened, and the mole immense wrought on
     Over the foaming deep high arched, a bridge
     Of length prodigious joining to the wall
     Immovable of this now fenceless world
     Forfeit to Death; from hence a passage broad,
305 Smooth, easy, inoffensive down to Hell.
     So, if great things to small may be compared,
     Xerxes, the liberty of Greece to yoke,
     From Susa his Memnonian palace high

Came to the sea, and over Hellespont
310   Bridging his way, Europe with Asia joined,
And scourged with many a stroke th' indignant waves.
Now had they brought the work by wondrous art
Pontifical, a ridge of pendent rock
Over the vexed abyss, following the track
315   Of Satan, to the selfsame place where he
First lighted from his wing, and landed safe
From out of Chaos to the outside bare
Of this round world: with pins of adamant
And chains they made all fast, too fast they made
320   And durable; and now in little space
The confines met of empyréan Heav'n
And of this world, and on the left hand Hell
With long reach interposed; three several ways
In sight, to each of these three places led.
325   And now their way to earth they had descried,
To Paradise first tending, when behold
Satan in likeness of an angel bright
Betwixt the Centaur and the Scorpion steering
His zenith, while the sun in Aries rose:
330   Disguised he came, but those his children dear
Their parent soon discerned, though in disguise.
He, after Eve seduced, unminded slunk
Into the wood fast by, and changing shape
To observe the sequel, saw his guileful act
335   By Eve, though all unweeting, seconded
Upon her husband, saw their shame that sought
Vain covertures; but when he saw descend
The Son of God to judge them, terrified
He fled, not hoping to escape, but shun
340   The present, fearing guilty what his wrath
Might suddenly inflict; that past, returned
By night, and list'ning where the hapless pair
Sat in their sad discourse, and various plaint,
Thence gathered his own doom, which understood
345   Not instant, but of future time. With joy
And tidings fraught, to Hell he now returned,
And at the brink of Chaos, near the foot

Of this new wondrous pontifice, unhoped
Met who to meet him came, his offspring dear.
350 Great joy was at their meeting, and at sight
Of that stupendous bridge his joy increased.
Long he admiring stood, till Sin, his fair
Enchanting daughter, thus the silence broke.
    O parent, these are thy magnific deeds,
355 Thy trophies, which thou view'st as not thine own;
Thou art their author and prime architect:
For I no sooner in my heart divined,
My heart, which by a secret harmony
Still moves with thine, joined in connection sweet,
360 That thou on earth hadst prospered, which thy looks
Now also evidence, but straight I felt
Though distant from thee worlds between, yet felt
That I must after thee with this thy son;
Such fatal consequence unites us three:
365 Hell could no longer hold us in her bounds,
Nor this unvoyageable gulf obscure
Detain from following thy illustrious track.
Thou hast achieved our liberty, confined
Within Hell gates till now, thou us empow'red
370 To fortify thus far, and overlay
With this portentous bridge the dark abyss.
Thine now is all this world, thy virtue hath won
What thy hands builded not, thy wisdom gained
With odds what war hath lost, and fully avenged
375 Our foil in Heav'n; here thou shalt monarch reign,
There didst not; there let him still victor sway,
As battle hath adjudged, from this new world
Retiring, by his own doom alienated,
And henceforth monarchy with thee divide
380 Of all things, parted by th' empyreal bounds,
His quadrature, from thy orbicular world,
Or try thee now more dang'rous to his throne.
    Whom thus the Prince of Darkness answered glad.
Fair daughter, and thou son and grandchild both,
385 High proof ye now have giv'n to be the race
Of Satan (for I glory in the name,

Antagonist of Heav'n's Almighty King)
Amply have merited of me, of all
Th' infernal empire, that so near Heav'n's door
390 Triumphal with triumphal act have met,
Mine with this glorious work, and made one realm
Hell and this world, one realm, one continent
Of easy thoroughfare. Therefore while I
Descend through darkness, on your road with ease
395 To my associate Powers, them to acquaint
With these successes, and with them rejoice,
You two this way, among these numerous orbs
All yours, right down to Paradise descend;
There dwell and reign in bliss; thence on the earth
400 Dominion exercise and in the air,
Chiefly on man, sole lord of all declared;
Him first make sure your thrall, and lastly kill.
My substitutes I send ye, and create
Plenipotent on earth, of matchless might
405 Issuing from me: on your joint vigour now
My hold of this new kingdom all depends,
Through Sin to Death exposed by my exploit.
If your joint power prevail, th' affairs of Hell
No detriment need fear; go and be strong.
410   So saying he dismissed them, they with speed
Their course through thickest constellations held
Spreading their bane; the blasted stars looked wan,
And planets, planet-strook, real eclipse
Then suffered. Th' other way Satan went down
415 The causey to Hell gate; on either side
Disparted Chaos overbuilt exclaimed,
And with rebounding surge the bars assailed,
That scorned his indignation: through the gate,
Wide open and unguarded, Satan passed,
420 And all about found desolate; for those
Appointed to sit there, had left their charge,
Flown to the upper world; the rest were all
Far to the inland retired, about the walls
Of Pandaemonium, city and proud seat
425 Of Lucifer, so by allusion called,

Of that bright star to Satan paragoned.
There kept their watch the legions, while the grand
In council sat, solicitous what chance
Might intercept their Emperor sent; so he
430   Departing gave command, and they observed.
As when the Tartar from his Russian foe
By Astrakhan over the snowy plains
Retires, or Bactrian Sophy from the horns
Of Turkish crescent, leaves all waste beyond
435   The realm of Aladule, in his retreat
To Tauris or Casbeen. So these the late
Heav'n-banished host, left desert utmost Hell
Many a dark league, reduced in careful watch
Round their metropolis, and now expecting
440   Each hour their great adventurer from the search
Of foreign worlds: he through the midst unmarked,
In show plebeian angel militant
Of lowest order, passed; and from the door
Of that Plutonian hall, invisible
445   Ascended his high throne, which under state
Of richest texture spread, at th' upper end
Was placed in regal lustre. Down a while
He sat, and round about him saw unseen:
At last as from a cloud his fulgent head
450   And shape star-bright appeared, or brighter, clad
With what permissive glory since his Fall
Was left him, or false glitter: all amazed
At that so sudden blaze the Stygian throng
Bent their aspéct, and whom they wished beheld,
455   Their mighty chief returned: loud was th' acclaim:
Forth rushed in haste the great consulting Peers,
Raised from their dark Divan, and with like joy
Congratulant approached him, who with hand
Silence, and with these words attention won.
460   Thrones, Dominations, Princedoms, Virtues, Powers,
For in possession such, not only of right,
I call ye and declare ye now, returned
Successful beyond hope, to lead ye forth
Triumphant out of this infernal pit

465 Abominable, accursed, the house of woe,
And dungeon of our Tyrant. Now possess,
As lords, a spacious world, to our native Heaven
Little inferior, by my adventure hard
With peril great achieved. Long were to tell
470 What I have done, what suffered, with what pain
Voyaged th' unreal, vast, unbounded deep
Of horrible confusion, over which
By Sin and Death a broad way now is paved
To expedite your glorious march; but I
475 Toiled out my uncouth passage, forced to ride
Th' untractable abyss, plunged in the womb
Of unoriginal Night and Chaos wild,
That jealous of their secrets fiercely opposed
My journey strange, with clamorous uproar
480 Protesting Fate supreme; thence how I found
The new created world, which fame in Heav'n
Long had foretold, a fabric wonderful
Of absolute perfection, therein man
Placed in a Paradise, by our exíle
485 Made happy: him by fraud I have seduced
From his Creator, and the more to increase
Your wonder, with an apple; he thereat
Offended, worth your laughter, hath giv'n up
Both his beloved man and all his world,
490 To Sin and Death a prey, and so to us,
Without our hazard, labour, or alarm,
To range in, and to dwell, and over man
To rule, as over all he should have ruled.
True is, me also he hath judged, or rather
495 Me not, but the brute serpent in whose shape
Man I deceived: that which to me belongs,
Is enmity, which he will put between
Me and mankind; I am to bruise his heel;
His seed, when is not set, shall bruise my head:
500 A world who would not purchase with a bruise,
Or much more grievous pain? Ye have th' account
Of my performance: what remains, ye gods,
But up and enter now into full bliss.

So having said, a while he stood, expecting
505   Their universal shout and high applause
To fill his ear, when contrary he hears
On all sides, from innumerable tongues
A dismal universal hiss, the sound
Of public scorn; he wondered, but not long
510   Had leisure, wond'ring at himself now more;
His visage drawn he felt to sharp and spare,
His arms clung to his ribs, his legs entwining
Each other, till supplanted down he fell
A monstrous serpent on his belly prone,
515   Reluctant, but in vain; a greater power
Now ruled him, punished in the shape he sinned,
According to his doom: he would have spoke,
But hiss for hiss returned with forkèd tongue
To forkèd tongue, for now were all transformed
520   Alike, to serpents all as áccessóries
To his bold riot: dreadful was the din
Of hissing through the hall, thick swarming now
With complicated monsters, head and tail,
Scorpion and asp, and amphisbaena dire,
525   Cerastes horned, hydrus, and ellops drear,
And dipsas (not so thick swarmed once the soil
Bedropped with blood of Gorgon, or the isle
Ophiusa); but still greatest he the midst,
Now dragon grown, larger than whom the sun
530   Engendered in the Pythian vale on slime,
Huge Python, and his power no less he seemed
Above the rest still to retain; they all
Him followed issuing forth to th' open field,
Where all yet left of that revolted rout
535   Heav'n-fall'n, in station stood or just array,
Sublime with expectation when to see
In triumph issuing forth their glorious chief;
They saw, but other sight instead, a crowd
Of ugly serpents; horror on them fell,
540   And horrid sympathy; for what they saw,
They felt themselves now changing; down their arms,
Down fell both spear and shield, down they as fast,

And the dire hiss renewed, and the dire form
Catched by contagion, like in punishment,
545   As in their crime. Thus was th' applause they meant,
Turned to exploding hiss, triumph to shame
Cast on themselves from their own mouths. There stood
A grove hard by, sprung up with this their change,
His will who reigns above, to aggravate
550   Their penance, laden with fair fruit like that
Which grew in Paradise, the bait of Eve
Used by the Tempter: on that prospect strange
Their earnest eyes they fixed, imagining
For one forbidden tree a multitude
555   Now ris'n, to work them further woe or shame;
Yet parched with scalding thirst and hunger fierce,
Though to delude them sent, could not abstain,
But on they rolled in heaps, and up the trees
Climbing, sat thicker than the snaky locks
560   That curled Megaera: greedily they plucked
The fruitage fair to sight, like that which grew
Near that bituminous lake where Sodom flamed;
This more delusive, not the touch, but taste
Deceived; they fondly thinking to allay
565   Their appetite with gust, instead of fruit
Chewed bitter ashes, which th' offended taste
With spattering noise rejected: oft they assayed,
Hunger and thirst constraining, drugged as oft,
With hatefullest disrelish writhed their jaws
570   With soot and cinders filled; so oft they fell
Into the same illusion, not as man
Whom they triúmphed once lapsed. Thus were they
              plagued
And worn with famine, long and ceaseless hiss,
Till their lost shape, permitted, they resumed,
575   Yearly enjoined, some say, to undergo
This annual humbling certain numbered days,
To dash their pride, and joy for man seduced.
However some tradition they dispersed
Among the heathen of their purchase got,
580   And fabled how the serpent, whom they called

Ophion with Eurynome, the wide-
Encroaching Eve perhaps, had first the rule
Of high Olympus, thence by Saturn driv'n
And Ops, ere yet Dictaean Jove was born.
585   Meanwhile in Paradise the hellish pair
Too soon arrived, Sin there in power before,
Once actual, now in body, and to dwell
Habitual habitant; behind her Death
Close following pace for pace, not mounted yet
590   On his pale horse: to whom Sin thus began.
        Second of Satan sprung, all conquering Death,
What think'st thou of our empire now, though earned
With travail difficult, not better far
Than still at Hell's dark threshold to have sat watch,
595   Unnamed, undreaded, and thyself half-starved?
        Whom thus the Sin-born monster answered soon.
To me, who with eternal famine pine,
Alike is Hell, or Paradise, or Heaven,
There best, where most with ravin I may meet;
600   Which here, though plenteous, all too little seems
To stuff this maw, this vast unhidebound corpse.
        To whom th' incestuous mother thus replied.
Thou therefore on these herbs, and fruits, and flow'rs
Feed first, on each beast next, and fish, and fowl,
605   No homely morsels, and whatever thing
The scythe of Time mows down, devour unspared,
Till I in man residing through the race,
His thoughts, his looks, words, actions all infect,
And season him thy last and sweetest prey.
610   This said, they both betook them several ways,
Both to destroy, or unimmortal make
All kinds, and for destruction to mature
Sooner or later; which th' Almighty seeing,
From his transcendent seat the saints among,
615   To those bright orders uttered thus his voice.
        See with what heat these dogs of Hell advance
To waste and havoc yonder world, which I
So fair and good created, and had still
Kept in that state, had not the folly of man

620 Let in these wasteful Furies, who impute
Folly to me, so doth the Prince of Hell
And his adherents, that with so much ease
I suffer them to enter and possess
A place so Heav'nly, and conniving seem
625 To gratify my scornful enemies,
That laugh, as if transported with some fit
Of passion, I to them had quitted all,
At random yielded up to their misrule;
And know not that I called and drew them thither
630 My Hell-hounds, to lick up the draff and filth
Which man's polluting sin with taint hath shed
On what was pure, till crammed and gorged, nigh burst
With sucked and glutted offal, at one sling
Of thy victorious arm, well-pleasing Son,
635 Both Sin, and Death, and yawning grave at last
Through Chaos hurled, obstruct the mouth of Hell
For ever, and seal up his ravenous jaws.
Then heav'n and earth renewed shall be made pure
To sanctity that shall receive no stain:
640 Till then the curse pronounced on both precedes.
    He ended, and the Heav'nly audience loud
Sung hallelujah, as the sound of seas,
Through multitude that sung: Just are thy ways,
Righteous are thy decrees on all thy works;
645 Who can extenuate thee? Next, to the Son,
Destined restorer of mankind, by whom
New heav'n and earth shall to the ages rise,
Or down from Heav'n descend. Such was their song,
While the Creator calling forth by name
650 His mighty angels gave them several charge,
As sorted best with present things. The sun
Had first his precept so to move, so shine,
As might affect the earth with cold and heat
Scarce tolerable, and from the north to call
655 Decrepit winter, from the south to bring
Solstitial summer's heat. To the blank moon
Her office they prescribed, to th' other five
Their planetary motions and aspécts

In sextile, square, and trine, and opposite,
660 Of noxious efficacy, and when to join
In synod unbenign, and taught the fixed
Their influence malignant when to show'r,
Which of them rising with the sun, or falling,
Should prove tempestuous: to the winds they set
665 Their corners, when with bluster to confound
Sea, air, and shore, the thunder when to roll
With terror through the dark aërial hall.
Some say he bid his angels turn askance
The poles of earth twice ten degrees and more
670 From the sun's axle; they with labour pushed
Oblique the centric globe: some say the sun
Was bid turn reins from th' equinoctial road
Like distant breadth to Taurus with the sev'n
Atlantic Sisters, and the Spartan Twins
675 Up to the Tropic Crab; thence down amain
By Leo and the Virgin and the Scales,
As deep as Capricorn, to bring in change
Of seasons to each clime; else had the spring
Perpetual smiled on earth with vernant flow'rs,
680 Equal in days and nights, except to those
Beyond the polar circles; to them day
Had unbenighted shone, while the low sun
To recompense his distance, in their sight
Had rounded still th' horizon, and not known
685 Or east or west, which had forbid the snow
From cold Estotiland, and south as far
Beneath Magellan. At that tasted fruit
The sun, as from Thyéstean banquet, turned
His course intended; else how had the world
690 Inhabited, though sinless, more than now,
Avoided pinching cold and scorching heat?
These changes in the heav'ns, though slow, produced
Like change on sea and land, sideral blast,
Vapour, and mist, and exhalation hot,
695 Corrupt and pestilent: now from the north
Of Norumbega, and the Samoed shore
Bursting their brazen dungeon, armed with ice

And snow and hail and stormy gust and flaw,
Boreas and Caecias and Argestes loud
700 And Thrascias rend the woods and seas upturn;
With adverse blast upturns them from the south
Notus and Afer black with thund'rous clouds
From Serraliona; thwart of these as fierce
Forth rush the levant and the ponent winds
705 Eurus and Zephyr, with their lateral noise,
Sirocco, and Libecchio. Thus began
Outrage from lifeless things; but Discord first,
Daughter of Sin, among th' irrational
Death introduced through fierce antipathy:
710 Beast now with beast gan war, and fowl with fowl,
And fish with fish; to graze the herb all leaving,
Devoured each other; nor stood much in awe
Of man, but fled him, or with count'nance grim
Glared on him passing: these were from without
715 The growing miseries, which Adam saw
Already in part, though hid in gloomiest shade,
To sorrow abandoned, but worse felt within,
And in a troubled sea of passion tossed,
Thus to disburden sought with sad complaint.
720   O miserable of happy! is this the end
Of this new glorious world, and me so late
The glory of that glory? who now, become
Accursed of blessèd, hide me from the face
Of God, whom to behold was then my heighth
725 Of happiness: yet well, if here would end
The misery; I deserved it, and would bear
My own deservings; but this will not serve;
All that I eat or drink, or shall beget,
Is propagated curse. O voice once heard
730 Delightfully, *Increase and multiply*,
Now death to hear! for what can I increase
Or multiply, but curses on my head?
Who of all ages to succeed, but feeling
The evil on him brought by me, will curse
735 My head, Ill fare our ancestor impure,
For this we may thank Adam; but his thanks

Shall be the execration; so besides
Mine own that bide upon me, all from me
Shall with a fierce reflux on me redound,
740   On me as on their natural centre light
Heavy, though in their place. O fleeting joys
Of Paradise, dear bought with lasting woes!
Did I request thee, Maker, from my clay
To mould me man, did I solicit thee
745   From darkness to promote me, or here place
In this delicious garden? as my will
Concurred not to my being, it were but right
And equal to reduce me to my dust,
Desirous to resign, and render back
750   All I received, unable to perform
Thy terms too hard, by which I was to hold
The good I sought not. To the loss of that,
Sufficient penalty, why hast thou added
The sense of endless woes? inexplicable
755   Thy justice seems; yet to say truth, too late,
I thus contest; then should have been refused
Those terms whatever, when they were proposed:
Thou didst accept them; wilt thou enjoy the good,
Then cavil the conditions? and though God
760   Made thee without thy leave, what if thy son
Prove disobedient, and reproved, retort,
Wherefore didst thou beget me? I sought it not:
Wouldst thou admit for his contempt of thee
That proud excuse? yet him not thy election,
765   But natural necessity begot.
God made thee of choice his own, and of his own
To serve him; thy reward was of his grace;
Thy punishment then justly is at his will.
Be it so, for I submit, his doom is fair,
770   That dust I am, and shall to dust return:
O welcome hour whenever! why delays
His hand to execute what his decree
Fixed on this day? why do I overlive,
Why am I mocked with death, and lengthened out
775   To deathless pain? how gladly would I meet

Mortality my sentence, and be earth
Insensible, how glad would lay me down
As in my mother's lap! there I should rest
And sleep secure; his dreadful voice no more
780 Would thunder in my ears, no fear of worse
To me and to my offspring would torment me
With cruel expectation. Yet one doubt
Pursues me still, lest all I cannot die,
Lest that pure breath of life, the spirit of man
785 Which God inspired, cannot together perish
With this corporeal clod; then in the grave,
Or in some other dismal place, who knows
But I shall die a living death? O thought
Horrid, if true! yet why? it was but breath
790 Of life that sinned; what dies but what had life
And sin? the body properly hath neither.
All of me then shall die: let this appease
The doubt, since human reach no further knows.
For though the Lord of all be infinite,
795 Is his wrath also? be it, man is not so,
But mortal doomed. How can he exercise
Wrath without end on man whom death must end?
Can he make deathless death? that were to make
Strange contradiction, which to God himself
800 Impossible is held, as argument
Of weakness, not of power. Will he draw out,
For anger's sake, finite to infinite
In punished man, to satisfy his rigour
Satisfied never? that were to extend
805 His sentence beyond dust and Nature's law,
By which all causes else according still
To the reception of their matter act,
Not to th' extent of their own sphere. But say
That death be not one stroke, as I supposed,
810 Bereaving sense, but endless misery
From this day onward, which I feel begun
Both in me, and without me, and so last
To perpetuity; ay me, that fear
Comes thund'ring back with dreadful revolution

815   On my defenceless head; both Death and I
     Am found eternal, and incorporate both,
     Nor I on my part single; in me all
     Posterity stands cursed. Fair patrimony
     That I must leave ye, sons; O were I able
820   To waste it all myself, and leave ye none!
     So disinherited how would ye bless
     Me now your curse! Ah, why should all mankind
     For one man's fault thus guiltless be condemned,
     If guiltless? But from me what can proceed,
825   But all corrupt, both mind and will depraved,
     Not to do only, but to will the same
     With me? how can they then acquitted stand
     In sight of God? Him after all disputes
     Forced I absolve: all my evasions vain
830   And reasonings, though through mazes, lead me still
     But to my own conviction: first and last
     On me, me only, as the source and spring
     Of all corruption, all the blame lights due;
     So might the wrath. Fond wish! couldst thou support
835   That burden heavier than the earth to bear,
     Than all the world much heavier, though divided
     With that bad woman? Thus what thou desir'st,
     And what thou fear'st, alike destroys all hope
     Of refuge, and concludes thee miserable
840   Beyond all past example and future,
     To Satan only like both crime and doom.
     O conscience, into what abyss of fears
     And horrors hast thou driv'n me; out of which
     I find no way, from deep to deeper plunged!
845   Thus Adam to himself lamented loud
     Through the still night, not now, as ere man fell,
     Wholesome and cool, and mild, but with black air
     Accompanied, with damps and dreadful gloom,
     Which to his evil conscience represented
850   All things with double terror: on the ground
     Outstretched he lay, on the cold ground, and oft
     Cursed his creation, Death as oft accused
     Of tardy execution, since denounced

The day of his offence. Why comes not Death,
855 Said he, with one thrice ácceptáble stroke
To end me? Shall Truth fail to keep her word,
Justice divine not hasten to be just?
But Death comes not at call, Justice divine
Mends not her slowest pace for prayers or cries.
860 O woods, O fountains, hillocks, dales and bow'rs,
With other echo late I taught your shades
To answer, and resound far other song.
Whom thus afflicted when sad Eve beheld,
Desolate where she sat, approaching nigh,
865 Soft words to his fierce passion she assayed:
But her with stern regard he thus repelled.
　　Out of my sight, thou serpent, that name best
Befits thee with him leagued, thyself as false
And hateful; nothing wants, but that thy shape,
870 Like his, and colour serpentine may show
Thy inward fraud, to warn all creatures from thee
Henceforth; lest that too Heav'nly form, pretended
To Hellish falsehood, snare them. But for thee
I had persisted happy, had not thy pride
875 And wand'ring vanity, when least was safe,
Rejected my forewarning, and disdained
Not to be trusted, longing to be seen
Though by the Devil himself, him overweening
To overreach, but with the serpent meeting
880 Fooled and beguiled; by him thou, I by thee,
To trust thee from my side, imagined wise,
Constant, mature, proof against all assaults,
And understood not all was but a show
Rather than solid virtue, all but a rib
885 Crookèd by nature, bent, as now appears,
More to the part siníster from me drawn,
Well if thrown out, as supernumerary
To my just number found. O why did God,
Creator wise, that peopled highest Heav'n
890 With Spirits masculine, create at last
This novelty on earth, this fair defect
Of nature, and not fill the world at once

With men as angels without feminine,
Or find some other way to generate
895   Mankind? this mischief had not then befall'n,
And more that shall befall, innumerable
Disturbances on earth through female snares,
And strait conjunction with this sex: for either
He never shall find out fit mate, but such
900   As some misfortune brings him, or mistake,
Or whom he wishes most shall seldom gain
Through her perverseness, but shall see her gained
By a far worse, or if she love, withheld
By parents, or his happiest choice too late
905   Shall meet, already linked and wedlock-bound
To a fell adversary, his hate or shame:
Which infinite calamity shall cause
To human life, and household peace confound.
    He added not, and from her turned, but Eve
910   Not so repulsed, with tears that ceased not flowing,
And tresses all disordered, at his feet
Fell humble, and embracing them, besought
His peace, and thus proceeded in her plaint.
    Forsake me not thus, Adam, witness Heav'n
915   What love sincere, and reverence in my heart
I bear thee, and unweeting have offended,
Unhappily deceived; thy suppliant
I beg, and clasp thy knees; bereave me not,
Whereon I live, thy gentle looks, thy aid,
920   Thy counsel in this uttermost distress,
My only strength and stay: forlorn of thee,
Whither shall I betake me, where subsist?
While yet we live, scarce one short hour perhaps,
Between us two let there be peace, both joining,
925   As joined in injuries, one enmity
Against a foe by doom express assigned us,
That cruel serpent: on me exercise not
Thy hatred for this misery befall'n,
On me already lost, me than thyself
930   More miserable; both have sinned, but thou
Against God only, I against God and thee,

And to the place of judgement will return,
There with my cries importune Heaven, that all
The sentence from thy head removed may light
935 On me, sole cause to thee of all this woe,
Me me only just object of his ire.
     She ended weeping, and her lowly plight,
Immovable till peace obtained from fault
Acknowledged and deplored, in Adam wrought
940 Commiseration; soon his heart relented
Towards her, his life so late and sole delight,
Now at his feet submissive in distress,
Creature so fair his reconcilement seeking,
His counsel whom she had displeased, his aid;
945 As one disarmed, his anger all he lost,
And thus with peaceful words upraised her soon.
     Unwary, and too desirous, as before,
So now of what thou know'st not, who desir'st
The punishment all on thyself; alas,
950 Bear thine own first, ill able to sustain
His full wrath whose thou feel'st as yet least part,
And my displeasure bear'st so ill. If prayers
Could alter high decrees, I to that place
Would speed before thee, and be louder heard,
955 That on my head all might be visited,
Thy frailty and infirmer sex forgiv'n,
To me committed and by me exposed.
But rise, let us no more contend, nor blame
Each other, blamed enough elsewhere, but strive
960 In offices of love, how we may light'n
Each other's burden in our share of woe;
Since this day's death denounced, if aught I see,
Will prove no sudden, but a slow-paced evil,
A long day's dying to augment our pain,
965 And to our seed (O hapless seed!) derived.
     To whom thus Eve, recovering heart, replied.
Adam, by sad experiment I know
How little weight my words with thee can find,
Found so erroneous, thence by just event
970 Found so unfortunate; nevertheless,

Restored by thee, vile as I am, to place
Of new acceptance, hopeful to regain
Thy love, the sole contentment of my heart,
Living or dying, from thee I will not hide
975 What thoughts in my unquiet breast are ris'n,
Tending to some relief of our extremes,
Or end, though sharp and sad, yet tolerable,
As in our evils, and of easier choice.
If care of our descent perplex us most,
980 Which must be born to certain woe, devoured
By Death at last, and miserable it is
To be to others cause of misery,
Our own begotten, and of our loins to bring
Into this cursèd world a woeful race,
985 That after wretched life must be at last
Food for so foul a monster, in thy power
It lies, yet ere conception to prevent
The race unblest, to being yet unbegot.
Childless thou art, childless remain:
990 So Death shall be deceived his glut, and with us two
Be forced to satisfy his rav'nous maw.
But if thou judge it hard and difficult,
Conversing, looking, loving, to abstain
From love's due rites, nuptial embraces sweet,
995 And with desire to languish without hope,
Before the present object languishing
With like desire, which would be misery
And torment less than none of what we dread,
Then both ourselves and seed at once to free
1000 From what we fear for both, let us make short,
Let us seek Death, or he not found, supply
With our own hands his office on ourselves;
Why stand we longer shivering under fears,
That show no end but death, and have the power,
1005 Of many ways to die the shortest choosing,
Destruction with destruction to destroy.
    She ended here, or vehement despair
Broke off the rest; so much of death her thoughts
Had entertained, as dyed her cheeks with pale.

1010 But Adam with such counsel nothing swayed,
To better hopes his more attentive mind
Labouring had raised, and thus to Eve replied.
        Eve, thy contempt of life and pleasure seems
To argue in thee something more sublime
1015 And excellent than what thy mind contemns;
But self-destruction therefore sought, refutes
That excellence thought in thee, and implies,
Not thy contempt, but anguish and regret
For loss of life and pleasure overloved.
1020 Or if thou covet death, as utmost end
Of misery, so thinking to evade
The penalty pronounced, doubt not but God
Hath wiselier armed his vengeful ire than so
To be forestalled; much more I fear lest death
1025 So snatched will not exempt us from the pain
We are by doom to pay; rather such acts
Of contumácy will provoke the Highest
To make death in us live: then let us seek
Some safer resolution, which methinks
1030 I have in view, calling to mind with heed
Part of our sentence, that thy seed shall bruise
The serpent's head; piteous amends, unless
Be meant, whom I conjecture, our grand Foe
Satan, who in the serpent hath contrived
1035 Against us this deceit: to crush his head
Would be revenge indeed; which will be lost
By death brought on ourselves, or childless days
Resolved, as thou proposest; so our Foe
Shall 'scape his punishment ordained, and we
1040 Instead shall double ours upon our heads.
No more be mentioned then of violence
Against ourselves, and wilful barrenness,
That cuts us off from hope, and savours only
Rancour and pride, impatience and despite,
1045 Reluctance against God and his just yoke
Laid on our necks. Remember with what mild
And gracious temper he both heard and judged
Without wrath or reviling; we expected

Immediate dissolution, which we thought
1050 Was meant by death that day, when lo, to thee
Pains only in child-bearing were foretold,
And bringing forth, soon recompensed with joy,
Fruit of thy womb: on me the curse aslope
Glanced on the ground; with labour I must earn
1055 My bread; what harm? Idleness had been worse;
My labour will sustain me; and lest cold
Or heat should injure us, his timely care
Hath unbesought provided, and his hands
Clothed us unworthy, pitying while he judged;
1060 How much more, if we pray him, will his ear
Be open, and his heart to pity incline,
And teach us further by what means to shun
Th' inclement seasons, rain, ice, hail and snow,
Which now the sky with various face begins
1065 To show us in this mountain, while the winds
Blow moist and keen, shattering the graceful locks
Of these fair spreading trees; which bids us seek
Some better shroud, some better warmth to cherish
Our limbs benumbed, ere this diurnal star
1070 Leave cold the night, how we his gathered beams
Reflected, may with matter sere foment,
Or by collision of two bodies grind
The air attrite to fire, as late the clouds
Justling or pushed with winds rude in their shock
1075 Tine the slant lightning, whose thwart flame driv'n down
Kindles the gummy bark of fir or pine,
And sends a comfortable heat from far,
Which might supply the sun: such fire to use,
And what may else be remedy or cure
1080 To evils which our own misdeeds have wrought,
He will instruct us praying, and of grace
Beseeching him, so as we need not fear
To pass commodiously this life, sustained
By him with many comforts, till we end
1085 In dust, our final rest and native home.
What better can we do, than to the place
Repairing where he judged us, prostrate fall

Before him reverent, and there confess
Humbly our faults, and pardon beg, with tears
1090 Watering the ground, and with our sighs the air
Frequenting, sent from hearts contrite, in sign
Of sorrow unfeigned, and humiliation meek.
Undoubtedly he will relent and turn
From his displeasure; in whose look serene,
1095 When angry most he seemed and most severe,
What else but favour, grace, and mercy shone?
     So spake our father penitent, nor Eve
Felt less remorse: they forthwith to the place
Repairing where he judged them prostrate fell
1100 Before him reverent, and both confessed
Humbly their faults, and pardon begged, with tears
Watering the ground, and with their sighs the air
Frequenting, sent from hearts contrite, in sign
Of sorrow unfeigned, and humiliation meek.

BOOK XI

The Argument

The Son of God presents to his Father the prayers of our
first parents now repenting, and intercedes for them: God
accepts them, but declares that they must no longer abide in
Paradise; sends Michael with a band of Cherubim to dispossess
5   them; but first to reveal to Adam future things: Michael's
coming down. Adam shows to Eve certain ominous signs; he
discerns Michael's approach, goes out to meet him: the angel
denounces their departure. Eve's lamentation. Adam pleads,
but submits: the angel leads him up to a high hill, sets before
10   him in vision what shall happen till the Flood.

Thus they in lowliest plight repentant stood
Praying, for from the mercy-seat above
Prevenient grace descending had removed
The stony from their hearts, and made new flesh
5   Regenerate grow instead, that sighs now breathed
Unutterable, which the spirit of prayer
Inspired, and winged for Heav'n with speedier flight
Than loudest oratory: yet their port
Not of mean suitors, nor important less
10   Seemed their petition, than when th' ancient pair
In fables old, less ancient yet than these,
Deucalion and chaste Pyrrha to restore
The race of mankind drowned, before the shrine
Of Themis stood devout. To Heav'n their prayers
15   Flew up, nor missed the way, by envious winds
Blown vagabond or frustrate: in they passed
Dimensionless through Heav'nly doors; then clad
With incense, where the golden altar fumed,
By their great Intercessor, came in sight
20   Before the Father's throne: them the glad Son

Presenting, thus to intercede began.
   See Father, what first fruits on earth are sprung
From thy implanted grace in man, these sighs
And prayers, which in this golden censer, mixed
With incense, I thy priest before thee bring.
Fruits of more pleasing savour from thy seed
Sown with contrition in his heart, than those
Which his own hand manuring all the trees
Of Paradise could have produced, ere fall'n
From innocence. Now therefore bend thine ear
To supplication, hear his sighs though mute;
Unskilful with what words to pray, let me
Interpret for him, me his advocate
And propitiation, all his works on me
Good or not good ingraft; my merit those
Shall perfect, and for these my death shall pay.
Accept me, and in me from these receive
The smell of peace toward mankind, let him live
Before thee reconciled, at least his days
Numbered, though sad, till death, his doom (which I
To mitigate thus plead, not to reverse)
To better life shall yield him, where with me
All my redeemed may dwell in joy and bliss,
Made one with me as I with thee am one.
   To whom the Father, without cloud, serene.
All thy request for man, accepted Son,
Obtain, all thy request was my decree:
But longer in that Paradise to dwell,
The law I gave to Nature him forbids:
Those pure immortal elements that know
No gross, no unharmonious mixture foul,
Eject him tainted now, and purge him off
As a distemper, gross to air as gross,
And mortal food, as may dispose him best
For dissolution wrought by sin, that first
Distempered all things, and of incorrupt
Corrupted. I at first with two fair gifts
Created him endowed, with happiness
And immortality: that fondly lost,

60 This other served but to eternize woe;
    Till I provided death; so death becomes
    His final remedy, and after life
    Tried in sharp tribulation, and refined
    By faith and faithful works, to second life,
65 Waked in the renovation of the just,
    Resigns him up with heav'n and earth renewed.
    But let us call to synod all the blest
    Through Heav'n's wide bounds; from them I will not hide
    My judgements, how with mankind I proceed,
70 As how with peccant angels late they saw;
    And in their state, though firm, stood more confirmed.
        He ended, and the Son gave signal high
    To the bright minister that watched; he blew
    His trumpet, heard in Oreb since perhaps
75 When God descended, and perhaps once more
    To sound at general doom. Th' angelic blast
    Filled all the regions: from their blissful bow'rs
    Of amarantine shade, fountain or spring,
    By the waters of life, where'er they sat
80 In fellowships of joy: the sons of light
    Hasted, resorting to the summons high,
    And took their seats; till from his throne supreme
    Th' Almighty thus pronounced his sov'reign will.
        O sons, like one of us man is become
85 To know both good and evil, since his taste
    Of that defended fruit; but let him boast
    His knowledge of good lost, and evil got,
    Happier, had it sufficed him to have known
    Good by itself, and evil not at all.
90 He sorrows now, repents, and prays contrite,
    My motions in him; longer than they move,
    His heart I know, how variable and vain
    Self-left. Lest therefore his now bolder hand
    Reach also of the Tree of Life, and eat,
95 And live for ever, dream at least to live
    For ever, to remove him I decree,
    And send him from the garden forth to till
    The ground whence he was taken, fitter soil.

Michael, this my behest have thou in charge,
100 Take to thee from among the Cherubim
Thy choice of flaming warriors, lest the Fiend
Or in behalf of man, or to invade
Vacant possession some new trouble raise:
Haste thee, and from the Paradise of God
105 Without remorse drive out the sinful pair,
From hallowed ground th' unholy, and denounce
To them and to their progeny from thence
Perpetual banishment. Yet lest they faint
At the sad sentence rigorously urged,
110 For I behold them softened and with tears
Bewailing their excess, all terror hide.
If patiently thy bidding they obey,
Dismiss them not disconsolate; reveal
To Adam what shall come in future days,
115 As I shall thee enlighten; intermix
My cov'nant in the woman's seed renewed;
So send them forth, though sorrowing, yet in peace:
And on the east side of the garden place,
Where entrance up from Eden easiest climbs,
120 Cherubic watch, and of a sword the flame
Wide waving, all approach far off to fright,
And guard all passage to the Tree of Life:
Lest Paradise a réceptácle prove
To Spirits foul, and all my trees their prey,
125 With whose stol'n fruit man once more to delude.
He ceased; and th' Archangelic Power prepared
For swift descent, with him the cohort bright
Of watchful Cherubim; four faces each
Had, like a double Janus, all their shape
130 Spangled with eyes more numerous than those
Of Argus, and more wakeful than to drowse,
Charmed with Arcadian pipe, the pastoral reed
Of Hermes, or his opiate rod. Meanwhile
To resalute the world with sacred light
135 Leucothea waked, and with fresh dews embalmed
The earth, when Adam and first matron Eve
Had ended now their orisons, and found

Strength added from above, new hope to spring
Out of despair, joy, but with fear yet linked;
140   Which thus to Eve his welcome words renewed.
　　Eve, easily may faith admit, that all
The good which we enjoy from Heav'n descends;
But that from us aught should ascend to Heav'n
So prevalent as to concern the mind
145   Of God high-blest, or to incline his will,
Hard to belief may seem; yet this will prayer,
Or one short sigh of human breath upborne
Ev'n to the seat of God. For since I sought
By prayer th' offended Deity to appease,
150   Kneeled and before him humbled all my heart,
Methought I saw him placable and mild,
Bending his ear; persuasion in me grew
That I was heard with favour; peace returned
Home to my breast, and to my memory
155   His promise, that thy seed shall bruise our Foe;
Which then not minded in dismay, yet now
Assures me that the bitterness of death
Is past, and we shall live. Whence hail to thee,
Eve rightly called, mother of all mankind,
160   Mother of all things living, since by thee
Man is to live, and all things live for man.
　　To whom thus Eve with sad demeanour meek.
Ill worthy I such title should belong
To me transgressor, who for thee ordained
165   A help, became thy snare; to me reproach
Rather belongs, distrust and all dispraise:
But infinite in pardon was my Judge,
That I who first brought death on all, am graced
The source of life; next favourable thou,
170   Who highly thus to entitle me vouchsaf'st,
Far other name deserving. But the field
To labour calls us now with sweat imposed,
Though after sleepless night; for see the Morn,
All unconcerned with our unrest, begins
175   Her rosy progress smiling; let us forth,
I never from thy side henceforth to stray,

Where'er our day's work lies, though now enjoined
Laborious, till day droop; while here we dwell,
What can be toilsome in these pleasant walks?
180   Here let us live, though in fall'n state, content.
　　　So spake, so wished much-humbled Eve, but Fate
Subscribed not; Nature first gave signs, impressed
On bird, beast, air, air suddenly eclipsed
After short blush of morn; nigh in her sight
185   The bird of Jove, stooped from his airy tow'r,
Two birds of gayest plume before him drove:
Down from a hill the beast that reigns in woods,
First hunter then, pursued a gentle brace,
Goodliest of all the forest, hart and hind;
190   Direct to th' eastern gate was bent their flight.
Adam observed, and with his eye the chase
Pursuing, not unmoved to Eve thus spake.
　　　O Eve, some further change awaits us nigh,
Which Heav'n by these mute signs in Nature shows
195   Forerunners of his purpose, or to warn
Us haply too secure of our discharge
From penalty, because from death released
Some days; how long, and what till then our life,
Who knows, or more than this, that we are dust,
200   And thither must return and be no more.
Why else this double object in our sight
Of flight pursued in th' air and o'er the ground
One way the self-same hour? Why in the east
Darkness ere day's mid-course, and morning light
205   More orient in yon western cloud that draws
O'er the blue firmament a radiant white,
And slow descends, with something Heav'nly fraught.
　　　He erred not, for by this the Heav'nly bands
Down from a sky of jasper lighted now
210   In Paradise, and on a hill made halt,
A glorious apparition, had not doubt
And carnal fear that day dimmed Adam's eye.
Not that more glorious, when the angels met
Jacob in Mahanaim, where he saw
215   The field pavilioned with his guardians bright;

Nor that which on the flaming mount appeared
In Dothan, covered with a camp of fire,
Against the Syrian king, who to surprise
One man, assassin-like had levied war,
220 War unproclaimed. The princely hierarch
In their bright stand, there left his powers to seize
Possession of the garden; he alone,
To find where Adam sheltered, took his way,
Not unperceived of Adam, who to Eve,
225 While the great visitant approached, thus spake.
    Eve, now expect great tidings, which perhaps
Of us will soon determine, or impose
New laws to be observed; for I descry
From yonder blazing cloud that veils the hill
230 One of the Heav'nly host, and by his gait
None of the meanest, some great Potentate
Or of the Thrones above, such majesty
Invests him coming; yet not terrible,
That I should fear, nor sociably mild,
235 As Raphael, that I should much confide,
But solemn and sublime, whom not to offend,
With reverence I must meet, and thou retire.
He ended; and th' Archangel soon drew nigh,
Not in his shape celestial, but as man
240 Clad to meet man; over his lucid arms
A military vest of purple flowed
Livelier than Meliboean, or the grain
Of Sarra, worn by kings and heroes old
In time of truce; Iris had dipped the woof;
245 His starry helm unbuckled showed him prime
In manhood where youth ended; by his side
As in a glistering zodiac hung the sword,
Satan's dire dread, and in his hand the spear.
Adam bowed low; he kingly from his state
250 Inclined not, but his coming thus declared.
    Adam, Heav'n's high behest no preface needs:
Sufficient that thy prayers are heard, and Death,
Then due by sentence when thou didst transgress,
Defeated of his seizure many days

255 Giv'n thee of grace, wherein thou may'st repent,
And one bad act with many deeds well done
May'st cover: well may then thy Lord appeased
Redeem thee quite from Death's rapacious claim;
But longer in this Paradise to dwell
260 Permits not; to remove thee I am come,
And send thee from the garden forth to till
The ground whence thou wast taken, fitter soil.
        He added not, for Adam at the news
Heart-strook with chilling gripe of sorrow stood,
265 That all his senses bound; Eve, who unseen
Yet all had heard, with audible lament
Discovered soon the place of her retire.
        O unexpected stroke, worse than of Death!
Must I thus leave thee Paradise? thus leave
270 Thee native soil, these happy walks and shades,
Fit haunt of gods? where I had hope to spend,
Quiet though sad, the respite of that day
That must be mortal to us both. O flow'rs,
That never will in other climate grow,
275 My early visitation, and my last
At ev'n, which I bred up with tender hand
From the first op'ning bud, and gave ye names,
Who now shall rear ye to the sun, or rank
Your tribes, and water from th' ambrosial fount?
280 Thee lastly nuptial bower, by me adorned
With what to sight or smell was sweet; from thee
How shall I part, and whither wander down
Into a lower world, to this obscure
And wild, how shall we breathe in other air
285 Less pure, accustomed to immortal fruits?
        Whom thus the angel interrupted mild.
Lament not Eve, but patiently resign
What justly thou hast lost; nor set thy heart,
Thus over-fond, on that which is not thine;
290 Thy going is not lonely, with thee goes
Thy husband, him to follow thou art bound;
Where he abides, think there thy native soil.
        Adam by this from the cold sudden damp

Recovering, and his scattered spirits returned,
295   To Michael thus his humble words addressed.
     Celestial, whether among the Thrones, or named
Of them the highest, for such of shape may seem
Prince above princes, gently hast thou told
Thy message, which might else in telling wound,
300   And in performing end us; what besides
Of sorrow and dejection and despair
Our frailty can sustain, thy tidings bring,
Departure from this happy place, our sweet
Recess, and only consolation left
305   Familiar to our eyes, all places else
Inhospitable appear and desolate,
Nor knowing us nor known: and if by prayer
Incessant I could hope to change the will
Of him who all things can, I would not cease
310   To weary him with my assiduous cries:
But prayer against his absolute decree
No more avails than breath against the wind,
Blown stifling back on him that breathes it forth:
Therefore to his great bidding I submit.
315   This most afflicts me, that departing hence,
As from his face I shall be hid, deprived
His blessèd count'nance; here I could frequent,
With worship, place by place where he vouchsafed
Presence divine, and to my sons relate;
320   On this mount he appeared, under this tree
Stood visible, among these pines his voice
I heard, here with him at this fountain talked:
So many grateful altars I would rear
Of grassy turf, and pile up every stone
325   Of lustre from the brook, in memory,
Or monument to ages, and thereon
Offer sweet smelling gums and fruits and flow'rs:
In yonder nether world where shall I seek
His bright appearances, or footstep trace?
330   For though I fled him angry, yet recalled
To life prolonged and promised race, I now
Gladly behold though but his utmost skirts

Of glory, and far off his steps adore.
　　To whom thus Michael with regard benign.
335　Adam, thou know'st Heav'n his, and all the earth,
Not this rock only; his omnipresence fills
Land, sea, and air, and every kind that lives,
Fomented by his virtual power and warmed:
All th' earth he gave thee to possess and rule,
340　No déspicáble gift; surmise not then
His presence to these narrow bounds confined
Of Paradise or Eden: this had been
Perhaps thy capital seat, from whence had spread
All generations, and had hither come
345　From all the ends of th' earth, to celebrate
And reverence thee their great progenitor.
But this pre-eminence thou hast lost, brought down
To dwell on even ground now with thy sons:
Yet doubt not but in valley and in plain
350　God is as here, and will be found alike
Present, and of his presence many a sign
Still following thee, still compassing thee round
With goodness and paternal love, his face
Express, and of his steps the track divine.
355　Which that thou may'st believe, and be confirmed
Ere thou from hence depart, know I am sent
To show thee what shall come in future days
To thee and to thy offspring; good with bad
Expect to hear, supernal grace contending
360　With sinfulness of men; thereby to learn
True patience, and to temper joy with fear
And pious sorrow, equally inured
By moderation either state to bear,
Prosperous or adverse: so shalt thou lead
365　Safest thy life, and best prepared endure
Thy mortal passage when it comes. Ascend
This hill; let Eve (for I have drenched her eyes)
Here sleep below while thou to foresight wak'st,
As once thou slept'st, while she to life was formed.
370　　　To whom thus Adam gratefully replied.
Ascend, I follow thee, safe guide, the path

Thou lead'st me, and to the hand of Heav'n submit,
However chast'ning, to the evil turn
My obvious breast, arming to overcome
375   By suffering, and earn rest from labour won,
If so I may attain. So both ascend
In the visions of God; it was a hill
Of Paradise the highest, from whose top
The hemisphere of earth in clearest ken
380   Stretched out to the amplest reach of prospect lay.
Not higher that hill nor wider looking round,
Whereon for different cause the Tempter set
Our second Adam in the wilderness,
To show him all earth's kingdoms and their glory.
385   His eye might there command wherever stood
City of old or modern fame, the seat
Of mightiest empire, from the destined walls
Of Cambalu, seat of Cathayan Khan
And Samarkand by Oxus, Temir's throne,
390   To Paquin of Sinaean kings, and thence
To Agra and Lahore of Great Mogul
Down to the golden Chersonese, or where
The Persian in Ecbatan sat, or since
In Hispahan, or where the Russian Czar
395   In Moscow, or the Sultan in Bizance,
Turkéstan-born; nor could his eye not ken
Th' empire of Negus to his utmost port
Ercoco and the less marítime kings
Mombaza, and Quiloa, and Melind,
400   And Sofala thought Ophir, to the realm
Of Congo, and Angola farthest south;
Or thence from Niger flood to Atlas mount
The kingdoms of Almansor, Fez and Sus,
Morocco and Algiers, and Tremisen;
405   On Europe thence, and where Rome was to sway
The world: in spirit perhaps he also saw
Rich Mexico the seat of Motezume,
And Cusco in Peru, the richer seat
Of Atabalipa, and yet unspoiled
410   Guiana, whose great city Geryon's sons

Call El Dorado: but to nobler sights
Michael from Adam's eyes the film removed
Which that false fruit that promised clearer sight
Had bred; then purged with euphrasy and rue
415 The visual nerve, for he had much to see;
And from the Well of Life three drops instilled.
So deep the power of these ingredients pierced,
Even to the inmost seat of mental sight,
That Adam now enforced to close his eyes,
420 Sunk down and all his spirits became entranced:
But him the gentle angel by the hand
Soon raised, and his attention thus recalled.
    Adam, now ope thine eyes, and first behold
Th' effects which thy original crime hath wrought
425 In some to spring from thee, who never touched
Th' excepted tree, nor with the snake conspired,
Nor sinned thy sin, yet from that sin derive
Corruption to bring forth more violent deeds.
    His eyes he opened, and beheld a field,
430 Part arable and tilth, whereon were sheaves
New reaped, the other part sheep-walks and folds;
I' th' midst an altar as the landmark stood
Rustic, of grassy sward; thither anon
A sweaty reaper from his tillage brought
435 First fruits, the green ear, and the yellow sheaf,
Unculled, as came to hand; a shepherd next
More meek came with the firstlings of his flock
Choicest and best; then sacrificing, laid
The inwards and their fat, with incense strewed,
440 On the cleft wood, and all due rites performed.
His off'ring soon propitious fire from heav'n
Consumed with nimble glance, and grateful steam;
The other's not, for his was not sincere;
Whereat he inly raged, and as they talked,
445 Smote him into the midriff with a stone
That beat out life; he fell, and deadly pale
Groaned out his soul with gushing blood effused.
Much at that sight was Adam in his heart
Dismayed, and thus in haste to th' angel cried.

450   O teacher, some great mischief hath befall'n
To that meek man, who well had sacrificed;
Is piety thus and pure devotion paid?
    T' whom Michael thus, he also moved, replied.
These two are brethren, Adam, and to come
455 Out of thy loins; th' unjust the just hath slain,
For envy that his brother's offering found
From Heav'n acceptance; but the bloody fact
Will be avenged, and th' other's faith approved
Lose no reward, though here thou see him die,
460 Rolling in dust and gore. To which our sire.
    Alas, both for the deed and for the cause!
But have I now seen death? Is this the way
I must return to native dust? O sight
Of terror, foul and ugly to behold,
465 Horrid to think, how horrible to feel!
    To whom thus Michaël. Death thou hast seen
In his first shape on man; but many shapes
Of death, and many are the ways that lead
To his grim cave, all dismal; yet to sense
470 More terrible at th' entrance than within.
Some, as thou saw'st, by violent stroke shall die,
By fire, flood, famine; by intemperance more
In meats and drinks, which on the earth shall bring
Diseases dire, of which a monstrous crew
475 Before thee shall appear; that thou may'st know
What misery th' inabstinence of Eve
Shall bring on men. Immediately a place
Before his eyes appeared, sad, noisome, dark;
A lazar-house it seemed, wherein were laid
480 Numbers of all diseased, all maladies
Of ghastly spasm, or racking torture, qualms
Of heart-sick agony, all feverous kinds,
Convulsions, epilepsies, fierce catarrhs,
Intestine stone and ulcer, colic pangs,
485 Demoniac frenzy, moping melancholy
And moon-struck madness, pining atrophy,
Marasmus, and wide-wasting pestilence,
Dropsies, and asthmas, and joint-racking rheums.

Dire was the tossing, deep the groans; Despair
490 Tended the sick busiest from couch to couch;
And over them triumphant Death his dart
Shook, but delayed to strike, though oft invoked
With vows, as their chief good, and final hope.
Sight so deform what heart of rock could long
495 Dry-eyed behold? Adam could not, but wept
Though not of woman born; compassion quelled
His best of man, and gave him up to tears
A space, till firmer thoughts restrained excess,
And scarce recovering words his plaint renewed.

500 O miserable mankind, to what fall
Degraded, to what wretched state reserved!
Better end here unborn. Why is life giv'n
To be thus wrested from us? rather why
Obtruded on us thus? who if we knew
505 What we receive, would either not accept
Life offered, or soon beg to lay it down,
Glad to be so dismissed in peace. Can thus
Th' image of God in man created once
So goodly and erect, though faulty since,
510 To such unsightly sufferings be debased
Under inhuman pains? Why should not man,
Retaining still divine similitude
In part, from such deformities be free,
And for his Maker's image sake exempt?

515 Their Maker's image, answered Michael, then
Forsook them, when themselves they vilified
To serve ungoverned appetite, and took
His image whom they served, a brutish vice,
Inductive mainly to the sin of Eve.
520 Therefore so abject is their punishment,
Disfiguring not God's likeness, but their own,
Or if his likeness, by themselves defaced
While they pervert pure Nature's healthful rules
To loathsome sickness, worthily, since they
525 God's image did not reverence in themselves.

I yield it just, said Adam, and submit.
But is there yet no other way, besides

These painful passages, how we may come
To death, and mix with our connatural dust?
530   There is, said Michael, if thou well observe
The rule of *Not too much*, by temperance taught
In what thou eat'st and drink'st, seeking from thence
Due nourishment, not gluttonous delight,
Till many years over thy head return:
535 So may'st thou live, till like ripe fruit thou drop
Into thy mother's lap, or be with ease
Gathered, not harshly plucked, for death mature:
This is old age; but then thou must outlive
Thy youth, thy strength, thy beauty, which will change
540 To withered weak and grey; thy senses then
Obtuse, all taste of pleasure must forgo,
To what thou hast, and for the air of youth
Hopeful and cheerful, in thy blood will reign
A melancholy damp of cold and dry
545 To weigh thy spirits down, and last consume
The balm of life. To whom our ancestor.
    Henceforth I fly not death, nor would prolong
Life much, bent rather how I may be quit
Fairest and easiest of this cumbrous charge,
550 Which I must keep till my appointed day
Of rend'ring up, and patiently attend
My dissolution. Michaël replied,
    Nor love thy life, nor hate; but what thou liv'st
Live well, how long or short permit to Heav'n:
555 And now prepare thee for another sight.
    He looked and saw a spacious plain, whereon
Were tents of various hue; by some were herds
Of cattle grazing: others, whence the sound
Of instruments that made melodious chime
560 Was heard, of harp and organ; and who moved
Their stops and chords was seen: his volant touch
Instinct through all proportions low and high
Fled and pursued transverse the resonant fugue.
In other part stood one who at the forge
565 Labouring, two massy clods of iron and brass
Had melted (whether found where casual fire

Had wasted woods on mountain or in vale,
Down to the veins of earth, thence gliding hot
To some cave's mouth, or whether washed by stream
570   From underground); the liquid ore he drained
Into fit moulds prepared; from which he formed
First his own tools; then, what might else be wrought
Fusile or grav'n in metal. After these,
But on the hither side a different sort
575   From the high neighbouring hills, which was their seat,
Down to the plain descended: by their guise
Just men they seemed, and all their study bent
To worship God aright, and know his works
Not hid, nor those things last which might preserve
580   Freedom and peace to men: they on the plain
Long had not walked, when from the tents behold
A bevy of fair women, richly gay
In gems and wanton dress; to the harp they sung
Soft amorous ditties, and in dance came on:
585   The men though grave, eyed them, and let their eyes
Rove without rein, till in the amorous net
Fast caught, they liked, and each his liking chose;
And now of love they treat till th' ev'ning star
Love's harbinger appeared; then all in heat
590   They light the nuptial torch, and bid invoke
Hymen, then first to marriage rites invoked;
With feast and music all the tents resound.
Such happy interview and fair event
Of love and youth not lost, songs, garlands, flow'rs,
595   And charming symphonies attached the heart
Of Adam, soon inclined to admit delight,
The bent of nature; which he thus expressed.
     True opener of mine eyes, prime angel blest,
Much better seems this vision, and more hope
600   Of peaceful days portends, than those two past;
Those were of hate and death, or pain much worse,
Here nature seems fulfilled in all her ends.
     To whom thus Michael. Judge not what is best
By pleasure, though to nature seeming meet,
605   Created, as thou art, to nobler end

Holy and pure, conformity divine.
Those tents thou saw'st so pleasant, were the tents
Of wickedness, wherein shall dwell his race
Who slew his brother; studious they appear
610 Of arts that polish life, inventors rare,
Unmindful of their Maker, though his Spirit
Taught them, but they his gifts acknowledged none.
Yet they a beauteous offspring shall beget;
For that fair female troop thou saw'st, that seemed
615 Of goddesses, so blithe, so smooth, so gay,
Yet empty of all good wherein consists
Woman's domestic honour and chief praise;
Bred only and completed to the taste
Of lustful appetence, to sing, to dance,
620 To dress, and troll the tongue, and roll the eye.
To these that sober race of men whose lives
Religious titled them the sons of God,
Shall yield up all their virtue, all their fame
Ignobly, to the trains and to the smiles
625 Of these fair atheists, and now swim in joy,
(Erelong to swim at large) and laugh; for which
The world erelong a world of tears must weep.
        To whom thus Adam of short joy bereft.
O pity and shame, that they who to live well
630 Entered so fair, should turn aside to tread
Paths indirect, or in the mid-way faint!
But still I see the tenor of man's woe
Holds on the same, from woman to begin.
        From man's effeminate slackness it begins,
635 Said th' angel, who should better hold his place
By wisdom, and superior gifts received.
But now prepare thee for another scene.
        He looked and saw wide territory spread
Before him, towns, and rural works between,
640 Cities of men with lofty gates and tow'rs,
Concourse in arms, fierce faces threat'ning war,
Giants of mighty bone, and bold emprise;
Part wield their arms, part curb the foaming steed,
Single or in array of battle ranged

645   Both horse and foot, nor idly must'ring stood;
     One way a band select from forage drives
     A herd of beeves, fair oxen and fair kine
     From a fat meadow ground; or fleecy flock,
     Ewes and their bleating lambs over the plain,
650   Their booty; scarce with life the shepherds fly,
     But call in aid, which makes a bloody fray;
     With cruel tournament the squadrons join;
     Where cattle pastured late, now scattered lies
     With carcasses and arms th' ensanguined field
655   Deserted: others to a city strong
     Lay siege, encamped; by battery, scale, and mine,
     Assaulting; others from the wall defend
     With dart and jav'lin, stones and sulphurous fire;
     On each hand slaughter and gigantic deeds.
660   In other part the sceptred heralds call
     To council in the city gates: anon
     Grey-headed men and grave, with warriors mixed,
     Assemble, and harangues are heard, but soon
     In factious opposition, till at last
665   Of middle age one rising, eminent
     In wise deport, spake much of right and wrong,
     Of justice, of religion, truth and peace,
     And judgement from above: him old and young
     Exploded, and had seized with violent hands,
670   Had not a cloud descending snatched him thence
     Unseen amid the throng: so violence
     Proceeded, and oppression, and sword-law
     Through all the plain, and refuge none was found.
     Adam was all in tears, and to his guide
675   Lamenting turned full sad; O what are these,
     Death's ministers, not men, who thus deal death
     Inhumanly to men, and multiply
     Ten thousandfold the sin of him who slew
     His brother; for of whom such massacre
680   Make they but of their brethren, men of men?
     But who was that just man, whom had not Heav'n
     Rescued, had in his righteousness been lost?
        To whom thus Michael. These are the product

Of those ill-mated marriages thou saw'st:
685   Where good with bad were matched, who of themselves
Abhor to join; and by imprudence mixed,
Produce prodigious births of body or mind.
Such were these giants, men of high renown;
For in those days might only shall be admired,
690   And valour and heroic virtue called;
To overcome in battle, and subdue
Nations, and bring home spoils with infinite
Manslaughter, shall be held the highest pitch
Of human glory, and for glory done
695   Of triumph, to be styled great conquerors,
Patrons of mankind, gods, and sons of gods,
Destroyers rightlier called and plagues of men.
Thus fame shall be achieved, renown on earth,
And what most merits fame in silence hid.
700   But he the seventh from thee, whom thou beheld'st
The only righteous in a world perverse,
And therefore hated, therefore so beset
With foes for daring single to be just,
And utter odious truth, that God would come
705   To judge them with his saints: him the Most High
Rapt in a balmy cloud with wingèd steeds
Did, as thou saw'st, receive to walk with God
High in salvation and the climes of bliss,
Exempt from death, to show thee what reward
710   Awaits the good, the rest what punishment;
Which now direct thine eyes and soon behold.
   He looked, and saw the face of things quite changed;
The brazen throat of war had ceased to roar,
All now was turned to jollity and game,
715   To luxury and riot, feast and dance,
Marrying or prostituting, as befell,
Rape or adultery, where passing fair
Allured them; thence from cups to civil broils.
At length a reverend sire among them came,
720   And of their doings great dislike declared,
And testified against their ways; he oft
Frequented their assemblies, whereso met,

Triumphs or festivals, and to them preached
Conversion and repentance, as to souls
725   In prison under judgements imminent:
But all in vain: which when he saw, he ceased
Contending, and removed his tents far off;
Then from the mountain hewing timber tall,
Began to build a vessel of huge bulk,
730   Measured by cubit, length, and breadth, and heighth,
Smeared round with pitch, and in the side a door
Contrived, and of provisions laid in large
For man and beast: when lo a wonder strange!
Of every beast, and bird, and insect small
735   Came sevens, and pairs, and entered in, as taught
Their order: last the sire, and his three sons
With their four wives; and God made fast the door.
Meanwhile the south wind rose, and with black wings
Wide hovering, all the clouds together drove
740   From under heav'n; the hills to their supply
Vapour, and exhalation dusk and moist,
Sent up amain; and now the thickened sky
Like a dark ceiling stood; down rushed the rain
Impetuous, and continued till the earth
745   No more was seen; the floating vessel swum
Uplifted; and secure with beakèd prow
Rode tilting o'er the waves, all dwellings else
Flood overwhelmed, and them with all their pomp
Deep under water rolled; sea covered sea,
750   Sea without shore; and in their palaces
Where luxury late reigned, sea-monsters whelped
And stabled; of mankind, so numerous late,
All left, in one small bottom swum embarked.
How didst thou grieve then, Adam, to behold
755   The end of all thy offspring, end so sad,
Depopulation; thee another flood,
Of tears and sorrow a flood thee also drowned,
And sunk thee as thy sons; till gently reared
By th' angel, on thy feet thou stood'st at last,
760   Though comfortless, as when a father mourns
His children, all in view destroyed at once;

And scarce to th' angel utter'dst thus thy plaint.
   O visions ill foreseen! better had I
Lived ignorant of future, so had borne
765 My part of evil only, each day's lot
Enough to bear; those now, that were dispensed
The burd'n of many ages, on me light
At once, by my foreknowledge gaining birth
Abortive, to torment me ere their being,
770 With thought that they must be. Let no man seek
Henceforth to be foretold what shall befall
Him or his children, evil he may be sure,
Which neither his foreknowing can prevent,
And he the future evil shall no less
775 In apprehension than in substance feel
Grievous to bear: but that care now is past,
Man is not whom to warn: those few escaped
Famine and anguish will at last consume
Wand'ring that wat'ry desert: I had hope
780 When violence was ceased, and war on earth,
All would have then gone well, peace would have crowned
With length of happy days the race of man;
But I was far deceived; for now I see
Peace to corrupt no less than war to waste.
785 How comes it thus? unfold, celestial guide,
And whether here the race of man will end.
To whom thus Michael. Those whom last thou saw'st
In triumph and luxurious wealth, are they
First seen in acts of prowess eminent
790 And great explóits, but of true virtue void;
Who having spilt much blood, and done much waste
Subduing nations, and achieved thereby
Fame in the world, high titles, and rich prey,
Shall change their course to pleasure, ease, and sloth,
795 Surfeit, and lust, till wantonness and pride
Raise out of friendship hostile deeds in peace.
The conquered also, and enslaved by war
Shall with their freedom lost all virtue lose
And fear of God, from whom their piety feigned
800 In sharp contést of battle found no aid

Against invaders; therefore cooled in zeal
Thenceforth shall practise how to live secure,
Worldly or dissolute, on what their lords
Shall leave them to enjoy; for th' earth shall bear
805   More than enough, that temperance may be tried:
So all shall turn degenerate, all depraved,
Justice and temperance, truth and faith forgot;
One man except, the only son of light
In a dark age, against example good,
810   Against allurement, custom, and a world
Offended; fearless of reproach and scorn,
Or violence, he of their wicked ways
Shall them admonish, and before them set
The paths of righteousness, how much more safe,
815   And full of peace, denouncing wrath to come
On their impenitence; and shall return
Of them derided, but of God observed
The one just man alive; by his command
Shall build a wondrous ark, as thou beheld'st,
820   To save himself and household from amidst
A world devote to universal wrack.
No sooner he with them of man and beast
Select for life shall in the ark be lodged,
And sheltered round, but all the cataracts
825   Of heav'n set open on the earth shall pour
Rain day and night, all fountains of the deep
Broke up, shall heave the ocean to usurp
Beyond all bounds, till inundation rise
Above the highest hills: then shall this mount
830   Of Paradise by might of waves be moved
Out of his place, pushed by the hornèd flood,
With all his verdure spoiled, and trees adrift
Down the great river to the op'ning gulf,
And there take root an island salt and bare,
835   The haunt of seals and orcs, and sea-mews' clang.
To teach thee that God áttribútes to place
No sanctity, if none be thither brought
By men who there frequent, or therein dwell.
And now what further shall ensue, behold.

840　　He looked, and saw the ark hull on the flood,
　　　Which now abated, for the clouds were fled,
　　　Driv'n by a keen north wind, that blowing dry
　　　Wrinkled the face of deluge, as decayed;
　　　And the clear sun on his wide wat'ry glass
845　　Gazed hot, and of the fresh wave largely drew,
　　　As after thirst, which made their flowing shrink
　　　From standing lake to tripping ebb, that stole
　　　With soft foot towards the deep, who now had stopped
　　　His sluices, as the heav'n his windows shut.
850　　The ark no more now floats, but seems on ground
　　　Fast on the top of some high mountain fixed.
　　　And now the tops of hills as rocks appear;
　　　With clamour thence the rapid currents drive
　　　Towards the retreating sea their furious tide.
855　　Forthwith from out the ark a raven flies,
　　　And after him, the surer messenger,
　　　A dove sent forth once and again to spy
　　　Green tree or ground whereon his foot may light;
　　　The second time returning, in his bill
860　　An olive leaf he brings, pacific sign:
　　　Anon dry ground appears, and from his ark
　　　The ancient sire descends with all his train;
　　　Then with uplifted hands, and eyes devout,
　　　Grateful to Heav'n, over his head beholds
865　　A dewy cloud, and in the cloud a bow
　　　Conspicuous with three listed colours gay,
　　　Betok'ning peace from God, and cov'nant new.
　　　Whereat the heart of Adam erst so sad
　　　Greatly rejoiced, and thus his joy broke forth.
870　　　O thou who future things canst represent
　　　As present, Heav'nly instructor, I revive
　　　At this last sight, assured that man shall live
　　　With all the creatures, and their seed preserve.
　　　Far less I now lament for one whole world
875　　Of wicked sons destroyed, than I rejoice
　　　For one man found so perfect and so just,
　　　That God vouchsafes to raise another world
　　　From him, and all his anger to forget.

But say, what mean those coloured streaks in heav'n,
880   Distended as the brow of God appeased,
Or serve they as a flow'ry verge to bind
The fluid skirts of that same wat'ry cloud,
Lest it again dissolve and show'r the earth?
     To whom th' Archangel. Dextrously thou aim'st;
885   So willingly doth God remit his ire,
Though late repenting him of man depraved,
Grieved at his heart, when looking down he saw
The whole earth filled with violence, and all flesh
Corrupting each their way; yet those removed,
890   Such grace shall one just man find in his sight,
That he relents, not to blot out mankind,
And makes a covenant never to destroy
The earth again by flood, nor let the sea
Surpass his bounds, nor rain to drown the world
895   With man therein or beast; but when he brings
Over the earth a cloud, will therein set
His triple-coloured bow, whereon to look
And call to mind his cov'nant: day and night,
Seed time and harvest, heat and hoary frost
900   Shall hold their course, till fire purge all things new,
Both heav'n and earth, wherein the just shall dwell.

BOOK XII

The Argument

The angel Michael continues from the Flood to relate what shall succeed; then, in the mention of Abraham, comes by degrees to explain, who that Seed of the Woman shall be, which was promised Adam and Eve in the Fall; his Incarnation,
5 Death, Resurrection, and Ascension; the state of the Church till his second coming. Adam, greatly satisfied and recomforted by these relations and promises descends the hill with Michael; wakens Eve, who all this while had slept, but with gentle dreams composed to quietness of mind and submission.
10 Michael in either hand leads them out of Paradise, the fiery sword waving behind them, and the Cherubim taking their stations to guard the place.

As one who in his journey baits at noon,
Though bent on speed, so here the Archangel paused
Betwixt the world destroyed and world restored,
If Adam aught perhaps might interpose;
5 Then with transition sweet new speech resumes.
　　Thus thou hast seen one world begin and end;
And man as from a second stock proceed.
Much thou hast yet to see, but I perceive
Thy mortal sight to fail; objects divine
10 Must needs impair and weary human sense:
Henceforth what is to come I will relate;
Thou therefore give due audience, and attend.
This second source of men, while yet but few,
And while the dread of judgement past remains
15 Fresh in their minds, fearing the Deity,
With some regard to what is just and right
Shall lead their lives, and multiply apace,
Labouring the soil, and reaping plenteous crop,

Corn wine and oil; and from the herd or flock,
20 Oft sacrificing bullock, lamb, or kid,
With large wine-offerings poured, and sacred feast,
Shall spend their days in joy unblamed, and dwell
Long time in peace by families and tribes
Under paternal rule; till one shall rise
25 Of proud ambitious heart, who not content
With fair equality, fraternal state,
Will arrogate dominion undeserved
Over his brethren, and quite dispossess
Concord and law of Nature from the earth,
30 Hunting (and men not beasts shall be his game)
With war and hostile snare such as refuse
Subjection to his empire tyrannous:
A mighty hunter thence he shall be styled
Before the Lord, as in despite of Heav'n,
35 Or from Heav'n claiming second sov'reignty;
And from rebellion shall derive his name,
Though of rebellion others he accuse.
He with a crew, whom like ambition joins
With him or under him to tyrannize,
40 Marching from Eden towards the west, shall find
The plain, wherein a black bituminous gurge
Boils out from under ground, the mouth of Hell;
Of brick, and of that stuff they cast to build
A city and tow'r, whose top may reach to Heav'n;
45 And get themselves a name, lest far dispersed
In foreign lands their memory be lost,
Regardless whether good or evil fame.
But God who oft descends to visit men
Unseen, and through their habitations walks
50 To mark their doings, them beholding soon,
Comes down to see their city, ere the tower
Obstruct Heav'n tow'rs, and in derision sets
Upon their tongues a various spirit to raze
Quite out their native language, and instead
55 To sow a jangling noise of words unknown:
Forthwith a hideous gabble rises loud
Among the builders; each to other calls

Not understood, till hoarse, and all in rage,
As mocked they storm; great laughter was in Heav'n
60 And looking down, to see the hubbub strange
And hear the din; thus was the building left
Ridiculous, and the work Confusion named.
  Whereto thus Adam fatherly displeased.
O execrable son so to aspire
65 Above his brethren, to himself assuming
Authority usurped, from God not giv'n:
He gave us only over beast, fish, fowl
Dominion absolute; that right we hold
By his donation; but man over men
70 He made not lord; such title to himself
Reserving, human left from human free.
But this usurper his encroachment proud
Stays not on man; to God his tower intends
Siege and defiance: wretched man! what food
75 Will he convey up thither to sustain
Himself and his rash army, where thin air
Above the clouds will pine his entrails gross,
And famish him of breath, if not of bread?
  To whom thus Michael. Justly thou abhorr'st
80 That son, who on the quiet state of men
Such trouble brought, affecting to subdue
Rational liberty; yet know withal,
Since thy original lapse, true liberty
Is lost, which always with right reason dwells
85 Twinned, and from her hath no dividual being:
Reason in man obscured, or not obeyed,
Immediately inordinate desires
And upstart passions catch the government
From reason, and to servitude reduce
90 Man till then free. Therefore since he permits
Within himself unworthy powers to reign
Over free reason, God in judgement just
Subjects him from without to violent lords;
Who oft as undeservedly enthrall
95 His outward freedom: tyranny must be,
Though to the tyrant thereby no excuse,

Yet sometimes nations will decline so low
From virtue, which is reason, that no wrong,
But justice, and some fatal curse annexed
100   Deprives them of their outward liberty,
Their inward lost: witness th' irreverent son
Of him who built the ark, who for the shame
Done to his father, heard this heavy curse,
Servant of servants, on his vicious race.
105   Thus will this latter, as the former world,
Still tend from bad to worse, till God at last
Wearied with their iniquities, withdraw
His presence from among them, and avert
His holy eyes; resolving from thenceforth
110   To leave them to their own polluted ways;
And one peculiar nation to select
From all the rest, of whom to be invoked,
A nation from one faithful man to spring:
Him on this side Euphrates yet residing,
115   Bred up in idol-worship; O that men
(Canst thou believe?) should be so stupid grown,
While yet the patriarch lived, who 'scaped the Flood,
As to forsake the living God, and fall
To worship their own work in wood and stone
120   For gods! Yet him God the Most High vouchsafes
To call by vision from his father's house,
His kindred and false gods, into a land
Which he will show him, and from him will raise
A mighty nation, and upon him show'r
125   His benediction so, that in his seed
All nations shall be blest; he straight obeys,
Not knowing to what land, yet firm believes:
I see him, but thou canst not, with what faith
He leaves his gods, his friends, and native soil
130   Ur of Chaldea, passing now the ford
To Haran, after him a cumbrous train
Of herds and flocks, and numerous servitude;
Not wand'ring poor, but trusting all his wealth
With God, who called him, in a land unknown.
135   Canaan he now attains, I see his tents

Pitched about Sechem, and the neighbouring plain
Of Moreh; there by promise he receives
Gift to his progeny of all that land;
From Hamath northward to the desert south
140 (Things by their names I call, though yet unnamed)
From Hermon east to the great western sea,
Mount Hermon, yonder sea, each place behold
In prospect, as I point them; on the shore
Mount Carmel; here the double-founted stream
145 Jordan, true limit eastward; but his sons
Shall dwell to Senir, that long ridge of hills.
This ponder, that all nations of the earth
Shall in his Seed be blessèd; by that Seed
Is meant thy great Deliverer, who shall bruise
150 The Serpent's head; whereof to thee anon
Plainlier shall be revealed. This patriarch blest,
Whom *faithful Abraham* due time shall call,
A son, and of his son a grandchild leaves,
Like him in faith, in wisdom, and renown;
155 The grandchild with twelve sons increased, departs
From Canaan, to a land hereafter called
Egypt, divided by the river Nile;
See where it flows, disgorging at seven mouths
Into the sea: to sojourn in that land
160 He comes invited by a younger son
In time of dearth, a son whose worthy deeds
Raise him to be the second in that realm
Of Pharaoh: there he dies, and leaves his race
Growing into a nation, and now grown
165 Suspected to a sequent king, who seeks
To stop their overgrowth, as inmate guests
Too numerous; whence of guests he makes them slaves
Inhospitably, and kills their infant males:
Till by two brethren (those two brethren call
170 Moses and Aaron) sent from God to claim
His people from enthralment, they return
With glory and spoil back to their promised land.
But first the lawless tyrant, who denies
To know their God, or message to regard,

175 Must be compelled by signs and judgements dire;
     To blood unshed the rivers must be turned,
     Frogs, lice, and flies must all his palace fill
     With loathed intrusion, and fill all the land;
     His cattle must of rot and murrain die,
180 Botches and blains must all his flesh emboss,
     And all his people; thunder mixed with hail,
     Hail mixed with fire must rend th' Egyptian sky
     And wheel on th' earth, devouring where it rolls;
     What it devours not, herb, or fruit, or grain,
185 A darksome cloud of locusts swarming down
     Must eat, and on the ground leave nothing green:
     Darkness must overshadow all his bounds,
     Palpable darkness, and blot out three days;
     Last with one midnight stroke all the first-born
190 Of Egypt must lie dead. Thus with ten wounds
     The river-dragon tamed at length submits
     To let his sojourners depart, and oft
     Humbles his stubborn heart, but still as ice
     More hardened after thaw, till in his rage
195 Pursuing whom he late dismissed, the sea
     Swallows him with his host, but them lets pass
     As on dry land between two crystal walls,
     Awed by the rod of Moses so to stand
     Divided, till his rescued gain their shore:
200 Such wondrous power God to his saint will lend,
     Though present in his angel, who shall go
     Before them in a cloud, and pillar of fire,
     By day a cloud, by night a pillar of fire,
     To guide them in their journey, and remove
205 Behind them, while th' obdúrate king pursues:
     All night he will pursue, but his approach
     Darkness defends between till morning watch;
     Then through the fiery pillar and the cloud
     God looking forth will trouble all his host
210 And craze their chariot wheels: when by command
     Moses once more his potent rod extends
     Over the sea; the sea his rod obeys;
     On their embattled ranks the waves return,

And overwhelm their war: the race elect
215 Safe towards Canaan from the shore advance
Through the wild desert, not the readiest way,
Lest ent'ring on the Canaanite alarmed
War terrify them inexpért, and fear
Return them back to Egypt, choosing rather
220 Inglorious life with servitude; for life
To noble and ignoble is more sweet
Untrained in arms, where rashness leads not on.
This also shall they gain by their delay
In the wide wilderness, there they shall found
225 Their government, and their great senate choose
Through the twelve tribes, to rule by laws ordained:
God from the mount of Sinai, whose grey top
Shall tremble, he descending, will himself
In thunder lightning and loud trumpet's sound
230 Ordain them laws; part such as appertain
To civil justice, part religious rites
Of sacrifice, informing them, by types
And shadows, of that destined Seed to bruise
The Serpent, by what means he shall achieve
235 Mankind's deliverance. But the voice of God
To mortal ear is dreadful; they beseech
That Moses might report to them his will,
And terror cease; he grants what they besought
Instructed that to God is no accéss
240 Without mediator, whose high office now
Moses in figure bears, to introduce
One greater, of whose day he shall foretell,
And all the prophets in their age the times
Of great Messiah shall sing. Thus laws and rites
245 Established, such delight hath God in men
Obedient to his will, that he vouchsafes
Among them to set up his tabernacle,
The Holy One with mortal men to dwell:
By his prescrípt a sanctuary is framed
250 Of cedar, overlaid with gold, therein
An ark, and in the ark his testimony,
The records of his Cov'nant; over these

A mercy-seat of gold between the wings
Of two bright Cherubim; before him burn
255   Seven lamps as in a zodiac representing
The Heav'nly fires; over the tent a cloud
Shall rest by day, a fiery gleam by night,
Save when they journey, and at length they come,
Conducted by his angel to the land
260   Promised to Abraham and his seed: the rest
Were long to tell, how many battles fought,
How many kings destroyed, and kingdoms won,
Or how the sun shall in mid heav'n stand still
A day entire, and night's due course adjourn,
265   Man's voice commanding, Sun in Gibeon stand,
And thou moon in the vale of Aialon,
Till Israel overcome; so call the third
From Abraham, son of Isaac, and from him
His whole descent, who thus shall Canaan win.
270   Here Adam interposed. O sent from Heav'n,
Enlight'ner of my darkness, gracious things
Thou hast revealed, those chiefly which concern
Just Abraham and his seed: now first I find
Mine eyes true op'ning, and my heart much eased,
275   Erewhile perplexed with thoughts what would become
Of me and all mankind; but now I see
His day, in whom all nations shall be blest,
Favour unmerited by me, who sought
Forbidden knowledge by forbidden means.
280   This yet I apprehend not, why to those
Among whom God will deign to dwell on earth
So many and so various laws are giv'n;
So many laws argue so many sins
Among them; how can God with such reside?
285   To whom thus Michael. Doubt not but that sin
Will reign among them, as of thee begot;
And therefore was law given them to evince
Their natural pravity, by stirring up
Sin against law to fight; that when they see
290   Law can discover sin, but not remove,
Save by those shadowy expiations weak,

The blood of bulls and goats, they may conclude
Some blood more precious must be paid for man,
Just for unjust, that in such righteousness
295 To them by faith imputed, they may find
Justification towards God, and peace
Of conscience, which the law by ceremonies
Cannot appease, nor man the moral part
Perform, and not performing cannot live.
300 So law appears imperfect, and but giv'n
With purpose to resign them in full time
Up to a better cov'nant, disciplined
From shadowy types to truth, from flesh to spirit,
From imposition of strict laws, to free
305 Acceptance of large grace, from servile fear
To filial, works of law to works of faith.
And therefore shall not Moses, though of God
Highly beloved, being but the minister
Of law, his people into Canaan lead;
310 But Joshua whom the Gentiles Jesus call,
His name and office bearing, who shall quell
The adversary Serpent, and bring back
Through the world's wilderness long wandered man
Safe to eternal Paradise of rest.
315 Meanwhile they in their earthly Canaan placed
Long time shall dwell and prosper, but when sins
National interrupt their public peace,
Provoking God to raise them enemies:
From whom as oft he saves them penitent
320 By judges first, then under kings; of whom
The second, both for piety renowned
And puissant deeds, a promise shall receive
Irrevocable, that his regal throne
For ever shall endure; the like shall sing
325 All prophecy, that of the royal stock
Of David (so I name this king) shall rise
A son, the Woman's Seed to thee foretold,
Foretold to Abraham, as in whom shall trust
All nations, and to kings foretold, of kings
330 The last, for of his reign shall be no end.

But first a long succession must ensue,
And his next son for wealth and wisdom famed,
The clouded ark of God till then in tents
Wand'ring, shall in a glorious temple enshrine.
335   Such follow him, as shall be registered
Part good, part bad, of bad the longer scroll,
Whose foul idolatries, and other faults
Heaped to the popular sum, will so incense
God, as to leave them, and expose their land,
340   Their city, his temple, and his holy ark
With all his sacred things, a scorn and prey
To that proud city, whose high walls thou saw'st
Left in confusion, Babylon thence called.
There in captivity he lets them dwell
345   The space of seventy years, then brings them back,
Rememb'ring mercy, and his Cov'nant sworn
To David, 'stablished as the days of Heav'n.
Returned from Babylon by leave of kings
Their lords, whom God disposed, the house of God
350   They first re-edify, and for a while
In mean estate live moderate, till grown
In wealth and multitude, factious they grow;
But first among the priests dissension springs,
Men who attend the altar, and should most
355   Endeavour peace: their strife pollution brings
Upon the temple itself: at last they seize
The sceptre, and regard not David's sons,
Then lose it to a stranger, that the true
Anointed King Messiah might be born
360   Barred of his right; yet at his birth a star
Unseen before in heav'n proclaims him come,
And guides the eastern sages, who inquire
His place, to offer incense, myrrh, and gold;
His place of birth a solemn angel tells
365   To simple shepherds, keeping watch by night;
They gladly thither haste, and by a choir
Of squadroned angels hear his carol sung.
A virgin is his mother, but his sire
The power of the Most High; he shall ascend

370   The throne hereditary, and bound his reign
With earth's wide bounds, his glory with the Heav'ns.
    He ceased, discerning Adam with such joy
Surcharged, as had like grief been dewed in tears,
Without the vent of words, which these he breathed.
375   O prophet of glad tidings, finisher
Of utmost hope! now clear I understand
What oft my steadiest thoughts have searched in vain,
Why our great expectation should be called
The Seed of Woman: virgin mother, hail,
380   High in the love of Heav'n, yet from my loins
Thou shalt proceed, and from thy womb the Son
Of God Most High; so God with man unites.
Needs must the Serpent now his capital bruise
Expect with mortal pain: say where and when
385   Their fight, what stroke shall bruise the Victor's heel.
    To whom thus Michael. Dream not of their fight,
As of a duel, or the local wounds
Of head or heel: not therefore joins the Son
Manhood to Godhead, with more strength to foil
390   Thy enemy; nor so is overcome
Satan, whose fall from Heav'n, a deadlier bruise,
Disabled not to give thee thy death's wound:
Which he, who comes thy Saviour, shall recure,
Not by destroying Satan, but his works
395   In thee and in thy seed: nor can this be,
But by fulfilling that which thou didst want,
Obedience to the law of God, imposed
On penalty of death, and suffering death,
The penalty to thy transgression due,
400   And due to theirs which out of thine will grow:
So only can high justice rest apaid.
The law of God exact he shall fulfil
Both by obedience and by love, though love
Alone fulfil the law; thy punishment
405   He shall endure by coming in the flesh
To a reproachful life and cursèd death,
Proclaiming life to all who shall believe
In his redemption, and that his obedience

Imputed becomes theirs by faith, his merits
410 To save them, not their own, though legal works.
For this he shall live hated, be blasphemed,
Seized on by force, judged, and to death condemned
A shameful and accursed, nailed to the cross
By his own nation, slain for bringing life;
415 But to the cross he nails thy enemies,
The law that is against thee, and the sins
Of all mankind, with him there crucified,
Never to hurt them more who rightly trust
In this his satisfaction; so he dies,
420 But soon revives, death over him no power
Shall long usurp; ere the third dawning light
Return, the stars of morn shall see him rise
Out of his grave, fresh as the dawning light,
Thy ransom paid, which man from death redeems,
425 His death for man, as many as offered life
Neglect not, and the benefit embrace
By faith not void of works: this Godlike act
Annuls thy doom, the death thou shouldst have died,
In sin for ever lost from life; this act
430 Shall bruise the head of Satan, crush his strength
Defeating Sin and Death, his two main arms,
And fix far deeper in his head their stings
Than temporal death shall bruise the Victor's heel,
Or theirs whom he redeems, a death like sleep,
435 A gentle wafting to immortal life.
Nor after resurrection shall he stay
Longer on earth than certain times to appear
To his disciples, men who in his life
Still followed him; to them shall leave in charge
440 To teach all nations what of him they learned
And his salvation, them who shall believe
Baptizing in the profluent stream, the sign
Of washing them from guilt of sin to life
Pure, and in mind prepared, if so befall,
445 For death, like that which the Redeemer died.
All nations they shall teach; for from that day
Not only to the sons of Abraham's loins

Salvation shall be preached, but to the sons
Of Abraham's faith wherever through the world;
450   So in his seed all nations shall be blest.
Then to the Heav'n of Heav'ns he shall ascend
With victory, triúmphing through the air
Over his foes and thine; there shall surprise
The Serpent, prince of air, and drag in chains
455   Through all his realm, and there confounded leave;
Then enter into glory, and resume
His seat at God's right hand, exalted high
Above all names in Heav'n; and thence shall come,
When this world's dissolution shall be ripe,
460   With glory and power to judge both quick and dead,
To judge th' unfaithful dead, but to reward
His faithful, and receive them into bliss,
Whether in Heav'n or earth, for then the earth
Shall all be Paradise, far happier place
465   Than this of Eden, and far happier days.
    So spake the archangel Michaël, then paused,
As at the world's great period; and our sire
Replete with joy and wonder thus replied.
    O goodness infinite, goodness immense!
470   That all this good of evil shall produce,
And evil turn to good; more wonderful
Than that which by creation first brought forth
Light out of darkness! full of doubt I stand,
Whether I should repent me now of sin
475   By me done and occasioned, or rejoice
Much more, that much more good thereof shall spring,
To God more glory, more good will to men
From God, and over wrath grace shall abound.
But say, if our Deliverer up to Heav'n
480   Must reascend, what will betide the few
His faithful, left among th' unfaithful herd,
The enemies of truth; who then shall guide
His people, who defend? will they not deal
Worse with his followers than with him they dealt?
485   Be sure they will, said th' angel; but from Heav'n
He to his own a Comforter will send,

The promise of the Father, who shall dwell
His Spirit within them, and the law of faith
Working through love, upon their hearts shall write,
490   To guide them in all truth, and also arm
With spiritual armour, able to resist
Satan's assaults, and quench his fiery darts,
What man can do against them, not afraid,
Though to the death, against such cruelties
495   With inward consolations recompensed,
And oft supported so as shall amaze
Their proudest persecutors: for the Spirit
Poured first on his apostles, whom he sends
To evangelize the nations, then on all
500   Baptized, shall them with wondrous gifts endue
To speak all tongues, and do all miracles,
As did their Lord before them. Thus they win
Great numbers of each nation to receive
With joy the tidings brought from Heav'n: at length
505   Their ministry performed, and race well run,
Their doctrine and their story written left,
They die; but in their room, as they forewarn,
Wolves shall succeed for teachers, grievous wolves,
Who all the sacred mysteries of Heav'n
510   To their own vile advantages shall turn
Of lucre and ambition, and the truth
With superstitions and traditions taint,
Left only in those written records pure,
Though not but by the Spirit understood.
515   Then shall they seek to avail themselves of names,
Places and titles, and with these to join
Secular power, though feigning still to act
By spiritual, to themselves appropriating
The Spirit of God, promised alike and giv'n
520   To all believers; and from that pretence,
Spiritual laws by carnal power shall force
On every conscience; laws which none shall find
Left them enrolled, or what the Spirit within
Shall on the heart engrave. What will they then
525   But force the Spirit of grace itself, and bind

His consort Liberty; what, but unbuild
His living temples, built by faith to stand,
Their own faith not another's: for on earth
Who against faith and conscience can be heard
530 Infallible? yet many will presume:
Whence heavy persecution shall arise
On all who in the worship persevere
Of spirit and truth; the rest, far greater part,
Will deem in outward rites and specious forms
535 Religion satisfied; truth shall retire
Bestuck with sland'rous darts, and works of faith
Rarely be found: so shall the world go on,
To good malignant, to bad men benign,
Under her own weight groaning, till the day
540 Appear of respiration to the just,
And vengeance to the wicked, at return
Of him so lately promised to thy aid,
The Woman's Seed, obscurely then foretold,
Now amplier known thy Saviour and thy Lord,
545 Last in the clouds from Heav'n to be revealed
In glory of the Father, to dissolve
Satan with his perverted world, then raise
From the conflagrant mass, purged and refined,
New heav'ns, new earth, ages of endless date
550 Founded in righteousness and peace and love,
To bring forth fruits joy and eternal bliss.
        He ended; and thus Adam last replied.
How soon hath thy prediction, seer blest,
Measured this transient world, the race of time,
555 Till time stand fixed: beyond is all abyss,
Eternity, whose end no eye can reach.
Greatly instructed I shall hence depart,
Greatly in peace of thought, and have my fill
Of knowledge, what this vessel can contain;
560 Beyond which was my folly to aspire.
Henceforth I learn, that to obey is best,
And love with fear the only God, to walk
As in his presence, ever to observe
His Providence, and on him sole depend,

565 Merciful over all his works, with good
Still overcoming evil, and by small
Accomplishing great things, by things deemed weak
Subverting worldly strong, and worldly wise
By simply meek; that suffering for truth's sake
570 Is fortitude to highest victory,
And to the faithful death the gate of life;
Taught this by his example whom I now
Acknowledge my Redeemer ever blest.
    To whom thus also th' angel last replied:
575 This having learnt, thou hast attained the sum
Of wisdom; hope no higher, though all the stars
Thou knew'st by name, and all th' ethereal Powers,
All secrets of the deep, all Nature's works,
Or works of God in Heav'n, air, earth, or sea,
580 And all the riches of this world enjoy'dst,
And all the rule, one empire; only add
Deeds to thy knowledge answerable, add faith,
Add virtue, patience, temperance, add love,
By name to come called charity, the soul
585 Of all the rest: then wilt thou not be loath
To leave this Paradise, but shalt possess
A paradise within thee, happier far.
Let us descend now therefore from this top
Of speculation; for the hour precise
590 Exacts our parting hence; and see the guards,
By me encamped on yonder hill, expect
Their motion, at whose front a flaming sword,
In signal of remove, waves fiercely round;
We may no longer stay: go, waken Eve;
595 Her also I with gentle dreams have calmed
Portending good, and all her spirits composed
To meek submission: thou at season fit
Let her with thee partake what thou hast heard,
Chiefly what may concern her faith to know,
600 The great deliverance by her Seed to come
(For by the Woman's Seed) on all mankind,
That ye may live, which will be many days,
Both in one faith unanimous though sad,

With cause for evils past, yet much more cheered
605 With meditation on the happy end.
   He ended, and they both descend the hill;
Descended, Adam to the bow'r where Eve
Lay sleeping ran before, but found her waked;
And thus with words not sad she him received.
610   Whence thou return'st, and whither went'st, I know;
For God is also in sleep, and dreams advise,
Which he hath sent propitious, some great good
Presaging, since with sorrow and heart's distress
Wearied I fell asleep: but now lead on;
615 In me is no delay; with thee to go,
Is to stay here; without thee here to stay,
Is to go hence unwilling; thou to me
Art all things under Heav'n, all places thou,
Who for my wilful crime art banished hence.
620 This further consolation yet secure
I carry hence; though all by me is lost,
Such favour I unworthy am vouchsafed,
By me the promised Seed shall all restore.
   So spake our mother Eve, and Adam heard
625 Well pleased, but answered not; for now too nigh
Th' Archangel stood, and from the other hill
To their fixed station, all in bright array
The Cherubim descended; on the ground
Gliding metéorous, as ev'ning mist
630 Ris'n from a river o'er the marish glides,
And gathers ground fast at the labourer's heel
Homeward returning. High in front advanced,
The brandished sword of God before them blazed
Fierce as a comet; which with torrid heat,
635 And vapour as the Libyan air adust,
Began to parch that temperate clime; whereat
In either hand the hast'ning angel caught
Our ling'ring parents, and to th' eastern gate
Led them direct, and down the cliff as fast
640 To the subjected plain; then disappeared.
They looking back, all th' eastern side beheld
Of Paradise, so late their happy seat,

Waved over by that flaming brand, the gate
With dreadful faces thronged and fiery arms:
645 Some natural tears they dropped, but wiped them soon;
The world was all before them, where to choose
Their place of rest, and Providence their guide:
They hand in hand with wand'ring steps and slow,
Through Eden took their solitary way.

NOTES

In these notes references to critics are usually by surname only. For bibliographical details see Further Reading. The abbreviation *Var.* refers to the *Variorum Commentary on the Poems of John Milton* (6 vols., 1970–). I have used the following abbreviations of specific manuscripts and editions of Milton's works:

BMS	Bridgewater Manuscript of *A Masque*
Ed I	*Paradise Lost*. First edition (1667)
Ed II	*Paradise Lost*. Second edition (1674)
MS	The Manuscript of *Paradise Lost* i
TMS	The Trinity Manuscript
1637	*A Maske Presented at Ludlow Castle* (1637)
1638	*Justa Edouardo King naufrago* (1638)
1645	*Poems of Mr. John Milton* (1645)
1671	*Paradise Regain'd. A Poem in IV Books. To which is added Samson Agonistes* (1671)
1673	*Poems, &c. Upon Several Occasions* (1673)

The following abbreviations are used for titles of works by Milton.

CD	*Christian Doctrine* (*De Doctrina Christiana*)
DDD	*Doctrine and Discipline of Divorce*
Ep. Dam.	*Epitaphium Damonis*
Nativity	*On the Morning of Christ's Nativity*
PL	*Paradise Lost*
PR	*Paradise Regained*
Q Nov	*In Quintum Novembris*
RCG	*Reason of Church Government*
REW	*Ready and Easy Way*
SA	*Samson Agonistes*
TKM	*Tenure of Kings and Magistrates*
YP	*The Complete Prose Works of John Milton*, edited by Don M. Wolfe *et al.*, 8 vols. (New Haven, 1953–82)

The following abbreviations are of works by other authors:

Ariosto, *Orl. Fur.*	*Orlando Furioso*
Boiardo, *Orl. Inn.*	*Orlando Innamorato*
Claudian, *De Rapt. Pros.*	*De Raptu Proserpinae*
Dante, *Inf.*, *Purg.*, *Par.*	*Inferno, Purgatorio, Paradiso*
Fletcher, *CV*	*Christs Victorie, and Triumph*
Hesiod, *Theog.*, *WD*	*Theogony, Works and Days*
Homer, *Il.*, *Od.*	*Iliad, Odyssey*
Lucretius, *De Rerum Nat.*	*De Rerum Natura*
Ovid, *Her.*, *Met.*	*Heroides, Metamorphoses*
Spenser, *FQ, Shep. Cal.*	*Faerie Queene, Shepheardes Calender*
Sylvester, *DWW*	Joshuah Sylvester, *The Divine Weeks and Works of Guillaume de Saluste, Sieur du Bartas*
Tasso, *Gerus. Lib.*	*Gerusalemme Liberata*
Virgil, *Aen.*, *Ecl.*, *Georg.*	*Aeneid, Eclogues, Georgics*

Unless otherwise stated, all biblical citations are from the Authorized Version (A.V.). LXX refers to the Septuagint (the Greek version of the Old Testament (O.T.)) and Junius-Tremellius refers to *Testamenti Veteris Biblia Sacra* (1581), the Protestant Latin version of the O.T. by Franciscus Junius and Immanuel Tremellius.

Abbreviations of academic journals used are:

CLS	*Comparative Literature Studies*
EC	*Essays in Criticism*
ELH	*A Journal of English Literary History*
ELR	*English Literary Renaissance*
JEGP	*Journal of English and Germanic Philology*
JHI	*Journal of the History of Ideas*
MLN	*Modern Language Notes*
MLR	*Modern Language Review*
MQ	*Milton Quarterly*
MS	*Milton Studies*
N&Q	*Notes and Queries*
PMLA	*Publications of the Modern Language Association of America*
RES	*Review of English Studies*
SEL	*Studies in English Literature*
SP	*Studies in Philology*
UTQ	*University of Toronto Quarterly*

An asterisk signifies that the word or sense so marked is the earliest recorded instance in the *Oxford English Dictionary*. See Note on the Text, pp. liii–lv.

PARADISE LOST

M.'s great epic is the culmination of two ambitions. Since his youth M. had wanted to write an epic. He refers to the hope in *Elegia VI, Mansus, Epitaphium Damonis* and elsewhere – but his plan had been to write an Arthuriad. He had also planned to write a tragedy about the Fall of Man. Edward Phillips reports that part of Satan's address to the sun (iv 32–41) was shown to him 'several Years before the Poem was begun', when it was intended to be 'the very beginning' of a tragedy (Darbishire 72). Aubrey reports that M. began writing *PL* in earnest in about 1658 and finished in about 1663 (Darbishire 13). The invocation to book vii was clearly written after the Restoration.

When first published in 1667, *PL* was a poem of ten books. Critics often see this ten-book scheme as a vestige of M.'s original dramatic design, a double five-act structure. An alternative model is Tasso's twenty-book epic *Gerusalemme Liberata*, to which M. often alludes in *PL*. For the second edition of 1674, M. split books vii and x into two, thus creating a twelve-book epic. His model here is Virgil's twelve-book *Aeneid*. Homer's *Iliad* and *Odyssey* each have twenty-four books, so the second edition of *PL* has the same relation to them as the first edition had had to *Jerusalem Delivered*.

The Verse, line 4. *invention of a barbarous age* Latin poets first began to use rhyme in Christian hymns of the fifth and sixth centuries.
line 14. *apt numbers* appropriate rhythm.
  quantity number.
line 21. *the first in English* An exaggeration. The Earl of Surrey, who introduced blank verse into England, had used it in his translation of selections of Virgil's *Aeneid* (an *heroic poem*).

BOOK I

The Argument, line 9. *centre* (centre of) the earth.
line 10. *yet not made* Our universe was created after Satan fell from Heaven (vii 131–5), but before he escaped from Hell (ii 830–32, 1004–6).
line 11. *utter* utter and outer.
line 23. *angels . . . Fathers* Cp. *CD* i 7: 'many of the Greek Fathers, and some of the Latin, were of the opinion that angels . . . existed long before this world' (trans. Carey, *YP* 6. 313). Fathers who shared M.'s view included Jerome, Origen, Gregory of Nazianzen, Basil, and Chrysostom.

1. *man's* mankind's and Adam's (*Adam* in Hebrew means 'man').

fruit including 'consequences'.

4. *one greater man* Christ, the Second Adam (Romans 5. 19). Homer (*Od.* i 1) and Virgil (*Aen.* i 1) had sung of one 'man'; M. will sing of two.

6–16. The identity of M.'s *Muse* remains a mystery, despite attempts to see her as Father, Son, or Holy Spirit. M.'s widow identified her as 'God's grace, and the Holy Spirit' (Newton lvi). See below, *17n*. See also iii *19n*, vii 1–12, and ix 21–4.

8. *That shepherd* Moses, the supposed author of Genesis. He was tending sheep on Mount Horeb (*Oreb*), when God called him (Exod. 3. 1). He later received the Law on Horeb, or Sinai, one of Horeb's spurs (Exod. 19. 20).

10. *out of Chaos* M. believed that God created the universe out of unformed matter, not out of nothing. See *CD* i 7.

Sion hill Mount Zion, the site of Solomon's Temple.

11. *Siloa's brook* a spring near the Temple. Jesus cured a blind man with its waters (John 9. 7).

12. *oracle* the sanctuary housing the ark of the Covenant in Solomon's Temple (I Kings 6. 19).

15. *Aonian mount* Helicon, sacred to the Muses. Porter (45–7) sees a specific allusion to Hesiod, whom the Muses visited while he tended his flocks on Helicon. Hesiod sang how 'from the beginning', 'heaven and earth and all things rose out of Chaos' (*Theog.* 115–16).

16. *Things . . . rhyme* translating Ariosto, *Orl. Fur.* i 2: *Cosa non detta in prosa mai, né in rima.* Cp. also Horace, *Odes* III i 2–3: 'songs never heard before'.

17. *Spirit* the Holy Spirit, despite M.'s insistence in *CD* i 6 that the Holy Spirit is never invoked in the Bible (*YP* 6. 295). *Dove-like* (21) points to the doves of Mark 1. 10, Luke 3. 22 and John 1. 32, which even *CD* identifies with 'the actual person of the Holy Spirit, or its symbol' (trans. Carey, *YP* 6. 285). If *chiefly* refers to *thou*, Spirit and Muse are distinct; if to *Instruct* (19), they are identical.

19. *Instruct* Latin *instruere*, 'to build', linking *temples* and *heart*.

21–2. *brooding* Cp. Gen. 1. 2. M. follows Junius-Tremellius (*incubabat*) rather than A.V. ('moved') and so preserves the image of a brooding dove.

24. *argument* subject-matter (*OED* 6).

25. *assert* defend, take the part of (*OED* 2).

26. *justify* both 'justify to men' and 'ways of God to men'.

28. *what cause* echoing Virgil, *Aen.* i 8: *Musa mihi causas memor* ('tell me the cause, O Muse').

29. *grand* pre-eminent (*OED* 3a) and all-inclusive (*OED* 6), as in 'grand total'.

30. *fall off* of friends: to become estranged. Of subjects: to revolt, withdraw from allegiance (*OED* 'fall' 92e), with overtones of 'the Fall'.

33. *Who first seduced them* Cp. Homer's question as to who sowed discord among the Greeks (*Il.* i 8).

34. *infernal Serpent* Cp. Rev. 12. 9: 'that old serpent, called the Devil, and Satan'.

35–6. *deceived / The mother of mankind* There may be a pun on 'dis-Eved'. See Gen. 3. 20: 'Adam called his wife's name Eve; because she was the mother of all living'. 'Eve' meant 'life', and M. relates the name to prelapsarian immortality (xi 161–171). Cp. *PR* i 51–2.

36. *what time* when (*OED* 10a), not a Latinism.

38–49. *aspiring . . . arms* echoing several biblical accounts of Satan's fall. Cp. Isa. 14. 12–15, Luke 10. 18, II Pet. 2. 4, Jude 6, Rev. 20. 1–2.

43. *impious war* Latin *bellum impium*, 'civil war'.

46. *ruin* falling from a height (*OED* 1b), Latin *ruina*.
   combustion confusion, tumult (*OED* 5b) and conflagration.

48. *adamantine chains* Satan was bound with 'chains of darkness' (Jude 6, II Pet. 2. 4) or 'a great chain' (Rev. 20. 1–2). Cp. also Phineas Fletcher, *The Purple Island* (1633) xii 64: 'the Dragon . . . bound in adamantine chain'. Adamant was a mythical substance of impenetrable hardness.

50. *space* extent of time (*OED* 3) and linear distance (*OED* 5a). The devils *Lay* for *Nine* days after their fall, which also lasted nine days (vi 871). Hesiod's Titans fell for nine days and nights from heaven to earth and nine more from earth to Tartarus (*Theog.* 720–25).

52. *fiery gulf* Satan is chained on a fiery lake. See lines 184 and 210, and cp. Rev. 19. 20: 'a lake of fire burning with brimstone'.

56. *round he throws his baleful eyes* Cp. Ariosto's description of the Saracen Rodomonte: *Rivolge gli occhi orribili* (*Orl. Fur.* xviii 18).

57. *witnessed* bore witness to (his own *affliction*) and beheld (his followers').

59. *angels' ken* angels' range of sight. The early texts do not use apostrophes, so *ken* might be a verb.

66. *hope never comes* recalling the inscription over Dante's Hell: *Lasciate ogne speranza, voi ch' intrate* (*Inf.* iii. 9); 'Abandon every hope, you who enter'. Cp. also Euripides, *Troades* 681.

68. *Still* always.

71. *those*] *Ed I, Ed II*; these *MS*.

72. *utter* utter and outer (cp. Matthew 25. 30).

74. *the centre* the earth (*OED* 2b).
   pole celestial pole. M. here measures the distance from Heaven to Hell as thrice the radius of the universe. At ii 1051–3 our whole universe is a speck in Chaos. Homer and Hesiod place Hades as far below earth as heaven is above it (*Il.* viii 16, *Theog.* 722–25). Virgil places Tartarus 'twice' as far below (*Aen.* vi 577).

81. *Beëlzebub* Hebrew 'Lord of the Flies', one of many forms of the Philistine sun-god Baal ('prince of the devils' in Matt. 12. 24). Notice that

Beëlzebub will not get that name until *long after* (80). See below, i 361–5*n*.

82. *Satan* Hebrew 'Enemy'. This is Satan's name *in Heav'n*, not Hell. The devils see God, not Satan, as the 'great Enemy' (ii 137). Satan lost his 'former name' when he rebelled (v 658). He acknowledges his new name only at x 386.

84. *how fall'n! how changed* Cp. Isa. 14. 12 ('How art thou fallen . . . O Lucifer') and Virgil, *Aen* ii. 274–5 (*quantum mutatus ab illo / Hectore*). Satan is unable to put any name to his companion. Cp. Dryden's revision in *The State of Innocence* (1677): 'Ho, *Asmaday*, awake, / If thou art he: But, ah! how chang'd from him!' (20).

93. *He with his thunder* The devils repeatedly avoid naming 'God'. See e.g. i 122, 161–2, ii 59, etc. Contrast iii 695, where Uriel at once names God.

102. *me preferring* liking me better and putting me forward.

105–6. *What . . . lost* Cp. Satan's boast in Fairfax's translation (1600) of Tasso, *Gerus. Lib.* iv 15: 'We lost the field, yet lost we not our heart'.

107. *study of* effort to achieve.

109. *And . . . overcome* 'What else does "not being overcome" mean?'

114. *Doubted* feared for.

116. *Fate* imagined by Satan to be an independent force, but cp.*CD* i 2: 'fate or *fatum* is only what is *fatum*, spoken, by some almighty power' (trans. Carey, *YP* 6. 131).

  gods angels. Even God calls angels 'gods' (iii 341).

117. *empyreal* of the highest Heaven.

123. *triúmphs* prevails, exults, rides in pomp (as in a Roman triumph).

126. *racked*] *Ed I*, *Ed II*; wracked *MS*. Satan is wrecked, ruined (*OED* 'wrack' 2, 3), but *In pain* gives priority to *racked*.

128. *Powers*] *MS*; Powers, *Ed I*, *Ed II*. Richardson (who was unaware of *MS*) noted in 1734: 'the Comma after Powers, as in all Editions we have Noted, perplexes the Sense. 'twas not *Satan*, but Those Powers that led the *Seraphim* to War under His Conduct. One of these Powers is This Bold Companion who Here under a Compliment he makes to *Satan* Proudly Insinuates his Own Merit.' *Powers* and *Seraphim* (129) are two of nine angelic orders, the others being Cherubim, Thrones, Dominations, Virtues, Principalities, Archangels, Angels.

134. *event* outcome.

139. *perish* including 'incur spiritual death' (*OED* 1b).

141. *glory* effulgence, bliss of heaven, halo (*OED* 6, 7a, 9).
  extinct extinguished.

144. *Of force* perforce and due to the force.

146. *entire* unimpaired, undiminished (*OED* 4c).

147. *support* endure, undergo, esp. with fortitude or without giving way (*OED* 1b).

148. *suffice* satisfy.

152. *deep* Chaos (the usual meaning in *PL*).

153–5. *What . . . punishment?* 'What can it avail us that our strength is undiminished, and that our being is eternal, if our punishment is also eternal?'

156. *Arch-Fiend coined on the analogy of 'Archangel'.

158. *Doing or suffering* acting or enduring. Satan anticipates the famous words of Mutius Scaevola as he thrust his hand into a flaming brazier as a demonstration of Roman courage. See ii 199*n* and cp. *PR* iii 194–5.

159–68. *To do aught good . . . aim* contrast God's power to bring good out of evil (xii 470–8).

166. *succeed* ensue (with *evil* as subject).

167. *if I fail not* unless I am mistaken. *Fail* means 'err' (*OED* 11), but the sequence *succeed . . . fail* also hints at Satan's ultimate failure.

    disturb forcibly divert.

168. *destined* intended (*OED* 2) – but the sense of 'destiny' tells against Satan's boast.

173. *The fiery*] Ed I, Ed II; This fiery *MS*.

178. *slip* let slip.

180. *dreary* **dismal, gloomy (*OED* 4), dire, horrid, (*OED* 2).

182. *livid* of a bluish leaden colour (*OED* 1). Virgil (*Aen.* vi 320) and Statius (*Thebaid* i 54) describe the rivers of Hades as *livida*.

183–91. The rhymes signal a change of scene (as in a blank verse drama) and create an impression of order emerging from destruction.

185. *There rest, if any rest* Cp. Shakespeare, *Richard II* V i 5–6: 'Here let us rest, if this rebellious earth / Hath any resting for her true king's queen'.

186. *afflicted powers* routed armies.

187. *offend* strike so as to hurt (*OED* 6).

196. *rood* either a linear measure (6–8 yards) or a measure of land (about a quarter of an acre).

198–9. *Titanian . . . Typhon* Titans and Giants were *Earth-born* monsters who rebelled against *Jove* and were confined in Tartarus, the classical hell. In Homer and Hesiod, the hundred-armed *Briareos* is Zeus's ally, but Virgil makes him a Titan (*Aen.* vi 287, x 565). *Typhon* (Typhoeus) was a Giant with a hundred serpent-heads. At first the gods fled his attack (see i 481*n*), but Jove crushed him under Mount Etna (Ovid, *Met.* v 346–53). M. often compares these rebellions to Satan's (see i 50, 480–81, 510, 576, 778, ii 539, vii 605).

201. *Leviathan* a whale, but the name was also associated with Satan. Cp. Isa. 27. 1: 'the Lord . . . shall punish leviathan the piercing serpent, even leviathan the crooked serpent; and he shall slay the dragon that is in the sea'. The story of the illusory island was a commonplace often applied to Satan. See J. H. Pitman, 'Milton and the Physiologus', *MLN* 40 (1925)

439. Contrast the undeceptive Leviathan at vii 412–16. Boiardo and Ariosto tell how the paladin Astolfo mistook a whale for an island and was carried off (*Orl. Inn.* II xiv 3, *Orl. Fur.* VI 37–43).

202. *Océan stream* the river Ocean, described by Homer as encircling the world. Homer locates such strange and wonderful creatures as the Pygmies and the Cimmerians 'by the stream of Ocean'. See e.g. *Il.* i 423, *Od.* iv 567.

204. *night-foundered* engulfed in night. (The vessel is also about to founder.)

207. *lee* shelter (from wind) given by neighbouring object.

208. *Invests* wraps, covers.

224. *horrid* dreadful and bristling (with *spires*).

226. *incumbent* pressing with his weight upon (*OED* 1a).

227. *unusual weight* Cp. Spenser's dragon, whose flight 'did forcibly divide / The yielding aire, which nigh too feeble found / Her flitting partes, and element unsound, / To beare so great a weight' (*FQ* I xi 18).

228. *lights* alights, with overtones of 'lessens the weight' (*OED* v^1 1).

229–30. *MS* pointing. *Ed I* and *Ed II* (semicolon after *fire*, comma after *hue*) focus the simile exclusively on *hue*. *MS* likens the flying Satan to a flying *hill*.

230–37. *force . . . smoke* Cp. the descriptions of *Etna* in Virgil, (*Aen.* iii 570–82), Ovid (*Met.* v. 346–58), and Tasso (*Gerus. Lib.* iv 8). The Giant Encaladus was buried under Etna after the Giants' revolt. See above, 198–9n. M. combines imagery of birth (*conceiving*) and excretion (*wind, entrails, bottom, stench*).

231. *subterranean wind* the cause of earthquakes in classical and Renaissance seismology. Cp. Ovid, *Met.* xv 296–305.

232. *Pelorus* Cape Faro, near Mount Etna in Sicily.

235. *Sublimed* converted directly from solid to vapour by volcanic heat.

236. *involved* enveloped, wreathed.

239. *Stygian* black as the river Styx.

244. *change for* take in exchange for.

254–6. *The mind . . . the same* Amalric of Bena's heresy that Heaven and Hell are states of mind had been condemned in 1204, but continued to attract seventeenth-century sects. Satan's boast takes an ironic twist at iv 75.

257. *all but less than* eliding the idioms 'all but equal to' and 'only less than'.

263. *Better to reign in Hell, than serve in Heav'n* The thought was proverbial (as was its opposite). See e.g. Ps. 84. 10, Homer, *Od.* xi 488, Aeschylus, *Promethus Bound* 965. M.'s version is close to Phineas Fletcher, *The Apollyonists* (1627) i 20: 'To be in heaven the second he disdaines: / So now the first in hell, and flames he raignes'. Cp. *The Purple Island* (1633) vii 10.

265. *associates* companions in arms (*OED* B 2). *Copartners, loss* and *share* also evoke the image of a failed business venture.

266. *astonished* including 'thunderstruck' (Latin *extonare*).

oblivious causing oblivion.

276. *edge* critical moment (*OED* 6b), line of battle (*OED* 5a). Cp. Latin *acies* and 'rough edge of battle' (vi 108).

282. *pernicious* destructive, ruinous.

284–7. *shield . . . moon* Cp. Achilles' shield, from which 'the light glimmered far, as from the moon' (Homer, *Il.* xix 574).

285. *Ethereal temper* tempered in Heaven and tempered in celestial fire (Greek *aithein*, 'to burn').

288. *Tuscan artist* Galileo. He studied the moon with a telescope (*optic glass*). M. had visited him in Florence in 1638 or 1639. He is the only one of M.'s contemporaries to be named in *PL*. Cp. iii 588–90, v 261–3. *Fesole* (Fiesole) overlooks *Valdarno* (the valley of the Arno).

292–4. *spear . . . wand* Cp. Homer's simile likening Polyphemus's club to the mast of a 'black ship of twenty oars' (*Od.* ix 322). M. implies relative magnitudes ('spear is to pine as pine is to wand'), but also evokes an image of Satan hobbling on a light walking-stick or twig (*OED* 'wand' 1c, 2a). See Fish (159).

294. *ammiral* flagship. M.'s spelling 'gives the true etymology, from *emir* . . . not from admire' (Ricks). Cp. Satan as 'Sultan' (i 348).

296. *marl* soil.

299. *Nathless* nevertheless.

302. *autumnal leaves* Similes comparing the passing generations (or numberless dead) to falling leaves are frequent in epic. Cp. Homer, *Il.* vi 146, Virgil, *Aen.* vi 309–10, Dante, *Inf.* iii 112–15, Ariosto, *Orl. Fur.* xvi 75. The image is especially apt to fallen angels. Cp. Isa. 34. 4: 'all the host of heaven . . . shall fall down, as the leaf falleth off from the vine'.

303. *Vallombrosa* a wooded valley in Tuscany (Etruria), which M. may have visited. The name ('valley of shadows') evokes 'valley of the shadow of death' (Ps. 23).

304. **overarched* M. repeats the neologism at ix 1107.

sedge seaweed. Cp. Isa. 57. 20: 'The wicked are like the troubled sea, when it cannot rest, whose waters cast up mire and dirt'. Homer likens the routed Achaians to seaweed cast up by a storm (*Il.* ix 5–9).

305. *Orion* The constellation (representing an armed giant) was associated with stormy weather (see Amos 5. 8, Virgil, *Aen.* i 535 and vii 719, Apollonius Rhodius, *Argonautica* i 1202).

306. *vexed* disturbed.

307. *Busiris* a mythical Pharaoh who sacrificed strangers. He was commonly identified with the Pharaoh of Exod. 1. M. identifies him with the Pharaoh of Exod. 14 who pursued the Israelites (*sojourners of Goshen*) through the Red Sea.

312. *Abject* cast down (literal and metaphorical).

314. *deep*] *Ed I, Ed II*; deeps *MS*.

315. *Princes, Potentates* suggesting 'Principalities' and 'Powers' (see above, 128*n*).

320. *virtue* strength. M. pointedly withholds the title of the angelic order of 'Virtues'. See ii 310–13, v 772–4, x 460–62 for further examples of such taunting with titles.

324. **Seraph* M. coined the singular on the analogy of *Cherub* and *Cherubim* (*OED*).

328–9. *thunderbolts / Transfix us* Cp. Virgil, *Aen*. i 44, where Oilean Ajax is pierced through the chest (*transfixo pectore*) by a thunderbolt which impales him to a rock.

339. *Amram's son* Moses, who summoned a plague of locusts with his *rod* (Exod. 10. 12–15).

340–41. *pitchy cloud / Of locusts* echoing Sylvester, *DWW* (1592–1608), *The Lawe* (1606): 'a sable Clowde / Of horned *Locusts*' (533–4).

341. *warping* rising, swarming, whirling through the air (*OED*).

345. *cope* vault or canopy like that of the sky (*OED* 7d).

348. *Sultan* the title of the Ottoman emperors. The word carried a smear of despotism in M.'s time.

351–5. *the populous North . . . sands* refers to the Goths, Huns, and Vandals who inundated the Roman Empire and plunged Europe into the Dark Ages. For Satan's association with the North, see v 689*n*.

353. *Rhene, Danaw* Rhine, Danube.

361–5. *their names . . . new names* Contrast Rev. 3. 12, where it is the righteous who get a 'new name'. Here the *new names* are those of future devils. The *blotted* angelic names never appear in *PL*. Cp. i 80–81, v 658, vi 373–85. For God's blotting of names, see Exod. 32. 33 and Rev. 3. 5: 'He that overcometh . . . I will not blot out his name out of the book of life'. M. has *Books* (not 'Book') to suggest the great number of angels. 'Blot out' implies 'annihilate, destroy' (*OED* 5), as in xi 891: 'to blot out mankind'.

366. *sufferance* divine permission (*OED* 6c).

372. *gay* showy, specious, immoral (*OED* 3, 5, 2).

religions rites (*OED* 3a).

373. *devils to adore for deities* Cp. Deut. 32. 17: 'They sacrificed unto devils, not to God'. Justin Martyr, Tertullian, Origen, Lactantius, and Augustine had argued that pagan gods were fallen angels, and the belief continued uninterrupted until the Renaissance. Cp. *Nativity* 173ff. and see C. A. Patrides, 'The Cessation of the Oracles: The History of a Legend' (*MLR* 60, 1965, 500–507).

376. *who first, who last* Cp. Homer, *Il*. v 703 ('who then was the first and who the last that they slaughtered?') and Virgil, *Aen*. xi 664 ('whom first, whom last, fierce maid, did you strike down with your dart?'). Catalogues of warriors are frequent in epic. Cp. Homer, *Il.* ii 484–877, Virgil, *Aen.* vii 641–817, Ariosto, *Orl. Fur.* xiv.

380. *promiscuous* indiscriminate.

386. *Thund'ring out of Sion* Joel 3. 16 and Amos 1. 2 prophesy how God 'shall roar out of Zion'.

387. *Between the Cherubim* a common phrase in the O.T. (see e.g. M.'s translation of Psalm 80. 1). There were images of Cherubim on the ark of the Covenant and more Cherubim flanked the ark in the Holy of Holies (Exod. 25. 18–21, I Kings 6. 23, 8. 6–7).

391. *affront* insult and face in defiance.

392. *Moloch* Hebrew 'king'. A god of the Ammonites, whose capital was *Rabba*, 'city of waters' (II Samuel 12. 27). Hollow brass idols depicted Moloch enthroned, with arms outstretched, wearing a crown on his calf's head. Children were sacrificed by being placed in his red-hot arms.

395. *passed through fire* Cp. II Kings 23. 10: 'that no man might make his son or daughter to pass through the fire to Molech'. A marginal comment in the Geneva Bible explains that Moloch's worshippers 'smote on the tabret [timbrel] while their children were burning, that their crye shulde not be heard'. See also Lev. 18. 21.

403. *opprobrious hill* the Mount of Olives. See below, 416*n*.

   grove Groves are associated with idolatry throughout the O.T. See Deut. 16. 21: 'Thou shalt not plant thee a grove of any trees near unto the altar of the Lord thy God'. Cp. I Kings 14. 23, I Kings 16. 33, I Kings 18. 19, II Kings 21. 7, II Kings 23. 4, and see *PR* ii 289 and note.

404. *Hinnom* a valley adjacent to Jerusalem. Patrick Hume, the earliest editor of *PL* (1695), derived the name from a Hebrew verb meaning 'cry out through excessive torment'.

   Tophet from Hebrew *toph*, 'a timbrel'. See lines 394–5.

405. *Gehenna* Greek, 'valley of Hinnom', translated in the A.V. (e.g. at Matt. 5. 29) as 'Hell'.

   Type symbol (*OED* 1).

406. *Chemos* Moabite fertility-god, identified by Jerome with the phallic god Priapus. See Num. 25 for Israel's *wanton rites* (414) and the plague (*woe*) that followed.

407–11. *Aroer, Hesebon, Sibma* and *Elealè* were northern Moabite towns. *Nebo* was in the *Abarim* mountains in the south.

409. *Seon* the Amorite King Sihon, conqueror of Moab, conquered in his turn by Moses (Num. 21. 21–30).

411. *Asphaltic pool* the Dead Sea, which has deposits of bitumen.

416. *hill of scandal* the Mount of Olives, where Solomon built temples for Chemos and Moloch (I Kings 11. 7).

417. *lust hard by hate* The context invites a priapic pun.

418. *Josiah* a reforming King of Judah. He destroyed the groves and idols of Moloch and Chemos (II Kings 23. 10–14).

422. *Baälim and Ashtaroth* plural forms of 'Baal' and 'Ashtoreth'. 'Baal' means 'lord' and is prefixed to proper names (e.g. Baal-Peor, Baal-Zebub). Cp. Judges 10. 6: 'the children of Israel . . . served Baalim and Ashtaroth'.

425. *uncompounded* undifferentiated into members. Cp. vi 350–53.

429. *Dilated* enlarged. Cp. iv 986.

432. *these*] *MS*; those *Ed I, Ed II*. *MS* is supported by line 437.

438–9. *Astoreth . . . Astarte* the Phoenician (*Sidonian*) original of Aphrodite, called *queen of Heav'n* at Jer. 44. 19. She had a bull's head above her own head, from which sprang lunar *crescent horns* (cp. *Nativity* 200).

443. *offensive mountain* the Mount of Olives, where the *uxorious king* Solomon built a temple for Astoreth to please his wives (II Kings 23. 13, I Kings 11. 4–5).

444. *heart . . . large* intellect . . . capacious. Cp. I Kings 4. 29: 'God gave Solomon . . . largeness of heart'. The Hebrew word translated as 'heart' in A.V. means 'intellect' (*OED* 'large' 3c).

446–52. *Thammuz . . . wounded* Thammuz follows Astarte because they were lovers (identified with Venus and Adonis). Here *Adonis* is a river in Lebanon, discoloured every July with reddish mud (supposedly Thammuz's blood). This *annual wound* was the occasion of a religious festival. See *Nativity* 204.

452–7. *love-tale . . . Judah* Cp. Ezek. 8. 14: 'Then he brought me to the door of the gate of the Lord's house which was toward the north; and, behold, there sat women weeping for Thammuz'.

457–61. *Next . . . fell flat* The Philistines placed the ark of the Covenant (which they had captured) in Dagon's temple. When they entered the temple the next morning, 'behold, Dagon was fallen upon his face to the ground before the ark of the Lord: and the head of Dagon and both the palms of his hands were cut off upon the threshold; only the stump of Dagon was left to him' (I Sam. 5. 4).

460. *grunsel* groundsel, threshold.

462–3. *upward . . . fish* John Selden had derived Dagon's name from Hebrew *dag*, 'fish' (*De Dis Syris* ii 3).

464–6. The five main Philistine cities were *Azotus* (or Asdod), *Gath, Ascalon, Accaron* (or Ecron), and *Gaza* (or Azza). M. employs the variant forms in *SA*.

467. *Rimmon* the chief Syrian god.

471. *A leper once he lost* Elisha told the Syrian general Naaman he would be cured of leprosy if he washed in the Jordan. At first Naaman scoffed ('Are not Abana and Pharpar, rivers of Damascus, better than all the waters of Israel?'), but he obeyed, was healed, and renounced Rimmon for God (II Kings 5. 8–19).

gained a king King Ahaz of Judah defeated Syria, then converted to Rimmon's cult (II Kings 16. 7−17).

472. *sottish* foolish.

478. *Osiris, Isis, Orus* Egyptian gods represented with the heads of beasts (respectively a bull, a cow, and a falcon).

479. *abused* deceived (*OED* 4a).

481. *disguised in brutish forms* Ovid tells how the Olympian gods fled from Typhon into Egypt, hiding in bestial forms that the Egyptians later worshipped (*Met.* v 319−31). See above, 198−9*n*. Cp. also Virgil, *Aen.* viii 698, where Egypt's 'monstrous gods' fight for Antony at Actium.

484. *calf in Oreb* Aaron made the 'calf in Horeb' (Ps. 106. 19) while Moses was receiving the Law (Exod. 32). The gold had been *borrowed* from Egypt (Exod. 12. 35), and the calf was traditionally identified with the Egyptian Apis.

rebel king Jeroboam, who led ten tribes of Israel in revolt against Solomon's son Rehoboam (I Kings 12. 12−23). The oxymoron implies that kingship is a kind of rebellion. Cp. vi 199, xii 36. In *Defensio* (1651) M. denies that Jeroboam was a rebel (*YP* 4. 406).

485. *Doubled* repeated (*OED* 3) and made twice as many (*OED* 1). Jeroboam set up two calves, 'the one in Bethel, and the other . . . in Dan' (I Kings 12. 29).

486. *Lik'ning . . . ox* Cp. Ps. 106. 20: 'they changed their glory into the similitude of an ox that eateth grass'.

487−9. *Jehovah . . . gods* God smote the Egyptian firstborn, 'both man and beast', at the passover (Exod. 12. 12).

490. *Belial* Hebrew 'worthlessness'. The word is not a name, and 'Belial' was never worshipped as a god. But the biblical phrase 'sons of Belial', common in the O.T., encouraged personification, as in II Cor. 6. 15. M.'s Belial is a coward. He comes *last*, in contrast to soldier Moloch, who came 'First' (392).

495. *Eli's sons* Cp. I. Sam. 2. 12: 'the sons of Eli were sons of Belial'. Although priests, they 'lay with the women that assembled at the door of the tabernacle' (I Sam. 2. 22).

498. *luxurious* given to luxury, and lascivious, unchaste (*OED* 1).

499. *riot* wanton revel (*OED* 2), debauchery (*OED* 1).

500. *injury* including 'offensive speech, reviling' (*OED* 2).

outrage including 'violent clamour, outcry' (*OED* 2b).

502. *flown* swollen, in flood (*OED* 'flow' 11b), often used figuratively of persons, as in Spenser, *FQ* II ii 36: 'In wine and meats she flowd above the bancke'.

504−5. *when . . . rape* following *Ed II. MS* and *Ed I* read 'when hospitable doors / Yielded their matrons to prevent [*MS* avoid] worse rape'. Both versions allude to Gen. 19 and Judges 19, but *Ed II* gives priority to Judges.

At Gen. 19. 8 Lot begs the Sodomites to rape his daughters rather than his angel guests. No rape took place and the angels destroyed Sodom. At *Gibeah* a Levite escaped *worse* (homosexual) *rape* by surrendering his concubine to 'certain sons of Belial'. The woman's fate could not have been worse. She was abused 'all the night' and died the next morning – possibly at the Levite's hands (Judges 19. 28–9). The change from 'Yielded' to *Exposed* might imply a moral judgement. Cp. Adam's 'To me committed and by me exposed' (x 957).

508. *Javan* Noah's grandson, ancestor of the Ionian Greeks (Gen. 10. 1–5).

509. *Heav'n and Earth* Uranus and Gaea, progenitors of the gods.

510. **boasted* OED's earliest participial instance.

510–13. *Titan . . . found* The Christian Lactantius (*Divine Institutes* I xiv) tells how *Titan*, the eldest son of Uranus and Gaea (*Heav'n and Earth*), was deposed by his brother *Saturn*, who was in turn deposed by his son *Jove*.

513. *measure* retribution (OED 15).

514–15. *Crete . . . Ida* Jove (Zeus) was born and secretly raised in a cave on Mount Ida in Crete.

516. *middle air* the second of three supposed layers of the atmosphere, extending only to the mountain-tops. Satan was associated with this region, on account of his title 'prince of the power of the air' (Eph. 2. 2). See *PR* i 39–47.

517. *Delphian cliff* the site of Apollo's oracle.

518. *Dodona* the site of Zeus's oracle, in northern Greece.

519. *Doric land* Greece.

519–21. *Saturn . . . isles* Following his defeat by Jove, Saturn fled over *Adria* (the Adriatic) to *th' Hesperian fields* (Italy), and thence to *the Celtic* fields (France) and *the utmost isles* (Britain).

523. *damp* dazed, stupefied (OED 2).

525. *found themselves not lost* Cp. Matt. 10. 39: 'He that findeth his life shall lose it'. The angels' newly-found selves are not the ones they have lost (see i 361–5n).

527. *doubtful* both 'full of apprehension' (OED 5) and 'giving cause for apprehensions' (OED 4).

528. *recollecting* remembering and pulling (himself) together.

530. *fainting*] Ed II; fainted MS, Ed I.

532. *clarions* shrill trumpets used in war.

534. *Azazel* Hebrew 'God strengthens'. Cabbalistic lore made him one of four standard-bearers in Satan's army. 'Azazel' was sometimes thought to be his original name (see Bernard Bamberger, *Fallen Angels*, 1952, 278), but M.'s rebels have lost their angelic names. See i 80–81, 361–3, v 658 and cp. vi 371–85. In the Hebrew version of Lev. 16. 8, the word translated as 'scapegoat' means 'goat for Azazel', a wicked spirit.

536. *advanced* raised, elevated (*OED* 4).

541. *upsent Cp. the neologisms 'upwhirled' (iii 493) and 'upgrown' (ix 677).

542. *concave* vault.

543. *reign* realm (*OED* 2).

546. *orient* lustrous and rising.

548. *serried pressed close together, shoulder to shoulder.

550. *phalanx* Greek and Macedonian battle formation consisting of heavy infantry presenting an impenetrable thicket of spears. Greek phalanxes were usually eight ranks deep; Satan's is *Of depth immeasurable* (549).

550–59. *Dorian . . . minds* Cp. Plutarch's description of Spartans marching to *flutes*: 'it was a sight at once solemn and terrifying to see them marching in step to the pipes, creating no gap in the phalanx nor suffering any disturbance of spirit, but approaching the confrontation calmly and happily in time to the music' (*Lycurgus* 22). Plato describes the *Dorian mood* (mode) as 'the note or accent which a brave man utters in the hour of danger and stern resolve, or when his cause is falling, and he is going to wounds or death' (*Republic* iii 399, trans. Jowett).

556. *swage* assuage, relieve.

560–61. *Breathing . . . silence* Cp. Homer's Achaians marching 'silently, breathing valour, / stubbornly minded each in his heart to stand by the others' (*Il.* iii 8). *Breathing* also suggests wind instruments such as *flutes*. Cp. vi 63–8.

563. *horrid* bristling (Latin *horridus*) with spears.

568. *traverse* across the ranks (having looked down the *files*).

573. *since created man* since man was created (Latin idiom).

575. *small infantry* Pygmies. On the war of Pygmies and cranes see Homer, *Il.* iii 3–6. Notice the pun on *infantry*.

577. *Phlegra* The war between the gods and the Giants began at Phlegra in Macedonia and ended at Phlegra in Italy.

579. *auxiliar* assisting, with a mocking pun on *auxilia* (foreign, low-paid troops in the Roman army).

580. *Uther's son* King Arthur, some of whose knights were Breton (*Armoric*).

583. *Aspramont* 'the dark mountain': a mountain in Calabria. Romantic epics tell how Charlemagne defeated a Saracen army there. See Andrea da Barbarino's *Aspromonte* and Ariosto, *Orl. Fur.* i 30, xvii 14, xxvii 54. *Montalban* 'the white mountain': the home of the paladin Rinaldo.

584. *Damasco* Damascus. Christians and Saracens joust there in Ariosto, *Orl. Fur.* xvii.

Trebizond a Byzantine city on the Black Sea, famous for tournaments.

585. *Biserta* Bizerte, a port in Tunisia, from which Boiardo's Troiano leads a Muslim invasion of Spain (*Orl. Inn.* ii).

586–7. *Charlemagne . . . Fontarabbia* There is no known source for Charlemagne's *fall* at *Fontarabbia* (Fuenterrabia, on the Spanish coast), though Charlemagne's paladin Roland made a famous last stand at Ronces-valles, some forty miles away. M. may be alluding to the events of August 1659, when Charles II visited Fuenterrabia in an attempt to muster French and Spanish support (Fowler).

588. *observed* including 'reverenced, honoured' (*OED* 4b). The syntax allows either Satan or his troops to be the observer.

594. *glory* see above, i 141*n*.

594–9. *sun . . . monarchs* Charles II's censor objected to these lines – and with reason. An eclipse had provoked *fear of change* on the day of Charles's birth, 29 May 1630. Royalists officially claimed the event as a good omen (see e.g. Dryden, *Astraea Redux*, 288–91), but M.'s nephew, Edward Phillips, remembered it as a portent of the Interregnum. See *Chronicle of the Kings of England* (1665), 498. See also Edward Chamberlayne, *Anglia Notitiae* (1669), 127: 'the Sun suffered an Eclipse, a sad presage as some then divined, that this Prince's Power should for some time be eclipsed, as it hath been'. Cp. Tasso's comparison of Argantes to a comet that 'tidings sad of death and mischief brings / To mighty lords, to monarchs, and to kings' (*Gerus. Lib.* vii 52).

595. *horizontal* on the horizon.

597. *disastrous* ill-starred (Latin *dis* + *astrum*), with a hint that 'Lucifer' has been 'dis-starred'. See v 708, vii 131, x 425.

599. *Perplexes* puzzles and torments.

601. *intrenched* wounded (*OED* 'entrench' 3), *furrowed (*OED* 'intrench' 1, earliest instance 1754).

603. *courage*] *Ed I, Ed II*; valour *MS*.

considerate prudent, deliberate (*OED* 2), as in 'the willing and considerate murderer' (1597); from Latin *considerare*, 'to watch the stars'.

609. *amerced / Of* *deprived of (*OED* 2d). 'Amerce' meant 'fine' and one was amerced 'in' or 'with' (not 'of') a sum. M.'s usage puns on the root *amercié*, 'at the mercy of'.

615. *blasted heath* echoing Shakespeare, *Macbeth* I iii 77.

620. *Tears such as angels weep* Angels were usually thought to be incapable of weeping, but cp. Shakespeare, *Measure for Measure* II ii 121–2, where 'proud man' is said to play 'such fantastic tricks before high heaven / As makes the angels weep'. M.'s good angels eat (v 434–5), make love (viii 620–29), and maybe weep (xi 23–5), so Satan's tears need not reveal a coarsened nature, though they might express a tyrant's sentimentality. Newton in 1749 saw an allusion to the Persian King Xerxes, who wept while reviewing his 'vast army, and reflecting that they were mortal, at the time that he was hast'ning them to their fate, and to the intended destruction of the greatest people in the world, to gratify his own vain glory'. Cp. x 307–11n.

624. *event* outcome.

632. *puissant* powerful.

636. *different* perhaps 'deferent', in the sense 'protracted, lingering' (*OED* 'defer' 4b).

646. *work* plan (*OED* 11).

    close design secret scheming.

650. *Space* *stellar depths (*OED* 8), but even this sense is too small. Satan is referring to Chaos (not just our universe), and *worlds* here means 'universes'. Cp. ii 916, 1004, 1052, iii 74, vii 191, 209, etc. Nicholas of Cusa and Giordano Bruno had argued for an infinite universe with many habitable worlds. The theory had neo-Platonic and Epicurean sources, but it was still a 'a fringe belief' in M.'s time (Marjara 77). Cp. Lucretius, *De Rerum Nat.* ii 1048–89.

651. *fame* rumour. See ii 346–52, 830, x 481–2 for the rumour of man's creation, and see vii 150–56n for God's motives in creating us.

654. *favour equal* Raphael later speaks of God's 'equal love' for men and angels (viii 228). Beëlzebub will soon claim that man is 'favoured more' (ii 350).

656. *eruption* breaking out (suggesting Hell's volcanoes).

662. *Open or understood* overt or covert. Cp. Belial's 'open or concealed' (ii 187). Belial wants to escape God's notice; Satan wants God to know his enemy.

666–7. *highly* haughtily (*OED* 5) and loudly (*OED* 3c). The paronomasia (*highly . . . Highest*) is typical of M. Cp. i 642, iv 181, v 869, ix 11, etc.

672. *scurf* sulphurous deposit (suggesting also a diseased body).

673. *his womb* 'the perverted body-landscape of Hell' (Ricks) – but this nuance might have been weaker in M.'s time, when *his* served for *its*. M. uses 'its' only three times in his poetry.

676. *pioneers* military engineers.

678. *Mammon* an Aramaic word for 'riches', personified at Matt. 6. 24 and Luke 16. 13. Medieval tradition identified Mammon with Plutus, the god of wealth, and so with Pluto, god of the underworld. Burton made him prince of the lowest order of devils (*Anatomy of Melancholy* I ii I 2).

679. *erected* high-souled (*OED* 2) and upright (in posture).

684. *vision beatific* mystical experience of seeing God.

685. *suggestion* devilish temptation (*OED* 1).

686. *centre* (centre of) the earth.

686–8. *impious . . . hid* Cp. Ovid's description of men rifling earth's bowels (*viscera terrae*) in search of riches (*Met.* i 137–40); also Spenser, *FQ* II vii 17, where 'a cursed hand' seeking 'hid treasures' wounds the 'wombe / Of his great Grandmother'; also Phineas Fletcher, *The Apollyonists* (1627) v 4: 'The earth (their Grandame Earth) they fierce invade, / And all her bowels search, and rent, and tear'. The oxymoron *precious bane* (692) recalls Giles Fletcher, *CV* (1610) ii 54, where men wound 'their mothers side' while searching for 'pretious perills'.

690. *ribs* veins of ore (technical term). Pearce in 1733 compared viii 465–9 where God opens Adam's side and extracts 'a rib . . . wide was the wound'. *admire* marvel.

694. *Babel* the Tower of Babel (xii 38–62).

works of Memphian kings the Egyptian pyramids.

703. *founded*] MS, *Ed I*; found out *Ed II*. The devils had found the ore in lines 688–90. Now they melt it.

704. *bullion dross* boiling dregs.

711. *Rose like an exhalation* Exhalations were thought to cause comets, meteors (both bad omens), and pestilence. See ix 180*n*, x 692–4.

712. *dulcet symphonies and voices sweet* Pandaemonium, like Troy and Thebes, arises to the sound of music.

713. *pilasters* square columns or pillars.

714. *overlaid* surmounted.

715. *architrave* the lowest member of the entablature in a classical temple: the main beam that rests on the columns.

716. *Cornice* the uppermost member of the entablature, surmounting the frieze.

bossy carved in relief.

717. *fretted* adorned with carved or wrought patterns.

718. *Alcairo* Cairo (ancient Memphis).

720. *Belus* a Babylonian god. Herodotus describes his temple as a series of eight towers placed one on top of another (i 181).

Serapis a god of Ptolemaic Egypt (composite of Osiris and Apis).

728. *cressets* iron baskets hung from the ceiling.

729. *naphtha and asphaltus* oil and pitch, to be placed in *lamps* and *cressets* respectively.

731. *Admiring* marvelling.

732–5. *architect . . . residence* Cp. the gods' palaces built by Hephaestos (Homer, *Il.* i 605–8) and Mulciber (Ovid, *Met.* ii 1–4).

738. *his name* Hephaestos (in *Greece*), or *Mulciber* (or Vulcan) in Italy (*Ausonian land*). His angelic name has been blotted out and M. never speaks it.

740–46. *how he fell . . . isle* Cp. the daylong fall of Homer's Hephaestos (*Il.* i 591–5): '[Zeus] caught me by the foot and threw me from the magic threshold, / and all day long I dropped helpless, and about sunset / I landed in Lemnos'.

745. *zenith* highest point of the celestial sphere (*OED* 1, referring to

Mulciber's fall) and culminating point of a heavenly body (*OED* 2, referring to *sun*).

746. *Aégean* For accent cp. *PR* iv 238 and Fairfax's Tasso (i 61): 'O'er Aegean Seas by many a Greekish hold'.

750. *engines* plots (*OED* 3) and machines used in warfare (*OED* 5).

756. **Pandaemonium* Greek 'seat of all demons (or *daimones*)'. The original spelling allows the devils to see themselves as classical *daimones* rather than demons (though *daimones* still suggests demons through N.T. usage). Cp. *PR* ii 122.

capital] *Ed I*, *Ed II*; 'Capitoll' corr. to 'Capitall' (in a different hand) *MS*.

757. *peers* nobles. Pandaemonium has a King and House of Lords, but no Commons (see below, i 792*n*). Cp. ii 507 ('grand infernal Peers') and contrast i 39 and v 812, where 'peers' means 'equals'. Satan exploits the ambiguity at ii 445.

759. *place* rank, official position.

choice promotion or election from the ranks.

764. *Wont* were wont to.

Soldan's Sultan's.

765. *paynim* pagan.

768–75. *bees . . . affairs* Homer's Achaians marching to a council (*Il.* ii 87–90), Virgil's busy Carthaginians (*Aen.* i 430–35) and Virgil's dead awaiting reincarnation (*Aen.* vi 707–9) are all likened to bees. Seventeenth-century apiarists would kill off a swarm by lowering the hive into a flaming sulphur pit. This fiery end could serve as a warning to those who praised the swarm's Royalist politics (see John Simons, *MQ* 21. 1, March 1987, 21–2). Virgil (*Aen.* xii 583–92) and Apollonius Rhodius (*Argonautica* ii 130–34) liken panic-stricken defenders of a city to bees whose hive is filled with smoke. See also Virgil, *Georg.* iv 149–227.

769. *Taurus* the zodiacal sign of the Bull (hence *rides*).

774. *expatiate* both 'wander at will' and 'speak at length'. The word adds mock grandeur to the devils.

780. *that Pygméan race* See above, 575*n*. The Pygmies were supposed to live beyond the Himalayas (*the Indian mount*).

781–8. *faery elves . . . rebounds* Encounters with elves are frequent in folklore. Aubrey tells of a shepherd who came across dancing elves: 'He sayd the ground opened, and he was brought into strange places under ground where they used musicall Instruments, violls, and Lutes.' Such encounters bring *joy* at the time, but 'never any afterwards enjoy themselves' (*Remaines*, 1686–7, 204). A medieval tradition held that the less sinful fallen angels were allowed to haunt earth's forests, where they were known as 'elves'.

782. *midnight revels* Cp. Shakespeare, *A Midsummer Night's Dream*, II i

141 ('moonlight revels'), but M.'s elves are quite un-Shakespearean.

783–4. *sees,* / *Or dreams he sees* Cp. Virgil, *Aen.* vi 751–4, where Aeneas glimpses Dido's shade 'as one who sees . . . or thinks to have seen, the moon / Rising through cloud'.

785. *arbitress* witness (lit. 'one who goes to see', *ad* + *bito*).

790. *at large* free, uncramped – with a play on the other sense of 'large'. Ricks remarks that 'nothing could more effectively belittle the devils' than this 'superbly contemptuous pun' (*Milton's Grand Style*, 15).

792. *Court* The royal connotation is ominous. Parliament was also a 'court', but there is no House of Commons in Pandaemonium, where Satan sits enthroned amidst *Lords*.

795. *close recess* secret and secluded place.

conclave secret assembly (*OED* 4), suggesting 'the assembly of Cardinals met for the election of a Pope' (*OED* 3). In Phineas Fletcher's *The Apollyonists* (1627) jesuitical devils conceive the Gunpowder Plot after meeting in 'deepe Conclave' (i 17).

797. *Frequent* crowded.

798. *consult* a secret meeting for purposes of sedition (*OED* 2).

BOOK II

1–6. *High . . . eminence* Cp. the bright throne of Spenser's Lucifera (*FQ* I iv 8); also M.'s description in *Defensio* of Charles I enthroned (*YP* 4. 506).

2. *Ormus* Hormuz, an island town in the Persian Gulf, famous for jewels.

5. *merit* desert of either good or evil (*OED* 2a).

7. *high uplifted beyond hope* both 'lifted high above (his) hope' and 'lifted high in a place so low as to be beyond all hope'. Cp. i 66, iv 160.

9. *success* outcome (with a wry pun on the modern sense).

11. *Powers and Dominions* angelic orders (Col. 1. 16).

10. *imaginations* schemes, plots (*OED* 2a).

15. *Virtues* the angelic order, with overtones of 'manliness, valour' (*OED* 'virtue' 7).

24–40. *The happier . . . assured us* Lewis (98) calls Satan's argument 'nonsense', since its corollary is that 'every approach to victory must take away the grounds on which victory is hoped'. Waldock (69–70) replies that Satan's speech is rhetoric, not logic, and should be judged 'by its effect'.

41. *open war or covert guile* Cp. Tasso's Satan urging 'open force, or secret guile' (*Gerus. Lib.* iv 16, trans. Fairfax). Notice that Satan asks the devils to debate how (not whether) to return.

43. *Moloch* As at i 392, Moloch is first on his feet. The contrast between

the bellicose Moloch and the eloquent coward Belial has epic precedent in the contrasts between Virgil's Turnus and Drances (*Aen.* xi 336f.) and Tasso's Argantes and Orcanes (*Gerus. Lib.* x 35f.). See below, 109*n.*

50. *recked* cared.

thereafter accordingly.

51. *sentence* judgement.

52. *More unexpért* less experienced.

63. *horrid* horrifying and bristling (with *flames*).

65. *engine* machine of war (God's thunder).

69. *Tartarean* of Tartarus, the classical hell.

strange fire Cp. Lev. 10. 1–2: 'the sons of Aaron . . . offered strange fire before the Lord, which he commanded them not. And there went out fire from the Lord, and devoured them, and they died'.

73. *drench* soporific potion (*OED* 2) and *act of drenching (*OED* 4, earliest instance 1808, but the verb had existed since medieval times).

74. *forgetful* causing oblivion.

75. *in our proper motion we ascend* Moloch is proved wrong when Satan encounters a 'vast vacuity' in Chaos and plummets downward (ii 932–5). The devils may have lost their angelic buoyancy, but Marjara (148–9) sees M. as confirming the New Philosophy of Galileo and debunking Aristotelian physics.

79. *Insulting* making assaults (*OED* 3) and exulting.

81. *ascent is easy* Contrast Virgil, *Aen.* vi 126–9: 'the descent to Avernus is easy . . . but to retrace one's steps and escape to the upper air, this is the task, this is the toil'. See also ii 432–3, iii 19–21, 524.

82. *event* outcome.

89. *exercise* vex, afflict (*OED* 4b).

90. *vassals of his anger* Cp. Spenser, *Tears of the Muses* 126: 'vassals of Gods wrath, and slaves of sin'; also Romans 9. 22: 'vessels of wrath fitted to destruction'. In *The Hierarchie of the Blessed Angels* (1635), Thomas Heywood had identified 'vessels of wrath' as a demonic order commanded by Belial (436). Moloch's pun might therefore be a jibe at Belial, who styles himself 'vessel', but is really a 'vassal'.

92. *penance* punishment (*OED* 5), suggesting Roman Catholic mortification of the flesh (notice *scourge*).

94. *What doubt we* Why do we hesitate.

97. *essential* essence (adj. for noun).

99–101. *if . . . nothing* 'if we are indeed indestructible, we are already in the worst possible state, which is not annihilation'.

104. *fatal* upheld by Fate and deadly.

106. *denounced* portended.

109. *Belial* See i 490*n.* M.'s cowardly orator resembles Tasso's Orcanes, who makes a disguised plea for capitulation in the Saracen council (*Gerus.*

Lib. x 48). Cp. also Virgil's Drances, who in council was 'valiant of tongue, though his hand was cold for battle' (*Aen.* xi 337–8).

110. *person* person of rank (*OED* 2c) and mask (Latin *persona*). Notice *false and hollow.*

114. *reason* argument.

116. *To vice industrious* Cp. Sylvester, *DWW* (1592–1608), *Eden* (1598) 304: 'To vertue dull, to vice ingenious'.

123. *success* outcome (with a wry pun on the modern sense).

124. *fact* feat of valour (*OED* 1b).

127. *scope* target.

139. *ethereal mould* that which is fashioned of pure fire (in contrast to Moloch's *baser fire*).

148. *thoughts . . . eternity* Cp. Lucretius, *De Rerum Nat.* ii 1044–7: 'the mind seeks to discover what exists out there in the infinity of space beyond the walls of the world, where the intellect longs to peer, and the mind flies free by its own projection'.

    wander a recurrent word in *PL*, where it has 'almost always a pejorative, or melancholy connotation' (MacCaffrey 188). See e.g., i 365, ii 561, iii 667, vii 50, ix 1136, and Fish (130–41).

150. *wide womb of uncreated Night* Cp. Spenser, *FQ* III vi 36: 'in the wide wombe of the world there lyes, / In hatefull darkenesse and in deepe horrore, / An huge eternall *Chaos*'.

151. *Devoid of sense and motion* Cp. Claudio's dread of death that ends 'This sensible warm motion' (Shakespeare, *Measure for Measure* III i 120).

152. *Let this be good* 'supposing this were desirable'.

156. *Belike* in all likelihood.

    impotence lack of self-restraint (*OED* 3), sarcastically contrasted with God's omnipotence.

159–63. *Wherefore . . . worse* Referring to Moloch's question 'what can be worse / Than to dwell here?' (85–6).

160. *they who* Belial avoids naming Moloch, who is in any case nameless (see i 361–5). The 'courteously impersonal form' (Fowler) is appropriate to Parliamentary debate, where names were (and still are) prohibited.

165. *amain* at full speed.

170–74. *What if . . . What if* The coward's question. Cp. Tasso's Orcanes: 'But what if that appointed day they [the pagan reinforcements] miss? / Or else, ere we expect, what if they came?' (*Gerus. Lib.* x 44, trans. Fairfax).

170. *breath that kindled* Cp. Isa. 30. 33: 'the pile [of Hell] is fire and much wood; the breath of the Lord, like a stream of brimstone, doth kindle it'.

170–71. *fires . . . sevenfold* Cp. the fiery furnace into which Nebuchadnezzar cast Shadrach, Meshach, and Abed-nego. The furnace was heated 'seven times more than it was wont to be heated' (Dan. 3. 19).

174. *red right hand* Cp. Horace's image of Jove exciting civil war in Rome by hurling thunderbolts with a 'red right hand', *rubente dextera* (*Odes* I ii 1-4).

176. *cataracts* flood-gates (Latin, *cataractae*). At Gen. 7. 11, the Vulgate and Junius-Tremellius describe Noah's Flood as coming from *cataractae*. See xi 824*n*. Our *firmament* rained water, Hell rains fire.

182. *racking* both 'torturing' and 'driving'.

184. *converse with* both 'talk by means of' and 'dwell with'.

185. *Unrespited, unpitied, unreprieved* M. is fond of triple collocations of the prefix 'un-'. See e.g. iii 231, v 899.

187. *open or concealed* Cp. 'open or understood' (i 662) and 'open war or covert guile' (ii 41).

188-9. *what can . . . With him* How can force or guile hurt him?

191. *motions* proposals.

199. *To suffer, as to do* echoing the famous words spoken by Mutius Scaevola, when he burned his hand so as to give the Etruscan Porsenna a demonstration of Roman fortitude: *Et facere et pati fortia Romanum est* (Livy ii 12). Belial manages to sound like Scaevola, but his whole purpose is to avoid *the flames* (172). Cp. i 158 and *PR* iii 195.

212. *mind* be concerned about (*OED* 8), be aware of (*OED* 4). The latter sense casts doubt on God's omniscience.

214. *his breath . . . flames* See above, 170*n*.

215-19. *Our . . . pain* Belial considers three possibilities: (1) the angels' *purer essence* will prevail over Hell's flames and so remove pain at its source, (2) the angels will get used to Hell, though neither they nor it will change, (3) Hell's flames will cause the angels' *purer essence* to change, and so deprive the angels of their ability to feel pain. Belial prefers a comfortable life to his angelic essence, but at least he is concerned for his essence. Mammon is indifferent about it at ii 276-7, where he welcomes Belial's (3) as the angels' best hope.

216. *inured* accustomed, but M.'s voice behind Belial may play on 'burn in' (*OED* 'inure' v²) as in 'He . . . inures the Marke of the Beast, the Devills Flesh-brand, upon one or other part of the body' (1646). Belial's *purer essence* will also be 'burned away' (Latin *inurere*, 'remove by burning').

218. *temper* physiological temperament (the mixture of humours determining one's physical and mental constitution).

220. *light* both 'lightly borne' and 'luminous'.

224. *For happy* as for happiness.

233. *strife* between *Fate* and *Chance* (Bentley), or God and the devils (Pearce). 'There may also be an allusion to the Empedoclean notion of a universal Strife' (Fowler).

243. *Forced* both 'compulsory' and 'produced with effort'.

hallelujahs an imperative (Hebrew 'praise Jah'). Cp. 'unfeignèd halleluijahs' (vi 744).

lordly   both 'haughty' and 'as Lord'.

245. **Ambrosial*   divinely fragrant (*OED* 1c).

250. *by leave obtained*   if God were to grant us permission.

256. *easy yoke*   Cp. Matt. 11. 28–30: 'Come unto me . . . For my yoke is easy'. Cp. also Samson's contempt for those who prefer 'Bondage with ease' to 'strenuous liberty' (*SA* 271).

263–7. *How oft . . . throne*   Cp. Ps. 18. 11: 'He made darkness his secret place; his pavilion round about him were dark waters and thick clouds of the skies'. See also II Chron. 6. 1: 'The Lord hath said that he would dwell in thick darkness'.

275. *our elements*   both 'elements composing our bodies' and 'our places of abode' (*OED* 'element' 12). Demons were thought to dwell in the four elements (see *Il Penseroso* 93–4). Augustine had denied that devils could assume bodies of Hell-fire (*City of God* xxi 10), but M. allows more to Mammon's hopes. The irony lies in Mammon's shameful readiness to relinquish his *purer essence* (see above, 215–19*n*).

277. *temper*   proportionate mixture of elements (*OED* 1), bodily constitution (*OED* 8).

278. *The sensible*   *the element (in a spiritual being) that is capable of feeling (*OED* B 3, sole instance). Cp. M.'s use of 'speakable' in the active sense 'able to speak' (ix 563).

281. *Compose*   set in order (*OED* 15).

282. *where*] *Ed I*; *were Ed II*.

285. *hollow rocks*   imitating *cava saxa*, a stock phrase in Latin verse (cp. Virgil, *Aen*. iii 566, Lucan, *Pharsalia* iv 455). M.'s simile also recalls Tasso's description of the Christian army at prayer: 'Such noise their passions make, as when one hears / The hoarse sea waves roar, hollow rocks betwixt' (*Gerus. Lib.* iii 6, trans. Fairfax). See also *Gerus. Lib.* ix 22.

288. *o'erwatched*   worn out with watching (*OED* 3).

297. *policy*   statecraft, including the bad sense 'crafty device, stratagem' (*OED* 4b).

302. *front*   forehead or face (*OED* 1, 2).

306. **Atlantéan*   Poets often likened statesmen to the Titan Atlas, whom Jove condemned to bear the heavens on his shoulders. See e.g. Spenser's Sonnet to Lord Burleigh prefaced to *FQ*.

312. *style*   ceremonial title. Cp. Satan's preoccupation with titles at v 772–7, x 460–2, and *PR* ii 121–5.

324. *first and last*   Cp. Rev. 22. 13: 'I am Alpha and Omega, the beginning and the end, the first and last'.

327. *iron sceptre*   Cp. Rev. 19. 15 ('he shall rule them with a rod of iron') and M.'s translation of Ps. 2 (line 20): 'With iron sceptre bruised'. Cp. also Abdiel's distinction between God's 'golden sceptre' and 'iron rod' (v 886–7). God's *golden* (328) and *iron* sceptres symbolized Mercy and Justice. Cp.

Fletcher, *CV* (1610) i 75, where Mercy begs the Father not to use the 'yron scepter' of Justice against man.

329. *What* Why.

330. *determined us* put an end to us (*OED* 1) and decided our course (*OED* 16).

336. *to* to the limit of.

337. *reluctance* struggling (*OED* 1).

349–50. *less / In power* Cp. Ps. 8. 5: 'thou hast made him a little lower than the angels, and hast crowned him with glory and honour'.

350. *favoured more* Beëlzebub's *more* might be petulant. Satan and Raphael both say that men and angels are 'equal' in God's favour (i 654, viii 228). Flannagan suggests that *favoured more* might mean 'resembling his father more, as in the idiom "He favored his father" '. M. never says that angels were made in God's image, but iv 567 implies that they were.

352–3. *oath . . . shook* Cp. Isa. 13. 12–13: 'I will make a man more precious than fine gold; even a man than the golden wedge of Ophir. Therefore I will shake the heavens'. Cp. also Heb. 6. 17 and 12. 26, Homer, *Il.* i 530, Virgil, *Aen.* ix 106.

355. *mould* bodily form (*OED* sb³ 10b), with overtones of 'earth regarded as the material of the human body' (*OED* sb¹ 4).

357. *attempted* both 'try with temptations' (*OED* 'attempt' II 5) and 'try with violence, make an attack upon' (*OED* III).

367. *puny* including 'born since us' (French *puis né*).

368. *their God* not 'our God' or 'God'. This is the first time in *PL* that any devil has spoken the name.

369–70. *repenting . . . Abolish* Cp. Gen. 6. 7: 'And the Lord said, I will destroy man . . . for it repenteth me that I have made them'. Cp. iii 162–6 and ix 945–51.

374. *partake with us* both 'share our fate' and 'take our side'.

375. *original*] *Ed II*; originals *Ed I*. Some editors prefer 'originals' because it more obviously refers to both Adam and Eve. But 'original' could mean 'derivation, parentage' (*OED* sb 1) as well as 'progenitor' (*OED* sb 2), and it might also mean 'pattern, archetype' (*OED* sb 3), and so imply a sneer at God as the original of man's image.

376. *Advise* consider, ponder (*OED* 3).

377. *sit in darkness* Cp. Ps. 107. 10–11: 'Such as sit in darkness and in the shadow of death, being bound in affliction and iron; Because they rebelled against the words of God'.

378. *Hatching vain empires* Cp. God's Spirit *brooding* on the abyss (i 20–22, vii 233–40).

383. *one root* Adam and Eve (root of our family tree) and the forbidden Tree, 'root of all our woe' (ix 645).

387. *States* dignitaries, nobles (*OED* 24). Editors infer a reference to the three Estates of the Realm (Lords, Clergy, Commons), but Pandaemonium has no Commons. See i 792*n*.

391. *Synod* assembly (usually of clergy, so *Synod of gods* is satirical, cp. vi 156).

404. *tempt* attempt (Satan will also 'tempt' God by testing how far he can go).

405. *abyss* Greek, 'bottomless'.

406. *obscure* *darkness (*OED* B 1, adj. as noun). *Palpable obscure* recalls Exod. 10. 21: 'darkness which may be felt' (Junius-Tremellius: *palpare possit tenebras*).

407. *uncouth* unknown.

409. *abrupt* *precipice (*OED* B, earliest instance of the adj. used as a noun). Corns (88) sees these coinages as reflecting the 'abortive gulf' (ii 441) of Chaos: 'readers too are left groping for some familiar substantive to fix upon: we find instead the shaky premise of a new noun'.

410. *happy isle* The first of a series of 'metaphors and similes in which Satan is a voyager or trader, and earth an island' (Fowler). Cp. ii 636–42, 1043–4, iv 159–65, ix 513–16. The phrase also hints at the Fortunate Isles of Greek myth (cp. iii 568–70 and note).

412. *senteries* sentries.

415. *Choice in our suffrage* care in our vote (which never takes place).

418. *suspense* attentive, in suspense, hanging (*OED* a 1, 2, 4).

420. *all sat mute* So 'all stood mute' when God called for a volunteer to die for man (iii 217). Most critics see Satan's heroic offer (ii 426–66) as a parody of the Son's (iii 222–65). Cp. Homer, *Il.* vii 92–3, where Hector challenges any Greek to single combat, and all sat 'silent, / ashamed to refuse him, and afraid to accept his challenge'.

425. *proffer* volunteer (oneself) and offer (the *voyage*) to someone else (and so be seen to decline it).

432–3. *long . . . light* Another echo of the Sibyl's warning to Aeneas (see above, 81*n*). Cp. also Dante, *Inf.* xxxiv 95 ('long is the way, and arduous the road').

435. *Outrageous to devour* violently destructive.

436. *gates . . . adamant* Cp. the adamantine gates of Virgil's Tartarus (*Aen.* vi 552). On adamant, see i 48*n*.

439. *unessential* *possessing no essence (*OED* 1). Cp. 'uncreated Night' (ii 150) and 'unsubstantial' night in *PR* iv 399.

441. *abortive* Chaos is a 'womb' (ii 150, 911, x 476) containing *embryon atoms* (ii 900) and *pregnant causes* (913). Satan may also think of Chaos 'as a miscarrying womb . . . from which the traveller may never be born, or which may render him as if unborn' (Fowler).

444. *escape.*] *Ed I, Ed II, Ed III*; escape? *Ed IV*. The earlier pointing admits no doubt about the magnitude of the dangers Satan is facing.

445. *Peers* nobles (cp. i 757, ii 507), but with overtones of 'companions', 'equals' (*OED* 3, 1). Satan had 'set himself in glory above his peers' (i 39), so he is naturally evasive as to whether Hell's Peers are equal to each other or to him. M. and Salmasius had debated the precise meaning of 'Peer' (Latin, *parem*). See *Defensio* (*YP* 4. 463).

450–56. *Wherefore . . . honoured sits?* Cp. the heroic speech of Homer's Sarpedon: 'Glaukos, why is it you and I are honoured before all others / with pride of place, the choice meats and the filled wine cups / in Lykia . . . ? Therefore it is our duty in the forefront of the Lykians / to take our stand, and bear our part in the blazing of battle' (*Il.* xii 310–16).

452. *Refusing* 'if I refuse'.

457. *intend* occupy yourselves with (*OED* 12). *Go* invites a pun on 'start on a journey' (*OED* 'intend' 6b), contrasting Satan's heroic voyage with the passive adventurism of those who *intend at home*.

461. *deceive* wile away (*OED* 5).

467. *prevented* pre-empted.

468. *raised* made bold.

478. *reverence* bow (*OED* 2).

prone bending forward and downward (*OED* 1). Fowler understands 'grovelling' (*OED* 4), and contrasts the good angels' obeisance (iii 349). But *Towards him they bend* need not imply prostration. Even good angels bow 'low' to 'superior Spirits' (iii 736–8).

485. *close* secret.

varnished speciously tricked out.

488–95. *As when . . . rings* Cp. Ariosto's lovely simile likening Olimpia's tearful face to sunlight after a shower, when birds sing in 'beams of light' (*Orl. Fur.* xi 65).

490. *louring element* threatening sky.

496–7. *Devil with devil damned / Firm concord holds* Cp. Matt. 12. 25–6: 'Every kingdom divided against itself is brought to desolation . . . if Satan cast out Satan, he is divided against himself; how shall then his kingdom stand?'

504. *enow* enough.

507. *Peers* nobles, Peers of the Realm.

508. *Paramount* Lord paramount, supreme ruler.

509. *Antagonist* translating 'Satan', which means 'enemy', 'adversary' or 'antagonist'. Cp. x 386–7.

512. *globe* body of soldiers (Latin *globus*). Flying angels might also adopt a spherical formation. Cp. vi 399, *PR* iv 581, and Fletcher, *CV* (1610) iv 13: 'A globe of winged Angels'.

fiery Seraphim Seraphs were associated with fire on account of Hebrew *saraph*, 'to burn'. Cp. v 807.

513. **emblazonry* heraldic devices.

*horrent bristling.

515. *result* outcome of deliberations (*OED* 3a).

517. *alchemy* brass (trumpets).

520. *acclaim shout of applause (coined from the verb).

521. *raised* encouraged.

522. *rangèd powers* armies drawn up in ranks.

526. *entertain* while away (*OED* 9b).

527. *his*] Ed I; *this* Ed II.

528–55. *Part . . . audience* Athletic games and musical contests are frequent in classical epic. Cp. Homer, *Il.* ii 774–9, xxiii 262ff., *Od.* viii 100ff., Virgil, *Aen.* v 104ff., Apollonius Rhodius, *Argonautica* ii 1ff., Statius, *Thebaid* vi 255ff. M.'s infernal games most closely resemble *Aen.* vi 642–59.

528. *sublime* raised aloft (*OED* 1) and elated (*OED* 3b).

530. *Pythian fields* The Pythian games (supposedly instituted by Apollo after he had killed the serpent Python) took place at Delphi.

531. *shun the goal* swing tight around the turning-pole in a chariot race. Cp. Homer, *Il.* xxiii 318–41.

532. *fronted* confronting each other (in mock battle).

533–8. *to warn . . . burns* Armies appeared in the sky above Jerusalem before it fell to Antiochus (II Macc. 5. 1–4), and again before it fell to the Romans (Josephus, *De Bellis* VI v 3). Armies were also seen fighting in England's skies in 1640, 1643, 1648, 1659, 1660 and 1661. M.'s nephew, Edward Phillips, recalled that the Civil War had been portended by battles 'in the Ayre'. Radical pamphlets saw such battles as a warning against the Restoration. *Mirabilis Annus* (1661) likens airy battles over London to those preceding Jerusalem's fall. Patrick Hume in 1695 recognized that M. was alluding to 'our Civil Wars'. See John Leonard, ' "To Warn Proud Cities": a Topical Reference in Milton's Airy Knights Simile', *Renaissance and Reformation* 19 (1995) 63–71.

536. *Prick* spur.

couch lower to the attack position.

538. *welkin* sky.

539. *Typhoean See i 197–200n. Typhoeus's name was associated with 'typhoon' and meant *whirlwind* (541).

540. *ride the air* torment the air (cp. vi 244) by riding on whirlwinds. Cp. Ps. 18. 10 and Shakespeare, *Macbeth*, 'Cherubins, hors'd / Upon the sightless couriers of the air' (I vii 22–3).

542–6. *Alcides . . . Euboic Sea* Hercules (*Alcides*) had killed the centaur Nessus by shooting him with an arrow dipped in the Hydra's poisonous blood. Mortally wounded, Nessus told Hercules' wife, Deianeira, that she should soak a robe in his blood. The robe, he said, would revive Hercules' love. Not suspecting treachery, Deianeira soaked a robe in the now *envenomed* blood, and presented it to Hercules after he returned from another victory at *Oechalia*. Tormented by the robe's corrosive touch,

Hercules threw his friend *Lichas* (who had innocently brought the robe) from the top of Mount *Oeta* in Thessaly into the Euboean Sea. See Ovid, *Met.* ix 134f., Sophocles, *Trachiniae*, and Seneca, *Hercules Furens*.

550. *complain* compose a musical lament (*OED* 1b) and grumble.

552. *partial* both 'polyphonic' and 'prejudiced'.

554. *Suspended* riveted the attention of (*OED* 5a) and deferred. The parenthesis 'suspends as it were the event' (Newton).

took captivated, charmed.

557. *retired* 'in Thought, as well as from the Company' (Richardson).

561. *in wand'ring mazes lost* echoing Virgil, *Aen.* v 590 (on the Cretan labyrinth) and Ariosto, *Orl. Fur.* xiii 50 (on the maze palace of Atlante). Mazes are a recurrent image in *PL*. Cp. iv 239, v 620-24, ix 499, x 830.

564. *apathy* the Stoic virtue of freedom from passion.

568. *obdur̀ed* hardened, especially 'in wickedness or sin' (*OED* 1). Cp. vi 785.

570. *gross* massed.

575-81. The epithet attached to each river translates its Greek name.

591. *pile* massive building.

592. *Serbonian bog* Lake Serbonis, on the Egyptian coast. Diodorus Siculus tells how 'whole armies' had been engulfed in its quicksands, 'for as the sand is walked upon it gives way but gradually, deceiving with a kind of malevolent cunning those who advance upon it' (I xxx 5-7). Apollonius Rhodius tells how the monster Typhon was whelmed beneath Serbonis after warring against Zeus (*Argonautica* ii 1210-15). For other bog similes, see ii 939 and ix 634-45.

594. *parching* withering with cold (*OED* 'parch' 2b).

595. *frore* frozen. Hell's icy torments were traditional. Cp. Dante, *Inf.* xxxii.

596. *Harpy-footed* taloned. Harpies (monsters with women's faces) carried souls off to the avenging *Furies* (Homer, *Od.* xx 77, Virgil, *Aen.* iii 211f.). *haled*] hailed *Ed I*, *Ed II*. This is a region of *hail* (589), so the early spelling may be a pun.

600. *starve* die by freezing.

604. *Lethean sound* Lethe, river of forgetfulness. Virgil's dead, after suffering for a thousand years, are permitted to drink from Lethe before being reincarnated (*Aen.* vi 748-51). M.'s devils have no second chance.

611. *Medusa* the snaky-haired Gorgon whose look turned men to stone.

613. *wight* person.

614. *Tantalus* was 'tantalized' in Hades by being set in a pool from which he could not drink, and under trees whose fruit he could not eat (Homer, *Od.* xi 582-92). Cp. x 556-77.

628. *Gorgons, Hydras ... Chimeras* The Hydra was a venomous serpent with nine heads, the Chimera a fire-breathing monster. For Gorgons, see above, 611*n*. Aeneas is threatened by the shades of Gorgons and the Chimera in Virgil's hell (*Aen.* vi 288–9).

631. *toward*] Ed I; towards *Ed II*.

632. *Explores* makes proof of (a Latinism).

634. *shaves* barely escapes touching.

637. *Hangs in the clouds* Ships seen in a mirage appear to fly. The simile suits the master of illusions who burdens the air with 'unusual weight' (i 227).

equinoctial at the equator.

638. *Close sailing* sailing close to the wind.

Bengala Bengal. The ships are sailing south and west from India around the Cape of Good Hope (641). At iv 159–65 Satan is likened to ships sailing in the opposite direction.

639. *Ternate and Tidore* Spice Islands in the Moluccas.

640. *spicy drugs* any spice or medicinal substance.

641. *Ethiopian* Indian Ocean.

642. *Ply* beat up against the wind (*OED* v² II 6).

stemming holding course (*OED* v³ 1e).

645. *thrice threefold* overgoing the 'threefold' bronze wall encircling Hesiod's Tartarus (*Theog.* 726–33).

647. *impaled* fenced in.

650–9. *seemed woman . . . unseen* Phineas Fletcher in *The Apollyonists* (1627) depicts 'Sin' (Satan's daughter by Eve) as half woman, half serpent, and makes her 'Porter to th' infernall gate' (i 10–12). Cp. also Phineas Fletcher's Hamartia in *The Purple Island* (1633) xii 27–31, Virgil's Scylla (*Aen.* iii 424–8), Ovid's Scylla (*Met.* xiv 59–67), and Spenser's Errour (*FQ* I i 14f.). M. does not name Sin until line 760.

652. *Voluminous* consisting of many coils (*OED* 1).

654. *cry* pack.

655. *Cerberean* From Cerberus, the many-headed watchdog of hell.

660. *Scylla* a once beautiful nymph, whose lower parts were changed into a ring of barking dogs when Circe poured poison into the bay where she bathed (Ovid, *Met.* xiv 50–74). Scylla then preyed on sailors (see below, ii 1019*n*). Chrysostom had likened Sin to Scylla in *Homily on I Corinthians* ix 9. See M. J. Edwards, *N&Q* n.s. 42 (December 1995) 448–50.

661. *Trinacrian* Sicilian.

662. *night-hag* Hecate, Scylla's mother and goddess of witchcraft. Her approach was signalled by howling dogs.

Lapland famous for witchcraft.

665. *labouring* eclipsed (*OED* 3b), but suggesting also pains of childbirth (*womb*, *infant*). Lucan (*Pharsalia* vi 499–506, 554–8) describes witches causing lunar eclipses (*labores*) and drinking *infant blood*.

677. *admired* wondered.

679. *Created thing* The heretical implication that God and his Son were creatures shocked Bentley, but M. did believe the Son was created. See *CD* i 5 (esp. *YP* 6. 211).

683. *miscreated front* misshapen face. Cp. the 'miscreated mould' of Spenser's monster Disdayne (*FQ* II vii 42). Guyon is about to fight Disdayne, when Mammon 'did his hasty hand withhold, / And counseld him abstaine from perilous fight: / For nothing might abash the villein bold'. Sin offers similar advice to Satan (810–14).

686. *taste* know.

proof experience.

688. *goblin* evil spirit.

692. *Drew . . . the third part* Cp. Rev. 12. 4: '[the dragon's] tail drew the third part of the stars of heaven, and did cast them to the earth'. Cp. v 710.

693. *Conjúred* sworn together (*OED* 1), constrained by oath (*OED* 3), bewitched (*OED* 7).

694. *God* Death's readiness to name God sets him apart from the devils, who call God anything but 'God' (see i 93*n*). Death has not yet committed himself to Satan, but his own claim to rule Hell (698) implicitly defies God (see ii 327).

701. *whip of scorpions* Cp. Rehoboam's threat to Israel: 'my father hath chastised you with whips, but I will chastise you with scorpions' (I Kings 12. 11). A 'scorpion' was thought to be a studded whip.

708–11. *comet . . . war* Cp. Tasso's simile likening Argantes to a comet that brings death 'To mighty lords, to monarchs, and to kings' (*Gerus. Lib.* vii 52, trans. Fairfax). Cp. also Virgil, *Aen.* x 272–5 and Spenser, *FQ* III i 16, where Aeneas's plumed helmet and Florimell's hair are likened to comets. Comets were bad omens. One appearing in Ophiucus in 1618 was thought to have presaged the Thirty Years War (Fowler).

709. *Ophiucus* The constellation of the Serpent Bearer in the northern sky. Cp. Satan as 'Infernal Serpent' raising rebellion in the North (i 34, v 689).

710. *horrid* bristling (Latin *horridus*).

hair playing on the etymology of 'comet' (Greek κομήτης, 'long-haired').

714–16. *two black clouds . . . Caspian* Boiardo likens Orlando and Agricane to clashing thunderclouds (*Orl. Inn.* I xvi 10). Tasso likens Argantes to thunderclouds over the *Caspian* (*Gerus. Lib.* vi 38).

722. *foe* the Son of God (see Heb. 2. 14 and I Cor. 15. 26).

735. *pest* plague.

752–61. *All . . . me* Sin's birth from Satan's head is modelled on Athene's birth from the head of Zeus, which theologians had compared to God's generation of the Son.

755. *left side* Eve was created from Adam's left (or 'sinister') side (viii 465, x 886).

758–9. *amazement seized / All th' host of Heav'n* echoing Hesiod, *Theog.*

(588), where 'amazement seized' men and gods as they beheld the first woman, whom Hephaestos had made to punish men for stealing fire. Cp. Eve as Pandora (iv 714).

760. *Sign* portent (*OED* 9) and mere semblance (*OED* 8b). The paronomasia suggests that *Sin* received her name because she was a portentous *sign*.

772. *pitch* summit.

778–87. *my womb . . . Death* Cp. James 1. 15: 'Then when lust hath conceived, it bringeth forth sin: and sin, when it is finished, bringeth forth death'.

809. *so Fate pronounced* Cp. *CD* i 2: 'fate or *fatum* is only what is *fatum*, spoken, by some almighty power' (trans. Carey, *YP* 6. 131).

813. *dint* blow from a weapon.

825. *pretences* claims (*OED* 1), with overtones of the modern sense (cp. vi 421).

829. *unfounded* bottomless.

833. *purlieus* outskirts (*OED* 3).

836. *surcharged* overpopulated (*OED* 5c).

842. *buxom* yielding (*OED* 2). The phrase *the buxom air* echoes Spenser. Spenser's dragon, wounded by Redcrosse, whips 'the buxome aire' with his tail (*FQ* I xi 37), and Spenser's Jove, disguised as an eagle, spreads 'wide wings to beat the buxome ayre' (III xi 34).

embalmed balmy, fragrant (with ominous overtones of death and decay).

850. *due* just title.

869–70. *right hand . . . without end* Sin parodies the Nicene creed: 'We believe in . . . Jesus Christ . . . who sitteth on the right hand of the Father, and . . . of whose kingdom there shall be no end'.

875. *powers* armies.

877. *wards* the ridges inside a lock and the incisions on a key corresponding to them.

883. *Erebus* hell.

885. **bannered*.

889. *redounding* billowing.

890–1039. In *CD* i 7 M. argues that God created the universe out of primal matter (not nothing). This matter 'was good, and it contained the seeds of all subsequent good' (trans. Carey, *YP* 6. 308). Many critics have nevertheless doubted whether Chaos is good in *PL*. Schwartz (22–4) sees 'Hell and Chaos' as 'allied' against God. Adams (76) sees Chaos as the common enemy of God and Satan. M.'s Chaos seems hostile partly because it continues to exist after the Creation (ii 911, iii 418–26). Contrast Ovid, *Met.* i 19f., where Chaos is all used up. See A. B. Chambers, 'Chaos in *Paradise Lost*', *JHI* 24 (1963) 55–84 (p. 83). See further, v 472*n*.

891. *secrets* secret places (*OED* B 5), with a hint of 'secret parts', sexual organs (*OED* B 6). Chaos is a 'womb' (ii 150, 911).

hoary ancient (*OED* 1c) and hory ('foul, filthy'). At Job 41. 32, Leviathan surges through the sea so that 'one would think the deep to be hoary' (greyish white).

898. *Hot, Cold, Moist, and Dry* The four contraries. In the universe they combine to form the four elements, while in the human body they form the four humours. The union of hot and dry produces fire and choler; that of hot and moist, air and blood; of cold and moist, water and phlegm; of cold and dry, earth and melancholy. In the universe, we encounter the contraries only in their combined forms. Satan meets them raw.

900. *embryon atoms* indivisible units of matter that are the seeds of everything. Cp. *pregnant causes* (913). Atomist philosophers held that the universe was formed of an infinite number of atoms that had collided with each other while falling through infinite space. Atoms were of various shapes and sizes: hooked (*sharp*) ones formed solids, while round (*smooth*) ones formed fluids. There was no Creator, and all was brought together by Chance (Lucretius, *De Rerum Nat.* ii). Marjara (93) sees M. as confining the atoms to Chaos, since 'Chaos is the only place where such atomies could exist'.

903−6. *unnumbered . . . wings* The *sands* correspond to atoms and the *winds* to the four contraries. Ariosto uses the same simile as an image for Fortune (*Orl. Fur.* xxxiii 50).

904. *Barca . . . Cyrene* cities in the Libyan desert.

905. *Levied* lifted up (on the wind) and enlisted as troops.

   poise add weight to (*OED* 4a).

909. *arbiter* judge, with an overtone of capricious arbitration.

910. *Chance governs all* 'The only important school of philosophy which attributed chance to nature was atomism' (Marjara 92).

910−18. *Into . . . Stood* Bentley in 1732 objected to Satan's standing *Into this wild abyss*. Strictly, Satan stands and looks. But M.'s syntax, and the absence of the expected verb of motion, mime Satan's hesitation.

910. *abyss* The literal meaning ('bottomless') suggests that Satan is looking down even though he means to ascend. Vertigo is to be expected in Chaos (see 893−4).

911. *The womb . . . grave* translating Lucretius, *De Rerum Nat.* v 259. Lucretius is speaking of the earth, not Chaos.

916. *more worlds* other universes. See i 650n.

919. *frith* firth, estuary.

921. *ruinous* falling, crashing (as of towers).

921−2. *to compare / Great things with small* a Virgilian formula (*Ecl.* i 24, *Georg.* iv 176), but Virgil's 'small things' really are small (puppies, bees). M.'s *small* things (the sacking of a city, the distintegration of the universe) would be great in any other poem. Cp. vi 310, x 306, and *PR* iv 563−4.

922. *Bellona* Roman goddess of war.

927. *vans* *wings (*OED* sb¹ 3).

932. *vast vacuity* Porter (58) compares Hesiod's 'great chasm' in Tartarus, through which a man might fall for a year, buffeted by whirlwinds (*Theog.* 740–43). Satan might fall for thousands of years (*to this hour*).

933. *pennons* *wings (from Latin *pennae* or English 'pinion').

936. *rebuff* *repelling blast (*OED* 2), with a play on 'snub'. Even Chaos rejects Satan.

937. *instínct* *impelled, inflamed (*OED* 2). Thunder and lightning were thought to arise when earth's hot sulphurous vapours mixed with cold nitrous vapours in the atmosphere. Chaos 'spontaneously forms gunpowder' (Schwartz 27).

939. *boggy Syrtis* The Syrtes were two shifting sandbanks off the north coast of Africa between Cyrene and Carthage. Lucan (*Pharsalia* ix 303f.) describes Cato of Utica's heroic journey through the greater Syrtis, which Nature had left 'ambiguous between sea and land'. Tasso (*Gerus. Lib.* xv 18) names Syrtis alongside Mount Casius and Damietta (the site of M.'s Serbonian bog, ii 592–3). Apollonius Rhodius describes Syrtis as a misty wasteland (*Argonautica* iv 1235f.). The Trojan fleet encounters the Syrtes in Virgil, *Aen.* i 111.

943–7. *gryphon . . . gold* Gryphons (or griffins) were monsters (part lion, part eagle) that guarded the gold of Scythia against the one-eyed Arimaspians (Herodotus iii 116).

944. *moory* marshy.

945. *Arimaspian* Earlier authors used the form 'Arimasp'.

948–50. *O'er bog . . . flies* The monosyllables, which 'cannot be pronounced but slowly, and with many pauses' (Newton), mime the difficulty of Satan's voyage.

952. *stunning* deafening. *OED*'s earliest participial instance.

954. *vehemence* including 'mindlessness' (Latin *vehe-mens*).

964. *Orcus and Ades* variant names for Pluto (Hades).

965. *Demogorgon* Lucan (*Pharsalia* vi 744–9) and Statius (*Thebaid* iv 516) depict the gods of the underworld as dreading a mysterious being whose name causes the earth to shake. A medieval scribe supplied the name 'Demogorgon', perhaps in error for *Demiourgos* (the Creator in Platonic philosophy). Demogorgon passed into literature through Boccaccio's *De Genealogiis Deorum*. See e.g. Spenser, *FQ* I i 37 and IV ii 47. In *Prolusion i* M. identifies Demogorgon 'with the Chaos of the ancients' (*YP* 1. 222).

971–2. *disturb / The secrets* Bentley wanted to emend *disturb* to 'disclose', but *secrets* means 'secret places' (*OED* 5) and Satan is hinting at his own disruptive powers, which even Chaos might notice.

977. *Confine with* border on.

980. *I travel this profound, direct my course* The comma (common to all seventeenth-century editions) allows *direct* to act as both adjective and verb and so permits Satan to be evasive as to whether he is asking for directions. Satan is reluctant to admit that he is more than *half lost* (975).

982. *behoof* advantage.

988. *Anarch Chaos, ruler of anarchy (and so no ruler).

989. *incomposed* agitated and disarranged.

990. *I know thee, stranger, who thou art* Cp. Mark 1. 24 and Luke 4. 34, where a devil addresses Christ: 'I know thee who thou art, the Holy One of God'.

999. *serve* suffice.

1000. *so* in this way (by residing on the frontiers).

1001. *[y]our* our *Ed I, Ed II.* Zachary Pearce proposed the emendation in 1733. Chaos does have *intestine broils* (civil wars), but these cannot *weaken* him, for they are the means 'By which he reigns' (908−9). Heaven's civil war has *encroached* on Chaos by bringing Hell and our universe into being (1002−5). *Intestine broils* echoes Marlowe, *Hero and Leander* (1598) i 252: 'And with intestine broils the world destroy'.

1004. *heaven* the universe surrounding our earth, as distinct from *Heaven* (1006), the abode of God.

1005. *golden chain* see below, 1051*n*.

1007. *walk* Satan 'swims or sinks, or wades, or creeps, or flies' through Chaos, but he never takes a *walk*. Empson (118) hears Chaos as jeering, but the understatement also implies a haughty compliment.

1008. *speed* both 'meet with success' and 'make haste'; perhaps also 'destroy, kill' (*OED* 9c).

1013. *pyramid* spire, flame-shape (supposedly derived from Greek *pyr*, 'fire').

1018. *justling rocks* the Symplegades ('clashing ones') − rocks through which the Argonauts passed in search of the golden fleece (Apollonius Rhodius, *Argonautica* ii 552−611).

1019−20. *Ulysses . . . steered* The monsters Scylla and Charybdis threatened any sailor passing through the Straits of Messina between Italy and Sicily. On Circe's advice, Odysseus chose the lesser evil of Scylla in preference to the *whirlpool* of *Charybdis*. Scylla devoured six of his men as he passed under her rock (*Od.* xii 234−59). Homer does not place Scylla in a *whirlpool*.

1019. *larboard* port (opposite of starboard).

1024−8. *Sin and Death . . . a bridge* See x 293−305.

1024. *amain* with main force and at full speed.

1034. *influence* astral influence (see iv 669*n*), here used as a metaphor for Heaven's light streaming into Chaos.

1039. *works* fortifications (*her* refers to *Nature*).

1043. *holds* holds a course for.

1044. *shrouds* the standing rigging of a ship (*OED* sb² 1).

　　tackle torn Cp. Shakespeare, *Coriolanus* IV v 67−8 (Aufidius addressing the disguised Coriolanus): 'Though thy tackle's torn, / Thou show'st a noble vessel.' 'Tackle' is the running rigging used to work a ship's sails (*OED* 2a).

1046. *Weighs* keeps steady.

1048. *undetermined . . . round* Heaven is so *wide*, that Satan can only guess at its shape.

1050. *living* native, unhewn.

1051. *golden chain* The golden chain with which Zeus threatens to pull gods, earth and sea (Homer, *Il.* viii 18–27) was from ancient times interpreted as an allegory of universal concord. See e.g. Plato (*Theaetetus* 153D), Chaucer (*The Knight's Tale* I (A) 2987–93), Spenser (*FQ* II vii 46), and M.'s *Prolusion ii* (*YP* 1. 236). From this tradition Fowler concludes that M.'s image has the effect of 'binding and ordering' the turmoil of Chaos. Ricks, noting the proximity of *chain* to *pendent*, draws the opposite inference that 'the universe is like a beautiful jewel or "pendent", liable to be stolen'.

1052. *pendent world* The whole universe, hanging in space. Cp. Shakespeare, *Measure for Measure* III i 124–5: 'blown with restless violence round about / The pendent world'.

1053. *magnitude* one of the classes into which astronomers ranked the fixed stars according to brilliancy. The simile makes the universe appear much smaller than it had seemed at i 74 or ii 999–1006.

1054. *fraught with* big with the menace of (*OED* ppl. a 3b). Cp. the nautical imagery in 1043–4).

1055. *he hies* he makes haste. M. opens book iii with the same alliteration.

BOOK III

1. *Light* physical light alone (Kelley 91–4, Bauman 214–32) or a metaphor for the Son of God (Hunter[2] 149–56). Either light could be *first-born* (see Gen. 1. 3 and Col. 1. 15).

2–3. *Or . . . unblamed* 'Or may I, without committing blasphemy, describe you as being co-eternal with God?' M. in *CD* i 5 denies that the Son is co-eternal with the Father.

3. *God is light* I John 1. 5.

4. **unapproachèd* inaccessible (see ix 5*n*). God dwells 'in the light which no man can approach unto' (I Tim. 6. 16).

6. *effluence* emanation.

7. *hear'st thou rather* 'Would you rather be called'. Cp. the cautious addressing of divine beings in vii 1–2 and *Ep. Dam.* 208.

    ethereal consisting of ether, the subtlest element. See vii 244*n*.

7–8. *stream . . . fountain* Cp. Lactantius, *Divine Institutes* IV xxix: 'the [Father] is as it were an overflowing fountain, the [Son] as a stream flowing forth from it: the former as the sun, the latter as it were a ray extended from the sun' (*cit.* Hunter[2] 150). See also iii 375.

10. *invest* cover.

11. *world of waters dark and deep* Cp. Spenser, *FQ* I i 39: 'the world of waters wide and deepe'.

12–16. The *void and formless infinite* and *middle darkness* are Chaos; the *Stygian pool* and *utter* darkness are Hell.

17. *Orphéan lyre* Orpheus sought his dead wife Eurydice in Hades, and his singing moved Pluto to release her. M. sings with *other notes* because his song is not intended to charm the ears of Hell. Orpheus was the supposed author of the Orphic *Hymn to Night*, which sees Night as a beneficent deity. M.'s Night is malevolent. See A. B. Chambers, 'Chaos in *Paradise Lost*', *JHI* 24 (1963), 55–84 (p. 75).

19. *Taught by the Heav'nly Muse* M. 'speaks *to* the light *about* the Muse', so the Light is not the Muse (Bauman 230).

20–21. *The dark descent . . . hard and rare* another echo of the Sibyl's warning to Aeneas. See ii 432–3*n*.

25. *quenched* *destroyed the sight of the eye (*OED* 1c). Eyes were thought to emit beams and M. imagines these as having been extinguished.

25–6. *drop serene . . . suffusion* translating *gutta serena* and *suffusio nigra*, medical terms for ocular diseases.

29. *Smit with the love of sacred song* Cp. Lucretius, *De Rerum Nat.*, i 922–5: 'high hope of renown has . . . struck into my heart sweet love of the Muses . . . I love to approach virgin springs'. Cp. also Virgil, *Georg.* ii 475–7.

30. *Sion* the sacred mountain (as opposed to Helicon or Parnassus). Cp. i 10–12.

32. *nor sometimes forget* often remember.

34. *So were I* Would that I were.

35. *Thamyris* a legendary Thracian poet, punished with blindness for boasting that he could outsing the Muses (Homer, *Il.* ii 594–600).
  Maeonides Homer.

36. *Tiresias* the blind Theban prophet. Cp. Marvell's 'On Mr Milton's *Paradise Lost*': 'Just heaven thee, like Tiresias, to requite, / Rewards with prophecy thy loss of sight' (43–4).
  Phineus a Thracian prophet, blinded by the gods.

37. *voluntary* freely (as in a musical 'voluntary', chosen by the performer). *move* put forth, utter (*OED* 4).

38. *numbers* verses.
  wakeful bird nightingale.

39. *darkling* in the dark.

47. *Book of Knowledge* the Book of Nature, God's revelation in his creatures.

48. *blank* void (*OED* 7), but *expunged* and *razed* also suggest a blank page in Nature's book. The Romans *expunged* writing on waxed tablets by covering it with little pricks, or *razed* it by shaving the tablets clean.

60. *sanctities* angels.

61. *his sight* seeing him, and being seen by him.

62. *his right* Heb. 1. 2–3: 'His Son . . . sat down on the right hand of the Majesty on high'.

67. *fruits* playing on Latin *fruitio*, 'enjoyment'.

71. *this side Night* that part of Chaos between Heaven and the universe.

72. *dun* dusky.

sublime aloft.

73. *stoop* descend from a height (*OED* 5a) and descend swiftly on prey (*OED* 6, hawking term).

74. *world* universe. The *bare outside* is a hard outer shell.

75. *without* both 'on the outside of' and 'not having'. The *land* on the *outside* of our *firmament* is unsheltered by any firmament. The oxymoron *imbosomed without* implies the vulnerability of a universe imbosomed in nothing but itself.

76. *Uncertain . . . air* Satan cannot tell whether the universe is surrounded by ocean or air.

81. *Transports* both 'conveys' and 'carries away' (with hate).

Adversary the literal meaning of *Satan* (see i 82*n*).

83. *main* vast, uninterrupted. Cp. 'Main ocean' (vii 279).

84. *Wide interrupt* forming a wide breach.

93. *glozing* flattering.

119. **unforeknown* M. in *CD* i 3 argues that future events are certain for no other reason than that God foreknows them (*YP* 6. 164–5). In his anxiety to acquit his *foreknowledge*, God now says that the Fall would have been *certain* even if he had not foreknown it. This statement can only damage God's (and M.'s) theodicy, for it inadvertently concedes that the certainty (not just the possibility) of the Fall is grounded in something other than divine foreknowledge.

120. *impúlse* instigation, esp. a strong suggestion supposed to come from a good or evil spirit (*OED* 3).

129. *first sort* fallen angels.

suggestion prompting from within (*OED* 1b), devilish temptation (*OED* 1a). See v 702*n*.

136. *Spirits elect* unfallen angels. Cp. I Tim. 5. 21: 'the elect angels'.

140. *Substantially* M. in *CD* i 5 argues that God imparted to the Son his 'divine substance', but not his 'total essence' (trans. Carey, *YP* 6. 211–12).

153–4. *That be . . . from thee* Cp. Abraham's plea for the Sodomites: 'That be far from thee to do after this manner, to slay the righteous with the wicked: and that the righteous should be as the wicked, that be far from thee' (Gen. 18. 25).

158. *naught* nothing, nought (*OED* 1) and wickedness (*OED* 2).

166. *blasphemed* reviled, defamed.

169. *Son of my bosom* Cp. John 1. 18: 'the only begotten Son, which is in the bosom of the Father'.

170. *my . . . effectual might* Cp. I Cor. 1. 24: 'Christ the power of God'. Cp. also Venus's words to Cupid at *Aen.* i 664: 'Son, who art alone my strength, my mighty power'. Patristic tradition had applied Virgil's line to Christ.

177. *exorbitant* forsaking the right path (*OED* 3), immoderate (*OED* 4a), abnormal (*OED* 2c).

178. *yet once more* See Heb. 12. 26–7 and *Lycidas* 1.

180. *know how frail* Cp. Ps. 39. 4: 'That I may know how frail I am'.

183. *peculiar grace* M. rejects Calvinist predestination in *CD* i 4 (*YP* 6. 181), but here God implies that some are predestined to be saved. Danielson (82–3) compares Richard Baxter's *Catholick Theologie* (1675), which distinguishes between 'sufficient Grace' (offered to everyone) and 'efficient Grace' (given to a few). Thus no one is predestined to damnation but some are predestined to salvation.

186. *betimes* in time.

189. *stony hearts* 'I will take the stony heart out of their flesh, and will give them an heart of flesh' (Ezek. 11. 19).

200. *hard be hardened* M. in *CD* i 8 says that 'hardening of the heart . . . is usually the last punishment' inflicted on sinners 'in this life' (trans. Carey, *YP* 6. 336–7).

206. *Affecting* aspiring to.

208. *sacred* *set apart (*OED* 2b), accursed (*OED* 6).

  devote consigned to destruction (*OED* 'devoted' 3).

211. *Some other able* Immortal angels are presumably *able* to redeem man by choosing to *be mortal* (214). But see below, 281*n*.

212. *rigid* strict (also suggesting *rigor mortis*).

  satisfaction the theological term for Christ's sacrifice.

215. *just th' unjust to save* Cp. I Pet. 3. 18: 'the just for the unjust'.

217. *stood mute* Cp. ii 418–29, where the devils 'sat mute' until Satan volunteered to undertake the voyage to earth.

219. *Patron* advocate.

224. *doom* Judgement.

225. *fulness dwells* Cp. Col. 2. 9: 'For in him dwelleth all the fulness of the Godhead bodily'.

231. *unprevented* before being prayed for. Cp. 'Prevenient grace' (xi 3).

233. *dead in sins* Cp. Eph. 2. 4: 'when we were dead in sins'.

234. *meet* fitting, adequate.

241. *wreck* wreak, give vent to (*OED* v² 2), but suggesting too that the Son is a rock on which Death's rage will wreck itself. Cp. iv 11 ('wreck on innocent frail man').

244. *Life in myself forever* Cp. John 5. 26: 'For as the Father hath life in himself; so hath he given to the Son to have life in himself'.

247–9. *Thou wilt not . . . corruption* Cp. Ps. 16. 10: 'Thou will not leave my soul in hell; neither wilt thou suffer thine Holy One to see corruption'.

250. *I shall rise* The Son's confidence might not emerge from easy foreknowledge. In *CD* i 5 M. denies omniscience to the Son (*YP* 6. 265–6).

251–4. *spoiled . . . triumph* Cp. Col. 2. 15: 'And having spoiled principalities and powers, he made a shew of them openly, triumphing over them'.

251. *spoil* prey (*OED* 4), with overtones of 'spoils of war'. Human nature, exalted by the Resurrection, 'was very often referred to as "spoil"' (Fowler, ix 147–51n).

252–3. *Death . . . sting* Cp. I Cor. 15. 55: 'O death, where is thy sting?'

255. *lead Hell captive* Cp. Eph. 4. 8: 'he led captivity captive'.

maugre in spite of.

258. *ruin* hurl to the ground and destroy.

259. *Death last* Cp. I Cor. 15. 26: 'The last enemy that shall be destroyed is death'.

261. *long absent* The Son seems to imagine a longer absence than thirty-three years. See Empson (127–9).

271. *Admiration* astonishment and veneration.

276. *complacence* pleasure, delight (*OED* 2).

281–2. *Thou . . . join* 'Therefore join to thy nature the nature of those whom thou alone canst redeem'.

281. *thou only canst redeem* At line 211 God had implied that angels were 'able' to redeem us. Are we now to infer that God was then deliberately misleading the angels (as he does at vi 44–55)?

286. *The head* Cp. I Cor. 11. 3: 'The head of every man is Christ'.

287–8. *As in him . . . restored* Cp. I Cor. 15. 22: 'as in Adam all die, even so in Christ shall all be made alive'.

291. *Imputed* attributed vicariously (*OED* 2, theological term).

293. *transplanted* continuing the horticultural image begun in *seed* and *root* (284, 288). Cp. *CD* i 21, 'Of Ingrafting in Christ', where M. defines ingrafting as 'the process by which God the Father plants believers in Christ. That is to say, he makes them sharers in Christ, and renders them fit to join, eventually, in one body with Christ' (trans. Carey, *YP* 6. 477).

299. *Giving* submitting.

300. *dearly* lovingly and at great cost.

307. *fruition* pleasurable possession (*OED* 1). 'Christ is ready to renounce *God-like fruition* for man, but man will not renounce the fruit that makes him Godlike' (Fowler).

quitted renounced (*OED* 6b), left (*OED* 7), redeemed, set free (*OED* 1a), remitted a debt (*OED* 4).

309. *By merit* Cp. Satan 'by merit raised' (ii 5).

317–18. *all power / I give thee* Cp. Matt. 28. 18: 'All power is given unto me'.

320. *Thrones . . . Dominions* The four angelic orders named at Col. 1. 16 (with *Princedoms* for 'principalities').

321–2. *All knees . . . earth* Cp. Phil. 2. 10: 'at the name of Jesus every knee should bow, of things in heaven, and things in earth, and things under the earth'.

324–9. *Shalt in the sky appear . . . rouse their sleep* See Revelation, Matt. 24. 30–31, and I Cor 15. 51–2.

327. *cited* summoned, roused.

330. *saints* all the elect.

331. *arraigned* accused.

334. *The world shall burn* See II Peter 3. 10–13.

340. *need* be needed.

341. *God shall be All in All* Empson (130) takes God to mean that he is 'going to abdicate', but see I Cor. 15. 28: 'then shall the Son also himself be subject unto him that put all things under him, that God may be all in all'. Cp. vi 730–33.

342–3. *Adore him . . . as me* Cp. John 5. 23: 'All men should honour the Son, even as they honour the Father'.

347. *rung* probably a transitive verb, with *multitude of angels* (345) the subject, and *Heav'n* the object.

348. *jubilee* jubilation. Fowler hears a play on the Hebrew Jubilee – a ritual celebration occurring every fifty years, when slaves were freed. It was a 'type' of the Atonement.

   hosannas Hebrew 'save now' or 'save, pray'.

351–2. *down . . . crowns* Cp. Rev. 4. 10, where the twenty-four elders 'cast their crowns before the throne'.

353. *amarant* Greek 'unfading': a legendary immortal flower. The crown of glory 'that fadeth not away' (I Pet. 1. 4) is in the Greek said to be *amarantinon*. Clement of Alexandria says that the righteous will be awarded crowns of amarant in Heaven (*Paedagogus* II viii 78). Cp. *Lycidas* 149.

363. *sea of jasper* Cp. Rev. 4. 6: 'before the throne there was a sea of glass like unto crystal'. See also iii 518–19.

367. **preamble* musical prelude.

370. *exempt* excluded.

373. *Immutable, immortal, infinite,* a direct lift from Sylvester, *DWW* (1592–1608), I i 45. M. often uses triple negatives. See e.g. ii 185, iii 231, *PR* iii 429.

375. *Fountain of light* see above, iii 7–8n.

377. *but* except.

378–80. *cloud . . . dark* At the dedication of the Temple 'the house was filled with a cloud, even the house of the Lord; for the glory of the Lord had filled the house of God. Then said Solomon, The Lord hath said that he would dwell in thick darkness' (II Chron. 5. 13 – 6. 1). Cp. ii 263–7.

381. *that* so that.

382. *veil their eyes* Isa. 6. 2.

383. *of all Creation first* Cp. Col. 1. 15: 'the firstborn of every creature'.

385. *without cloud* Contrast the Father, who appears *through a cloud* (378).

387. *Whom else no creature can behold* Cp. John 1. 18: 'No man hath seen God at any time; the only begotten Son, which is in the bosom of the Father, he hath declared him'.

388. **effulgence* coined from Latin *effulgens*.

392. *Dominations* an angelic order ('Dominions' at iii 320 and Col. 1. 16).

405. *much more to pity inclined* The clause could refer either to the Father (402) or the Son.

412–15. *Hail . . . disjoin* echoing many pagan hymns, which end with a hailing of the god and a promise to resume his praises. Cp. the Homeric hymn to Delian Apollo.

412. *thy name* The name 'Christ' never appears in *PL*.

413. *my song* Bentley wanted to emend to 'our songs', but the shift to the first person allows M. to refer to his own poem.

418. *opacous* opaque.

419. *first convéx* the outer shell encompassing the universe.

422. *alighted* both 'landed' and 'illumined' (*OED* 'alight' v³ 1). Satan and the shell on which he walks are dimly lit by the reflected light of Heaven (427–30).

429. *vexed* tossed about.

431. *Imaus* mountains extending from the Himalayas to the Arctic Ocean.

432. *roving Tartar* Nomadic Mongols had ravaged Asia and Europe under Genghis Khan and Tamerlane. Ricks hears a pun on Tartarus (*Milton's Grand Style*, 126). Martindale (128) finds the pun 'far-fetched', but it had been a commonplace since 1237, when Friar Julian of Hungary referred to Mongol Tatars as *Tartari*, 'people of hell'. *Tartar* was also a variant of 'Tartarus' (*OED* 'Tartar' sb⁴).

434. *yeanling* newborn. Fowler associates the *lambs* and *kids* with the sheep and goats separated at the Last Judgement (Matt. 25. 32–3).

436. *Hydaspes* now the river Jhelum, which rises in Kashmir.

438. *Sericana* China. Travellers' reports of *cany wagons* reached a wide audience through Mendoza's *Historie of the Great and Mightie Kingdome of China* (trans. Parke, 1588).

*cany made of cane or bamboo.

441. *Walked up and down* Cp. Job 1. 7: 'Whence comest thou? Then Satan answered the Lord, and said, From going to and fro in the earth, and from walking up and down in it'.

444–97. M.'s *Paradise of Fools* is indebted to Ariosto's Limbo of Vanity on the moon (*Orl. Fur.* xxxiv 73ff.). Ariosto's Limbo is less satirical than M.'s, but it includes one anti-ecclesiastical stanza (on the Constantine Donation) that M. translated.

444. *store* plenty (*OED* 4b) and a body of persons (*OED* 3).

446. *vain* empty, foolish (*OED* 2, 3).

449. *fond* infatuated and foolish.

452. *painful* painstaking.

456. *Abortive* prematurely born (see line 474) and failing of the intended effect.

  unkindly unnaturally.

457. *fleet* glide away, flit, vanish (*OED* 10). Of the soul: to pass away from the body (*OED* 10b).

459. *some* Ariosto. See above, 444−97*n*.

461. *Translated saints* holy men removed from earth by God. Such were Enoch (Gen. 5. 24) and Elijah (II Kings 2. 11). Cp. xi 705−10. Although M. scorns Ariosto's notion of the moon's inhabitants, M.'s own speculation is indebted to *Orl. Fur.* xxxiv 58−68, where Astolfo ascends to the moon in Elijah's chariot.

461−2. *middle . . . kind* M.'s contemporaries were excited by the possibility of extraterrestrial life. See e.g. John Wilkins, *The Discovery of a World in the Moone* (1638). Wilkins paraphrases Nicholas of Cusa: 'the inhabiters of the Sunne are like the nature of that Planet, more cleare and bright, more intellectual and spirituall than those in the Moone, . . . and those of the earth . . . more grosse and materiall than either, so that these intellectuall natures in the Sun, are more forme than matter, those in the earth more matter than forme, and those in the Moone betwixt both' (194). There was much curiosity as to whether aliens would be infected by Adam's sin (Wilkins 189−90). M. hints strongly that they would not (iii 568−71, viii 144−58).

463−4. *ill-joined . . . Giants* Gen. 6. 4 describes how the Sons of God begot a race of Giants on the daughters of men. M. returns to the story in xi 573−627 and (with a different interpretation) in *PR* ii 178−81.

467. *Sennaär* the LXX and Vulgate form of 'Shinar' (Gen. 11. 2). M. returns to the Babel story in xii 38−62.

470. *fondly* foolishly.

471. *Empedocles* a pre-Socratic philosopher who threw himself into Etna so as to conceal his mortality. His plan was frustrated when the volcano threw up one of his sandals.

473. *Cleombrotus* a youth who drowned himself so as to enjoy the immortality promised in Plato's *Phaedo*.

474. *Embryos and idiots* were consigned by Franciscan theologians to a limbo above the earth. M. satirizes this doctrine by placing the *friars* in their own limbo.

474. *eremites* hermits.

475. *White, black and grey* Carmelites, Dominicans, Franciscans.

trumpery religious ornaments (*OED* 2c), imposture (*OED* 1).

477. *Golgotha* Calvary, where Christ was crucified and buried. Cp. Luke 24. 5–6: 'Why seek ye the living among the dead? He is not here but is risen'.

479. *weeds* robes.

481–3. *They . . . moved* Moving outward through the Ptolemaic system, the traveller from earth would pass the seven planetary spheres, the *fixed* stars, the ninth (*crystálline*) sphere, and the *primum mobile* (*first moved*). The *trepidation* (oscillation) of the eighth sphere had been added to Ptolemy's system so as to account for the precession of the equinoxes; it was much debated (*talked*) in M.'s time. *Balance* and *weighs* allude punningly to Libra, the Scales: a point of reference for measuring the trepidation or 'libration' (Fowler).

484. *wicket* not the *palace gate* of line 505, but 'a small door made in, or placed beside, a large one, for ingress and egress when the large one is closed' (*OED* 1). The image implies that Roman superstition seeks clandestine ingress.

485. *keys* Matt. 16. 19 (cp. *Lycidas* 110).

489. *devious* off the main road (*OED* 1), erring, straying (*OED* 3); also a transferred epithet implying the Friars' deviousness.

491. *beads* rosaries.

492. *dispenses* dispensations.

bulls papal decrees.

493. **upwhirled* Cp. the neologisms 'upsent' (i 541) and 'upgrown' (ix 677).

494. *backside* lower hemisphere of the universe – with a scatological pun (notice *winds*).

496. *Paradise of Fools* The phrase 'fool's paradise' had long been proverbial.

501. *travelled* including travailed, wearied.

502. *degrees* steps or rungs of a stairway or ladder (*OED* 1a). Since *each stair mysteriously was meant* (516), there is also a play on degrees of dignity or rank. See below, 516*n*.

506. *frontispiece* pediment over a door (*OED* 2).

507. *orient* lustrous, sparkling.

510–15. *Jacob . . . gate of Heav'n* Jacob fled to Padan-Aram (in Syria) after cheating his brother Esau out of their father's blessing. While sleeping in Luz, he had a dream of angels ascending and descending a ladder reaching to Heaven (Gen. 28. 10–17). Fowler sees a parallel between Jacob and Satan, who has 'fled retribution and is at a parting of the ways where he could still repent'. But God has said that the devils will not find grace (iii 129–32) and the ladder confronts Satan with his *exclusion* (525).

513. The *Ed I* and *Ed II* pointing (comma after *Luz*, not *Padan-Aram*) creates the false impression that Padan-Aram is in the field of Luz. Luz is in the Judaean hills, not Syria.

516. *mysteriously* allegorically. D. C. Allen (*MLN* 68, 1953, 360) shows that Jacob's ladder was sometimes identified with Zeus's golden chain (see ii 1051*n*) and interpreted as a symbol of the Chain of Being. M.'s stairway may be the 'golden chain' of ii 1051, but here it is retractable.

518. *Viewless* invisible.

sea the waters that flow 'above the firmament' (Gen. 1. 7). H. F. Robins (*PMLA* 69, 1954, 903–14) argues that this sea envelops the whole *primum mobile*, even though Satan had walked on 'firm land' at iii 75 and 418. But the sea flows only *underneath* the stairway, 'about' its foot (Argument to book iii).

519. *liquid* including 'clear, transparent, bright' (*OED* 2).

521. *Wafted by angels* refers to Lazarus, who was 'carried by the angels into Abraham's bosom' (Luke 16. 22).

522. *Rapt . . . fiery steeds* Elijah ascended to Heaven in a *chariot* drawn by 'horses of fire' (II Kings 2. 11).

524. *easy ascent* Cp. 'Th' ascent is easy' (ii 81) and contrast Virgil, *Aen.* vi 126 ('the descent . . . is easy . . . but to retrace one's steps . . . this is the task'). See ii 432–3, iii 19–21.

528. *A passage down to th' earth* Since the passage opens *just o'er* Paradise, and Satan views the universe in *breadth* from *pole to pole* (561–2), Satan is standing at some point on the celestial equator, not at a celestial pole. The *primum mobile* is constantly rotating, so one of two conclusions must follow: (1) the passage is also rotating and just happens to be below the stairway when Satan reaches it, or (2) the shell on which Satan stands is a motionless sphere exterior to the *primum mobile*. In either case, the universe 'is lying, as it were, on its side' (Fowler), with earth's axis parallel to Heaven's floor.

534. *and* and so did.

choice careful in choosing (*OED* 3a).

535. *Paneas* Greek name for the city of Dan, the northernmost city of Canaan.

536. *Beërsaba* Beersheba, the southernmost city of Canaan. The phrase 'from Dan even to Beersheba' is common in the O.T.

543. *scout* The military sense suggests that Satan has come to conquer the cosmic *metropolis*.

546. *Obtains* reaches (*OED* 5) and occupies (*OED* 6).

547. *discovers* reveals.

552. *though after Heaven seen* though he had seen Heaven.

556–7. *circling . . . shade* the earth's shadow rotating around the universe. It does not extend beyond the sphere of the moon, and beyond it the sky is blue, with stars, sun, and planets clearly visible.

556. *canopy* Canopies over beds or thrones were often conical in shape.

558. *fleecy star* Aries, the Ram.

559. *Andromeda* a constellation adjacent to Aries. In Greek myth Andromeda was a beautiful princess menaced by a dragon.

562. *world's first region* the vast space between the universe's outer shell and the earth's atmosphere.

563. *precipitant* rushing headlong.

564. *marble* gleaming, sparkling (Greek *marmareos*).

567. *happy isles* alluding to the Fortunate Isles, or Islands of the Blest, in Greek mythology. Cp. ii 410, where the devils speak of man's 'happy isle'. Here the plural implies that inhabitants of *other worlds* may have escaped man's Fall.

568. *Hesperian gardens* a paradise beyond the western ocean, where a dragon guarded golden apples. Hercules killed the dragon and stole the apples. See iv 250n. The allusion might imply that aliens were created with their own forbidden fruit, and so did not fall with Adam and Eve. See iii 461–2.

571. *above them* Fowler notes that the sun is above the stars *in splendour* (572), but below them in space. Since Satan does not know whether he is moving *up or down*, M. might intend both senses of *above*.

575. *By centre or eccentric* by a centric or eccentric orbit. A centric orbit has the earth (or sun) at its centre; an eccentric orbit does not. M. avoids choosing between the Ptolemaic and Copernican systems. Cp. viii 83.

576. *longitude* the distance he flew (measured by degrees of arc) along the ecliptic.

578. *distance due* Cp. Satan's contemptuous reference to the courtier angels' 'practised distances' about God's throne (iv 945).

580. *numbers that compute* rhythms that measure.

581. *Days . . . years* Cp. Gen. 1. 14: 'Let there be lights in the firmament of the heaven to divide the day from the night; and let them be for signs, and for seasons, and for days, and years'. See also Plato, *Timaeus* (38–40).

582–3. *turned / By his magnetic beam* Kepler's theory that the sun's magnetism was responsible for planetary motions was popular in M.'s time. See Marjara (123–7).

588–90. *a spot . . . saw* Galileo had observed sun-spots through his telescope (*optic tube*) in 1610.

592. *metal*] medal *Ed I*, *Ed II*. The case for emending is clinched by the repetition of *metal* and *stone* in lines 595–6.

596. *carbuncle* any red gem, including 'a mythical gem said to emit a light in the dark' (*OED* 1).

chrysolite any green gem.

597. *to the twelve* 'up to and including all the twelve'. See Exod. 28. 17–20 for the jewels in *Aaron's breastplate*.

598. *a stone* the Philosopher's Stone. Alchemists had identified it with the *urim* on Aaron's breastplate (Exod. 28. 30). The stone allegedly had the power to heal all diseases and restore Paradise, as well as transmute base metals into gold. See Lyndy Abraham, *Marvell and Alchemy* (1990) 16.

599. *Imagined . . . seen* 'elsewhere imagined more often than seen'.

601. *Philosophers* magicians, alchemists (*OED* 2).

603. *volátile* able to fly (*OED* 2a) and evaporating rapidly (*OED* 3a).

The winged god Hermes symbolizes the element mercury, used by alchemists in their quest for the Philosopher's Stone. Alchemists would *bind* mercury by sealing it in a *limbeck* (alembic) and solidifying it.

604. *Proteus* the shape-shifting sea-god (from ancient times a symbol of matter). Alchemists can dissolve matter into its *native form*, but they cannot recompose the four contraries of this primal matter (see ii 898) into the Philosopher's Stone. The allusion to shape-shifting prepares for Satan's first metamorphosis (634).

606. *here* in the sun.

607. *elixir* the liquid form of the Philosopher's Stone, capable of curing all diseases and prolonging life.

608. *Potable* drinkable.

virtuous energizing.

609. *arch-chemic* chief of the alchemists. The sun's rays were thought to penetrate the earth and generate precious metals and stones. Cp. *A Masque* 732–6.

610. *humour* moisture.

617. *equator* the celestial equator, where (before the Fall) the sun would *culminate* or reach its highest point. After the Fall, *direct* (and therefore shadowless) beams occur only at the points where ecliptic and equator coincide.

620. *visual ray* The eye was thought to emit a beam onto the object perceived.

622. *ken* range of vision.

623. *The same whom John saw* Cp. Rev. 19. 17: 'I saw an angel standing in the sun'.

625. **beaming* *OED*'s earliest instance of the participial adjective.

tiar crown.

627. *Illustrious* lustrous, gleaming.

634. *casts* schemes (*OED* 43) and casts off (his present shape).

636–9. *Cherub . . . feigned* Cp. II Cor. 11. 14: 'Satan himself is transformed into an angel of light'.

637. *prime* prime rank, with overtones of 'prime of life'.

643. *succinct* *scant, close-fitting (*OED* 3a).

644. *decent* comely (*OED* 2).

648. *Uriel* Hebrew 'Light (or fire) of God'. The name is not biblical, but it appears as the name of an angel in the apocryphal II Esdras (4. 1) and the pseudepigraphal I Enoch (22. 2). Uriel is also prominent in cabbalistic lore.

one of the seven See Rev. 1. 5, 8. 2, and Tob. 12. 15 for the seven angels before God's throne. The Bible does not name them, but I Enoch lists them as Uriel, Raphael, Raguel, Michael, Zerachiel, Gabriel, Remiel. Other lists exist, but this is the only one to place Uriel *first* (656).

650. *are his eyes* Cp. Zech. 4. 10: 'those seven . . . are the eyes of the Lord which run to and fro through the whole earth'.

655. *God* The disguised Satan now speaks the name for the first time.

656. *authentic* authoritative (*OED* 1).

Interpreter one who makes known the will of another; a title of Mercury as messenger of the gods (*OED* 3). Cp. vii 72.

664. *favour* favourite (*OED* 1d), perhaps also 'resemblance'. See ii 350*n*.

667. *wand'ring* See ii 148*n*.

671–2. *That I may . . . behold* Cp. Herod's question to the Magi concerning the Second Adam: 'when ye have found him, bring me word again, that I may come and worship him also' (Matt. 2. 8).

694. *tends* inclines.

709. *mould* substance.

716. *quintessence* the fifth element, of which the heavenly bodies were made.

717. *spirited with various forms* presided over by various angelic spirits or Intelligences. Cp. Plato, *Timaeus* 41E.

718. *rolled orbicular* referring both to the spherical shape of the newly-created stars and the orbits that they follow.

726. *Night* earth's night (but with a glance at Chaos and Night, who *would invade* the universe).

730. *triform* alluding to the moon's phases; but ancient poets called the lunar goddess *triformis* because of her triple nature (Luna in heaven, Diana on earth, and Hecate or Proserpina in hell). Virgil associates 'threefold Hecate' with Chaos (*Aen.* iv 510–11).

731. *Hence* from here (the sun).

fills and empties M. often imagines light as a liquid. Cp. iii 7–8 and vii 359–65.

732. *checks the night* holds night in check. Ricks hears a pun on ' "chequers, variegates with its rays" as in Robert Greene: "checkt the night with golden rays" (1590, *OED*)'.

738. *reverence* including 'obeisance, bow' (*OED* 2).

740. *ecliptic* the sun's orbit around the earth.

sped including 'prospered' (*hoped success*).

742. *Niphates* a mountain on the border of Armenia and Assyria.

BOOK IV

3. *second rout* St John prophesies a second battle in Heaven at Rev. 12. 3–12.

5. *Woe . . . earth* Cp. Rev. 12. 12: 'Woe to the inhabiters of the earth and of the sea! for the devil is come down unto you, having great wrath, because he knoweth that he hath but a short time'.

10. *Accuser* translating Greek *diabolos*. Cp. Rev. 12. 10: 'the accuser of our brethren is cast down, which accused them before our God day and night'.

11. *wreck* wreak, avenge (*OED* v² 3) and ruin (*OED* v¹ 4). Wreaking vengeance, Satan will ruin both man and himself. Cp. iii 241.

17. *engine* cannon and plot. Cp. i 750, ix 172–4.

18. *distract* drive mad (*OED* 6), draw in different directions (*OED* 1).

20. *Hell within him* Contrast Satan's boast at i 254–5, and cp. the words of Marlowe's Mephostophilis in *Doctor Faustus* I iii 76: 'Why, this is hell, nor am I out of it'. Cp. also II i 121–2: 'where we are is hell, / And where hell is, there must we ever be'.

27. *Eden* Hebrew 'delight' (contrasting with *grieved*, *sad*).

31. *revolving* pondering.

32–113. *O thou . . . know* M.'s nephew and biographer Edward Phillips reports that this soliloquy (at least lines 32–41) was written 'several Years before the Poem was begun', and was intended to begin a tragedy on the Fall (Darbishire 72). Cp. the opening addresses to the sun in Aeschylus, *Prometheus Bound*, and Euripides, *Phoenissae*.

33. *Look'st* both 'survey' and 'seem to be'.

sole unique (and suggesting *sol*, 'the sun').

36–7. *thy name / O sun* See Leonard 102 for the pun on 'Son' and the suggestion of *Satan* ('Enemy') in *no friendly*. Satan never openly names the Son after his expulsion from Heaven.

37. *hate thy beams* Cp. John 3. 20: 'Every one that doeth evil hateth the light'.

43. *he created what I was* Satan had claimed to be 'self-begot' (v 860). He might have been lying, or he might now be suddenly convinced of his creatureliness. See Empson, 64–5.

45. *Upbraided none* Cp. James 1. 5: 'God, that giveth to all men liberally, and upbraideth not'.

50. *'sdained* disdained.

51. *quit* requite, pay.

53. *still . . . still* continually . . . continually (but in line 56 *still* includes 'nevertheless').

56. *By owing owes not* The first 'owe' means 'acknowledge as belonging to oneself' (*OED* 1c). Thus a *grateful mind*, simply by acknowledging a debt, ceases to owe it. Fowler traces the idea to Cicero, *Pro Plancio* xxviii 68. See also *Ad Patrem* 111–14.

61. *Power* celestial being (*OED* 7).

66, 67, 71. *thou* Satan himself.

75. *myself am Hell* See above, 20*n*.

79. *O then at last relent* The Church Father Origen had thought that Satan might be saved through *repentance* (80), but M.'s God excludes the rebel angels from grace at iii 129–32 and v 615. Cp. Matt. 25. 41, Rev. 20. 10.

79–80. *is there no place / Left for repentance* Cp. Heb. 12. 17: 'when he [Esau] would have inherited the blessing, he was rejected: for he found no place of repentance, though he sought it carefully with tears'.

81. *that word* 'submission'.

87. *abide* pay the penalty for (erroneous form of 'abye') and abide by, remain true to.

94. *grace* unmerited favour of God. *Act of grace* was also a legal term meaning 'formal pardon, *spec.* a free and general pardon, granted by an Act of Parliament' (*OED* 15b).

97. *violent* not free or voluntary (*OED* 5b).

110. *Evil be thou my good* Cp. Isa. 5. 20: 'Woe unto them that call evil good, and good evil'. Satan need not be pledging himself to evil as an absolute. Stephen Fallon compares the moral relativism of Hobbes in *Leviathan* (1651) 24: 'these words of Good, Evil, and Contemptible, are ever used with relation to the person that useth them: There being nothing simply and absolutely so; nor any common Rule of Good and Evill, to be taken from the nature of the objects themselves'. For Satan, 'good' is 'the arbitrarily imposed "good" of God, who first gave names to things' (Fallon 219).

112. *reign* govern.

115. *pale* pallor.

116. *borrowed* assumed, counterfeit (*OED* 2a).

118. *distempers* disorders arising from an imbalance of the four humours. Cp. ii 218, 276–7.

122–4. *practised . . . practised* plotted evil (*OED* 9b) . . . become proficient.

123. *couched* lying hidden.

125. *warned* summoned to duty (*OED* 7a), a military term.

126. *Assyrian mount* Niphates (iii 742).

132. *delicious Paradise* 'Paradise of delights', translating the Vulgate's *in Paradiso deliciarum* (Gen. 2. 15), which the A.V. renders as 'the garden of Eden'.

134. *champaign head* treeless plateau.

135. *hairy sides* 'The Freudian idea that the happy garden is an image of the human body would not have frightened Milton in the least' (Lewis 47). *Mound* (134) even suggests the *mons veneris*. A myrtle-clad mount in

Spenser's Garden of Adonis has precisely this significance (*FQ* III vi 43).

136. *grotesque* *of landscape: romantic, picturesque (*OED* B 2b), from 'grotto'.

140. *sylvan scene* echoing Virgil, *Aen.* i 164 (*silvis scaena*).

141. *woody theatre* Cp. Spenser, *FQ* III v 39: 'And mighty woods, which did the valley shade, / And like a stately Theatre it made'.

149. *enamelled* bright and variegated in colour.

151. *humid bow* rainbow.

153. *of* out of (both Satan's emergence and the transformation of *pure* into *purer air*).

154. *inspires* infuses (*joy*) and breathes in (*air*).

156. *gentle gales* breezes.

158-9. *stole / Those balmy spoils* Cp. Ariosto's earthly Paradise: 'From flowers, fruit and grass the breezes stole / The varied perfumes' (*Orl. Fur.* xxxiv 51).

159-65. *As . . . smiles* Cp. Diodorus Siculus's description of the fragrant breezes of Arabia Felix wafting out to sea (III xlvi 4); also Ariosto's account of spice-laden breezes delighting 'sailors out at sea' (*Orl. Fur.* xviii 138, xv 16).

160. *Hope* Good Hope (contrasting with Satan's *despair*).

162. *Sabéan* of Saba (the biblical Sheba).

163. *Araby the blest* Arabia Felix (modern Yemen).

165. *grateful* pleasing.

old Ocean the Titan Oceanus.

167. *bane* destroyer, murderer.

168-71. *Asmodéus . . . bound* In the apocryphal Book of Tobit, Tobias (*Tobit's son*) travelled to Media and married Sarah, whose previous seven husbands had been killed on their wedding night by the demon Asmodeus. Instructed by the angel Raphael, Tobias burned the heart and liver of a fish. Smelling the *fishy fume*, Asmodeus 'fled into the utmost parts of Egypt, and the angel bound him' (Tob. 8. 3). Tobias later cured his father's blindness with the fish's gall (Tob. 11. 8). Cp. v 221-3.

170. *with a vengeance* with great violence (*OED* 4b) and with a curse (*OED* 4a).

172. *savage* wild, wooded.

175. *brake* thicket.

176. *had perplexed* would have entangled.

181. *bound . . . bound* The contemptuous pun looks back to *fast bound* (171).

182. *sheer* entirely and perpendicularly.

183-7. *wolf . . . fold* Cp. John 10. 1: 'He that entereth not by the door into the sheepfold, but climbeth up some other way, the same is a thief and a robber'. Cp. also Ariosto's Saracen Rodomonte leaping the moat of Paris 'with one bound' like a hunting dog (*Orl. Fur.* xiv 130, xvi 20). Once in the city, he slaughters Christians like a wolf among sheep (*Orl. Fur.* xvi 23). Cp. also Virgil, *Aen.* ix 59–64, 563–5.

186. *hurdled cotes* sheep-pens of wattled fences.

secure overconfident (*OED* 1), with a wry pun on 'safe'.

191. *In at the window climbs* Cp. Spenser's Kirkrapine, a 'sturdie thiefe / Wont to robbe Churches' who 'in at the window crept' (I iii 17). Spenser and M. both echo Joel 2. 9, where the *thief* is an avenging army: 'they shall climb up upon the houses; they shall enter in at the windows like a thief'. The army turns 'the garden of Eden' into 'a desolate wilderness' (2. 3).

188. **unhoard* take out of a hoard.

192. *clomb* archaic past tense of 'climb'.

193. *lewd* unprincipled (*OED* 5), with a play on 'not in holy orders' (*OED* 1). Thus *lewd hirelings* implies that a paid clergy is not a real clergy. M. thought that ministers should support themselves. See his *Considerations Touching the Likeliest Means to Remove Hirelings Out of the Church* (1659) and his condemnation of 'hireling wolves' in his sonnet *To the Lord General Cromwell* (14).

196. *cormorant* a seabird noted for gluttony, hence a symbol for human rapaciousness (*OED* 2). At Isa. 34. 11 the cormorant is associated with the day of God's vengeance when Edom will lie waste: 'The cormorant and the bittern shall possess it'. Contrast Raphael as phoenix, v 272.

198. *virtue* power, efficacy. M. is elsewhere evasive as to whether the Tree of Life was truly *life-giving*. See iv 219–20, xi 93–8 and notes.

200. *well used* i.e. by Adam and Eve. Satan *only used* the Tree of Life *for prospect* (lookout); Adam and Eve might have used it as a *pledge*.

211. *Auran* the province of Hauran on the eastern border of Israel (Ezek. 47. 18).

212. *great Seleucia* a city on the Tigris, built by Alexander's general Seleucus Nicator (called *great* to distinguish it from other cities of the same name). See *PR* iii 291.

213–14. *sons of Eden ... Telassar* Cp. II Kings 19. 11 and Isa. 37. 12, where the Assyrians destroy 'the children of Eden which were in Telassar'.

219. **ambrosial* divinely fragrant (*OED* 1c). The etymology (Greek *ambrotos*, 'immortal') suggests that the Tree of Life might bestow immortality, but see xi 93–6.

220. *vegetable gold* Fowler hears an echo of 'potable gold' (see iii 680*n*) and 'vegetable stone' – both forms of the elixir of life or Philosopher's Stone. Cp. also Virgil's description of the golden bough (*Aen.* vi 143–4).

222. *Knowledge ... ill* Cp. *CD* i 10: 'It was called the tree of knowledge of good and evil because of what happened afterwards: for since it was tasted, not only do we know evil, but also we do not even know good except through evil' (trans. Carey, *YP* 6. 352). Cp. ix 1070–73, xi 84–9.

223. *a river* the Tigris (identified at ix 71).

228. *kindly* natural.

233. **main streams* Cp. Gen. 2. 10: 'And a river went out of Eden . . . and became into four heads'.

237. *crispèd* rippling.

239. *error* wandering; 'the evil meaning is consciously and ominously excluded' (Stein 66). Cp. vii 302.

241. *nice* fastidious.

242. *knots* flower-beds laid out in intricate designs (*OED* 7).

boon bountiful.

246. **Embrowned* darkened (*OED* 1).

248. *odorous gums* Cp. Spenser's Garden of Adonis, where a grove of myrtles dropped 'sweet gum' and 'Threw forth most dainty odours' (*FQ* III vi 43). Spenser's grove symbolizes the *mons veneris* (see above, 135*n*).

250. *amiable* desirable.

Hesperian fables See iii 568*n*. Ralegh in *The History of the World* (1614) notes that the dragon guarding the apples of the Hesperides was 'taken from the Serpent, which tempted Evah' (86).

255. *irriguous* well-watered.

256. *without thorn* a traditional inference from Gen. 3. 18.

257. *umbrageous* shady.

258. *mantling* enveloping (*OED* 2).

262–3. *Myrtle* and *mirror* are attributes of Venus, goddess of love and gardens.

264. *airs* breezes and melodies.

266. *universal Pan* A spurious etymology (Greek πᾶν, 'all') encouraged the notion that the wood-god Pan was a symbol of universal nature.

267. *Graces* three naked goddesses (Euphrosyne, Aglaia, Thalia) who attended Venus.

Hours the Horai, three goddessed who presided over the seasons.

268. *eternal spring* There are no seasons until earth is tilted on its axis, after the Fall (x 651–91). Ovid, *Met.* v 391, describes *Enna*, where *Proserpine* was ravished, as a land of *perpetuum ver*, 'eternall Spring' (trans. Sandys).

269–72. *Enna . . . world* Ovid tells how *Dis* (Pluto, Hades) snatched *Proserpine*, daughter of the grain-goddess *Ceres*, from the Sicilian meadow of *Enna*. The earth grew barren while Ceres searched for her daughter. Jove promised that Proserpine should be restored if she had eaten no food in Hades, but she had eaten seven pomegranate seeds and so had to stay in Hades half the year (*Met.* v 385ff., *Fasti* iv 420ff.). Sandys notes that Proserpine's pomegranate 'is held to have a relation' to the apple that 'thrust *Evah* out of Paradice'. See George Sandys, *Ovid's Metamorphosis* (1632), 195.

270. *Herself a fairer flow'r* Cp. ix 432: 'Herself, though fairest unsupported flow'r'; also Ovid, *Met.* v 398–401, where Proserpine's gathered flowers (*collecti flores*) fall from her robe, and she grieves for them even as she herself is abducted. M. often alludes to Proserpine's abduction in *PL*. See 381–5n below, ix 396, 838–42n.

273–4. *Daphne* a grove of laurels on the river *Orontes* in Syria. It had a *Castalian spring* named for that of the Muses on Mount Parnassus, and an oracle of Apollo (hence *inspired*).

275–9. *Nyseian . . . eye* Diodorus Siculus (III lxvii–lxx) tells how King *Ammon* of Libya had a son, *Bacchus*, by the nymph *Amalthea*. Fearing his jealous wife *Rhea*, Ammon hid Amalthea and Bacchus on Nysa, an island in *the river Triton* near modern Tunis. Christian commentators identified Jupiter-Ammon with Noah's son Ham (*Cham*).

278. *florid* ruddy (Bacchus was the god of wine).

281. *Amara* a mountain-top fastness where Abyssinian kings raised their sons (*issue*) among secluded gardens and palaces. Peter Heylyn in his *Cosmographie* (1652) says it was 'a dayes journey high', adding 'some have taken (but mistaken) it for the place of *Paradise*' (iv 64).

282. *Ethiop line* equator.

286. **undelighted all delight* 'Eden' means 'delight'.

291. *worthy* here probably an adverb (*OED* B) signifying that Adam and Eve really were what they *seemed* to be.

293. *severe* austerely plain ('like a severe style in music or architecture', Lewis 118). Cp. xi 1144, 1169.

295. *Whence* from God's image.

296. *their sex not equal seemed* Joseph Wittreich in *Feminist Milton* (1987) 86 argues valiantly but unpersuasively that Adam and Eve *seem* unequal only because we are seeing them through Satan's eyes. Raphael and the Son both insist upon Adam's headship (viii 561–78, x 145–56), as does M. in his prose (*YP* 2. 589–90, 6. 355).

299. *He . . . him* Cp. I Cor. 11. 3: 'the head of every man is Christ; and the head of the woman is the man; and the head of Christ is God'.

300. *front* forehead.

   sublime of lofty aspect.

301. *hyacinthine* Cp. Odysseus's hair that 'hung down like hyacinthine petals', shining like 'gold on silver' (Homer, *Od.* vi 231–2).

301–8. *locks . . . sway* Cp. I Cor. 11. 14–15: 'Doth not even nature itself teach you, that, if a man have long hair, it is a shame unto him? But if a woman have long hair, it is a glory to her: for her hair is given her for a covering'. The A.V. marginal gloss explains that the woman's 'covering' is a 'sign that she is under the power of her husband'.

306. *wanton* sportive, luxuriant (*OED* 3, 7a), but with proleptic overtones of the pejorative sense, which M. often uses elsewhere (e.g., i 414, 454, iv 768, ix 1015).

310. *coy* shyly reserved (*OED* 2), not 'coquettish'.

312. *mysterious* secret, awe-inspiring (as in a religious rite). See 743n below.

The etymology (Greek *muein*, 'to close lips or eyes') is paradoxical when nothing is hidden. Contrast Donne, 'Elegy 19': '[women] are mystic books, which only we . . . May see revealed' (41–3).

313. *dishonest* including 'dishonourable', 'unchaste' and 'unseemly to the sight' (*OED* 1, 2, 3).

321. *hand in hand* a recurrent motif. Cp. iv 488–9, 689, 739, ix 385–6, 1037, xii 648.

323. *goodliest* most handsome and well-proportioned.

323–4. *since . . . sons* The syntax was not unidiomatic. Bush cites Browne, *Pseudodoxia* I i: 'he [Adam] was the wisest of all men since'.

329. *recommend cool Zephyr* 'make a cool breeze welcome' (Zephyr was god of the west wind).

332. *Nectarine* sweet as nectar (*OED*), though the nectarine peach was also known.

compliant including *'pliant' (*OED* 2).

333. *recline recumbent (sole instance in *OED*).

334. *damasked* woven with rich designs, variegated (*OED* 1, 3).

336. *brimming OED's earliest participial instance.

337. *purpose* conversation (*OED* 4b).

*endearing OED's earliest participial instance.

338. *Wanted* were lacking.

dalliance caressing (*OED* 2).

341. *chase* unenclosed parkland (*OED* 3) and (ominously, since there were no carnivores) hunted animals (*OED* 4a).

343. *ramped* stood on his hind legs – 'a threatening posture' (*OED* 'ramp' 3a), but here benign. Cp. vii 466.

344. *Dandled the kid* Cp. Isa. 11. 6: 'the leopard shall lie down with the kid; and the calf and the young lion and the fatling together'.

ounces lynxes.

pards leopards.

348. *Insinuating* winding (Latin *insinuare*), with a proleptic hint of 'dark suggestions' (ix 90).

Gordian twine coils as convoluted as the Gordian knot, which only Alexander could disentangle (by cutting it with his sword).

352. *ruminating* chewing the cud.

353. *prone career* descending course and headlong gallop (the chariot of the sun).

354. *Ocean Isles* the Azores (identified in line 592).

ascending Scale The sun is in Aries (x 329), so the stars 'rise in Libra, the Scales, the portion of the sky exactly opposite' (Fowler).

358–62. *What . . . Little inferior* Cp. Ps. 8. 4–5 (and Heb. 2. 6–7): 'What is man, that thou art mindful of him . . . / For thou hast made him a little lower than the angels, / And hast crowned him with glory and honour'.

359. *room* place. Cp. 'vacant room' (vii 190).

360. *mould* bodily form (*OED* sb³ 10b) and earth regarded as the material of the human body (*OED* sb¹ 4). Cp. ii 355.

370. *so happy* such happiness.

376. *strait* intimate (*OED* 14) and strict, severe (*OED* 6).

381. *freely give* Satan parodies Matt. 10. 8: 'freely ye have received, freely give'.

381–3. *Hell . . . kings* Cp. Isaiah's prophecy of the fall of Babylon: 'Hell from beneath is moved for thee to meet thee at thy coming: it stirreth up the dead for thee, even all the chief ones of the earth; it hath raised up from their thrones all the kings of the nations' (Isa. 14. 9). This analogue suggests that Satan is gloating, but cp. also Claudian, *De Rapt. Pros.* ii 276–306, where Pluto genuinely tries to console the abducted Proserpine by telling her that Hades is spacious. He concludes: 'kings in purple robes will kneel at your feet' (300). Cp. iv 269, ix 432, and ix 838–42.

382. *entertain* an ambiguous word, which could mean 'treat in (any) specified manner' (*OED* 8), even torture, as in 'entertained with all variety of persecution' (1611). Satan plays on 'receive', 'show hospitality to' (*OED* 12, 13), but Hell's *gates* will also 'admit and contain' mankind (*OED* 11). Cp. Satan's offer to prepare 'Fit entertainment' for the Messiah (v 690).

387. *for* in place of.

393–4. *necessity, / The tyrant's plea* Cp. M.'s contempt in *Eikonoklastes* for Royalist appeals to 'the necessity of the times' (*YP* 3. 373). But 'necessity' was really Cromwell's word. Legend later had it that he had stood over the body of King Charles and muttered 'Cruel necessity!' He pleaded 'accident and necessity' against the Levellers, 'providence and necessity' when trying the King, and *la necessité* when dissolving the Rump. M. approved of these acts, but he may have had misgivings when Cromwell 'saw it was necessary' to dissolve the Barebones Parliament (as they were debating tithes) and become Lord Protector, assuming regal pomp 'of necessity'. See Antonia Fraser, *Cromwell: Our Chief of Men* (1973), 210, 229, 274, 293, 423, 447, 449, 462–3.

402. *A lion now he stalks* Cp. I Pet. 5. 8: 'your adversary the devil, as a roaring lion, walketh about, seeking whom he may devour'. Contrast the playful lion of line 343.

404. *purlieu* outskirts of a forest (*OED* 1).

410. *Turned him all ear* Adam's words turned Satan all ear. Fowler thinks that *all ear* might be M.'s coinage, but Drummond had used the phrase in his Sonnet XXV. Cp. also *A Masque* 560.

411. *Sole . . . sole* only . . . chief (with a pun on 'soul').

423–4. *Tree / Of Knowledge* In accordance with Gen. 2. 16–17, the name 'Tree of Knowledge of Good and Evil' antedates the Fall (cp. viii 323–33). Some biblical commentators had thought that so deceptive a name must be Satan's invention. Cp. ix 1070–73 and see Arnold Williams, *The Common Expositor* (1948) 105–7.

425. *whate'er death is*   Adam and Eve as yet barely grasp the notion of annihilation (cp. ix 695, 775). After the Fall they have difficulty in thinking of death as anything else (see ix 826–33, x 770–816).

427. *pronounced*   both 'passed sentence' and 'uttered a vocal sound'. *Death* is as yet an empty word in Paradise. Contrast ii 788 where 'Hell trembled at the hideous name'.

447. *odds*   the amount by which one thing exceeds another (*OED* 1b). Eve means that Adam is superior, but her syntax allows herself to be *Pre-eminent* in enjoying him.

451. *of*]   *Ed II*; on *Ed I*.

459. *lake*   not a 'pool', though critics repeatedly write of 'Eve at the pool'. Eve's *liquid plain* (455) is a genuine geographical feature (260–63), far grander than the small woodland pool in which Narcissus lost himself (*Met.* iii 407–12). Sandys uses 'liquid plain' to translate Ovid's *campoque . . . aquae* (*Met.* i 41–2): a description of earth's primeval ocean. See further, McColley (77).

460–68. *As . . . thyself*   The allusion to Ovid's proud Narcissus (*Met.* iii 402–510) need not convict Eve of sinful pride. Eve did not know that the beautiful face was her own, and (unlike Narcissus) she turned from her reflection when she learned the truth. Bush cites a tradition that 'some of the newly created angels looked up to God, others fell in love with themselves'. But cp. also the Self-love of Spenser's 'High Eternal Power': 'It loved itself because itself was fair; / (For fair is loved)' (*An Hymn of Heavenly Love* 29–30).

466. *vain*   futile. There may be overtones of 'indulging in personal vanity', but *OED* does not cite that sense before 1692. Cp. Spenser's Britomart gazing into Merlin's 'glassie globe': 'Her selfe a while therein she vewd in vaine' (*FQ* III ii 22).

467. *a voice*   belonging to God (viii 485–6) or possibly an angel (iv 712).

470. *stays*   awaits (*OED* 14) and hinders. The former sense refers to Adam, the latter to Eve's reflection.

472. *shall*   So all early editions. Many editors emend to 'shalt', and so make *thou* the sole subject of *enjoy*. But *shall enjoy* could be governed by *he* (with *thy soft embraces* as object). See Adams (90).

474–5. *thence be called / Mother of human race*   Cp. Gen. 3. 20: 'And Adam called his wife's name Eve; because she was the mother of all living'. 'Eve' means 'life'. In Genesis, Adam names 'Eve' only after the Fall, when he and she are subject to death. Some commentators thought that Adam chose the name in defiance of God. Others associated it with misery and sin. M. rejects this misogynistic tradition by giving 'Eve' prelapsarian status. Adam bestows the name in line 481. Cp. v 385–8, xi 156–71.

476–91. Cp. Adam's recollection of these events at viii 481–520.

478. *platan* plane tree.

486. *individual* both 'inseparable' (*OED* A 2) and 'distinguished by attributes of [her] own' (*OED* A 4).

488. *other half* Cp. Plato, *Symposium* 189d–193e.

493. *unreproved* irreproachable. See ix 5n.

499–500. *Jupiter . . . clouds* Jupiter was god of the sky and Juno goddess of the air, and their union was sometimes allegorized as the marriage of Aether and Aer. See e.g. Natale Conti, *Mythologiae* (1567) II iv. Conti cites *Iliad* xiv 346–51, where Zeus and Hera make love under a cloud. Notice, however, that M.'s Jupiter *impregns the clouds*, not Juno. The substitution of clouds for Juno is troubling because it recalls Ixion, who fathered the centaurs on a cloud that he mistook for Juno. M. compares Eve with Ixion's cloud in *Tetrachordon* (*YP* 2. 597–8).

507. *happier Eden* See 27n above.

511. *pines* torments.

515. *knowledge forbidd'n* Satan speaks here as if he believed the fruit really could give knowledge. Contrast x 485–7.

522. *ruin* fall (Latin *ruina*), but *foundation* and *build* also suggest the paradox of building ruins.

530. *A chance but chance* 'An opportunity, even if only a fortuitous one'.

538. **roam* act of wandering (coined from the verb).

539. *utmost longitude* uttermost west.

541. *with right aspéct* directly.

548. *Still* continually.

549. *Gabriel* Hebrew 'Strength of God'. Muslim and cabbalistic lore made Gabriel a 'warrior' (576); M. might also have known a tradition (embodied in I Enoch 20. 7) which gave Gabriel charge of Paradise and the Cherubim.

552. *unarmèd* Cp. the devils' more warlike games (ii 532–8).

555–6. *gliding . . . star* Cp. Tasso, *Gerus. Lib.* ix 62, where an angel descends to earth as 'in the stillness of a moonshine even / A falling star so glideth down from Heaven' (trans. Fairfax); also Homer, *Il.* iv 75–9.

555. *even* both 'evening' and 'nearly *even* sunbeam' (Empson[2] 157). See below, 590n.

557. *thwarts* both 'traverses' (*OED* 1) and 'frustrates'. Cp. 'checks the night' (iii 732).

vapours fired ignited exhalations (thought to cause shooting stars).

567. *God's latest image* God's first image was the Son. M. neither denies nor explicitly states that angels bear God's image.

described traced (*OED* 5) with the eye. Uriel had given Satan directions (iii 722–35), but he is here referring to what he saw, not what he said. Adams therefore urges modernizing editors to print 'descried'. He points out that 'descry' and 'describe' were often confused in the seventeenth century. No editor has followed Adams's advice, though most agree that Uriel means 'descried'. I retain *described* because it suggests that Uriel never took his eye off Satan, whom he closely *marked*. 'Descry' would imply that Uriel merely caught sight of Satan.

568. *gait* journey (*OED* 'gate' sb² 6) and manner of flying.

572. *shade* trees.

580. *vigilance* vigilant guards.

590. *beam* sunbeam and balance beam (*now raised* because the sun has set, allowing Uriel to slide *downward*).

592–5. *whether . . . there* As at iii 573–6, M. does not commit himself to either the Ptolemaic or the Copernican system. *Ed I* and *Ed II* spell 'whither' thus admitting a pun.

592. *prime orb* either the sun or the *primum mobile* (both move with *incredible* speed in the Ptolemaic system).

594. *Diurnal* in the space of one day.

volúble moving rapidly (*OED* 3) and capable of ready rotation on its axis (*OED* 2).

600. *accompanied* both 'joined their company' and 'played a musical accompaniment'.

603. *descant* warbled song, melodious strain (*OED* 3).

605. *Hesperus* Venus, the evening star.

608. *Apparent* plainly seen (*OED* 1), with a play on 'heir apparent' (notice *queen*). Cp. Ariosto's erotic description of the moon breaking through clouds: 'The moon at this petition parts the cloud . . . As fair as when she offered herself nude / To Endymion' (*Orl. Fur.* xviii 185).

617. *unemployed* *idle (*OED* 2a). *OED*'s earliest instance modifying sentient creatures.

620. *regard* observant attention and esteem.

627. *walk*] *Ed II*; walks *Ed I*.

628. *manuring* cultivating of plants (*OED* 2b) and inhabiting (*OED* 1b) of Paradise.

632. *Ask riddance* need to be cleared.

635. *author* one who gives existence (*OED* 1) and one who has authority (*OED* 5).

disposer ruler (*OED* 2).

640. *seasons* times of day.

641–56. *Sweet . . . sweet* Many critics liken Eve's embedded lyric to a sonnet, but M.'s rhetorical figure has a closer analogue in Hector's farewell to Andromache (Homer, *Il.* vi 447–55). Like Eve, Hector lists the things that are dear to him, then he repeats his list with negatives, before directly addressing his spouse in the second person. In both cases it is the direct address that turns the preceding double *enumeratio* into a declaration of love.

642. *charm* the blended singing of many birds (*OED*).

648. *solemn bird* the nightingale (see line 602).

660. *accomplished* complete, perfect.

661. *Those* Perhaps a misprint for 'these' (as editors since Newton have conjectured), but Adam might well prefer to look at Eve than at the stars.

664. *light prepared* Ps. 74. 16 (see below, 724–5*n*).

668. *kindly* natural and benign.

669. *influence* an etherial fluid flowing from stars and planets and 'influencing' man's character and destiny. (p. vii 375, vii 513, ix 105–6 etc.)

foment cherish with heat.

670. *Temper* heal or refresh by restoring the proper 'temper' of elements or humours (see ii 276–7).

674. *unbeheld.

676. *want . . . want* lack . . . lack.

685. *rounding* walking the rounds (see line 862) and singing 'rounds' (*responsive each to other's note*).

688. *Divide the night* both 'divide the night into watches' and 'perform with musical "divisions"' (*OED* 11a). Cp. *Passion* 4.

690. *blissful bower* recalling Spenser's Bower of Bliss (*FQ* II xii), but cp. also Venus's 'blisfull bowre of joy above' (*FQ* III vi 95).

691. *Planter* Cp. Gen. 2. 8: 'God planted a garden'. God is also the planter of a new world colony. Cp. i 650–53 and see J. M. Evans, *Milton's Imperial Epic* (1996) 4: 'God . . . is "the sovran Planter", a periphrasis that links him with the royal patron of England's first transatlantic colony'.

694. *Laurel and myrtle* emblems of Apollo and Venus.

698. *jessamine* jasmine.

699. *flourished* luxuriant, adorned with flowers.

701. *Crocus, and hyacinth* The same plants spontaneously arise when Hera seduces Zeus on Mount Ida (Homer, *Il.* xiv 347–9).

703. *emblem* ornament of inlaid work (*OED* 1), with a play on the emblematic properties of the flowers: 'the humility of the *violet*, prudence of the *hyacinth*, amiability of the *jessamine*' (Fowler).

705. *shadier*] *Ed I*; shady *Ed II*.

707–8. *Pan or Silvanus . . . Faunus* wood-gods represented as half man, half goat. All were fertility gods and Silvanus was also associated with gardens and limits.

708. *close* secret.

711. *hymenean* wedding hymn. Hymen was the ancient god of marriage. Cp. *L'Allegro* 125 and *Elegia V* 105–8.

712. *genial* presiding over marriage and generation. At viii 484–7 Eve is led by her Maker, not an *angel*.

714. *Pandora* Greek 'all gifts', the first woman, created at Jove's command. Prometheus ('Forethought') and Epimetheus ('Afterthought') were sons of

Iapetus (*Japhet*). Prometheus stole Jove's fire for man. Jove, *to be avenged*, sent Hermes to Epimetheus with Pandora as a gift. She came with a sealed jar containing the world's ills. In Renaissance versions, Epimetheus opened the jar, but Hesiod credits Pandora with the act (*WD* 93). In *Theog.* he dispenses with the jar, as if woman were punishment enough. M.'s simile is compatible with any of these versions.

717. *Japhet* Noah's son (Gen. 9–10). His identification with the Titan Iapetus was traditional.

719. *authentic* belonging to himself (*OED* 7), original (*OED* 4).

724. *pole* sky.

Thou also mad'st Eighteenth-century critics applauded the 'masterly transition' whereby the poet's voice 'passes into' that of Adam and Eve (Addison, *Spectator*, no. 231). The effect is lost when quotation marks are placed before *Thou*.

724–5. *the night . . . the day* Cp. Ps. 74. 16: 'The day is thine, the night also is thine: thou hast prepared the light and the sun'.

730. *wants* lacks.

735. *gift of sleep* Ps. 127. 2, Homer, *Il.* ix 712–13, Virgil, *Aen.* ii 268–9.

739. *Handed* *joined hand in hand (*OED* 3), a sense coined by M. in *DDD*: 'if any two be but once handed in the Church'.

741. *ween* surmise.

743. *Mysterious* awe-inspiring, sacred. St Paul calls the union of husband and wife 'a great mystery' (Eph. 5. 32), dignified by Christ's marriage to his Church. Cp. also the 'mysterious rites' of marriage in Jonson, *Hymenaei* 137.

744–9. *hypocrites . . . foe* Cp. I Tim. 4. 1–3: 'in the latter times some shall depart from the faith, giving heed to seducing spirits, and doctrines of devils; speaking lies in hypocrisy; having their conscience seared with a hot iron; forbidding to marry'. M. dignifies sex by having Adam and Eve make love before the Fall.

747. *commands to some* I. Cor. 7. 1.

748. *Our Maker bids increase* Gen. 1. 28.

751. *propriety* right of possession or use (*OED* 1a). Before the Fall, monogamous marriage was the only property right.

756. *charities* *feelings or acts of affection (*OED* 2b).

761. *bed is undefiled* Cp. Heb. 13. 4: 'Marriage is honourable in all, and the bed undefiled'.

762. *patriarchs* By including them in his hymn to wedded love, M. might be hinting at polygamy, which they had practised and he defended in *CD*. See A. Rudrum, 'Polygamy in *Paradise Lost*', *EC* 20 (1970), 18–23.

763. *Love* Cupid, whose golden arrows (*shafts*) kindled love.

764. *purple* brilliant and imperial (notice *Reigns*).

766. *unendeared both 'devoid of affection' and 'lacking value'. 'Endear' could mean 'enhance the value of' (*OED* 2), as in 'love endeareth the meanest things' (1594).

768. *masque* masquerade, masked ball.

769. *starved* perished with cold (*OED* 4), from standing outside the mistress's door. See e.g. Ovid, *Amores* i 6, 9; iii 11a. Serenades were sung at night, in the open air (*in sereno*).

773. *repaired* replaced (with new roses).

774. *Blest pair* Cp. Virgil, *Aen.* ix 446, on the intimate friends Nisus and Euryalus: *Fortunati ambo!*

776. *shadowy cone* earth's shadow rotating around the earth (see iii 556–7). When the shadow is *Half way* between the horizon and the zenith it is nine o'clock.

777. *sublunar* beneath the moon.

778. *ivory port* ivory gate – the source of false dreams in Homer (*Od.* xix 562f.) and Virgil (*Aen.* vi 893f.). True dreams issued from a gate of horn. Fowler notes that M.'s Cherubim use the ivory gate because they 'are to interrupt a false dream'. Others might feel that the allusion implies that the good angels will fail. Homer says that dreams issuing from the ivory gate are ineffectual, 'their message is never accomplished' (*Od.* xix 565).

782. *Uzziel* Hebrew 'My strength is God'. A man at Exod. 6. 18, but cabbalistic tradition attributed the name to one of seven angels before God's throne (West 154).

785. *shield . . . spear* left . . . right.

788. *Ithuriel* Hebrew 'Discovery of God'. The name is not biblical. R. H. West (*SP* 47, 1950, 211–23) conjectures that M. may have made 'this one up' (219), but Ithuriel is an angel in Moses Cordovero's *Pardes Rimmonim* (Cracow, 1592) and other sixteenth-century tracts. See Gustav Davidson, *A Dictionary of Angels* (1967) 152. M. did not coin angels.

Zephon Hebrew 'a looking out'. Zephon is a man at Num. 26. 15, and a devil in Selden's *De Dis Syris* (1617), I iii 43. He may yet emerge as an angel.

791. *secure* free from anxiety (*OED* 1).

793. *Who* one who.

802. *Fancy* the faculty of forming mental images. Were Satan able to reach Eve's Fancy, he would enjoy greater freedom to form *illusions* than if he just had access to her *spirits*, which produce more abstract *hopes* and *desires*.

805. *animal spirits* the highest of three kinds of fine vapours produced in the human body. The liver and heart produced natural and vital spirits, which rose to the brain to become animal spirits (Latin *anima*, 'soul'). These then imparted motion to the body and conveyed sense data to the reason. At v 485 Raphael speaks of still higher 'intellectual' spirits, which may be M.'s invention. Hunter (46–55) cites many sources to show that Satan has no direct access to Eve's reason.

807. *distempered* vexed (by an imbalance of the four 'humours').

809. *conceits* notions (*OED* 1), with overtones of *pride*. The context (*Blown up, engend'ring*) also suggests a sexual impregnation. Satan might be parodying the immaculate conception, which was thought to have taken place through Mary's *ear* (800).

812. *celestial temper* both the weapon, 'tempered Heav'nly' (ii 813), and Ithuriel's angelic 'temperament' (ii 218, 277).

815. *Lights* alights and kindles.

   nitrous powder gunpowder.

816. *tun* barrel.

   magazine storehouse for explosives.

817. *Against* in preparation for.

   *rumoured OED's earliest participial instance.

   smutty black. Smut is a fungous disease that turns cereal grains into a black powder.

821. *grisly King* Moloch's epithet at *Nativity* 209.

828. *Know ye not me* Satan does not know himself, for he appeals to an identity that is no longer his. *There sitting* recalls the unfallen Lucifer, who aspired to 'sit also on the mount of the congregation' (Isa. 14. 13). Satan will not acknowledge the name 'Satan' until x 386.

840. *obscure* lowly (answering *unknown*, *lowest*) and gloomy.

848. *pined* mourned.

856. *Single* in single combat (*OED* 15) and simple, honest, sincere (*OED* 14).

868. *shade* trees.

869. *port* bearing.

870. *wan* gloomy, sad, sickly.

873. *lours* scowls.

879. *transgressions* including 'crossing the bounds' (*OED* 1b).

   charge both the responsibility and those whom Gabriel is responsible for (Adam and Eve).

880. *approve* test by experience (*OED* 8) and commend. The former sense draws Satan's contempt (see line 895).

886. *esteem of wise* reputation for wisdom.

892–3. *change . . . with* exchange . . . for.

893–4. *recompense / Dole with delight* 'replace grief with joy'. But Satan also hints punningly at his true purpose, which is 'delightfully to deal out death'. *Recompense* includes 'mete out in requital' (*OED* 3) and *dole* includes 'distribution of gifts' (*OED* sb² 5), including 'death' (*OED* sb² 5b). Cp. Samson 'dealing dole among his foes' (*SA* 1529).

895. *To thee no reason* Since Gabriel has never experienced pain, he cannot understand the need to escape it.

896. *object* put forward as an objection.

899. *durance* imprisonment.

thus much what So much in answer to what.

904. *O . . . wise* 'O what a loss to Heaven to lose such a judge of wisdom as you!'

911. *However* in any way he can.

918. *all Hell broke loose* already proverbial (*OED* 'hell' 10).

926. *stood* withstood.

928. *The*] Ed I; *Thy Ed II*.

929. *seconded* both 'assisted' and 'taken the place of a defeated combatant' (*OED* 2c).

930. *at random* wide of the mark. A military metaphor: guns fired 'at random' when firing at long range (*OED* 5b).

932. *assays* afflictions, efforts, attacks (*OED* 2, 14, 15).

939. *afflicted powers* downcast armies (cp. i 186).

940. *mid air* Satan will become 'prince of the power of the air' (Eph. 2. 2).

942. *gay* brilliantly good (used ironically, *OED* 6b), showily dressed (*OED* 4).

945. *practised distances* Satan contemptuously draws a parallel between the good angels' court etiquette (which prescribes various *distances* from the *throne*) and their keeping at a safe distance in battle. *Distances* also plays on 'musical intervals' (*OED* 5c) kept in *songs*.

959. *fawned . . . adored* Waldock (81) dismisses Gabriel's 'unsupported calumny'; Empson (111) takes it as proof that Heaven was 'unattractive' even 'before Satan fell'. But Satan *servilely adored* God on the day of the Son's exaltation, when he 'seemed well-pleased' (v 617).

962. *aread* advise.

avaunt begone.

965. *drag thee chained* Cp. Rev. 20. 1–3: 'an angel . . . having . . . a great chain in his hand . . . laid hold on the dragon . . . and bound him a thousand years, and cast him into the bottomless pit'.

967. *facile* easily moved.

969. *waxing more in rage* both 'growing more angry' and 'growing bigger in his anger' (*OED* 'more' 1). See lines 985–8.

971. *limitary* both 'stationed on the boundary' (*OED* 2) and 'subject to limits' (*OED* 1).

976. *road of Heav'n* not the Milky Way (as editors claim) but a *star-paved* road in Heaven that Raphael likens to the Milky Way at vii 577–81. A *progress* is a state procession.

978. *moonèd horns* crescent formation (for *phalanx* see i 550n).

980. *ported spears* not as in 'port arms', but 'With their Spears borne pointed towards him' (Hume, 1695). Cp. Randle Holme, *The Academy of Armory* (1688): 'Port your pike, is in three motions to . . . beare it forward aloft' (III xix 147). The blades therefore face Satan, whose *stature reached the sky* (988).

980–85. *field . . . chaff* Empson[2] (172) claims that the simile 'makes the good angels look weak', and epic precedent supports his view. Homer (*Il.* ii 147–50), Tasso (*Gerus. Lib.* xx 60), Apollonius Rhodius (*Argonautica* iii 1386f.) and Ariosto (*Orl. Fur.* xvi 68) compare demoralized armies to a wind-tossed cornfield. Cp. also Phineas Fletcher's simile likening devils escaped from Hell to a tempest descending on corn: 'the Plowmans hopes new-eard / Swimme on the playne' (*The Apollyonists* ii 40). In Ps. 1. 4 it is the ungodly who are 'like the chaff which the wind driveth away'.

981. *Ceres* corn (Ceres being goddess of agriculture).

983. *careful* anxious.

985. *alarmed* called to arms.

987. *Teneriffe or Atlas* mountains in the Canary Islands and Morocco. Atlas was also a rebel Titan (see ii 306*n*). Cp. Tasso's Solimano, who resists a Christian assault as a mountain assailed with storms 'Doth unremovèd, steadfast, still withstand / Storm, thunder, lightning, tempest, wind and tide' (*Gerus. Lib.* ix 31, trans. Fairfax).

    unremoved unremovable (see ix 5*n*).

989. *Horror* from Latin *horrere*, to bristle.

992. *cope* vault.

997. *Scales* the constellation Libra. M. also alludes to Zeus weighing the fates of pagan epic combatants (Homer, *Il.* viii 68–77, xxii 208–13, Virgil, *Aen.* xii 725–7). In pagan epics the loser's fate sinks downward; Gabriel declares Satan to be *light* (1012). Cp. Dan. 5. 27: 'TEKEL; Thou art weighed in the balances, and found wanting'.

998. *Astraea* goddess of justice. She lived on earth during the Golden Age, but human wickedness drove her to the heavens, where she was stellified as Virgo (Ovid, *Met.* i 149f.). Cp. *Nativity* 141–3.

999–1000. *he weighed . . . air* God uses a balance in Creation at Job 28. 24 and Isa. 40. 12.

1001. *ponders* weighs in the scales (*OED* 1) and considers.

BOOK V

2. *orient* sparkling (*OED* 2) and eastern.

5. *bland* *gentle, balmy, soothing (*OED* 2). Contrast the 'exhilarating vapour bland' produced by the forbidden fruit (ix 1047).

    only mere.

6. *Aurora's fan* leaves stirred by the morning breeze. Aurora was goddess of morning.

12. *cordial* heartfelt.

15. *peculiar graces* charms all her own. An echo of iii 183 ('chosen of peculiar grace') might imply that Eve's grace 'is out of the ordinary, excessive, and, as in Calvin's scheme, irresistible. It is grace out of proportion to merit' (Rumrich[2] 140).

16. *Zephyrus on Flora* the west wind over flowers. The flower-goddess Flora is Zephyr's consort in Ovid, *Fasti* v 197.

17–25. *Awake . . . sweet* Cp. Song of Sol. 2. 10–12: 'Rise up, my love, my fair one, and come away . . . . The flowers appear on the earth; The time of the singing of birds is come'. Like Solomon, Adam wakens his love with an aubade. Contrast Satan's serenade (v 38–47), which is a parody of Song of Sol.

21. *prime* first hour of the day, beginning at six o'clock.

22. **tended OED*'s earliest participial instance.

blows blooms.

23. *balmy reed* balsam.

34. *offence* including 'occasion of unbelief or doubt' (*OED* 2).

38. *Why sleep'st thou* See below, 673*n*.

44. *heav'n wakes with all his eyes* Cp. Giles Fletcher on the Nativity, *CV* (1610) i 78: 'heav'n awaked all his eyes, / To see another Sunne, at midnight rise'. The *eyes* are stars.

47. *still* continually.

56–7. *dewy . . . Ambrosia* Cp. Virgil's Venus: 'her ambrosial hair exhaled divine perfume' (*Aen.* i 403–4).

60. *god* angel. Some modernizing editors retain the early editions' 'God'. Cp. v 117.

61. *reserve* restriction (*OED* 6), self-restraint (*OED* 9), knowledge withheld from one person by another (*OED* 10).

66. *vouched with* backed by.

72. *Communicated* shared (*OED* 4). The context (*divine, gods, Taste*) also suggests 'partake of the Holy Communion' (*OED* 6b). Cp. ix 755.

79. *as we* Zachary Pearce noted in 1733 how these words are placed so as to refer either to *Ascend to Heaven* or to *in the air*. Empson[2] (163) sees 'a natural embarrassment' in Satan's implied doubt 'as to whether he could go to Heaven himself'. Contrast Raphael's unequivocal 'as we' (v 499), and see i 516*n* for Satan's confinement to the air.

84. *savoury* appetizing, but the word derives from Latin *sapere* meaning both 'taste' and 'know'. The noun 'savour' could still mean 'perception, understanding' (*OED* 5). In biblical usage (e.g., Gen. 8. 21), 'savour' was used of sacrifices that God found pleasing (*OED* 2c), so Eve's dream implies that God wants her to eat the apple.

86. *Could not . . . Forthwith* Eve dreams of the consequences of eating, but the crucial act is absent from her dream – perhaps because Satan cannot 'make her go through the motions of disobedience, even in her fancy' (Fish 222).

94. *sad* grave, serious (*OED* 4a).

98. *uncouth* strange (*OED* 3) and distasteful (*OED* 4).

99. *harbour* lodge; often with some notion of lurking or concealment (*OED* 7). Evil may *come and go*, but cannot reside, in unfallen minds (117).

102. *Fancy* the mental faculty which produces images. See iv 802*n*.

104. *represent* bring clearly before the mind (*OED* 2a).

106. *frames* directs to a certain purpose (*OED* 5c).

109. *cell* compartment of the brain.

115. *our last evening's talk* either the discussion about the prohibition (iv 421ff.) or Eve's question about the stars (iv 657–8), to which her dream has offered a flattering answer (v 44–7). Satan did not overhear Eve's question (he exited at iv 535), so the dream-answer (v 44–5) might not be his. Eve's own *Fancy* may have played a part, as Adam surmises.

117. *god* probably 'angel' (see above, 60*n*), but maybe God, whose omniscience extends to evil.

118. *so* so long as it remains.

   unapproved *not sanctioned (*OED* 3) and not put to the proof (*OED* 'approve' 8).

123. *wont* are accustomed.

131. *wiped them with her hair* echoing Luke 7. 38, where Mary Magdalene washes Jesus's feet with her tears and 'did wipe them with the hairs of her head'. See also x 910–12.

136. *cleared* including 'freed from the imputation of guilt'.

137. *arborous.

142. *Discovering* revealing.

145. *orisons* prayers.

146–7. *various style . . . holy rapture* formal elaboration . . . extempore effusion. Anglicans preferred the former, Puritans the latter. Adam and Eve have both.

147. *wanted* lacked.

150. *numerous* rhythmic, harmonious (*OED* 5).

151. *tuneable* melodious, sweet-sounding (*OED* 1).

153–208. The morning hymn imitates Ps. 148 and the Song of the Three Holy Children (35–66), an apocryphal song set for Matins in the 1549 Book of Common Prayer as the Canticle *Benedicite*.

158–9. *these declare/Thy goodness* Cp. Ps. 19. 1: 'The heavens declare the glory of God'.

165. *Him . . . end* Cp. Rev. 22. 13 ('I am Alpha and Omega, the beginning and end') and Jonson, 'To Heaven' 10 ('First, midst, and last, converted one and three').

166. *Fairest of stars* Venus or Lucifer, the morning star.

last in the train of night Lucifer is the last star to disappear in the morning, and (as Hesperus) the first to appear in the evening.

174. *fall'st* The setting sun was commonly said to 'fall' (*OED* 7e), but here the word is proleptic.

178. *song* the Music of the Spheres, audible to unfallen man (see *Nativity* 125–8, *Arcades* 63–73).

181. *quaternion* group of four.

198. *singing up to heaven gate* Cp. Shakespeare, *Sonnet* XXIX (11–12) and *Cymbeline* II iii 20.

205. *still* always.

213. *overwoody* having too many branches.

214. *pampered* overloaded – with a pun on French *pampre*, 'vine-branch'.

215–19. *vine . . . leaves* The *elm* traditionally 'wedded' the *vine* in an emblem of 'masculine strength' and 'feminine softness' (Fowler). Cp. ix 217 and Horace, *Odes* II xv 4, IV v 30, but notice also the matriarchal possibilities in *adopted* (218).

221. *Raphael* Hebrew 'Health of God'. The angel Raphael appears in the apocryphal Book of Tobit, to which M. alludes in lines 222–3. Raphael helped Tobit's son Tobias win a wife (see iv 168–71*n*) and he told Tobias how to cure Tobit's blindness (Tob. 11. 7–14). As in *PL*, God sends Raphael to earth in answer to a prayer: 'The prayer of both was heard in the presence of . . . God' (Tob. 3. 16).

229. *friend with friend* So God spoke to Moses, 'face to face, as a man speaketh unto his friend' (Exod. 33. 11).

238. *secure* overconfident (*OED* 1).

244. *pretend* plead, offer as an excuse.

249. *ardours* bright angels (from Latin *ardere*, 'to burn').

250. *Veiled . . . wings* Cp. iii 382 and Isa. 6. 2.

261–2. *glass / Of Galileo* telescope. Galileo is the only contemporary of M. to be named in *PL*.

262–3. *less assured . . . Imagined lands* Cp. i 288–91, where M. has more faith in Galileo's observations of lunar 'lands, / Rivers, or mountains'. Philosophers since Plutarch had conjectured that the moon's spots were seas or mountains; Galileo claimed that the telescope revealed them more clearly.

264. *Cyclades* an archipelago in the south Aegean. *Delos* was the traditional centre, but here appears as a *spot* to a *pilot* sailing from *amidst* the group. Since Delos is compared to the earth (260), this displacement from centre to periphery might hint at a Copernican universe: Delos was famous for having floated adrift (see x 296). *Samos* lies outside the Cyclades, off the coast of Asia Minor.

265. *kens* discerns.

266–76. *Down . . . lights* Raphael's descent to earth is modelled on the earthward descents of Virgil's Mercury (*Aen.* iv 238–58) and Tasso's Michael (*Gerus. Lib.* ix 60–62). Cp. also Satan's descent at iii 562–90.

266. *prone* bent forward.

269–70. Having sailed through interstellar space with *steady wing*, Raphael now beats earth's yielding (*buxom*) atmosphere with *quick fan*.

272. *phoenix* a mythical bird that existed one at a time (hence *sole*). It was consumed by fire every 500 years, but would rise from its ashes (*relics*), which it then carried to the temple of the sun at Heliopolis in Egypt (Ovid, *Met.* xv 391–407). The phoenix symbolized friendship, marriage, and resurrection. Cp. *SA* 1699–1707. Virgil's Mercury, alighting in Libya, is likened to a seabird (*Aen.* iv 254).

277. *six wings* like the Seraphim in Isa. 6. 2.

279. *mantling* covering as with a mantle. Raphael is naked but for his *wings*.

281. *zone* belt.

282. *Skirted* bordered.

284. *mail* plumage (*OED* 5), suggesting also scale-armour (*OED* 2).

285. *grain* dye.

  Maia's son Mercury, messenger of the gods.

286. *shook . . . fragrance* So, in Fairfax's Tasso, Gabriel descending 'shook his wings with rory [dewy] May dews wet' (*Gerus. Lib.* i 14).

288. *state* rank and stateliness of bearing.

289. *message* mission, errand.

293. *odours* aromatic substances.

  cassia a cinnamon-like spice.

  nard spikenard, source of an aromatic ointment.

  balm balsam.

295. *Wantoned . . . prime* Cp. Shakespeare, *Sonnet* XCVII: 'Bearing the wanton burthen of the prime' (7). *Wantoned* means 'revelled', but the pejorative sense has appeared often enough (e.g. i 414, iv 768) for its exclusion to be ominous.

  played at will both 'freely acted out' and 'sported amorously with carnal desire' (*OED* 'play' 10c, 'will' 2).

297. *enormous* both 'immense' and 'unfettered by rules' (*OED* 1), with proleptic overtones of 'wicked, outrageous' (*OED* 2).

299. *in the door* Cp. Gen. 18. 1–2: '[Abraham] sat in the tent door in the heat of the day; and he lift up his eyes and looked, and, lo, three men stood by him'. Adam's entertainment of Raphael is modelled on Abraham's entertainment of the three angels.

300–302. *mounted . . . womb* The sexual metaphor is probably intended. Cp. Earth's erotic invitation to Phoebus in *Elegia V* 81f. The sun's rays were thought to penetrate the earth (see iii 609*n*).

306. **nectarous.*

milky often applied to the fruit juices (*OED* 1b), and here modifying *Berry* and *grape* as well as *stream*.

321. *mould* model, pattern (*OED* sb³ 5) and earth regarded as the material of the human body (*OED* sb¹ 4).

Adam (Hebrew, 'red') was thought to have been named for the red earth (Hebrew *adamah*) from which he was made (Gen. 2. 7).

322. *inspired* given the breath of life.

store . . . store reserve . . . abundance.

324. *frugal* economical (from Latin *fruges*, 'fruits').

327. *gourd* any fruit of the melon family.

335. *inelegant* *wanting in aesthetic refinement (*OED* 2) and ill-chosen (from Latin *eligere*, to select). Cp. ix 1017.

336. *upheld* sustained, continued.

kindliest most natural.

338. *Earth all-bearing Mother* translates the Greek and Latin titles Παμμήτορ γῆ, Magna Mater and Omniparens.

339. *India* Indies.

339–41. *middle shore* includes *Pontus*, the south coast of the Black Sea (abundant in grain, fruit and nuts) and the *Punic* (Carthaginian) coast of the Mediterranean, famous for figs.

341. *Alcinous* King of the Phaeacians on the mythical island of Scheria. His gardens contained trees that never failed to bear fruit, winter or summer (Homer, *Od.* vii 112–32).

342. *rined* rinded ('rine' was a variant form of 'rind').

345. *must* unfermented grape-juice.

meaths (non-alcoholic) mead.

348. *Wants* lacks.

349. *unfumed* naturally scented, not burned for incense.

350. *primitive* original (*OED* 1), as in 'Adam in his primitive estate' (1630).

353. *state* stateliness of bearing (*OED* 18a), bodily form (*OED* 9a), imposing display (*OED* 17a).

354–7. *tedious . . . *agape* M. contrasts Adam's naked majesty with the kind of pomp that accompanied Charles II's entry into London on 29 May 1660. From his hiding-place in Bartholomew Close, M. would have heard what John Evelyn saw: 'a Triumph of above 20,000 horse & foote, brandishing their swords and shouting with unexpressable joy: The wayes straw'd with flowers, the bells ringing, the streetes hung with Tapissry, fountaines running with wine: The Major [Mayor], Aldermen, all the Companies in their liver[ie]s, Chaines of Gold, banners; Lords & nobles, Cloth of Silver, gold & vellvet every body clad in, the windos & balconies all set with Ladys, Trumpets, Musick, & myriads of people flocking the streetes & ways as far as *Rochester*, so as they were 7 houres in passing the Citty'.

354. *solemn* awe-inspiring (*OED* 7).

360. *bowing low* Abraham 'bowed himself toward the ground' before angels (Gen. 18. 2), but when St John fell at an angel's feet 'to worship him', the angel said: 'See thou do it not: I am thy fellow servant' (Rev. 19. 10). Cp. ii 478n.

365. *want* miss, be parted from.

371. *Virtue* Raphael was a 'Seraph' at line 277 and will be an 'Archangel' at vii 41. M. uses these titles freely, in accordance with Protestant tradition.

378. *Pomona* Roman goddess of fruit-trees. Cp. ix 393–4.

381–2. *fairest . . . strove* alluding to the judgement of Paris, who chose Venus over Juno and Minerva as the most beautiful goddess. Venus's prize was the apple of discord. Cp. Marlowe, *Hero and Leander* (1598): 'Where Venus in her naked glory strove' (i 12).

384. *virtue-proof* armoured in virtue, but the counter-inference 'proof *against* virtue' also suggests itself. Fowler hears a further nuance: 'proof against Raphael, *the angelic virtue* (line 371)'. Raphael and Eve are both naked (see above, 279n), so Eve is to be doubly commended for not needing a *veil*.

no thought infirm Cp. Spenser, *Epithalamion*: 'That suffers not one looke to glaunce awry, / Which may let in a little thought unsownd' (236–7).

385–7. *Hail . . . second Eve* Cp. Luke 1. 28: 'Hail, thou that art highly favoured, the Lord is with thee: blessed art thou among women'. A Roman Catholic tradition derived *Ave* from *Eva* (inverted because Mary restored what Eve lost). M. celebrates Eve's nature, by placing her *un*inverted name alongside the word that had supposedly inverted it. Cp. Adam's hailing of Eve at xi 158.

388. *mother of mankind* Cp. Gen. 3. 20: 'Adam called his wife's name Eve; because she was the mother of all living'.

396. *No fear lest dinner cool* Fire was discovered only after the Fall (cp. ix 392, x 1070–78). M.'s vegetarian joke might also make a political point. John Simon, in *N&Q* n.s. 31 (September 1984), 326–7, hears an allusion to Shakespeare's *Timon of Athens* III vi 67–8: 'Make not a city feast of it, to let the meat cool ere we can agree upon the first place'. Simon notes: 'another consequence of the Fall was the jockeying for place and preferment to be found in courts'. Cp. M.'s contempt for marshalled (carefully ranked) feasts in ix 37.

397. *author* ancestor (*OED* 2a).

406. *of* by.

407. *No ingrateful* pleasant (with a hint that God's gifts should be gratefully accepted).

408. *Intelligential substances* angels. Cp. viii 181.

412. *concoct, digest, assimilate* Three stages of digestion.

417. *fires* heavenly bodies, of which the *moon* is *lowest*.

419–20. *spots . . . turned* Contrast i 287–91, where M. follows Galileo's theory that lunar spots are landscape features.

424. *alimental* nourishing.

429. *mellifluous* honey-flowing.

430. *pearly grain* manna. Cp. Exod. 16. 14.

433. *nice* difficult to please.

434. *nor seemingly* not just in appearance. In insisting that Raphael really did eat, M. follows Gen. 18. 8 and 19. 3 ('they did eat') rather than Tob. 12. 19, where Raphael says: 'I did neither eat nor drink, but ye did see a vision'. Most Reformers shared M.'s interpretation of Genesis, but not his materialist view that angels need food (414).

435. *in mist* both 'mystically' (*OED* 'mist' sb²) and 'in vapour'. Orthodox *theologians* saw angels as immaterial beings that took bodies of air. See e.g. Donne, 'Air and Angels'.

gloss both 'deceptive appearance' (*OED* sb² 1b) and 'comment inserted in the margin' (*OED* sb¹ 1).

437. *concoctive* digestive (*OED* 1), with overtones of the alchemical sense 'bring to a perfect or mature state by heat' (*OED* 'concoct' 2).

438. *transubstantiate* convert from one substance into another (*OED* 1). By using the word of digestion M. mocks the doctrine of 'transubstantiation' and the *real* (437) presence championed by Catholic *theologians*.

redounds remains undigested.

transpires passes out as vapour through the pores (*OED* 3a).

440. *empiric* experimental (*OED* 1b), with overtones of the pejorative sense 'impostor, charlatan' (*OED* 2b).

445. *crowned* filled to the brim (a classical metaphor, see e.g. Homer, *Il.* i 470).

446–8. *if ever . . . sight* Gen. 6. 2 tells how the 'sons of God saw the daughters of men that they were fair; and they took them wives of all which they chose'. The *sons of God* were usually identified as human sons of Seth (see xi 622*n*), but M. here follows a patristic tradition identifying them with angels (see *PR* i 179–81 and note).

449. **unlibidinous* not given to lust (sole instance in *OED*).

467. *yet what compare?* 'yet how can one begin to compare them?'

468. *hierarch* **commander of a celestial hierarchy (*OED* 2).

472. *one first matter* M.'s universe was created out of Chaos (ii 916, vii 233), not out of nothing. In *CD* i 7 M. argues that the primal matter was good and had its origin in God: 'it was good, and it contained the seeds of all subsequent good. It was a substance, and could only have been derived from the source of all substance. It was in a confused and disordered state at first, but afterwards God made it ordered and beautiful' (trans. Carey, *YP* 6. 308). Many critics have nevertheless doubted whether the Chaos of *PL* is good. See ii 890–1039*n*. M. in *CD* does not call the primal matter

'Chaos', and in *PL* he does not say that Chaos came from God. He describes Chaos as 'eternal' and 'unoriginal' (ii 896, iii 19, x 477).

478. *bounds* both 'limits' and 'leaps'. Notice *Springs* (480). M.'s universe is both hierarchical and dynamic.

479–83. The *root, stalk, leaves, flow'r* and *fruit* are literal and metaphorical, providing an image for the universe and one illustration of its dynamism. Raphael is also justifying his eating of *fruit*.

481. *consummate* complete, perfect.

483. *gradual scale* The etymologies (Latin *gradus*, 'step', *scala*, 'ladder') point to the *scala naturae* or cosmic ladder. See lines 509–12 and cp. iii 501–25.

sublimed elevated (*OED* 2a), refined (*OED* 2b). The word had alchemical overtones.

484. *spirits* See iv 805*n*. The usual hierarchy (in ascending order) was natural, *vital* and *animal* spirits, with the immaterial soul distinct from all three. Stephen Fallon (104) notes that M. omits natural spirits and adds *intellectual* spirits, which are 'his own invention'. Since the soul receives *her being* from the spirits (487), M. implies that the soul is material.

488. *Discursive, or intuitive* Aquinas had distinguished angelic intuition (the immediate apprehension of truth) from human reason (the arguing from premisses to conclusions). M. acknowledges that this distinction holds *most* of the time, but his angels sometimes reason (see e.g. v 831f.), while Adam and Eve sometimes intuit (see viii 354, xii 610–13).

493. *proper* my own.

497–500. *Your bodies . . . dwell* a clear indication that God did not intend the prohibition to last for ever. Adam and Eve are on probation in the Garden until they have proved their worthiness to *ascend*. Cp. vii 157–61 and see Lewis (68), Danielson (178).

498. *tract* duration, lapse.

499. *as we* See v 79 and note. Unlike the dream-angel, Raphael is clear that he can ascend to Heaven.

502. *entire* including 'wholly devoted', 'sincere' (*OED* 3c, 10).

505. *incapable* unable to contain (*OED* 1).

509. *scale of Nature* the *scala naturae* (ladder of Nature) or 'Chain of Being', extending from God down to the lowest dregs of the universe (see e.g. Macrobius, *In Somnium Scipionis* I xiv 15). It was often identified with Jacob's ladder and M. makes this connection at iii 510–18.

518. *apprehend* feel emotionally (*OED* 7).

525. *persevere* including 'continue in a state of grace' (*OED* 1e).

538. *surety* ground of certainty or safety (*OED* 6).

547. *Cherubic songs* See iv 680–88.

552. *yet* in addition, besides (*OED* 1a).

557. *Worthy of sacred silence* translating Horace, *Odes* II xiii 29–32: *sacro* *digna silentio*. Horace describes Alcaeus and Sappho singing in Hades. Alcaeus sang of war and the expulsion of tyrants. M. cites Horace's lines approvingly in his *Defensio* (*YP* 4. 441).

558. *large day* most of the day.

566. *remorse* pity, compassion (*OED* 3a).

571. *dispensed* permitted (*OED* 5b).

574–6. *earth . . . like* The doctrine that our world is but a *shadow* of the divine is from Plato, *Republic* x. M. stresses the likeness of the two worlds, not their differences.

578–9. *earth . . . poised* echoing Sandys's Ovid (*Met.* i 12): 'the self-poiz'd Earth'.

580–82. *For time . . . future* M.'s belief that time existed before the creation of our universe runs counter to a long philosophical tradition. Plato (*Timaeus* 37–8), Aristotle (*Physics* iv 11–12), and Augustine (*City of God* xi 5–6) all argue that time began with the universe. In *CD* i 7 M. conjectures that Satan fell before 'the first beginnings of this world. There is certainly no reason why we should conform to the popular belief that motion and time, which is the measure of motion, could not, according to our concepts of "before" and "after", have existed before this world was made' (trans. Carey, *YP* 6. 313–14).

583. *Great Year* the cycle completed by the heavenly bodies when they have returned to their original positions (Plato, *Timaeus* 39D). A common estimate was 36,000 years.

583–4. *empyreal . . . imperial* Raphael's pun carefully preserves imperial authority for God. Contrast Beëlzebub's 'imperial Powers' (ii 310).

588. *Ten thousand thousand* Cp. Dan. 7. 10: 'ten thousand times ten thousand stood before him'.

589. *gonfalons* banners hanging from cross-bars, often used in ecclesiastical processions.

598. *flaming Mount* Exod. 19. 19.

599. *Brightness . . . invisible* Cp. 'darkness visible' (i 63).

600. *progeny of Light* The angels were created by the Son (v 835– 7), so *Light* probably refers to him. Cp. iii 1–8.

603. *This day I have begot* echoing Ps. 2. 7 ('Thou art my Son; this day have I begotten thee') and Heb. 1. 5 ('For unto which of the angels said he at any time, Thou art my Son, This day have I begotten thee?'). M. in *CD* i 5 takes these verses to mean that 'God begot the Son in the sense of making him a king'. Thus the 'begetting' is metaphorical and refers to the Son's 'exaltation above the angels' (trans. Carey, *YP* 6. 207). Many have thought that M.'s interpretation is strained, but it has biblical precedent in Acts 13. 33 and Heb. 5. 5. M. believed that the Son was created before the angels, whom he created (see v 835–40 and note).

605. *anointed* Cp. M.'s *Brief Notes Upon a Late Sermon* (1660): 'who is

[God's] *Anointed*, not every King, but they only who were anointed or made Kings by his special command' (*YP* 7. 475).

606. *head* Cp. Col. 2. 9: 'ye are complete in him, which is the head of all principality and power'.

607. *by myself have sworn* Cp. Gen. 22. 16: 'By myself have I sworn, saith the Lord'.

607–8. *bow / All knees* Cp. Phil. 2. 9–11: 'at the name of Jesus every knee should bow, of things in heaven, and things in earth, and things under the earth'.

609. *vicegerent* exercising God's authority (*OED* 2).

610. *individual* indivisible (*OED* 1).

611. *him who disobeys* 'whoever disobeys him'.

614. *utter* outer and total.

618. *solemn* of days or seasons: set apart for religious ceremonies (*OED* 2).

621. *fixed* the fixed stars.

622. *mazes intricate* Cp. Virgil's *Aen.* v 575f., where Iulus leads the Trojan boys in a mazelike ride on horseback, 'interweaving circle with alternate circle', tracing a course like the Cretan labyrinth. Heaven's mazes have their counterpart in the 'wand'ring mazes' of Hell (ii 561).

623. *Eccentric* an off-centre planetary orbit (see viii 83*n*).
   *intervolved intertwined.

625. *their* refers both to angels and planets and so associates angelic singing with the Music of the Spheres. Cp. Job 38. 7: 'the morning stars sang together, and all the sons of God shouted for joy'.

627. *now* Added in *Ed II*.

637–40. *They . . . show'red*] *Ed I* reads: 'They eat, they drink, and with refection sweet / Are filled, before th' all bounteous King, who show'red'.

637. *communion* fellowship, esp. 'an organic union of persons united by common religious faith' (*OED* 4).

639. *full measure only bounds* only full measure bounds.

642. *ambrosial night* Cp. Homer, *Il.* ii 57: 'a divine dream came to me through the ambrosial night'. The allusion is ominous, since Agamemnon's dream lured him into a disastrous attack. See below, 673*n*.

645. *night comes not there* Cp. Rev. 21. 25: 'There shall be no night there'.

646. *roseate* *rose-scented (*OED* 3), with a pun on Latin *ros*, 'dew'.

652. *living streams . . . Trees of Life* Cp. Rev. 22. 2: 'On either side of the river, was there the tree of life'.

657–8. *but not so waked / Satan* Cp. Virgil's description of Dido's sleeplessness (*Aen.* iv 529). It was night, and all other creatures were sleeping, 'but not the soul-wracked Phoenician queen' (*at non infelix animi Phoenissa*).

658. *former name* Patristic tradition took Isa. 14. 12 to mean that Satan's original name was 'Lucifer'. Raphael likens Satan to Lucifer the morning star (v 708, 762, vii 131), but he never says that Satan was named 'Lucifer'.

Satan's former name has been blotted from the books of life (i 361–5) and so is *heard no more*.

659–60. *of the first, / If not the first* Raphael's ambiguous wording leaves open the question of Satan's precise rank.

664. *Messiah* Hebrew 'anointed'.

669. *dislodge* leave a place of encampment (*OED* 2b) and drive a foe out of his position (*OED* 1c). The latter sense has God's *throne* (670) as object.

671. *subordinate* Raphael never names him. He lost his original name when he rebelled (i 361–5), and he will not be known as 'Beëlzebub' until 'long after' man's Fall (i 81).

673. *Sleep'st thou* echoing many previous epics, where heroes and villains are roused from sleep by a voice which lures them into rash or adventurous acts. Cp. Dream waking Agamemnon (Homer, *Il.* ii 23), Mercury waking Aeneas (Virgil, *Aen.* iv 560), Allecto waking Turnus (*Aen.* vii 421), Ismeno waking Solimano (Tasso, *Gerus. Lib.* x 8) and Satan waking the Pope in M.'s *Q Nov* 92. Cp. also above, 38n, where Eve (unusually) does not wake when Satan asks 'Why sleep'st thou?'

680. *minds* purposes, intentions (*OED* II), esp. 'the way in which one person is affected towards another' (*OED* II 15b).

681. *debate* both 'discuss' and 'contend, fight for' (*OED* 2).

685. *Tell them that by command* Satan has received no command and he does not clearly say that he has. His own command (*Tell them*) arrogates the commanding voice of God. See below, 699n.

689. *North* the traditional site of Lucifer's throne (Isa. 14. 13).

690. *Fit entertainment* a Satanic ambiguity, since 'entertain' could have the military sense 'engage an enemy's forces' (*OED* 9c), as in: 'Porus had prepared an Army to entertain [Alexander]' (1654). Cp. iv 382, vi 611.

695. *Bad influence* Satan as 'Lucifer' sheds malignant astral 'influences'. See iv 669n.

699. *the Most High* God, but also Satan, who is *commanding*. Cp. Lucifer's words at Isa. 14. 14: 'I shall be like the most High'.

702. *suggested* falsely imputed (*OED* 2) and insinuated (*OED* 4). The former sense refers to God's supposed command, which Satan pretends to be obeying (v 768–9); the latter sense refers to Satan's real motive of rebellion. The angels fall at 'their own suggestion' (iii 129) because they are free to hear the *Ambiguous words* (703) either as a genuine proposal to welcome the Messiah or as a call to rebellion. Abdiel hears only the innocent sense (v 883). See Leonard (149–59). 'Suggest' implies 'seduce, tempt away' (*OED* 2).

703. *jealousies* including 'suspicions, apprehensions of evil' (*OED* 5).

 sound make trial of (*OED* v² 6b) and convey an impression of (*OED* v¹ 4). The subordinate conveys a false impression of his own *integrity* while sounding out others. *Sound* also implies 'healthy, untainted'. Cp.

II Tim. 1. 13: 'hold fast the form of sound words which thou hast heard of me'.

704. *integrity* including 'innocence, sinlessness' (*OED* 3), as in 'Adam in his integritie should have wrought, but without wearinesse' (1622).

706. *Potentate* ruler, with overtones of angelic 'Potentates' or 'Powers' (Latin *potestates*). Cp. v 749.

707. *name* fame (*OED* 6), but suggesting also Satan's 'former name' (658).

708. *count'nance* including 'feigned appearance' (*OED* 2b), 'show of feeling towards another' (*OED* 7), 'repute in the world' (*OED* 9), 'position, standing, dignity' (*OED* 10).

morning star 'Lucifer, son of the morning' (Isa. 14. 12). Virgil likens Pallas to Lucifer the morning star in *Aen.* viii 589.

710. *Drew after him* Marching in the van of his host, Satan acts like the evening star, not the *morning star*, which appears 'last in the train of night' (v 166). Bentley wanted to emend to 'evening star', but (as Empson² 185 notes) 'the inversion acts as part of the conflict of feeling'. Lucifer-Satan leads his stellar angels 'only towards night'. Cp. *Nativity* 74.

third part Cp. Rev. 12. 4: 'And his tail drew the third part of the stars of heaven, and did cast them to the earth'. Cp. ii 692.

712. *Abstrusest* most secret.

713. *golden lamps* Cp. Rev. 4. 5: 'There were seven lamps of fire burning before the throne, which are the seven Spirits of God'. These lamps are perhaps identical with the seven angels of iii 648 or the seven planetary Intelligences (Empson² 184).

716. *sons of morn* angels. Cp. Job 38. 7: 'when the morning stars sang together, And all the sons of God shouted for joy'.

721. *Nearly* closely, particularly.

724–5. *foe / Is rising* 'Satan' means 'foe' (see i 82n).

725–6. *erect his throne . . . North* Cp. Isa. 14. 12–13: 'How art thou fallen from heaven, O Lucifer . . . ! For thou hast said in thine heart, I will . . . exalt my throne above the stars of God: I will sit also upon the mount of the congregation, in the sides of the north'.

736–7. *derision . . . Laugh'st* Cp. Ps. 2. 4: 'He that sitteth in the heavens shall laugh: / The Lord shall have them in derision'.

739. *Illústrates* renders illustrious (*OED* 4).

740. *in event* by the outcome.

741. *dextrous* including 'situated on the right side' (*OED* 1), alluding to the Son's position at God's 'right hand' (iii 279, v 606, vi 892). Cp. ii 174 ('His red right hand').

743. *powers* armies (*OED* 9) or angelic 'Powers', here standing for all angelic orders. Cp. vi 898.

745–6. *stars . . . dew-drops* Cp. Rev. 12. 3–4, where Satan as dragon cast a third of 'the stars of heaven' to earth. Cp. also Hos. 6. 4: 'O Judah . . . your goodness is as a morning cloud, and as the early dew it goeth away'. Cp. also Marvell, 'On a Drop of Dew' (printed 1681).

748. *regencies* *districts under the control of a regent (*OED* 4).

750. *triple degrees* 'Dionysius the Areopagite' had distinguished nine orders in three groups of three: Seraphim, Cherubim, Thrones; Dominions, Virtues, Powers; Principalities, Archangels, Angels. M. uses these titles, but follows Protestant tradition in rejecting Dionysius's strict hierarchy. Many of M.'s highest angels (including Michael and Satan) are 'Archangels', and some angels have more than one title.

to in comparison with which.

753–4. *globose . . . longitude* globe projected onto a flat plane.

758. *pyramids* Cp. M.'s description of the 'pyramidal figure' of prelacy in *RCG*: 'her pyramid aspires and sharpens to ambition . . . it is the most dividing, and schismaticall forme that Geometricians know of' (*YP* 1. 790).

760. *Lucifer* the morning star. Raphael is not naming Satan's 'former name', but using a metaphor to *interpret* it. See above, 658n, and cp. vii 131–3, x 425.

761. *dialect of men* Homer also distinguishes human from divine names (*Il.* xiv 291, xx 74), but where Homer confidently names both ('Xanthus to the gods, to men Scamander'), M. declines to intrude upon God's mysteries.

763. *Affecting* aspiring to (*OED* 1) and assuming a false appearance of (*OED* 6a).

764. *that Mount* the 'flaming mount' of line 598.

766. *Mountain of the Congregation* Cp. Lucifer's boast at Isa. 14. 13: 'I will sit also upon the mount of the congregation'. Isaiah's Lucifer aspires to God's own mountain; Satan claims the name.

773. *magnific titles* Titles like 'Power' and 'Domination' might seem to support Satan's argument, but Protestants understood angelic titles to refer to essences, not offices. See e.g. Thomas Heywood, *The Hierarchie of the Blessed Angels* (1635) 210. Satan therefore errs in inferring *power* from *Powers*.

775. *engrossed* monopolized (*OED* 4).

776. *eclipsed* Cp. i 597 and vii 364–8.

778. *hurried *OED*'s earliest participial instance.

786. *yoke* Cp. Matt. 11. 29–30: 'Take my yoke upon you, and learn of me; for I am meek and . . . my yoke is easy'.

799. *much less for this to be our Lord* Satan's contemptuous *this* pointedly withholds the name 'Messiah'. Cp. Luke 19. 14: 'We will not have this man to reign over us'.

805. *Abdiel* Hebrew 'Servant of God'. Abdiel is an angel in the *Sepher Raziel* (West 154).

821. *unsucceeded with no successor.

835–40. *by whom . . . Powers* Cp. Col. 1. 16–17: 'By him [Christ] were all things created . . . whether they be thrones, or dominions, or principalities, or powers: all things were created by him, and for him: And he is before all things'. M. believed that God created the Son, who then created the angels. See above, 603*n*.

839. *Crowned . . . glory* Cp. Ps. 8. 5: 'Thou hast . . . crowned him [man] with glory'. This verse was taken as a prophecy of the Incarnation, so Abdiel might hint at an angelic Incarnation (*One of our number*). See Danielson (219–24).

860. **self-begot* Satan at iv 43 had admitted that God created him, but that speech is subsequent to this one in time, so we cannot conclude that Satan is now lying. Satan might genuinely doubt God's claims until the Son expels him from Heaven. See Empson (64–5). Satan claims to be his own creator in Prudentius, *Hamartigenia* 171–2 (Evans 113).

864. *Our puissance is our own* Cp. Ps. 12. 4: 'Our lips are our own: who is lord over us?'

864–5. *right hand / Shall teach* Cp. Ps. 45. 4: 'Thy right hand shall teach thee terrible things'. Cp. also Virgil's blasphemous Mezentius, whose only deity is his own right hand, *dextra mihi* (*Aen.* x 773).

868. *Address* both 'dutiful approach' (*OED* 9) and (military) 'skill, dexterity' (*OED* 4), as in 'His Royal Highness employs all his Address in alarming the enemy' (1710).

875. *flaming Seraph* Hebrew *saraph*, 'to burn'.

883. *indulgent laws* the laws of line 693 (which the Messiah has never threatened or promised).

886–7. *golden sceptre . . . iron rod* See ii 327*n*.

890. *wicked tents* So Moses warns the Israelites not to join Korah's rebellion: 'Depart, I pray you, from the tents of these wicked men . . . lest ye be consumed' (Num. 16. 26). Cp. also Ps. 84. 10: 'I had rather be a doorkeeper in the house of my God, than to dwell in the tents of wickedness'.

　　devoted doomed (*OED* 3), but the other sense 'faithful, loyal' attaches itself to *I* (889).

903. *single* including 'simple, honest' (*OED* 14).

906. *retorted* flung back (scorn) – with a play on Latin *retortus*, 'turned back' (*his back he turned*).

907. *swift destruction* Cp. II Pet. 2. 1: 'there shall be false teachers among you, who privily shall bring in damnable heresies, even denying the Lord that bought them, and bring upon themselves swift destruction'.

BOOK VI

1. *dreadless angel* Abdiel.

2. *champaign* plain.

3. *Hours* the Horae, goddesses of the seasons and gatekeepers of heaven (Homer, *Il.* v 749, Spenser, *FQ* VII vii 45).

rosy hand the Homeric 'rosy-fingered' (*Il.* i 477).

4. *Unbarred the gates of light* Cp. Ovid, *Met.* ii 112–14: 'Aurora . . . opened wide her purple gates'. The allusion is proleptic of Satan's defeat, for Ovid continues: 'the stars all flee away, and Lucifer closes their ranks as, last of all, he departs from his watchtower in the sky' (114–15).

4–8. *There is a cave . . . day and night* Cp. Hesiod's abysm where Day and Night hold alternate residence: 'Night and Day approach and greet each other as they pass in and out over the great bronze threshold' (*Theog.* 744–54). M. inverts Hesiod by placing the cave in Heaven, not Hell, and by describing it before, not after, the celestial battle. See Porter (60).

8. *Grateful vicissitude* delightful change.

10. *Obsequious* following dutifully.

12. *twilight* Cp. Rev. 21. 25: 'there shall be no night there'.

15. *Shot through* variegated in colour; the military context also suggests 'pierced'.

orient resplendent.

16. *embattled* set in battle array.

19. *in procinct* ready for battle (Latin *in procinctu*). Cp. also Chapman's Homer, *Il.* xi 89: 'in all procinct of warre'.

24. *of so many myriads . . . one* Cp. Ovid's Deucalion and Pyrrha, survivors of the Greek flood (*Met.* i 325–6): 'Jove saw that of so many thousands, one man was left; and of so many thousands, one woman'.

29. *Servant of God, well done* echoing the parable of the talents: 'Well done, thou good and faithful servant' (Matt. 25. 21). 'Abdiel' means 'servant of God'.

29–30. *fought . . . fight* Cp. I Tim. 6. 12: 'fight the good fight'.

33–4. *borne . . . reproach* Cp. Ps. 69. 7: 'for thy sake I have borne reproach'.

42. *Right reason* conscience, planted by God in all men.

44. *Michael* Hebrew 'Who is like God?' See Rev. 12.7f. for Michael's role in the war (and cp. Dan. 10. 13 and 12. 1). Following Jewish and patristic tradition, M. makes Michael prince of angels. Most Protestants identified him with Christ.

49. *Equal* perhaps 'at least equal' (*OED* 1a). Only a third of the angels rebelled (ii 692, v 710), so Michael's army might outnumber Satan's two to one. Cp. Satan's words at vi 166 ('I see that most . . . had rather serve') and see Empson (41).

54. *Tartarus* hell.

56-7. *clouds. . . smoke* Mount Sinai was covered with clouds and 'altogether on a smoke' when God issued the Ten Commandments (Exod. 19. 18).

58. *reluctant* *writhing (*OED* 1). There may be a play on the modern sense, which M. also coined (*OED* 2b).

60. *gan* began to.

62. *quadrate* square formation.

64-5. *In silence . . . breathed* Cp. the fallen angels marching silently to Dorian flute music (i 550-59). Both angelic armies are adapted from Plutarch's Spartans (*Lycurgus* 22) and Homer's Achaians (*Il.* iii 8). See i 550-59*n*, i 560-61*n*.

69. *obvious* in the way.

70. *strait'ning* hemming in.

73-6. *as when . . . of thee* Similes comparing armies to birds are common in epic (see e.g. Homer, *Il.* ii 459f., Virgil, *Aen.* vii 699f.), but Raphael chooses similes that fit Adam's experience. See Gen. 2. 20: 'And Adam gave names to all cattle and to the fowl of the air, and·to every beast of the field'. Cp. also viii 349-54.

78. *terrene* *the earth (*OED* 5a).

80. *fiery region* Cp. Homer, *Il.* ii 455-8: 'As obliterating fire lights up a vast forest / along the crests of a mountain, and the flare shows far off, / so as they marched, from the magnificent bronze the gleam went / dazzling all about through the upper air to the heaven'.

81. *battailous* warlike.

82. *beams* The initial sense 'rays of light' changes to 'shafts of spears'. Satan promises a new morning, but brings only war. (*OED* has no instance of 'beam' meaning 'spear', but cp. Spenser, *FQ* III vii 40 and I Sam. 17. 7.)

84. *argument* heraldic devices.

86. *expedition* warlike enterprise (*OED* 2a) and speed (*OED* 5).

90. *fond* foolish.

93. *hosting* hostile encounter (*OED*) and entertaining as guests (*OED* 'host' v² 1). *Fierce hosting* is an oxymoron when war is *strange*. Cp. 'Fit entertainment' (v 690).

   wont were accustomed.

96. *Hymning *OED*'s earliest instance of the verb. The noun dates from Anglo-Saxon times.

101-2. *enclosed / With flaming Cherubim* Satan enthroned is an *Idol* of the Father (see i 387*n*).

107. *cloudy* gloomy, frowning (*OED* 6).

108. *edge* line of battle (*OED* 5a). Cp. i 276*n*.

115. *realty* sincerity, honesty (*OED* 2).

118. *to sight* seemingly.

120. *tried* proved by trial.

129. *prevention* obstruction (*OED* 4).

130. *securely* confidently.

137–9. *out of smallest things . . . armies* echoing Matt. 3. 9 ('God is able of these stones to raise up children unto Abraham') and Matt. 26. 53. Cp. also Cromwell's assurance at Naseby 'that GOD would do great things, by small means; and by things that are not, bring to nought things that are' (Joshua Sprigge, *Anglia Rediviva* (1647) 43).

141. **Unaided.*

147. *sect* a politically charged word in M.'s time, when it was used to smear Puritan schismatics. Like Abdiel, M. is proud of the designation. See *Eikonoklastes* (1649): 'I never knew that time in *England*, when men of truest Religion were not counted Sectaries' (*YP* 3. 348).

153. *assay* attack, assault (*OED* 15).

156. *synod* assembly (usually ecclesiastical, so a synod of *gods* is absurd). Cp. ii 391.

161. *success* fortune (i.e. ill – but Abdiel will be more 'successful' than Satan expects).

163. *Unanswered . . . boast* 'Lest you boast I was unable to answer you'.

165. *all one* one and the same (*OED* 'all' 5b).

167–8. *Minist'ring . . . minstrelsy* Satan's contemptuous pun brings out the common etymology: *ministerium*, 'office, service'. Cp. Heb. 1. 14: 'Are they not all ministering spirits?'

169. *Servility* both 'obsequiousness' and 'the condition of being in bondage' (*OED* 1). Abdiel's word *servitude* (175) ignores the charge of obsequiousness.

174. *deprav'st* pervert the meaning of (*OED* 3), vilify (*OED* 4).

182. *lewdly* wickedly (*OED* 2), ignorantly (*OED* 1).

183–4. *Reign . . . Heav'n* Contrast Satan's words at i 263: 'Better to reign in Hell, than serve in Heav'n'.

193. *ruin* including 'swift descent'.

196. *Winds under ground* the supposed cause of earthquakes (cp. i 230–37).

197. *pushed a mountain from his seat* Contrast Satan as an irremovable mountain at iv 985–7. Cp. also vi 643f.

199. *Thrones* a synecdoche for all angelic orders. The oxymoron *rebel Thrones* is also politically suggestive. Cp. 'rebel king' (i 484) and Michael's revelation that the first king derived his name from 'Rebellion' (xii 36).

209. *brayed* made a loud harsh jarring sound (*OED* 3).

210. *madding* furiously whirling.

215. *cope* sky (*OED* sb¹ 7) and shock of combat (*OED* sb²).

216. *battles main* the main bodies of the armies (as distinct from van and wings).

222. *These elements* the earth and its atmosphere, realm of the four elements.

223. *regions* divisions of the universe (*OED* 3a).

225. *combustion* confusion, tumult (*OED* 5b).

232-3. *yet ... chief* 'yet each single warrior seemed like a commander-in-chief'.

234. *sway* force bearing its object in a certain direction (*OED* 3), as in 'Push'd and yielding to superior sway ... the Spartan ranks gave way' (1757).

236. *ridges of grim war* Probably 'ranks' (*when to close*), but cp. the Homeric phrase πολέμοιο γέφυραι (*Il.* iv 371, xi 160, etc.), which might refer to the space between two battle lines.

239. *moment* moment of a balance (*OED* 5), hence 'deciding factor'. Notice *sway* (234) and *even scale* (245).

243. *main* strong, vigorous.

244. *Tormented* agitated (*OED* 3).

248. **attack* OED's earliest instance of the noun.

254. *orb* circle (*OED* 1).

255. *adamant* a mythical substance of impenetrable hardness, usually identified with diamond or steel. M. here imagines it to be a metal folded back on itself ten times (*tenfold*).

259. *Intestine war* civil war.

262-3. *evil ... Unnamed* Contrast Adam's statement that 'Evil into the mind of god or man / May come and go' (v 117-19). Michael speaks as one who has been a complete stranger to evil.

272. *casts* throws and vomits (*OED* 25).

274. *Brooks* endures, 'stomachs' (*OED* 3).

282. *Adversary* translates 'Satan'.

284-8. *Hast ... hence* 'Have you turned the weakest of my host to flight, or to fall, but that they rise unconquered? And do you think that I am easier to deal (*transact*) with than they are? Are you so imperious as to try to chase me away with threats?'

288. *Err not* Don't imagine.

296. *parle* parley.

addressed made ready (*OED* 3a).

305. *two broad suns* Cp. Euripides, *The Bacchae* 918 and Virgil, *Aen.* iv 470. When Pentheus denied Dionysus's divinity, he was maddened and lured to his destruction by a vision of two suns blazing in the heavens.

306. *Expectation* personifying the other angels' apprehension. Cp. Shakespeare, *Troilus and Cressida* Prol., and *Henry V* II Prol.: 'now sits Expectation in the air'.

311. *Great things by small* See ii 921-2n.

broke broken.

313-14. *aspéct ... opposition* astrological terms denoting the relative position of the heavenly bodies. Two *planets* were in 'opposition' when they occupied opposite signs. Their influence on men was then *malign*.

315. *jarring spheres confound* refers both to physically colliding *planets* (313) and discordant celestial music. *Jarring* means 'striking' and 'out of tune', *spheres* means 'planets' (*OED* 10b) and 'music of the spheres' (*OED* 2b), *confound* means 'smash' (*OED* 1d) and 'throw into confusion'. Cp. x 412–14.

318. *determine* decide the matter.

need repeat need to be repeated.

319. *As not of power* since it would be impossible to repeat such a blow.

at once refers back to *determine*.

320. *prevention* anticipation.

321. *armoury of God* Cp. Jer. 50. 25: 'The Lord hath opened his armoury, and hath brought forth the weapons of his indignation'.

325. *in half cut sheer* 'Overgoing Virgil: Turnus' sword merely shatters in fragments' (Fowler). See *Aen.* xii 741.

326. *shared* cut into parts, cut off (*OED*).

328. *convolved* *contorted (*OED* 3). The older sense 'coiled' (*OED* 2) anticipates Satan's serpent metamorphosis (x 504f.).

329. *griding cutting keenly (earliest participial instance).

*discontinuous gaping (*OED* 1).

332. *nectarous humour* Cp. the divine ichor that flows from Aphrodite's hand when Diomedes wounds her. Homer explains that the gods have no blood, for they do not eat food or drink wine (*Il.* v 339–42). M.'s angels (who drink nectar) bleed *nectarous* fluid (*humour*). *Sanguine* means 'blood-red' (*OED* 1), but also suggests the sanguine *humour* which in Renaissance physiology gave rise to courage. Thus Satan's loss of this humour implies a loss of morale.

344. *Yet soon he healed* Cp. Pope's parody: 'But airy substance soon unites again' (*The Rape of the Lock* iii 152).

346. *reins* kidneys.

352. *limb provide themselves with limbs (*OED* v 2, sole instance).

353. *likes* pleases.

condense or rare dense or airy.

355. *the might of Gabriel* the mighty Gabriel (Homeric diction); *Gabriel* means 'Strength of God'.

356. *ensigns* either 'standard bearers' (*OED* 7) or 'companies serving under one standard' (*OED* 6). As many as 500 men might serve in an 'ensign'.

357. *Moloch* The name is not supposed to exist until after man's Fall (see i 364–5). Raphael might foreknow the names of future devils (cp. xii 140), but to name them here implies the failure of his mission. He had withheld 'Beëlzebub' from book v (see v 671*n*), but now allows many devils' names to infiltrate book vi. See below, 371–85*n*.

359–60. *Holy One . . . blasphémous* Cp. II Kings 19. 22: 'Whom hast thou reproached and blasphemed . . . ? the Holy One of Israel'.

360. *Refrained* from Latin *refrenare*, 'to bridle'. The early spelling 'refreined' (*Ed I, Ed II*) might pun on 'reins'. Notice *chariot* (358). Moloch's tongue runs away with him.

362. *uncouth* unfamiliar (*OED* 2), unpleasant (*OED* 4).

bellowing Cp. Ares bellowing when Diomedes wounds him (Homer, *Il.* v 860). Moloch's bellowing is also 'typical of a bull god' (Flannagan).

365. *Adramelech* 'King of fire', a Sepharvite god worshipped at Samaria with human sacrifice (II Kings 17. 31).

Asmadai Asmodeus ('creature of judgement'), a Persian god who will encounter Raphael again (see iv 167–71).

369. *annoy* injure.

370. *atheist* *impious (*OED* B).

371–85. *Ariel* ('lion of God'), *Arioch* ('lion-like'), and *Ramiel* ('thunder of God') are devils, but Raphael might be naming their *Cancelled* angelic names. All three names had been used of good as well as bad angels in pseudepigraphal, rabbinical and demonological texts. See Harris Fletcher, *Milton's Rabbinical Readings* (1930) 268–79 and R. H. West, *SP* 47 (1950) 211–23 (pp. 215–17). The names are troubling however we take them. Raphael should not name *Cancelled* angelic names (see i 362, v 659), but he cannot name devils without presupposing man's Fall (see above, 357*n*).

379. *Cancelled* blotted out (*OED* 3a). Cp. i 362, v 658.

382. *Illaudable* unworthy of praise.

383. *ignominy* including 'namelessness' (Latin *in*, 'not' + *nomen*, 'name').

386. *battle* army (*OED* 8).

swerved gave way (*OED* 4).

391. *what stood* those who resisted.

392. *Satanic.*

393. *Defensive scarce* scarcely able to defend themselves.

399. *cubic phalanx* See i 550*n*. Angels might fly in a cube formation. The cube symbolized 'virtue and stability' (Fowler). Contrast the rebels' 'hollow cube' (vi 552).

entire unwearied (*OED* 4e), with unbroken ranks (*OED* 5b), honest, upright (*OED* 9).

404. *unobnoxious* not liable (*OED* 1).

407. *Inducing* drawing, overspreading (*OED* 7).

411. *prevalent* victorious.

413. *Cherubic . . . fires* overgoing Homer (*Il.* viii 553f.), where the victorious Trojans merely attend camp-fires.

415. *dislodged* shifted his quarters (*OED* 1b, military term).

416. *Potentates* either 'leaders' or a synecdoche for all angelic orders.

416. *council called by night* Nocturnal councils in which a defeated army recovers its morale are frequent in epic. See e.g. Homer, *Il.* ix *passim*, xix 243–314, and Virgil, *Aen.* ix 224–313.

421. *mean pretence . . . affect* modest ambition . . . aspire to. But M.'s voice behind Satan plays on 'base pretext . . . assume a false appearance of'.

429. *Of future* In the future.

430. *Omniscient* 'Omnipotent' would better suit the context, but Satan is mocking God. A God who knows about Satan's plans might still be powerless to thwart them.

432. *known as soon contemned* no sooner known than despised.

438. *valid* strong, powerful (*OED* 3).

440. *worse* injure (*OED* 2) and worst, get the better of.

444. *sound* unaffected by injury (*OED* a 2) and search into.

447. *Nisroch* an Assyrian god (II Kings 19. 37). According to Stephanus's *Dictionary* (1621), the Hebrew name means 'Flight' or 'Delicate temptation'. See Dewitt T. Starnes and Ernest William Talbert, *Classical Myth and Legend in Renaissance Dictionaries* (1955), 268.

455. **impassive* not feeling pain (*OED* 1), from the theological term 'impassible'.

456–7. *avails / Valour* Both words are from Latin *valere*, 'to be worth, or strong', so Nisroch 'sharply implies that valour ceases to be itself when . . .' (Ricks).

458. *remiss* slack, weak.

464. *He who* whoever (hinting that Nisroch might seek a new leader).

invent Nisroch means 'plan' (*OED* 2a), as in 'a plot invented . . . by Cacodaemons' (1641), but the technological sense existed and Satan plays upon it in line 470 when he announces his invention of gunpowder.

465. *offend* attack (*OED* 5), injure (*OED* 6).

467. *to me* in my opinion.

471. *main* highly important.

472–81. *Which . . . light* The sun was thought to generate precious metals and gems within the earth. Cp. iii 608–12 and *A Masque* 732–6.

473. **ethereous* 'a new word for a new way of looking at matter as instinct not with heavenly spirit but with chemical power' – James Mengert in *MS* 14 (1980), 95–115 (108). The usual word is 'ethereal'.

477. *mind* give heed to.

478. *crude* raw, unripe.

479. *spiritous* refined (*OED* 1).

spume frothy matter produced in the refining of metals.

479–81. *touched . . . light* Svendsen (119) notes how the images (*touched, tempered, shoot, opening*) anticipate the invention of gunpowder.

483. *infernal flame* Satan means 'fire from underground', but M.'s voice behind him anticipates Hell-fire.

484. *engines* machines of war (*OED* 5a). The diabolic invention of gunpowder has many epic precedents. Cp. Ariosto, *Orl. Fur.* ix 28f., ix 91, xi 21–8, Spenser, *FQ* I vii 13, Daniel, *Civil Wars* (1609) vi 26–7. Erasmo di Valvasone had introduced the invention of artillery into his angelic war in *L'Angeleida* (1590). See Kirkconnell (81). Notice that Raphael never names Satan's weapons as 'cannon'. Cp. *Orl. Fur.* ix 28–9, where the innocent Olimpia describes 'a strange new weapon' without naming it. Ariosto in his own voice later names many kinds of artillery (*Orl. Fur.* xi 24–5). Our perspective is that of Ariosto; Adam's is that of Olimpia.

485. *other bore* the touch-hole.

touch contact (with *fire*) and touch-powder (gunpowder over the touch-hole). The same pun recurs at vi 520, 566, 584.

486. *infuriate raging.

488. *implements* playing on Latin *implementum*, 'a filling up'.

489. *To pieces* to confusion (*OED* 1c) and 'to smithereens'.

491. *only* unique, peerless (*OED* 5).

496. *cheer* mood, spirits.

498. *admired* marvelled at.

504. *machination* both 'plotting' and 'mechanical appliance for war' (*OED* 4).

511. *originals* original elements (*OED* 6a).

512. *nitrous foam* saltpetre (an ingredient in gunpowder).

514. *Concocted and adusted* heated and dried up (alchemical terms).

518. *found* cast (in a foundry).

519. *missive* missile (adj.).

incentive reed kindling match.

520. *pernicious* destructive (*OED* a^1, from Latin *perniciosus*) and swift (*OED* a^2, from Latin *pernix*).

521. *conscious* privy to (*OED* 2) and guilty (*OED* 4b). Night is personified as an accomplice.

535. *Zophiel* Hebrew 'Spy of God'. The name is not biblical, but it appears in *The Zohar* where Zophiel is one of two angelic chieftains under Michael (Numbers 154a).

536. *in mid air earliest instance of 'mid air' and 'in mid air' (*OED*). Cp. ii 718, iv 940.

541. *Sad* steadfast, firm (*OED* 2).

secure confident.

545. *conjecture* prognosticate, gather from signs (*OED* 1).

548. *impediment* military baggage (*OED* 3).

549. *Instant without disturb* urgent without panic.

took alarm took up arms.

550. *embattled* drawn up in battle formation.

553. *Training* hauling.

enginery artillery.

impaled surrounded for defence (*OED* 1c, military term).

555. *At interview* in mutual view (*OED* 2).

560. *composure* settlement of disputes (*OED* 4) and constructing (*OED* 1) of weapons. See also 613*n*, below.

breast heart (*OED* 5a) and broad front of a moving company (*OED* 7). *Peace* might contain a pun on 'piece' meaning 'cannon' (*OED* 11).

562. *overture* opening of negotiations (*OED* 3) and aperture, hole (*OED* 1) – the cannons' 'hideous orifice' (577). There may be a further pun on 'overthrow' (*OED* 8) referring both to the previous day's defeat and the expected victory.

perverse peevish (*OED* 3), with a pun on Latin *perversus*, 'turned the wrong way' (*turn not back*).

564–6. *discharge . . . charge* 'perform our duty' and 'discharge our explosives'.

567. *propound* There may be a pun on 'pound' meaning 'fire heavy shot (*OED* v^1 4a), but *OED* has no instance before 1815. 'Crush by beating, pulverize' (*OED* 1) was current.

568. *ambiguous words* Satan's puns may cause us to groan, but they are not at first obvious to the good angels who have never heard of artillery.

572. *triple-mounted* either 'arranged in three rows' (see 605, 650) or 'having three barrels mounted on one stock'. M. may be thinking of the kind of ordnance called 'organs' or *orgues*, which could fire several barrels at once.

576. *mould* moulded out of (*Brass,* etc.).

578. *hollow* insincere – with a pun on *hollowed* cannon (574).

580. *suspense* cautious (*OED* 3), in suspense.

581. *amused* including the military sense: 'divert the attention of the enemy from one's real designs' (*OED* 5).

586–9. *deep-throated . . . disgorging* Cp. the scatological body-landscape of Hell (eg: i 230–37, 670–74).

587. *Embowelled* disembowelled (*OED* 2), or filled the bowels (*OED* 3) to breaking point (*entrails tore*).

589. *chained* The devils are using chain-shot, linked cannonballs capable of felling whole ranks.

594. *Angel on Archangel rolled* Angels are the lowest, and Archangels the second lowest, order in Pseudo-Dionysius's hierarchy. M. uses such titles freely, but the present line does imply some kind of hierarchy.

597. *quick contraction or remove* See i 777–80 and iv 810–19 for the angels' ability to change size.

598. *dissipation* scattering, dispersal (*OED* 1).

599. **serried* pressed together, in close order.

601. *indecent* shameful.

605. *posture* position of a weapon in drill or warfare (*OED* 2b).

displode fire, discharge.

tire volley (*OED* 3).

611. *entertain* punning on the military sense 'engage an enemy' (*OED* 9c). Cp. v 690.

open front candid face (*OED* 'open' 16, 'front' 3a) and divided front rank (*OED* 'front' 5a). See vi 569–70: 'the front / Divided'. *With open front* implies 'with open arms', but also the now obsolete phrase 'with open face' meaning 'brazenly' (*OED* 'open' 5b), as in: 'with open face ... vent Blasphemies' (1650).

613. *composition* truce (*OED* 23b), with a possible pun on 'chemical composition' (gunpowder).

614. *vagáries* frolics (*OED* 3a) and rambling from the subject under discussion (*OED* 2).

615. *As they would dance* Cp. Aeneas's taunt to Meriones in Homer, *Il.* xvi 617.

619. *result* outcome of deliberations (*OED* 3a) and action of springing back to a former position (*OED* 1).

620–27. Belial's puns are obvious except for *amused* (see above, 581*n*), *stumbled* ('nonplussed' and 'tripped up'), and *understand* ('comprehend' and 'prop up' *OED* 9).

635. *Rage prompted them* Cp. *Aen.* i 150: *furor arma ministrat*, 'rage supplies them with arms'. The allusion prepares for the Messiah's entry, for Virgil is describing rioters who hurl stones until a noble man pacifies them.

644–6. The hurling of *hills* as missiles recalls the war between the gods and Giants, which M. has already likened to the War in Heaven (cp. i 50, 197–200, 230–37). See esp. Claudian, *Gigantomachia* 70f.: 'One giant brandishes Thessalian Oeta in his mighty hand, another gathers all his strength and hurls Pangaeus at the foe, Athos with his snows arms another; this one roots up Ossa, that tears out Rhodope . . .' Cp. also Hesiod, *Theog.* 713–20 and Ovid, *Met.* i 151–62.

646. *amaze* astonishment, panic (*OED* 3).

654. *Main* of great bulk (*OED* 3), formed of solid rock (*OED* 4b).

655. *oppressed* crushed in battle (*OED* 1a).

657. *pent* closely confined.

664. *hills . . . hills* Cp. Tasso, *Gerus. Lib.* xvi 5: 'hill gainst hill, and mount gainst mountaine smote' (trans. Fairfax); also Virgil's simile describing the ships at Actium (*Aen.* viii 692): *montis concurrere montibus altos* ('high mountains clashed with mountains').

665. *jaculation* throwing.

667. *civil* orderly, humane, refined, non-military (*OED*), with a pun on 'Civil War'.

668. *To* compared with.

668–9. *confusion . . . confusion* Cp. ii 996: 'Confusion worse confounded'. The war threatens to reduce Heaven to Chaos.

671–3. *Almighty Father . . . sum of things* echoing Ovid, *Met.* ii 300, where Earth begs Jove, the *pater omnipotens*, to place the public interest first (*rerum consule summae*) and kill Phaethon so as to save the world from conflagration.

674. *advised* having considered (*OED* 1).

677. *declare* manifest, show forth.

679. *Assessor* *one who sits beside (*OED* 1).

680. *Effulgence radiance.

681–2. *invisible . . . Visibly* Cp. Col. 1. 15: 'the image of the invisible God'.

684. *Second omnipotence* Cp. John 5. 19: 'The Son can do nothing of himself, but what he seeth the Father do'. M. in *CD* i 5 cites this verse to show that the Son derives his power from the Father (*YP* 6. 266).

692. *Insensibly* imperceptibly.

698. *main* whole continent of Heaven.

701. *suffered* permitted.

709. *unction* anointing (iii 317, v 605).

712. *war* *instruments of war (*OED* 6a).

714. *Gird . . . thigh* Cp. Ps. 45. 3: 'Gird thy sword upon thy thigh, O most mighty'.

728. *well pleased* Cp. Matt. 3. 17: 'my beloved Son, in whom I am well pleased'.

731–2. *resign . . . All in All* See iii 341n.

734. *whom thou hat'st, I hate* Cp. Ps. 139. 21: 'Do not I hate them, O Lord, that hate thee?'

738. *prepared ill mansion* Hell. Contrast John 14. 2: 'In my Father's house are many mansions . . . I go to prepare a place for you'.

739. *th' undying worm* Mark 9. 44.

744. *Unfeignèd hallelujahs* Cp. 'forced hallelujahs' (ii 243).

748. *sacred morn* Cp. Homer, *Il.* xi 84.

749–59. The Messiah's living chariot, with its four-faced Cherubim, is taken from Ezekiel 1 and 10.

752. *instínct* *impelled, moved, animated (*OED* 2).

753. *four faces* of man, lion, ox and eagle (Ezek. 1. 10) or cherub, man, lion and eagle (Ezek. 10. 14).

759. *show'ry arch* rainbow. See Ezek. 1. 28.

761. *urim* Hebrew 'lights': gems worn by Aaron in his breastplate (Exod. 28. 30). Cp. iii 598 and *PR* iii 13–15.

762. *Victory* M.'s personification is modelled on Nike, the winged Greek goddess.

763–4. The *eagle* was Jupiter's bird and *thunder* his weapon.

765. *effusion* copious emission of smoke (*OED* 1c).

766. *bickering* *coruscating, quivering (*OED* 3) and skirmishing with arrows (*OED* 'bicker' 1b). Messiah's chariot shoots 'arrows' of 'fire' (see vi 845–50 and Ezek. 1. 13).

769–70. *twenty thousand . . . Chariots* Cp. Ps. 68. 17: 'The chariots of God are twenty thousand'.

771. *on wings of Cherub* Cp. Ps. 18. 10: 'He rode upon a cherub, and did fly'.

sublime lifted up.

773. *Illustrious* shining.

776. *his sign* anticipating the Second Coming: 'And then shall appear the sign of the Son of man in heaven' (Matt. 24. 30).

777. *reduced* led back (*OED* 2b).

778. *circumfused* spread around.

785. *obdured* obdurate, hardened in sin. See iii 200*n*.

788. *In . . . dwell* Cp. *Aen.* i 11 (Virgil's wonder at Juno's malice): 'Can such anger dwell in heavenly hearts?' Satan will echo the same line when tempting Eve (ix 729–30).

789–91. *what signs . . . hardened* Cp. God's hardening of Pharaoh's heart to all his *signs* (Exod. 14. 4–8).

794. *re-embattled* drawn up again in battle array.

801–2. *Stand still . . . this day* echoing Moses' words when God destroyed the Egyptians in the Red Sea: 'Fear ye not, stand still, and see the salvation of the Lord which he will shew to you this day' (Exod. 14. 13).

808. *Vengeance is his* a biblical commonplace. See e.g. Rom. 12. 19: 'Vengeance is mine; I will repay'.

809. *Number . . . not ordained* Messiah will defeat the rebels unaided. M. may also be alluding to the numerological commonplace that One is not a number (Fowler).

815. *Kingdom . . . glory* Cp. the Lord's Prayer (Matt. 6. 13).

827. *the Four* the 'four Cherubic shapes' of line 753.

832. *Gloomy as Night* So Hector, shining in bronze, breached the Achaians' rampart 'with dark face like sudden night' (Homer, *Il.* xii 462). Heaven's night is not gloomy (v 645, vi 11–12), so the Son must be dark as Chaos – but even Chaos pales before him (vi 862–6).

833. *steadfast Empyrean shook* So Olympus shook when Zeus went out to fight Typhoeus (Hesiod, *Theog.* 842–3). Cp. also Isa. 13. 12: 'I will shake the heavens'. God's throne remains unshaken (834), so Satan was lying when he said that he 'shook his throne' (i 105).

838. *Plagues* blows, wounds (*OED* 1), divine punishments, often with reference to 'the ten plagues' of Egypt (*OED* 2). Cp. the allusions to Pharaoh in lines 789–91 and 801–2. The Great Plague of 1665 killed 60,000 Londoners.

840. *O'er . . . rode* Cp. M.'s description in *An Apology* of Zeal ascending 'his fiery Chariot' drawn by beasts that resemble 'those four' seen by Ezekiel: 'with these the invincible warriour Zeale shaking loosely the slack reins drives over the heads of Scarlet Prelats . . . brusing their stiffe necks under his flaming wheels' (*YP* I. 900).

842–3. *mountains . . . shelter* Cp. Rev. 6. 16, where the damned cry 'to the mountains and rocks, Fall on us, and hide us from the face of him that sitteth on the throne, and from the wrath of the Lamb'. See also Luke 23. 30, Hos. 10. 8.

846. *Distinct* adorned (*OED* 4).

849. *pernicious* destructive and swift.

853. *half his strength* Contrast Hesiod's Zeus, who 'no longer checked his might', but 'put forth all his strength' to quell the Titans (*Theog.* 685–7).

857. *goats or timorous flock* Cp. Homer's comparison of fleeing Trojans to 'fawns' (*Il.* xxii 1). Cp. also the parable of the sheep and goats (Matt. 25. 33). The goats were sent 'into everlasting fire, prepared for the devil and his angels' (25. 41).

859. *furies* with overtones of 'Furies' – the avenging goddesses of Greek myth (see ii 596*n*).

861. *Rolled inward* Cp. Rev. 6. 14 on the Last Judgement: 'And the heaven departed as a scroll when it is rolled together'.

862. *wasteful* desolate, uninhabited, void (*OED* 3) and laying waste (*OED* 1).

868. *ruining* falling headlong.

871. *Nine days they fell* Hesiod's Titans fall for nine days from heaven to earth and for a further nine days from earth to Tartarus (*Theog.* 720–25). The angels' nine-day fall precedes their nine-day stupor in Hell (i 50).

873. *rout* uproar, disreputable crowd, defeated army.

874. *Encumbered* blocked up (*OED* 6), harassed, pressed hardly upon (*OED* 3b), burdened.

874–5. *Hell . . . Yawning . . . closed* Cp. Isa. 5. 14: 'hell hath enlarged herself, and opened her mouth without measure: and their glory, and their multitude, and their pomp, and he that rejoiceth, shall descend into it'.

884. *jubilee* joyful shouting (*OED* 5b).

885. *palm* an emblem of victory presaging apocalyptic triumphs (Rev. 7. 9).

892. *right hand* '[The Son] sat down on the right hand of the Majesty on high' (Heb. 1. 3).

898. *powers* armies (*OED* 9) or 'Powers', standing for all angelic orders. Cp. v 743.

909. *Thy weaker* Eve (the 'weaker vessel' of I Pet. 3. 7). It is odd that Raphael should speak about her as if she were absent. M. will soon tell us that she has been 'attentive' to the whole story (vii 50–51). Raphael might

be ignoring Eve in compliance with God's instruction that he 'Converse
with Adam' (v 230), or (as Jean Gagen suggests) M. might be inconsistent
as to how much Eve hears. See ix 275-6n.

BOOK VII

1-50. M.'s third invocation in *PL*. The first two were at i 1-49 and iii 1-
55. Most critics see ix 1-47 as a fourth invocation, but M. does not address
his Muse after book vii. See ix 1-47n.

1. *Descend from Heav'n* echoing Horace's invocation of the Muse Calliope:
Descende caelo (*Odes* III iv 1).

Urania one of the nine Muses (the Muse of astronomy in late Roman
times). The name means 'heavenly'. Du Bartas in *L'Uranie* had made
Urania the Muse of Christian poetry. M. invokes *the meaning, not the name*
(5) because he invokes a truly heavenly source of inspiration.

2. *If rightly thou art called* Cp. the cautious addressing of divine beings in
iii 7 and *Ep. Dam.* 208.

3. *Olympian hill* M. diminishes pagan epic by calling Mount Olympus 'a
mere hill' (Fowler). The distinction between hill and mountain was well
established (see *OED* 'hill' 1a).

4. *Pegasean* The winged horse Pegasus was a symbol for inspired poetry.
He had created the Muses' spring, Hippocrene ('horse spring'), with a
stamp of his hoof. He was also associated with Bellerophon (see below, 18-
20n).

8-12. *Before . . . song* Cp. Prov. 8. 24-31, where *Wisdom* tells of her origins
before Creation: 'When there were no depths, I was brought forth; when
there were no fountains abounding with water. Before the mountains were
settled, before the hills was I brought forth . . . Then I was by him, as one
brought up with him; was daily his delight, rejoicing always before him'.
Wisdom was often identified as the Son, but M. in *CD* i 7 takes her to be
a personification of the Father's wisdom.

9. *converse* keep company (*OED* 2).

10. *play* M. follows the Vulgate (*ludens*) rather than A.V. ('rejoicing')
or Junius-Tremellius (*laetificans*). There may be a musical pun on *play*,
suggesting that Wisdom and Urania play instruments to accompany their
song (12).

15. *Thy temp'ring* 'the air tempered (made suitable) by you'; also implying
that the Muse has 'guided' and 'attuned' M. himself (*OED* 'temper' 7, 15).

18-20. *Bellerophon . . . forlorn* Bellerophon killed the Chimera (see ii 628)
and defeated the Solymi and Amazons, but he incurred the gods' anger
when he tried to fly to heaven upon Pegasus. Zeus sent an insect to
sting the horse, and Bellerophon fell down to the *Aleian field* ('plain of

wandering'). Cp. Homer, *Il.* vi 200–202. Natale Conti, in *Mythologiae* (1567) IX iv, says that Bellerophon was blinded in his fall.

18. *clime* region, atmosphere; with a pun on 'climb'.

20. *Erroneous* straying (physical and moral).

22. *diurnal sphere* the visible universe, which appears to rotate daily.

23. *rapt* transported, enraptured.

pole celestial pole.

24–5. *unchanged / To hoarse or mute* M. would be *hoarse* if he were to become a turncoat, and *mute* if he were censored.

25–7. *evil days . . . dangers* M. probably wrote these lines shortly after the Restoration, when he was in *danger* of being dismembered like Orpheus (32–8). Several of his old republican colleagues, including Sir Henry Vane, were hanged, drawn and quartered. M. was spared that fate by the Act of Oblivion (August 1660). See Lieb² 70–80.

27. *darkness* M. had been totally blind since 1652.

29. *Visit'st . . . nightly* Cp. Ps. 17. 3: 'thou hast visited me in the night'. M.'s early biographers report that he composed at night or in the early hours of the morning. See Darbishire (33) and cp. iii 32 and ix 22.

32. *barbarous dissonance* The same phrase occurs in *A Masque* (550), again in the context of Bacchic revelry. Here *Bacchus and his revellers* are probably the Royalists, whom M. in *REW* calls 'these tigers of Bacchus' (*YP* 7. 452).

34. *Thracian bard* Orpheus. Bacchus's Maenads dismembered him after he rejected their love. See *Lycidas* 58–63, Virgil, *Georg.* iv 485–527, Ovid, *Met.* xi 1–66.

35. *Rhodope* a mountain range in Thrace.

36. *rapture* ecstasy (a sense coined by M. in *Nativity* 98), with overtones of 'seizing and carrying off as prey' (*OED* 1).

37. *the Muse* Calliope, the Muse of epic poetry.

46. *touch* Cp. Gen. 3. 3: 'neither shall ye touch it, lest ye die'.

50. *wand'ring* innocent meandering – but the hint of moral aberration is strong after *Erroneous there to wander* (20). Cp. vii 302.

consorted both 'accompanied' and 'wedded'.

50–51. *Eve . . . heard* M. here insists that Eve heard the whole story of Satan's rebellion, but Eve later speaks as if she had been absent. See ix 275–8 and note.

52. *admiration* astonishment.

muse meditation (*OED* sb²).

57. *redounded* flowed back (*OED* 4), from Latin *unda*, 'a wave'. Cp. the allusion to the whelming of Pharaoh in vi 800.

59. *repealed* abandoned (*OED* 2). For Adam's *doubts* see v 554.

63. *conspicuous* visible (in contrast to the invisible Heaven).

66. *drouth* thirst. Cp. Dante, *Purg.* xviii 4, where Dante thirsts for more of Virgil's discourse.

67. *current* running.

72. *Divine interpreter* echoing Mercury's title as messenger of the gods, *interpres divum* (Virgil, *Aen.* iv 378).

79. *end* final purpose.

83. *seemed* seemed good (*OED* 7e).

88. *yields or fills / All space* 'The air *yields* to solid bodies or *fills* the space they leave vacant' (Fowler). *Space* might also refer to 'outer space', before which *the ambient air* (earth's atmosphere) *yields* or gives way.

90. *florid* flowery, resplendent, flourishing (*OED* 1, 4, 6).

90−91. *what cause / Moved* Cp. i 28−30: 'what cause / Moved our grand parents . . . to fall off ?'

92. *late* recently (*OED* 4); perhaps also 'at a late date' − but Milton in *CD* i 7 says only a fool would ask 'what God did before the creation of the world' (trans. Carey, *YP* 6. 299).

94. *Absolved* completed (*OED* 2).

    unforbid unforbidden.

97. *magnify* glorify. Cp. Job 36. 24: 'magnify his work'.

98−100. *And . . . hears* Appeals to continue a narrative are common in epic. See esp. Homer, *Od.* xi 372−6, where Alcinous asks Odysseus to go on speaking until the dawn.

99. *suspense* attentive (*OED* 1), hanging (*OED* 4), *held back (*OED* 5).

102. *His generation* 'how he was created'.

103. *unapparent deep* invisible Chaos.

106. *watch* stay awake (*OED* 1).

109. *illustrious* including 'bright, shining' (*OED* 1).

116. *infer* *make, render (*OED* 1c, sole instance).

121. *inventions* speculations.

    hope hope for, aspire to.

126−30. *knowledge . . . wind* Cp. Davenant, *Gondibert* (1651) II viii 22: 'If knowledg, early got, self vallew breeds, / By false digestion it is turn'd to winde'.

131. *Lucifer* the morning star, substituting for Satan's 'former name', which is now 'heard no more' (v 659). Notice that Satan was *brighter* among the angels than Lucifer among the stars (not merely 'as bright as Lucifer' or even 'as bright relative to the angels as Lucifer is to the stars'). Cp. v 760, x 425.

142. *us dispossessed* 'once he had dispossessed us'.

143. *fraud* *the state of being defrauded (*OED* 5) − a passive usage unique to M., from Latin *fraus*. Cp. ix 643, *PR* i 372.

144. *place . . . more* Cp. Job 7. 10: 'He [that dies] shall return no more to his house, neither shall his place know him any more'.

150−56. *But . . . innumerable* Empson (56) infers that God 'creates us to spite the devils' − a view Satan shares (ix 147−9). Whatever God's motive for creating us, he does not make the number of men tally with that of the rebel angels. Notice *men innumerable* (156) and cp. Augustine, *City of God*, xxii 1: 'God is gathering a people so numerous that from them he may fill the places of the fallen angels and repair their number. Thus that beloved Heavenly City will not be deprived of its full number of citizens, and might even rejoice in a still more numerous population'. Cp. iii 289.

152. *fondly* foolishly.

154. *in a moment* See below, 176*n*.

159. *long obedience* God did not intend the prohibition to last for ever. Adam and Eve and their descendants might have worked their way up to Heaven. See v 493–500.

162. *inhabit lax* spread out, occupy the now vacant territories.

165. *overshadowing* Cp. Gabriel's words to Mary: 'the power of the Highest shall overshadow thee' (Luke 1. 35).

Spirit Editors cite *CD* i 7 as proof that M. must mean 'God's power' not 'the Holy Spirit'. But even *CD* allows the Spirit of Gen. 1. 2 to be a 'person' – provided it remain 'subordinate' to the Father (*YP* 6. 304). Cp. i 17*n*.

169. *nor vacuous* M.'s God creates out of Chaos, not out of nothing (see ii 890–1039*n* and v 472*n*). Chaos is infinite because God fills it, but God withholds his *goodness* (171) from Chaos until he uses it for Creation.

170. *uncircumscribed* Dante celebrates God as *non circunscritto* in *Purg.* xi 2. Nicholas of Cusa had described God as a circle whose centre is everywhere and whose circumference is nowhere. Cp. ix 107–8.

172. *Necessity and Chance* 'Necessity' was especially associated with Aristotle's notion of creation, which M. saw as a limit on God's omnipotence (see *CD* i 2). The atomist philosophers Democritus and Empedocles made 'Chance' the cause of all things. M. limits Chance to the uncreated atoms of Chaos. See ii 895–910 and Marjara (93).

173. *what I will is Fate* In *CD* i 2 M. points out that 'Fate' means 'that which is spoken' (from Latin *fari*, 'to speak'). See i 116*n* and cp. *PR* iv 316–17.

176. *Immediate are the acts of God* Augustine had argued for an immediate Creation (*De Genesi* i 1–3). The literal-minded Satan sneers at God for requiring six days (ix 136–9).

179. *earthly notion* human understanding.

182–3. *Glory . . . men* Luke 2. 14.

191. *worlds* ages (*OED* 5) or universes (*OED* 9), of which God might create an *infinite* number. Cp. i 650, ii 916, vii 209, x 362.

199–201. *chariots . . . brazen mountains* Cp. Zech. 6. 1: 'there came four chariots out from between two . . . mountains of brass'.

200. *armoury of God* Cp. Jer. 50. 25: 'The Lord hath opened his armoury'.

204. *within . . . lived* Cp. the animated chariot of vi 845–50.

205-6. *Heav'n opened . . . gates* Cp. the self-opening gates of Ps. 24. 7 (cit. below, 565-7*n*).

212. *Outrageous* enormous (*OED* 1) and violent (*OED* 2).

wasteful desolate (*OED* 3) and devastating (*OED* 1).

217. **omnific* all-creating.

221. *him* the Son.

224. *fervid* burning.

225. *compasses* Cp. Prov. 8. 27: 'he set a compass upon the face of the depth'. See also Dante, *Par.* xix 40: 'He that turned His compass round the limit of the world'.

230. *Thus . . . bounds* Cp. Job 38. 11: 'Hitherto shalt thou come, but no further: and here shall thy proud waves be stayed'.

231. *just* exact (*OED* 9), suitable (*OED* 7).

world universe.

233. *Matter unformed and void* Cp. Gen. 1. 2: 'the earth was without form, and void'. Cp. also Plato's account of Creation from formless matter (*Timaeus* 50).

235. *brooding* See i 21-2*n*.

236. *vital virtue* life-giving power.

237-42. *downward . . . hung* Cp. the differentiation of the four elements in Ovid, *Met.* i 21-31, Lucretius, *De Rerum Nat.* v 432ff., and Claudian, *De Rapt. Pros.* i 248-53. According to these poets, heavy elements sank to the centre to form the earth. M.'s *cold infernal dregs* sink beneath the universe rather than to its heart. Thus M.'s universe is wholly good (no part is *Adverse to life*), but Chaos still threatens it from outside. See ii 890-1039*n*.

238. *tartareous* crusty, gritty (*OED* a² 2), with a play on Tartarus, hell.

239. *founded* attached (*OED* v² 5).

conglobed gathered into (concentric) spherical regions.

242. *earth . . . hung* Cp. Ovid, *Met.* i 12-13: *pendebat in aere tellus / ponderibus librata suis* ('the earth hangs poised by her own weight in the air'). Cp. also Job 26. 7: 'He . . . hangeth the earth upon nothing'.

244. *Ethereal* Ancient cosmologists thought of ether as a fifth element (*quintessence*). It filled all space beyond the sphere of the moon, and stars and planets were composed of it. See iii 7 ('pure ethereal stream') and iii 716.

248. *she* light (see line 360).

tabernacle Cp. Ps. 19. 4: 'he set a tabernacle for the sun'.

254. *orient* eastern, shining, rising like the dawn.

255. *Exhaling* rising as vapour (*OED* 2).

256. *joy and shout* Cp. Job 38. 7, where the angels 'shouted for joy' as they witnessed Creation.

261-3. *firmament . . . Waters* Cp. Gen. 1. 6: 'And God said, Let there be a firmament in the midst of the waters, and let it divide the waters from

the waters'. M. identifies the 'firmament' with the space between the earth
and the universe's outer shell. Others identified it with the shell itself. The
waters below the firmament are earth's seas. The waters above the firmament
form an *ocean* (271) on the universe's shell. See below, 271*n*.

264. *expanse* from Latin *expansum*, which correctly translates the Hebrew
word rendered as 'firmament' in A.V.

   liquid clear, bright, transparent (*OED* 2).

266–7. *convéx . . . round* vault . . . universe.

269. *world* universe.

271. *Crystálline ocean* not the crystalline sphere of iii 482, but the jasper sea
of iii 518–19, that flows about the foot of the stair leading to Heaven. See
iii 518*n*.

273. *distemper* disturb the due proportion of elements (*OED* 1), and so
reduce them to their raw 'contraries' (see ii 898*n*).

277. *embryon* embryo. Earth is both *the Great Mother* about to *conceive*
(281), and the foetus enveloped (*involved*) in protective *waters*. *Magna Mater*
was a title of Cybele, mother of the gods (cp. v 338).

279. *Main* uninterrupted.

280. *Prolific humour* generative liquid. Earth's seas now act as penetrating
seed as well as nursing fluid. Cp. i 21–2*n*.

281. *Fermented* (from Latin *fervere*, 'to boil') has alchemical overtones
(*OED* 1b), as in: 'Ferments . . . Seminal sparks hidden in matter . . . put
into motion, and by the variety of that motion producing the variety of
bodies' (1677).

282. *genial* generative.

288. *tumid* swollen.

291. *precipitance* headlong fall (*OED* 1).

292. *conglobing* gathering into spheres. At lines 239–40 the entire universe
'conglobed'. As above, so below. Cp. Marvell, 'On a Drop of Dew', 5–8.

293. *crystal wall* anticipating the parting of the Red Sea. See xii 197: 'two
crystal walls'.

   ridge direct surge forward in waves.

296. *of armies thou hast heard* Raphael again chooses a simile to fit Adam's
understanding. Cp. vi 73–6.

299. *rapture* force of movement (*OED* 2) and joy.

302. *serpent error wand'ring* All three words evoke the Fall for the fallen
reader, but Adam and Eve hear only the innocent meaning. Thus *error*
implies 'moral trangression' (*OED* 5) but means 'winding course' (*OED* 1).
Serpent might be nothing more than a present participle (from Latin *serpere*,
'to creep'). See Stein (66), Ricks (110), Fish (130–41).

308. *congregated* echoing the Junius-Tremellius version of Gen. 1. 10:
congregationem vero aquarum vocavit maria.

321. *swelling*] smelling *Ed I, Ed II*. Bentley's emendation has been widely accepted.

322. *and*] *Ed II*; add *Ed I*.

humble low-growing.

323. *implicit* entangled (*OED* 1).

325. *gemmed* put forth blossoms (*OED* 1a), from Latin *gemmare*, but suggesting also 'adorned with gems'.

331–3. *not yet rained . . . mist* Gen. 2. 5–6.

332. *till the ground* Cp. Gen. 2. 5: 'there was not a man to till the ground'. 'Till' might include any kind of cultivation (*OED* 4). Ploughing was unknown before the Fall.

338. *recorded* bore witness to (*OED* 10).

348. *altern* *in turns (*OED* 4).

351. *vicissitude* reciprocal succession (*OED* 4).

356. *of ethereal mould* fashioned from ether, which is naturally luminous (iii 7, vii 244).

357. *every magnitude* every class of brightness into which the stars are ranked by astronomers.

360. *cloudy shrine* the 'cloudy tabernacle' of line 248.

362–4. *liquid light . . . fountain* Cp. Lucretius, *De Rerum Nat.* v 281: *liquidi fons luminis, aetherius sol* ('the ethereal sun, fountain of liquid light'). *Liquid* includes 'clear, bright, transparent' (*OED* 2).

364. *other stars* Raphael's first hint that our sun might be one of many stars. He will develop the idea in viii 148–58.

366. *his*] *Ed I*; her *Ed II*. 'His' points to 'Lucifer', 'her' to 'Venus'. Fowler prefers 'her' since 'his' introduces an 'inappropriate association' with Satan. But book vii is full of such prolepses (see eg. 302, 412, 427–31, 494–8). Raphael had explicitly named the *morning planet* as 'Lucifer' at vii 131 (cp. v 760, x 425). He never names 'Venus'. Lucifer has *horns* in accordance with Galileo's observations.

367. *tincture* active principle emanating from afar (*OED* 6b), with overtones of the alchemical 'universal tincture', the elixir (*OED* 6a). See iii 600–612 for the sun's alchemical powers. The context (*fountain, urns*) also evokes the etymology, from Latin *tingere*, 'to dip'.

368. *small peculiar* own small light. Kepler and Boyle shared M.'s belief that stars and planets shone with their own light as well as with the reflected light of the sun (Marjara 66–7). See further viii 150*n*.

370. *First in his east the* Flannagan emends to 'First in the east his', but the *Ed I* and *Ed II* phrasing suggests the freshness of Creation. The new sun does not just arise 'in the east': it defines the east by arising there for the first time.

372. *jocund to run* Cp. Ps. 19. 4–5: 'he set a tabernacle for the sun. Which is as a bridegroom coming out of his chamber, and rejoiceth as a strong man to run a race'.

374–5. *Pleiades . . . sweet influence* Cp. Job 38. 31: 'Canst thou bind the sweet influences of the Pleiades?'

379. *In that aspéct* i.e. when full.

382. *dividual* *shared (*OED* 3).

388. *Reptile* creeping animal (*OED* 1), translating Junius-Tremellius, *reptilia animantia* (Gen. 1. 20). A.V. has 'moving creature'.

403. *Bank the mid sea* The fish are so numerous as to form living banks – shelving elevations in the sea where fish gather.

406–10. *Show . . . play* Fowler notes that *waved, coats, dropped,* and *bended* are heraldic terms. Cp. the 'mantling' swan (439) and 'rampant' lion (466) and contrast the haughty impreses of vi 84 and ix 34–7.

406. *waved* both 'glimpsed through the waves' and 'striped with "wavy" heraldic markings' (*OED* 1c).

dropped spotted.

407. *attend* watch for.

409. *smooth* a stretch of calm water (*OED* 1c, nautical term).

410. *bended* suggesting the dolphin's curved shape as it leaps, but playing also on the heraldic term 'bendy' (i.e. divided into diagonal lines).

411. M.'s eighteenth-century editors noted how the scansion ('Wállowing / unwíeld/y, enór/mous in/ their gáit') is mimetically unwieldy.

412. *Leviathan* Cp. the Satanic Leviathan of i 200–208. It is surprising to re-encounter the simile 'amidst the joyful numbering of God's created' (Fish 150), but this Leviathan is not treacherous, for he resembles a *moving land,* not an 'island' (i 205).

419. *kindly* natural.

420. *callow* unfledged.

fledge fledged.

421. *summed their pens* brought their feathers to full growth.

422. *clang* harsh cry (Latin *clangor*).

despised looked down upon.

422–3. *under . . . prospect* The ground seemed to be under a cloud (of birds).

425. *loosely* separately.

region sky.

426. *wedge* *fly in a wedge formation (*OED* 4c).

427. *Intelligent of seasons* There are no seasons until x 651–707, when God sends his angels to tilt the earth on its axis. Do the *prudent* (430) birds sense the imminent Fall? Cp. Jer. 8. 7: 'the stork in the heaven knoweth her appointed times; and the turtle and the crane and the swallow observe the time of their coming; but my people know not the judgment of the Lord'.

429. *mutual wing* Birds flying in formation were thought to support each other with their wings (Svendsen 158).

432. *Floats* undulates.

434. *Solaced* *made cheerful.

439. *mantling* forming a mantle.

439–40. *rows / Her state* The swan is monarch, royal barge, and rowers all in one.

441. *dank* pool, mere (*OED* 2).

tow'r soar aloft into (*OED* 5).

444. *other* peacock.

451. *soul*] foul *Ed I* and *Ed II*. Bentley's emendation has been widely accepted ('fowl' were created on the previous day).

452. *Cattle* domestic livestock (not just bovine animals).

454. *teemed* gave birth to (*OED* 1).

456. *full-grown No hyphen in *Ed I* or *Ed II*.

457. *wons* dwells.

461. *Those . . . these* wild beasts . . . cattle. Future carnivores are already distinguished from their prey. The former rise in *pairs* (459), the latter in *flocks* or *herds* (461–2).

rare spread out at wide intervals (*OED* 3a).

466. *brinded* tawny with streaks (*OED*).

ounce lynx.

467. *libbard* leopard.

470. *mould* earth and pattern by which something is shaped.

471. *Behemoth* a huge biblical beast (Job 40. 15), identified with the elephant. A marginal note in the Geneva Bible also identifies him with the Devil (Hughes).

474. *river horse* translating the Greek 'hippopotamus'.

475. *creeps* *creeps along (*OED* 5a).

476. *worm* any creeping animal, including serpents.

482. *Minims* smallest forms of animal life (*OED* 4).

483. *involved* coiled.

484. *wings* Cp. Isa. 30. 6: 'fiery flying serpent'.

485. *parsimonious emmet* thrifty ant. M. in *REW* celebrates the ant as an example 'of a frugal and self-governing democratie or Commonwealth; safer and more thriving in the joint providence and counsel of many industrious equals, then under the single domination of one imperious Lord' (*YP* 7. 427). Cp. i 768–75, where the monarchical beehive is associated with Hell.

486. *large heart* capacious intellect. See i 444*n*. Cp. also Virgil's description of bees as having *ingentis animos angusto in pectore*, 'huge souls in tiny breasts' (*Georg.* iv 83).

488. *popular* populous (*OED* 3) and plebeian (*OED* 2b).

489. *commonalty* common people, with overtones of 'a self-governing commonwealth, a republic' (*OED* 1b).

493. *gav'st them names* See viii 342–54 and Gen. 2. 19–20.

494–8. *Needless . . . call* Fish (156) comments: 'with every other reader I am condemned to see in this praise of the serpent an ominousness that is simply not there'.

497. *hairy mane* Cp. the maned sea-serpents that emerge from the sea to devour Laocoon and his sons and so ensure Troy's fall (Virgil, *Aen.* ii 203–7).

*terrific terrifying.

502. *Consummate* complete, perfect.

504. *Frequent* in throngs.

505–10. *There wanted yet . . . Govern the rest* Cp. Ovid, *Met.* i 76–7: 'The nobler Creature, with a mind possest, / Was wanting yet, that should command the rest' (trans. Sandys, 1632). Ovid also celebrates man's erect stature (i 84–6).

505. *end* completion and purpose.

508–9. *erect / His stature* both 'stand upright' and 'elevate his condition' (*OED* 'erect' 2, 'stature' 4), as in 'Erect my spirite into thy blisse' (1589). Man's erect stance is a sign that he was created for Heaven. See viii 259–61, and contrast Mammon, 'the least erected Spirit' (i 679).

509. *front* brow or face.

510. **self-knowing* Cp. the Platonic and Delphic maxim 'Know thyself'. See xi 531*n*.

511. *Magnanimous* great-souled, nobly ambitious, lofty of purpose.

correspond both 'be in harmony' and 'hold communication'.

528. *Express* exact, truly depicted (*OED* 1a), well-framed (*OED* 1b). Cp. Heb. 1. 3, where the Son is made in 'the express image' of God. Cp. also Shakespeare, *Hamlet* II ii 286f.: 'What a piece of work is a man . . . how express and admirable, in action how like an angel, in apprehension how like a god!'

536. *thence* both 'from there' (the world outside Paradise) and 'for that cause' (to subdue the earth).

537. *delicious* delightful. See iv 132*n*.

544. *Thou may'st not* 'Taste' is understood, the abrupt omission being mimetic of restraint.

547. *Surprise* *betray into doing something not intended (*OED* 4b), over-power the will (*OED* 1b), catch in the act (*OED* 3). Cp. the dictionary definition given by Edward Phillips (M.'s nephew): 'to lead a man into an Error, by causing him to do a thing over hastily' (1696).

557. *Idea* Platonic Form (the sole occurrence of the word in M.'s English poetry).

559. *Symphonious* harmonious.

tuned performed.

563. *stations*] *Ed I*; station *Ed II*. The singular limits the meaning to 'appointed place'; the plural plays on 'station' as 'the apparent standing still of a planet' (*OED* 5). Cp. vii 98−102, where Adam says the sun will 'delay' to hear of its Creation.

564. *pomp* triumphal procession (*OED* 2).

jubilant from Latin *jubilare*, 'to shout with joy'. There may be overtones of the Hebrew 'Jubilee' (see iii 348*n*), with which *jubilare* was associated. Cp. vi 884.

565. *Open, ye everlasting gates* Cp. Ps. 24. 7: 'Lift up your heads, O ye gates; and be ye lift up, ye everlasting doors; and the King of glory shall come in'. Cp. also Fletcher, *CV* (1610) iv 15: 'Tosse up your heads ye everlasting gates, / And let the Prince of glorie enter in'.

575. *blazing portals* Fowler identifies these with the signs of Capricorn and Cancer, but the Messiah has now left our universe. Raphael likens Heaven's *road* to our *Milky Way* in a simile (577−9). Thus M. overgoes Ovid, *Met.* i 168−71, where the Milky Way is the gods' highway to Jove's hall. **578.** *pavement stars* Cp. iv 976: 'the road of Heav'n star-paved'.

580. *zone* *belt of the sky (*OED* 5).

588−90. *(for . . . Omnipresence]* *Ed I* and *Ed II* have two opening brackets (before *for* and *such*). Most editors remove the first, and so identify the *Father* as *Author and end*. Fowler removes the second and cites Heb. 12. 2 ('author and finisher') as evidence that the Son is *Author and end*. All editors assume that there can be only one opening bracket, but it is just possible that M. is breaking the rules of punctuation to suggest God's omnipresence and to imply that both Father and Son are Author and end.

596. *dulcimer* the bagpipe of Dan. 3. 5, rendered as 'dulcimer' in A.V.

597. *fret* bar on the finger-board of a stringed instrument.

598. *Tempered* brought into harmony.

599. *Choral or unison* in parts or in unison.

605. *Giant angels* The allusion to the Giants' revolt against Jove implies that the Greek myth is a garbled memory of the angels' rebellion. Cp. i 50, 199−200, 230−37, vi 643−66.

619. *hyaline* transliterating the Greek word for 'glassy', used in Rev. 4. 6 ('a sea of glass like unto crystal'). Cp. 'sea of jasper' (iii 518−19) and 'crystálline ocean' (vii 271).

620. *immense* immeasurable.

621. *Numerous* both 'of great number' and 'that can be numbered' (*OED* 4). Cp. Ps. 147. 4: 'He telleth the number of the stars; he calleth them all by their names'.

622. *destined habitation* See iii 667−70 and v 500 for further hints that men might colonize other worlds. At iii 566−72 and viii 146−8 M. conjectures that other worlds might already be inhabited.

623. *seasons* Cp. Acts i. 7: 'it is not for you to know the times or the seasons, which the Father hath put in his own power'.

624. *nether Ocean* the earth's seas, or 'waters below the firmament', as distinct from the 'clear hyaline', or 'waters above the firmament'.

631–2. *thrice happy if they know / Their happiness* Cp. Virgil on the happiness of simple peasants: 'O, happy, if he knew his happy state' (*Georg.* ii 457, trans. Dryden). Elsewhere M. implies that Adam and Eve lost their happiness by knowing it. See viii 282, ix 1072, xi 89 and esp. iv 774–5: 'O yet happiest if ye seek / No happier state, and know to know no more'.

632. *persevere* including the theological sense: 'continuance in a state of grace until it is succeeded by a state of glory' (*OED* 'perseverance' 2).

634. *hallelujahs* Hebrew, 'praise the Lord'.

636. *face of things* echoing v 43: 'Shadowy sets off the face of things'.

BOOK VIII

1–4. *The . . . replied* These lines were added in *Ed II*, when M. divided the original book vii into the present books vii and viii. *Ed I* vii 641 reads: 'To whom thus Adam gratefully replied'.

2. *charming* spellbinding.

3. *still stood fixed* So in Apollonius Rhodius, *Argonautica* i 512–16, Orpheus holds his audience spellbound while he sings of Creation. Cp. also Homer, *Od.* xiii 1–2.

7. *Historian* including 'storyteller' (*OED* 2).

9. *condescension* consent (*OED* 4), courteous disregard of rank (*OED* 1). 'A beautiful word, which we have spoiled' (Lewis 79).

14. *solution* explanation (*OED* 1b).

15–38. *When I behold . . . fails* Cp. Eve's question about the stars (iv 657–8). Adam is now dissatisfied with the answer he had given Eve (iv 660–88).

15. *this goodly frame* the universe (echoing Shakespeare, *Hamlet* II ii 310).

17–18. *spot . . . atom* Astronomers since antiquity had been aware that the earth was a mere speck in the universe.

19. *numbered* numerous and reckoned by number. Cp. Ps. 147. 4: 'He telleth the number of the stars; he calleth them all by their names'.

22. *officiate* minister, supply (*OED* 4a).

23. *opacous* dark.

punctual point-like (*OED* 3a), but the modern sense existed and prepares for the idea that the earth has timely motions (128–40).

25. *admire* marvel.

30. *For aught appears* so far as can be seen.

32. *sedentary* *motionless (*OED* 3b), slothful (*OED* 2b).

33. *compass* circular course (*OED* 11a).

36. *sumless* incalculable.

45. *visit* inspect (*OED* 9).

46. *nursery* nursery-garden and the activity of tending it.

51. *auditress The *OED* cites 'auditor' from the fourteenth century.

52–8. *Her husband . . . joined* The emphasis on Eve's choice (*preferred*, *chose*) softens, but does not remove, the hierarchical implication from I Cor. 14. 35: 'if they will learn any thing, let them ask their husbands at home: for it is a shame for women to speak in the church'.

61. *pomp* procession, train. The *Graces* attended Venus.
   still continually.

65. *facile* affable, courteous (*OED* 4).

67. *Book of God* a traditional metaphor for the heavens.

74. *scanned* discussed minutely (*OED* 3a), with a play on Latin *scandere*, 'to climb'.

75. *admire* marvel.

78. *quaint* ingenious (*OED* 1a).
   wide wide of the mark.

80. *calculate* predict the motions of (*OED* 2), frame (*OED* 5).
   wield direct, guide, hold in check (*OED* 4).

82. *save appearances* reconcile hypotheses with observed facts. To 'save (or salve) the appearances' was a scholastic term, borrowed from the Greeks. It need not be pejorative. See *OED* 'salve' v² 1, 'save' 12a.

83. *centric and eccentric* orbits with the earth (or sun) at the centre or off-centre respectively.

84. *epicycle* a smaller orbit whose centre corresponds to a fixed point on the circumference of the main orbit. A planet had a forward motion when on the outer part of the epicycle, and a retrograde motion when on the inner part. Both the Ptolemaic and Copernican systems had epicycles.

91. *infers* implies (*OED* 4).

99. *officious* attentive, dutiful (*OED* 1, 2a).

100. *speak* bespeak (but cp. Ps. 19. 1: 'The heavens declare the glory of God').

102. *line . . . far* Cp. Job 38. 5, where God asks, about the earth: 'Who hath laid the measures thereof, if thou knowest? or who hath stretched the line upon it?'

108. *numberless* incalculable (*swiftness*) and innumerable (*circles*, stellar orbits).

110. *Speed almost spiritual* the speed of angelic Intelligences (cp. 'the speed of thought').

122. *advantage* including 'place of vantage, elevation' (*OED* 3).

123. *world* universe.

other stars another hint (cp. vii 364) that the sun might be one of many stars. Raphael develops the idea in lines 148–58.

124. *attractive virtue* power of attraction. Kepler had theorized that the sun attracted the planets by magnetism. See iii 582–3n.

125. *rounds* circles and circular dances.

126. *wand'ring* 'Planet' is derived from Greek πλανήτης, 'wanderer'.

127. *retrograde* See above, 84n.

128. *six* Mercury, Venus, Mars, Jupiter, Saturn, and the moon. In Ptolemaic astronomy, the seventh planet is the sun; in Copernican, the earth.

130. *three different motions* The first two are daily and yearly. Editors disagree about the third. If Raphael refers to the precession of the equinoxes, he does so proleptically, for there was no precession before the Fall (see x 668f.). Fowler therefore identifies the third motion with Copernicus's 'motion in declination', whereby the earth's axis was thought to swivel so as to point always in the same direction.

131. *several spheres* Even with his epicycles, Ptolemy was obliged to posit a ninth sphere beyond the fixed stars. Aristotle had imagined fifty-six spheres.

132. *thwart obliquities* oblique paths that cross each other. There may be a pun on 'obliquity of the ecliptic' (*OED* 1), referring to the inclination of the equator to the ecliptic. The pun would have to be proleptic, for equator and ecliptic coincided before the Fall.

134. *rhomb* Greek 'wheel' or 'spinning top'. Raphael is referring to the *primum mobile*, which revolved around the universe in twenty-four hours, carrying the lower spheres with it. Copernicus dispensed with this first-moved sphere.

142. *terrestrial moon* both 'earth's moon' and 'earth-like moon'.

144–8. *if land . . . there* Cp. i 290–91, iii 460–62 and v 418–22.

148. *other suns* Nicholas of Cusa had conjectured that the fixed stars were suns with planetary systems, and that suns, planets, and moons were inhabited. Kepler rejected the idea, but Bruno and Descartes were among those who accepted it. M. imagines that stars might be inhabited at iii 566–71, 606–12, vii 621–5. See also i 650 and note.

149. *moons* any satellites (including planets) *attendant* on a sun. Cp. Wilkins, *The Discovery of a World in the Moon* (1638) Proposition xi: 'as their world is our Moone, so our world is their Moone'.

150. *male and female* original and reflected. Raphael associates gender with *light*, not specific heavenly bodies, so it is misleading to speak of 'male suns and female moons' or to invoke Apollo and Diana. *Moons* (planets) exchange female light reciprocally (140–44), and they also have some 'peculiar' light of their own (vii 368). Even *suns* might borrow some female light from their stellar neighbours (vii 364–9). See vii 368n.

151. *animate the world* endow the universe with life (by sustaining life on neighbouring heavenly bodies).

152. *Stored* including 'provide for the continuance of a race or breed' (*OED* 'store' 2a).

157. *this habitable* imitating a phrase used by the Greeks to distinguish their world from barbarian lands. Since it occurs in the context of what is *obvious* (open) *to dispute*, Raphael might hint that other worlds are civilized.

164. *inoffensive* unobstructed (Latin *inoffensus*) and harmless (*OED* 1).

sleeps *spins with imperceptible motion (*OED* 3c, used of spinning tops, earliest instance 1854).

167. *Solicit* disturb, disquiet (*OED* 1), with an etymological play on 'put the whole in motion' (Latin *sollus, ciere*).

168. *Leave . . . fear* 'Fear God, and keep his commandments: for this is the whole duty of man' (Eccles. 12. 13).

181. *Intelligence* angelic spirit.

187. *wand'ring thoughts* Cp. Belial's 'thoughts that wander through eternity' (ii 148).

194. *fume* something unsubstantial, transient, imaginary (*OED* 5), something which goes to the head and clouds the reason (*OED* 6). Cp. ix 1050.

195. *fond impertinence* foolish irrelevance.

197. *still to seek* always searching.

198. *pitch* summit.

202. *sufferance* (divine) permission.

209. *Fond* foolish.

218. *Nor are thy lips ungraceful* Cp. Ps. 45. 2: 'Grace is poured into thy lips: Therefore God hath blessed thee'.

*ungraceful The *OED* also credits M.'s nephew, Edward Phillips, with the earliest instance of 'ungracefulness'.

225. *fellow servant* When St John tried to worship an angel, the angel said: 'I am thy fellow servant' (Rev. 22. 9).

228. *equal love* Contrast Beëlzebub's jealous claim that men are 'favoured more' than angels (ii 350). Cp. also i 651.

229–40. *For . . . obedience* Raphael's explanation does not reflect well on God. A God who would mar Creation in a fit of temper or go out of his way to disappoint his angels seems neither omnipotent nor good. See Empson (110).

230. *uncouth* strange, desolate, unpleasant.

239. *state* ceremony.

inure strengthen by exercise.

243–4. *Noise . . . rage* Cp. Aeneas outside the gate of Tartarus, hearing cries of torment (Virgil, *Aen.* vi 557–9); also Astolfo listening to the howls of the damned (Ariosto, *Orl. Fur.* xxxiv 4).

246. *sabbath ev'ning* the evening that began the seventh day. Following Hebrew custom, Milton reckons days from sunset to sunset.

251. *who himself beginning knew* Cp. v 859–63. Like Satan, Adam cannot remember his origins, but where Satan takes this as proof that he was not created, Adam infers the existence of a *Maker* (278).

256. *reeking* steaming (*OED* 2), without unpleasant associations. *OED*'s earliest instance of the sense 'smell unpleasantly' is from 1710 (*OED* 3).

263. *lapse* *gliding flow (*OED* 6), with proleptic overtones of 'the Fall' (*OED* 2b), as in 'thy original lapse' (xii 83).

268. *went* walked.

269. *as*] *Ed I*; and *Ed II*.

272. *readily could name* Adam's ability to intuit true names indicates his native wisdom (see below, 352–3n).

276. *live and move* Cp. Acts 17. 28: 'For in him we live, and move, and have our being'.

282. *happier than I know* Cp. iv 774–5: 'O yet happiest if ye seek / No happier state, and know to know no more'. Both statements imply that to know one's happiness is to lose it. Cp. also ix 1070–73, and contrast vii 631–2: 'thrice happy if they know / Their happiness'.

288. *oppression* weighing down.

292. *stood at my head a dream* Homer's Oneiros ('Dream') stands at Agamemnon's head while falsely promising speedy victory (*Il.* ii 20). M. had earlier associated Dream with Satan (see v 38, 642, 673 and notes). Cp. *PR* iv 407.

296. *mansion* dwelling-place. Gen. 2. 8 and 2. 15 make clear that Adam was created outside Paradise, which he received as a gift, not a birthright.

300–314. *by the hand ... divine* Cp. Eve's dream of flying (v 86–93). Adam's flight is *real* (310) and his *guide* (312) does not abandon him. Contrast v 91: 'My guide was gone'.

311. *lively* vividly (*OED* 4).

316. *Whom ... I am* Cp. God's reply when Moses asks for his name: 'I AM that I AM. . . . Thus shalt thou say unto the children of Israel, I AM hath sent me unto you' (Exod. 3. 14).

320. *till and keep* In the A.V. Adam's task was to 'dress' the garden (Gen. 2. 15). God commands him to 'till the ground' (Gen. 3. 23) after the Fall. M. follows the Hebrew, Greek (LXX) and Latin versions, which dignify work by using the same word in both verses.

324. *Knowledge ... ill* M. follows Gen. 2. 17 in making God, not Satan, author of the Tree's name. See iv 423–4n, ix 1072n.

331. *From that day mortal* a traditional solution to Gen. 2. 17, where God tells Adam that he will die on 'the day' he eats. (Adam lived to be 930.)

332. *lose* Fowler and Campbell retain the *Ed I* and *Ed II* spelling 'loose' because it indicates 'violate' (*OED* 8) or 'break up, do away with' (*OED*

7a) as well as 'lose'. But 'lose' must be dominant when God warns Adam about the loss of Paradise in a poem called *Paradise Lost*. 'Lose' could in any case include 'destroy, be the ruin of' (*OED* 2a). Cp. viii 553, ix 959.

334. *interdiction* prohibition.

337. *purpose* conversation (*OED* 4).

350. *two and two* The animals had been created in 'broad herds' (vii 462). Now as Adam names them they shrink to more manageable proportions. Cp. Gen. 7. 9 ('two and two unto Noah into the ark').

351. *stooped* bowed to a superior authority (*OED* 2a).

350. *cow'ring* the quivering of young hawks, who shake their wings, in sign of obedience to the old ones (*OED* 1b).

352–3. *named . . . nature* Cp. *Tetrachordon* (1645): 'Adam who had the wisdom giv'n him to know all creatures, and to name them according to their properties, no doubt but had the gift to discern perfectly' (*YP* 2. 602); also *CD* i 7: 'he could not have given names to the animals in that extempore way, without great intelligence' (trans. Carey, *YP* 6. 324). The idea that Adam had named things 'rightly' (439) was supported by Gen. 2. 19 ('whatsoever Adam called every living creature, that was the name thereof') and by Plato's *Cratylus*. Cp. also Bacon, *Of the Interpretation of Nature*: 'when man shall be able to call the creatures by their true names he shall again command them'.

354. *sudden* extempore (*OED* 7), of mental faculties: quick, sharp (*OED* 4b).

355. *found not* Cp. Gen. 2. 20: 'for Adam there was not found an help meet'. M. takes Genesis to mean that Adam (not God) failed to find what he was looking for.

357. *O by what name* Cp. Moses' question at Exod. 3. 13 ('What is his name?') and God's reply (cit. above, 316*n*). Cp. also Prov. 30. 4: 'What is his name, and what is his son's name, if thou canst tell?' Lieb (172) cites *CD* i 5: 'the giving of a name is always acknowledged to be the function of a superior, whether father or lord' (trans. Carey, *YP* 6. 261).

371. *Replenished* abundantly stocked (*OED* 1).

373. *Their language* Hughes and Fowler cite the pseudepigraphal Book of Jubilees, which states that animals spoke in Paradise (3. 28). But M.'s animals were created 'mute to all articulate sound' (ix 557). *Language* here means 'inarticulate sounds used by the lower animals' (*OED* 1c). God is testing Adam's appreciation of human language, which was made for rational conversation. Adam would not deserve Eve if he were to be content with animals' language.

379–80. *Let . . . speak* Cp. Abraham's plea at Gen. 18. 30: 'Oh let not the Lord be angry, and I will speak'.

383–4. *Among unequals what . . . delight* Adam requests an equal, and God promises to give him his 'wish exactly' (viii 451). But Raphael, the Son, and M. himself (both in *PL* and in his prose) deny that Eve was Adam's equal. See iv 296*n*.

384. *sort* suit, fit, be in harmony (*OED* 18).

387. *intense . . . remiss* taut . . . slack. The image is of strings in a musical instrument. Man's string is too taut and that of the animals too slack for there to be *harmony* between them.

390. *participate* share with others (*OED* 2).

392. *consort* both 'spouse' and 'harmonious music' (*OED* sb² 3b).

396. *converse* associate familiarly (*OED* 2) and have sexual intercourse (*OED* 2b). Adam has not yet asked for the 'meet and happy conversation' that M. saw as the 'noblest end of mariage' (*DDD*, *YP* 2. 246), and God will not grant his request until he does so. The entire episode is a test of Adam's ability to give 'conversation' its fully human meaning. See lines 412, 418, 432.

399. *nice* fastidious, with overtones of 'lascivious' (*OED* 2).

402. *in pleasure* including 'in Eden' (*Eden* being Hebrew for 'pleasure').

406–7. *none . . . less* Cp. Horace's Jove, who 'has created nothing greater than himself, nor alike, nor second' (*Odes* I xii 17–18). M. substitutes *equal* for 'greater'.

417. *But in degree* except relatively (Adam is a *perfect* man, but does not have God's *absolute* perfection).

419. *solace* *alleviate, assuage (*OED* 1c).

421. *through all numbers absolute* perfect in all parts (*OED* 'absolute' 4, Latin *numerus*) and complete in all numbers (*OED* 'absolute' 5b). 'The divine monad contains all other numbers' (Fowler). Critics disagree as to whether Adam is conversing with the Father or the Son. The present line implies that the distinction is unimportant for unfallen man. Contrast x 55–6.

423. *single imperfection* imperfection of being single.

426. *Collateral* mutual (lit. 'side by side'). Cp. iv 741: 'Straight side by side were laid'.

427. *secrecy* retirement, seclusion (*OED* 2b).

427–8. *alone . . . accompanied* echoing Cicero's famous description of Scipio Africanus: *Numquam minus solum, quam cum solus* ('never less alone than when alone'), *De Officiis* III i 1.

433. *complacence* pleasure, delight, satisfaction (*OED* 2).

435. *Permissive* allowed.

445. *Knew . . . alone* Cp. Gen. 2. 18: 'And the Lord God said, It is not good that the man should be alone'.

450. *thy fit help, thy other self* M. expands Gen. 2. 18 ('an help meet for him') in accordance with his own gloss in *Tetrachordon*: 'The originall here is more expressive then other languages word for word can render it . . . God as it were not satisfy'd with the naming of a help, goes on describing *another self, a second self, a very self it self'* (*YP* 2. 600). *Other self* translates Greek and Latin terms for intimate friends.

453. *earthly* earthly nature. Cp. Dan. 10. 17: 'For how can the servant of this my lord talk with this my lord? for as for me, straightway there remained no strength in me, neither is there breath left in me'.

454. *stood under* been exposed to (*OED* 77b).

460. *Mine eyes he closed* Contrast the open-eyed *trance* at Num. 24. 4: 'He ... saw the vision of the Almighty, falling into a trance, but having his eyes open'.

461. *Fancy* Cp. Adam's account of Fancy's role in dreams (v 102-9).

462. *Abstráct* withdrawn, removed (*OED* 2).

462-82. *methought . . . dream* alluding to M.'s own *Sonnet XIX* ('Methought I saw my late espousèd Saint'), in which the blind poet awakens to *dark*, *loss*, and despair ('I waked, she fled, and day brought back my night'). Adam wakes to behold Eve *Such as I saw her in my dream.*

465. *left side* The Bible does not specify from which side Eve was taken (Gen. 2. 21), but the left was a traditional inference, since that was the side nearest Adam's heart (cp. iv 484). See ii 755 and x 884-8 for the 'sinister' implications.

466. *cordial spirits* vital spirits from the heart.

471-3. *so lovely . . . summed up* Fowler hears an ominous echo of Marino's description of Helen: 'So well does beauty's aggregate / In that fair face summed up unite, / Whatever is fair in all the world / Flowers in her' (*L'Adone* ii 173).

476. *air* mien, look (*OED* 14a), breath (*OED* 9), inspiration (*OED* 10), as in 'a kind of divine ayre informing men of their truth' (1660).

476-7. *inspired / The spirit* including 'breathed the breath'.

481-520. See iv 440-491 for Eve's version of these events.

481. *When out of hope* when I had given up hope.

484. *amiable* lovely.

494. *enviest* give reluctantly (*OED* v 3).

495-9. *Bone . . . soul* Cp. Gen. 2. 23-4: 'And Adam said, This is now bone of my bones, and flesh of my flesh: she shall be called Woman because she was taken out of Man. Therefore shall a man leave his father and his mother, and shall cleave unto his wife: and they shall be one flesh'. M. adds *one heart, one soul* in accordance with his view that marriage is more than a fleshly union. Cp. *Tetrachordon, YP* 2. 605-14.

502. *conscience* internal conviction (*OED* 1a).

504. *obvious* bold, forward (*OED* 2).

*obtrusive forward, unduly prominent (*OED* 2).

508. *she what was honour knew* Cp. Heb. 13. 4: 'Marriage is honourable in all, and the bed undefiled'.

509. *obsequious* compliant with the will of a superior (*OED* 1).

511. *blushing like the Morn* Lewis (124) objects to unfallen Eve's 'female bodily shame' and finds it 'most offensive' that her blush should be 'an incentive to male desire'. But not all blushes signify shame. See line 619. M.'s syntax even leaves open 'some tender possibility . . . that Adam too is blushing' (Christopher Ricks, *Keats and Embarrassment*, 1974, 22).

513. *influence* See iv 669n. Stars will not shed malignant influences until after the Fall. See x 661–4.

514. *gratulation* rejoicing and congratulation. Cp. Homer, *Il.* xiv 347–51, where the *earth* puts forth flowers as Zeus and Hera make love.

515. *gales* winds.

airs breezes and melodies. Cp. iv 264.

518. *amorous bird of night* the nightingale.

519. *ev'ning star* Hesperus (Venus), whose rising was the traditional sign for lighting the *bridal lamp* and bringing the bride to the bridegroom. Cp. xi 588–91, Catullus, *Carmina* lxii and Spenser, *Epithalamion* 286–95.

521. *state* original, flourishing, prosperous condition (*OED* 6a), exalted position (*OED* 16).

526. *vehement* both 'ardent' and 'deprived of the mind' (from Latin *vehe mens*).

530. *Transported* enraptured, but 'transport' could also mean 'banish' (*OED* 2c), so Adam speaks with dramatic irony.

531. *Commotion* mental perturbation, excitement (*OED* 5).

535. *proof* impervious.

sustain withstand (*OED* 8a).

536. *subducting* subtracting.

539. *exact* finished, refined, perfect (*OED* 1).

547. *absolute* complete, perfect (*OED* 4), independent (*OED* 7).

553. *Looses* becomes unstable (*OED* 5), as in: 'the hole frame of the joyntes of his body dissolved and losed' (1526). Many editors modernize to 'loses', but Adam's point is that he goes to pieces even when he wins an argument with Eve.

556. *Occasionally* incidentally (*OED* 2b), on the occasion of Adam's request. Eve was made for Adam, but not as an afterthought.

consúmmate make perfect (*OED* 3).

562. *diffident* mistrustful (*OED* 1).

563–4. *she . . . her* Wisdom.

565–6. *things / Less excellent* Eve is less excellent than Adam (570–75), but her *outside* (568) is also less excellent than her own inner wisdom (578).

569–70. *thy love / Not thy subjection* i.e. 'love her, don't subject yourself to her'. See x 153 and note.

572. **self-esteem OED*'s earliest instance is from 1657, but M. coined the term in *An Apology for Smectymnuus* (1642), where he boasts of his 'honest

haughtinesse, and self-esteem either of what I was, or what I might be'
(*YP* 1. 890).

574. *head* Cp. I Cor. 11. 3: 'the head of the woman is the man'.

576. *adorn adorned (sole adjectival instance in *OED*).

577. *awful* awe-inspiring.

578. *who sees . . . wise* See x 925–7 and xi 163 for instances of Eve's wisdom.
Cp. also Ariosto's view that a woman's intuition is a special gift from
Heaven (*Orl. Fur.* xxvii 1).

583. *divulged* **imparted generally (*OED* 3, sole instance), with overtones
of 'reveal a secret' (love-making as a 'mystery'). See below, 599*n*.

590. *heart enlarges* including 'makes wise'. See i 444*n*.

591. *scale* ladder (the neo-Platonic ladder of love).

598. *genial* nuptial, generative. Cp. iv 712.

599. *mysterious* St Paul describes marriage as 'a great mystery' (Eph. 5.
32), patterned after Christ's union with his Church. Cp. iv 743.

601. *decencies* **decent or becoming acts (*OED* 4).

607. *subject not* do not make me subject to her.

608. *foiled* overcome.

609–10. *from . . . representing* variously represented to me by the senses.

611. *Approve . . . approve* Cp. Ovid's Medea committing herself to evil: 'I
see the better, I approve it too: / The worse I follow' (*Met.* vii 20–21,
trans. Sandys).

617. *virtual* in essence or effect, though not actually (*OED* 4a).

  immediate involving actual contact (*OED* 2a). Virtual love-making would
be limited to *looks*; immediate love-making would include *touch*.

619. *proper* distinctive, morally commendable, comely. M. approved of
both sexes blushing in the context of love. See above, 511*n*. Critics have
disapproved of Raphael's blush, and Waldock (108) mocks it; but Raphael's
blush is 'a delightful touch' (Flannagan), and a natural response to Adam's
embarrassing question.

624. *In eminence* eminently, surpassingly.

626. *Easier . . . embrace* Devils had been thought to mate with women (see
v 446–50*n*), but amorous encounters between angels were rare in angelology.
Editors compare Henry More, *The Immortality of the Soul* (1659), where
angels are 'mutual Spectators of the perfect pulchritude of one anothers
persons' (III ix 4), but this is at best *virtual* rather than *immediate* love-
making. West (172) finds no 'hint' of 'amorous . . . penetration' in More.

628. *restrained conveyance* restricted mode of expression. Raphael might
be thinking of monogamy as well as physical *bars* of *joint* or *limb*. Cp. Mark
12. 25: 'the angels which are in heaven' 'neither marry, nor are given in
marriage'. Cp. M.'s covert allusion to polygamy at iv 762.

631. *green cape* Cape Verde.

  verdant isles the Cape Verde Islands, off West Africa.

632. *Hesperian* in the west (*OED* 1), suggesting also the Hesperian Isles, with which the Cape Verde Islands were sometimes identified.

634–5. *love . . . command* Cp. I John 5. 3: 'this is the love of God, that we keep his commandments'.

637. *admit* permit (*OED* 2a).

639. *persevering* continuing in a state of grace (*OED* 1e).

641. *arbitrament* free choice (*OED* 1).

642. *require* call upon, look for (*OED* 9).

649. *condescension* See above, 9n.

BOOK IX

1–47. The induction to book ix refers to the Muse in the third person (21), but never invokes her. Contrast the invocations at i 1–49 and vii 1–50, and cp. iii 1–55, where M. invokes Light but not the Muse (see iii 19n).

1. *No more of talk* both 'no more talk about conversation' and 'no more conversation'.

2. *familiar* both 'on a family footing' (*OED* 2) and 'familiar (guardian) angel' (*OED* 2d).

5. *Venial* permissible, blameless (*OED* 3). Orgel and Goldberg object that *unblamed* 'would make no sense' if Adam were blameless. They conclude that Adam 'is at fault', though 'not seriously', for his 'inquisitiveness about astronomy'. But *unblamed* is a Latin use of the past participle and means 'unblameable'. Cp. iii 4, iv 493, 987 and *A Masque* 793. M. also plays on Latin *venialis*, 'gracious'.

6. *breach* breaking of a command (*OED* 3) and break-up of friendly relations (*OED* 5b).

9. *distance* including 'aloofness'.

   distaste aversion and disrelish.

13 (and 28). *argument* subject-matter (*OED* 6).

14–15. *wrath . . . Achilles* Homer's subject in the *Iliad* (i 1). See *Il.* xxii 136f. for Achilles' pursuit of Hector.

16–17. *rage / Of Turnus* Turnus, King of the Rutuli, was a suitor of *Lavinia*, daughter of King Latinus. He made war on the Trojans when Latinus gave Lavinia to Aeneas (Virgil, *Aen.* vii).

17. **disespoused* *OED*'s sole instance.

18. *Neptune's ire* Odysseus (*the Greek*) incurred Poseidon's anger when he blinded Poseidon's son, Polyphemus (Homer, *Od.* ix 526–35).

   or Juno's Juno hated Aeneas because his mother Venus (*Cytherea*) had defeated her in the beauty contest judged by Paris (see v 381–2n).

19. *Perplexed* *tormented (*OED* 1b).

20. *answerable* fitting, corresponding.

22. *nightly visitation* See vii 29*n*.

   **unimplored*.

26. *long choosing, and beginning late* See headnote to *PL* (p. 711).

29. *dissect* both 'cut to pieces' and 'anatomize'. Classical and Italian epics give precise details in describing wounds.

33. *races and games* See ii 528–55*n*.

34–7. Turning from the classical epic, M. now rejects medieval romances and Renaissance romance epics.

34. *tilting furniture* accoutrements for jousting.

   **emblazoned* OED*'s earliest participial instance.

35. *Impreses* heraldic devices (often with a motto).

   quaint cunningly designed (*OED* 3), haughty (*OED* 9).

   caparisons ornamental coverings (or armour) for horses.

36. *Bases* cloth coverings for horses (*OED* sb³ 1).

   tinsel trappings Spenser equips the horses of Duessa (*FQ* I ii 13) and Florimell (*FQ* III i 15) with 'tinsell trappings'.

37. **marshalled feast* a feast with the guests placed at table according to rank (*OED* 'marshal' 2). *OED*'s earliest participial instance.

38. *sewers* attendants at a feast who supervised the seating of the guests. *seneschals* stewards.

39. *artifice* *mechanic art, artificer's work (*OED* 1b).

43. *raise* both 'evoke' and 'raise to a new level'.

44. *That name* of epic.

   age too late In his poem *Naturam non pati senium* M. had argued against the theory that the world is decaying, but in *RCG* he fears that something 'advers in our climat, or the fate of the age' might inhibit the epic poet (*YP* 1. 814).

44–5. *cold / Climate* Aristotle had said that cold climates dull intelligence (*Politics* VII vii 1) and the idea troubles M. in *Mansus* 24–9, *RCG* and *Of Education* (*YP* 1. 814, 2. 383).

45. *years* M. was fifty-eight in 1667.

   damp stupefy, benumb (*OED* 2) and dampen (*cold Climate*).

   intended both 'purposed' and 'outstretched' (*wing*).

46. *Depressed* lowered (*wing*) and dejected (spirits).

49. *Hesperus* Venus, the evening star.

54. *improved* augmented, made worse (*OED* 4).

56. *maugre* despite.

63. *seven continued nights* Satan experiences a week of darkness by flying in the earth's shadow, thus eluding the eye of Uriel in *the sun* (60). But M. nods when he places Satan in darkness *From pole to pole*. Earth's poles were in perpetual daylight before the Fall (x 680–87). Fowler sees a 'deliberate prolepsis' as Satan describes 'a fallen world', but even in the fallen world darkness extends only to one pole at a time.

65. *car of Night* the earth's shadow (conceived as the chariot of Nox, goddess of night).

66. *colure* one of two great circles intersecting at right angles at the poles and dividing the equinoctial circle into four equal segments.

67. *coast averse* side turned away. The sentries are stationed in the east of Paradise (iv 542); Satan enters from the north (iv 223).

77. *Pontus* the Black Sea.

78. *Maeotis* the Sea of Azov. The *river Ob* flows from Siberia into the Arctic Ocean.

80. *Orontes* a river in Syria.

  ocean barred God sets 'bars and doors' for the sea at Job 38. 10.

81. *Darien* Panama.

87. *irresolute* undecided.

89. *Fit vessel* Cp. Rom. 9. 22: 'What if God, willing to shew his wrath, and to make his power known, endured with much longsuffering the vessels of wrath fitted to destruction'. See also Acts 9. 15, and II Tim. 2. 21.

89. *imp* child of the Devil (*OED* 4a), evil spirit (*OED* 4b).

90. *suggestions* temptations.

95. *Doubt* suspicion.

104–5. *officious . . . for thee alone* Contrast Raphael's words at viii 98–9: 'Yet not to earth are those bright luminaries / Officious, but to thee earth's habitant'.

107–8. *God . . . extends to all* Fowler compares the Renaissance commonplace that 'God is an infinite sphere, whose centre is everywhere, whose circumference nowhere'. Cp. vii 170.

110. *Not . . . appears* Contrast iii 606–12 where the sun's 'elixir pure' arises from its own 'rivers', 'fields and regions'. See also iii 565–71, viii 148–58.

112. *gradual* gradated, in steps.

113. *growth, sense, reason* the vegetable, animal, and rational souls (see v 484–5).

118. *Rocks, dens, and caves* Satan's celebration of the earth's beauty carries a melancholy echo from Hell: 'Rocks, caves, lakes, fens, bogs, dens, and shades of death' (ii 621).

120–1. *siege / Of contraries* Satan is besieged by *Pleasures* which throw his *Torment* into acute contrast. Thus M. inverts the allegorical siege, in which it was 'Satan, with pleasure as his ally, who beleaguered the human soul' (Fowler). One such allegorical siege is found in Spenser, *FQ* II xi 6, where Maleger besieges the castle of Alma with various pleasures, deploying them 'Where each might . . . his contrary obiect most deface' (*FQ* II xi 6).

123. *Bane* poison, destruction, woe.

144. *to repair his numbers* God does create us to 'repair' a 'detriment' (vii 152–3), but Satan does not constrain our *numbers*. See iii 289 and vii 150–56*n*.

145. *virtue* power.

148–9. *into our room . . . earth* So Tasso's Satan despises 'Vile man, begot of clay, and born of dust' who will possess Heaven 'in our place' (*Gerus. Lib.* iv 10), trans. Fairfax (1600).

150. *original* origin.

151. *spoils* Satan means 'spoils of war', but Fowler notes a secondary meaning whereby he 'unwittingly prophesies' the Incarnation. Exalted human nature was 'often referred to as "spoil"'. The context evokes a third meaning: 'skin of a snake' (*OED* 6). Man's 'spoil' is exalted, Satan's debased.

156. *flaming ministers* Cp. Ps. 104. 4 ('his . . . ministers a flaming fire') and Heb. 1. 14 ('Are they not all ministering spirits?').

164. *Gods* Most modernizing editors read 'gods' (angels), but Satan is more likely referring to the Father and the Son, for it is they who *sit the highest*. Cp. Lucifer's words at Isa. 14. 13–14: 'I will sit also upon the mount of the congregation . . . I will be like the most High'.

  constrained compressed, forced, imprisoned (*OED* 7, 1, 8).

166. *incarnate* the Satanic counterpart to the Messiah's Incarnation.

170. *obnoxious* exposed, liable to punishment (*OED* 1a, 2). Satan is also 'injurious' (*OED* 5) to the serpent, whom he makes noxious or *nocent* (186).

172–4. *recoils . . . well aimed . . . fall short* Cp. the 'devilish engine' that 'recoils' on Satan at iv 17.

173. *reck* care.

174. *higher I fall short* 'I fall short when I aim higher'.

176. *despite* both (God's) 'spite' (*OED* 4) and (Satan's) 'contempt' (*OED* 1).

180. *black mist low creeping* Cp. Lucretius's description of a spreading plague (*De Rerum Nat.* vi 1120–21): *aer inimicus serpere coepit, / ut nebula ac nubes paulatim repit* ('the baleful air begins to creep, and glides like mist or cloud'). The connection with Satan is fortified by *inimicus* and *serpere*. Cp. x 695, where postlapsarian exhalations are 'pestilent'.

183. *labyrinth* home of the monstrous Minotaur.

186. *Nor*] *Ed II*; Not *Ed I*.

  nocent both 'harmful' and 'guilty' (*OED* 1, 2), the opposite of 'innocent'.

188. *brutal* animal.

191. *close* concealed, confined, stifled.

197. *grateful* pleasing, and full of gratitude.

198–9. *choir . . . wanting voice* the musical silence of Paradise. Cp. iv 600–604.

200. *airs* breezes and melodies.

204. *Eve . . . began* Eve has never before spoken *first*. Her plain *Adam* (205) is also unprecedented.

205. *still* continually.

209. *Luxurious* luxuriant (*OED* 4), but the pejorative sense (cp. i 498, 722, xi 711, 784) adds an ominous overtone taken up by *wanton* (211).

213. *hear*] *Ed I*; bear *Ed II*.

216–17. *direct . . . where to climb* i.e. around the masculine elm. In her new spirit of independence, Eve speaks dismissively about an emblem of wifely dependence. Contrast v 215–16 where she and Adam 'led the vine / To wed her elm'.

218. *spring* grove of young trees.

219. *redress* set upright (*OED* 1a).

227. *Sole . . . sole* Unrivalled . . . only. The same pun as at iv 411, but here the context also suggests 'unaccompanied by another' (*OED* 2a), so *associate sole* is an oxymoron.

229. *motioned* proposed.

249. *solitude . . . society* See viii 427–8n.

265. *Or* whether.

270. *virgin majesty* Puritans extended the term 'virginity' to marriage. Philip Stuubes in *Anatomie of Abuses* (1583) calls marriage 'pure virginitie' (sig. G8).

272. *composure* *calmness, collectedness. The extant sense (*OED* 11). Earlier senses included 'temperament' (*OED* 6c) and 'posture, pose' (*OED* 7).

275–6. *by thee informed . . . overheard* Eve had been 'attentive' to all of Raphael's story about Satan (vii 51), so it is odd that she should now speak as if she had heard only his *parting* words – especially since Raphael did not mention Satan at viii 630–43. Raphael's final warning (*overheard* by Eve?) was about Adam's passion for Eve. Gagen argues that M. is inconsistent about how much Eve heard (*MQ* 20, March 1986, 17–22). See also vi 909n.

292. *entire* unblemished, blameless (*OED* 8).

293. *diffident* mistrustful.

296. *asperses* bespatters, vilifies.

310. *Accéss* increase.

318. *domestic* concerned for his family.

320. *Less* too little.

322–41. *If this . . . exposed* Cp. M.'s *Areopagitica*: 'I cannot praise a fugitive and cloister'd vertue, unexercis'd & unbreath'd, that never sallies out and sees her adversary' (*YP* 2. 515). Eve anticipates *Areopagitica*, but M. had never intended his argument to apply to the unfallen state, but to the 'state of man' as it 'now is' (*YP* 2. 514).

325. *like* equal (to each other and to Satan's attack).

326. *still* always.

328. *affronts* both 'insults' and 'confronts face to face' (*OED* 7). *Front* (330) means 'face'.

329. *integrity* sinlessness (*OED* 3). Eve herself is breaking integrity in the sense 'undivided state' (*OED* 1).

334. *event* outcome.

335. *what is . . . virtue* Cp. *Areopagitica*: 'what were vertue but a name?' (*YP* 2. 527).

341. *no Eden* including 'no pleasure'. See iv 27*n*.

343. *O woman* Adam gently reminds Eve of his authority: 'she shall be called Woman, because she was taken out of Man' (Gen. 2. 23, cp. viii 496–7).

353. *still erect* always alert (*OED* 'erect' 3), and suggesting man's 'Godlike erect' posture, sign of *reason* (vii 508).

358. *mind . . . mind* remind . . . pay heed to. Perhaps also *take care of (*OED* 11a, cited from 1694).

359. *subsist* stand firm (*OED* 7).

361. *specious* deceptively attractive (*OED* 2). There may be a pun on 'species' (which is etymologically related).

suborned procured in an underhand manner (*OED* 3).

367. *approve* prove.

371. *securer* more careless, overconfident.

386. *light* light-footed, with overtones of 'fickle, ready of belief' (*OED* 16), 'wanton' (*OED* 14b) and 'frivolous' (*OED* 14a), as in 'A sober grave matron . . . will never be light' (1631).

387. *Oread or Dryad* mountain- or wood-nymph. Oreads were mortal and Dryads 'perished with the trees over which they presided' (Fowler).

Delia Diana (who was born on Delos).

388. *Betook her to the groves* a prolepsis, since 'groves' in the O.T. are associated with idolatry. See i 403*n* and cp. *PR* ii 289.

388–9. *Delia's self / In gait surpassed* Porter (111) sees a 'strong allusion' to the ill-fated Dido, whom Virgil likens to Diana leading her Oreads out to the hunt (*Aen.* i 500–501): 'she carries her quiver on her shoulder and, stepping along, surpasses those goddesses' (*gradiensque deas supereminet*). See also below, 783*n*, 1000–1001*n*.

392. *Guiltless* *having no experience of (*OED* 3). Adam discovers fire only after the Fall (x 1070–80), and it is associated with guilt in the Prometheus story (iv 715–19).

393. *Pales* goddess of flocks and pastures.

Pomona goddess of fruit-trees. The wood-god *Vertumnus* wooed her, changing his shape in order to seduce her. Ovid makes her a nymph and says that she surrendered with 'answering passion' (*Met.* xiv 623–771).

394. *Likeliest*] *Ed II*; Likest *Ed I*. *Likeliest* is preferable because 'likely' includes 'seemly, becoming, appropriate' (*OED* 6) as well as 'resembling' (*OED* 1). *Likeliest* might also imply that Eve 'is likely to get in trouble' (Adams 84). Cp. 'where likeliest he might find' (ix 414).

395. *prime* prime of youth, springtime, and first age of the world (*OED* 6b). Autumn and winter were unknown until *Ceres* lost *Proserpina*. See iv 269–72*n*.

404–5. *O much . . . return* Direct address of a character is a Homeric formula. Cp. *Il.* xvi 787: 'there, Patroklos, the end of your life was shown forth'. Martin Mueller, *CLS* 6 (1969), 292–316 (302), argues that M. has modelled Adam and Eve's parting on that of Achilles and Patroclus. Patroclus entreated 'his own death' when he asked to enter the battle wearing Achilles' armour. Achilles prayed in vain for Patroclus's safe return (Homer, *Il.* xvi 47, 246–52).

405. *event perverse* unexpected outcome (Latin *perversus*, 'turned the wrong way'). Cp. *SA* 737: 'perverse event'.

413. *Mere* entirely and only.

425. **fragrance* The older form was 'fragrancy'.

431. *mindless* heedless.

432. *Herself . . . flow'r* echoing iv 270 ('Herself a fairer flow'r'). For Eve as Proserpine, see iv 269–72n and below, 838–42n, and cp. ix 395.

436. *voluble* gliding, undulating (*OED* 3), with proleptic overtones of 'glib, fluent' (*OED* 5a).

437. *arborets* shrubs, small trees.

438. *hand* handiwork.

440. *Adonis* a hunter loved by Venus. After he was killed by a boar, Jupiter (or Proserpine) *revived* him at Venus's request and he spent half the year with Venus and half with Proserpine. Since ancient times, small plots of fast-fading flowers had been called 'gardens of Adonis'. Spenser's Garden of Adonis is a paradise of perpetual spring, but even it is subject to mortality (*FQ* III vi 39–42).

441. *Laertes' son* Odysseus, who visits the miraculous gardens of Alcinous in Homer, *Od.* vii 112–35.

442. *mystic* allegorical (*OED* 1), perhaps also 'mythical'.

sapient king Solomon.

443. *Egyptian spouse* Solomon married Pharaoh's daughter (I Kings 3. 1). See Song of Sol. 6. 2 for his garden.

446. *annoy* *make noisome (not in *OED*, but 'annoy' and 'noisome' are etymologically related).

450. **tedded* spread out to dry (as hay).

kine cows.

453. *for* because of.

456. *plat* plot of ground.

459–66. *Her graceful . . . revenge* Cp. the effect of the Lady's chastity and beauty on Comus (*A Masque* 244–65).

461. *rapine* like 'rapture' and 'rape', from Latin *rapere*, 'to seize'. The would-be ravisher (393–411) is ravished.

463. *abstracted* drawn off, removed from (*OED* 1).

465. *Stupidly* *in consequence of stupefaction (*OED* 1b), but the modern sense existed (cp. xii 116) and M. might play on it to suggest that Satan is incapable of any positive good. When 'the Arch-Enemy' is *of enmity disarmed* he loses the only identity he has.

471. *recollects* remembers and summons by effort.

472. *gratulating* greeting (*OED* 1), with *thoughts* as object.

474. *transported* both 'entranced' and 'conveyed' (*hither brought us*). Cp. iii 81: 'what rage / Transports our Adversary'.

480. *Occasion* opportunity.

481. *opportune* conveniently exposed to attack (*OED* 4).

484. *haughty* of exalted courage (*OED* 4).

485. *mould* bodily form (*OED* sb³ 10b) and earth regarded as the material of the human body (*OED* sb¹ 4).

486. **informidable* Cp. the neologism 'undesirable' (ix 824), which also occurs in a litotes.

488. *to* in comparison with.

490. *terror be in love* Cp. Song of Sol. 6. 4: 'Thou art beautiful, O my love . . . Terrible as an army with banners'. Cp. also *PR* ii 160.

496. *indented* zigzagged.

500. *carbuncle* any red stone, esp. 'a mythical gem said to emit a light in the dark' (*OED*).

501. *erect* upright and alert (*OED* 3). Some biblical exegetes argued that the serpent went upright until God cursed it; others argued that it 'assumed an upright posture only while being used as an instrument by Satan' (Fowler). *As since* (497) favours the former view, but Satan's erectness still implies a novel self-awareness and phallic potency.

502. *spires* coils of a serpent (*OED* 1a).

503. *redundant* *in swelling waves (*OED* 3a) and *copious, plentiful (*OED* 2, citing *SA* 568 as earliest instance).

506. *Cadmus* the legendary founder of Thebes. He was changed into a serpent when he went to *Illyria* in his old age. His wife Harmonia (*Hermione*) became a serpent when she caressed his metamorphosed body (Ovid, *Met.* iv 563f.).

506–7. *god . . . Epidaurus* Aesculapius, god of healing, had a temple in Epidaurus from which he travelled in serpent form to end a plague in Rome (Ovid, *Met.* xv 622–744). Like Satan, he was erect (674), crested (669), and glided fold above fold (721).

508. *Ammonian Jove* Plutarch relates that Philip II of Macedon found his wife *Olympias* in bed with a serpent. The Delphic oracle identifed the serpent as Zeus-Ammon (*Alexander* 2). The historical Olympias did keep pet snakes in her bed – a hazard 'calculated to put even the toughest bridegroom off his stroke' (Peter Green, *Alexander of Macedon, 356–323 BC: a Historical Biography*, 1991, 30).

508–10. *Capitoline . . . Rome* Livy and others relate that Jupiter Capitolinus took serpent form to father Scipio Africanus, who defeated Hannibal.

510–14. Paul J. Klemp (*MQ* 11, 1977, 91–2) sees a deliberate acrostic S-A-T-A-N working in the same *sidelong* manner as the hidden tempter. Satan's name does not appear elsewhere in the temptation. Cp. the possible acrostic M-A-R-S in Virgil, *Aen.* vii 601–4.

510. *tract* course.

513–15. *a ship . . . sail* Cp. the earlier nautical similes with Satan as tenor (ii 636–42, 1043–4, iv 159–65).

517. *wanton* sportive (*OED* 3c), with proleptic overtones of the fallen sense. See Ricks, *Milton's Grand Style*, 112.

522. *Circean . . . disguised* The witch Circe changed men into animals, who fawned on Odysseus's crew like dogs on their master (Homer, *Od.* x 212–19).

525. *enamelled* variegated in colour.

530. *Organic* serving as an organ or instrument (*OED* 1).

impúlse Both 'impelling' (of *air*) and 'suggestion from an evil spirit' (*OED* 3a).

532. *Wonder not* Satan's entreaty not to marvel 'is calculated to produce precisely the opposite effect' (Steadman 108).

536. *I thus single* Satan's apology for coming alone prepares for his dismissal of Adam: *one man . . . what is one?* (545–6).

549. *glozed* fawned, talked smoothly and speciously (*OED* v¹ 3).

proem prefatory part of a speech.

553–4. *What . . . expressed?* M.'s Eve is shrewder than her biblical counterpart, who shows no surprise at hearing a serpent speak. Some exegetes blamed Eve for her lack of surprise. Fish (254) blames M.'s Eve for being surprised. M. recognizes that Eve's surprise is only natural, and ethically neutral.

558. *demur* hesitate about.

563. *speakable* *able to speak (*OED* 2).

576. *A goodly tree* Satan does not at first name the tree and so allows Eve to hope that it might not be the forbidden one.

579. *savoury* See v 84*n*.

580. *Grateful* pleasing.

581. *fennel . . . teats* Fennel and milk sucked from animals' teats were popularly supposed to be the favourite food of serpents.

582. *ewe* Le Comte (80) hears a pun on 'you'. Incubi (lustful demons) were thought to suck animals' *teats* and women's breasts. See Harry Blamires, *Milton's Creation: a Guide through 'Paradise Lost'* (1971) 225.

586. *defer* delay.

584–99. *To satisfy . . . Strange alteration* Satan's most cunning lie (and M.'s most significant addition to Genesis) is to have the serpent claim that it can speak because it ate the fruit. There were rabbinic versions in which the serpent ate the fruit in front of Eve to reassure her that it was safe to do so, but the serpent in these versions did not claim to have acquired knowledge by eating. Evans (276-7) cites Joseph Beaumont's *Psyche* (1648) as the sole precedent.

585. *apples* Satan alone speaks of 'apples' in *PL*. The good characters always refer to 'fruit', which includes 'consequences'.

601. *Wanted* were lacking.

605. *middle* the air between.

612. *universal dame* mistress of the universe.

613. *spirited* including *possessed by an evil spirit (*OED* 4).

616. *virtue* efficacy.
  proved tested.

623. *their provision* what is provided for them.

624. *her bearth* what she bears. The spelling (*Ed I*, *Ed II*) was unusual even in M.'s time.

625. *adder* any serpent (*OED* 1). Satan was often called 'the adder' in medieval times.

629. *blowing* blooming.

632. *made*] *Ed II*; make *Ed I*.

634-42. *wand'ring fire . . . lost* Cp. *A Masque* 205-9, 433, and the earlier bog similes in *PL* (ii 592-4, 939-40).

635. *Compact . . . vapour* composed of oily gas. Milton gives a scientific explanation for the *ignis fatuus*, or will-o'-the-wisp, before turning to the supernatural.

637. *agitation* friction (of gases) and (evil Spirit's) scheming (*OED* 6), as in 'crafty and subtill agitations' (1606).

640. *amazed* including 'led through a maze'. Cp. Shakespeare, *A Midsummer Night's Dream* II i 39: 'Mislead night-wanderers, laughing at their harm'.

642. *swallowed up and lost* echoing Belial: 'swallowed up and lost / In the wide womb of uncreated Night' (ii 149-50).

643. *fraud* *state of being defrauded (*OED* 5) – a passive usage unique to M., from Latin *fraus*. Cp. vii 143, *PR* i 372.

644-5. *tree / Of prohibition* both 'prohibited tree' and 'tree of *all* prohibition' (Ricks, *Milton's Grand Style*, 76).

645. *root* the same silent pun as at ii 383.

648. *Fruitless . . . excess* See Ricks, *Milton's Grand Style*, 73 on the 'jaunty levity' of Eve's pun on *Fruitless*. M.'s voice behind Eve puns on *excess* as 'violation of law', 'intemperance in eating' and 'unrestrained grief' (*OED* 4a, 5b, 2). Cp. xi 111: 'Bewailing their excess'.

653. *daughter of his voice* a Hebraism, *Bath Kol*, 'daughter of a voice'. Hunter (23) cites sources showing that *Bath Kol* (or *filia vocis*) was an inferior form of revelation, lacking real authority. Thus Eve understates the command, which had come from God's own voice and resounded dreadfully in Adam's (but not Eve's) ear (viii 335).

654. *Law to ourselves* Cp. St Paul on the virtuous Gentiles who 'are a law unto themselves' (Rom. 2. 14).

668. *Fluctuates* moves like a wave (*OED* 1).

act including Latin *actio*, an orator's exterior bearing.

669. *Raised* both in posture and rhetoric.

673. *in himself collected* both mentally and physically (the serpent's coils).
part both 'dramatic role' and 'part of the body'

674. *Motion* gesture, mime, with overtones of 'puppet show' (*OED* 13a).
audience attention.

675. *in heighth* the high, impassioned style usually reserved for the climax of an oration.

677. *to heighth *upgrown* both 'standing upright' and 'elevated in rhetorical style'.

680. *science* knowledge.

683–7. *highest agents . . . the Threat'ner* The serpent begins to avoid naming 'God'.

687. *To* both 'in addition to' and 'eventuating in'.

692. *incense* excite, kindle (*OED* v² 2).

694. *virtue* courage (*OED* 7), which Satan identifies with moral virtue.

695. *denounced* threatened.

whatever thing death be Satan had learned about death at ii 781–816. He now feigns innocence. Cp. Adam's 'whate'er death is' (iv 425), but even Adam knew death to be 'Some dreadful thing'.

698–9. *if what is evil / Be real* Many theologians had argued that evil is a privation of good, and so has no real existence. Satan perverts this doctrine into the easy inference that evil is nothing to worry about. He also hints that if evil is real, it must have been created by a malevolent God.

701. *Not just, not God* Satan's final naming of 'God' argues him out of existence. Henceforward he will speak of 'gods' (708–25).

713–14. *putting off . . . gods* Satan perverts a biblical metaphor. See e.g. Col. 3. 9–10: 'ye have put off the old man with his deeds; And have put on the new man'.

717. *participating* partaking of.

722. *they all* i.e. they produce all.

729–30. *can envy dwell / In Heav'nly breasts* echoing Virgil on Juno's anger: *tantaene animis caelestibus irae?* (*Aen*. i 11). Raphael had echoed the same line when describing the devils' desperate resistance in battle (vi 788).

732. *humane* both 'human' and 'benevolent' (the spellings were not yet distinguished). The oxymoron 'human goddess' looks back to 'human gods' (712).

739. *noon* Eve had promised Adam that she would 'be returned by noon' (401).

741. *savoury* See v 84n.

742. *Inclinable* disposed (modifying *desire*) and bending down (modifying *fruit*). Fowler rules out the latter sense, but cp. iv 332 and viii 308. Cp. also Spenser, *FQ* II xii 54 and Marvell, 'The Garden' (printed 1681) 33–40.

754. *infers* implies.

the good Eve omits 'evil', yet evil is what the tree will bring. See below, 1072*n*.

755. *communicated* See v 72*n*.

want lack.

758. *In plain* in plain words.

761. **after-bands* subsequent bonds.

770. *envies* begrudges.

771. *author* authority, informant (*OED* 4).

unsuspect above suspicion.

776. *cure of all* Eve means 'remedy', but M. puns on Latin *cura*, 'grief'. Cp. 'all our woe' (i 3, ix 645).

781. *ate*] eat *Ed I*, *Ed II* (past tense, pronounced 'et').

783. *signs of woe* Porter (112) sees an allusion to Virgil, *Aen.* iv 165–70, where earth gave a sign (*signum*) of woe at the moment of Dido's 'fall': 'Primal Earth and nuptial Juno gave the sign; lightning flashed and Heaven was witness to the marriage, and nymphs howled on the mountain-top. That was the first day of death, the first cause of woe.'

792. *knew not eating death* The syntax includes: 'she did not experience death while she ate', 'she did not know that she was eating death', 'she did not acquire knowledge while she ate death', and 'she did not know death, which devours' (Latin *mors edax*).

793. *boon* jolly, jovial.

795. *virtuous, precious* most powerful, most precious (Greek and Latin idiom: the positive for the superlative).

797. *sapience* both 'knowledge' and 'tasting' (Latin *sapere*). Cp. Adam's pun at ix 1018.

infamed slandered.

800. *each morning . . . due praise* Eve now offers the tree the kind of morning hymn she had once offered God (v 153–208).

804. *gods* Editors infer that Eve means 'God' and that she has picked up the plural from Satan (712, 716). But Eve's gods might be 'angels' (cp. v 70), whom she distinguishes from unspecified *others* (the Father and Son).

810–11. *secret . . . secret* uncommunicative (*OED* 2a) . . . hidden. Rather than face the disappointing fact that wisdom is still uncommunicative, Eve takes comfort in the thought that her own doings might be hidden from God. Cp. Ps. 10. 11: 'He [the wicked man] hath said in his heart, God hath forgotten: / He hideth his face; he will never see it'.

815. *safe* both 'not endangered' and 'not at present dangerous'.

820. *odds* equalizing allowance (*OED* 4c), advantage (*OED* 4b).

821. *copartner* both 'sharer' and 'equal' (*OED* 3), as in 'Without a Co-Partner, or any Parallel' (1660).

wants is lacking.

824. **undesirable* See above, 486*n*.

827. *I shall be no more* A new concept for Eve, who had had no notion of death as annihilation at iv 425 or ix 695. The fruit has brought her some kind of knowledge.

832. *all deaths* Eve is being hyperbolical, but her plural has ominous resonances. The 'second death' was a theological term for damnation. M. in *CD* i 11–13 distinguishes four deaths: guiltiness, spiritual death, extinction of body and soul, and final damnation. Cp. x 770–844.

835. *low reverence* deep bow.

837. *sciential* granting knowledge.

sap including a pun on Latin *sapere*, 'to know'. See above, 797*n*.

838–42. *Adam . . . harvest queen* Cp. Claudian's Proserpina in Enna: 'she made a flower crown and put it on her brow, / but she did not see this grim prophecy of marriage' (*De Rapt. Pros.* ii 142–3). Cp. also the *garland* worn by Pandora when she comes to Epimetheus full of 'Lies and persuasive words and cunning ways' (Hesiod, *WD* 79). Bush compares Andromache embroidering flowers for Hector, unaware that he is dead (Homer, *Il.* xxii 437f.). See below, 892–3*n*.

845. *divine of* divining (with proleptic overtones of 'divinity', cp. ix 1010). *Misgave him* with proleptic overtones of 'bestow amiss' (*OED* 3). Cp. 'She gave him' (ix 996).

846. *falt'ring measure* Adam's heartbeat; also the 'measured motion' of 'unsteady Nature' (*Arcades* 70–74), which has just been thrown out of rhythm (782–4). *Ed I* and *Ed II* punningly spell 'fault'ring'.

852. *ambrosial* *fragrant (*OED* 1c), and recalling 'nectar, drink of gods' (line 838).

854. *apology* justification (not regret).

855. *bland* mildly coaxing (*OED* 1), flattering (Latin *blandus*).

864–5. *nor to evil unknown / Op'ning the way* i.e. 'this tree does not open the way to evil, which remains unknown', but Eve's syntax admits the opposite meaning: 'this tree is known to evil, to which it opens the way'.

868. *Or . . . or* either . . . or.

876. *erst* formerly.

887. *distemper* disordered state arising from disturbance of bodily humours, intoxication (*OED* 4, 4d).

890. *Astonied* stunned, paralysed (with a pun on 'as stone').

blank discomfited, deprived of speech, resourceless (*OED* 5) and pale (*OED* 1).

892–3. *From his slack hand . . . dropped* Cp. Homer, *Il.* xxii 448, where

Andromache hears the sound of mourning and realizes that Hector is dead: 'her limbs spun, and the shuttle dropped from her hand to the ground'. Cp. also Statius, *Thebaid* vii 148–50, where Bacchus, fearing the destruction of Thebes, drops his thyrsus, and unspoiled grapes fall from his garlanded head.

893. *faded roses* 'The first instance of decay in Paradise' (Fowler), but cp. the 'show'red roses' at iv 773.

901. *deflow'red* Cp. Eve as 'unsupported flow'r' (ix 432). Her temptation has also been presented as a sexual seduction (ix 386–96).

devote doomed (*OED* 'devoted' 3). Porter (111) compares Dido, *pesti devota futurae*, 'doomed to impending ruin' (Virgil, *Aen.* i 712).

905. *unknown* modifies *fraud*, not *Enemy*. Adam knows that Satan beguiled Eve, but he doesn't yet know how he did it. Cp. ix 1172, where Adam clearly knows who 'the lurking enemy' was. Adam has always referred to Satan as 'the Enemy'.

906–7. *with thee . . . to die* Waldock (52) and Empson (189) applaud Adam's decision as springing from 'protectiveness' and 'true love', but Adam chooses to die *with* Eve, for his own sake. He does not die for her. Cp. Eve's selfless offer at x 930–36.

919. *what seemed remédiless* Lewis (123) takes *seemed* to imply that Adam might have found a remedy, and Burden (168) infers that 'the remedy is divorce'. Other critics suggest that Adam, like the Son, might have risked himself to save Eve. See Fish (261–72), Danielson[2] (121–4), and Leonard (213–32).

922. *hath*] *Ed II*; *hast Ed I*. *Hast* goes better with line 921, but Adam might shift to a more general thought so as not to confront Eve's particular case.

923–5. *to eye . . . touch* Gen. 3. 3 and *PL* vii 46 confirm the *ban* on *touch*, but Adam's claim that it was perilous even to look at the fruit is nowhere supported.

924. *sacred* *set apart, exclusively appropriated (*OED* 2b), with overtones of 'consecrated', 'entitled to veneration' (*OED* 3b). Adam is making an idol of the fruit.

928. *fact* both 'crime' (*OED* 1c) and 'a thing done' (*OED* 1a).

946–50. *loath . . . next* Cp. the Son's plea at iii 156–64.

947. *Adversary* Satan. Adam still refers to him as *the Foe* (951), but now fails to pursue his earlier insight that serpent and 'enemy' are one and the same (see above, 905*n*).

953. *Certain* resolved.

954. *death is to me as life* Cp. Satan's 'Evil be thou my good' (iv 110), but Adam (who did not understand death at iv 425) might not see the paradox. He intends a witty play on *life* as the meaning of Eve's name: 'if death consort with you, then death is to me like Eve'. By *Consort* Adam means 'associate', but the sense 'have sexual commerce with' (*OED* 2) is grimly appropriate to the lustful Death of book ii.

959. *to lose thee were to lose myself* The *Ed I* and *Ed II* spelling 'loose' could indicate 'lose' or 'loose'. *Bond* (956) invites a pun, but the implications are ambiguous. 'Loose' could mean 'set free' (*OED* 1b), 'redeem' (*OED* 10), or 'dissolve, do away with' (*OED* 7a).

961. *O . . . love* Cp. iii 410 ('O unexampled love').

973. *good . . . good* Eve still omits 'evil' from the name 'Tree of Knowledge of good and evil'. Cp. lines 754–9, 864–5.

980. *oblige* make liable to a penalty.

  fact crime, deed.

984. *event* outcome.

994–5. *recompense . . . recompense* compensation for a loss . . . retribution for an offence (*OED* 2, 5). Cp. Adam's bitter cry at 1163: 'Is this the love, is this the recompense?'

994. *compliance* unworthy submission (*OED* 6b).

998. *not deceived* Cp. I Tim. 2. 14: 'Adam was not deceived'.

1000–1001. *Earth . . . second groan* Cp. earth's groan at the 'fall' of Dido and Aeneas (Virgil, *Aen.* iv 165–70). See above, 783*n*. Cp. also the mournful groan (*gemitus lacrimabilis*) that comes from beneath the tree plucked by Aeneas at *Aen.* iii 39.

1003–4. *sin / Original* the theological doctrine that all of Adam's descendants 'committed sin in Adam' (*CD* i 12, *YP* 6. 395, trans. Carey). Cp. x 729f.

1016. *dalliance* amorous toying (*OED* 2). Contrast the innocent 'youthful dalliance' of iv 338.

1018. *sapience* wisdom and taste. See above, 797*n*.

1019. *each meaning savour* tastiness (*OED* 1b) and understanding (*OED* 5). Cp. v 84.

  we] *Ed I*; me *Ed II*.

1021. *purveyed* provided food.

1026. *forbidden ten* proleptic of the Ten Commandments.

1027. *play* have sex (*OED* 10c).

1028. *meet* appropriate, with a pun on 'meat' ('human body regarded as an instrument of sexual pleasure', *OED* 3e, cited from 1595). Contrast Eve as a 'help meet' (Gen. 2. 21) and unfallen Adam's judging 'of fit and meet' (viii 448).

1029–32. *For never . . . now* echoing Zeus's amorous invitation to Hera (Homer, *Il.* xiv 314–16) and Paris's to Helen (*Il.* iii 442): 'Never before as now has passion enmeshed my senses'. Zeus and Hera make love on a bed of flowers (including *hyacinth*, *Il.* xiv 346–51), and Zeus falls asleep when *wearied*.

1030–31. *adorned / With all perfections* Flannagan hears a pun on 'Pandora', 'all gifts'. Cp. iv 714–15.

1034. *toy* light caress (*OED* 1).

1037. *a shady bank* Before the Fall Adam and Eve had made love in their bower at night-time (see iv 741). Now they do it anywhere, at any time.

1042-4. *their fill . . . solace* Cp. Prov. 7. 18, where a woman 'with the attire of an harlot' accosts a youth: 'Come, let us take our fill of love until the morning: let us solace ourselves with loves'. Contrast the 'solace' of marriage before the Fall (iv 486, viii 419, ix 844).

1043. *seal* a legal metaphor enlivened by a bawdy pun. Cp. Donne, 'Elegy 19': 'To enter in these bonds, is to be free; / Then where my hand is set, my seal shall be' (32-3).

1047. *bland* *pleasing to the senses (*OED* 2). Contrast the 'temperate vapours bland' that before the Fall bred 'airy light', not *grosser*, sleep (v 5).

1050. *unkindly* unnatural.

   conscious guilty (*OED* 4b).

1058. *he* i.e. Shame (who is personified, see line 1097).

1059. *Danite* Samson was of the tribe of Dan (Judges 13. 2). M. in *SA* takes *Dalila* (Delilah) to be Samson's wife, not a *harlot*.

1062. *they* M. likens both Adam and Eve to Samson. Eve is not Adam's Dalila.

1067. *Eve . . . evil* Adam's pun is *constrained* (1066), 'forced as opposed to natural' (*OED* 2). 'Eve' means 'life', and Adam will reaffirm this meaning at xi 159-61.

1068. *of whomsoever taught* Having suppressed his recognition of Satan (see above, 905*n*), Adam is now genuinely ignorant. But recognition is still within his grasp. See ix 1172-3.

1072. *good lost, and evil got* M. follows most commentators in deriving the tree's name from the event. Cp. iv 222, 774-5, xi 84-9 and *CD* i 10: 'since it was tasted, not only do we know evil, but also we do not even know good except through evil' (trans. Carey, *YP* 6. 352-3).

1078. *evil store* evil in abundance.

1079. *the first* the evil that caused the *shame*.

1083. *this earthly* earthly nature. Cp. viii 453.

1087. *umbrage* shadow, foliage, protective screen (*OED* 1, 2c, 5) and false show (*OED* 6), as in 'Truth will appear from under all the false glosses and umbrages that men may draw over it' (1693). Notice *Hide me*.

1091. *plight* including 'offence, sin' (*OED* sb^1 2) and 'pleat', 'attire' (*OED* sb^2 1, 8). The pun may be borrowed from Spenser (see below, 1116*n*).

1092-3. Following *Ed I*. *Ed II* wrongly transposes *for* and *from*.

1094. *obnoxious* exposed (*OED* 1a), with possible overtones of the modern sense, which *OED* cites from 1675.

1101. *fig-tree* the banyan (*ficus religiosa*). In fact it has small leaves, but M.

has taken his details from contemporary encyclopedists. The *loopholes* (1110) and the Amazon simile (1111) are found in Gerard's *Herbal* (1597) 1330.

1103. *Malabar* south-west coast of India.

Deccan southern India.

1106. *mother tree* Cp. the feminization of the Tree of Knowledge (ix 581–2, 680).

1111. *Amazonian targe* an Amazon's shield.

1115. *naked glory* Cp. Marlowe, *Hero and Leander* (1598), i 12–13: 'Venus in her naked glory strove / To please the careless and disdainful eyes / Of proud Adonis'.

1116. *Columbus . . . girt* Cp. Spenser's simile likening Fancy to a sunburned Indian clad in 'painted plumes' and 'proudest plight' (*FQ* III xii 8). American Indians were sometimes seen as untainted by the Fall, but M. associates them with ruined innocence. See Evans[3] 94f.

1117. *cincture* belt.

1121. *sat them down to weep* Cp. Ps. 137. 1: 'By the rivers of Babylon, there we sat down, yea, we wept, when we remembered Zion'.

1131. *distempered* See above, 887*n*.

1132. *estranged* changed from his normal self (*OED* 4) and alienated (from Eve).

1140. *approve* test.

1141. *owe* both 'own' and 'owe'.

1144. *What words . . . thy lips* echoing Homer (*Il.* xiv 83). Eve is referring specifically to Adam's word *wand'ring* (1136) which has now assumed its fallen meaning. See ii 148*n* and Fish (140).

severe another tainted word. It had meant 'austerely simple' (iv 283–4, 845, v 807), but Eve now means 'harsh'. Adam laments the new meaning in line 1169.

1155. *the head* I Cor 11. 3 (cit. above, viii 574*n*).

1164. *expressed* modifies both (Eve's) *love* (1163) and *mine for thee*. Eve's love was 'declared'; Adam's was 'manifested in actions' (*OED* 'express' 7).

1175. *confidence* overboldness (*OED* 4a).

secure overconfident.

1183–4. *women . . . her* The grammatical inconsistency is 'in keeping with Adam's agitation' (Bush).

1188. *fruitless* Cp. Eve's pun in line 648.

1189. *no end* inverting 'No more' (ix 1).

BOOK X

3. *perverted* including 'turned from a true to a false religious belief' (*OED* 3b).

10. *Complete* fully equipped (*OED* 5), as in 'complete steel'. Notice *armed* and cp. *A Masque* 420.

12. *still* always.

16. *manifold in sin* sinful in many ways.

19. *by this* by this time.

28–30. *they . . . vigilance* 'Accountable for their actions, they (the *guards*) hasted to the supreme throne to make plain their utmost vigilance with a righteous plea.'

31. *approved* confirmed (*OED* 2). Cp. Argument, 'approve their vigilance, and are approved'.

40. *speed* be successful.

45. *moment* slightest weight sufficient to tip a *scale*.

48. *rests* remains.

49. *denounced* formally proclaimed.

49–52. *that day . . . immediate stroke* God had told Adam that he would die 'in the day' he ate (Gen. 2. 17). See viii 331*n.*

53. *Forbearance no acquittance* 'abstinence from enforcing a debt is not release from the debt' (proverbial expression, *OED* 'forbearance' 3).

54. *Justice . . . scorned* 'My justice must not be scorned as my generosity has been'.

56–7. *to thee . . . All judgement* John 5. 22.

58. *might*] Ed II; may Ed I.

70–71. *in me . . . well pleased* Matt. 3. 17.

77. *derived* diverted (*OED* 2) and passed on by descent (*OED* 4).

78. *illústrate* set in the best light.

79. *Them* justice and mercy.

80. *Attendance none shall need* no retinue will be necessary.

    train attendants.

82. *the third* Satan.

83. *Convict* proved guilty (*OED* a 2).

    rebel to all law M. had called Charles I a 'rebell to Law' (*YP* 3. 230).

84. *Conviction* both 'proof of guilt' and **'condition of being convinced of sin' (*OED* 8). *OED* cites the latter sense only from 1675, but it was well established in the verb. See John 8. 9 and *PR* iv 308.

86. *collateral* side by side.

87. **ministrant* Cp. Heb. 1. 14: 'Are they not all ministering spirits?'

89. *coast* region of the earth (*OED* 6).

90–91. *the speed . . . winged* The Son's descent is timeless. Raphael had taken most of the morning to travel from Heaven to earth (viii 110–15).

92. *cadence* sinking, with a musical pun taken up by *airs* (Ricks). Cp. iv 264–6.

106. *obvious* coming in the way (*OED* 3), thus 'coming out to meet'. Cp. viii 504.

107–8. *what change . . . what chance* Cp. ii. 222–3 ('what chance, what change / Worth waiting').

112. *apparent* manifest.

120. *still* always.

128. *other self* See viii 450*n*.

135. *Devolved* caused to fall upon.

137–43. *This woman . . . did eat* Cp. Gen. 3. 12: 'The woman whom thou gavest to be with me, she gave me of the tree, and I did eat.' Biblical commentators detected a hint of resentment in 'thou gavest'. To this M. adds irony (*so good, / So fit*), tactlessness (*so divine*) and self-exculpation (*I could suspect no ill*). Contrast Eve's humble directness in lines 159–62.

147. *or but equal* or even equal. Cp. viii 568–75.

151. *real* both 'true' and 'royal' (*OED* a¹).

155–6. *part / And person* role and character (theatrical terms).

157. *few* few words.

165. *unable* modifies *serpent*.

167. *end* purpose.

171. *at last* including 'on the last day' (see line 190).

173. *mysterious* mystical (see x 1030–40).

183. *second Eve* a common patristic idea. Cp. v 385–7.

184. *Satan . . . lightning* When the disciples told Jesus how they had subjected devils, he replied: 'I beheld Satan as lightning fall from heaven. Behold, I give unto you power to tread on serpents and scorpions, and over all the power of the enemy' (Luke 10. 18–19).

185. *Prince of the Air* Satan is 'prince of the power of the air' in Eph. 2. 2. Cp. *PR* i 39–47.

186–7. *Spoiled . . . show* Col. 2. 14–15.

188. *Captivity led captive* Ps. 68. 18, Eph. 4. 8.

190. *tread . . . under our feet* Cp. Rom. 16. 20: 'the God of peace shall bruise Satan under your feet shortly'.

195–6. *thy husband's . . . rule* Cp. Gen. 3. 16: 'thy desire shall be to thy husband, and he shall rule over thee'. Adam has always ruled over Eve in *PL*. See iv 441–8, viii 561–75, x 145–56, etc. M. in *CD* i 10 argues that Adam's authority became 'still greater after the Fall' (trans. Carey, *YP* 6. 355).

210. *denounced* announced as a calamitous event about to take place (*OED* 1b).

214. *the form of servant* Phil. 2. 7.

215. *he washed his servants' feet* John 13. 5.

217. *or ... Or* either ... or. If the beasts were *slain*, the Son is 'the immediate cause' of 'the first instance of actual death' (Fowler).

222. *robe of righteousness* Cp. Isa. 61. 10: 'he hath covered me with the robe of righteousness'. Notice the pun *Opprobrious ... robe*.

236. *author* father (*OED* 2a) and prompter, instigator (*OED* 1d).

241. *avengers*] *Ed II*; avenger *Ed I*.

  like so well as.

243-4. *Methinks ... Wings growing* Cp. *PL* ix 1009-10, where the fallen and intoxicated Adam and Eve 'fancy that they feel / Divinity within them breeding wings'. Fowler notes that Sin's wings may grow 'simultaneously' with Adam and Eve's, for M. has just taken us back in time. See line 229. M. thus presents us with the Fall 'twice in the poem, and this second time it is horrific' (Rushdy 130).

246. *sympathy* affinity drawing two things together.

  connatural force innate force linking us.

249. *conveyance* communication.

253-323. Prodigies of building or engineering are traditional in epic. In *PL* we have seen Pandaemonium and the Creation. Examples in earlier epics include the wall around the Greek ships (Homer, *Il.* vii 433f.), Carthage (Virgil, *Aen.* i 423f.), Caesar's causeway over the port of Brindisi (Lucan, *Pharsalia* ii 660-79), and Goffredo's siege engines (Tasso, *Gerus. Lib.* xviii).

254. *impervious* through which there is no way (*OED* 1).

257. *main* ocean (of Chaos).

260. *intercourse* passing back and forth.

261. *transmigration* permanent emigration (to earth), but suggesting also 'passage from this life, by death' (*OED* 3). Sin and Death's bridge opens our way to Hell as readily as it opens Hell's way to us.

264. *meagre* emaciated (*OED* 1).

272. *snuffed* *detected by inhaling an odour (*OED* v² 4). *OED*'s earliest instance (from Dryden, 1697) is an obvious imitation of Milton.

274-8. *ravenous fowl ... bloody fight* Cp. Satan as vulture at iii 431-9. Cp. also Lucan's description of vultures following the Roman armies to Pharsalia (*Pharsalia* vii 831-7).

275. *Against* in anticipation of.

277. *designed* set apart, destined.

279. *feature* form, shape (*OED* 1c).

281. *Sagacious* acute in sense of smell (*OED* 1), with a play on 'wise'. Cp. Adam and Eve's puns on 'savour' and 'sapience' (ix 797, 1018-10).

284. *diverse* in different directions.

285. *Hovering upon the waters* Sin and Death travesty the dove-like Spirit of God at Creation. See i 21-2, vii 235-40.

288. *shoaling* crowding together (*OED* v³ 2).

290. *Cronian Sea* the Arctic Ocean (solid with ice).

291. *th' imagined way* the north-east passage to Cathay. Hudson had tried to find it in 1608, but his way was blocked by ice.

292. *Petsora* Pechora, a river in Siberia.

293. *Cathayan* Milton distinguished Cathay (North China) from China proper. See xi 386–8.

294. **petrific* that turns things to stone.

cold and dry See ii 898*n* for the four contraries: Hot, Cold, Moist, and Dry. Death employs the qualities productive of melancholy and associated with decay. Fowler contrasts the Son's use of Hot and Moist in Creation (vii 236–9).

296. *Delos floating once* Pregnant by Jupiter (and persecuted by Juno) Latona could find no place in which to give birth to Apollo and Diana until Neptune *fixed* the floating island of *Delos* with his *trident* (Callimachus, *Hymns*, iv, Hyginus, *Fables*, cxl). Cp. v 262–6.

297. *Gorgonian* The Gorgon Medusa turned anything she looked at into stone. See ii 611.

Rigor stiffness, harshness, coldness, straight course (Latin *rigor*).

298. *asphaltic slime* bitumen, pitch. Cp. i 729 and xii 40–44.

300. *mole* massive pier or bridge.

302. *wall* the hard outer shell of the universe (see ii 1023–33).

305. *inoffensive* free from obstacles (Latin *inoffensus*), with a play on *fenceless* (303).

307–11. *Xerxes . . . waves* In 480 BC King Xerxes of Persia built a bridge of ships over the Hellespont so that his army could invade Greece. He ordered the sea to be whipped when it destroyed this bridge. As his army passed over a second bridge, Xerxes wept at the thought that all his soldiers would be dead within a hundred years (Herodotus vii 46). Cp. i 620*n*. Quint (7) traces M.'s simile to Lucan, who compares Caesar's causeway over the port of Brindisi to Xerxes' bridging of 'Europe and Asia' (*Pharsalia* ii 672–7). Quint also notes a pun on *Hellespont* as 'Hell's pont'.

308. *Susa* the biblical Shushan, winter palace of the Persian kings. It was called *Memnonia* after its mythical ruler Memnon, the Ethiopian king who fought for Priam at Troy and was killed by Achilles.

313. *Pontifical* *bridge-building (*OED* 6), with a pun on 'papal' (*OED* 2) or 'episcopal' (*OED* 1). The Pope's title *Pontifex* was taken to mean that he was a bridge-builder between this world and the next. See below, 348*n*.

314. *vexed* turbulent.

321. *confines* boundaries.

322. *the left* the 'sinister' evil side. Cp. ii 755, x 886 and Matt. 25. 33.

323. *three several ways* the stair linking the universe to Heaven, the bridge joining the universe to Hell, and the passage through the universe down to the earth (iii 526–39).

327. *Satan . . . bright* Cp. II Cor. 11. 14: 'Satan himself is transformed into an angel of light'.

328. *Betwixt the Centaur and the Scorpion* If *the Centaur* is Sagittarius, Satan is steering his way through Anguis, the Serpent constellation. If *the Centaur* is Centaurus, Satan is steering through Lupus, the Wolf. M. likens Satan to a wolf at iv 181-3.

332. *unminded* unnoticed.

334. *sequel* consequence.

335. *unweeting* unaware.

337. *covertures* garments (see ix 1110-15), concealments (*OED* 7), justifications (*OED* 8; see x 115-17).

342-5. *list'ning . . . future time* refers to Adam's recollection of the curse on Satan (x 1030). Thus x 720-1104 precedes x 345-609 in chronological time. See further below, 716n.

344. *understood* (he) understood.

347. *foot* the end of the slope of the bridge (*OED* 18b).

348. **pontifice* bridge (*OED* sb², sole instance), coined from Latin *pons* on the model of 'edifice' – but 'pontifice' (*OED* sb¹) already existed as a variant of 'Pontifex' meaning 'Bishop' or 'Pope'. In this sense, Satan himself is the *wondrous pontifice*.

359. *Still* always.

364. *consequence* relationship of cause to effect.

366. **unvoyageable*.

370. *fortify* grow strong (*OED* I 6) and erect fortifications (the bridge).

371. *portentous* marvellous (*OED* 2) and ominous (*OED* 1).

372. *virtue* manliness, courage, valour (*OED* 7), the only virtue Satan's followers recognize.

374. *odds* advantage, profit.

375. *foil* defeat (*OED* sb²). A 'foil' in wrestling was 'a throw not resulting in a flat fall' (*OED* sb² 1), so Sin punningly hints that Satan's 'foil' was not a 'Fall'. 'Foil' could also mean 'tread under foot' (*OED* v¹ 1) and so anticipate Satan's ultimate fate (cp. x 175-81).

378. *doom* Judgement.

381. *quadrature* Cp. Rev. 21. 16, where the New Jerusalem is 'foursquare'. The sphere was thought to be more perfect than the cube, so Sin's antithesis between God's square and Satan's *orbicular* realm implies a 'subtle sneer' (Fowler). Heaven was 'undetermined square or round' at ii 1048.

382. *try* find by experience to be (*OED* 13).

386. *Satan . . . the name* This is the first and only time that Satan speaks his name in *PL*.

387. *Antagonist* 'Satan' means 'enemy', 'adversary' or 'antagonist'. The latter word originally signified a competitor in athletic games (as in *SA*

1628), so Satan might be looking back to Sin's word 'foil' (375) and boasting of his prowess as a wrestler.

390. *Triumphal . . . triumphal* Sin and Death celebrate Satan's triumph by building a triumphal arch. Cp. *PR* iv 37.

397. *these*] *Ed II*; those *Ed I*.

404. *Plenipotent* having full power.

408. *prevail*] *Ed I*; prevails *Ed II*.

409. *No detriment* echoing the formula by which the Roman Senate would give dictatorial power to two Consuls: *ne quid respublica detrimenta capiat* ('that the state suffer no harm').

go and be strong So Moses tells Joshua to take possession of the Promised Land: 'Be strong and of a good courage: for thou must go with these people' (Deut. 31. 7).

412. *bane* poison, destruction.

blasted stricken by malignant astral influences (*OED* 1).

413. *planet-strook* stricken by the malign influence of an adverse planet (*OED*); suggesting also a physical collision. Cp. vi 310–15.

real eclipse not just an obscuration by an intervening body, but a diminution of light at its source.

415. *causey* causeway, arched viaduct (*OED* 2c).

420. *those* Sin and Death.

425. *Lucifer* the morning star. Cp. v 760, vii 131.

allusion metaphor (*OED* 3).

426. *paragoned* compared (*OED* 1).

427. *the grand* 'the grand infernal Peers' (ii 507).

428. *solicitous* anxious (*OED* 1).

431–3. *Tartar . . . Retires* The simile implies Satanic cunning, since Tartars were famous for shooting arrows to the rear while feigning retreat. Cp. Spenser, *FQ* II xi 26, and Phineas Fletcher, *The Purple Island* (1633): 'As when by Russian Volga's frozen banks / The false-back Tartars fear with cunning feign, / And posting fast away in flying ranks, / Oft backward turn, and from their bows down rain / Whole storms of darts; so do they flying fight: / And what by force they lose, they winne by sleight' (xi 48).

432. *Astrakhan* a Tartar khanate on the lower Volga annexed by Ivan the Terrible in 1556. Astrakhan was a mere remnant of the once mighty Golden Horde, so the name implies the devils' decline. But they remain a threat. In 1571 the Tartars 'broke into *Russia*' and 'burnt *Mosco* to the ground' (M.'s *History of Muscovia*, *YP* 8. 515).

433. *Bactrian Sophy* Persian Shah.

433–4. *horns . . . crescent* referring both to the Turkish battle formation and emblem.

435. *realm of Aladule* Armenia (Aladule being the last Persian ruler before the Turkish conquest).

436. *Tauris* Tabriz, in north-west Persia.

Casbeen Kazvin, north of Teheran.

438. *reduced* led back (*OED* 2), drawn together (*OED* 25), and diminished.

439. *metropolis* including 'parent state of a colony' (*OED* 3). Satan will soon provide *foreign worlds* to colonize (441).

441-55. *he ... returned* Satan's *invisible* entry, his remaining *unseen*, and his *sudden* blazing *as from a cloud* are taken from Tasso, *Gerus. Lib.* x 32–50, where the Sultan Solimano enters a Saracen council of war concealed in a cloud, and 'Unseen, at will did all the prease behold' (x 35). When morale is at its lowest, Solimano tears the cloud 'like a veil' and 'amid the press he shined' (x 49). M.'s *whom they wished beheld* (454) directly echoes Fairfax's translation of Solimano's first words on becoming visible: 'Of whom you speake behold the Soldan here' (x 50). Cp. also Homer, *Od.* vii 37–145 and Virgil, *Aen.* i 411–14, 579–94.

444. *Plutonian infernal, from Pluto, god of the underworld.

445. *state* canopy.

451. *permissive* permitted (by God).

453. *Stygian* Styx, the river of hate in Hades. Cp. ii 506, 577.

457. *Divan* Turkish Council of State. Satan was a 'Sultan' at i 348 and he has just appeared in the manner of Tasso's Sultan Solimano.

458. *Congratulant saluting (*OED* 'congratulate' 5).

458-9. *with hand / Silence* Cp. Lucan's hero-villain Caesar commanding his legions' attention before leading them into revolt: *dextraque silentia iussit*, 'with his right hand commanded silence' (*Pharsalia*, i 298).

460-62. *Thrones ... of right* Satan's distinction between *right* and *possession* accords with seventeenth-century notions of ruling *de jure* (by law) or *de facto* (by possession). Thus Charles II claimed to rule *de jure* throughout the Interregnum, but did not rule *de facto* until 1660. See v 773*n* for Satan's fallacy in arguing from angelic titles.

471. *unreal* formless (Chaos has matter but not form).

475. *uncouth* strange and desolate (*OED* 2b, 5).

477. *unoriginal having no origin, uncreated (*OED* 1, sole instance in this sense).

477-8. *Chaos ... opposed* Critics object that Chaos and Night did not oppose Satan, and 'Chaos even helped him' (Fowler). But Chaos the place was a formidable obstacle (ii 910–50).

480. *Protesting* both 'appealing to' (*OED* 6) and 'protesting against'. Satan equivocates as to whether *Fate* was for him or against him.

481-2. *fame ... foretold* See i 651–6, ii 345–76.

487. *an apple* Satan alone speaks of 'apples' in *PL*. Cp. ix 585. The poem's good characters speak of 'fruit', which relates actions to consequences. Cp. i 1, iii 67, etc.

496-7. *that ... enmity* This is the nearest Satan ever comes to naming

himself to the other devils. The Hebrew word translated as 'enmity' at Gen.
3. 15 is not etymologically related to 'Satan', but see x 1030–34 and note.

503. *bliss* Satan's last word in the poem is answered with a rhyming *hiss*
(508, 518).

511–14. *His visage . . . prone* Cp. the serpent metamorphoses in Ovid, *Met.*
iv 572–603 (alluded to at ix 506) and Dante, *Inf.* xxiv and xxv.

513. *supplanted* tripped up (*OED* 1) and made to fall from power (*OED*
2). The etymology (Latin *sub*, 'under + *planta*, 'sole of the foot') anticipates
the crushing of Satan's head (x 181).

515. *Reluctant* struggling, writhing.

517. *doom* judgement (the curse of x 175–81).

521. *riot* rebellion.

523. *complicated* *composite (*OED* 4), tangled (*OED* 2).

524. *amphisbaena* Greek 'going both ways': a mythical snake with a head
at either end of its body (Lucan, *Pharsalia* ix 719).

525. *Cerastes* a snake with four horns. The *hydrus* and *ellops* are mythical
water snakes.

526. *dipsas* a mythical snake whose bite caused raging thirst. Lucan describes
how one of Cato's soldiers, bitten while crossing the Libyan desert, searched
for water deep in the sand, drank sea-water ('but there was not enough'),
and finally opened his veins so as to drink blood (*Pharsalia* ix 737–60). Cp.
the devils' *scalding thirst* (556).

526–7. *soil . . . Gorgon* When Perseus flew over Libya, drops of blood
falling from Medusa's severed head became snakes. Lucan and Ovid cite
the story to explain why snakes are so abundant in Libya (*Pharsalia* ix 620–
732, *Met.* iv 617–20).

528. *Ophiusa* Greek 'full of snakes'. The name was anciently given to
several islands.

529. *dragon* Cp. Rev. 12. 9. In Joost van den Vondel's *Lucifer* (1654),
Lucifer becomes a dragon at the moment of his expulsion from Heaven
(Kirkconnell 414). Cp. also Phineas Fletcher, *The Purple Island* (1633) vii
10–11.

529–31. *the sun . . . Python* The monstrous serpent *Python*, slain by Apollo,
was born of the *slime* deposited by Deucalion's flood (Ovid, *Met.* i 438–
40). The *Pythian vale* is Delphi.

535. *in station* at their posts.

in just array on parade.

536. *Sublime* *exalted in feeling, elated (*OED* 3b).

540. *sympathy* both 'compassion' and 'corresponding condition'.

546. *exploding* *OED*'s earliest participial instance. The sense includes
'hoot (an actor) off the stage', 'reject with scorn', 'expose the hollowness
of' and 'drive out air' (*OED* 1, 2, 3, 4).

550. *penance* punishment (*OED* 5).

fair fruit] *Ed I*; fruit *Ed II*.

560. *Megaera* one of three snaky-haired Furies, goddesses and avengers of crime. Cp. ii 596.

562. *bituminous lake* the Dead Sea, identified as the site of *Sodom* on the authority of II Esdras 5. 7. Josephus claimed that fruit growing near the Dead Sea contained Sodom's ashes and would dissolve into ashes when plucked (*De Bellis* IV viii 4). M. alludes to this story in *Eikonoklastes*, where he compares King Charles's rhetoric to 'the Apples of *Asphaltis*' that look appealing to the eye, 'but touch them, and they turne into Cinders' (*YP* 3. 552). Cp. Deut. 32. 32: 'their vine is of the vine of Sodom . . . Their wine is the poison of dragons, / And the cruel venom of asps'.

565. *gust* relish.

568. *drugged* *nauseated (*OED* 2b).

572. *triúmphed* triumphed over.

once both 'as soon as' (man fell) and 'a single time' (in contrast to the devils' *oft*-repeated error).

575. *some say* No source has been found for M.'s story of an annual metamorphosis.

579. *purchase* both 'plunder' (*OED* 8) and 'annual return or rent from land' (*OED* 10), 'alluding to the *annual* punishment of the devils' (Fowler). See lines 575-6.

581. *Ophion with Eurynome* the first king and queen of Olympus, overthrown by *Saturn* and *Ops* (Cronus and Rhea), who were ousted in their turn by *Jove* (Apollonius Rhodius, *Argonautica* i 503-9). *Ophion* means 'serpent' and *Eurynome* means 'wide-ruling' (though *wide-Encroaching* suggests 'wide of the law'). Claudian describes Ophion as a serpent and includes him among the Giants who fought against Jove (*De Rapt. Pros.* iii 332-56). The association with Satan was traditional.

584. *Dictaean* Zeus was raised in Crete, either on Mount Dicte or in the Dictaean cave in Mount Ida (see i 515).

587. *actual* 'Actual sin' is a theological term for sin that is freely chosen (as opposed to 'original sin', which is inherited).

in body physically present (Sin's body) and habitually rooted (in all other bodies).

590. *pale horse* Cp. Rev. 6. 8: 'behold a pale horse: and his name that sat on him was Death, and Hell followed with him'.

593. *travail* labour and travel.

595. *Unnamed* Sin had named Death at ii 787, but the name has hitherto been an empty sound in Paradise. See iv 427*n*.

599. *ravin* prey.

601. *unhidebound *OED*'s sole instance. A 'hidebound' animal is one that is so emaciated as to have the 'skin clinging closely to the back and ribs' (*OED* 1). Death is so ravenous that he can never fill his skin.

611. **unimmortal* The neologism implies that mortality is not a natural state but a privation.

616–17. *dogs . . . havoc* Cp. Shakespeare, *Julius Caesar* III i 273: 'Cry "Havoc" and let slip the dogs of war'. 'Havoc' was the signal permitting a victorious army to pillage.

624. *conniving* shutting one's eyes to a thing that one dislikes but cannot help (*OED* 'connive' 1).

627. *quitted all* handed everything over (*OED* 'quit' 5b). Cp. iii 307, where God praises the Son for having 'quitted (i.e. "renounced", "redeemed", "remitted") all'.

630. *draff* dregs.

633. *at one sling* Cp. I Sam. 25. 29: 'The souls of thine enemies, them shall he sling out, as out of the middle of a sling'.

638. *heav'n and earth renewed* II Pet. 3. 7–13.

640. *precedes* both 'takes precedence' and 'goes before'.

642. *hallelujah, as the sound of seas* Rev. 19. 6.

644. *Righteous are thy decrees* Rev. 16. 7.

645. *extenuate* disparage, diminish in honour (*OED* 5).

651. *sorted* suited.

656. *blank* white, pale (*OED* 1).

658. *aspécts* astrological positions (*OED* 4).

sextile, *square*, *trine*, and *opposite* are positions of 60, 90, 120, and 180 degrees respectively.

661. *synod* astrological conjunction.

fixed fixed stars.

664. *tempestuous* productive of storms. Cp. i 305–6.

668–78. *Some say . . . seasons* M. imagines that the earth's equator had coincided with the ecliptic, producing the prelapsarian 'eternal spring'. He gives both a heliocentric and a geocentric explanation to account for the loss of this pristine state. Copernican astronomers assume that the earth's axis is now tilted (668–71); Ptolemaic astronomers assume that the plane of the sun's orbit is tilted (671–8). M. typically declines to choose between the two systems.

671. *centric globe* the earth (pivoted on its centre).

672. *equinoctial road* the earth's equator.

673. *Like distant breadth* a like declination (23.5°).

673–7. *Taurus . . . Capricorn* The sun had been in Aries. Now it travels through the zodiac. In spring and summer, it passes through *Taurus* (which includes the Pleiades or *sev'n / Atlantic Sisters*), Gemini (*the Spartan Twins*), and Cancer (*the Tropic Crab*), where it reaches the summer solstice. In late summer and autumn, it moves through *Leo*, *Virgo* (*the Virgin*), *Libra* (*the Scales*), eventually reaching the winter solstice in *Capricorn*.

675. *amain* at full speed.

679. *vernant* flourishing in spring.

682. **unbenighted* not overtaken by the darkness of night.

686. *Estoliland* northern Labrador.

687. *Magellan* the straits at the tip of South America.

688. **Thyestean banquet* Thyestes seduced the wife of his brother Atreus. In revenge, Atreus killed one of Thyestes' sons and served him to Thyestes as food. The sun turned from the banquet in horror (Seneca, *Thyestes* 776-8).

693. *sideral blast* malign stellar influence.

694. *exhalation* vapour productive of meteors (see i 710-12).

695. *pestilent* See ix 180n for the tradition that mists carried the plague.

696. *Norumbega* northern New England and maritime Canada.

   Samoed north-eastern Siberia.

697. *brazen dungeon* the cave in which Aeolus imprisoned the winds (Virgil, *Aen.* i 50-59).

698. *flaw* sudden squall.

699-700. *Boreas*, *Caecias*, *Argestes*, and *Thrascias* are winds from the N, NW and NE; opposing them are *Notus* (S) and *Afer* (SW), while blowing across (*thwart*) them are *Eurus* (ESE), *Zephyr* (W), *Sirocco* (SE) and *Libecchio* (SW).

703. *Serraliona* Sierra Leone (on the west coast of Africa).

704. *levant . . . ponent* east and west (lit. 'rising' and 'setting'). In the Mediterranean, a 'levant' (or 'levanter') was a strong easterly wind from the Levant.

707-8. *Discord . . . Daughter of Sin* The classical Discordia (Eris) was Death's sister. She was depicted with serpents wreathed about her head.

716. *Already in part* Adam has not yet witnessed the *miseries* of lines 650-715. He first sees animals pursue each other at xi 185-90. Sin and Death have not yet entered our universe, and Satan has not yet left it. Satan is still in Paradise, eavesdropping, at the end of book x. See above, 342-5n.

718. *troubled sea* Cp. Isa. 57. 20: 'The wicked are like the troubled sea, when it cannot rest, whose waters cast up mire and dirt'. Cp. i 304-6, iv 19.

729. *propagated* handed down from one generation to another (*OED* 1d), extended (*OED* 4), increased and multiplied (*OED* 2).

738. *own* own curses.

   bide upon stick to (*OED* 2b).

739. *redound* flow back (*OED* 4) and cast opprobrium (*OED* 8b).

740. *light* both 'alight' and 'not heavy'. *Light / heavy* is a paradox. According to Aristotelian science (still current in M.'s day), heavy objects lost their heaviness, and their tendency to move, once they reached their *natural centre*, the centre of the earth. The curses of Adam's descendants should therefore become light once they reach Adam. Instead, Adam will continue to feel them as *heavy*.

743. *Did I request . . . from my clay* Cp. Isa. 45. 9: 'Woe unto him that striveth with his Maker! Let the potsherd strive with the potsherds of the earth. Shall the clay say unto him that fashioneth it, What makest thou?'

748. *equal* equitable, just.

758. *Thou* Adam himself. In lines 743–55 *thou* referred to God.

760–64. *what if . . . proud excuse* Cp. Isa. 45. 10: 'Woe unto him that saith unto his father, What begettest thou?'

764. *election* choice.

778. *mother's lap* Cp. Spenser, *FQ* V vii 9: 'mother Earths deare lap'. Adam's desire is more poignant for the fact that earth is his only mother.

782–814. *Yet . . . perpetuity* Adam considers three possibilities: (1) the soul will survive the body (782–89), (2) body and soul will both die (789–808), (3) body and soul will survive in *endless misery* (808–16). Editors often confuse (2) with M.'s 'mortalist heresy', which held that body and soul died together, and were resurrected together on the last day (*CD* i 13). Adam intuits the first part of this doctrine, but fails to imagine resurrection or damnation. Even when he speaks of *endless misery* (810), it is misery in Paradise that daunts him. Adam has forgotten (or blocks out) Raphael's warning about 'eternal misery' in Hell (vi 904).

783. *all I* all of me.

795. *be it* even if it is.

804–8. *that . . . sphere* Adam employs a scholastic argument, which held that the action of any agent is limited by the recipient's powers to be acted upon. So while God's *anger* might be *infinite*, man (as a *finite* creature) cannot suffer infinitely.

814. *revolution* recurrence.

815–16. *Death and I / Am* Adam's ungrammatical *Am* reflects his realization that he and death are *incorporate*, 'united in one body' (*OED* 1).

827. *they then*] Ed II; they Ed I.

831. *conviction* both 'proof of guilt' and *'the condition of being convinced of sin' (*OED* 8). See above, 84*n*.

832. *me, me only* Adam echoes the Son's offer to die for man: 'Behold me then, me for him' (iii 236). See also x 936.

834. *So might the wrath* 'would that the wrath were so confined'.

836. *world* universe.

842–4. *abyss . . . plunged* Cp. Satan's descent into the 'lower deep' of an internal Hell (iv 75–9).

847. *black air* Cp. Satan as a pestilent 'black mist' (ix 180).

853. *denounced* proclaimed as a threat or warning.

860–62. *O woods . . . other song* Adam recalls the morning hymn of v 153–208 (see esp. 203–4).

867. *thou serpent* Clement of Alexandria and Eusebius had claimed that 'Eve' aspirated means 'serpent'. See D. C. Allen, *MLN* 74, 1959, 681–3. Elsewhere in *PL* M. follows a rival tradition which took 'Eve' to mean 'life'. See iv 474–5*n*, v 385–7*n*, xi 159–61*n*. Adam now invents a bad pun and a misogynistic tradition. Cp. ix 1067, where Adam puns on 'Eve' and 'evil'. See further, Leonard 229–30.

869. *wants* is missing.

872. *pretended* held in front as a cover (*OED* 1), with overtones of 'feigned'.

878–9. *him . . . overreach* overconfidently thinking that you could outwit him.

884–5. *rib / Crookèd by nature* a commonplace of misogynistic diatribes. Cp. Joseph Swetnam, *The Araignment of Lewd, idle . . . women* (1615): 'a ribbe is a crooked thing . . . and women are crooked by nature' (1).

886. *sinister* left side (with evil overtones). Cp. Sin's birth from 'the left side' of Satan's head (ii 755).

887. *supernumerary* Calvin and other commentators believed that Adam had been created with an extra rib for the purpose of forming Eve.

888–95. *O why . . . Mankind* echoing the misogyny of Euripides' Hippolytus (*Hippolytus* 616–19) and Ariosto's Rodomonte (*Orl. Fur.* xxvii 120).

890. *Spirits masculine* M. in his own voice has told us that Spirits assume 'either sex . . . or both' (i 424).

891. *defect / Of nature* Aristotle had called the female a defective male.

898. *strait* close, intimate, hard-pressing, tightly-drawn (used of bonds and embraces, *OED* 2). The *Ed I* and *Ed II* spelling 'straight' plays on 'honest, free from crookedness' (*OED* 6a) to contrast honest men with *Crooked* women (885).

   conjunction union, including 'marriage', 'sexual union' (*OED* 2a, 2b).

910–13. *tears . . . plaint* Cp. Mary Magdalene washing Jesus's feet with her hair and tears (Luke 7. 38). Cp. v 130–31.

917. *deceived* perhaps including a pun on 'dis-Eved'. Cp. i 35, ix 904, and *PR* 1 52 ('Eve / Lost Paradise deceived'). Adam has just wrenched 'Eve' from 'life' to 'serpent' (x 867).

917–18. Eve acts like a *suppliant* in Greek epic or tragedy, clasping Adam's *knees* in a plea for protection.

926. *doom* the judgement at x 175–81. It is fitting that Eve bring this up, since the *enmity* was to be 'between the *woman* and the serpent' (Fowler). Eve does not yet recognize her *foe*, but her words open the way for Adam's recognition in line 1034.

931. *God . . . and thee* Cp. iv 299: 'He for God only, she for God in him'.

936. *Me me only* Eve's cry combines Adam's guilt ('On me, me only', x

832) with the Son's love ('Behold me then, me for him', iii 236). Cp. Abigail's plea for her husband: 'Upon me, my lord, upon me let this iniquity be' (I Sam. 25. 24). Cp. also the plea of Nisus for Euryalus (Virgil, *Aen.* ix 427).

965. *derived* passed on by descent.

969. *event* outcome.

976. *extremes* extremities, hardships.

978. *As in our evils* considering our afflictions.

979. *descent* descendants.

perplex torment.

987. *prevent* forestall, cut off in advance.

989–90. *Childless . . . two* So the first five editions. Most subsequent editions move *So Death* back to the previous line. Fowler argues that the metrical irregularity may 'be intended to mime first the deficiency of childlessness (line 989 defective), then the glut denied to Death (line 990 hypermetrical)'.

990. *deceived* cheated out of.

991. *forced* including 'fattened, crammed with food' (*OED* v^3 2).

993. *Conversing* cohabiting, with overtones of 'have sexual intercourse' (*OED* 2b) even though this is what Eve proposes to abstain from.

996. *the present object* Eve herself.

1000. *make short* lose no time.

1009. *dyed*] 'di'd' *Ed I*, *Ed II*, with an obvious pun.

1027. *contumácy* wilful disobedience, contempt of a court of law.

1028. *make death in us live* M.'s voice behind Adam is referring to eternal damnation, *mors aeterna*. Cp. 'living death' (788).

1030–34. *calling . . . Satan* Recovering his insight of ix 904–6 and ix 1172–3, Adam at last names Eve's tempter. He owes his recognition partly to Eve, who at x 925–7 reminded him of their 'one enmity / Against a foe by doom express assigned us, / That cruel serpent'. Adam now matches *Foe* with *Satan* and with the curse of enmity on the serpent. Justin Martyr and Irenaeus had interpreted *Satan* as *Sata-nas*, 'apostate serpent'. See Leonard (231) and L. W. Barnard, *Justin Martyr: his Life and Thought* (1967), 108.

1045. *Reluctance* resistance, struggling against (*OED* 1).

1051–2. *Pains . . . joy* Adam unwittingly prophesies the Second Coming. Cp. Christ's metaphor at John 16. 20–21: 'ye shall be sorrowful, but your sorrow shall be turned into joy. A woman when she is in travail hath sorrow, because her hour is come: but as soon as she is delivered of the child, she remembereth no more the anguish, for joy that a man is born into the world'.

1053. *Fruit of thy womb* another unwitting allusion to the Son. Cp. Luke 1. 42.

1058. **unbesought.*

1061. *to pity incline* Cp. iii 402, 405.

1066. *shattering* scattering, causing to fall.

1068. *shroud* shelter.

cherish keep warm (*OED* 6).

1069. *this diurnal star* the sun. The thought that our sun is a star now implies man's insignificance. Cp. 'other suns' (viii 148), where the emphasis is on God's glory.

1071. *sere* dry.

foment heat, with a play on Latin *fomes*, 'kindling wood'.

1073. *attrite* ground down by friction.

1075. *Tine* ignite.

thwart slanting.

1078. *supply* serve as a substitute for.

1081-2. *of grace / Beseeching him* both 'asking him for grace' and 'beseeching him, having been given the grace to do so'.

1086-1104. *to the place . . . meek* The repetition of 1086-92 in 1098-1104 is a Homeric formula (cp. *Il.* ix 122-57, 264-99), but M. does not repeat 1093-6 and so refrains from presuming that God will *relent and turn from his displeasure.* Adam and Eve have yet to be expelled from Paradise.

1103. *Frequenting* filling.

BOOK XI

1. *stood* Adam and Eve were 'prostrate' at x 1099, but now their *port* is not of *mean suitors* (9). They had stood to pray at iv 720.

2. *mercy-seat* the golden covering of the ark of the Covenant (Exod. 25. 17-22) – a type of divine intercession.

3. *Prevenient grace* grace that is antecedent to human will (theological term).

4. *stony . . . flesh* Cp. Ezek. 11. 19: 'I will take the stony heart out of their flesh, and will give them a heart of flesh'.

6. *Unutterable . . . prayer* Cp. Rom. 8. 26: 'we know not what we should pray for as we ought: but the Spirit itself maketh intercession for us with groanings which cannot be uttered'.

8-9. *port . . . important* Both words are from Latin *portare*, 'to carry'.

12. *Deucalion* the Greek Noah. He and his wife *Pyrrha* survived a universal flood by building an ark. They then prayed to *Themis*, goddess of justice, who told them to restore mankind by throwing stones behind them. The stones became men and women. Notice *stony* and *made new flesh* (4).

15. *envious* malicious, spiteful (*OED* 2).

17. **Dimensionless* without physical extension (*OED* 1a).

18. *incense* Rev. 8. 3.

28. *manuring* cultivating (*OED* 2).

33–4. *advocate / And propitiation* Cp. I John 2. 1: 'We have an advocate with the Father, Jesus Christ the righteous: And he is the propitiation for our sins'.

35. *ingraft* Rom. 11. 16–24. Cp. iii 293*n*.

44. *Made . . . one* Cp. John 17. 22–3: 'that they may be one, even as we are one: I in them, and thou in me'.

52. *purge him off* Cp. ii 141, where Belial predicts that Heaven would 'purge off the baser fire' of Hell (ii 141).

53. *distemper* imbalance of the four humours (*OED* 3) resulting in death and decay.

55. *dissolution* death, with overtones of 'dissolute living'.

59. *fondly* foolishly.

65. *renovation* renewal of the body at the resurrection (*OED* 1b).

67. *synod* assembly.

70. *peccant* sinning.

74. *trumpet . . . Oreb* A trumpet sounded on Mount Horeb when God delivered the Ten Commandments (Exod. 19. 19).

76. *general doom* the Last Judgement. See Matt. 24. 31, I Thess. 4. 16 and I Cor. 15. 52: 'the trumpet shall sound, and the dead shall be raised incorruptible'.

78. **amarantine* See iii 352*n*.

86. *defended* forbidden (*OED* 3).

91. *motions* stirrings of the soul (*OED* 9b). Cp. *PR* i 290, *SA* 1382.

93. *Self-left* if left to itself.

93–8. *Lest . . . taken* Cp. Gen. 3. 22–3: 'And now, lest he put forth his hand, and take also of the tree of life, and eat, and live for ever: therefore the Lord God sent him forth from the garden of Eden, to till the ground from whence he was taken'. M.'s addition *dream at least to live* implies that Adam could not have cheated God.

102. *Or . . . or* either . . . or.

   in behalf of man Empson[2] (165) cites the phrase as evidence of Satan's altruism, but it might mean 'with regard to man' (*OED* 'behalf' 1d) or 'in man's name' (*OED* 2a) rather than 'for man's benefit' (*OED* 2b).

102–3. *invade / Vacant possession* encroach on untenanted property.

105. *remorse* pity, compassion (*OED* 3a).

106. *denounce* announce.

108. *faint* lose heart.

111. *excess* violation of law (*OED* 4), intemperance in eating (*OED* 5b).

126. **Archangelic.*

128–30. *four faces . . . eyes more numerous* Ezek. 1. 18.

129. *double Janus* Janus, the Roman god of gateways, had two faces. Janus

Quadrifrons had four faces corresponding to the four seasons and four quarters of the earth.

131. *Argus* a hundred-eyed giant. Juno set him to watch Io, whom Jove had disguised as a heifer. Mercury (*Hermes*) killed him after charming him to sleep with his *pipe* and sleep-inducing wand (*opiate rod*). See Ovid, *Met.* i 568–779.

135. *Leucothea* goddess of the dawn and a protectress of children.

144. *prevalent* potent, influential.

157–8. *Assures . . . past* echoing the last words of Agag, King of the Amalekites, spoken just before Samuel cut him to pieces: 'surely the bitterness of death is past' (I Sam. 15. 32). Like Agag, Adam has 'spoken too soon' (Fowler), but his hope that Eve's *seed* will bring eternal life is not groundless.

158. *hail to thee* anticipating 'the holy salutation used / Long after to blest Mary, second Eve' (v 386–7).

159–61. *Eve . . . all things live* Cp. Gen. 3. 20: 'And Adam called his wife's name Eve; because she was the mother of all living'. 'Eve' (Hebrew *Chava*) is cognate with *chai*, 'life'. The biblical Eve is not so named until after the Fall. Before then she was 'the woman'. M.'s Adam had named Eve at iv 481. He now affirms that the name was *rightly* given. See iv 474–5*n*, v 385–7*n*.

185. *bird of Jove, stooped* the eagle, having swooped.

   tow'r lofty flight.

187. *beast . . . woods* lion.

188. *brace* pair.

196. *too secure* overconfident.

205. *orient* both 'bright' and 'eastern'. The latter sense is paradoxical, for Michael's squadron appears *in yon western cloud*. Cp. Raphael appearing as 'another morn' in the east of Paradise (v 310), and Satan's army arising as a 'fiery region' on Heaven's northern horizon (vi 79–82).

208. *by this* by this time.

209. *lighted* both 'alighted' and 'shone' (*OED* v² 1).

210. *made halt* came to a halt (military term).

214. *Mahanaim* Hebrew 'armies', 'camps' (hence *pavilioned*). Jacob gave the name to the place where he saw an army of angels (Gen. 32. 1–2).

216–20. *flaming . . . unproclaimed* The *Syrian king* besieged the city of *Dothan* in an attempt to capture Elisha (*One man*). When Elisha's servant expressed fear at the Syrian 'horses and chariots', Elisha prayed to God, asking him to open the servant's eyes 'that he may see. And the Lord opened the eyes of the young man; and he saw: and, behold, the mountain was full of horses and chariots of fire' (II Kings 6. 17).

221. *stand* station (military term).

powers army.

227. *determine* make an end.

237. *thou retire* Contrast v 383 where Eve 'Stood to entertain her guest from Heaven'; but even before the Fall Eve 'sat retired' while Adam and Raphael conversed (viii 41).

240. *Clad to meet man* Raphael had been covered by his wings, but had not worn clothes (v 277–85).

lucid bright.

242. *Meliboean* The Thessalian town of Meliboea was famous in antiquity for its purple dye.

243. *Sarra* Tyre, also famous for its dye (*grain*).

244. *Iris . . . woof* Cp. the Attendant Spirit's 'sky-robes, spun out of Iris' woof' (*A Masque* 83).

247. *zodiac* belt of constellations.

249. *state* stateliness of bearing.

254. *Defeated of* cheated of (*OED* 7).

his seizure what he had seized.

256–7. *one . . . cover* Cp. I Peter 4. 8: 'for charity shall cover the multitude of sins'.

264. *gripe* spasm or pang of grief (*OED* sb¹ 2a).

267. *Discovered* revealed.

retire withdrawal.

270. *native soil* Unlike Adam, Eve was created in Paradise.

272. *respite* delay, extension (*OED* 1).

277. *gave ye names* Eve's naming of the flowers, like Adam's naming of the animals, implies special knowledge (see viii 352–3*n*). M. here departs from traditional interpretations of Gen. 2. 19, where Adam alone gives names.

283. *to* compared with.

293. *by this* by this time.

damp stupefied condition (*OED* 4).

298. *Prince among princes* Cp. Dan. 10. 13: 'Michael, one of the chief princes'.

309. *can* both 'knows' (*OED* 1) and 'can perform'.

316. *from . . . hid* Cp. Cain's response to his curse: 'from thy face shall I be hid; and I shall be a fugitive and a vagabond in the earth' (Gen. 4. 14).

323. *grateful* both 'pleasing' and 'expressing gratitude'. Patriarchs built altars where God had spoken to them. See e.g. Gen. 12. 7.

331. *promised race* the human race, whose 'promised Seed' will bruise Satan's head (xi 155, xii 623).

336. *Not this rock only* Cp. Jesus's warning to the woman of Samaria not to localize worship 'in this mountain' (John 4. 21).

338. *Fomented* nurtured, cherished.

virtual potent.

357. *To show . . . future days* Prophetic visions are frequent in epic. See e.g. Virgil, *Aen.* vi 754–854 (Aeneas's vision of Rome), Ariosto, *Orl. Fur.* xiii 53–74 (Bradamante's vision of the House of Este), and Spenser, *FQ* III iii 29–49 (Britomart's vision of Britain). An angelic subordinate of Michael relates future events to Daniel in Dan. 10–12.

367. *drenched* overwhelmed (*OED* 6). A 'drench' was a soporific potion. Cp. ii 73.

373. **chast'ning OED*'s earliest participial sense.

374. *obvious* exposed, vulnerable (*OED* 2).

377. *visions . . . hill* Cp. Ezek. 40. 2: 'In the visions of God brought he me into the land of Israel, and set me upon a very high mountain'.

379. *ken* view.

380. *the amplest*] *Ed II*; amplest *Ed I*.

381–4. *that hill . . . glory* When Satan tempted Christ he took 'him up into an exceeding high mountain' (Matt. 4. 8). See also Luke 4. 5 and *PR* iii 251ff.

388. *Cambalu* capital of Cathay (north China). M. imagines China and Cathay to be distinct, but the *Cathayan khan* Kubilai had ruled all China from Cambalu (Beijing).

389. *Temir* Timur (Tamburlaine), a descendant of Genghis Khan. His capital *Samarkand* was near the *Oxus* river in modern Uzbekistan.

390. *Paquin* Peking (Beijing).

*Sinaean Chinese.

391. *Agra and Lahore* Mogul capitals in northern India and the Punjab (Pakistan).

Great Mogul the Mogul emperor.

392. *golden Chersonese* a vaguely defined area east of India, fabled for its wealth. See *PR* iv 74 and note.

393. *Ecbatan* Ecbatana, capital of Media and a summer residence of the Persian kings. Isfahan (*Hispahan*) replaced Kazvin as the Persian capital in the sixteenth century (hence *since*).

395. *Bizance* Byzantium (Constantinople, Istanbul), capital of the Ottoman Empire after falling to the Turks in 1453.

396. *Turkéstan-born* The Ottoman Turks traced their tribal origins to Turkestan, in central Asia between Mongolia and the Caspian.

397. *Negus* title of the Abyssinian emperors.

398. *Ercoco* Arkiko, a Red Sea port in modern Ethiopia.

399. *Mombaza* Mombasa, in Kenya.

Quiloa Kilwa, in Tanzania.

Melind Malindi, in Kenya. All Muslim colonies on the east African coast.

400. *Sofala* a port in Mozambique, sometimes identified with the biblical *Ophir*, the source of Solomon's gold.

402. *Niger* a river in west Africa.

Atlas the Atlas Mountains in Morocco.

403. *Almansor* Various Muslim rulers were called 'Al-Mansur' ('the victorious'). Here it may be a title (cp. *Khan, Ksar, Great Mogul, Negus*) or a name (cp. *Motezume, Atabalipa*). M. may be thinking of Abu'Amir al Ma-Ma'afiri, Caliph of Cordova (r. 976–1002), known to European writers as 'Almanzor', or Abu Yusuf Ya'qub al-Mansur (r. 1184–99). Both ruled north Africa and much of Spain.

Fez in Morocco.

Sus Tunis.

404. *Tremisen* Tlemcen, part of Algeria.

406. *in spirit* because of the earth's curvature.

407. *Motezume* Montezuma II, the last Aztec ruler. His capital Tenochtitlán (*Mexico*) fell to Cortez in 1520.

409. *Atabalipa* Atahuallpa, the last Inca ruler, murdered in 1533 by Pizarro, who sacked his capital Cuzco (in Peru).

410. *Geryon's sons* the Spanish. Geryon was a mythical three-headed monster (killed by Hercules) who inhabited an island off the Spanish coast. Spenser made him an allegory of the 'huge powre and great oppression' of Spain (*FQ* V x 9).

411. *El Dorado* a mythical city in the New World. Ralegh, who tried to find it in 1595, wrote in *The Discoverie of Guiana*: 'I have beene assured by such of the Spanyardes as have seen *Manoa* the emperiall Citie of *Guiana*, which the *Spanyardes* call *el Dorado*, that for the greatness, for the riches, and for the excellent seat, it farre exceedeth any of the world' (10).

412. *the film removed* So Athena removes the mist from Diomedes' eyes (Homer, *Il.* v 127), Venus clears the eyes of Aeneas (Virgil, *Aen.* ii 604), and Michael clears those of Goffredo (Tasso, *Gerus. Lib.* xviii 92f.).

414. *euphrasy and rue* herbs thought to sharpen the eyesight. Fowler notes that Greek *euphrasia* means 'cheerfulness' and *rue* means 'sorrow', so the two names pun on the 'joy' and 'pious sorrow' (xi 361–2) of Adam's visions.

416. *Well of Life* Cp. Ps. 36. 9: 'With thee is the fountain of life: in thy light shall we see light'.

426. *excepted* forbidden.

427. *that sin*] *Ed I*; that *Ed II*. *Sinned thy sin* is biblical idiom (Exod. 32. 30, John 5. 16).

429–60. See Gen. 4 for the story of Cain and Abel. Adam never hears these names in book xi, where all his visions are of unnamed persons. Michael speaks names only after recounting the Confusion of tongues (see xii 140*n*).

430. *tilth* cultivated land.

432. *landmark* boundary marker.

436. *Unculled picked at random (unlike Abel's 'choicest' offering, 438).

441. *fire from heav'n* Acceptable sacrifices were often consumed by 'fire from heaven' (Lev. 9. 24, I Kings 18. 38, etc.). God 'had respect unto Abel and his offering' (Gen. 4. 4).

442. *nimble glance* quick flash.

grateful pleasing.

443. *sincere* including 'unmixed, uncontaminated' (*OED* 2).

455. *Out of thy loins* As progenitor of all mankind, Adam need not realize that Cain and Abel will be his own sons.

457. *fact* evil deed, crime.

469. *his grim cave* Cp. the 'deep cave' leading to Virgil's underworld (*Aen.* vi 237). Within the cave dwell Grief, Cares, Diseases, Age, Death and other horrors (*Aen.* vi 273f.).

dismal including 'malign, fatal' (*OED* 2).

476. *inabstinence OED cites 'abstinence' from 1382.

477−90. Adam's vision of future diseases has no one biblical source.

479. *lazar-house* a hospital for those suffering leprosy or other infectious diseases, named for Lazarus (Luke 16. 20).

485−7. *Demoniac . . . pestilence* Added in *Ed II*. It is odd that *Ed I* should make no mention of *wide-wasting pestilence*. The Great Plague had just killed 60,000 Londoners.

486. *moon-struck madness* lunacy.

487. *Marasmus* wasting away of the body.

496. *not of woman born* Cp. Shakespeare, *Macbeth* IV i 80, V viii 13.

497. *best of man* manliness, courage. Cp. Shakespeare, *Macbeth* V viii 18. When Macduff tells Macbeth that he was not born of woman, Macbeth replies that the news has 'cowed my better part of man'.

502. *Better . . . unborn* a commonplace in classical literature. See e.g., Sophocles, *Oedipus at Colonus* 1224−6, Theognis 425, and Seneca, *Ad Marciam: De Consolatione* xxii 3.

512−14. *Retaining . . . Maker's image* Cp. *CD* i 12: 'it cannot be denied that some traces of the divine image still remain in us' (trans. Carey, *YP* 6. 396).

516. *vilified* lessened in worth, made morally vile (*OED* 1, 1b).

519. *Inductive mainly to* strongly inducing (a repetition of).

528. *passages* deaths (*OED* 2b).

531. *Not too much* This maxim (*rule*) was carved in Apollo's temple at Delphi alongside the inscription 'Know thyself' (Plato, *Protagoras* 343B).

535−7. *ripe . . . mature* The comparison of peaceful death to the dropping of *ripe fruit* goes back to Cicero, *De Senectute* (19). Cyriack Skinner (who is now known to have written the anonymous *Life*) reports that M. died 'with so little pain or Emotion, that the time of his expiring was not perceiv'd by those in the room' (Darbishire 33).

Harshly plucked recalls Eve's Fall: 'she plucked, she ate' (ix 781f.).

536. *mother's lap* Cp. x 778.

544. *damp* depression of spirits (*OED* 5), noxious vapour (*OED* 1).

551–2. So *Ed II*. *Ed I* has only the one line: 'Of rend'ring up. Michael to him replied'.

551. *attend* wait for.

553. *Nor love thy life, nor hate* a classical commonplace. Cp. Martial: 'neither dread thy last day, nor hope for it' (*Epigrams* X xlvii 13).

556–97. Adam's third vision is based on Gen. 4. 19–22 and Gen. 6. 2–4.

557–8. *tents . . . cattle* An indication (to us, not Adam) that these are Cain's descendants: 'such as dwell in tents, and . . . such as have cattle' (Gen. 4. 20). Adam learns the truth at xi 607–10.

560. *who* Jubal, Cain's descendant and 'the father of all such as handle the harp and organ' (Gen. 4. 21).

561. *volant* moving rapidly.

562. *Instinct* *impelled (*OED* 2).

   proportions musical rhythms or harmonies (*OED* 10).

563. *fugue* From Latin *fuga*, 'flight'. Notice *Fled*. 'Jubal's race is the fugitive race of Cain' (Fowler). See Gen. 4. 12: 'a fugitive . . . shalt thou be'.

564. *one* Tubal-Cain, Jubal's brother and 'an instructor of every artificer in brass and iron' (Gen. 4. 22).

566. *casual* accidental (*OED* 1).

573. *Fusile* formed by melting or casting.

574. *a different sort* the descendants of Seth. They dwell on the *hither side* because Cain had migrated to 'the east of Eden' (Gen. 4. 16).

578–9. *works / Not hid* Josephus (*Antiquities* I ii 3) credits Seth's descendants with discovering astronomy. M. implicitly contrasts this lawful science with Tubal-Cain's metallurgy – a delving after 'treasures better hid' (i 688). At viii 166 even astronomy is full of 'matters hid'.

584. *amorous ditties* ominously recalling the 'amorous ditties' of i 449.

588. *ev'ning star* Venus, planet of love (cp. viii 519).

591. *Hymen* god of marriage. Cp. *L'Allegro* 125–9.

593. *interview* including 'glance' (*OED* 3b), 'mutual view of each other' (*OED* 2).

   event outcome.

595. *symphonies* harmonies.

   attached laid hold of (*OED* 3).

607–8. *tents / Of wickedness* Cp. Ps. 84. 10: 'I had rather be a doorkeeper in the house of my God, than to dwell in the tents of wickedness'. Jabal was the father of 'such as dwell in tents' (Gen. 4. 20). Cp. also v 890.

618. *completed* *accomplished, fully equipped (*OED* 3).

619. *appetence* appetite, desire.

620. *troll* not 'wag' (as most editors) but *'move (the tongue) volubly' (*OED* 4b). The gesture implies *lustful appetance*.

622. *sons of God* Cp. Gen. 6. 2: 'the sons of God saw the daughters of men that they were fair; and they took them wives of all which they chose'. M. here follows a patristic tradition identifying the sons of God with Seth's descendants. Elsewhere he adopts a rival tradition that saw the sons of God as fallen angels. See v 446–50 and *PR* ii 178–81 and notes.

624. *trains* wiles, snares (*OED* sb² 1, 2). Cp. *SA* 533.

625. *swim in joy* The expression was idiomatic (cp. 'swim in mirth' ix 1009). Michael's pun (not understood by Adam) resembles Satan's puns on artillery (vi 338–67) which the good angels had at first not understood.

632–3. *man's woe . . . woman* Like his earlier puns on 'Eve' (ix 1067, x 867), Adam's pun on 'woman' is based on a false etymology and is motivated by self-exculpation. It was also a cliché.

638–73. Adam's fourth vision is an elaboration of Gen. 6. 4. The details imitate scenes on the shields of Achilles (Homer, *Il.* xviii 478–540) and Aeneas (Virgil, *Aen.* viii 626–728). Homer begins with a wedding-feast but soon proceeds to an assembly, siege, cattle-raid and pitched battle.

641. *Concourse* hostile encounter (*OED* 1b).

642. *Giants* A hint to the reader (but not to Adam) that Adam is witnessing the consequences of the marriages of lines 585–97. Cp. Gen. 6. 4: 'There were giants in the earth in those days; and also after that, when the sons of God came in unto the daughters of men, and they bare children to them, the same became mighty men which were of old, men of renown'.

  emprise martial prowess.

643. *Part . . . steed* Cp. the chivalric devils in Hell: 'Part curb their fiery steeds' (ii 531).

644. *ranged* drawn up in ranks.

651. *makes*] *Ed II*; tacks *Ed I*. The earlier reading may be an error or an aphetic of 'attacks'.

654. **ensanguined* blood-stained (*OED* 1).

656. *scale* scaling-ladder.

665. *one* Enoch, identified more clearly in lines 700 and 707.

669. *Exploded* mocked, drove away (*OED* 1).

670. *a cloud . . . snatched him* Gen. 5. 24 states that God 'took' Enoch, but never mentions a cloud. M. may have had indirect access to the pseudepigraphical I Enoch where Enoch says 'clouds invited me' (14. 8).

678. *Ten thousandfold* One of Enoch's prophecies was that 'the Lord cometh with ten thousands of his saints, to execute judgment upon all' (Jude 14).

689–90. *might . . . virtue* 'Virtue' could mean 'physical strength', 'manliness' (*OED* 6, 7), and Latin *virtus* (from *vir*, 'man') meant 'valour'. Contrast 'true virtue' (790).

698. *renown on earth* The biblical giants were 'men of renown' (see above, 642*n*).

700. *seventh from thee* Jude 14 calls Enoch 'the seventh from Adam'. See also Gen. 5. 1–22.

706. *balmy* including alchemical 'balm' – a mythical substance thought to preserve life.

wingèd steeds Cp. the 'horses of fire' that translated Elijah (II Kings 2. 11). Ariosto places Enoch and Elijah together in the earthly Paradise where they dwell 'far beyond our pestilential air' (*Orl. Fur.* xxxiv 59). The *climes of bliss* are presumably Heaven, but at iii 461 M. had conjectured that 'Translated saints' might dwell on the moon.

707. *walk with God* Cp. Gen. 5. 24: 'Enoch walked with God: and he was not; for God took him'.

712–53. Adam's vision of the Flood is based on Gen. 6. 9 – 9. 17. Cp. also Jesus's account at Luke 17. 26–7: 'They did eat, they drank, they married wives, they were given in marriage, until the day that Noe entered into the ark, and the flood came'. The details of lines 738–53 follow Ovid's account of Deucalion's flood (*Met.* i 262–347).

715. *luxury* including 'lust'.

riot debauchery, wanton revel. Cp. i 498–500.

717. *passing fair* both 'pre-eminent beauty' and 'women passing by'.

719. *reverend sire* Noah (like the other biblical characters Adam sees in book xi, he is never named).

724–5. *to souls / In prison* So Christ 'preached unto the spirits in prison' (I Pet. 3. 19). Peter goes on to liken Christ to Noah (3. 20–21).

734. *and insect* M. places insects in the ark in accordance with Gen. 6. 20 ('every creeping thing'). Some commentators thought that insects grew from putrefaction and so need not have been saved by Noah.

740. *supply* assistance (*OED* 1).

741. *exhalation dusk* dark mist.

742. *amain* with main force.

749–50. *sea . . . without shore* Cp. Ovid, *Met.* i 292: 'For, all was Sea, nor had the Sea a shore' (trans. Sandys, 1632).

750–52. *palaces . . . stabled* Cp. Ovid, *Met.* i 299–300: 'Where Mountaine-loving Goats did lately graze, / The Sea-calfe now his ugly body layes' (trans. Sandys).

753. *bottom* boat.

754. *How didst thou grieve then, Adam* The direct address of a character is a Homeric formula. See ix 404–11 and note.

756–7. *flood, / Of tears* The conceit is common in Donne. See 'A Valediction of Weeping' and 'Holy Sonnet 5'.

765–6. *each . . . bear* Cp. Matt. 6. 34: 'Sufficient unto the day is the evil thereof'.

777. *Man is not whom* 'There is no one left'.

797–806. *The conquered . . . depraved* M. is probably alluding to the backsliding Englishmen who had betrayed the English Commonwealth in 1660. Cp. *SA* 268–77.

797. *enslaved* *OED*'s earliest participial sense. The verb 'enslave' first appeared in English at the time of the Civil War (*OED*'s earliest instance is from 1643).

815. *denouncing* proclaiming.

821. *devote* doomed.

824. *cataracts* following the Junius-Tremellius version of Gen. 7. 11. Where A.V. speaks of 'windows of heaven', Junius-Tremellius has *cataractae*, 'flood-gates'. Cp. ii 176.

831. *hornèd flood* Greek and Roman river-gods were depicted as bull-like because of their strength (Homer, *Il*. xxi 237, Virgil, *Georg*. 373, *Aen*. viii 77).

833. *the great river* Cp. Gen. 15. 18: 'the great river, the river Euphrates'.
gulf the Persian Gulf.

834. *salt* barren (biblical diction). The description and location of dislodged Paradise suit the island of Hormuz, which M. had associated with Satan at ii 2. Paradise is obliterated by the Flood in Sylvester, *DWW* (1592–1608), *Eden* 185–92.

835. *orcs* sea-monsters. Cp. Satan as Leviathan (i 200–202).
sea-mews' clang harsh cries of gulls.

840. *hull* float adrift.

842. *north wind* Gen. 8. 1, Ovid, *Met*. i 328.

843. *Wrinkled . . . decayed* The sea's *face* is wrinkled as with age until it mirrors the sun's *clear* (unwrinkled) face. Fowler hears a pun on *glass* (844) as 'mirror' and 'drinking vessel'. Notice *thirst* and cp. the sun's supping with the ocean at v 426.

847. *tripping* running.

851. *some high mountain* 'the mountains of Ararat' (Gen. 8. 4). See above, 429–60n for M.'s avoidance of names in book xi.

854. *retreating* *OED*'s earliest participial instance.

864. *Grateful* expressing gratitude and pleasing.

866. *three listed colours* the primary colours (red, yellow, blue) arranged in bands.

867. *cov'nant* The rainbow signifies God's covenant with mankind never again to flood the earth (Gen. 9. 8–17).

870. *who*] *Ed II*; *that Ed I*.

880. *Distended* 'spread out' and so 'not contracted in anger' (God's *brow*).

881. *verge* limiting or bounding belt (*OED* 16).

886–7. *repenting . . . Grieved* Cp. Gen. 6. 6: 'And it repented the Lord that he had made man on the earth, and it grieved him at his heart'.

888–9. *violence . . . Corrupting* Cp. Gen. 6. 11: 'The earth also was corrupt before God, and the earth was filled with violence'.

899. *Seed time and harvest* Cp. Gen. 8. 22: 'neither will I again smite any more every thing living, as I have done. While the earth remaineth, seedtime and harvest'.

900. *till fire purge all things new* II Pet. 3. 6–7.

BOOK XII

1–5. *As . . . resumes* These lines were added in 1674 when book x of *Ed I* became books xi and xii of *Ed II*.

1. *baits* of travellers: stops at an inn (*OED* 7).

7. *second stock* Noah, but glancing too at Christ, in whom believers were 'ingrafted'. See iii 293*n*.

24. *one* Nimrod (identified obliquely in lines 30 and 36).

30–32. *Hunting . . . tyrannous* Cp. Gen. 10. 8–10: 'Nimrod . . . began to be a mighty one in the earth. He was a mighty hunter before the Lord. . . . And the beginning of his kingdom was Babel'. Nimrod was the archetypal tyrant. M. in *Eikonoklastes* (1649) calls him 'the first King' (*YP* 3. 598) and John Vicars in *God in the Mount* (1646) praises Cromwell for resisting 'the mighty Nimrods and hunting Furies of our time' (273). Even Salmasius admitted that kingship began with Nimrod, who won his power by 'arms' (see *YP* 4. 1027).

34. *Before the Lord* M. offers two possible interpretations of the phrase (Gen. 10. 9). Either Nimrod openly defied God (*in despite of Heav'n*) or he claimed divine right (*second sov'reignty*), like the Stuart kings.

36. *rebellion . . . name* An ancient (but false) etymology derived 'Nimrod' from Hebrew *marad*, 'to rebel'. M. often employs the paradox that kings are rebels. Cp. 'rebel king' (i 484) and 'rebel Thrones' (vi 199). In *TKM* M. calls Charles I a 'rebell to Law' (*YP* 3. 230).

38–62. See Gen. 11. 1–9 on the Tower of Babel. Genesis does not say that Nimrod built the tower, though it associates him with Babel (10. 10). Josephus first made Nimrod responsible for the Confusion (*Antiquities* I iv 2).

41. **gurge* whirlpool (coined from Latin *gurges*).

42. *mouth of Hell* Cp. Sylvester, *DWW* (1592–1608), *Babilon* (1598): 'there, for their firme foundations / They digg to hell' (154–5).

43. *cast* determine (*OED* 44), scheme (*OED* 43), and throw (anything fluid) into a particular shape (*OED* 49).

45. *get themselves a name* Cp. Gen. 11. 4: 'And they said, Go to, let us build us a city and a tower, whose top may reach unto heaven; and let us make us a name, lest we be scattered abroad upon the face of the whole earth'. *Name* means 'reputation' but also suggests the proper names 'Nimrod' and 'Babel', to which Michael alludes in lines 36 and 62. Cp. the devils who 'got them new names' (i 365).

52. *in derision* Cp. Ps. 2. 4: 'the Lord shall have them in derision'.

53. *various* *'calculated to cause difference' (*OED* 5b).

55. *jangling noise* Cp. Sylvester, *DWW* (1592–1608), *Babilon* (1598): 'Through all the worke . . . A jangling noyse' (190–91).

56–60. *gabble . . . hubbub* The nonsense words suggest 'Babel', but M. avoids the obvious pun 'babble'. 'Hubbub' was a Gaelic interjection of contempt (*OED*), so the builders (like the metamorphosed devils) cast scorn 'on themselves from their own mouths' (x 546).

62. *Confusion named* Cp. Gen. 11. 9: 'Therefore is the name of it called Babel; because the Lord did there confound the language of all the earth'. *Babel* (Babylon) means 'gate of the gods' but was punningly related to Hebrew *balal*, 'confound'. See Josephus, *Antiquities* (I iv 3) and A.V. marginal gloss.

81. *affecting* aspiring.

82–101. *yet know . . . inward lost* Michael roots political in psychological *servitude*. The whole passage implicitly blames the English people for capitulating to monarchy in 1660. Cp. *SA* 268–71.

84. *right reason* conscience, planted by God in all men.

85. *dividual* separate, distinct.

101. *irreverent son* Ham, who looked on the nakedness of his drunken father, Noah. Noah then cursed Ham's son Canaan and all his descendants: 'Cursed be Canaan; a servant of servants shall he be unto his brethren' (Gen. 9. 25).

104. *vicious* depraved.

race descendants (*OED* 1), tribe (*OED* 2b). *OED* records 'one of the great divisions of mankind' only from 1774, so M. is probably thinking of the Canaanites rather than black Africans (who were also classed among Ham's descendants). But Noah's curse was used to justify black slavery and M. is untroubled by the persecution of '*Slaves* and *Negro's*' in *Of Reformation* (*YP* 1. 617).

111. *peculiar* specially chosen. Cp. Deut. 14. 2: 'the Lord hath chosen thee to be a peculiar people unto himself'.

113. *one faithful man* Abraham. Lines 113–63 are based on Gen. 11. 27–25. 10.

115. *Bred up in idol-worship* Abraham's father Terah 'served other gods' (Josh. 24. 2).

117. *the patriarch* Noah, who lived for 350 years after the Flood (Gen. 9. 28).

119. *their own work in wood and stone* Cp. Jeremiah's scorn for those who say 'to a stock, Thou art my father; and to a stone, Thou hast brought me forth' (Jer. 2. 27). M. now gives no hint that pagan gods were devils (cp. i 365–75).

125–6. *seed . . . blest* Cp. Gen. 12. 3: 'in thee shall all families of the earth be blest'. At line 148 Michael connects God's promise with the Messiah.

127. *Not knowing . . . believes* Cp. Heb. 11. 8: 'By faith Abraham . . . went out, not knowing whither he went'.

130. *Ur* a city on the west bank of the Euphrates.

131. *Haran* a city east of the Euphrates, north-west of Ur.

132. *servitude* slaves and servants.

139–45. *From . . . eastward* The Promised Land is bounded to the north by *Hamath*, a city on the Orontes (Num. 34. 8, Josh. 13. 5), to the south by the *desert* of Zin (Num. 34. 3), to the west by the Mediterranean (Num. 34. 6), and to the east by the *Jordan* (Num. 34. 12) or *Mount Hermon* (Josh. 13. 5).

140. *names . . . yet unnamed* Cp. Virgil, *Aen.* vi 776: 'Names to be heard for places nameless now'.

144. *Mount Carmel* on the Mediterranean, near modern Haifa.

double-founted M. follows an incorrect tradition that the Jordan springs from two streams, named 'Jor' and 'Dan'.

146. *Senir* a peak of Mount Hermon, depicted on seventeenth-century maps as a *ridge*.

152. *faithful Abraham* italicized in *Ed I*, perhaps (as Flannagan notes) to emphasize a phrase instituted by God at Gal. 3. 9. God renames Abram at Gen. 17. 5: 'Neither shall thy name any more be called Abram, but thy name shall be Abraham; for a father of many nations have I made thee'. Cp. Gen. 12. 2: 'I will bless thee, and make thy name great'. 'Abraham' is the first personal name Michael has revealed.

153. *son* Isaac.

grandchild Jacob.

160. *younger son* Joseph (see Gen. 45–6).

161–96. As at i 306–7, M. identifies the Pharaoh of Exod. 1 (who enslaved the Israelites) with the Pharaoh of Exod. 14 (who pursued them).

165. *Suspected to* mistrusted by (*OED* 1b).

sequent successive (to Joseph's Pharaoh) and pursuing (Moses). Latin *sequor* could mean 'pursue'.

166. *overgrowth* too rapid growth.

inmate foreign (*OED* 1b).

168. *kills their infant males* Exod. 1. 16–22.

173. *denies* refuses.

179. *murrain* cattle plague.

180. *Botches* boils, tumours.

blains pustules.

188. *Palpable darkness* See ii 406n.

190. *ten wounds* the ten plagues (Exod. 7–12).

191. *The*] *Ed II*; *This Ed I*.

river-dragon Pharaoh is called 'the great dragon that lieth in the midst of his rivers' at Ezek. 29. 3. Cp. Satan as dragon (x 529) and Leviathan (i 201).

197. *two crystal walls* Cp. Exod. 14. 22: 'the waters were a wall unto them on their right hand, and on their left'. Cp. also vii 293 ('crystal wall') and M.'s version of Ps. 136 (line 49): 'walls of glass'. Sylvester in *DWW* (1592–1608), *The Lawe* (1606) describes the Red Sea dividing into 'walls of cristall' (690).

199. **rescued* *OED*'s earliest participial instance.

200. *saint* holy person (Moses).

202–3. *Before . . . fire* Exod. 13. 21–4. M.'s view that God was *present in his angel*, not in his own person, is based on Exod. 33. 2–4. See further *CD* i 5 (*YP* 6. 254).

205–13. *king pursues . . . waves return* Exod. 14. 23–31. Cp. i 306–11.

207. *defends* repels, prevents (*OED* 1, 2).

210. *craze* shatter (*OED* 1).

214. *war* *soldiers in fighting array (*OED* 6b).

216. *not the readiest way* M.'s explanation for the Israelites' detour through the desert (lasting thirty-eight years) is from Exod. 13. 17–18.

217. *alarmed* called to arms.

225. *great senate* the Seventy Elders (Exod. 24. 1–9, Num. 11. 16–30). M. in *REW* exalts 'the supreme councel of seaventie call'd the *Sanhedrim*' as a model republican government (*YP* 7. 436).

227–30. *God . . . laws* Exod. 19. 16–20.

232. *types* any person, event or object in the O.T. prefiguring a Christian counterpart. Cp. Heb. 8 and see below, 238–44*n*.

236–8. *they beseech . . . terror cease* Cp. Exod. 20. 19: 'Speak thou with us and we will hear: but let not God speak with us, lest we die'.

238. *what they besought*] *Ed II*; them their desire, *Ed I*.

238–44. Moses is a type or *figure* of Christ in his office as *mediator*. See Deut. 18. 15–19, Acts 3. 22 and cp. *CD* i 15: 'the office of mediator is also ascribed to Moses, as a type of Christ' (trans. Carey, *YP* 6. 431).

247. *tabernacle* See Exod. 25–6 and Heb. 9.

255. *as in a zodiac* Josephus says the candlestick had *seven lamps* in imitation of the seven planets (*Antiquities* III vi 7).

256–8. *over the tent . . . journey* Exod. 40. 34–8.

263–7. *the sun . . . overcome* When Joshua defeated the Amorites he said: 'Sun, stand thou still upon Gibeon; and thou, Moon, in the valley of Ajalon. And the sun stood still, and the moon stayed, until the people had avenged themselves upon their enemies' (Josh. 10. 12–13). *Gibeon* and *Aialon* were a few miles north of Jerusalem.

264. *adjourn* The context (*a day*) invites a play on French *jour*.

267. *the third* Jacob, named *Israel* ('he wrestles with God') at Gen. 32. 28.

274. *eyes true op'ning* Contrast the false eye-openings of ix 708, 875, 985, 1071, x 1053, xi 412. *True* is an adverb (*OED* C).

277. *His day* Adam means 'Abraham's day', but M.'s voice behind him alludes to John 8. 56: 'Your father Abraham rejoiced to see my day'. When asked if he had seen Abraham, Jesus replied: 'Before Abraham was, I am' (8. 58). Adam will learn the meaning of Abraham's *seed* (273) at xii 446–50.

287. *evince* make evident (*OED* 5). 'Overcome' (*OED* 1) is a momentary possibility, but it cannot survive line 290 (*law* can reveal sin, but not *remove* it). Cp. Rom. 3. 20: 'by the deeds of the law there shall no flesh be justified in his sight: for by the law is the knowledge of sin'.

288. *natural pravity* Original Sin (theological term).

291–2. *shadowy . . . goats* Cp. Heb. 10. 4: 'it is not possible that the blood of bulls and of goats should take away sins'. Blood sacrifices under the law were 'a shadow of good things to come' (Heb. 10. 1).

293. *blood more precious* I Pet. 1. 18.

294. *Just for unjust* I Pet. 3. 18.

295. *imputed* attributed vicariously (*OED* 2, theological term).

297–8. *law . . . Cannot appease* Cp. Gal. 2. 16: 'A man is not justified by the works of the law, but by the faith of Jesus Christ'.

301. *resign* make over, yield up (*OED* 2).

307–10. *not Moses . . . Joshua* Deut. 34, Josh. 1. Cp. *CD* i 26: 'The imperfection of the law was made apparent in the person of Moses himself. For Moses, who was a 'type' of the law, could not lead the children of Israel into the land of Canaan, that is, into eternal rest. But an entrance was granted to them under Joshua, that is, Jesus' (trans. Carey, *YP* 6. 519).

310. *Joshua . . . Jesus* 'Jesus' is the Greek equivalent of 'Joshua' ('saviour'). Thus the O.T. Joshua was a type of Christ. See above, *232n* on typology.

316. *but* except.

319. *he saves them penitent* ambiguous, since *penitent* could mean 'relenting' (*OED* 2) and so modify *he* as well as *them*. *OED* cites the Douay Bible (1609): 'Thou art our Lord, most highe, benigne, long-suffering, and very merciful, and penitent upon the wickednes of men'.

322–4. *promise . . . endure* See II Sam. 7. 16 for Nathan's promise to David: 'thy throne shall be established for ever'.

325–7. *royal stock . . . son* Messianic prophecies about David's line are frequent in the O.T. (e.g. Isa. 11. 10, Ps. 89. 36) and are applied to Jesus in the N.T. (e.g. Luke 1. 32).

329–30. *of kings / The last* M. in *TKM* (1649) argues that Christ's kingship made other kings redundant (*YP* 3. 256).

332. *next son* Solomon. See I Kings 5–8, II Chron. 2–4 on the Temple. The ark is *clouded* because God spoke from amidst clouds (Exod. 24. 16)

and a cloud of glory filled the Temple when the ark was placed there
(I Kings 8. 10).

338. *Heaped . . . sum* 'Added to the sum total of the people's sins'.

339–45. *expose . . . seventy years* See II Kings 25, II Chron. 36 and Jer. 39
on the Babylonian Captivity and the destruction of the Temple (sixth
century BC). Jeremiah prophesied seventy years of captivity (Jer. 25. 12).

348–50. *Returned . . . re-edify* The Persian kings Cyrus, Darius and Artax-
erxes permitted the Jews to return and rebuild the Temple (Ezra, Neh. 1–
6).

349. *disposed* put into a favourable mood (*OED* 6).

353–7. *priests . . . sceptre* The apocryphal II Macc. 4–6 tells how *strife*
between the priests enabled the Seleucid King Antiochus IV to sack
Jerusalem and pollute the Temple, which he dedicated to Zeus (169 BC).
They (356) are the priestly dynasty of the Maccabees (Hasmoneans), one
of whom, Aristobulus I, proclaimed himself king in 104 BC, becoming the
first king since the Babylonian Captivity.

357. *sons* descendants.

358. *stranger* Antipater the Idumean. The Romans made him governor of
Jerusalem in 61 BC and procurator of Judaea in 47 BC. He was Herod the
Great's father.

364. *solemn* holy (*OED* 1), awe-inspiring (*OED* 7).

367. *squadroned *OED*'s earliest participial instance.

370–71. *bound . . . Heav'ns* Cp. Ps. 2. 8 (which was referred to Christ): 'I
shall give thee . . . the uttermost parts of the earth'. Christ's *reign* on *earth*
will last throughout the Millennium – the 1,000 years following his Second
Coming (Rev. 20). See *CD* i 33 (*YP* 6. 623–4). Cp. also Virgil's prophecy
that Augustus will bound his 'empire with Ocean, his glory with the stars'
(*Aen.* i 287).

373. *Surcharged* overwhelmed (*OED* 4b) and weighed down with moisture
(*OED* 3c). Cp. *SA* 728.

379. *virgin mother, hail* Luke 1. 28. Cp. v 385–7, xi 158.

383. *capital* on the head (*OED* 1), fatal (*OED* 2d).

393. *recure* heal a wound (*OED* 2).

394. *destroying . . . works* Cp. I John 3. 8: 'For this purpose the Son of God
was manifested, that he might destroy the works of the devil'.

396. *want* lack.

401. *apaid* satisfied.

402. *exact* rigorous, strict (*OED* 4, 5) and perfect (*OED* 1).

403–4. *love . . . law* Cp. Rom. 13. 10: 'Love is the fulfilling of the law'.

406. *cursèd death* Cp. Gal. 3. 13 (citing Deut. 21. 23): 'Christ hath redeemed
us from the curse of the law, being made a curse for us: for it is written,
Cursed is every one that hangeth on a tree'.

409. *Imputed* attributed vicariously (*OED* 2, theological term).

410. *though legal works* 'though their works accorded with the (Mosaic) law'. M. shared the general Protestant belief in Justification by Faith. See *CD* i 22.

415–16. *to the cross he nails ... sins* Col. 2. 14.

419. *satisfaction* payment of penalty (theological term).

422. *stars of morn* literal stars and angels. Cp. Job 38. 7: 'the morning stars sang together'. Christ was also called 'morning star' (Rev. 22. 16), though Michael here presents the resurrected Son as a rising sun (*dawning light*).

432. *in ... stings* Cp. I Cor. 15. 55: 'O death, where is thy sting?' Flannagan notes that Sin's sting returns to its source in Satan's *head*. Cp. ii 752–8.

433. *temporal* temporary (*OED* 1). M. believed that body and soul died and were resurrected together.

442. *profluent* flowing. M. believed that baptism should be performed in running water (*CD* i 28, *YP* 6. 544).

450. *So ... blest* Michael now reveals the meaning of God's promise to Abraham that all nations will be blessed in his seed (xii 277, Gen. 12. 3). The *seed* is Christ. Cp. Gal. 3. 8: 'the scripture, foreseeing that God would justify the heathen through faith, preached before the gospel unto Abraham, saying, In thee shall all nations be blessed'.

454. *prince of air* Satan is 'prince of the power of the air' at Eph. 2. 2 and is led captive 'up on high' at Eph. 4. 8. He is led *in chains* at Rev. 20. 1.

460. *quick* living. The N.T. often speaks of judging 'the quick and dead' (e.g. Acts 10. 42, II Tim. 4. 1).

467. *period* consummation, end (*OED* 5).

469–78. *O goodness ... abound* Much debated. Many hear Adam as articulating the paradox of the 'Fortunate Fall', but Adam says only that God's bringing good out of evil is *more wonderful* than his bringing light out of darkness. He does not say that man will be more happy for sinning. Contrast Fletcher, *CV* (1610) iii 12: 'Such joy we gained by our parentalls, / That good, or bad, whither I cannot wiss, / To call it a mishap, or happy miss / That fell from Eden, and to heav'n did rise'. M. never implies that the Fall is a precondition for man's ascent to Heaven. Adam and Eve could have reached Heaven without sinning (see v 496–503, vii 155–61) and the Son could have become incarnate without man's Fall (see v 839*n* and Danielson 215–27).

469. *immense* unmeasured, infinite (*OED* 1).

478. *wrath ... abound* Cp. Rom. 5. 20: 'Where sin abounded, grace did much more abound'.

486. *Comforter* the Holy Spirit (John 15. 26).

488–9. *law ... love* Rom. 3. 27, Gal. 5. 6.

491–2. *spiritual armour ... fiery darts* Cp. Eph. 6. 11–17: 'Put on the whole armour of God ... taking the shield of faith, wherewith ye shall be able to quench all the fiery darts of the wicked'.

493. *What . . . afraid* Cp. Ps. 56. 11: 'In God have I put my trust: I will not be afraid / What man can do unto me'.

501. *To speak all tongues* Cp. Mark 16. 17 ('they shall speak with new tongues') and the fulfilment of this promise in Acts 2. 4–7.

505. *race well run* A Pauline metaphor (I Cor. 9. 24, II Tim. 4. 1, etc.) used by M. in *Areopagitica*: 'the race, where that immortall garland is to be run for' (*YP* 2. 515).

508. *grievous wolves* Cp. Acts 20. 29: 'For I know this, that after my departing shall grievous wolves enter in among you, not sparing the flock'. Cp. iv 183–7, *Lycidas* 113–31, and M.'s sonnet *To the Lord General Cromwell* 14.

511. *lucre* Cp. I Pet. 5. 2: 'Feed the flock of God . . . not for filthy lucre, but of a ready mind'. M. was opposed to a stipendiary clergy.

511–14. *the truth . . . understood* a typical Protestant assertion of the Christian's right to interpret scripture guided solely by the inner light.

515. *names* titles of rank or dignity (*OED* 2b).

520. *pretence* assertion of a right or title (*OED* 1), with overtones of the modern sense.

523. *enrolled* written (in the Bible).

525. *force the Spirit* M. in *CD* i 30 denounces the forcing of conscience as 'a yoke not only upon man but upon the Holy Spirit itself' (trans. Carey, *YP* 6. 590).

526. *His consort Liberty* II Cor. 3. 17.

527. *living temples* Cp. I Cor. 3. 16: 'Know ye not that ye are the temple of God?'

529–30. *Who . . . Infallible* M. attacks papal claims to 'infallibilitie over both the conscience and the scripture' in *A Treatise of Civil Power* (*YP* 7. 248). The doctrine of papal infallibility was not instituted until 1870.

532–3. *worship . . . truth* John 4. 23.

534. *Will*] *Ed I*; Well *Ed II*.

536. *works of faith* See *CD* i 22 for M.'s view that faith is a work and 'not merely infused' (trans. Carey, *YP* 6. 489). Cp. also 'faith not void of works' (xii 427).

539. *groaning* Cp. Rom. 8. 22: 'For we know that the whole creation groaneth and travaileth in pain together until now'.

540. *respiration* respite, breathing space (*OED* 3).

546. *dissolve* not 'annihilate' (as Fowler) but 'destroy the binding power of' (*OED* 11). Annihilation would be a mercy to the devils (ii 155–9), whom God had said that he would punish 'without end' (v 615). M. in *CD* i 33 confirms that Hell is a place of 'endless punishment' and rejects the view that Hell might be destroyed in the final conflagration: 'If this were to happen it would be very nice for the damned, no doubt!' (trans. Carey,

YP 6. 630). Michael had earlier said that the Son would destroy Satan by destroying his works. See xii 394–5.

547. **perverted* turned from the right way. *OED*'s earliest participial instance.

548–9. *conflagrant . . . earth* See II Pet. 3. 6–13 on the destruction by fire. See Rev. 21. 1 on the *New heavens, new earth.*

551. *fruits* playing on Latin *fruitio*, meaning *joy* or *bliss.*

555. *Till time stand fixed* At Rev. 10. 5–6 an angel swears 'that there should be time no longer'. Cp. *On Time* 1.

559. *this vessel* the entire human nature (mind and body).

565. *Merciful . . . works* Cp. Ps. 145. 9: 'his tender mercies are over all his works'.

566. *overcoming evil* Cp. Rom. 12. 21: 'overcome evil with good'.

567–8. *weak . . . strong* Cp. I Cor. 1. 27: 'God hath chosen the weak things of the world to confound the things which are mighty'. See also vi 137–9*n.*

576–7. *all the stars . . . by name* Cp. Ps. 147. 4: 'He telleth the number of the stars; he calleth them all by their names'.

581–4. *only add . . . charity* II Pet. 1. 5–7.

587. *paradise within* Cp. Satan's 'Hell within' (iv 20).

588–9. *top / Of speculation* both 'hill of extensive view' and 'summit of theological speculation'.

592. *motion* military deployment (*OED* 5).

593. *remove* signal for departure (*OED* 5b).

602. *many days* Adam lived to be 930 (Gen. 5. 5).

608. *found her waked* The Argument to book xii says that Adam 'wakens Eve'.

611. *God is also in sleep* Cp. Num. 12. 6: 'If there be a prophet among you, I the Lord will make myself known unto him in a vision, and will speak unto him in a dream'.

615–18. *with thee . . . all places thou* Cp. Ruth 1. 16: 'And Ruth said, Intreat me not to leave thee, or to return from following after thee: for whither thou goest, I will go; and where thou lodgest, I will lodge: thy people will be my people, and thy God my God'. See also Eve's love poem at iv 641–56.

629. **metéorous* raised on high (*OED*). A 'meteor' was any atmospheric phenomenon (*OED* 1) and 'meteoric' meant 'pertaining to the region of mid-air' (*OED* 1a). Richardson contrasts the good angels' lofty, luminous *mist* with Satan as a 'black mist low creeping' (ix 180).

630. *marish* marsh.

631. *the labourer's heel* Adam is now a labourer, and his *heel* is vulnerable to the serpent (Flannagan).

635. *adust* scorched. Patristic tradition interpreted the 'flaming sword' of Gen. 3. 24 as the heat of the uninhabitable torrid zone (hence *Libyan*).

637–8. *In either hand . . . ling'ring parents* Michael's conduct of Adam and Eve recalls the angels' conduct of Lot's family from Sodom: 'And while he lingered, the men laid hold upon his hand, and upon the hand of his wife, and upon the hand of his two daughters; the Lord being merciful unto him: and they brought him forth, and set him without the city' (Gen. 19. 16).

640. *subjected* lying below.

643. *brand* sword (*OED* 8b) or lightning (*OED* 3d). Cp. Gen. 3. 24: 'a flaming sword which turned every way'.

644. *dreadful faces thronged* Martindale (134) compares 'the supreme moment of terror' in Virgil's *Aeneid*, when Venus clears Aeneas's sight and he sees the gods' 'dreadful forms' (*dirae facies*) menacing Troy (ii 622).

648. *hand in hand* See iv 321n.

648–9. *wand'ring . . . way* Cp. Ps. 107. 4: 'They wandered in the wilderness in a solitary way; they found no city to dwell in.' But the psalm continues: 'Then they cried unto the Lord . . . and he delivered them out of their distresses. / And he led them forth by the right way' (6–7).

THE STORY OF PENGUIN CLASSICS

Before 1946 ...'Classics' are mainly the domain of academics and students, without readable editions for everyone else. This all changes when a little-known classicist, E. V. Rieu, presents Penguin founder Allen Lane with the translation of Homer's *Odyssey* that he has been working on and reading to his wife Nelly in his spare time.

1946 *The Odyssey* becomes the first Penguin Classic published, and promptly sells three million copies. Suddenly, classic books are no longer for the privileged few.

1950s Rieu, now series editor, turns to professional writers for the best modern, readable translations, including Dorothy L. Sayers's *Inferno* and Robert Graves's *The Twelve Caesars*, which revives the salacious original.

1960s The Classics are given the distinctive black jackets that have remained a constant throughout the series's various looks. Rieu retires in 1964, hailing the Penguin Classics list as 'the greatest educative force of the 20th century'.

1970s A new generation of translators arrives to swell the Penguin Classics ranks, and the list grows to encompass more philosophy, religion, science, history and politics.

1980s The Penguin American Library joins the Classics stable, with titles such as *The Last of the Mohicans* safeguarded. Penguin Classics now offers the most comprehensive library of world literature available.

1990s The launch of Penguin Audiobooks brings the classics to a listening audience for the first time, and in 1999 the launch of the Penguin Classics website takes them online to a larger global readership than ever before.

The 21st Century Penguin Classics are rejacketed for the first time in nearly twenty years. This world famous series now consists of more than 1300 titles, making the widest range of the best books ever written available to millions – and constantly redefining the meaning of what makes a 'classic'.

The Odyssey continues ...

The best books ever written

PENGUIN (🐧) CLASSICS

SINCE 1946

Find out more at www.penguinclassics.com